JOE K

A BIOGRAPHY OF JOE KASBERGER

BY

DENNIS A. JOYCE

Published by Newark Abbey Press
First Paperback Edition

Library of Congress Cataloging-in-Publication Data
pending

Joyce, Dennis A. 1943 –

  Joe K: A Biography of Joe Kasberger / by Dennis A, Joyce

Includes index

ISBN 0-9664459-2-9

Edited by Robert M. Huntington, Ph. D.

Designed by Rory Morgan Joyce

Production by Herald Publishing Company, Houston, TX

Printed in United States of America by Quinn-Woodbine, Inc.,
Woodbine, NJ

DEDICATION

In his own words, Joe Kasberger attributed his success to three factors. First, the rabbit's foot he kept in his pocket. Second, he was a stickler for details. Third, Joe had more than his share of talented players and associates. Accordingly, this book is dedicated to all of Joe's assistant coaches, team managers and players at Mt. Angel College, Mt. Angel Academy and Normal School and St. Benedict's Prep.

I want each of Joe's players, even if your name does not appear in these pages, to know of the contributions that you made. Every effort has been made to list all lettermen in the Appendix. You played for a great coach with a nationally significant record. Rightfully, you can take pride in contributing to the awesome numbers that Joe compiled over more than four and one-half decades of coaching baseball, basketball and football. I sincerely regret that I am unable to identify and provide a picture of every player .

Much of Joe's national significance as a coach is connected to his tenure at St. Benedict's Prep in Newark, NJ. It is necessary, therefore, to recognize another key reason for his coaching successes – the Milbauer Family in Newark. It all began at Notre Dame in 1924 when Joe was befriended by Frank A. Milbauer. Several years later, Frank's parents, Louise and Frank W. Milbauer, made Joe Kasberger a part of their family. Their daughter, Claire Milbauer, would become akin to Joe's younger sister and an expert on much of Joe's post-1930 life. The Milbauer family provided Joe a Newark home away from his family home in The Dalles, OR for nine months of every year for twenty-five years. The enduring nature of these bonds is truly exceptional.

It was while living with the Milbauers that Joe achieved most of his greatest records. As the research reveals, and this book attempts to convey, Joe was first and foremost an Oregonian. The fact that he stayed in Newark, for as long as he did, certainly appears to have much to do with his "adopted" family. For this reason, a two-part dedication for this book is gratefully made.

TABLE OF CONTENTS

PHOTO/DOCUMENT CREDITS

I. JOE KASBERGER'S EARLY YEARS

(Bernard Sandoz) P. 19, (Bernard Sandoz) P. 20 upper, (Bernard Sandoz) P. 20 middle, (Bernard Sandoz) P. 20 lower, (Bernard Sandoz) P. 21 upper, (Joe Kasberger) P. 21 middle, (Joe Kasberger) P. 21 lower, (Joe Kasberger) P. 23, (Msgr. William Stone) P. 25, (Msgr. William Stone) P. 26, (The Dalles HS) P. 28 upper, (The Dalles HS) P. 28 lower, (Marilyn Ericksen) P. 29, (Joe Kasberger) P. 30, (Joe Kasberger) P. 32, (Bernard Sandoz) P. 33, (William Murray) P. 36, (*The Dalles Chronicle*) P. 38, (Joe Kasberger) P. 40.

II. JOE AS A STUDENT AT MT. ANGEL COLLEGE

(Joe Kasberger) P. 49 upper, (Joe Kasberger) P. 49 lower, (Joe Kasberger) P. 52, (Joe Kasberger) P. 53, (Bernard Sandoz) P. 55, (Mt. Angel Abbey) P. 57, (Mt. Angel Abbey) P. 58, (Joe Kasberger) P. 59, (Joe Kasberger) P. 60, (Mt. Angel Abbey) P. 61 upper, (Joe Kasberger) P. 61 lower, (Joe Kasberger) P. 62 upper, (Joe Kasberger) P. 62 lower, (Joe Kasberger) P. 63 upper, (Joe Kasberger) P. 63 lower, (Joe Kasberger) P. 64, (Bernard Sandoz) P. 65, (Bernard Sandoz) P. 66, (Bernard Sandoz) P. 71, (Joe Kasberger) P. 74, (Joe Kasberger) P. 77, (Joe Kasberger) P. 78, (Mt. Angel Abbey) P. 79, (Mt. Angel Abbey) P. 80.

III. JOE AT OAC BEFORE AND AFTER THE WAR

(Oregon State University) P. 88, (University of Oregon) P. 94 upper, (Bernard Sandoz) P. 94 lower, (Bernard Sandoz) P. 95, (Southern Oregon University) P. 96, (Bernard Sandoz) P. 97, (University of Oregon) P. 100, (University of Oregon) P. 103, (University of Oregon) P. 106, (Oregon State University) P. 109, (Oregon State University) P. 110, (Oregon State University) P. 114, (Oregon State University) P. 116, (Oregon State University) P. 117, (Oregon State University) P. 118, (Oregon State University) P. 119, (Oregon State University) P. 121, (Oregon State University) P. 124.

IV. JOE AS A COACH AT MT. ANGEL COLLEGE

(Bernard Sandoz) P. 126, (Mt. Angel Abbey) P. 128, (Joe Kasberger) P. 129, (Mt. Angel Abbey) P. 130, (Joe Kasberger) P. 131, (Joe Kasberger) P. 134, (University of Notre Dame) P. 135, (Joe Kasberger) P. 141, (The Dalles HS) P. 142, (University of Notre Dame) P. 144, (Mt. Angel Abbey) P. 145, (Mt. Angel Abbey) P. 149, (Mt. Angel Abbey) P. 150, (Mt. Angel Abbey) P. 153, (Mt. Angel Abbey) P. 154, (Bernard Sandoz) P. 162 upper, (Bernard Sandoz) P. 162 lower, (Joe Kasberger) P. 163 upper, (Bernard Sandoz) P. 163 lower, (M. Claire Milbauer) P. 164 upper, (Mt. Angel Abbey) P. 164 lower, (Mt. Angel Abbey) P. 165.

V. AFTERMATH OF THE FIRE

.

VI. THE POST-GRADUATE (PG) ATHLETIC ERA

VII. COACHING WITHOUT POST-GRADUATES (PGs)

Abbey) P. 330, (Betty Hellberg) P. 331 upper, (Newark Abbey) P. 331 lower, (Ben Scotti) P. 332, (M. Claire Milbauer) P. 334 upper, (M. Claire Milbauer) P. 334 lower, (Bernard Sandoz) P. 335, (Newark Abbey) P. 336 upper, (Newark Abbey) P. 336 lower, (Newark Abbey) P. 337, (Newark Abbey) P. 338 upper, (Newark Abbey) P. 338 lower, (M. Claire Milbauer) P. 339 upper, (Newark Abbey) P. 339 lower, (Rory Joyce) P. 340, (*Newark News*) P. 343.

VIII. APPENDIX/COVER

APPENDIX: (University of Oregon) P. 361, (Oregon State University) P. 362. COVER: (Harold Morgan) left inside flap, (Betty Hellberg) front cover lower overlay, (Newark Abbey) back cover overlay, panoramic background (Joe Kasberger).

Permission to use these materials is appreciated by the author.

FOREWORD

From the beginning of time, scholars, authors, historians, and newsmen have attempted to capture the life and ways of those special people who enter our lives, stay a while, and leave us the better for it. Dennis Joyce does precisely this in his epic work on Joe Kasberger. Joyce does a most scholarly and meticulous job of researching and documenting all aspects of the coach who became a legend in his time.

Joe Kasberger, a quiet, soft-spoken, "laid back," Westerner learned his football at Notre Dame. It was there that he met Frank Milbauer, then one of the seven "mules" for the "Four Horsemen." They became lifelong friends.

Kasberger, from the town of The Dalles, Oregon, came East in 1930 on his way to complete a Master's Degree in Physical Education at Columbia University. During his sojourn at Columbia, the football/baseball coaching position at St. Benedict's Prep opened, and Frank Milbauer persuaded Joe to take it. This he did, and held the position until the late 1960s.

I was fortunate to play for Joe in 1932-33 and was immediately enamored with this wonderful guy. Kasberger was a masterful coach and teacher, with unlimited concern for his players and students. He was not only a great role-model, but for me a father-figure as well. He counseled me long and well in helping me make my decision to attend Columbia University. Dennis Joyce must have had a similar experience when he played baseball for Joe in 1959.

After over thirty-five years of coaching, studying films, and discussing football with Joe Kasberger, I am certain that he would have been successful at any level of football, be it college or professional. Some have wondered why he did not move up from St. Benedict's. I believe that Joe, a religious man of simple needs and one who never sought the limelight, and a man who lived on his own terms, found at St. Benedict's his "Home Plate" from which to operate, and the freedom to use the entire "Length of the Field" in which to accomplish his goals.

In his "home away from home" with the Milbauers, he was very comfortable. In addition to Frank Milbauer, he developed a steadfast relationship with Claire Milbauer, Frank's sister. Joe was her "older brother." Claire, a wonderful and caring lady, personally supervised all of Joe's medical care during his illness.

Then too, St. Benedict's, a preparatory school for college, each year had an influx of great athletes which added in perpetuity to Kasberger's remarkable coaching record. I feel that Joe vicariously got many of his "college coaching kicks" through Spec Keene, his Phi Delta Theta fraternity brother at OAC, once a very successful football coach at Willamette University in Salem, OR. From the very start, Kasberger sent many of his best players to play for Keene. The most noteworthy of these was Dick Weisgerber of East Orange, NJ. With Weisgerber at running back, Willamette won three conference titles in the three years that he played for Keene. Weisgerber was All-American and later played for the Green Bay Packers under Curley Lambeau – and Joe enjoyed every minute of it!

Athletics, for its participants, renders a most vibrant and exhilarating experience. However, it is not necessarily for all, but only for those who wish to compete and be tested in the public arena. In the hands of the "right" coach (Joe Kasberger), it becomes an exceptional educational tool for teaching the facts of life – and more.

Participants who do not prepare themselves well (mentally and physically) for the contest, not only will lose, but can be humiliated before the crowd. Experience gained from athletics is lifelong and invaluable.

About football, Pudge Heffelfinger, the great Yale immortal, once said, "A game that can keep you young and vibrant and all steamed up is a precious thing." American football is truly that. At a time when some youths are developing traits of irresponsibility, disloyalty, and other selfish, self-centered characteristics, this thrilling competitive sport remains as one of the last strongholds for the persistent development of self-discipline, loyalty to a cause, and respect for others – attributes that are also American traditions.

Yes, there are other coaches of the cut of Joe Kasberger, but Dennis Joyce chose to wonderfully immortalize OUR "Joe," and he did it well – very well.

Joe Kasberger entered our lives in 1930, stayed a while as football/baseball coach, departed in 1969, and we were definitely much the better for it.

The coach passed away on October 1, 1969 after a bout with cancer. On October 4, his body, accompanied by his close friend Reverend Father Nicholas Collins, emplaned for the family burial plot on the outskirts of that quaintly named town, The Dalles, in his beloved Oregon.

Thank you, Dennis, for bringing Joe back to us once again.

Thank you Joe for coming the first time – God Bless, Rest Well.

With much affection,
John F. Bateman, St. Benedict's Prep, Class of 1934

PREFACE

Joe Kasberger is probably the last man who would want a book written about himself. There are several reasons why a book about Joe is appropriate: a nationally significant coaching record; his influence as a teacher and coach that touched thousands; a positive, accomplished, and exemplary life; and, the fact that he is in the Newark and New Jersey sports halls of fame.

Joe's life spanned the two coasts of the continent. The irony is that many on the West Coast knew little about his East Coast accomplishments and vice versa. Joe made a tremendous impact on so many young men in New Jersey and Oregon, with feats familiar to the children and grandchildren of those who knew him. Numerous disciples in the coaching ranks found a role model in Joe for their chosen professions. Surely this is a man who left his mark on sports, enriched schools, and changed young lives. In researching Joe, it is surprising how little was known about him despite the presence of significant Oregon material.

Would Joe have garnered more attention if he had gone to the pros as his former New Jersey coaching colleague, Vince Lombardi did? Did the parade pass Joe by, or was there something else to this gentle but powerful man who was never one to reveal much of himself, even to those who seemed to know him?

Conflicting accounts of Joe's life and career create a biographer's challenge in separating facts and fables. Since he is of legendary proportions, there are many stories, not all verifiable. Source material from his Oregon years abounds, but there is not as much on his Newark career. The legendary tales were many, but the facts few! Who was this man? Where did he come from? How did he get here? If he was so good, why did he stay?

Much of Joe's stature is derived from his baseball and football coaching career at St. Benedict's Prep in Newark, NJ. What many do not realize is that Joe was a successful college coach at his alma mater, Mt. Angel College, in St. Benedict, OR. Before its destruction, Joe was the athletic director and head coach in football, basketball, and baseball. Afterwards, Joe was the head women's basketball coach at Mt. Angel Academy and Normal School in Mt. Angel, OR. With so many career head-coaching games, it is important to put Joe's record into perspective. Thus, Joe's career head-coaching record at Mt. Angel College from September, 1922 through June, 1926 is approximated as follows:

	W	L	T
Football	17	9	1
Basketball	48	12	0
Baseball	36	18	0 (54 games played, assuming he won at least two-thirds)
TOTAL	101	39	1

When Joe's St. Benedict's Prep career-record is combined with his Mt. Angel College and Mt. Angel Academy and Normal School career-records, results are reckoned as follows:

	W	L	T
Mt. Angel College	101	39	1
Mt. Angel Academy and Normal School	10	1	0
St. Benedict's Prep	793	202	18
TOTAL	904	242	19

Data compiled from yearbooks, student newspapers, and Joe's notes on schedules appear in the Appendices, but vary with several published career totals of wins, losses, and ties that appeared after Joe's death. The author does not wish to diminish Joe's record; but rather to present it as factually as possible.

Joe told a former player, John Thomas, that "sports publicity is like perfume; it should be sniffed and never inhaled."[1] Self-promotion was not Joe's style, and by today's standards, he was old-fashioned, and possibly repelled news reporters. Nevertheless, the impressive records stand. Thanks to two Newark reporters, Lloyde S. Glicken of the *Star-Ledger* and Paul Horowitz of the defunct *Evening News*, there are excellent stories on which to base research. Horowitz, in particular, discussed Joe's coaching style insightfully.

> As a school sports reporter in the Depression years of the 1930s, I came to know the man with the booming voice, Kasberger, best among St. Benedict's coaches. Nicknamed Oregon Joe, Kasberger was an extraordinary man who had a profound effect upon the athletes he coached. He never used profanity, nor did he smoke or drink. He was a stern disciplinarian, yet a considerate coach.

As an early observer of Joe, Horowitz is important in putting his record into a local perspective. Horowitz saw and compared the many football teams observed over his career, and concluded after Joe's death that:

> ... some of the St. Benedict's teams I saw in the '30s were as good or better than Bill Foley's contemporary teams at Bloomfield High School – and they were the best high schools in New Jersey scholastic history.[2]

Joe's baseball and football teams were dynasties in New Jersey, affording him fame in the New York and Philadelphia metropolitan areas. His national prominence is significant, also, but obscure. In 1988, Bruce L. Howard, director of publications and communications for the National Federation of State High School Associations, placed Joe's coaching records on a national stage, by stating that St. Benedict's Prep's baseball 64-game win streak from 1946-50 "is tied for fourth on the all-time list," ranking behind the following schools: "Briarwood Archbishop Molloy, New York, 68 (1963-66); Oklahoma City Capitol Hill, Oklahoma, 66 (1952-54), and Waxahachie, Texas, 65 (1924-27)."

For career baseball wins, Howard wrote that Joe's 610 victories rank him fourth on the all-time list, with the national record held by Vince Meyer with 1,105 from 1935 to 1981. For Joe's combined career baseball and football records, Howard replied as follows.

We do not keep any combined-sport coaching records, so I do not know how his 799-202-18 overall record ranks. The 207 football victories does not rank in the top 10, which is as deep as we go in any category.[3]

If there were combined records, nationally, it is doubtful there would be many coaches in Joe's select company. Similarly, in New Jersey it is unlikely that any other coach has his combined career baseball and football records, despite superior football records. Emphasizing Joe's great St. Benedict's Prep record are the prep school and college freshman and junior varsity teams that he faced. It is unlikely that coaches ranked ahead of Joe faced this calibre of competition.

For Joe, winning or losing was not as important as sportsmanship. Yet, his job as a coach and athletic director was to win. How was he able to balance these objectives? Joe's career-successes raise questions about his personality and background. What made him the winner that he was? Also, what kept Joe going for so long? Was he pursuing something that only he understood?

At St. Benedict's Prep, Joe's competition had great variation, ranging from college junior-varsity and freshman teams, to prep schools with postgraduate players, to conventional high schools. Joe was blessed with talented and motivated student-athletes who allowed him to implement his coaching philosophy with great results in many eras and under different conditions. Some changes that Joe faced were subtle, while others were profound, yet all appear to have been taken in stride. The younger reader, who did not know Joe, must understand the milieu in which he performed. Thus, the stability that Joe created seems very important in understanding him. Also fascinating about Joe were his mannerisms, and ways of doing things, all part of the legend.

Returning home each summer gave Joe a chance to maintain youthful and early coaching-career relationships. How Joe is remembered in Oregon, therefore, is as important as how he is remembered in Newark. In Oregon, however, Joe's lasting impression was as a Mt. Angel College and Oregon State University athletic star. Joe never stopped being an Oregonian, even in Newark, which made him alluring to those who encountered him.

Joe's life span saw him experience many major events that marked the period. He arrived too late to be a "pioneer" on the Oregon Trail, but he was an early sports pioneer as an all-around student-athlete, before becoming a successful coach. Joe was unusual in that while others went West to pursue dreams, he went East and found his fame. In its most basic version, Joe's life begins and ends in The Dalles, OR. In between there were several stops that must be recognized to better understand him as a developing coach.

In today's world of tarnished sports celebrities, Joe may provide a reminder of what sports should be. Perhaps this research will convince Oregonians that their native son's glory is augmented by his East Coast performance. With renewed interest and a fresh look, "Oregon Joe" may achieve a hall of fame selection in Oregon when the facts are better known.

ACKNOWLEDGEMENTS

Thanks are owed a multitude of people responsible for this book. Over the years that went into its research and writing, many friendships have blossomed. An alphabetical list of nearly one-hundred and fifty people with whom I have communicated about Joe Kasberger follows. All of the following have contributed something and they deserve immense thanks for their time and effort.

John M. Allen, Alan Archambault, Dawn Barron, John F. Bateman, Ph.D., Joyce Baudenstill, Bill Bennett, Pat Bernard, Dinesh Bhatt, Bill Blauvelt, Ernest Ben Blood, Matthew Bolger, Jim Booth, Lorenzo Bouie, Robert Buob, Patricia Brandt, Robert Braun, John Brookhouse, Steve Bungum, Rt. Rev. Martin Burne, O.S.B., Anthony Candelmo, Peter Carlesimo, Ruth Cavallaro, Mary Jane Cedar Face, James P. Clark, Rt. Rev. Brian Clarke, O.S.B., Gerald Clarke, Carl Cluff, Kevin Colley, Frank Cosentino, Charles Cummings, Karen Cummings, Rev. Augustine Curley, O.S.B., John Dalton, Sharla Davis, Hugh Devore, Sister Alberta Dieker, O.S.B, Bob DiQuollo, Harry Durkin, George Edmonston, Lorna Elliott, Joshua Ellison, George Enderle, Marilyn Gronewald Ericksen, Rev. Hugh Feiss, O.S.B., David Fenk, Rev. Jerome Fitzpatrick, O.S.B., Anthony Fraiola, Jerry Froelich, Gilbert Gaul, Lloyde Glicken, Mary Grant, John Grembowiec, Joe Grum, Christine Harris, Holly Hazwell, Betty Hellberg, Joseph P. Hellberg, Wiles Hellock, Ayne Helwig, Alfred Helwig, Alfred Helwig, M.D., Gilbert Hewson, Charlotte Hook, Bruce Howard, Rev. Theodore Howarth, O.S.B., Roger Hull, Robert M. Huntington, Ph.D., William Jamieson, Bob Jenny, William Johnston, Pam Jones, Anthony Joyce, Diane Joyce, Edward Joyce, Elizabeth Joyce, Jeremy Joyce, Julia Joyce, Rory Joyce, Jennifer Kasberger, Josephine Kasberger, Sister Rosemarie Kasper, S.N.J.M., Frank Kern, George Koeck, Peter Kowalski, Charles Lamb, Rebecca Landis, Harriet Langfeldt, Rev. Edwin Leahy, O.S.B., Vince Liddy, Jay Locey, Richard Lorenzo, Marguerite L. Mount Loretangeli, Terence Loughery, Sandy Macomber, Susan McGonigal, Chris McKinley, Frank McKinley, John McKinley, Bernard McTigue, David Ment, M. Claire Milbauer, Frank Milbauer, Jr., Helen Mondell, Virginia Moore, Harold Morgan, Rosemary Morgan, Bill Murray, Richard Nazareta, Elizabeth Nielsen, Francis O'Brien, Kathleen Milbauer O'Hare, Paul Olsen, Rob Pasquinucci, Michael Petriella, M.D., Alan Pfeifer, Rev. Martin Pollard, O.S.B., Andrew Purcell, Walter D. Ray, Al Reinoso, Bill Richardson, Laurie Rogerson, Rich Rosenthal, Marilyn Roth, Bernard (Bud) Sandoz, Charles Sandoz, Goldie Sandoz, Jim Sandoz, Jim Scarpone, Eugene Schiller, Christopher Seelen, Ben Scotti, Fred Scotti, Tony Scotti, Connie Shrope, Rev. Edmund Smith, O.S.B., Adam Spiegel, Scott Spiegelberg, Bill Steinman, Edward Stiso, Msgr. William Stone, Jenny Thomas, John F. Thomas, Joseph R. Thomas, Paul Thornton, Bruce Thorson, Rev. Boniface Treanor, O.S.B., Rev. Benedict Tyler, O.S.B., Cliff Voliva, Julia Wallace, Vincent Walsh, Rev. Joe Walter, S.J., William Wassersug, Rt. Rev. Joseph Wood, O.S.B.

From among the aforementioned, several valuable textual and photo contributions were made. Others proofed rough, early versions of Joe's story as it unfolded. Previously unpublished text was provided by Claire Milbauer, Bud Sandoz, John Bateman, Ph.D., Kathleen O'Hare Milbauer, Frank Milbauer, Jr., Christopher Seelen, Michael Petriella, M.D., Ben Scotti, Bill Murray, Robert M. Huntington, Ph.D., Marilyn Gronewald Ericksen, Msgr. William Stone, John Thomas, Joe and Betty Hellberg, Joe Thomas, John Allen, Rev. Jerome Fitzpatrick, O.S.B., Rt. Rev. Martin Burne, O.S.B., George Koeck, Tony Fraiola, John Brookhouse, Rev. Martin Pollard, O.S.B., Joe Grum, and Patricia Brandt.

Previously published material has come from many institutional resources thanks to archivists, librarians, and others. They include: Elizabeth Nielsen, Oregon State University Archives; Rev. Hugh Feiss, O.S.B., Mt. Angel Abbey Archives; Rev. Augustine Curley, O.S.B., Newark Abbey/St. Benedict's Prep Archives; Charles Lamb and Kevin Colley, University of Notre Dame Archives; Cliff Voliva, Paul Olsen, and Jim Booth, Willamette University; Rich Rosenthal and Mary Jane Cedar Face, Southern Oregon State College; Alan Archambault, Fort Lewis Military Museum; Lorna Elliott, The Dalles-Wasco County Library; Lorenzo Bouie, US Army Records Center; Sister Alberta Dieker, O.S.B., Queen of Angels Monastery, Mary Grant, Archdiocese of Portland; Sister Rosemarie Kasper, S.N.J.M., Sisters of The Holy Names; Steve Bungum, The Dalles HS; Marguerite Mount Loretangeli, Bordentown, NJ Historical Society; Frank Kern, San Diego Hall of Champions; Joyce Baudenstill and Rob Pasquinucci, Phi Delta Theta Fraternity; Susan McGonigal, Notre Dame Sports Information; Pam Jones, Mississippi State University Sports Information; David Ment, Holly Hazwell, Bill Steinman, and Dinesh Bhatt, all of Columbia University; Laurie Rogerson and Sandy Macomber, the *Oregonian*. Notre Dame student, Walter D. Ray, is especially thanked for finding elusive correspondence between Joe and Knute Rockne, as well as other Rockne correspondence, to answer many questions about Joe's Notre Dame experience.

Providing early review and comment after reading rough text that was compiled from the research findings were the following: Julia Joyce, Edward Joyce, John Grembowiec, Helen Mondell, Liz Joyce, Jeremy Joyce, and many of the contributors enumerated above. Initial editing and organizing of the material was done by my sister, Diane Joyce Cogan.

Reproducing splendid photos and text editing have been performed by my wife, Rory Morgan Joyce. Printing technology is often beyond my comprehension, but she made me a believer with a suggestion to include as many photos as possible to make Joe's story come alive. Rory's employers, Jeanne and Joe Samuels of Herald Publishing Company are deeply thanked for use of their state-of-the-art computer equipment, which made an idea a reality.

Finally, my editor, Robert M. (Robin) Huntington, Ph.D. was there when I needed help in finalizing good research material into this final draft. It was not easy to plow through a large amount of rough material but he did, and I am grateful for his time, effort, and expertise. Any errors of omission or commission are solely those of the author. In the pages that follow, Joe's life is presented to the extent it has been revealed by those acknowledged here.

I. JOE KASBERGER'S EARLY YEARS

A Prophecy Deferred

Joe's roots in The Dalles, Oregon were deep. Except for two summers, Joe is thought to have been in The Dalles for at least a part of every year in his life. You could take Joe out of The Dalles, but you could never take The Dalles out of Joe. Since The Dalles is so significant in Joe's life, its influences merit close scrutiny. They shaped Joe for the road of life that he journeyed, as the place of initial departure and of final return.

The Dalles, Oregon

Joseph Michael Kasberger's home town changed since its founding a half century earlier, becoming more civilized than the frontier outpost that some might envision. Yet The Dalles in 1896 was not too far removed from its earliest days, with a pioneer spirit and rugged individualism to dominate the town's personality. These traits were required by those who settled the West. To succeed, despite the hardships encountered on the trail west, required physical and emotional strength. While the trail west was difficult in its own right, surviving upon arrival was no mean feat. There were no guarantees of success and happiness, only the hope of a better life. The children of these courageous men and women were reared with a full understanding of their heritage.

The Dalles is a river town on the Columbia River, about 85 miles east of Portland. Its history is as colorful as the subject of this research. Well before the Louisiana Purchase, the town's site was important to the native population. Native Americans lived on the banks of the bountiful and scenic Columbia River that separates Oregon from Washington. The natural beauty surrounding The Dalles remains relatively similar to its virgin origins. Located 35 miles northeast of Mount Hood, The Dalles is blessed with spectacular scenery. Yet, its location certainly could be described as transitional, because to the east one finds a very different climate that does not support the lush vegetation of the state's western side. The modest development of the town today reflects a delicate balance. On one hand there is a busy, but small, city that meets commercial, agricultural, and industrial needs. Noteworthy today are irrigated cherry orchards, and beyond them "dry" wheat ranches, that surround The Dalles.[1] Juxtaposed to this economic imperative is a reverence for the land that supports the lifestyle there.

President Thomas Jefferson purchased the Louisiana Territory from Napoleon of France for $15,000,000 in 1803, and immediately sent Lewis and Clark to explore the new acquisition. By Oct. 1805, these explorers were reported to have camped at Rock Fort in what is now The Dalles. The name "The Dalles" was derived from the French, loosely translated as "the narrows," a term used by explorers.[2]

The War of 1812 raised the issue of how the United States and England should divide the Pacific Northwest Territories. The Dalles' strategic military location was a major consideration in its development. In 1818, a joint occupation agreement between the United States and England went into effect, but failed to halt trade competition. Violence erupted over the lucrative fur trade with the Native Americans. From 1830-35, disease swept The Dalles and killed most of the remaining Native Americans downstream. With the diminished presence of Native Americans, settlement of the area by whites was more feasible.[3]

Religious groups were important in the early years of Oregon and The Dalles. In 1834, Oregon's capital city, Salem, was settled by Rev. Jason Lee and a small group of Methodist missionaries. They founded the Oregon Institute, now Willamette University, that is renowned as the oldest institution of higher learning in the West. In 1838, Rev. Daniel Lee founded the Methodist Church's Wascopum Mission. It was the first white settlement in the Columbia River Gorge, not far from The Dalles.[4]

By 1842 immigration to Oregon began from Independence, MO nearly 2,000 miles away, bringing 800 settlers to The Dalles in wagon trains over the Oregon Trail. Tensions between Native Americans and the new settlers resulted in the Whitman Mission Massacre, in 1847, about 120 miles from The Dalles. By 1848 the United States established the Oregon Territory, and, the remaining Native Americans signed peace treaties, that led to their great disadvantage. Unsurprisingly, there was a treaty violation in the mid-1850s, leading to the Yakima War and more bloodshed. After hostilities ended, The Dalles settlement was one of the largest in the Northwest because of the military presence.[5]

In 1850 the United States government enacted the Donation Land Act to promote settlement in the Oregon Territory. The government gave 320 acres of land to white males brave enough to make the trip. The first steamboat appeared on the Columbia River at about this time, making the trip from The Dalles safer and easier for settlers intent on proceeding to the Willamette River valley. On March 30, 1850 a regiment of Army regulars came from Fort Vancouver, directly across the Columbia River from Portland, to establish Camp Drum. This ten-square-mile military reservation was located at what is now The Dalles. The troops occupied the abandoned Methodist settlement and the Catholic mission that remained. In 1853 Camp Drum became known as Fort Dalles.[6]

Stability provided by the troops led to the establishment of Wasco County, Oregon Territories, the largest county ever created in the United States. With 130,000 square miles, it extended from Oregon into Idaho, Montana, and Wyoming. By 1856 Fort Dalles had emerged as the Wasco County seat of government, and as a city called The Dalles. In 1859 Oregon became a state and Wasco County was reduced in size, with new boundaries extending from the Idaho border to the east, and to the crest of the Cascade Mountains to the west. This Wasco County was later divided to form 17 Oregon Counties.[7]

Development in The Dalles was boosted in 1860 by gold discoveries in Eastern Oregon and Idaho. The economic boom was derived from The Dalles' location as an outfitting center and jumping-off point for miners. With economic prosperity came the need for schools to educate the settlers' children. By 1880 the Oregon Railway and Navigation Company began operating a railway in the Columbia River Gorge, establishing links with transcontinental railroads. Rail transportation provided a way to obtain needed supplies and a way to sell produce in distant markets. Wheat emerged as a major cash crop, then cattle and sheep.[8] It is at this point in the early 1880s that Joe's father, John Kasberger, arrived in the United States.

The Kasberger Family

John Kasberger, Joe's father, was born in 1858 and his mother, Anna Linsmeier Kasberger, was born in 1859. The Kasberger family's Bavarian roots were in Rabinstein bei Swiezel (River Swiezel), a small village in the Black Forest region. When and where they were married is not known. Wars and issues of German unification created economic problems that made migration to America attractive. John Kasberger is believed to have served in the military as a young man but became disenchanted. Thus his motivation to come to America is seen as part of the great exodus from Germany that began in the 1830s.[9]

John Kasberger arrived in the United States through New York City and immediately headed west. En route, he visited one of his two sisters in Traverse City, MI. It is believed that John came to The Dalles via Omaha, NB, where the Union Pacific Railroad had its headquarters. Presumably John Kasberger was hired in Omaha and sent to The Dalles as a new employee in 1885. Once John was settled, he sent for his wife and son, William, still in Bavaria, to join him.[10]

The Kasberger family was reunited in the mid-1880s and a second son, John, Jr., was born in 1888. The Kasbergers occupied temporary housing until their permanent homestead at 917 West Tenth Street in The Dalles was constructed. A third son, George, was born in 1889. The Kasbergers' first daughter, Anna, was born in 1892. She was followed by another son, Philip, in 1894. Joseph M. Kasberger was born on January 31, 1896, probably at home. The Kasbergers' fifth son, Max, followed in 1897. In 1899, a second daughter, Adelaide (Audie), arrived to complete the family. Another child, Frank, was born in 1902, but died five months after birth. [11]

The Kasberger residence was described as a European farm brought to the new country. The home had five bedrooms and was situated on one-half city block. This comprised approximately five lots of 5,000 square feet each, or a little more than one-half acre in size. Located on this site was a

Joe's grandparents and two aunts. The photo was probably taken in Bavaria.

mix of agricultural enterprises to insure food for the family. By one account, the Kasberger home had the following features:

> a barn, a one or two lot pasture to put the cow, a grainary, a chicken-house, a pigeon pen, a water well, a vegetable garden, fruit trees, and eventually a garage.[12]

Joe's father, John Kasberger, shortly after his arrival in The Dalles.

Truly, this German immigrant family was prepared for all eventualities. They had settled in the American West, but brought a lifestyle with them – "self-sufficiency moved from Europe to The Dalles." Despite farm stories associated with the legendary Joe, the Kasbergers were not a farming family *per se*. There were lots of farms in and around The Dalles. Thus, the Kasberger children took their work ethic and agricultural skills, learned at home, to earn money through farm work. In reality, however, the Kasbergers were a part of the Union Pacific railroad family. It is in this milieu that the son of a railroad man became associated with farming.[13]

John Kasberger worked as a hostler, servicing locomotives on the turntables of The Dalles' railyards. Union Pacific was an important employer in The Dalles economy, and Joe's father worked in their railroad shops until his retirement. He had an important job that required many hours to discharge his responsibilities, seven days a week. It was only on Sunday that he had time for relaxation for a few hours. On that weekly occasion, he got off two hours early. The Kasberger children, therefore, were depended upon to perform chores around the house. With such a

Joe's mother, Anna Linsmeier Kasberger, probably before leaving Germany for America.

large family, frugality was important and stressed to the children at an early age. Union Pacific paid its employees twice a month. For Anna Kasberger, the day after payday meant a trip to town to buy what was not grown at home.[14]

The Pacific Northwest presents a paradox of beauty, vastness, and remoteness. It is this physical splendor that makes it so important in American folklore. As

The Kasberger home in The Dalles as it looked when Joe was young.

the new world for an immigrant family, The Dalles was very different from East Coast "melting pot" cities as a home to European settlers. Even the much larger Oregon city of Portland, at that time, "retained many characteristics of the western frontier."[15] The remoteness and lower density of The Dalles, however, presented unique challenges to immigrants. There were no easy solutions for adapting in the new world, but the Kasbergers learned quickly about life in the American West. Their story of assimilation, while retaining their heritage, is seen in the development of their children.

The Dalles railroad yard roundtable.

Religion played a major role in Kasberger family life. Contrary to some accounts, Joe

Memorial Day Parade on Second Street in The Dalles.

came from a devoutly Roman Catholic background. With a strong family orientation in this religious tradition, Joe's adherence to his family's faith is not surprising, and all of the Kasberger children remained Catholics as adults. Their

Joe as a child.

faith was known to have "the strength of steel throughout their lives but they never spoke of it. There also was a vague and unspoken disapproval of anyone who was not Catholic." Joe as an adult, however, is not known to have had any prejudice against non-Catholics.[16]

Culturally, it can be argued that the Kasberger household was typically German. Unsurprisingly, therefore, rules were learned early in life and were difficult to change, even as children became older and more independent. Because of the family size and household responsibilities, behavior and lifestyle patterns were codified. By one account, rules of the

Kasberger household were "unstated but rigidly adhered to." Joe once remarked that "when he was growing up he always went to bed at 8 o'clock." Even as an adult, he went to bed around 8 o'clock: "it may not have been exactly that time but it was very early, and he never saw any reason to change it."[17]

Large households need schedules, not only for sleep and work, but also eating. Food preparation was a major chore for Anna Kasberger who was very organized in managing the Kasberger home. Her household "had a regularity to it the like of which I've never observed anywhere else," according to one account. With so many mouths to feed, she knew what her family liked. She could not accommodate every taste, but they knew what to expect on a given day. "Bread was made on Monday for the week's use, what had not been used by the following Sunday was made into German Potato Dumplings." [18]

John Kasberger's work schedule dictated when meals were served. The dinner meal was likely the only time his brood could be assembled to discuss family matters. The Sunday dinner was the highlight of the week, a tradition "that lasted until the last of the Kasberger children were dead and gone." This meal consisted of "potato dumplings, sauerkraut, pork roast and pickled beets" in vast quantities. In later years there was great regularity in the Kasberger household that centered on the Sunday dinner meal.

> Even if those children had their own homes they still returned on Sundays noon or evening to participate in that repast. Weekdays dinner was at noon, Sundays dinner was at 1:00; holidays, dinner was at 2:00, count on it.[19]

In such a household it is unsurprising that none of the Kasbergers liked change. They lived at a time that allowed them to engage in predictable behavior as a family unit. There were neighbors, but in the Kasberger family's early years, the parents shaped their children with few distractions from outside influences.

It is not known whether John and Anna Kasberger were bilingual prior to leaving Germany. As new immigrants, however, the language spoken in the Kasberger household was important. The language barrier may have created many problems initially, but had to be overcome for the family to succeed. John Kasberger must have become bilingual very early in his Union Pacific career. Anna Kasberger may have not been under the same pressure as her husband to learn English. She ventured from her home rarely, yet had to shop and communicate in English to some extent.

The Kasberger children grew up speaking both German and English. What may be surprising to some is that Joe "could speak German as well as he could speak English." This bilingual ability was shared by Joe's siblings. Because of the family's fluency in two languages, communication among them was never a problem. They had a family-decision rule, however, regarding the language spoken. "At home the language was German unless there were a non-German-speaking guest, then it was English." When the Kasberger family was away from home, "the spoken language was English." The language skills of the family were remarkable for their near perfection in English. It is recalled by Joe's nephew, Bud Sandoz, that "none of them, not even my grandfather, spoke English with any trace of a German accent." Also impressive was how the Kasberger children retained this ability. After John and Anna were dead, "they seldom spoke German but when it seemed appropriate to do so, they seemed not to have forgotten any of it."[20]

A traditional skill associated with Germans had a place of honor in the Kasberger household: glass blowing. Apparently in Bavaria, John Kasberger, Sr.'s father was a glass blower, a common craft in that part of the old country. The Dalles branch of the Kasberger family occasionally received "different little hand-tooled glass items [that] were sent from Germany." These glass works of art were "treasured items kept in the front room and were dusted and cleaned on a weekly basis." None of the Kasbergers were known to have practiced glass blowing in The Dalles.[21]

The Kasberger family in The Dalles maintained contact with their German relatives until the late 1940s. Thus, the young Kasberger family grew with a very strong sense of their heritage from the old world. New relationships were formed as children left the nest and became Americanized, retaining a very strong sense of family.

Did Joe grow up in a picture-postcard environment of scenic beauty? Was The Dalles a town that most of Joe's acquaintances from elsewhere would envy? Or, was his young life boringly tedious and hard with many chores. Moreover, was the atmosphere of The Dalles suffocating? The town's small size and lack of diversity could be perceived as presenting drawbacks by today's standards. What was life like for Joe in The Dalles at that time? There are no known

Joe as a young boy.

Kasberger diaries for this period, but insights recorded about Joe's contemporary, Linus Pauling, might help. Pauling was born a few years after Joe, in Condon, OR, approximately eighty miles southeast of The Dalles.

One of Pauling's biographers, David Newton, observed that "Condon is still a remote outpost with a population of less than 1,000." While The Dalles was two and one-half times larger than Condon in Joe's youth, Newton's description of life in Condon is insightful. It was characterized as being "probably much like what most young boys dream of: lots of free time, lots of outdoor life, and lots of sports."[22]

Another Pauling biographer, Anthony Serafini, provided a description that might assist in understanding Joe's development as a youth. Oregon's "remoteness in the early days of the century, coupled with its lack of entertainment . . . drove some to a lifetime affair with learning." [23]

Experiences outside the family are inevitable for children as they mature. In The Dalles, there were people from different ethnic groups and religions, as well as children whose fathers did not work for Union Pacific. Serafini described Oregon, then, as a place of great attraction for many young families. The common bond in most cases was that they sought the same opportunity as the

Kasbergers. Oregon was not a homogeneous environment and other fathers would "work on the cattle drives, build bridges and roads, and farm the rich soil."[24] Thus, the Kasberger children came to know the children of many backgrounds.

Probably, Joe led the life of most boys of that place and time. He performed chores that were not only work but also part of his education. He learned how to grow plants and raise animals. The Kasbergers' little homestead was not for show, but for food production. Also, he learned carpentry and how to play sports. One of the advantages of a large family was always having someone to play with. Naturally there were priorities, and sports, for Joe, came after other responsibilities were met.

Outside the home and neighborhood, the Kasberger children next encountered the church in their development. In The Dalles, St. Peter's Church was a splendid edifice, acclaimed for its gothic design. More important than its beauty was its role in serving Catholics from a variety of ethnic backgrounds, and its pastor did not have an easy job. It was, however, the focal point of the Catholic community in and around The Dalles. St. Peter's Church is partially responsible for Joe's strong Catholic convictions at an early age.

Monsignor William Stone's book, *The Cross in the Middle of Nowhere*, provides an exceptional view of Catholicism in Oregon and The Dalles. The realities of the immigrant Catholic experience, that the Kasberger family members surely shared as devout Catholics, are presented richly. For German Catholic immigrants, the Church was a stabilizing force. The faith and its traditions were mainstays for the Kasbergers. Its beliefs were a coherent tie to the life they left behind in Europe and bonded the Kasbergers with other German Catholics in and around The Dalles. Also, it introduced them to Catholic immigrants of different lands and cultures. The Catholic Church and its tradition of education shaped Joe early in life and remained with him always.

Saint Peter's Church

St. Peter's Parish in The Dalles had its origins as a mission founded in 1848 by Rev. L. Rousseau. In 1851, Fr. Toussaint Mesplie became the pastor, described as "one of the long line of 'characters' to labor in the Lord's vineyard in Eastern Oregon during the ensuing century and a half." Born in France in 1824, Fr. Mesplie "joined the Archdiocese of Oregon City [now Portland] as a cleric in 1847." Fr. Mesplie "completed his studies for the priesthood with the Archbishop at St. Paul (Oregon) and was ordained in 1850."[25]

Population growth in The Dalles required facilities to serve the faithful. Fr. Mesplie built two churches during his tenure: "one to replace the log structure which had burned down, and a second to accommodate its growing flock." It was in 1862 that Fr. Mesplie moved the church from the parish's original site, "west of the Fort." The new site was smaller, but had the advantage of being "near the Columbia River and closer to the center of the growing city." As a communicator, Fr. Mesplie proved to be very resourceful with his flock of many tongues.

At first he was unable to preach in English (all entries in the parish records were in French!) but he soon learned to do so under the tutelage of a young Irishman named John Halligan. He evidently knew how to communicate with the Indians whose camps were located at Celilo Falls, a few miles east of The Dalles, a prime fishing ground for tribes of the area. In his parish census of 1855 he counted 117 white people and 300 Indians in his charge.

Fr. Mesplie's stewardship of St. Peter's ended in 1863 when "Archbishop Blanchet transferred him to the Boise Basin to work among the gold miners . . . ."[26]

Presumably, all of the Kasberger children, except Willie, were baptized at St. Peter's Church. In a religiously mixed environment, such as The Dalles, with new arrivals from domestic and foreign locations, religious leadership was not an easy task. For the German Catholic families, their life was enhanced by Fr. Alphonse Bronsgeest, who, on July 14, 1881, "was transferred from Canyon City to The Dalles," to begin a stewardship of nearly four decades. A native of

Germany, Fr. Alphonse studied theology "at Innsbruck and the American College at the University of Louvain, in Belgium." As with his predecessor, Fr. Alphonse "was ordained for the Archdiocese of Oregon City on March 12, 1876." [27]

His first position, after ordination, was as the "assistant pastor at the Cathedral," for a brief period. It was not long before "he was appointed pastor of Canyon City in 1877." Fr. Alphonse was then transferred to The Dalles in 1881. As pastor of St. Peter's Church, he had

The oldest St. Peter's Church and St. Mary's Academy in the late 1800s.

additional duties beyond those concerning the flock located in the town. Resident pastors in several Oregon locations, besides The Dalles, served the outlying areas. For Fr. Alphonse, therefore, his parish was "throughout Eastern Oregon, so that, in effect, Bronsgeest's parish extended east as far as Condon and south to the Bend-Prineville area." In "regular visits to the interior," Fr. Alphonse travelled in a "two-horse buggy." When he arrrived at these remote outposts, "he offered Mass at ranch homes in places such as Shaniko, Antelope, Twickenham, Madras, Prineville and Bend." [28]

Thus, it was Fr. Alphonse's "custom to notify his parishioners in advance of his coming, and they responded by gathering for Mass and catechetical instruction." As technology evolved, he switched from horse and buggy to an automobile. Fr. Alphonse is distinct for being "one of the first citizens of The Dalles to own an automobile, an Apperson 'Jackrabbit.'" When he was not serving in a remote location, he "delighted in showing off the speed and maneuverability of his horseless carriage.'" Among his passengers in The Dalles were "parishioners and students of St. Mary's Academy," who frequently accompanied him "as he 'sped' to respond to sick calls in the environs of the City."[29]

Fr. Bronsgeest's building plans for a new St. Peter's Church reflected the continuing population growth experienced in The Dalles. His plans, however, were not easily implemented. At about this time Fr. Alphonse was made a monsignor for his work at St. Peter's and in eastern Oregon, but he encountered new challenges. The first was the devastating fire of 1891, "which destroyed much of The Dalles," and postponed "plans to build a new church." The church in use at that time, "the third in the history of the parish," was three decades old and in poor condition. Other problems emerged after a building committee, composed of "Max Vogt, Ed Fitzgerald and Jacob Fritz," began planning the new structure. The economic losses from the fire were soon compounded by two economic calamities. A depression resulting "from the removal of Union Pacific railroad shops, along with a severe crop failure, put a stop to the planning."[30]

The older St. Peter's Church extant in The Dalles, completed in the late 1890s.

After six years, and numerous delays, Fr. Bronsgeest's hopes were finally realized when "the cornerstone of the fourth church in The Dalles was laid by Archbishop Gross, July 29, 1897." The long-awaited church was spectacular.

> Father Louis Verhaag, in his monthly publication, *Reminiscences and Current Topics,* wrote in March, 1898, 'The dedication of this beautiful new Catholic Church at The Dalles, the finest in the Archdiocese, will take place on the Feast of St. Patrick next. Plans for the church, a gothic structure with a soaring steeple which is visible from virtually every part of the city, were obtained by Henry Herbring from his native Westphalia, in Germany.'[31]

Views of Catholics in The Dalles were not always kind. Two newspapers, the *Oregonian* and the *Catholic Sentinel,* reported controversy involving the pastor of St. Peter's Church. There was "a running battle between Monsignor Bronsgeest and a lawyer in The Dalles, named Bronaugh, who was a candidate for District Attorney for Wasco County." As a voice for the Catholics, Msgr. Bronsgeest was articulate and effective in challenging Mr. Bronaugh's bigotry in a battle that was waged in the newspapers.[32]

It is not known whether Joe was an altar boy, nor is it known whether he received the Sacrament of Confirmation at St. Peter's Church.

Saint Mary's Academy

The relationship between St. Peter's Church and St. Mary's Academy appears to have been close in their dual role of serving Catholic youth in The Dalles. Until Joe entered St. Mary's Academy in The Dalles, probably in Sept. 1903, there is no documentation about him except his Birth and Baptismal records. Due to the historical significance of Joe's first alma mater, a closer look appears warranted at this venerable institution with its rich tradition.

In Aug. 19, 1864, St. Mary's Academy was established in The Dalles by the Holy Names Sisters of Canada with "143 students," presumably boys and girls, at an unspecified grade-level. In 1871 it occupied a new structure on "Third and Lincoln Streets" to house a larger student body. By 1884, "a larger brick structure was erected and completed," that served as a civic "landmark for seventy-eight years." The top floor "had dormitories for fifty students." St. Mary's Academy then became exclusively a girls school until 1887.[33]

While St. Mary's Academy narrowly missed the flames that destroyed much of The Dalles in 1891, there was no escaping the flood of 1894 that left more than five feet of water on the school's first floor. After the waters subsided, the hard work began. "It took days to scrape the wet mud from the walls, to repaint and refurbish the building." Yet, St. Mary's Academy survived as "Oregon's first private school east of the Cascades." In the late 1800s and early 1900s, boys attended the primary school until it reverted to "an all-girl school (high school) until 1931. In that year boys were admitted to the high school." Due to its evolving role, there is confusion about St. Mary's Academy's long history in The Dalles, serving varying compositions of students at the primary and secondary levels.[34]

When Joe Kasberger attended St. Mary's Academy, it was operated by the Sisters of the Holy Names of Jesus and Mary with Oregon province headquarters in Marylhurst, OR, a Portland suburb. Then, it was a private school, independent of the diocese and parish, with tuition payments, as the revenue source. During Joe's elementary-school career at this institution, the only thing known is that he graduated from the eighth grade in 1910. All of the Kasberger children attended St. Mary's Academy for their primary education. The Kasberger girls, however, stayed and attended the secondary school, as well. The options for high-school-age boys in The Dalles were not as broad, and contrary to later accounts, Joe was not able to receive his secondary education here, for this reason.[35]

The Dalles High School

The next stop for Joe was The Dalles High School (TDHS). One of Pauling's biographers, Anthony Serafini, was not impressed by Oregon's secondary schools of this era. He characterized the system, then, as "worth nearly nothing, at least as far as science was concerned."[36] Under the circumstances of Oregon's early history when there may have been more important priorities than public education, it would not be surprising if this criticism were at least partially correct. The "general education" offered by "most of the high schools" in Oregon probably satisfied the needs of that era. In fairness to TDHS, it should be noted that public high schools were in their adolescence as Joe began his studies.

After all, there were few Linus Paulings in Oregon, despite the fact that Condon has the distinction of having had two Nobel Prize winners come out of its schools. The other was W. P. Murphy, in 1934.[37] Thus, high-school mathematics was described as "rudimentary." For cerebral students, "often only a college would provide courses beyond basic algebra."[38] If TDHS did not offer much of an academic challenge, Joe appears to have

Amaton Field and campus of The Dalles High School 1917.

been involved with its extracurricular offerings as a senior. There is no documentation of any prior participation. This seems significant due to the legend surrounding Joe's athletic history.

As a senior at TDHS, Joe exhibited the potential that he would fulfill. The *Crimson and Gray* yearbook for the Class of 1914 at TDHS provides valuable

Joe's photo from The Dalles HS 1914 yearbook.

insights into Joe. There are two photos of Joe Kasberger, as his name appears, along with the following activities: "Commercial Course; President of Student Body '14; Baseball Team,'14; Track Team, '14, and Class Play." Also, there is the quotation: "I awoke one morning and found myself famous."[39] It is not known whether Joe is being quoted by the yearbook editor. Or, did the yearbook editor think that the quotation suited Joe? His election as student body president in 1914 appears significant to the extent that there were religious tensions in The Dalles at that time. Joe's election may be seen as a positive dismantling of a social barrier.

Joe's first documented coach at TDHS was Alvin Edward Gronewald, known as Allie by all who knew him. The relationship between player and coach is not known, but they were linked by their German heritage and love of sports. Not following the Roman Catholicism practiced by the Kasbergers, the Gronewalds were Methodists. Due to Allie Gronewald's role, it seems appropriate to learn more about him. Gronewald, as a TDHS coach and German teacher, may have been Joe's first mentor in the secular world. Documentation is clear that Gronewald coached the 1914 TDHS baseball team on which Joe played.

There is a notion, however, that Robert L. (Bob) Murray may have been Joe's first coach at TDHS, since he is thought by some to have been the coach of all TDHS teams at that time.

Alvin Edward Gronewald was born on Nov. 4, 1886 in Faribault, MN. His parents, Herman and Rosina, already had a large family of five children when he was born as an identical twin to brother, Almon John. The twins were known as Jack and Allie. The German-speaking family learned English from their children as they attended local schools in Faribault. Allie graduated in 1905 from Baldwin Wallace College in Berea, OH and came to Pendleton, OR as a teacher. In 1907, he began coaching and teaching German and math at TDHS. Since he spoke German fluently it is no surprise that he taught this subject as well as coached baseball in 1914. Allie coached the women's basketball team at TDHS after Joe's graduation.[40]

Allie Gronewald

In a story from the June 4, 1914 The Dalles *Weekly Chronicle* that follows, there is an accompanying list of players' batting averages for the season. The numbers suggest that Joe was not much of a hitter. Yet, the story reveals him to be a good pitcher, despite his inexperience in organized baseball. The story headline reads: "Game goes to Columbia U – High School Players Best Contest of Season But Lose Out 5 to 2." (Columbia University in Portland was a Roman Catholic institution that is now known as the University of Portland and should not be confused with Columbia University in New York City). The text follows for the first revealed reference to Joe as an athlete:

> The Dalles high school baseball team closed its season here Saturday afternoon with its best exhibition of the season. The locals held the interscholastic champion of Portland, Columbia university, to the small score of 5 to 2.

It is common to find high school teams playing college teams in Oregon at this time. It is possible that the Columbia University team from Portland may have been from the prep school located on the Columbia campus. The story continues:

> One Joe Kasberger was largely responsible for the excellent showing made by Gronewald's men. He heaved a great game, and with a little better support would have won the battle. Moreover, he fielded his position in spectacular style, and made one of the locals' three hits, his hard single to left scoring one of the two runs made by The Dalles. Philpot safely hit twice in two times up, batting 1000 [sic]. He and Kasberger made all the hits of the locals.

In the paragraph that follows to continue the story, Duffy may have been Joe's friend, Matt Duffy, who appears in Joe's personal photo album.

Gronewald's men made their two scores in the second inning. Wilson walked. Duffy reached first on a fielder's choice, Wilson dying at second. Duffy took second on an under-throw to first. Elton struck out. Kasberger then made his first trip to the plate with the result he singled sharply to left, scoring Duffy from second. Kasberger stole second. Tyler walked. Kasberger stole third and scored when the Columbia pitcher booted Lewis' swift grounder.

The yearbook reference to Joe as a track man may be due to the speed shown here.

Kasberger struck out eight Columbia stickers, three in the first inning, in one, two, three order, and he walked only two. Columbia's pitcher struck out five and walked three. The Portlanders made eight hits, a couple of the scratch order.

Joe in The Dalles High School *baseball uniform.*

Transportation was a major consideration in athletic competition, as noted for this game. "The game was called at the end of the seventh to allow the Columbia players to catch train 17, at 4:20." The story ended with rewards given to TDHS athletes:

Seward Philpot made the best batting average for the season, 429 [sic], and won the $5 pair of shoes which was the prize offered by Blunt & Cates to the high school player ending the season as the leading sticker. The batting averages of the players follow:

Player	Games	AB	Hits	Av.
Philpot	6	21	9	.439
Wilson	5	16	6	.375
Harriman	6	22	7	.318
Wetle	6	19	6	.316
Lewis	5	16	5	.313
Elton	4	16	3	.187
Kasberger	6	19	3	.158
Duffy	6	21	3	.143
Mohr	6	15	2	.133
Tyler	6	16	1	.063

The batting average of the team is .254.[41]

The next story about Joe appeared in the 1914 edition of TDHS yearbook, *Crimson and Gray*. It is another version of the TDHS versus Columbia University game. Under the heading "High School Athletics" appears the following story of the May 30, 1914 encounter between TDHS in the season's last game against "Columbia University the champion of Portland's interscholastic baseball league."

The Dalles boys played well and for the first four innings were in the lead 2 to 0. However upon seeing D.H.S. in the lead Columbia picked herself up and would not let our boys make a score while they made 5 runs.

Despite the loss, there seemed to be pleasure with the team's performance.

> The score 5 to 2 shows it was a fight from the first. Both teams played splendid ball. D.H.S. lost we were proud of the good showing made [sic]. When the Class of 1914 left it took with it three men from the baseball nine. Two are out-fielders. Donald Lewis and Chris Wetle, and the pitcher Joe Kasberger [sic]. A great deal of praise should be given the ball tosser for it is his first year on the team and he pitched as none other in H.S. could.[42]

Joe's pitching must have impressed this account's writer, and possibly others.

As Joe's senior year ended, it is fortunate that there are other accounts of his activities. Besides baseball, Joe became an actor. This story mentioning Joe comes from the June 11, 1914 edition of The Dalles *Weekly Chronicle* with headline "Seniors Ably Present 2 Plays – Fig Leaf Quartette Has To Dodge Lemons But Never Misses Note." The text follows regarding the second play in which Joe made his acting debut:

> The 'Sympathy orchestra' opened the ceremonies of the evening at the Vogt theatre Tuesday when the senior class gave its class play. The medley of sounds produced by the boys, although various and unique, provided vast amusement for the hundreds of people present.

Both plays were reported as "given under the able direction of C.Y. Lamb, and both were exceedingly well done." During the intermission between plays, there was a performance by the "Fig Leaf Quartette," whose role appears to have been that of comedians.

> The 'Fig Leaf quartette,' Rorick, Bettengin, Flynn, and Hostetler, showed good judgement in dodging lemons volleyed at them from the gallery and the members of the aggregation never missed a note during the ordeal and rendered two popular selections and responded to a hearty encore between the shows.

The grand finale for the evening included Joe Kasberger to conclude the story.

> The second play was entitled 'That Rascal Pat,' and Pat, as depicted by Chris Wetle, was certainly a rascal and it was demonstrated that 'no man can serve two masters' and get away with it successfully, unless he is an Irishman and his name is Pat. The play went with a snap and vim that showed thorough and careful training and the droll stunts pulled by Pat in a most original way 'brought down the house.' Major Puffjacket, the rich old uncle, (Joe Kasberger) objected to the attentions of Charles Livingston, (Donald Lewis) who was poor but ambitious, to his niece Laura (Anna Brookhouse) but the irresistible 'Pat,' assisted by Laura's maid, Nancy, (Gertrude Crabtree) blundered into a solution

of the troubles of the lovers.[43]

The following flowery account of the 1914 commencement ceremony from TDHS provides a splendid "slice of life" account of The Dalles and its inhabitants. The story from The Dalles *Weekly Chronicle* issue of June 18, 1914 is headlined: "Twenty-Six Seniors Honored With High School Diplomas – Vogt Theatre, Whose Stage Presents Unusually Pretty Scene, Is Packed With Parents And Friends of Graduates – D.V. Poling Delivers Splendid Address Of Encouragement And Advice To Class – Lillie Turner And Mae Garrett Earn Special Honors." The text follows:

Joe's 1914 graduation photo from The Dalles High School.

'The true purpose of education is to cherish and unfold the seed of immortality already sown within us; to develop, to the fullest extent, the capacities of every kind with which God who made us has endowed us.'

The story continues as follows one paragraph later.

The curtain never went up at the Vogt on a prettier scene than that of Friday evening. The graduates were seated in a large semi-circle, extending, in two rows, entirely across the stage. The young ladies were all gowned in white, and each had a large bouquet of red roses, the class flower, in her lap, effecting a charming scene. Across the front of the stage had been built a small white trellis which formed the background for red roses and greenery. A tennis net, covered with ivy extended across the back of the stage, and in the center of this very pretty drapery red roses, outlined the large figures – '1914.' The class had adopted green and white as colors.

The story continues with the names of the graduates in the Class of 1914.

Those who were honored with diplomas last night are Lewis Burlingame, Prudence Bayley, Erma Bennett, Fayne Bell, Anna Brookhouse, Edna Chrisman, Curtis L. Corum, Gertrude Crabtree, Ica [sic] Derthick, Wilma Donnell, Jennie Darnall, Walter Eaton, Mae Garrett, Grace Gavin, Helen Gray, Joseph Kasberger, Donald Lewis, Earl L. Mann, Rhuea [sic] Micklam, Irene Palmer, Ruby Powell, Lillie Turner, Loya Van Norden, Kathryn Ward, Chris Wetle, Gus Weigelt.[44]

The composition by gender of the graduating class, "one of the largest" in TDHS's brief history, appears interesting. The numerical disparity between boys and girls in 1914 has been explained by one observer as follows:

The boys, destined to be all-purpose ranch-men, cowboys, lumbermen, etc. quit school and went to work. The girls – mainly responsible for culture on the frontier – stayed in school and graduated. Only boys who somehow knew they were destined for 'higher things' finished high school.[45]

College academic scholarships were a welcome reward for promising students and their parents. The story continued with the two recipients in the Class of 1914, who "had earned the highest honors."

The student who completed the four-year course with the best standing is Lillie Turner, who attained the high marking of 92.8. She wins the Whitman college scholarship. The other girl given special honor is Mae Garrett, whose standing was 92.3, and her reward is the scholarship offered by Pacific university.

Lillie Turner delivered the first oration of the evening. Her effort was a most creditable one, on the subject of 'Purpose of Education.' A very forceful and well-delivered oration was that of Earl Mann on 'Remedial Loans.' Fayne Bell won unusual honor for a high school student when she gave her oration 'The cry of the Children.' She showed careful thought and study in preparation and her delivery was excellent.[46]

The story concludes by noting "a splendid address," given to the graduates by Rev. D.V. Poling of Portland. Daniel Poling was the former pastor of the Congregational church in The Dalles, recalled as "a much admired and loved Congregational minister."[47]

With Joe's graduation, there are no written accounts of his activities until the autumn of 1915. It is believed he remained in The Dalles and worked for a local farmer, Fred Wetle, whose brother Chris was a teammate and classmate. Also, Joe

Five Kasberger sons: John, Joe, Philip, Max and George, in the cabbage patch.

may have played baseball during the summer of 1914, or summers of 1914-15, for The Dalles town team, probably coached by Bob Murray.[48]

While in The Dalles, Joe had a chance to observe what was described as Bob Murray's greatest team. The 1914 football season at TDHS provided a valuable learning opportunity and entertainment for Joe as an interested alumnus with personal knowledge of the players. Only one player, Matt Duffy, appears to have been a close friend of Joe's, based upon photos in his personal album. An interesting aspect of the 1914 football team is the perceived mix of nationalities represented. Coach Murray's ability to develop and blend young talent may have been one of his strengths as a coach. This appears to be an opportune place to digress and provide some background material, since the 1914-15 school year at TDHS seems important.

The Dalles Sports Tradition

The history of The Dalles is enriched by an unusual document, without title or date. One of the best sentences states that: "The Dalles had a long athletic history if only someone would take the time and effort to ferrit [sic] it out." The Dalles, in fact, has a proud and rich sports tradition. This anonymously-written document provides historical insights about the sports history of The Dalles.

Edward Sharp remembers when athletic events were held on the old fair grounds between Kelley Avenue and G and 10 and 12 streets, in the 1880's, which included baseball, horse racing and some track events. Home town teams like the firemen against the United Workmen or the Moose against the Eagles drew the crowds. Elmer Bettengin's father Al used to tell of the Mexican Bull fights that were held at 4th & Liberty by the Mexican pack train operators to the mines in 1859 to 1862 every Sunday in good weather. This gory event was very popular in The Dalles in those early days, nearly as popular as the free-for-alls fought out in the saloons with sawdust floors to absorb the blood, in the early years of The Dalles. The Irish soldiers from Old Fort Dalles never needed any reasons for a fight – all they needed was an opportunity.[49]

As an important stop on the immigrants' road west, The Dalles was naturally exposed to sports developed in the East. Baseball and football, in particular, were quickly embraced. The first coach of baseball and football in The Dalles was Arthur Stubling, emerging in the 1890s "before athletics was taken up in schools to any great extent."[50] The prevailing view of sports in schools before the turn of the century appears to be one of skepticism.

It was thought in those days that you went to school to get 'something in your head' and if you wanted or needed exercise there was always plenty of wood to chop, gardens to hoe or other chores for the boy big enough to play football or baseball.[51]

Sports in The Dalles appear to have been kept in perspective despite their popularity. "Athletic events were left to Sunday picnics, fairs or special occasions, at least there was no money for schools to 'spend on such foolishness.'" [52] Times changed, however, and more organized sports emerged.

The evolution of athletics in The Dalles may have led to a backlash by some residents with arguments pro and con over this issue. The school system had the delicate responsibility of balancing the academic curriculum with extracurricular activities. Sports may have interfered with chores for some children. For others, sports were perceived as necessary and beneficial.

> In the last 50 years the pendalem [sic] has swung over to the other side until today athletics comes [sic] first and education, if at all necessary in our higher schools, comes last. The high point in that trend seems to have been passed and we may look for economy demanding less attention to athletics and more to general education. [53]

The Bob Murray influence in The Dalles probably came at a time to make athletics socially acceptable. His achievements in this community made him a local leader, and Joe's introduction into organized athletics was probably due to him. As a youth, Joe was exposed to this great man and coach, even though he did not play football at TDHS. That missed opportunity, however, probably did not deter him from being a spectator. In observing Murray's players and teams, Joe was able to learn how to play the game.

The Murray-Kasberger linkage is fragile from the documentation available. Joe may have played for Bob's town baseball teams during the summers of his high school and college days. There is no clear documentation that Joe was ever coached by Bob Murray, unless Murray was the 1914 track coach at TDHS, when Joe is documented as a member of that team. There is a vague reference, presented later, to suggest that he was, since Joe is listed with former Murray players who had achieved stardom. Murray, therefore, appears to be critical in understanding Joe's athletic philosophy, at least initially, as a player and coach.

Bob Murray, as a significant force in Joe Kasberger's life and career, deserves a closer look. Murray's role in athletics began as a youth and went from playing to coaching over a career of thirty-five years. Fortunately, his story is documented from several sources. Jack Cross provided exceptional glimpses of Murray in stories that appeared in The Dalles *Chronicle*. Additional material comes from anonymous sources provided by The Dalles-Wasco County Library, and in The Dalles *Optimist*. The most significant body of knowledge comes from Bob's son, William C. Murray, in a 1988 paper.

The man who literally wrote the book on football in The Dalles was Robert L. Murray, born in The Dalles on Nov. 8, 1880. His parents, Cornelius and Nancy Robbins Murray, were pioneers who surmounted the trek west from Indiana and Iowa, with all that such a journey entails. They married near Champoeg, OR before coming to The Dalles in 1873. They were attracted there by Bob's grandfather, Dr. James Anderson Robbins, who "established a medical practice in The Dalles in that year." [54]

Cornelius Murray loved horses from childhood. He was a volunteer fireman

FOOTBALL FUNDAMEN̄ A . .
FOR STUDENTS OF
THE DALLES HIGH SCHO

COACH ROBERT L MURRAY

PRINTED BY HIGH SCHOOL PRINTERS, THE DALLES, ORE

Bob Murray as pictured on his football book.

in The Dalles, whose horses are believed to have been used "to draw both the steam engine and the hand pumper of the DFD" around 1879. Cornelius also worked for the Joe Peters Lumber Company, before dying suddenly in 1889. Cornelius' death was traumatic for his nine-year-old son, Bob. According to Bob Murray's son, Bill, "this event was probably as responsible as any single factor for my father's well-developed sense of independence."[55]

Bob Murray was educated in the public schools through 1892, when his "formal education ended with his graduation from grade school in The Dalles." Then, he took a job as a "callboy" for the Oregon Railroad and Navigation Company and later as a brakeman. In between these jobs, Bob worked as a "wool grader in the local scouring mill." Murray became a merchant later in the 1900s, as "proprietor of the Phillips and Murray Cigar Store," which may have had an influence in Joe Kasberger's college life. This establishment had a billiards table and was a focal point "for sports-interested men in town." Bob retained a "passion for athletics," which was reflected in his career as a player on the town's baseball and football teams.

To follow the various town teams through the 1890's and early 1900's is somewhat confusing because different teams of the town were formed under different auspices with different names. Bob appears to have played first for the Dalles Boys Club, but he later played quarterback for The Dalles Amateur Athletic Club and The Dalles Commercial and Athletic Club (the D.C. & A.C.). He also played for The Dalles High School. All of these involvements were volunteer. Through the first half of the first decade of the century the local town team was known as the Invincibles. We know that he was a player in the Multnomah Athletic Club vs. The Dalles game of 1896 when Multnomah won. At that time he was sixteen.[56]

Despite his youth and diminutive size, five-and-one-half feet tall, Murray quickly made a name for himself as head coach while playing quarterback for The Dalles town team at about the age of 14. Another account reports that he first began coaching The Dalles town team in 1904, while still a player. "In those days the rules of football was [sic] much different than now and the coach could BOTH play and coach the team."[57]

Scheduling games in The Dalles was a problem. "They played any teams they could find to play including different Portland teams, Hood River, Dufur, Heppner, Goldendale."[58] Getting to games may have been half the fun for players, despite the difficulties. For farmers dependent upon sons for labor, football was a difficult sport to support. Games in Hood River and Portland required the team to travel "both by rail and steamboat."[59] A game in Heppner saw the team travel "by rail." The most exciting trips, however, appear to have been to Goldendale and Dufur. For away games, "the team traveled by wagonette," described as "a large wagon drawn by 6 horses," as recalled in this story. On the Goldendale trip the team left before sundown, traveled all night, and arrived in Goldendale for breakfast and practice before the Sunday game. "Then they played a hard fast game, with no holts [sic] barred, literally walking all over their opponents."[60]

> Those were in the good old days of Jim Thorp [sic] when no one thought of getting hurt playing football! They had wooden ships and iron men, in those days, now we have iron ships and wooden men![61]

At game's end, players "went to quarters and cleaned up." Presumably, "quarters" were not the same as the boarding house where they went "for a bite to eat." With these concessions to bodily requirements, it was time to travel, and the team "clamored [sic] aboard the wagonette and drove back to The Dalles through the darkness of Sunday night so they would be ready for classes Monday morning!" The story ends with the belief that players loved the game. "They played for fun in those days, according to Guy Fagan and really enjoyed the trips." Traveling to a game in Antelope appeared to be special, going "by train to Shaniko and by stage from there to Antelope 'a short night ride' as the train got into Shaniko in the evening."[62]

Murray, in 1905, "organized the now famed 'invincible team' which was probably the strongest eleven ever developed in the city." The "invincible team" played against competition that was described by Cross as "all top teams in the Northwest." Murray's teams were so successful and became known as "the invincibles," because "they just couldn't be conquered!" The victory margins were substantial, with "over 300 points scored and was never scored upon," according to Cross. The invincibles "rolled over eight opponents and was never scored upon." The season's climax "came with a victory over Columbia university (now Portland University) in the final game." The names associated with Murray's first teams are reported as "all-around athletes," because "most all of them played baseball too." A few of the players recalled, besides Bob Murray, were "Guy Fagan, Guy Sexton, Nick White, Chas. Conroy and Ben Morgan." The record of the "invincibles" for the period 1906-1910 is not known.[63]

Art Sharp was one of the earliest football players from The Dalles to achieve national fame as a member of the 1913 and 1914 Notre Dame football teams. Art probably played for Bob Murray at TDHS before going to Columbia University in Portland. Sharp then transferred to Notre Dame where he played tackle at 5 feet, 11 inches and 190 pounds on the 1913 team. Knute Rockne was the captain of this team that posted a 7-0-0 record. In 1914, Notre Dame finished with a 6-2-0 record, with both teams coached by Jess Harper.[64]

Next, Coach Murray took his brand of football to a more organized level at TDHS. As a sophomore at TDHS in 1911, Joe Kasberger saw Murray orchestrate the transition from town football to a more formal approach. It was in 1911 when Murray, at the age of 31, "was appointed head coach at Dalles high where the school officially adopted football as a major sport." Murray "took over coaching duties for the school on a full-time basis, handling not only football but baseball and other school sports." 1911 was the year, "according to Bob Murray, when regular high school football schedules were lined up." Foes for TDHS were widely scattered in Portland, Hood River, Pendleton, Baker, and Dufur. The opposition mentioned here, "with some deviations from year to year, was the general picture."[65] Much of a coach's duties included getting a team to and from a game.

Despite these constraints, Murray's 1911 football squad won a chance to prove itself as Oregon's best high school team. It was a bittersweet ending, in the state championship game for the Indians, as TDHS was known. They were "defeated by a powerful Lincoln of Portland squad for the crown."[66] This was no disgrace since "Lincoln HS was probably Portland's oldest and drew on a vastly larger pool of athletes."[67]

One of the oddities about Murray's coaching career was the fact that he had no college education. Despite this shortcoming, Murray gained a reputation as being straightforward in his speaking and had many friends. With these personal traits, Murray became "famed as a molder of men, and responsible for development of many college sporting luminaries." Murray had a very simple philosophy of coaching: " 'Teach the boys the fundamentals well, and they won't lose many games.'"[68]

After two down seasons in 1912 and 1913, TDHS returned to the state championship game. In all fairness to TDHS and Coach Murray, it was not until the 1914 season that "he assumed full responsibility for the football season" with spectacular results. The 1914 "wonder team"

The famed Dalles high football team of 1914 – state champions – was probably the greatest squad ever coached by Bob Murray. The starting lineup that season was Backfield: John Harriman (qb); Benny Cohen (rh); Bill Steers (fb); Hollis Huntington (lf); Line: Henry Barnard (re); Matt Duffy (rt); Seward Philpot (rg); Virgil Egbert (c); Orville Gibson (lg); Harold Ganger (lt); and Guy Elton (le). Steers and Huntington later played starring roles in the Rose Bowl classic with Steers selected to the All-American squad. Above photo was taken on what is now known as Amotan field – then known as Murray [sic] field.

brought TDHS "its first championship." "It was in 1914 that Bob Murray's Dalles High school team first became what was acknowledged as Oregon State champions." It is Cross' contention that the 1914 team was "probably the best in school history," because of the six teams that it defeated.[69]

The first game was a 34-0 win over Portland Academy. Next to fall was Chemawa, "27-0 in spite of the presence on the Chemawa team of [Emil or Eric?] Hauser, a former O.A.C. star. We tromped Pacific U. 55 to 7." The next game was a 27-13 road win against Walla Walla. "The climax of the season's success was a Thanksgiving Day game on Amotan field when we beat Ashland 58 to 0." Oregon geography appears important in this game, since the Ashland team may have suffered from the long trip, "of several hundred miles."[70]

The culmination of the season was the Oregon state championship in the win over Ashland. Actually, TDHS claimed the "championship of Oregon, Eastern Washington and Idaho." The missing team on the 1914 schedule may have been Hood River, which by one account was victimized by TDHS in 1914 by a score of 114-0.[71] The other two games played in 1914 are missing from this account. Another story supplies one missing foe, St. James Athletic Club, possibly from Idaho.

Two players, Bill Steers and Hollis Huntington, were exceptional players, later achieving national fame in football. "Bill Steers was the heavy punter who generally always punted in the 70 yard bracket." Steers' kicking ability may have been the reason that the Indians "always kicked off first," as an essential part of their 1914 game-plan, described here.

> If the opponents steam rollered down the field, when The Dalles did get the ball Bill punted it back 72 yards or more so the opponents would wear themselves out bucking it back down the field again. After the opponents did that 3 or 4 times then The Dalles would open up on them. [72]

Steers was more than a great kicker. "It was said that Bill Steers had the longest 'stiff arm jab' of any football player in Oregon," according to one account. With his technique, "a man's whole face would disappear in the palm of his hand while the head of the opponent would snap back like it was on hinges." That was not all there was to Steers: "He could dodge, run fast, zig zag and change paces without effort, it seemed."[73] Moreover, Bill Steers yelled "raw beefsteak" as he plunged into the line. While Steers may have been the star of this "invincible team," he had help from his teammates. "The line could always drill a hole wherever the signals directed and the backfield was the '4-horsemen of 14.'"[74]

Clearly, this team was superior and Murray's athletes were attractive to colleges. Thus, Hollis Huntington and Bill Steers were lured to the University of Oregon, joining Hollis' older brother, Charles, who was known as "Shy." With Shy Huntington as quarterback, Oregon was a very good football team, and by the 1916 season had become a West Coast powerhouse. Shy had played for Bob Murray and his success was attributed to the fine coaching he had received.

Coach Murray was sensitive to issues of the sportsmanship displayed by his teams. "Most of the players of this team played baseball, basketball and went out for track so they too were 'all-around athletes' of the school." The players "learned their lessons from Bob Murray well and every player [sic] were afterwards fine citizens."[75] Nearly four decades later, Hollis Huntington reminisced in correspondence with Bob Murray about how innovative a coach he was. Hollis Huntington wrote that despite the "innovations" of the modern game, Coach Murray had taught his teams these same "new" strategies and formations in 1914. For this reason, Murray's undated book on football for his players at TDHS is a collector's item worthy of enshrinement in the Football Hall of Fame. While Bob Murray did not have much formal education, he wrote well and his philosophy of the game remains for posterity a highly literate work.

Surely, Joe was familiar with both the University of Oregon and its archrival, Oregon Agricultural College (OAC). It is not known, however, whether he was recruited by either. Among the Kasberger family's circle of friends in The Dalles was the Pashek family. Urban Pashek is shown in a photo with the Kasbergers. His wife Mary is recalled as a friend of Joe's mother. Their son, Gregory, was a year older than Joe, but the two were thought to be childhood friends. Pashek is believed to have attended St. Mary's Academy and TDHS. After graduating from TDHS, most likely in 1913, Gregory went to Mt. Angel College (MAC) and became an immediate star in all major sports.

Gregory Pashek, "Pelkey," the stellar line plunger.

Pashek's credibility with the Benedictine monks at MAC appeared to result in their recruitment of Joe. A few years later, the Oct. 1917 MAC newspaper, *Pacific Star*, alluded to Joe as a good player in The Dalles. An observer in a later news account of Joe remarked:

> 'Old reliable' Joe Kasberger . . . has more pep than the whole team put together,' was an expression uttered by a baseball scout sometime ago when he witnessed Kasberger play ball in The Dalles, Oregon. Joe did not lose his pep when he left the field but rather his spirits seemed to mount higher and higher every minute.[76]

What seems important to this sequence of events is Joe's age in 1915, nineteen, with no experience as a football player. Thus, Joe may not have been attractive to the larger colleges and universities as a football prospect.

Recruitment by the Benedictines

The legend of Joe Kasberger refers to an important episode in his life and career at about this time. Reportedly, Joe was picking grapes when two monks visited his parents in an effort to induce him to attend their college.[77] The representatives from MAC who came to The Dalles in pursuit of Joe, reportedly were Rev. Victor Rassier, O.S.B., the football coach and athletic director, and Rev. Hildebrand Melchior, O.S.B., the basketball coach.[78]

Fr. Victor's successful 1915 recruiting visit to The Dalles might be one of the most significant accomplishments of his career. Yet, Fr. Victor's lasting fame as a Benedictine was not in the realm of athletics. Not much older than Joe and the MAC players he coached, Fr. Victor was a very special man. Born in Little Falls, MN, John Rassier was one of eleven children. He received his secondary and college education at Conception, MO before arriving at Mt. Angel Seminary to continue his studies.[79]

Fr. Victor received the B.A. degree from MAC in 1911, and professed religious vows in 1912, taking the name Victor. During the period 1913-15, he was in Rome for Theological Studies and was later ordained at Collegeville, MN in 1915. Upon returning to Oregon, he was given two important positions: Director of Music and Athletic Director of the College. "Prefect of Discipline and later Rector of Mt. Angel College were Father Victor's other titles after ordination."[80] There are no insights about his athletic experiences as a player or coach.

Fr. Hildebrand was also a young monk when Joe first encountered him. He was born in 1888 in St. Paul, MN to a pioneering family that settled near Oregon's coast in Tillamook. From there, Fr. Hildebrand came to Mt. Angel in 1905, and entered Mt. Angel Seminary in 1909. After completing his studies, Fr. Hildebrand "was ordained as a Benedictine priest-monk at Mount Angel Abbey in 1915." His versatility made him a valuable member of the Benedictine community. "For five years after his ordination he taught at the monastery, drove its only car and coached basketball." [81]

Fr. Hildebrand was a great basketball player at MAC as a student. His career as MAC's basketball coach began even before ordination. An anonymous Dec. 9, 1916 story provides a glimpse about his fabled basketball playing career: "in his time [he] was one of the star guards of the state," reflecting highly on his talent. "Hildebrand led the Mt. Angel juniors through four consecutive seasons, playing 33 games without a loss." At the sub-varsity level, MAC is reported to have excelled as well. "The juniors in 1911 and 1912 won the junior championship of the state."[82]

Meeting the two monks from Mt. Angel may have raised immediate questions for Joe as he listened to their appeal. First, what is a Benedictine monk? Second, how did they get to Oregon? Despite the strong religious training received at home, St. Mary's Academy, and St. Peter's Parish, it is unlikely that Joe had ever dealt with Benedictines. Thus, it seems important to learn more about them as Joe may have investigated them.

Roman Catholicism is blessed with a variety of religious orders, established over its history, in the quest to seek and find God. The Benedictines are one of the Church's oldest and most distinguished orders. Their longevity and accomplishments give them great credibility. There is a brief description of the Benedictines in the *World Book* Encyclopedia.

The Benedictines follow the rule of life (Holy Rule) dictated by Saint Benedict of Nursia in Italy (circa 480-543). His plan was that each monastery should be a separate organization, and that for the monk, it should take the place of his family. The first monastery in Italy was established by Benedict at Subiaco; then came the famous foundation at Monte Cassino in 529.[83]

St. Benedict's life and teachings appealed to many young men over the centuries because they could identify with him. When St. Benedict became disillusioned with Roman city life, and found a cave to get away from it all, he made a statement understood over the ages. Isolation did not last and soon others flocked to him for wisdom. Before long a few followers became a larger group, requiring St. Benedict to formulate an organized approach to the life that they shared. St. Benedict taught his followers "the value of holy reading, of praying together and of manual labor."[84]

Because he had so many disciples, he wrote *The Rule of St. Benedict*, which has been widely followed throughout the history of religious life. Benedictines are those who follow the way of St. Benedict, with men called monks who live in monasteries. Nuns or sisters are the women who live in convents or priories. The Benedictine Order "spread rapidly," placing them "in the forefront of bringing Christianity and civilization to Western Europe during the next century." There are two important dimensions of the Benedictine Order: "piety and encouragement of learning." It was during the Middle Ages when the Benedictines made their most publicized contributions to Western civilization as "they neglected no branch of art or learning then known." The Benedictines are proclaimed to have "produced many of the books written before the invention of printing in Europe."[85] They also played a large part in preserving the traditions of Christianity. While their secular contributions are numerous, Benedictines have a dominant spiritual orientation that calls for them to be in the world but not of it.

It is important to understand the religious vows that Benedictines profess: Poverty, Chastity, Obedience to the Abbot, and Stability to the Abbey in which they are members unless directed otherwise. The meanings of most of these vows are self-evident, but a closer examination of "Stability to the Abbey" appears warranted. According to *Webster's New Collegiate Dictionary*, stability is "a vow binding a monk for life to a monastery." The Benedictines do not simply profess vows to the religious order, but profess vows to a place, a particular abbey, a vital concept in comprehending this religious order. [86]

Not all monks are ordained as priests of the Roman Catholic Church. For those who are ordained by the local bishop, there are many opportunities "to serve the community and the people of the diocese." Benedictines who are not priests, such as brothers, deacons, and lay oblates often work at the monastery where they begin the day at 5:15 with a multitude of activities. Work and prayer are the cornerstones of their life, and the spiritual life takes precedence over all other activities.

Five times during the day the monks gather in the church for common prayer. Each day they celebrate a Mass for the needs of the Church, their relatives, friends, and benefactors. Always included in the intentions for which the monks pray are the intentions of people who support the works of the monastery by their generosity.[87]

So much time is devoted by the Benedictines to prayer because *The Rule of St. Benedict* clearly states that "nothing is more important than what he called the 'Work of God.'" While not engaged in prayer, monks work hard. In a monastery the size of Mount Angel, there are many responsibilities to operate and maintain the facility, as well as other work to support their lifestyle. "Housekeeping chores, teaching in the school, caring for the elderly, and working on the grounds take up much of the monks' time."[88]

Most monasteries are in remote locations, not easily observed by the laity. Once discovered by outsiders, historically, *The Rule* and way of life provide a powerful allure to some. At Mt. Angel, prospective members "came to the new monastery looking for a place where they could work, pray and study together while seeking God." The notion of seeking God in a monastery has some appeal since Benedictines emphasize that their way of life is not based upon having found God, rather they seek God. Being suited for the religious life is a quality which needs testing, and provision is made for a trial period to determine if an individual is suited to be a member of the community. It is only after this trial that new members profess vows to become permanent members.[89]

Joe may have been curious to learn how these Benedictines came to Oregon. Possibly he discovered that they came from Switzerland and arrived in Oregon via Conception Abbey in Missouri in 1880. What is now known as Mount Angel Abbey was founded Oct. 30, 1882 as St. Benedict's Priory. Mount Angel's founders were Rev. Adelhelm Odermatt and a group of monks from the 800-year-old abbey of Engelberg in the Swiss Alps.[90]

Why were the Benedictines needed in Oregon? As evidenced in Joe's family, German-speaking immigrants had moved West and their numbers were expected to increase. For many, the Church was the nucleus of their community. The Swiss Benedictines spoke German, knew farming, and helped bridge the gap from the old country to the new. They were, therefore, an invaluable resource for the immigrating German pioneers. And, as the keepers of culture for Western civilization for so many years, they were ideal educators of those pioneers' children. Oneness with the land bonded the Benedictines to Catholic pioneers. They knew how to make the land produce and they understood farmers. The Benedictines initially came to serve the German immigrant communities on the East Coast. As German immigrants, among others, moved west, new monasteries were established to meet the needs of new communities that were settled.

Mt. Angel Abbey was originally a foundation of Engelberg Abbey in central Switzerland that was founded in 1120. Under Blessed Abbot Frowin, Engelberg was a "center of learning and religious life." Engelberg's enduring qualities are a result of good times and bad. "But one hundred years ago, the continued existence of the abbey seemed in doubt." In the mid-1800s, "a number of Swiss religious communities had been suppressed," and there was great concern at Engelberg. One response to these perceived threats came in 1854 when the Swiss Abbey of Einsieden "founded the monastery of St. Meinrad in Indiana," as "a place of possible refuge in a free land." By 1870, "it was not certain that Engelberg, even though it was located in an overwhelmingly Catholic area, would be spared."[91]

With a Swiss Benedictine presence established in Indiana, there were other incentives, besides self-preservation, that attracted the Engelberg monks westward.

> Abbot Boniface Wimmer of St. Vincent Abbey in Pennsylvania had been urging European monasteries to help minister to the religious needs of German-speaking Catholics in America. Missionary work among the Indians also beckoned the Swiss monks.[92]

Fathers Frowin Conrad and Adelhelm Odermatt were selected by their Engelberg Abbot, Anselm Villiger, to visit St. Meinrad in Indiana. From there they then went to Conception, MO, where a new monastery was under construction, and monks were being recruited from Switzerland. "Already by April 15, 1881, the monastery was firmly enough established to become an abbey and to form, with St. Meinrad Abbey, the Swiss-American federation." The two Engelberg monks "had to decide whether to transfer their vow of stability to the newly independent community or return to Engelberg."[93]

Fr. Adelhelm did not like these two options. Despite wanting to remain in America, "he did not wish to join the new American abbey" because he felt that Conception "departed too much from the venerable Swiss tradition," that he preferred. Fr. Adelhelm urged Abbot Anselm to consider a third option, an American version of Engelberg Abbey. Thus, if Engelberg were threatened, an American abbey based upon its tradition would provide a refuge. Abbot Anselm approved this request and Fr. Adelhelm and another Engelberg monk, Fr. Nicholas Frei, continued their travels west to find a site for a new monastery. "Eventually they came to Oregon; they had heard that the Rogue River Valley was a paradise, and Father Adelhelm wanted to see it." Upon arrival in Jacksonville, OR, the "inhabitants urged the Benedictines to settle there."[94]

Also wanting Benedictines was Archbishop Seghers in the Archdiocese of Oregon City. Prior to the Swiss monks' arrival, Archbishop Seghers "had been corresponding with Abbot Alexius Edelbrock of St. John's Abbey, Minnesota, a foundation of St. Vincent Abbey." After a trip to Oregon in Dec. 1881, Abbot Alexius "was not impressed: the climate was damp and dismal, the Catholic population meager, the number of clergy sufficient." Archbishop Seghers was not deterred and recalled a trip he had made a few months earlier to a little town by the name of Fillmore. He had visited on August 21 "to bless a new church built there by the citizens, who were tired of going seven miles to Gervais for Mass."

He took the opportunity to journey to the top of the nearby butte. There are several accounts of how he got there, but it seems certain that as he looked over the valley from the top of the butte, he was struck with what a suitable spot the hilltop was for a religious institute or seminary. Perhaps he was thinking of the Swiss Benedictines who were looking for a a monastic site.[95]

Fathers Adelhelm and Nicholas visited Archbishop Seghers in Oregon City. The archbishop asked the monks "to take care of the church in Fillmore over a weekend." There, they met the local Catholic leader, Mathias Butsch, who took them to the top of the butte near the town. "Father Adelhelm was convinced: this place with its beautiful view, fertile land and devout people was the site for a new Engelberg." Archbishop Seghers asked Fr. Adelhelm to remain for the winter and care for the new church in Fillmore and surrounding Catholic communities. Fr. Nicholas "went to San Francisco to learn English and to investigate possible locations for a monastery in California."[96]

When the winter of 1882 ended, Fr. Adelhelm returned to Engelberg on June 17 to get his abbot's approval for a new Oregon foundation. Also, Fr. Adelhelm sought "sisters to teach in Gervais and two Indian schools in Oregon, and recruits for his new foundation." His search was successful.

> On the way back across America he recruited Mother Bernadine Wachter, O.S.B., whom he had known in Missouri, and several other Benedictine Sisters who had come to America from the convents of Maria Rickenbach and St. Andrew (Sarnen) near Engelberg.[97]

When Fr. Adelhelm returned to Oregon on Oct. 28, 1882, he was accompanied by a traveling party of twenty-seven that included "the sisters, three priests, one lay brother, and some student candidates." The monks lived at the Gervais rectory until "the summer of 1884." During this period, Fr. Adelhelm was elevated to Prior, and "set about acquiring title to the hill near Fillmore, called 'Lone Butte' or 'Graves Butte.'" Besides buying the butte, Prior Adelhelm borrowed money to acquire farmland. "From 1882 to 1888 he purchased, at about $25 an acre, parcels of land amounting to over 1800 acres."[98]

Prior Adelhelm's foundation made "rapid progress," and changed the town's name from Fillmore to Mt. Angel. Plans were then made "to build a monastery with a church which would serve both towns and monks." To save money, rather than build on the hilltop, "the monastery and church were constructed on the first rise of the hill, near where the the abbey farm shops are today."[99]

Prior Adelhelm, next, began incorporating under Oregon law as a charitable corporation and in 1883 the Benedictines were recognized by the State of Oregon. "The articles of incorporation mentioned educational work, and state authorities urged the monks to undertake educational work in the local area." During the summer of 1884 the Benedictines occupied their new home. In addition to farming, the priests from St. Benedict Priory "served the Catholics in Gervais, Mount Angel and Sublimity."[100]

By 1887, Prior Adelhelm brought the founding of a college close to reality. A prospectus was issued for a college "which would offer a classical and commercial courses to boarding and day students (at a five-month fee of $90.00 and $50.00, respectively.)" With the assistance of Archbishop William H. Gross of the Diocese of Oregon City, MAC was founded in 1887. Also supportive was the Oregon legislature, which "granted a charter, with power to confer the usual academic honors."[101]

MAC's first year had fifty students "in a two-story college building measuring thirty by thirty-five feet." Enrollment nearly tripled in the second year and "the chapter voted to build a new college building." After receiving permission from Engelberg, the school year ended with the students "occupying their new, 150 by 50 feet, four-story building." MAC's initial success led to an expanded educational mission. As early as 1885, the Benedictines were urged by Archbishop William H. Gross to open a seminary. "The Mount Angel school catalogue for 1889-1890 announced that in accord with the latter's wishes, minor and major seminary divisions were to be opened that year." Due to demands associated with the schools, that enrolled 150 students, former parish duties in "Gervais and Sublimity were returned to the care of diocesan pastors in 1888 and 1889."[102] By 1889 Mt. Angel Seminary opened and is the oldest seminary west of the Rocky Mountains.

Despite the initial successes, Mt. Angel had difficulties within its first decade. "On May 3, 1892, the Monastery and Seminary buildings were destroyed by fire." Exacerbating the situation was debt "of about $200,000." No reference is made of insurance, but "there were no funds for rebuilding, there was even danger that the struggling community would lose its land." Prior Adelhelm turned to Archbishop Gross who approved an appeal "for help in Oregon." This effort was not a complete success, so Prior Adelhelm went "to the cities of the East to ask for funds." It was a time of great "physical hardships" as well as "worry and fear for the foundation's survival," which had to be shared "with the abbot and monks of Engelberg."[103]

Fortunately, "Prior Adelhelm's money-raising efforts were successful enough to give the community hope." Yet, his prolonged absences created problems that were recognized in Engelberg.

> In order to provide more leadership and financial management in the community, the Abbot of Engelberg sent out a new prior, Father Benedict Gottwald, one of the ablest monks at Engelberg. It was his task to guide the young community through some of its darkest days. He grappled with the heavy debt, the poor housing conditions, the disturbed monastic observance [sic].[104]

Fr. Benedict was a stern but sensitive man who performed his job in Oregon well. "After five years as prior, he returned to Switzerland, exhausted from his labors." His insights into St. Benedict Priory helped the abbot and Engelberg community prepare for the future in Oregon. The first matter to be resolved was the burned down priory church which was used by the parishioners in the town of Mt. Angel. It was decided "to build a new parish church closer to the center of town." The second matter to be addressed was where to rebuild the monastery? There was strong sentiment "to move to the top of the hill, while others argued vigorously for a more economical reconstruction on the original site."[105]

Before his death in 1901, Abbot Anselm of Engelberg appointed Abbot Frowin of Conception Abbey "as his delegate of visitation for Mount Angel." The purpose was "to conduct a thorough evaluation and study of Mount Angel's discipline and finances, and then to hold the election of a new prior." Fr. Thomas Meienhofer was elected on July 11, 1901 with an agenda for action. First he incorporated his community into the Swiss-American Federation in 1902. Next, he strove to complete the new hilltop monastery. The final task was to have his priory become an independent monastery.[106]

This 1892 fire was a severe setback but "by no means arrested the progress of the school."[107] Rebuilding began on this prominent natural site. By Christmas of 1903, a new college was occupied on the crest of Mt. Angel, composed of a "five-story quadrangle of buildings" that was the focal point of educational activities.

On Christmas Eve, 1903, the monks occupied their new hilltop home. The community thrived and in 1904 Mt. Angel sought independence from Engelberg. With the new monastery, "Prior Thomas felt that Mount Angel should become independent so that the local prior would have full authority." Thus, Abbot Frowin from Conception again came to Oregon to supervise "an election for the man to be presented to Rome for appointment as abbot of the newly independent community." After nine ballots, Fr. Thomas was elected as the first Abbot of St. Benedict Abbey.[108]

"On March 24, 1904, Pope Pius X made Mount Angel an abbey and appointed Father Thomas the first abbot." Independence from Engelberg and entry into the Swiss-American Federation made affairs in Oregon more stable, but the issue of indebtedness to Engelberg remained. "In 1904 these debts were consolidated on terms very favorable to the new abbey."[109] With these matters resolved, St. Benedict Abbey continued to grow.

> The enrollment in the abbey schools ranged between 90 and 150. Gradually other schools took over education of the youngest students, and the abbey concentrated its educational efforts in high school, college, and theology programs.[110]

By focusing on education, the Benedictines attracted more day students and boarders. The only distinction made among the boarding students was for the seminarians "who resided in separate wings," but attended classes with the lay students. Despite the successes, there were problems in the monastery that saddened and discouraged Abbot Thomas. "Eventually these put so much strain on him that on May 25, 1910, he resigned his position." After several months, a new abbot was elected on Aug. 30, 1910. "They chose Father Placidus Fuerst, who had been born in Germany in 1868." The second abbot of St. Benedict Abbey was among Fr. Adelhelm's "earliest recruits" to Oregon. He was proud of the

Swiss tradition and was known as an "accomplished musician and composer."

> At the time of his election, Abbot Placidus was pastor of Mount Angel parish. He accepted his new task out of a sense of duty to church and community, but he never was happy with the position.[111]

Returning to Joe Kasberger, the Mt. Angel monks with their youthfulness and athletic interests may have impressed him. Moreover, his parents may have been impressed that a Catholic college, with strong European ties, was interested in their son. Knowing Gregory Pashek's family may have made the decision to allow Joe to join the White and Gold Angels of MAC easy. The significance of this choice should not be lost on observers of Joe's life and career. Joe was the only member of his family privileged to attend college, at a time when such opportunities were available to very few youth. It is not known whether Joe received either an athletic scholarship or financial aid at MAC.

The parental concern that characterized the Kasberger's view of football at TDHS may have been alleviated by the Mt. Angel monks. Thus, more meaningful games were saved for the college level. A lifetime bond was forged between Joe and the Benedictines. The line between educating and preparing students for a religious life has always been fine and is important. Those professing a faith and unique lifestyle, such as Benedictines, are very powerful teachers to young students. It is impossible for monks, as teachers, to avoid inculcating certain values in their pupils. Even men who did not take vows to become Benedictines are affected by the values and ways of their teachers.

Gregory Pashek must have told the monks a glowing story about Joe's ability and potential. Why else would they make such a long trip? Also, they must have been confident that they could fetch young Joe for MAC. What else did they know of the subject for their visit? Possibly Joe's leadership skills as president of the student body at TDHS in 1914 impressed them. Also, Joe's devout religious convictions may have played a role. In any event, Joe proved to be a worthy prospect for both the short and long term.

Joe enrolled at MAC as an unheralded student-athlete, eternally grateful to the Benedictines for this opportunity. The level of competition was not the same as for Pacific Coast Conference schools, but it was a start.

II. JOE AS A STUDENT AT MT. ANGEL COLLEGE

"I Awoke One Morning and Found Myself Famous."

An individual is shaped by physical and geographical environments, and by the overall community of one's youth. The impact of family and schools, however, cannot be neglected in understanding how the person develops. There are explanations for individual behavior traits that are exhibited in value-systems and lifestyles. In the case of Joe Kasberger, this appears especially true for he learned the basics in The Dalles. At the age of 19, Joe was still relatively young and impressionable, so the experience of living away at college was as profound for him as it always is for others. As the crow flies, Mt. Angel was only about 100 miles from The Dalles. The terrain separating them, however, made for a lengthy trip in those days. One constant remained for Joe between these vastly different environments. Both shared a view of magnificent Mt. Hood that surely gave Joe a feeling of comfort and reassurance.

Joe as a young man, probably around the time he began his college years at Mt. Angel.

When Joe left The Dalles, he entered a life which changed him forever. At this Benedictine college, Joe found the best of all possible worlds. Even though he was away from home, he came to a place that reminded him of his past, yet built towards his future. On this campus he may have been amazed by the scope of activities that were a part of his new home. Now, as a young college student he was "formed" in two important elements of the Benedictine tradition: their scholasticism and their ties to the land. At MAC, Joe developed academically, socially, and athletically in a monastic environment. To know his student years here is to understand choices he made in his later life.

Foremost in any description of Mt. Angel are its paradoxical characteristics. On a map, Mt. Angel is just another small town in the flat, rich farm lands

Mt. Angel Abbey and College when Joe was a student.

of the Willamette River valley. The American landscape has many communities founded for religious reasons, so the town of Mt. Angel is not unusual *per se*. A visitor today sees a small, clean, and orderly mix of homes and businesses, not unlike what is found in other farming towns in America. Surrounding Mt. Angel is a "fertile plain, which is diversified by fields, meadows, groves, and orchards." Despite its rural location, Mt. Angel has easy access to two important cities. Salem, Oregon's state capital, is fourteen miles to the southwest. Oregon's largest city, Portland, is forty miles to the north.[1]

The town of Mt. Angel, however, lies at the base of an unusual topographical feature, a butte, now known as Mt. Angel. The site housing the monastic complex was described as "a beautiful, gently sloping hill, rising to a height of about 300 feet" above the land below. This is the "Mount of Communion," once known as Mt. Fillmore in the land of the "Setting Sun." This site was sacred to the Native Americans before the Benedictines.

> Long before the white man trod the forests of Oregon, this mount had been called by the Indians, Tap-a-Lam-a-Ho: the Mount of Communion. Years ago the famous cartoonist, Homer Davenport, related to Abbot Adelhelm, how his father had found the ruins of an old Indian temple on the summit of the mount. The Indians told him that from time immemorial they had gone up to the mount to pray, for they said, the Great Spirit dwells near the mountain top.[2]

Here, "the small Benedictine community continued the traditions of their Order and opened a much needed school of higher Christian Learning." The future looked bright.

> It seemed that the graces of God showered down more abundantly on the Benedictine community after the Abbey and College had been moved to the top of Tap-a-Lam-a-Ho, for since that time nothing has been able to check the progress of the institution.[3]

For a college campus, Mt. Angel has dramatic qualities of remoteness, beauty, and panoramic vistas of the surrounding areas that are spectacular. It was not the Swiss Alps, but the Benedictines may have felt very much at home. It provides a stimulating, yet serene, location for a religious foundation and educational institution. It affords a magnificent view of Oregon and Washington on the north, the long chain of the Cascade Range on the east, the Coast Range on the west, and the Waldo Hills with St. Mary's peak on the south. Rebuilding the college was not as easy. More importantly, perhaps, MAC brought to the Pacific Northwest the traditional work of the Benedictines for more than 1400 years: "Christian Education."[4]

With the durability of Benedictine education over the ages in view, it seems important to understand MAC's philosophy when Joe arrived as a student.

Mt. Angel College is a Catholic institution though it admits non-Catholics as well. Information and training in the truths and principles of religion is an influential factor in the educational system and program at Mt. Angel College. We believe that true education implies the training of the will, the control of the emotions, as well as the information of the mind. We hold that an adequate preparation for life consists more in the acquirement of inspirational ideals and Christian social attitudes than in the mastery of intellectual technique and memory skill. The primary purpose of the curricula offered is to prepare the young man for life rather than merely for a certain work in life.[5]

Despite holding a traditional liberal-arts college as the ideal, MAC had a practical view of students' interests besides the classical four-year program.

While the tendency of the time almost necessitates early specialization, Mt. Angel College still encourages its students to enroll, whenever possible, in the four-year Classical course leading to the A.B. degree. It is especially recommended as furnishing the highest and broadest mental culture and the best preparation for professional life. The course is prescribed for students preparing for the priesthood.[6]

During Joe's student years, MAC served multiple educational purposes as a college preparatory school, college, and seminary. Thus, there was a broad range of age groups that composed the student body of several hundred. Joe, and many classmates, were not enrolled in the classical curriculum. Thus, commercial and pre-professional classes appeared as popular with the lay students as the classical courses were for the seminarians. As a college student, Joe enrolled in the college's commercial department. Most students were in residence as boarders, rather than as commuters. Thus, the students were attuned to the monastery's rhythms and resonances. Perhaps Joe came to MAC to further his education. Perhaps he came to play sports. In any case, he came to a place where it was second nature to seek God.

1915-16 School Year

It is likely that Rev. Basil Schieber was the president of MAC when Joe arrived. It is not clear when Fr. Basil became president, but in one account he served as "acting president of Mt. Angel College for a series of years," until 1917. Unfortunately, Fr. Basil suffered from tuberculosis. "Failing health obliged the young priest to discontinue his college work and to seek rest and care in a southern climate." The year is not clear, but he returned to Mt. Angel, "physically renewed," one year later and "assumed his duties as the head of the oldest Catholic College in the Northwest."[7]

What is known about Fr. Basil comes primarily from a classmate, Fr. Leo Walsh. Joe's personal photo album has a picture of Fr. Leo with the caption "commonly known as Fr. Pat." Fr. Basil's ability is recalled to have "served him well in the splendid success achieved in the field of Catholic education." MAC's development had much to do with Fr. Basil. During his presidency, MAC "maintained its merited position among the schools of higher education in the state," among other accomplishments. There is more about a man who was "widely known and just as well liked." As an educator and administrator, he was admired for his "keen foresight and great intellectual acumen," so his activities "were chiefly educational and directive," while Joe was a student.[8]

As president, Fr. Basil assumed other roles. In the classroom, Fr. Leo observed that "he was a strict disciplinarian." Fr. Basil's sternness, however, was tempered with kindness, and his reputation, therefore, was one of strictness with an equal measure of "justice." Yet, Fr. Leo told that "you always knew he was running the school and he let you know it." Fr. Basil was truly a "hands-on" president whose style seems to have been profound in setting the tone for college and seminary students, as well as members of MAC's athletic teams. While Fathers Victor and Hildebrand were most directly linked to Joe on MAC's sports teams, Fr. Basil also appears influential and active with the athletic teams.[9]

Fr. Basil was very young for a college president, by today's standards. He was born on July 20, 1886 in Missouri into a family of three sisters and three brothers. A very bright student, he graduated from Conception College in 1904. One of his brothers, Rev. P. Odilo, O.S.B., remained in Missouri at Conception

Joe captioned this photo "our coach." It is thought to be MAC president Rev. Basil Schieber. "Notice the old form," was added by Joe.

Abbey when Fr. Basil came to Oregon. After entering the novitiate at St. Benedict Abbey, he made his holy profession of vows on Nov. 13, 1905 at Mt. Angel. As a seminarian, Fr. Basil was recalled as "one of the more outstanding students."[10]

This gifted student was allowed to proceed with his education at an advanced pace. When Fr. Basil finished his theology coursework, he was short "a few months of the canonical age for ordination," and needed a special dispensation. It was granted by the Most Rev. Archbishop Christie, D.D. who raised the young cleric to the priesthood on May 31, 1909. In view of his intellectual gifts, it was logical to consider him for the college presidency. Mt. Angel had many monks, but not all were fit to serve in this important role. Fr. Basil's abilities were seen by his peers, as well as by Abbot Placidus.[11]

Fr. Basil had other interests that gained him Joe's immediate attention. Mt. Angel's monks appear sports-loving and the college president was no exception. He not only liked athletics, but was an exceptional baseball player. When Fr. Basil came to Oregon, he was accompanied by Fr. Philip Growney, a baseball teammate. "They were a pitcher-catcher team." This monastic battery featured a powerfully-built pitcher, Fr. Basil, "tall and heavy set," and over six feet in height, weighing more than 200 pounds. Fr. Leo noted that Fr. Basil "could fill a door opening." His catcher, Fr. Philip, was diminutive. Fr. Basil used his size to great advantage and was a "marvelous pitcher," who could "hit his knees with his hands while standing erect." On the pitcher's mound, Fr. Basil "could reach almost half way to home plate when he pitched." As an intimidating presence who delivered the ball at high velocity, few batters "could stand up to his pitches." Opposing batters were fearful, and even his catcher, Fr. Philip, "would rock every time the ball would come in." Fr. Basil had another tool as a pitcher that made him unique. He "could throw anything with one hand or the other."[12]

Off the field, Fr. Basil used his pitching skills in the classroom. Fr. Leo recalled what Fr. Basil was capable of doing with large hands to an inattentive student. He grasped a book "in such a way that with little effort he could toss it and accurately hit the puple [sic] in the mug who was sitting in the last row." Fr. Basil's aim, however, was not always perfect.

Once in Monsignor's class a pupil just ahead of him was goofing off and Father Basil went to hit him with a book. The pupil ducked though and Monsignor got it full in the face and broke his nose. From this you can guess he was a strict man. But the students idolized him, especially for his baseball ability.[13]

Fr. Leo recalled Fr. Basil's teaching style. He did not teach from the teacher's desk. Rather, he sat on the pupil's desk "with his feet straddling the student and resting on his seat."[14] Another Fr. Basil story dealt with a social issue then afflicting Catholics.

Once when a delagation [sic] from the Silverton Ku Klux Klan came to the Abbey to inspect it on the assumption that we had a secret tunnel to the convent and was furthermore storing guns and ammunition in it [sic], Father Basil met them at the door. He told them if anyone came across the threshold he would throw them down the stairs. They backed down.[15]

Despite Fr. Basil's intimidating stature,

Joe and Fr. Philip Growney. Joe wrote under this photo in his album "I thought I was short."

Fr. Leo remembered a nice man who was well liked for the size of his "heart and mind." Moreover, he gave "forth from his magnanimous soul those admirable virtues of a priestly life, humility and charity." Throughout his priesthood, Fr. Basil's "goodness and grace" were recognized and he "earned the love and reverence of everyone that knew him."[16]

Arguably, one of the most significant men in Joe's career was Fr. Victor Rassier. This young monk was extremely versatile and his later career was far removed from the sports he enjoyed initially. As Joe's first football coach, Fr. Victor dealt with a talented and unheralded prospect with no organized-football experience. MAC's sports teams were known as "Angels," and the 1915 football squad had eight returning veterans. The Angels were led by their captain, Greg Pashek, Joe's friend from The Dalles. How Joe Kasberger would fit into this group was a question for Fr. Victor.

John Sohler, from Forest Grove, OR appears to have been an older player, returning to MAC after an absence following the 1912 season. Chas. "Charlie" Coghlan was a regular on MAC's previous football, basketball, and baseball squad. In football, Coghlan played end as a light, but speedy and intelligent, performer that made him a defensive stalwart. "One or two attempts at his side of the line usually sufficed to warn the opposition of the futility of attempting yardage there."[17] Bill Krebs is shown in Joe's personal photo album as "Tiny Bill Krebs," and another caption by Joe states: "Some Pal, Bill Krebs." Bill's role as a *Pacific Star* photographer showed this athlete to be sensitive with non-athletic interests.

> On Wednesday and Saturday afternoons Bill could be seen looking for one of nature's beauty spots and needless to say he never returned without a snapshot of some beautiful Oregon haunt.[18]

Possibly, some photos in Joe's personal photo album are by Krebs. As an athlete, Krebs was a star football player, "picked for two consecutive years on the All Star Non-Conference Football Team." In intramural basketball, Krebs "captained a quintet which captured the pennant for two successive years." To round out his college career, Krebs was acclaimed as an actor. "Before the footlights Billie was at his best and all plays staged at the College found him interpreting one of the leading characters."[19]

Charles Simon, a guard, was also the editor of the "College Note Department" of the *Pacific Star*. Simon "was a composer of the 'A' class, his stories being noted for their wit and humor." It was as an athlete, however, that Charlie gained campus fame and was awarded the coveted "A" sweater. "He holds the distinction of being a pick of the guard position for two years in the Northwest and Non-Conference squad."[20]

Hubert Melchior had physical tools and a disposition that made him an all-star tackle. In addition to being fast on his feet, Hubert was also "aggressive and fighting to the last ditch." This trait may have been the most important to his teammates. "He was never known to be a quitter, and it was his fighting spirit that won him a berth on the all-star team." Versatility appears prevalent among the MAC athletes. In "handball 'Hub' was the peer of them all and was a real star in playing single alley." He was part of a larger Melchior family at Mt. Angel. It is believed that Hubert was Fr. Hildebrand's younger brother. Hubert had two brothers who starred in basketball at MAC, one of whom was probably Fr. Hildebrand. Thus, "it remained for 'Hub' to add to the family's laurels by his prowess on the gridiron." In football, Hubert's specialty "was opening holes big enough for the proverbial wagon to go through."[21]

Greg Pashek was nicknamed "Pelky." As the 1915 football team's captain, Greg was described as a fullback who could both "buck the line and lead interference." Pashek was also a solid defensive player. "It will be a long time before Mt. Angel will again have a 'full' that will equal in any way the defensive ability of 'Pelk.'" Another story noted that he "hails from The Dalles, the home of many football stars of Oregon. Before coming to Mount Angel he played on The Dalles High school team."[22]

Lynn Fuller came to MAC after gaining experience as a "regular player with Portland Academy." Fuller was seen as "one of the prominent football and baseball athletes at Mount Angel College." His football ability in Portland was recognized when he was "chosen on the all-star inter-scholastic eleven."[23] There were other players on the 1915 MAC football team that is pictured here. Names of the players are not available.

1915 Mt. Angel College football team. Joe is second from right.

The first story on Joe Kasberger at MAC appeared in an Oct., 1915 *Pacific Star* football-season preview. As written by John Sohler, MAC's prospects were bolstered by his return along with that of Hubert Melchior. Sohler wrote that in addition to "our sturdy gridiron heroes of last year," there is "an abundant number of prospects among the new material," so hopes were high. Sohler speculated that "M.A.C. tends fair to put out one of the fastest foot-ball teams that ever graced the campus of the old Gold and White." Returning players were "old reliables," and included: "Capt. Pashek, Kronberg, Franciscovich, Krebs, Mattucci, Cook, Eckerlin [sic] and Albers." Sohler then addresses Joe.

Among the new material which is looming prosperous under the able guidance of Coach Rassier, one Joseph Kasberger, from The Dalles, is proving to be the find of the season, and with his cast iron constitution and grit tends fair to ably fill the shoes of the much lamente [sic] Quinn, the Cannibal Chieftain of last year's squad.

There are no insights on "Quinn, the Cannibal Chieftain." Sohler continued by adding that: "Pashek has been elected to succeed himself as captain of this season's squad." [24]

Joe's rival to be quarterback was a senior, Francis Franciscovich, who was "last year's reliable end." In the pre-season, Franciscovich "has been practicing at Quarter where he is showing up like a real veteran." Sohler opined that "no position is yet permanent," but a starting team was taking shape, and "those looking brightest for back field positions" are Pashek, Kasberger, Melchior, and Franciscovich. Kronberg and Sohler were listed as "probable ends." On the line, Bill Krebs "seems to have a cinch on his last year's position at center." Other players showing "real class" were: "Eckerlen, Cook, Albers, Pohndorf, Mattucci [sic], Coghlan, Duerst, Engertsberger, Spear, Terhaar and May." Sohler gave a hint of the schedule, described as including "some of the leading High Schools and Colleges in the state." Finally, the players were exhibiting a "wonderful spirit" with hopes that 1915 would be "a record-breaking year on the gridiron."[25]

Joe's name is mentioned next in the Nov., 1915 *Pacific Star* account of the game between MAC and Lebanon High School, believed to be Joe's first college game. Note that there is reference to a 1915 game between MAC and the Chemawa Indians that the Angels lost.[26]

MAC 42-Lebanon HS 0. Lebanon was a small town approximately fifty miles south of Mt. Angel. Except for mention in the lineup as quarterback for MAC, Joe was only noted as a kicker. There is great irony associated with Lebanon HS when a Kasberger protégé, Joe Hellberg, became a coach here. The game story is in the appendix.

Joe is mentioned, however, on the Humor Page of the *Pacific Star* in the "Ha!Ha!Ha! Section," as follows:

Kasberger (in a butcher shop): 'I want a pound of dog meat.'
Butcher: 'Will you eat it here or take it with you?'[27]

MAC 7-Pacific U. 27. Pacific University was founded in 1849 as an affiliate of the Congregational Church, that later evolved into the United Church of

Christ.[28] Located about 25 miles west of Portland in Forest Grove, Pacific was a convenient foe in terms of travel. The Dec., 1915 *Pacific Star* game-summary is in the Appendix. Other than a lineup reference, nothing was written about Joe.

MAC 20-Albany College 9. Albany College was located in Albany, OR, about thirty miles south of Mt. Angel. Joe's performance featured several "long end runs," as the quarterback. The Jan., 1916 *Pacific Star* game-summary is presented in the Appendix.

MAC 20-Oregon City 0. Oregon City is located about twenty miles north of Mt. Angel. It appears that this team was an Athletic Club, unaffiliated with an educational institution. In this game, Joe apparently scored his first touchdown on a ten-yard run. Joe's second touchdown was described as follows: "Two completed passes coupled with a series of line plunges enabled Kasberger to add another six points to the Angels' score in the same stanza." On this nasty-weather day, Kasberger, Simon, and Franciscovich "shared honors of the fray."[29] The full game story is in the Appendix.

The February, 1916 *Pacific Star* stated that the 1915 football team enjoyed "the most successful year ever experienced by the M.A.C. in this department of our annual pastime." Accordingly, the Angels claimed a championship.

By virtue of their overwhelming defeat of Albany College and their rejected challenge at the hands of Willamette University, Mt. Angel College lays claim to the Non-Conference championship of the State.[30]

For a young man who had never played organized football, Joe made a successful debut. Whether or not Joe liked the limelight, he was now famous. MAC's success seems remarkable with an inexperienced quarterback, a fact that was not lost in a *Pacific Star* story several years later. "Before coming to college Joe hailed from The Dalles, having there made a 'rep' in baseball." Also, Joe "easily swung into [the] quarterback position, though previous to his entrance at this college he had never played on the gridiron."[31]

Although the football season had ended, Joe's name appeared in the January, 1916 *Pacific Star.* Joe, "our plunging fullback, had the pleasure of a short visit from his sister and brother from The Dalles, during the first part

Joe in MAC football uniform, year unknown.

of December." They "were highly pleased with this section of the state, and we hope they will not forget to call again in the near future."[32]

The January, 1916 *Pacific Star* wrote about the "sumptuous" football banquet on Dec. 13 to celebrate the 1915 football season:

> The banquet hall was artistically decorated and immaculate tables groaned under the weight of the most delicious viands. Music was not wanting to make the event more hilarious, and the several vocal and instrumental numbers aided considerably in making the evening a very enjoyable one.[33]

The story mentioned that "pennants were distributed to the players by our congenial President, Rev. Fr. Basil," in appreciation for the team's success. Also announced was Joe being "elected captain of next year's foot-ball team," and hopes were high. "With Coach French at the helm and Capt. Kasberger on deck, great things may be expected from the 1916 squad."[34] Coach French suggests that Fr. Victor, as head coach, had an assistant. Or, was Fr. Victor a figurehead, with Coach French doing the coaching?

The Feb., 1916 *Pacific Star* had another story on the banquet and Joe. There appears to be confusion among *Pacific Star's* writers about Joe's position on the team. As noted in the lineups in the Appendix, Joe was the quarterback.

> Kasberger played half-back and called signals for the M.A.C. squad the past season, where he amply displayed his abilities which were no small factor in the wonderful record achieved by M.A.C. this year. Following the election each player voiced his sentiments concerning the game at M.A.C.; after which Coach French divulged a few remarks about his plans for the coming season. [35]

Abbot Adelhelm Odermatt

This *Pacific Star* account tempered enthusiasm for next year with a report that "a few of our stars will not be returning to school next year." It is not clear whether this was due to graduation or other reasons. The story concluded with the belief that "the majority have promised to be on hand for the opening of the 1916 season."[36]

In early 1916, Fr. Adelhelm was honored when he celebrated "his golden jubilee of profession," and he was made "titular abbot." Abbot Adelhelm lived an interesting life. "The venerated patriarch greatly appreciated this honor, and during his remaining years pontificated throughout the diocese with plenty of incense and ornate ceremony."[37]

His secular contributions were also recognized. An anonymous news story, dated Jan. 13, 1916, has the headline: "City Founder Honored – Mount Angel Council Gives Diploma To Father Odermatt. Beautiful Work of Art Given in Recognition of Man Who Established Educational Center." Mount Angel City Council, with Mayor P. S. Fuchs presiding, "held a special meeting." Brother Celestine, O.S.B.

was in attendance when city officials "signed the diploma appointing the Rt. Rev. Adelhelm Odermatt, O.S.B., an honorary citizen and recognizing him as founder of this place."[38] Abbot Adelhelm spent his last years as an assistant at St. Joseph parish in Portland. "He died in 1920, after suffering a stroke," but his remains were returned to Mt. Angel for burial.

Joe's emergence as a basketball player at MAC is surprising since there is no evidence that he played the sport at TDHS. Perhaps this is a first indication that Joe was a fine all-around athlete, and Fr. Hildebrand was as important to Joe's career as Fr. Victor. As Joe's first basketball coach, Fr. Hildebrand taught fundamentals that served him well.

MAC's winning basketball tradition was described in a June 3, 1926 *Pacific Star* story about the 1914-15 team. This team's photo is in Joe's personal photo album with the caption, "Some Team/Went to Frisco to Play for Championship."

> After winning 11 games in a state challenge, old M.A.C., under Coach William O'Rourke, was the only undefeated college team of its standing in the state, and was thus alone eligible to play for honors at the Panama Pacific International Exposition at San Francisco.[39]

Since basketball rules were not universal, the Angels "were finally eliminated there by Whittier College – one reason was that different playing rules were used in the South." It was the only loss, and the season ended "with 374 points for M.A.C. and 165 against."[40]

The February, 1916 *Pacific Star* presented the pre-season 1915-16

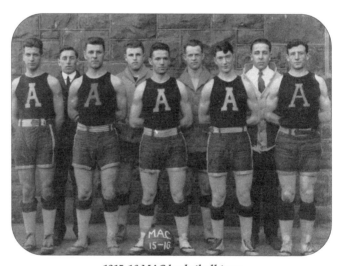

1915-16 MAC basketball team.

basketball team as having only one returning veteran from 1914-15. There was hope since there were many team candidates.

> Kronberg the only remaining player of last year's quintet has been elected captain; Franciscovich as manager is already fast on the trail of some of the leading colleges, and he promises to have a complete schedule. Among the games already on his list are Chemawa, Dalles, Holmes Business College, Salem, and others. Those showing up well in practice are Kronberg, Franciscovich, Pashek, Eckerlen, Sohler, Albers, Coghlan, Kasberger, Classic, Pohndorf, and Combs.[41]

The 1915-16 basketball team team finished with a 12-4 record. Game stories have not been revealed, but there is a season summary that indicates the team was competitive. Only Chemawa beat the Angels decisively by a score of 15-32. For the season, MAC outscored its opponents 383 to 294.[42]

A May, 1916 *Pacific Star* told of a "time honored custom" at MAC to celebrate the basketball season's end with a banquet for both varsity and intramural teams. It was held on March 28, "honored by the presence of Fathers Basil, Victor, and Hildebrand." Fr. Basil is described as the team "moderator" while Fathers Victor and Hildebrand were "honorary guests of the club." There is no description of the meal that was served.

> After adjusting a somewhat square meal in round stomachs, and while clouds of blue smoke curled fantastically from the best brand of havana [sic] cigars, Charles Simon in his congenial way introduced the toast master of the evening Joseph Kasberger. Joe showed himself able for the task and by his many pointed remarks and his genuine wit proved the hit of the evening.[43]

While Joe was a man of few words later in life, he appeared loquacious at MAC.

Joe's head baseball coach at MAC appears to have been Fr. Victor, possibly assisted in 1916 and 1917 by Fr. Basil. The names on the squad reveal several all-around athletes who performed on the football and basketball teams.

As a pitcher, Joe had a special relationship with his catcher, Guy Chapelle. Jack Sohler, also, appears to be a close friend as a pitcher on the Angel staff. For "Chappie," as he was known to Joe, it may have been a challenge to catch Joe, initially, as he made the transition to the college game. The 1916 baseball team had two men return from 1915, who were described as stalwarts: Greg Pashek and Lynn Fuller. An anonymous July, 1918 story reported that Pashek in the out-

field had a "perfect fielding percentage." An anonymous July, 1918 news story about Lynn Fuller in 1914 "held [him] as the best pinch hitter who ever attended the college." Chas. "Charlie" Coghlan was a real clutch player. "More than one game of baseball was won by Charles' ability to hit em [sic] hard when it meant runs." In the same anonymous story, Sohler was noted as having "twirled excellent ball" at Forest Grove in 1914.[44]

Baseball results for the 1916 Angels are unknown. The following summary is believed to pertain to the 1916 season. It appeared

John Sohler, Guy Chapelle and Joe. In his album, Joe captioned this photo "The Battery: Sohler, Chappy and Mooh."

June 17, in an anonymous paper, with the headline: "Mount Angel Tossers Win Most of Battles." MAC's season ended with a 9-4 record that was marked by "heavy and consistent hitting." The Angels' defense had "fast fielding" in support of fine pitching. Two newcomers on the pitching staff, Sohler and Kasberger, were described as "two able collegian twirlers," who showed "excellent ability on the mound." The story described

This undated and anonymous news photo of the 1916 team has the title "Mt. Angel College Possesses Winning Baseball Team." The caption reads "Team which won nine out of 13 games during the spring season. From left to right, upper row, the players are- Al [sic] R. Kronberg, captain; J. Sohler, J. Cook, Coach Victor, F. Albers, G. Pashek, F. Franciscovich. Lower row-M. Hannah, H. Ransom, N. Schandling [sic], J. Robinson, mascot; G. Cahaple [sic], J. Kasberger, C. Coghlan."

Sohler's pitching style as consisting of "a good display and variety of curves," in his arsenal. Joe was described as "a speedy tosser," who "depends upon his fastball." Coach Victor was credited for his "wise council and guiding hand" over the season. Praise was given, also, to MAC captain, Al Kronberg, as an "able man" who "bore an influential sway over his winning nine."[45]

Joe's personal photo album has many pictures from the MAC baseball team. One photo is captioned "The Coach With His Windcutting Crew." Another photo reveals Joe's affection for his catcher: "Old Chappie Boy"/The Best Little Catcher on Earth." Joe's nicknames appear to have been "Slouchy" and "Mooh," which may have stemmed from his cow milking ability, affirmed many years later. According to Joe, cow-milking was good for a pitcher by making the hands and arms strong. [46] The number of photos indicates that Joe had fond memories of playing Angels baseball.

The suggestion that Joe competed in track as a four-sport MAC athlete, does not appear credible in 1916. An anonymous story, dated March 17, without year, has the headline: "Mount Angel Not To Have Track Sports This Season." A meeting,

Joe on the sidelines with a fellow student and some Mt. Angel monks.

Joe captioned this photo from his album "Slouchy."

described as one of the "most important" in this school year, was held. The student body addressed track as a college sport because in recent years "Mount Angel college have [sic] not had a track team competing at the state events." The rationale was MAC's location, making it difficult "to attract many fans." Accordingly, "all unnecessary expenses must be curtailed." With these considerations, a final action was taken at this meeting. "The student body unanimously voted against the added expense." While there was no money for track, the same story reported that the president of the student body announced that "the regular May-day celebration would again be held."[47] The May Day celebration may have been the "M.A.C. Picnic" that is shown in Joe's personal photo album.

The end of the 1915-16 school year brought student awards and commencement exercises. The 1915-16 *Catalog* for Mt. Angel College and Seminary listed the graduates and award winning students. John Friedman of Alton, Iowa was the only graduate from the "Collegiate Department," and was awarded a Bachelor of Science Degree. Presumably certificates, rather than degrees, were awarded to the following students:

Joe at a Mt. Angel picnic.

Academic Department

Mr. Frank Albers, Cottonwood, Idaho
Mr. Charles Coghlan, Portland, Oregon
Mr. Francis Franciscovich, Astoria, Oregon
Mr. Aloysius May, Mt. Angel, Oregon
Mr. John Schroth, Portland, Oregon
Mr. Charles Simon, San Francisco, Cal.

Commercial Department

Mr. Raymond Combs, Haines, Alaska
Mr. Louis Growney, Maryville, Missouri
Mr. Joseph Kasberger, The Dalles, Oregon
Mr. Daniel Lyons, Oregon City, Oregon
Mr. Harold Ransom, Aumsville, Oregon
Mr. John Sohler, Forest Grove, Oregon

An uncaptioned photo from Joe's album may be of him pitching at MAC in 1916 or 1917.

Joe had an outstanding academic record to complement his performances as a three-sport varsity athlete. "The Gregg Teacher's Certificate" was awarded to two students: Louis Growney and Joe Kasberger. It is believed that this certificate enabled Joe to teach shorthand. In the category "GOLD MEDALS AND AWARDS" from the COMMERCIAL DEPARTMENT, Joe Kasberger received the award donated by "The Reverend B.C. Pffifner." The final award, most coveted by MAC's athletes, was the "A" Sweater and the recipients were as follows: "Mr. Guy Chapel, [sic] Vancouver, Washington; Mr. Joseph Kasberger, The Dalles, Oregon; Mr. Nathan Shanedling, Vancouver, Washington; and Mr. Charles Simon, San Francisco, California."[48]

Joe captioned this photo "Nuf sed." It was taken at the end of his freshman year when he received the gold medal.

When Joe came home in the summer of 1916, his vacation may have been both interesting and stressful. Everyone wanted to know about his college experiences. On a more somber side, there was World War I and the threat of a military draft. With five sons, and kin in Germany, this was not an easy time for John and Anna. Joe's personal photo album may provide an insight into how part of the vacation was spent in the calm before the storm.

The album has many photos from this era. One is captioned: "The Old Swimming Hole." A second photo of several young ladies in bathing suits is captioned: "The Mermaids." A third photo is captioned: "On the Beach About 6:00 PM." Finally, there are captions "In the Good Old Summer Time" and "Come in Boys the Water is Wet." The only individual who appears identifiable, besides Joe, is Matt Duffy, his teammate from TDHS. One photo is cap-

Joe swimming with friends at Mill Creek in The Dalles.

tioned "Duffy" and another is captioned "Duf and His Smoke." The caption "Not Guilty" may pertain to Duffy. Also, there are pictures of Joe's brothers wearing his "A" Sweater, without captions. Finally, there are pictures of Joe with male and female friends ("The Darlings," as captioned by Joe) swimming in what was probably the Columbia River or Mill Creek.[49]

While at home Joe was able to catch up on local news, especially high school football and the 1915 TDHS football team that had a rebuilding year.

1916-17 School Year

Joe returned to MAC at an uncertain time, so sports provided Joe and his classmates with a distraction from world events. When World War I began in August, 1914, German-Americans were cast in an awkward position due to their fatherland's military successes. On campus, there was a diversity of nationalities, with some students sharing either pro-German or anti-English persuasions. There were tensions in Oregon surrounding the volatile issues of World War I.

Msgr. Stone described "anti-Catholic sentiments" expressed by "organized groups of bigots." Catholics were "agents of a foreign government (the Vatican)," and to be distrusted. With increasing immigration from European countries, there was antagonism for those "regarded as 'Catholic.'" These sentiments became especially vocal prior to World War I, with German-Americans, in particular, targeted, and "bigotry focused on the clergy." Germans were not alone and Msgr. Stone observed that "Irish-Americans also came in for their share of the enmity because of their inborn antagonism toward the English government." The problem existed not only in large urban areas. Msgr. Stone noted that "Priests in Eastern Oregon felt the sting of this mentality."[50]

Accounts of Joe's second season as a MAC football player begin with an anonymous news story dated Sept. 30 with headline: "Mount Angel Squad Out – Two of Last Year's Stars Don Football Uniforms. Thirty Men Are Turning Out Daily for Practice – First Game Will Be With Vancouver, October 7." The mention of Coach French is interpreted to mean that he was Fr. Victor's assistant coach whose job it was to get the team ready. At the initial drills, Coach French "had the football squad running up and down the campus." Emphasis was given to "special teams," so Coach French devoted part of an afternoon to "punting and signal practice."[51]

The Oct., 1916 *Pacific Star* has another preseason football story written by John Engertsberger who introduces another MAC football coach for the 1916 season. Sept. 18th was the date practice began and Coach O'Neil's call for football candidates met with "hearty approval." A squad of twenty men, "filled with the old time 'pep' responded to the first call." Coach O'Neil, rather than Fr. Victor, "proceeded to mold his future stars into shape," after "the glad rags could be given out," suggesting that the uniforms were new. The story alludes to possible economic difficulties at MAC. "Athletic Association heedless of 'hard times' invested in completely new foot-ball togs." Perhaps the scarcity of cash required the story to emphasize safety.

> Coach O'Neil, a strong advocate of 'safety first,' took no chances of not securing the best, and did his own bargaining. To look at the new suits, hip pads, shoes, socks, shoulder pads and head gears, one could see that he was well acquainted with the needs of a football player, and likewise solicitous for the safety of the team.[52]

MAC's 1916 football "turnout this year is one of the best the school has had for many years, and several fast teams will no doubt be the result." Team captain, Joe Kasberger, was referred to as our "fighting fullback," giving Joe another nickname. "He is already known in our minds as 'Reliable Joe' and judging from present indications, this cognomen is not given amiss."[53] Other Angel players and their nicknames follow:

Uncaptioned 1916 MAC football team

Another old reliable, 'Speed' Sohler, after working during the summer months is back with the old time 'ginger' that always characterized his playing. 'Stonewall' Krebs, the coolheaded German and star of many games is again passing the ball.

Charlie Simon, last year's 'All Star' guard, has again donned his uniform to battle for the old White and Gold.

The following cryptic reference to Eckerlen's summer in Mexico is not explained as the story continues:

Eckerlen, the other 'All Star' guard, has been keeping in first class condition by training with our boys in Mexico. 'Hub' Melchior, our daring left tackle was one of the first to don his togs. 'Chas' Coghlan, our slippery right end is again in the game. 'Guisto' Mattacci [sic] has been keeping trim all summer and will fill a hole in the line that will make a steam roller look cheap.

Several new players were "showing up particularly well." They were: "Graser, Brophy, Brown, Glatt." The returning players "Kasberger, Sohler, Krebs, Mettucci [sic], Coghlan, Eckerlen, Melchior, Simon are showing up well in their old positions." The story lists these other players: "... Dean, ... Rassier, Wilfred, Engertsberger, Rassier, Steve, Brophy, ... Hannigan, Spear, Johnson, Hersy, Swall and Sullivan." The story continues with mention of a new football field, but practices were conducted "at the old grounds."[54]

MAC's 1916 football schedule included "the leading colleges and high schools," but there was doubt as to whether all players expected would report. "The return of two football stars of last year's squad, Eckerlen and Simon, has pleased Coach French." Both were valuable veterans who won postseason honors in 1915 from Edward Bailey, the Albany College coach who picked all-star teams. Bailey stated that for the guard position Eckerlen and Simon were chosen because they "are not equaled in any other college." Also mentioned are Joe and Bill Krebs, who had received postseason football honors in 1916 from Bailey. Krebs, as MAC's center, "was the most solid on any non-conference team." Joe, "the Mount Angel captain, was given praise for his plucky work in the backfield."[55]

Joe in a MAC football uniform.

One of the most variously spelled names of all the Angel players was "Guisto" or "Fighting" Mettucce [sic]. The correct spelling is provided later in the text, but for now it is presented as shown in the source story. The Angel squad was shaping up with both veterans and newcomers, with around "30 men . . . turning out daily for practice." The story speculates that MAC's roster would include the following men:

Krebs center, Eckerlen and Simon guards, with Schwall, a Forest Grove freshman, as sub; Coghlan and Brown, a Corvallis High School player, at ends; W. Rassier and Engertsberger will sub; 'Fighting' Mettucce [sic], Melchoir [sic], Meehan and Brophy are playing nip and tuck for the positions as tackles; Glatt, a former Oregon City boy, will undoubtedly be fullback; Sohler, of last year's squad, will retain his position as right halfback; Grazer, a 'dark horse,' is fighting hard for left half; Captain Kasberger, the heady and plucky quarterback, is going better than ever. Steve Rassier will sub in the backfield.[56]

An anonymous story, dated Sept. 23, is headlined: "Kasberger Is Captain – Mount Angel Team Expected to Give Good Account of Itself." Joe had high hopes and was confident that he has one of the "best collegiate football teams in the state." Yet, Joe was saddened that "Pashek, last year's fullback will not return, but he hopes to find a 'dark horse.'"[57]

The Oct. 1916 *Pacific Star* mentioned Joe in an article headlined "Athletic Association Re-Organized." On Oct. 2, the Athletic Association convened for the "semi-annual election of officers," and chose the following for the first semester: "John Sohler, President; Joseph Kasberger, Vice-President; and, William Krebs, Secretary-Treasurer." The results may have pleased the writer who added: "Nothing less than a most prosperous year is expected from three such capable men as the above-named." Also, Joe's name appeared again in the Oct. 1916 *Pacific Star's* "Ha!Ha!Ha!" Humor section:

Sohler: 'I believe there is quite a lot of truth in Honnigan.'
Kasberger: 'Why?'
Sohler: 'Because none ever comes out of him.'[58]

The Nov. 16 *Pacific Star* reported that the return of Greg Pashek and Lynn Fuller from the 1915 team, "although tardy, was welcomed by all." With Pashek and Fuller back, optimism grew with "every prospect for a very able team."[59] Besides football during the 1916 fall semester, Joe had another task – as reported in the Nov, 1916 *Pacific Star:*

'Old Reliable' Joe Kasberger, having been elected a member of the Athletic Association was chosen to attend to the wants of the students at the candy store. Joe feigned the idea of his being unfit for the task, nevertheless, a more competent student, or one that has the interest of the Association more at heart, could not be chosen in the discharge of this work. Stay with it, Joe.[60]

The Dec. 1916 *Pacific Star* presents football game accounts. With such high hopes for the 1916 season, the first game was a major disappointment.

MAC 2 - Vancouver A.C. 6. The game was played Oct. 18 in Vancouver, WA and Joe was one of the stars for the Angels. The Appendix has a complete game story.

MAC 13-Pacific U. 14. On Oct. 28, Joe had a tough day for the Angels. After

Greg Pashek scored the game's first touchdown, Joe "failed to kick goal by a few inches." Before the first half ended, Pacific scored a touchdown and converted the extra point for a 7-6 lead. In the third quarter, Coghlan scored a touchdown and Joe converted the extra point for a 13-7 Angel lead. After a valiant goal-line stand that lasted for three downs at the five yard line, Pacific scored a touchdown on its fourth try. Their extra point try was good and the Angels lost.[61] The complete game story is in the Appendix.

The next scheduled game for the Angels was against Willamette University, which had rejected in 1915, MAC's football game challenge. Located only 15 miles from Mt. Angel, Willamette was a perfect rival. Game details are unusual and feature Joe Kasberger.

MAC 0-Willamette 1. The Dec. 1916 *Pacific Star* has one of the most bizarre football stories that is imaginable. Perhaps the animosity stemmed from Willamette's 1915 rejection of MAC's challenge to a game. The Bearcats, as Willamette was known, began playing football in 1894. In their first football game in 1909, Willamette humiliated MAC 0-63; and the score was 0-47 in 1910. This was only the third game in this series.[62] The game story is in the Appendix.

MAC's forfeit-loss to Willamette prompted a letter to the editor in the Nov. 6, 1916 Salem *Sunday Journal* in response to what was perceived as biased reporting. The following headline appeared atop the letter: "Mt. Angel Explains Football Squabble."

> To the Sporting Editor of the *Journal* – In reply to the article appearing in your *Sunday Journal,* in which the Mount Angel college football team was announced to have left the 'field in a huff over an offside ruling,' during a game played last Saturday, November 4, on Willamette Field, I am requesting you to print this letter, which contains some of the facts of this game and which will help your readers to understand why Mount Angel left the field in a huff.
>
> To begin with, Mount Angel placed the ball three times within the shadow of Willamette's goal, only to lose it by timely penalties. Unexpectedly, Captain Kasberger evaded the referee's penalty when he went through tackle for 20 yards to a touchdown. With one more minute of play left in the third quarter, Halfback Sohler of Mount Angel intercepted a forward pass and raced 15 yards before being downed. Coach Matthews of Willamette, whom the officials of the game were unable to keep off the field of play, even during the progress of play, rushed up to the head linesman, and in plain English told him to call Mount Angel offside. Up to this time six penalties were inflicted on Mount Angel, five of them being 15-yard penalties and coming either after Mount Angel had made an appreciable gain or were nearing their opponents' goal. The Mount Angel captain, when asking the reason of the penalties, was told that the backfield men, when running interference for the man carrying the ball, did not keep their arms close enough to their body. On the other hand, Willamette had not been so much as penalized once.
>
> These few lines will help you to view the cause of Mount Angel's huff from their standpoint, and, I might add, from the standpoint of many of those who witnessed the game, as remarks, passed by and during the game and during the argument prior to the forfeiture indicated.

Thanking you for the courtesy, I am, respectfully yours, COACH FRENCH, Mount Angel College.[63]

The Jan. 1917 *Pacific Star* has a story on what appears to have been Joe's last game for the Angels. The Chemawa Indians conjure up images of Jim Thorpe and the Carlisle, PA Indian School a continent away. At about the same time as their Oregon counterparts, Carlisle became a famous East Coast football power. While Chemawa is not shown on contemporary Oregon road maps, it is believed to have been located in, or near, Salem. Whether the Chemawa Indians were a club team, or represented an educational institution, is not known. Chemawa, however, played against Pacific Coast Conference colleges, as well as smaller colleges, and even high schools. They were seen as a formidable opponent.

MAC 3 - Chemawa 0. Joe was the star, scoring the game's only points in the fourth quarter with a 38-yard field goal. The game story is in the Appendix. With MAC still smarting from the Willamette forfeit, the Jan. 1917 *Pacific Star* discusses the Chemawa game.

> The football game between Mt. Angel and Chemawa caused no little enthusiasm among the followers of the sport about the town of Mt. Angel. The spirit among the students was one of the notable features of the game. We shall venture here to extend our sincere thanks to Mr. Boreleske of Portland, who offered his services as referee. His straightforward and firm decisions were not only in strict accordance with the rules of football, but were, moreover, enforced in such a manner as not to distract from the interest taken in the game.[64]

The 1916 football season ended positively, but it was controversial and disappointing. With such high expectations, the Angels did not succeed as a team, yet team members were honored for their individual performances. When the all-star team was announced, several MAC players were selected. An anonymous news story dated Dec. 2 and bylined Albany, OR, without year, has the headline: "All-Stars Chosen – Non-Conference Team Picked by Albany College Coach. Grosvenor First Choice – French, of Albany; Lucas, of Pacific, and Kasberger of Mount Angel Are Selected as other Men Back of Line – COACH BAILEY'S ALL - NON -CONFERENCE ELEVEN." They are as follows:

Smith, Pacific U	Center
Krebs, Mount Angel	Right guard
Tohles, Albany College	Left guard
Tobie, Willamette	Right tackle
Livesay, Pacific U	Left tackle
Rexford, Willamette	Right end
Ratcliffe, Willamette	Left end
Kashberger [sic], Mt. Angel	Quarter
Grosvenor, Willamette	Right half
French, Albany College	Left half
Lucas, Pacific U	Fullback

Albany College's coach Bailey had selected an All-Star team for the last two years. His credibility as a judge of college football talent was based upon his experience as a player at the University of Oregon and with Portland's Multnomah Athletic Club. As a collegian, Bailey "was picked three seasons on the all-Northwest eleven." Excerpts of the story about Joe follow. The story in its entirety is presented in the Appendix.

> The quarterback position is given to Kasberger of Mount Angel. He is a good open-field runner, good at making interference and plays good defensive ball.[65]

An anonymous Dec. 20 news story is headlined: "Mount Angel Picks Captain – Joseph Kasberger, of The Dalles, is Chosen for Second Year." Excerpts of the text follow for the story on MAC's football banquet that was held the previous evening. The main news story was Joe's election as captain to lead the 1917 team. "He earned this position especially by his line plunging and his remarkable gains on his runs around the ends." The inference drawn from Joe's re-election is that he planned to return for his junior year. The story calls Joe a "star" basketball player with physical resilience. "During his two years of play at Mount Angel he has never been hurt during any of the athletic games."[66]

The Jan. 1917 *Pacific Star* described the Dec. 19 football banquet in the college refectory.

> It was an appetizing feast; everything from ham sandwiches to salt mackerel [sic] was served. Even that was not all; following the dinner some of the players being members of the elocution class were called upon to demonstrate their ability in that line. Stonewall Kasberger, captain of last year's team was called upon by the toastmaster to recall some of the team's achievements. He pictured the team as it appeared to him, and congratulated each member for the spirit displayed in every game. He exalted Coach French to whom he said all credit was due for the successful season just passed. [67]

Coach French "praised the players both for their college spirit and for their true sportsmanship." The banquet ended with "the unanimous election of Joe Kasberger as captain of the '17 team."[68] There is another Jan. 1917 *Pacific Star* story on the banquet.

> Many good speeches were given and jokes exchanged. Simon, the College orator, favored the select gathering with an excellent speech on College Spirit. Eckerlen, the toastmaster of the evening, was witty throughout and was very clever in introducing the different speakers. Father Basil and Coach Victor graced the occasion with their presence.[69]

Joe's reelection to be captain of the 1917 MAC football team appeared in another unidentified newspaper, probably the *Statesman-Journal* from Salem, OR. With an undated photo of Joe is the caption: "The Dalles Boy Will Captain Mount Angel College Team." Joe is described as "only a sophomore" from The

Dalles and "highly thought of by his teammates." The story concluded by stating that "Kasberger is a fighter from the ground up and prospects for a winning team are bright."[70]

The Jan. 1917 *Pacific Star* expressed gratitude to the 1916 football Angels, and warm sentiments about Joe:

Joe as a young man.

> All we can do is thank them collectively and to sing their praises for time to come. Our thanks are extended especially to one individual who was instrumental in the successful termination of the season, Coach Victor. Captain Kasberger is next in order. He, by right of position, but chiefly by his hard work deserves our special esteem. Last but by no means least, we wish to thank the second team, which so faithfully co-operated with the first and enabled Coach Victor to build up a team [of] which Mt. Angel is justly proud.[71]

In subsequent *Pacific Star* stories, it is apparent that Joe was very popular and multidimensional. In a small college environment, where everyone knows each other, there was no escape from the limelight. Opportunities abounded for Joe to grow as a student, rather than just as an athlete.

The Feb. 1917 *Pacific Star* described its annual New Year's eve celebration, the "*Pacific Star* Banquet." Joe's performance in a non-athletic role as a member of the student body appears important. In this regard, Frank Leipzig appears to have influenced Joe. According to the Feb. 1917 *Pacific Star*, the celebration was "somewhat tardy," presumably because it was held after New Year's Day in 1917.

> Frank Leipzig, our veteran ex-business manager, was toast master, and he went after it just as if he were getting ads. By noticing the advertising section you can see how well he accomplished this. Father Basil gave the boys a little address of thanks and discussed the *Star* pro and con, but mostly con. 'Doc' Friedman, editor-in-chief, poet, philosopher, and general authority for the M.A.C. Waiter's Union, had this to say, as did all the boys right on down the line, even unto 'Joe' Kasberger. Well, the banquet was superlatively good, the speaking was of the very best, and even the cigars were 'Optimos' (or were they 'Havana Taste')?[72]

The Banquet story's reference to Joe is presumed to deal with his candy store that also sold tobacco products. Glen Sullivan is not known to be either fact or fiction.

> Where is the band? What is it, a holiday? No, no, calm yourself, don't get flustrated [sic]; it's merely the return of Glen Sullivan, 'the red-headed ant eater.'

71

Wild and wooly 'Red' comes from that part of the country where the dogs bark at strangers and sage brush reigns supreme. The permission to smoke was one of the most appreciated Xmas presents, and for a few days he tried to smoke up all the cigars in the store; but having decided that 'Joe' can get them faster than he can smoke them, he undertook to let a pipe be his latest form of sacrifice at the altar of the goddess Nicotine.[73]

Joe's campus candy store may have generated revenues to support student activities, including athletics. Perhaps Bob Murray was Joe's cigar wholesaler! In this same *Pacific Star*, Joe is featured in another story, suggesting that MAC football heroes were not immune from media humor at their expense.

> Well, the ways of genius are always hard, even as is the road to heaven, and 'Joe' Kasberger must surely have thought he was on the way to both of them, for his trials have been many.
> But this is getting ahead of the story. It started this way: Joe had during Xmas vacation become attached to a flute possessed by his little brother, whom he had after much talking persuaded to part with. The instrument was brought to school and after much secret practising [sic] in his room, Joe finally decided to give a public recital for the benefit of the third floor East End. The hall was the chosen place for the exhibition, and the enraptured and amazed roomers formed the interesting audience. The music was sublime, and all took a turn at trying it. The results were amazing. Suddenly the air was electrified by a sharp 'Beat it!' The crowd dispersed like magic. Soon the conscientious Prefect put in an appearance, and the hunt for the mysterious instrument began in earnest. After much fruitless questioning and many inquiries, the culprit was located and the instrument of temptation removed.
> Our consolations, Joe, old boy! We give them freely.[74]

The same issue of the *Pacific Star* has a brief news item about Leipzig, whose departure created an opportunity for Joe to be a *Pacific Star* staff-member. Leipzig, due to a "scarcity of time and the necessity of devoting more attention to his studies, has resigned his position as Business Manager of the *Pacific Star*." To replace Leipzig in this important position, two students were required. "'Joe' Kasberger has been appointed to the place with Chas. J. Simon as assistant."[75]

In a related *Pacific Star* story, Leipzig's career with student activities is developed after his promotion from alumni editor to business manager. "Business manager is certainly a difficult position yet Frank found time to devote some attention to literary work." Also, "Frank was unanimously chosen president of the Athletic association for the last semester 1916-17." When Leipzig assumed the presidency, it was "heavily in debt." Frank, "with the help of his Vice-President, Secretary and Treasurer brought the amount within sight of a clear board." The other officers were John Sohler, Joe Kasberger, and William Krebs.[76]

Also significant about Leipzig is his MAC scrapbook, the source for many unidentified news stories that are presented here. From *Pacific Star* accounts, Leipzig had no athletic role as a player, but was prominent on campus and was featured in a *Pacific Star* story dated Feb. 1917.

We bow to Frank P. Leipzig the youth from Wisconsin but lately of Portland who built up our Alumni department, until today we frankly and truthfully say, we believe this department stands out superior to the Alumni department of any College Journal in the entire United States. Through the exertion of Father Thomas and Frank P. Leipzig hundreds of Alumni names have appeared on our lists and the present system employed in locating former students of Mount Angel is the form given to us by Frank.[77]

Joe's new *Pacific Star* duties coincided with the basketball season. How Joe found the time to play basketball, work at the *Pacific Star*, and maintain his academics is not discussed. It is known that he forged a close working relationship with Leipzig, to effectively perform this important function.

The following basketball stories about the 1916-17 basketball season are from an unknown newspaper. On Dec 8, the following headline appeared: "20 Turn Out At Mount Angel – Fight for Places on Basketball Team Promises to Be Lively." The story revealed that Fr. Hildebrand had twenty students report to pre-season tryouts.

With the return of Sohler and Kasberger, first-team men of last year, the quint will have a good foundation. Of the recruits Schwall, a freshman of Forest Grove, is showing ability. This same student in his first year at college easily made the first football team, and with his six feet two inches he looks mighty good as center of the basketball team. Of the other recruits Brown, of Albany High; Glatt, of Woodburn, and Spear, of Seaside, look good. Eckerlen, of Salem, is fighting hard for center or guard.[78]

Team manager John Sohler had the responsibility of arranging the schedule "with various colleges and high schools throughout the state." As late as mid-December, the schedule was not yet set, a possible indication that World War I was beginning to have an impact.[79]

An anonymous news story dated Dec. 9 has the headline: "Mt. Angel Basketers [sic] Now Under Training." This was Fr. Hildebrand's sixth year as coach, and after the first cuts, the original twenty players were reduced to ten. Kasberger played guard and Sohler forward; with these "two letter men of last year, the team looks good." One new player, William Spear, a sophomore from Seaside, OR, was "the dark horse of the season."[80]

The competition to start at center "was nip and tuck between Spear and Schwall, but during the past few days Spear is the favorite." Another player noticed was Ralph Classic from Portland, described as "a former junior of Christian Brothers" and "is easily the pick for the other forward position." Classic had all-around skills, particularly an "easy style of shooting" and an "ability to cover the floor are his chief abilities." Pashek and Eckerlen were seen as "fighting hard for the remaining guard position." A final player noted was Schwall, a Forest Grove freshman, who "will no doubt sub on the team."[81]

The prospects for the basketball team improved with the return of a key player from last year's team. On Dec. 9, the following headline appeared:

An anonymous news photo has the title: "Mount Angel Basketball Team," with 1916-1917 hand-written. The caption reads: "From left: Joseph Kasberger, guard; Gregory Pashek, guard; Ralph Classic, forward, Portland, junior; Coach Hildebrand; William Spear, center; Bernard Brost, spare, Portland, freshman; Captain Nat Shanedling [sic], former Jefferson star in the Inter-scholastic League, forward."

"Mount Angel Strengthened – Return of Nat Schanedling Changes Line-Up of Quintet." Nat, from Vancouver, WA, "considerably strengthened" the Angels squad. He was a "stellar forward of the Mount Angel team last year" and a "former Lincoln High star." He was described as a "running guard," and "equal to any in the state," with swiftness and an excellent shot.[82]

Classic remained set at the "first forward" position, but the other forward position was unsettled and was seen as a "tossup between Sohler and Brost." However, Sohler, "having played on the first team last year," was "not any too anxious to try out for the team," for unknown reasons. Thus, the forward position "is likely to go to Brost." Spear continued "doing well at center," with "ability in dribbling and his fine breast shot are his best qualities." Joe Kasberger remained set at one guard position. The other guard slot was described as a "merry tussle" between Glatt of Woodburn and Schwall of Forest Grove. Fortunately for Fr. Hildebrand, Pashek returned to play the other guard position.[83]

Nat appeared close to Joe from the captions recorded in his personal photo album. On the top of a photo, Joe captioned: "Dat A Pepper." On the bottom, Joe captioned: "Fat Shanedling, Best All Around Athlete For a Fat Man." Also, Nat was a member of the "Pig Shaved Crew," along with Spear, Simon, and Chapelle. After two weeks of practice, MAC appeared set to open their season.

An anonymous news story dated Dec. 16 has the headline: "Mount Angel To

Play Today – College Hoopers to Defend on Home Floor Against Molalla." Molalla, a small town located about twenty miles northeast of Mt. Angel, is believed to have had an Athletic Club team. Molalla was described as "fast," but had been unable to beat MAC in recent years. With three lettermen back from the 1916-17 team and the "addition of two second-team men of last year," the Angels felt "able to cope against the visitors."[84]

Fr. Hildebrand's starting lineup had Pashek and Kasberger as guards; Schanedling and Classic were the forwards; and the newcomer at center was Spear. MAC began the season with an impressive win and the game story is in the Appendix. Schanedling led all scorers with twenty points and Kasberger scored but two. Spear scored eight points and is a name to remember since it is believed that his brother, Chuck, became a famous MAC athlete in subsequent years.[85]

MAC 38-Woodburn AC 23. An anonymous Jan. 9 story has the headline: "Mt. Angel Wins From Woodburn A.C., 38-23 – Continues Winning Streak by Taking Lead at Start of Game." The highlight was Pashek starting the game "by tossing a goal from the center of the floor and a minute later Classic duplicated the feat."[86] The game story is in the Appendix.

MAC 55-Christian Brothers College 18. An anonymous Jan. 15 story has the headline: "Mt. Angel College Squad Beats C.B.C." The game's star was Ralph Classic, who "shot a spectacular basket from the 80-foot line," to lead MAC with 16 points, followed by Schanedling with 14 points. Joe Kasberger and Greg Pashek contributed 6 points each.[87] The game story is in the Appendix.

There are no other game stories for the 1916-17 basketball team. The season concluded with a limited schedule that found the Angels winning eight of the nine games played. The June 3, 1926 *Pacific Star* summarized the season in a brief story. "That few challengers came close to victory can be seen from the scores. Mt. Angel piled up 441 tallies to opponents 281."[88] The team that defeated the Angels is unknown. The March 1917 *Pacific Star* had the following brief story about MAC's basketball team. Obviously, expectations were not high when the 1916-17 season began. What the "Omega Oil" is has not been revealed.

> With our hats in our hands and our hearts filled with joy and thanks, we bow profoundly to our Basketball Coach, Father Hildebrand. Out of pessimists he has created a band of enthusiastic supporters. When the clarion sounded the first call to arms, we thought Basketball would be declared and proven a lost art. With a liberal supply of Omega Oil, Father lubricated the creaky joints of his Quintet and on first presentation and unanimous vote christened [sic] them, 'One of the best teams that Mt. Angel ever produced.'[89]

The limited basketball schedule reflected the threat of World War I. By season's end, United States entry into the war was a reality. Regardless, there was a basketball banquet.

In Feb. 1917 "Joe began managing the financial interests of the *Star*, proving himself the only one worthy to take the vacant place left by Frank P. Leipzig." Working in tandem, "Joe and Frank put their heads together, so to speak, and what one or the other didn't know, didn't amount to much." The story ends by noting that "Joe gained favor with the business men of the different cities advertising in our Magazine and seldom if ever was he refused an advertisement."[90]

The 1916-17 Mt. Angel College and Seminary *Catalog* provides an insight into the *Pacific Star*. It was an important MAC activity as the official news source not only for students and faculty, but also alumni and potential benefactors.

The *Pacific Star* is published monthly by the students. Its purpose is to aid their literary improvement, and to chronicle the news of the College and seminary. Being principally devoted to matters of local interest, it must rely for its patronage chiefly upon the students and the Alumni of the College and our friends. We urge all to give it their substantial support. Rev. Basil Schieber, O.S.B., Censor.

Editorial Staff
John Friedman, Editor-in-Chief
Frank P. Leipzig [No title]
Charles Coghlan, Literary Dept.
John L. Sohler, Alumni
John Engertsberger, Athletics
John Dunn, Exchanges
Charles Simon, College Notes
Alfred V. Dean, Pleasantries
William Krebs, Photographer
Joseph Kasberger, Business Manager[91]

In MAC's small environment, it is apparent that everyone was a potentially valuable member of the student body. There were many things to do and the opportunities presented were a challenge for personal growth and career development. There was no place to hide and become bored. How students did so much in the way of extracurriculars, in addition to academics, may be a tribute to their individual talents.

Student body elections were reported in the March, 1917 *Pacific Star*, as follows:

With the advent of the second semester, our Student Body held its bi-annual election of Officers. Great praise and credit are due the retiring President, Mr. John Sohler, his able Vice-President, Mr. Joseph Kasberger and the efficient Secretary, Mr. William Krebs. During their five months of incumbency, efficiency and zeal stamped their work as gilt edged.[92]

Announced were the new officers "who have pledged themselves to serve the Student-body for the ensuing five months," and are as follows: "Mr. Frank Leipzig, President; Mr. Chas. Simon, Vice-President; Mr. Joseph Kasberger, Secretary and Treasurer."[93]

An anonymous March 13 news story has the headline: "Kasberger Elected Captain – Mount Angel College Chooses Head for Basketball Team." Now, Joe faced the prospect of returning for his third year with responsibilities as captain for two major sports teams.

At the election held last evening by the five remaining regulars of the basketball quint of Mount Angel College, Joseph Kasberger was elected as captain for the five for next year. Joe is an all-around athlete and is making good at Mount Angel.

Joe's election implied that he still had every intention of returning for his junior year. The story added that he "has combined athletics with his classwork." The story concluded with a reference to Joe receiving "a gold medal for general excellence" the previous June.[94]

Coinciding with the demands of the basketball season, many MAC athletes found themselves involved in a musical endeavor. This event provided Fr. Victor a chance to broaden the college experiences for many of his athletes. Thus, MAC staged a Minstrel with several performances, the first given in January at Mt. Angel, and other performances planned in nearby cities. The March, 1917 *Pacific Star* described Fr. Victor's project as a Dramatic Club production to generate profits to defray athletic expenses. As future events proved, music was more important to Fr. Victor than sports. More impressive, however, were his persuasive powers with athletes that reflect highly on his leadership.

The Minstrel was also presented Feb. 17 and 18 in the Mt. Angel Parish Hall, "rehearsed and staged under the direction of Father Victor and the auspices of the Dramatic Club." Three MAC students "essayed the heavy roles." They were: "Lynn Fuller as Interlocutor, Charles Simon as Bones, and Charles Coghlan as Tambourine," accompanied by a much larger cast of students. The Minstrel required "faithful practice," and "able direction produced professional results." The review revealed that the "solo-work as well as the Chorus and Quartette selections bore a true musical ring."[95]

As the school year moved into its final phase, Joe's personal photo album reveals unofficial MAC activities. "Pillow Fighting" and "Night Shirt Parades" were saved for posterity by Joe. Campus grooming standards were probably challenged by Joe and several classmates as seen in a photo captioned "The Mustache Bunch/Two Months Work." A final photo of Mt. Angel Academy and Normal School, for women, suggests that Joe and his friends were occasional visitors to town. Another photo of Joe and

"The Mustache Bunch."

friends including a young lady who was probably a student at Mt. Angel Academy and Normal School, is captioned "Ensie, Some, You & Her."

MAC's 1917 baseball season appears limited due to World War I. An undated story, from an anonymous paper, pertains to the 1917 MAC baseball team and Joe's performance. There is no other information except pictures. "Kasberger

MAC baseball team, 1917. Joe captioned this photo "The Hop and Kickem Gang."

won three out of four games twirled on the local campus," and Joe "fanned 64 men in the games played and allowed only eight hits." Joe averaged sixteen strikeouts a game, which may have pleased Fr. Basil. Joe's "only defeat of the season was a victory for the Chemawa Indians in a 2-1 game of 14 innings."[96] Due to baseball schedule problems, it appears that the Angels played a prison team. There is a photo with the caption: "The State Pen Ball Club Outfit." Another photo caption has some fun with one of the coaches: "Give it to Him, i.e. Hot Air."

That story was the last to mention Joe as a MAC student from Sept. 1915 through June 1917. Another story mentioning Joe, however, appeared in the Oct. 1917 *Pacific Star*. This story pertains to a vacation trip taken by several monks in the summer of 1917. Their visit with Joe on July Fourth is a useful benchmark in his chronology.

To the tune of 'The Little Old Ford It Rambled Right Along' five of our professors, decked out in khaki touring suits, started for Yellowstone Park early on July fourth. No matter that a trailer was hooked behind the Ford; no matter that tent, blankets, and cooking utensils had to be carried; no matter that Fathers Hildebrand, Ildephonse, and Philip were already covering most of the sitting space of the cushions; there was still room for one more. Father Thomas, weighing only 204 pounds, could easily find place; but the poor Ford seemed to be on the point of breaking under its burden, when Father Basil piled on his 230 pounds of avoirdupois. Yet the crank was turned and THE LITTLE OLD

FORD RAMBLED RIGHT ALONG, and by nightfall had carried its ponderous load to The Dalles. Thanks to Jos. Kasberger of last year's foot-ball fame for the warm reception and genuine hospitality.

The travelers spent the night in The Dalles and excerpts of their trip story conclude as follows.

Frs. Victor, Hildebrand and Boniface.

In all 3000 miles were travelled. Once in a while Father Philip and Father Ildephonse took turns to ride on the train in the capacity of providing manager for the others, and oil amounted to sixty dollars, and on the home stretch the tires were worn. Fifteen 'blowouts' in the last two miles of travelling should vouch for that. To give the reader an idea of the route taken, we shall name some of the places gone through: Mt. Angel, Portland, The Dalles, Wasco, Heppner, Pendleton, Baker City, Payette, Boise, Blackfoot, Ashton, and Yellowstone. The return route was by way of Idaho Falls, Pocatello, Ogden, Salt Lake, Fremonton [sic – Tremonton, UT], Ontario, Burns, Bend, Eugene, Salem, and Mt. Angel. Though it was the end of July when the sightseers returned, still the little Ford had to ramble through snow in McKensie Pass and received the honor of being the third car of the season to plow the snow of said pass.[97]

There is ample evidence in Joe's personal photo album of warm relationships enjoyed with many monks. One photo is captioned: "Out For A Good Time/Fr. Ambrose, H. DeMartini, Fr. Bonaventure." Another is captioned: "You Can't Guess?/Frs. Victor, Hildebrand, Boniface." Finally, a photo is captioned: "Frs. Thomas & Ambrose."

On Aug. 1, 1914 World War I had begun but United States entry into the conflict did not occur until April, 1917. The war cast a dark cloud over the 1916-17 school year and created stress among many immigrant groups. Being a hyphenated American naturally made many draft-age young men uncomfortable. They reflected long and hard on the price of American citizenship. Also tested was their allegiance to the new homeland should the call to serve be sounded.

Joe was fortunate to have completed a year and a half of college when the United States entered the war. In retrospect, the impact at MAC appears to have been immediate and put a damper on an otherwise outstanding year in Joe's young life. During this tumultuous period, Joe made an important decision. Whether his decision-making process was war-related, or not, is unknown. The circumstances surrounding this decision, however, justify closer scrutiny.

As captain-elect of both football and basketball teams for the 1917-18 school year, Joe gave every indication of returning to MAC in September. There was no hint that Joe would do anything other than return.

"Tailgate party" 1917 style, at the Mt. Angel athletic fields.

Yet, *Pacific Star* stories in the spring of 1917 mentioned Joe's classmates withdrawing from school. While some enlisted in the armed forces, others presumably were forced home to work, perhaps because a sibling had been drafted.

There is no documentation to explain Joe's transfer from MAC to Oregon Agricultural College (OAC) for the 1917-18 school year. The visit of Mt. Angel monks to The Dalles on July Fourth appears to be a visit of convenience and a planned stop as part of their trip to Yellowstone. Based upon the information available, it is not viewed as an effort to persuade Joe to return to MAC. It can be reasoned, also, that MAC officials advised Joe to transfer to OAC, possibly due to its affiliation with the Student Army Training Corps (SATC). By transferring to OAC, Joe could continue his studies, perform athletically, and possibly defer entry into the Army until he qualified for Officer Candidate School.

On the home front, Joe's brothers were vulnerable to conscription into military service. If their father felt compelled to migrate from Germany because of discomfort with militarism, the summer of 1917 at the Kasberger home would have been difficult. It is ironic that his concern was now for his sons who might bear arms. In this climate, John Kasberger may have prevailed upon Joe to attend OAC and study agriculture as an expedient solution that served two purposes. First, Joe would please his father by studying agriculture. Second, he would prepare himself for military service without entry into active duty through enlistment or the draft. Of all the Kasberger sons, Joe was the only one who could earn officer-training status should there be no alternative to military service. To better understand the influences surrounding Joe because of World War I, it seems germane to examine the impact the conflict had on his MAC classmates.

The Oct. 1917 *Pacific Star* describes what happened to several that may have influenced Joe's thinking. The first student discussed is John Friedman, who in April "said goodbye to Mt. Angel and journeyed to Portland where he enlisted for overseas service." It was subsequently reported that Army life agreed with John "and from all indications we believe the insignia of Lieutenant will be his next title." John Sohler was in the Portland Office of Pacific Telephone as an auditor. "Chas. (Charlie) Coghlan is now a Sargent [sic] at Vancouver Barracks and last reports say he is sure in love with Army life." Billie Krebs left MAC in March "to manage a large tract of land in Southern Washington where he has remained ever since." Charles Simon was now completing his studies at the University of California. MAC's final athletic loss was Hubert Melchior, who "announced his intention of accepting the position of mechanic with the O-W.R.R.&N. at Portland." Finally, Frank Leipzig was studying theology at St. Patrick's Seminary in Menlo Park, CA.[98]

Faculty and administration changes at MAC also may have been an issue. An Oct. 1917 *Pacific Star* story dealt with Fr. Basil, describing him in athletics as "an organizer of the first type." The story expressed MAC's indebtedness to him for "the present standard of in and outdoor sports at this institution." Fr. Basil's sports knowledge was also noted as a former player and coach who brought to his presidency a valuable perspective.

> The 'ins' and 'outs' of Football, Baseball, and Basketball were not mysteries to him for his knowledge of the national pastimes placed him as coach of Football and Baseball in previous years.

The story concludes by mentioning Fr. Basil's new assignment, "guiding a little flock of devoted Catholics in Sacred Heart Parish, Tillamook, Oregon."[99] During Fr. Basil's illness while MAC president, Fr. Thomas Meier may have been groomed to succeed him.

The Oct., 1917 *Pacific Star* has two stories dealing with Joe that create some confusion. The first paragraph that describes the whereabouts of former MAC students, began with the phrase: "Like the previous mentioned boys" and continued as follows about Joe:

> Joe was a lover of out door sports being a prominent member of all three first teams. At football, Joe had no equal, he was a hero of the gridiron past-time and it is mainly due to his playing and headwork that Mt. Angel performed so well last year. He captained both Football and Basketball teams, pitched an excellent brand of ball for our baseball nine and on commencement day received as a reward for past services the 'A' Sweater. Joe is now at The Dalles, Oregon.[100]

The second *Pacific Star* story addresses more directly the absence of Joe, captain-elect of the 1917 team, in the following football preseason story. Prospects for the 1917 team "do not look so bright as last season," due to "the absence of many of our stellar players." The major loss was their anticipated captain.

> Principal among them is Joseph Kasberger, our sturdy captain. 'Reliable Joe,' as he is known among the students, was not only a field general of the highest order, but he was a line-plunger 'par excellence' as well; and in his breast there throbbed that indomitable spirit which was never on even speaking terms with the word 'quit.' His 'fight, fight, fight' has been the cause of many a victory, when the game seemed hopelessly lost.

Joe's transfer from MAC is reported as the story continues:

Joe is now a freshman at Oregon Agricultural College, and we are sure that Coach Pipal of that institution will thank his stars for the good fortune that guided the pride of M.A.C. to his fold; for under the persistent efforts of Coach Victor, Joe has developed into one of the best backfield men on the Coast.[101]

The same *Pacific Star* story revealed the whereabouts of other MAC players. Pashek, described as Joe's "faithful ally in the backfield," enlisted in the Navy. As events unfolded, another Pashek from The Dalles came to MAC. The story continues with the following updates and the impact the absence of these men was having on the 1917 football team.

Bill Krebs will be sadly missed from the ranks too. The fact that Bill was the universal choice for the position of center on the All-Star non-conference team is sufficient expression of the loss Mt. Angel feels at the thought of his no longer being among us. The name of Jack Sohler is a synonym for 'speed' in the vocabulary of the Mt. Angel boys. The question on the lips of the students during these days is, who will furnish them with the thrilling end runs this season as was Jack's wont in the seasons past? The departure of Chas. Simon for the University of California is leaving a hole in the old 'Stonewall' line which will be difficult to fill. Chas. was also one of those hustlers whose good work earned him a position on the mythical All-Star eleven.[102]

Apparently "Eck" was one of Joe's closer friends at MAC. There is a photo of Eck with Pashek and Medford Lester in Joe's personal photo album captioned: "All In and Out/Pelkey-Bo Peep-Eck." Pashek was "Pelkey," a shorter version of another photo caption by Joe. The longer version is captioned in another photo as "Pelkey Drake Greg. Pashek, 'The Stellar Line Plunger.'" Medford Lester was "Bo Peep." It is Eck's story, however, that is one of the more interesting of those presented.

When Uncle Sam's call sounded over the country appealing for volunteers Earnest Eckerlen was one of the first to respond. 'Eck' is now 'somewhere in France,' and perhaps, by this time charging trenches with the same success with which he charged the opponents' line; for be it understood that Earnest was No. 4 of last year's team who showed All-Star class.[103]

The impact of so many departures created a gloomy atmosphere on the hilltop that is reflected by the *Pacific Star's* final profile of an ex-football player.

From over the western hills comes the sad news that the last of the celebrated Melchior brothers will no longer be with us. 'Smiling' Hubert has been lured from Mt. Angel to stay by a very lucrative position as master mechanic in his own famous city, Tillamook.[104]

The Oct. 1917 *Pacific Star* noted the state of the preseason MAC football squad. Surprisingly MAC intended to field a team since many colleges suspended football programs. After the summer recess, it was reported that the campus "has again taken on the appearance of a lively athletic field," with football playing.[105]

Fr. Victor was again coaching the Angels and he was "well pleased with the early season's work." This account of the 1917 preseason football described the players as a "likely looking bunch...[that] numbered about twenty-five," and "already ploughing holes in the old field." In summarizing prospects for the 1917 Angel team, the *Pacific Star* opined: "This year's eleven promises to be light and fast, and for this reason will be very adaptable [sic] to Coach Victor's style of play." Optimistically, the story concluded "it appears that we are going to have a good team." [106]

But, there is a warning that "our team will not win and our hopes will not be realized unless we assist them with our entire and whole-souled support." Fan support was essential and more student participation appeared needed in 1917. "If we can afford to stand around and criticize, we can afford to get into a jersey and take a few knocks ourselves." For those who cannot play, they were urged to "boost" the team. There was a realization that only "eleven men out of one hundred and fifty can make the team, but the remainder can get out and root and boost." The story concluded with a call for "enthusiasm, 'pep,' and the old 'giniger' [sic]." The final sentence urged the Angels to "get out there and give all you have for the glory of the old White and Gold."[107]

There is, however, an anonymous September 14 news story that could pertain to the 1917-18 school year. It suggests that despite preseason practices, there might not be a football season.

> Nothing has been definitely settled at Mount Angel College in the athletic line for the coming season. During the past week college reopened with the largest enrollment it has had in years.[108]

During Joe's MAC student career, enrollment approximated one hundred and fifty students, and perhaps two dozen football players. It is surprising, therefore, that in spite of the war there was an enrollment increase. Fr. Victor may have been encouraged by the relatively large turnout of football players, even though so many experienced players did not return. There were enough football players to compete with other schools that did not suspend football. The results of the 1917 football season, however, are unknown.

Joe's decision to leave MAC is understandable, having distinguished himself in football as an all-star quarterback. Being one of the best backs on the coast, Joe was undoubtedly noticed by football coaches. Besides football, Joe was an all-star performer on the 1916-17 MAC basketball and baseball teams. It is not surprising, therefore, that Joe was now attractive to the bigger colleges in Oregon and on the West Coast.

Probably there were two considerations in Joe's decision to leave MAC. First, with his level of education, and attendance at an OAC-type college with military training in the curriculum, he would be called to active duty at a later time. This seems important, since Joe's two brothers, Philip and George, are believed to have been already called to active duty.

Second, OAC sought Joe with his reputation as a quality MAC athlete. OAC gave Joe several options. It afforded him a higher level of athletic competition. Also, it pleased his parents for him to study agriculture. Finally, OAC's Corvallis location was not much farther from home than Mt. Angel.[109]

As events unfolded, it does not appear that Joe's transfer to OAC from MAC involved any bridge-burning or hard feelings. Yet, the research does not reveal documentation of Joe's decision until after his arrival in Corvallis. The presumption is that Joe made the decision during the summer of 1917.

If personal photos are a testimonial for Joe's two college years on the hilltop, it can be argued that they may have been the two best years of his life.

III. JOE AT OAC
BEFORE AND AFTER THE WAR
"The man without a date"

What is now known as Oregon State University was Oregon Agricultural College (OAC) while Joe was in attendance. It had its beginnings as Corvallis College, a small private institution, founded in 1858. On Oct. 27, 1868 the school was designated as Oregon's Land Grant, state-assisted college by the State Legislature, the oldest public institution of higher learning in Oregon.[1]

OAC is located in Corvallis, Benton County, in the southern Willamette Valley. As the county seat, it is the center of government for the county, and of economic activity for the surrounding area. Corvallis was connected to Portland, 85 miles to the north, by rail service that took about 5 hours. San Francisco was 560 miles south. The OAC campus consisted of 500 acres, described as "a beautiful mix of broad green lawns, flowering trees, and ornamental shrubs." The pastoral campus is blessed by access to "the spectacular Oregon coast to the west and rugged Cascade mountains to the east." A moderate climate allows year-round recreation at nearby locations that range from "alpine and cross-country skiing to beachcombing, fishing, hiking, golf, and swimming." [2]

The former big man on the little MAC campus suddenly found himself in a new role as a freshman at OAC. The new Pacific Coast Conference offered Joe a major athletic challenge in the fall of 1917. At 21 years of age, he was distinctly different from today's incoming college freshman. As an experienced student-athlete, he was at least the equivalent of today's junior-college transfer.

Unlike today, those students were not considered as transfers entering colleges as juniors. Rather, they were entering as freshmen. The opportunities in the more secular OAC setting provided an atmosphere to broaden Joe considerably – with academic, social, and athletic achievements to serve him well for the rest of his life. Upon entering OAC, Joe may have expected to graduate in June, 1921, with three years of varsity eligibility athletics after his freshman year.

Joe's freshman year at OAC appears to have been one of relative obscurity. Besides his athletic prowess, Joe was an excellent student with an interest in other aspects of college life. OAC's student body was much larger than that of MAC. Another major difference was the fact that OAC was coeducational. The presence of women certainly was a novelty for Joe. A contemporary of Joe Kasberger at OAC was famed Nobel Prize-winner Linus Pauling. Student life at OAC was described in two books, *Linus Pauling, Scientist and Advocate* by David E. Newton, and *Linus Pauling, A Man and His Science*, a biography by Anthony Serafini. Serafini stated that "the vast majority of the students came from the great cattle ranches and wheat farms of eastern Oregon, others came from the coast and mountain regions." Also at OAC during this period were a surprising number of foreign students from "exotic" places.[3]

Serafini described OAC's academic programs then as consisting of "engineering, home economics, forestry, and business administration" as the primary fields of study, although agriculture should be mentioned unless Serafini considered agriculture as a non-academic program! Perhaps like Pauling, Joe was influenced to enter OAC because of cost considerations. As Pauling explained years later, tuition was free "and registration fees were only a few dollars, and books weren't very expensive.'" Pauling reportedly spent twenty dollars for second-hand books in his freshman year. [4]

Some OAC students worked to finance their educations. Pauling had a variety of jobs, "including working as a general handyman at a women's dormitory." If a student were not a big eater, Pauling stated that you could survive on fifty cents per day for meals. Serafini described Corvallis as having an environment that "was stark, functional, and working class." But there were good-times places, including watering holes beyond the campus. One in particular was known as "Five Corners," where Pauling was once seen "coming out of the place with a jug of wine in one hand, and a bag of goodies in the other."[5]

Despite being coeducational, complete with sororities and fraternities, OAC had a military presence, due to the Congressional Land Grant Act of 1862. OAC's *General Catalog* for 1917-18 described this relationship: "The General Government founded Agricultural and Mechanical Colleges to meet the conditions of both peace and war." Thus, OAC sought to train citizen-soldiers "for leadership."Accordingly, "the training at Agricultural and Mechanical Colleges coordinates closely with military training." OAC's *General Catalog* added that the objective was "to train the cadet to be able to perform the duties of an officer in enlisting, feeding, equipping, caring for, drilling, and training a company." [6]

Undergraduate males took a prescribed course of military studies, including drill "four periods a week throughout their undergraduate course." Academic credit was as follows: "One credit a semester is allowed for military drill, and grades are reported at the end of each semester the same as in any other subject."[7] The 1917-18 OAC *General Catalog* had a description of a new military program, "RESERVE OFFICERS' TRAINING CORPS." The essential provisions of "ROTC" were as follows:

> 1. **Object.** The primary object of the Reserve Officers' Training Corps is to qualify students by systematic and standard training methods for reserve officers, so that in time of national emergency men graduating from the College will be able to lead intelligently the units of large armies upon which the safety of the country depends.
> 2. **Eligibility.** All physically fit students of the College are eligible to membership.
> 3. **Basic Course.** The basic course, which comprises the first two years of military instruction at the College, is for all under classmen – vocationals, freshmen, or sophomores. Men taking this course do not bind themselves by any obligations not already required of them as College students. All members of the basic course are furnished, free of cost, by the Government, a complete military uniform, which includes the following articles, all of the regular-army quality of material: 1 pair breeches, 1 cap, 1 coat, 1 pair leggings, 1 set cap and collar ornaments, 1 pair russet shoes.[8]

OAC's 1921-22 *General Catalog* described ROTC for basic and advanced courses. For Basic Course, four hours of "military instruction each week are required for all men students," during the first two years. Over the final two college years, "five hours each week" are required in the Advanced Course. Additionally, there were "Military Credits for Graduation," dictating that a "minimum of 12 credits" in Military Science are required of all men for graduation." This requirement "comprises 6 credits for each of the first two years' basic work." Military service appeared to satisfy the military credits required for graduation. "If for any reason a student is relieved from the military requirements, other credits must be substituted for the military credits."[9] Clearly, Joe and his male cohorts received extensive military indoctrination and training as civilians.

Along with the new ROTC program, Joe was an early participant in a new league for inter-collegiate athletics, the Pacific Coast Intercollegiate Athletic Conference. At the time of Joe's arrival, this significant development in OAC and West Coast athletics was being implemented. The conference was formed Dec. 2, 1915 in Portland, OR by founders from the Universities of California, Oregon, Washington, and OAC. The Universities of Oregon and Washington, with OAC, had been members of the Northwest Conference. By 1916, at a meeting in Seattle, Stanford University and Washington State College applied for membership and were accepted. In the spring of 1917, the United States entered World War I and many colleges ceased regular intercollegiate athletic competition. For Pacific Coast Conference varsity teams, there were no conference games. The 1918 season, however, saw competition by member schools that are unrecognized in official conference records. The reason for this action was "S.A.T.C. [Student Army Training Corps] teams using non-student players."[10]

Eastern football had become a major campus sport in the West, spreading quickly after the first game was played in New Brunswick, NJ between Rutgers and Princeton Universities in 1869. That first college game was more akin to rugby than the football we know today, but the sport was popular, not only among students, but also with the public at large. As football evolved, the Eastern schools received increasing newspaper publicity, and intersectional play was an idea that came to fruition in the first Rose Bowl game. This New Year's Day classic in Pasadena, CA gave Western colleges a chance to test themselves against the best colleges from the East. The first games were played at California Institute of Technology (Cal-Tech's) stadium, known as Tournament Park.

In the 1916 Rose Bowl game, Washington State defeated Brown University, 14-0. Easterners were not convinced that West Coast football compared with their brand until the 1917 Rose Bowl game. When the University of Oregon, led by quarterback Shy Huntington, defeated the University of Pennsylvania 14-0, West Coast football received the respect it sought. The Quakers had been thought by many to be the nation's best team before the game. Two Penn players in that game were Bert Bell, future president of the National Football League, and Lou Little, future head football coach at Columbia University in New York City.

1917-18 School Year

1917 registration for OAC students was Oct. 12 and all previous enrollment records were exceeded. Joe's freshman year at OAC is documented to include his participation in four campus activities: Phi Delta Theta social fraternity, freshman football, freshman basketball and freshman baseball.[11]

Where Joe would live was an immediate issue. Housing was a problem for some students, especially freshmen, because dormitories were not common. For Joe's entire career at OAC, he lived in the Phi Delta Theta fraternity house, conveniently located at 610 Jefferson. This address placed Joe a few blocks from the heart of the campus. Fellowship and social activity made fraternity houses on college campuses popular then as an alternative to private boarding houses.[12]

In Sept. 1917, this house was a local fraternity, known as Kappa Sigma Nu, whose president was Roy Servais "Spec" Keene. In March 1918, Kappa Sigma Nu became a chapter of the national fraternity, Phi Delta Theta, founded at Miami University in Oxford, OH. The University of Oregon Chapter, Oregon Alpha, founded in 1912, was followed by Oregon Beta, at OAC in 1918. According to a Phi Delta Theta headquarters' account, the sequence of events began on Jan. 2, 1918 at the fraternity's Indianapolis Convention which granted OAC a charter on March 9, 1918.[13]

1922 **Beaver** *photo of the Phi Delta Theta fraternity house.*

According to fraternity records, Joe was a charter member, referred to as "Beta 048" in official records. Chronologically, Joe was the 48th brother initiated into the fraternity in March, 1918.[14] The Greek-letter social fraternities and sororities were common on many college campuses, public and private, after the Civil War. Brotherhood was as strong an incentive for many members as a decent place to live, eat, and socialize. After World War I, fraternity life may have been more serious due to the presence of more mature men. Thus, contemporary stereotypes of a fraternity may not be valid for that era. Joe and his brothers may have had lots of fun, but it is unlikely that they were "hell-raising party animals," a trait that emerged in future generations of younger Greeks.

Joe's link to Phi Delta Theta may have involved the Huntington brothers at the University of Oregon who had all grown up with him in The Dalles. A founding member of Phi Delta Theta at the University of Oregon was Walter Mills Huntington. Walter left TDHS in June 1907 to attend Allen Prep in Portland before entering the University of Oregon in Sept. 1908. Walter co-founded a local fraternity on the Eugene campus that subsequently became Phi

Delta Theta's "Alpha" Chapter in the State of Oregon. Walter was the older brother of Charles (Shy) and Hollis Huntington, who also were members of Phi Delta Theta.[15]

With a place to live and a new family to provide a sense of home, Joe began life as a student-athlete. Being a college athlete is not easy, due to the demands made on precious time. For a serious student-athlete, intent on getting an education, establishing priorities was probably no easier then than it is today. For Joe, the spiritual side may have been the most difficult aspect of leaving MAC. OAC's Catholic presence was furnished by a Newman Club, where students attended Mass and found fellowship.

It is not known whether athletic scholarships were offered then, or if Joe received a stipend for spending-money, room, board, and tuition. Pacific Coast Conference rules would have governed what member schools could give their athletes. In theory, then, all conference schools provided their athletes equal inducements. Competitive balance was important to the founders of the Pacific Coast Conference, and rules were established to insure fair competition. The issues of geography, travel, and expenses were critical on the West Coast. Compared to Eastern and Midwestern schools, located amid larger populations, the West Coast schools had to struggle, before and during World War I.

The head football coach was important for prospective players, as was the football program's record. For Joe, there may have been some anxiety about OAC's football history and the coaching situation. Joe's OAC career was marked by several coaches who continued an OAC tradition. To understand the 1917 coaching situation, it is helpful to see what had transpired earlier. OAC football coaches, prior to Sam "Rosey" Dolan, had Midwestern backgrounds. Dolan, however, was a native Oregonian from Albany, who played tackle on four Notre Dame teams from 1906-1909. Dolan graduated the year before Knute Rockne arrived to play on the 1910-1913 teams. As OAC's coach in 1911 and 1912 seasons, Dolan posted records of 5-2-0 and 3-4-0, respectively.[16]

After Dolan, several coaches followed in an unstable coaching climate. In 1913, E.J. "Doc" Stewart replaced Dolan for a brief period. This Western Reserve University (Ohio) alumnus lasted at OAC only through the 1915-16 school year. Stewart had an outstanding team in 1914 with a 7-0-2 record. Unfortunately, that one year was surrounded by less spectacular results. In 1913, OAC had a 3-2-3 season; and it had a 5-3-0 record in 1915 (the inaugural year of the Pacific Coast Conference) – which was not bad. It may not have been good enough, however, for OAC's alumni and administration. Why Stewart left is unknown, but he is distinctive for coaching both OAC varsity basketball and football teams. Through the 1915-16 season, Stewart spent five years as OAC's basketball coach. The coaching turnover may have been due to dual-sports coaching roles.[17]

The debut of Stewart's successor, Joseph Pipal, in 1916 resulted in a 4-5-0 record, with a 0-27 loss to Rose Bowl-bound Oregon. As opposed to OAC's instability with head coaches, the University of Oregon enjoyed both stability, success, and two Rose Bowl appearances from 1913-17, with Hugo Bezdek.[18]

Joe's first coach at OAC in 1917 was probably Joseph Pipal from Beloit

College in Wisconsin. This was feasible to the extent that Pipal coached both freshman and varsity football. Joe played on the frosh team (Aggie Rooks), while the varsity posted a 4-2-1 record. His assignment to the Aggie Rooks was due to Pacific Coast Conferences rules governing freshman eligibility, rather than athletic ability. The freshman team probably was used primarily by the varsity to prepare for its games. OAC sports teams were known as the "Beavers." [19]

There is only one game reported for the 1917 OAC Frosh, against Camp Lewis Army from Camp Lewis (now Fort Lewis), WA. In that game, Camp Lewis defeated the OAC Frosh 22-0 en route to a successful season. This game gave Joe important exposure that may have been rewarded with a future assignment. The season finale for this fine Camp Lewis team was the 1918 Rose Bowl game against the Mare Island Marines. That is the only information available about Joe's freshman year in football except for an anonymous Sept. 14, 1918 news story. "Those who saw him in action as quarterback on the freshman team were reminded of the style of Huntington, famous grid-iron player of Oregon University." [20]

OAC's 1917 varsity football team had a 1-2-1 record in Pacific Coast Conference competition. The big win was 14-7 over Oregon. Washington State led the conference with a 3-0-0 record, followed by California, 2-1-0, OAC, 1-2-1, Oregon, 1-2-0, and Washington, 0-2-1. Due to World War I, Washington State did not play in the 1918 Rose Bowl game, but the Rose Bowl tradition continued on New Year's Day with the best teams available. The Rose Bowl received permission for two service teams to play at Tournament Park, since the Rose Bowl Stadium was not built until several years later.[21]

Joe played basketball throughout his OAC career. OAC's early basketball history is well documented by James C. Heartwell's book, *The History of Oregon State College Basketball, 1901-02 – 52-53*. In 1915-16, only three Conference schools were on OAC's schedule, a distinct competitive advantage since the University of Oregon "had temporarily abandoned the sport." There were problems with scheduling, and dual league memberships in the Pacific Coast Conference and the Northwest Conference at this time.

These two Conferences had different athletic eligibility rules. Freshman could play in the Northwest Conference, but the Pacific Coast Conference had a "three year rule," which made freshman ineligible for varsity action. The situation improved in the 1916-17 school year when basketball returned at Oregon. Also, the addition of Washington State and Stanford permitted a six-team format, but created geography problems for coaches dealing with limited travel-budgets.

One interesting trip concerns the 1916-17 OAC basketball team. The Beavers mode of travel from Seattle, after playing the University of Washington, to San Francisco was by "steamer," or steamship. From San Francisco, games were played against Stanford and the University of California.[22]

The 1923 OAC yearbook, *Beaver,* reports Joe playing freshman basketball in the 1917-18 season. While Joe's name does not appear in Heartwell's book, he was probably familiar with the varsity while practicing against them. Thus, Heartwell's insights into the 1917-18 OAC varsity team are useful. Key individuals were head coach Everett May and team captain Howard "Hod" Ray. The 1917-18 team was affected by World War I, and several stars withdrew from OAC. Also, in 1917 Coach May left OAC to attend Officers' Training Camp. These setbacks did not deter the remaining players, who won a title and "completed the second of two undefeated seasons registered by Beaver teams in 50 years." [23]

This feat is more impressive when one realizes that OAC did not hire a basketball coach for the season. When Coach May departed, "no coach was hired for 1917-18 and the responsibility of this position fell on the shoulders of Capt. Ray." Although surrounded by inexperienced players, OAC played a limited schedule with a 10-0 record to lead the "Pacific Coast Conference's Northern Division." California and Stanford competed in the "California-Nevada League." After California beat Stanford twice in three games, they were declared champions. No effort was made to play a championship game between OAC and California, "due to the unsettled international conditions." [24]

The 1917-18 OAC basketball team is pictured in Heartwell's book with the caption "Second Undefeated Quintet in School's History." The team photo lists eight players: Butts Reardon, Cac Hubbard, Lee Bissett, Robby Robinson, Wayne Gurley, Jack Eakin, Dutch Krueger, Coach and Capt. Hod Ray. The 1917-18 OAC team's success, under unusual conditions, appears important. OAC played five games against teams that were not in the Pacific Coast Conference. With the exception of a close 10-9 win over Willamette, OAC dominated the smaller college teams, except Willamette, the only team that OAC "did not beat by at least 11 points." Other small college victims were Pacific College, 25-14 and 38-26; and Chemawa Indians, 34-16. Of interest to Joe had to be one game that the OAC varsity played against MAC. It was a 26-3 rout of the Angels. [25]

Individual honors went to OAC players at season's end. "Ray and Krueger at forwards and Reardon [sic] at guard were all-PCC selections in *Spalding's Guide*," as well as other all-star teams that were named. Along with Lee Bissett at center, these three OAC players were "the *Oregonian's* all-star west side choices." A fifth OAC player, Wayne Gurley, "was selected at forward on the *Oregonian's* second team." In recapping the 1917-18 OAC basketball season, Heartwell stated that the key was the team's desire to unify and win behind their captain Hod Ray. Their record was viewed as "a great tribute to the entire team and whenever outstanding OAC basketball accomplishments are discussed the 1917-18 season is always mentioned." Due to the war, however, this team did not reunite to repeat its accomplishments, since only Reardon would return. [26]

With the end of the basketball season, Joe began playing freshman baseball for OAC. It is likely that his first OAC baseball coach was Jimmie Richardson. There is no documentation of OAC freshman baseball and Joe's performance. In 1918 Pacific Coast Conference play, the OAC varsity had a 2-6 record, trailing Oregon, 6-2, California, 3-1, and Stanford, 1-3, in the final standings. The 1918 baseball season for Joe coincided with a new reality: male OAC students were now more vulnerable to active military duty.

The 1919 *Beaver* reported in its "Current Events" section, dated March 1, 1918, that "Many of the Frosh have gone into training." [27] Pauling's biographer,

Newton, addressed the war's impact on OAC's men at the end of the 1917-18 school year. Due to the SATC program, qualified students who were helped to stay in school now faced active duty. Serafini's account of the impact on Linus Pauling helps to explain Joe's situation. The mood was gloomy since "the specter of war cast shadows over the innocence of college life. It cramped Pauling's social life, but most of all his academic life."[28]

The end of the 1917-18 school year led to another adventure for Joe. At the age of 22, he was fortunate to have had the chance to complete his freshman year at OAC. The paradox is that World War I was ending, yet SATC led the young men to officers training school. Before that, however, there was summer work in defense-related positions. Mervyn Stephenson, and his cousin Linus Pauling, worked all summer in a Tillamook shipyard.[29]

News accounts of Joe and his MAC classmates during this period provide a glimpse into their lives. An anonymous news story dated July 13, with the year 1918 handwritten, has the headline: "Mount Angel Loyal – Many Students of St. Benedict College Are in Service – Present and Former Stars of College Diamond, Gridiron and Courts Scattered From Trenches to Training Camps." The story gives the whereabouts of Joe and many others, noting that "Mount Angel College has contributed more than its quota to the Nation's fighting forces."[30]

Pashek's Navy enlistment was noted without word of his location and duties. Ernest Eckerlen "entered the Marines and was sent to Mare Island. He remained here but a short time and was sent to France." Charles Coghlan was in "the Engineering Corps and promoted to sergeant. From that time on Mount Angel athletes poured into the Marines, Navy and Army." A "service flag" flew on the MAC campus as a tribute to its alumni now serving in the war. It "bore 156 stars, but the number of enlistments now far exceeds that total."

The story continues with news that "Joe Kasberger is another Mount Angel football star of last year who is now in khaki." Also mentioned was the drafting of William Terhaar who starred on MAC's 1917 football team. At Camp Lewis, Terhaar found other Angel alumni: George and Charles Fick, and George Merten.

The story continues with news about another football player from the Class of 1916, Harry Combs, described as a "Lieutenant at Camp Fremont, Cal." The story also described an unusual MAC alumnus who circumvented difficulty to serve.

William O'Rourke, the Midget Irishman, who recently was accepted by the Army officials because of his pluck in refusing to be discharged, was one of the cleverest handball players seen at College. O'Rourke, commonly known as 'Red' was also prominent in basketball.[31]

MAC president, Rev. Thomas Meier, "appointed Frank P. Leipzig, of Portland, chairman of a committee to keep track of the boys in service." Since graduating from MAC, he remained active with the college as the "alumni historian," while studying at St. Patrick's Seminary in Menlo Park, CA. Leipzig was also "stationed at Lents Junction for the Portland Railway, Light & Power Company," possibly as a summer job.[32]

An anonymous July 27 news story, with 1918 handwritten, has the headline: "Letters Sent to Mt. Angel Men – College Organizes Effort to Keep Former Students in Touch With Interests. Many Athletes in Army. Stars of Baseball and Football teams Are Doing Part in Making World Decent Place to Live In." The text of the story follows:

Letters are drifting in from 'over there' and from the Mount Angel alumni who are doing their bit in the American cantonments. Last Christmas Mount Angel College, due to the efforts of Rev. Thomas Meier, its president, organized a letter-writing system to all the old boys. Many of the old-timers have appreciated this work and the mail coming from the men who have enlisted or have been drafted all breathe the same spirit – thankfulness to the faculty for remembering them while they are fighting for Uncle Sam.

In response to letters received from MAC, alumni shared their military experiences. Lynn Fuller was in the Army, and mentioned that "athletics have been a great help to him in drilling men. Soon after his enlistment Lynn was made first sergeant in the 488th Aero Squad." Mention is made of Bill Krebs who had enlisted. Also, it was reported that John Sohler "during the past week has gone to Camp Lewis." Overall, the letter-writing campaign was successful. All but "two or three" from the famed 1916 football team had not been heard from regarding their enlistment status.[33]

Fr. Thomas Meier had his hands full as MAC's president during the war. Yet life on the hilltop went on for the 1917-18 school year. MAC "was one of the few colleges to keep athletics on the regular schedule when Uncle Sam decided to have war with Germany." The story observed that "the past school year has shown that it was a wise move to retain athletics." Not all schools were so fortunate in fielding athletic teams, but the "past year found Mount Angel arranging games in football and basketball with outside teams, but in baseball found the students played intramural games." The "baseball at home" experiment proved successful, "not only among the student body but financially," presumably due to no travel costs. The story concluded with the belief that "there is little doubt the Mount Angel athletic body will take to this new form of athletics very kindly next Spring."[34]

World War I had an impact throughout the United States. Bob Murray finally had a war in which he was old enough to fight, despite his size and age. His son, Bill, recalled his father's infatuation with the military.

Although it is hard to say how much Bob's military experience influenced his coaching, I'm sure it had an impact. He was eager to enlist in the Spanish-American War which began in the spring of 1898. He was not eighteen until the following November, and his mother opposed his enlistment. He served as private, corporal and first sergeant in the Oregon National Guard from 1899 to 1907.[35]

Even famous high school coaches were called to serve when the United

Shy Huntington

States entered World War I on April 6, 1917, and Bob Murray immediately applied for reserve officer training. In late June, Murray was inducted and sent to the Presidio in San Francisco for eight weeks of training, and was commissioned as a Second Lieutenant. On August 15, 1917 he was assigned to the Eighth Infantry Division at Camp Fremont, CA. "Assignment to this large training camp of 17,000 men was a disappointment since he wanted to go immediately to France." Bill Murray recalled his father's role.

During the war he was in much demand as a trainer of troops. His value in this way was unchallenged to the point that he was not permitted to leave Camp Fremont for any of the hot battles raging in France. He was also camp intelligence officer of this division-sized installation near Palo Alto.[36]

Also, Oregon's head coach, Hugo Bezdek, resigned after the 1917 season. He then coached the Mare Island Marines in the 1918 and 1919 Rose Bowl games. After the war he returned to academe and coached a third Rose Bowl team, Penn State, in 1923. He was succeeded by his quarterback in the 1917 Rose Bowl win over Penn, Shy Huntington.[37]

In the Army, Bob maintained his ties to football. With Shy Huntington as Oregon's new head coach, it is no coincidence that Murray was the referee in the Nov. 23, 1918 Oregon-California game. It ended in a 6-0 Golden Bear victory over the Ducks on a wet field, presumably in Berkeley.

He had been very active in inter-service officiating through his war experience – a linesman for the 1919 Mare Island game which was an inter-service competition and a harbinger of an interesting Rose Bowl game for January 1, 1920.[38]

Tasting the college game may have led Murray to give it a try after the war.

Joe's OAC and Army records document that he enlisted in the Army on August 28, 1918 and served at Camp Lewis, WA until his discharge on Feb. 21, 1919. His entry into the Army was reported in an anonymous Sept. 14 news story with the headline: "Kasberger In Service – Former Mount Angel Star is Now at Camp Lewis – All-Around Athlete is remembered as Great Football Player as Well as Baseball Moundsman."

Joe in Army uniform.

The Kasberger brothers in World War I Army uniforms: Max, left; George, top; Joe, right; and Philip, bottom.

News filtering down from Camp Lewis brings the report that Joseph Kasberger, ex-football, basketball, and baseball star, is doing his bit at that camp.[39]

It is believed that Joe reported to Camp Lewis with his brother Philip in August 191. His brothers Max and George were already serving in California, probably at Camp Fremont. For all practical purposes, however, hostilities in Europe were ending and American units were returning for deactivation.

Camp Lewis was located outside of Tacoma in a town called American Lake. Construction of this new "National Army Camp" had begun July 5, 1917, and it "was built for the lowest cost and in the shortest space of time of any cantonment in the country." It was "named Lewis, in honor of Captain Meriwether Lewis, Commander of the Lewis and Clark Expedition." In 1917, "Camp Lewis was the largest military post in the USA at the time." With United States entry into World War I, "Camp Lewis was the first National Army cantonment for draftee training to be opened." Even before construction was completed, it was used to support the war effort. "The first recruits arrived at Camp Lewis on 5 September 1917 and 37,000 officers, cadre, garrison, and trainees were on post by 31 December."[40]

Manpower problems for the Army were severe and time was of the essence. Enlistments were deferred since there were insufficient training facilities available. "A race for time ensued – the Army had only 25,000 regulars in 1917 and needed thousands more to fight in France." Thus, conscription, or the Draft, was revived to supplement those who volunteered. At Camp Lewis, many men who were "levied from Washington, Oregon, California, Idaho, Utah, Nevada, Wyoming and Montana, would have to be inprocessed, clothed, armed, and trained."[41] There is confusion about whether Joe was in the 91st Infantry Division, 75th Infantry Division, or the 13th Infantry Division.

> The 91st Infantry Division . . . trained at Camp Lewis from 5 September 1917 until it shipped out, on 21-24 June, 1918, for France, where it served with distinction.[42]

It is not believed that any members of the 91st Infantry Division remained at Camp Lewis after this unit went overseas. In its place, the 13th Infantry, "was organized at Camp Lewis in 1918 and was training in trench-warfare when the Armistice was signed, 11 November 1918." Despite the Armistice, concluding the "war to end all wars," it is reported that "the construction at Camp Lewis would continue until November 1919." Joe's Phi Delta Theta biography states that he was assigned to the 75th Infantry Division. Fort Lewis archives suggest that, since this was an East Coast unit at Camp Drum, NY, Joe may have been earmarked for this unit after Officers' Training.[43]

It is likely that Joe was assigned to an Officer Training unit as a member of the Camp Lewis football team. A 1929 news story reported that during "the World War he played Quarterback on the Army team at Camp Lewis," and the photo presented here may be from that experience.[44] The coach of the 1918 Camp Lewis football team that played in the 1919 Rose Bowl game against the Mare Island Marines was W.L. "Fox" Stanton. Before the war, he coached at Dickinson College in Pennsylvania. Camp Lewis' 1918 team was

Joe in Camp Lewis football uniform, 1918.

96

not as good as in 1917 and did not return to the 1919 Rose Bowl.

Mare Island Marines of Vallejo in Northern California were the competition for Camp Lewis in that Rose Bowl game won by Mare Island 19-7. Mare Island returned for the 1919 game to face the Great Lakes Naval team from Illinois that featured George Halas, who scored a touchdown. The service teams used college players, primarily. For the Mare Island Marines, their star in the 1918 and 1919 games was Hollis Huntington.[45]

At Camp Lewis, little else is known about Joe, other than playing on the 1918 football team. Why Joe was not discharged from active duty until Feb. 21, 1919 is probably due to his role in the demobilization effort after Armistice Day in November, 1918. Joe was honorably discharged as a corporal and the accompanying picture of the Kasberger brothers in uniform suggests that they were in The Dalles celebrating the war's conclusion. Thus, Joe lost only one semester; or two quarters, fall and winter, in the 1918-19 school year. Oregon State University records reveal that Joe did not return until autumn 1919.[46]

At home in The Dalles, a gathering of the Kasberger brothers in uniform.
Front : Max, Philip, Joe, George;
Back: Anna, Mr. Kasberger, Mrs. Kasberger, Julius Sandoz, Audie and a friend, Urban Pashek.

1918-19 School Year

The post-World War I mood at OAC was very different from the emotional climate of the previous school year. The return to normalcy possibly softened the harsher military dimension of the OAC experience. OAC, however, continued military training for men in ROTC. Since Joe did not serve for more than six months, he probably wore the uniform again while participating in drill and attending classes in military science. At worst, the Army had only been an inconvenience. Joe, however, had surely fallen behind any schedule to complete his undergraduate degree requirements in four calendar years.

While Joe was away from OAC the most significant thing he missed was the 1918 football season. OAC's 1918 football team, what there was of it, was led by new head-coach W.G. (Bill) Hargiss, from Emporia State College in Kansas. OAC fielded a football team with a 2-4-0 record, despite the 1918 competition being unrecognized and unreported by the Pacific Coast Conference. One game in the 1918 season stands out, a 6-21 loss suffered by OAC to Camp Lewis – where it is believed that Joe was the quarterback for the Army.[47]

Results of OAC's 1918-19 basketball team are not presented, except to say that it was not as good as in 1917-18. OAC hired a basketball coach for this season, or a football coach with added duties to coach basketball. Heartwell's account of this hiring shows the impact war continued to have. Few basketball teams face a season without at least one returning letterman. Poor Bill Hargiss, however, "didn't have a letterman to work with until Butts Rearden [sic] returned from the Army about the time the schedule started." Lee Bissett was elected OAC's team captain after the 1917-18 season. When Bissett did not return, Rearden became the captain. "This green squad started out with seven losses, then won three and closed the season with six more defeats."[48]

The only information available about the 1919 baseball season comes from the Pacific Coast Conference's season results. Washington was first with a 10-0 record, followed by Stanford 2-0, OAC 5-6, Washington State 1-5, Oregon 1-6, and California 0-2. After the 1918-1919 school year ended, it is possible that Joe attended the summer session, and may have worked in Corvallis as a business manager for a local physician. At some time during Joe's OAC career he was reported to have held such a position. This appears to be a plausible time, chronologically, for that event to occur.[49]

Coinciding with the negative effect of World War I was the national enactment of Prohibition. It was a problem for many immigrants, since the consumption of alcoholic beverages was an integral part of their cultures. With its introduction on July 1, 1919, alcoholic consumption was greatly curtailed. Joe was abstemious, but his father "drank beer, probably a bottle a day." Joe's brother John made home-brew for his father toward the end of Prohibition. Home-brewing was not always easy, as Bud Sandoz recalled. "Unfortunately it usually exploded before it could be used, but I'm sure that Grandpa could have his beer one way or another."[50]

But Joe did not abstain completely from alcohol. As an athlete, it is likely that he realized it was not good for him, and may have violated training rules. After his playing career, Joe was known to have a drink. By one account, "when offered on a special occasion he would have one drink and enjoy it." Joe's father "also smoked cigars, also probably one a day." Only George, of all the children, followed in this habit. None of the other Kasberger children cared for tobacco, an enduring family trait that was manifested in Joe's life.[51]

1919-20 School Year

When Joe returned to OAC in Sept., 1919 with 2,472 other students, he was a sophomore academically and for athletic eligibility.[52] As a returning veteran, and as a man aged 23, Joe certainly possessed considerable maturity. Yet many of Joe's OAC colleagues were probably more mature because of combat experiences. In this atmosphere, the Phi Delta Theta fraternity house was a welcome relief for some after trench warfare and barracks living.

To many college students, the fraternity or sorority house is the defining college experience. It can be argued that one had to be a Greek (fraternity member) to understand the bonds of brotherhood that the experience provides. For Joe, the relationships forged at Phi Delta Theta before the Army, brought him back to his OAC family away from home. Joe had some 59 initiated brothers at the end of the 1917-18 school year. When the 1918-19 school year began, the chapter had added another 26 members. Chapter president, Roy Keene, was so active in campus affairs that the Phi Delta Theta members had a role model who motivated others to get involved. Thus Joe began to branch out into many campus activities at this time. From this intimate house network, campus organizations, student government and athletic teams became filled with Phi Delta Thetas. [53]

Joe's sophomore year, according to the 1923 *Beaver*, began with varsity football and ended with varsity baseball. There was also intramural basketball as a member of the Phi Delta Theta team. In between these sports, Joe was a member of The Varsity "O" organization and the Vigilance Committee. Presumably the Vigilance Committee was most active early in the fall semester when committee members dealt with new students who were unfamiliar with OAC's traditions. "The rocky road of the Freshman is patrolled by the Vigilance Committee." For the recognized campus-enforcers of OAC's traditions, it appears that "Rooks" received many admonitions, per this warning: "Woe to the Rook who in his youthful exuberance oversteps the boundaries of O.A.C. tradition."[54] Being a group member may have been more honorary than functional during the football season, when Joe was consumed with football to the exclusion of other activities.

Bill Hargiss was Joe's first varsity football coach at OAC. Despite the earlier reference to Emporia State College, there is another account of Hargiss' background. "Hargiss came to O.A.C. from Kansas University, where he filled the position of coach for one year. He is a former U. of K. football hero."[55] As the veterans returned, college football became bigger and more popular than ever. In this climate of optimism, there are insights into Joe's 1919 teammates for his first varsity season.

> Henry [Reardon] is the captain of the team. His home is in Corvallis, Oregon. This is his last year on the team. Made all Northwest and All Coast in 1917. He played half for Mather Field Aviators last season. His regular position is quarterback.
>
> Ozbun G. Walker, left tackle is from Portland, Oregon, where he played four years on the Washington High School team. He plays tackle and was mentioned on Walter Camp's all-American team in 1917. He was in service last year.
>
> 'Cack' Hubbard, left end from Weiser, Idaho, has played three seasons for O.A.C. He is one of the best ends that O.A.C. has ever produced. He played with Camp Dick Aviators last season. His specialty is running down punts.
>
> Carl Lodell, left guard hails from Jefferson High School, Portland, Oregon. This is his third year on the varsity. Lodell has won great fame for his punting and open field running.

OAC 1919 football team – Top row: Kasberger, Heyden, Rose, Powell, Swan, Strohecker, McCart, Kirkenslager, Lodell, Walker, Stewart and Day; Bottom row: Asst. Coach Billie, Reynolds, Schroeder, Hodler, Van Hosen, Coach Hargiss, Reardon, Christensen, Johnson, Gill, Hubbard, Manager J. J. Richardson.

Clarence Johnson, right guard is another of Virgil Earl's protégés from Washington High School of Portland. This is his second year on the varsity. He is known as a real fighter when it comes to football.

Charles Rose, right end comes from Lincoln High School of Seattle, Washington. Chuck is noted for his wonderful defensive playing. He played with the Mather Field Aviators last season. This is his second year on the varsity.

Robert Stewart, center learned his first football at the Hill Military Academy of Portland, Oregon. This is his second year on the team, having played on O.A.C.'s service team last year.

George Powell, fullback is the one best bet O.A.C. has in the backfield. He is noted for his wonderful line plunging ability. He learned his first football at Franklin high school of Portland, Oregon.

Marion McCart, tackle makes a good running mate for Walker. He is heavy, fast and is possessed with an unusual amount of fight. His home is at Selma, California, where he played high school football for four years.

Albert Hodler, halfback came to O.A.C. from Columbia University of Portland. He is very shifty and a good ground gainer. He was picked on the mythical all-coast eleven last season. This is his second year on the team.

Joseph Kasberger, halfback whose home is in The Dalles, Oregon, played with Mt. Angel for two years previous to his entering O.A.C. He is a great halfback and a human corkscrew when it comes to going through the line.

Harry Swan, guard comes from Baker, Oregon. This is his second year on the varsity. He is big and husky and has wonderful possibilities.

W.W. Schroeder, quarter is another Portland product and learned his first football at James Johns High School. He is good at running back punts and handles the team very nicely. This is his first year on the squad. [56]

The season opened with a 0-0 tie against the Alumni, followed by a 21-0 win over the OAC Frosh (Rooks). The season became tougher after a 46-6 win over

Pacific. The promising start led to frustration when conference play began. Stanford came to Corvallis and defeated the Beavers 6-14. The next week, OAC was in Berkeley against California for another loss, 14-21. The losing streak continued at home against Multnomah Athletic Club (A.C.), 0-14, to set the scene for the season's big game. Oregon's hopes for a second Rose Bowl appearance were dimmed by an early-season loss to Washington State, 0-7, but there was still hope for a return trip to Pasadena.[57]

The University of Oregon Homecoming Week *Official Program* for the Oregon vs. OAC football game, November 15, 1919 "State Championship Football Game, 2:30 P.M.," provides insights into the rivalry, teams and players. In a hot series that began in 1894, Oregon led OAC 14-4-4. OAC's 14-7 win in 1917 over Oregon was its first since beating the Ducks 4-0 in 1907. The game story's text is headlined: "The Rival Football Teams."

No more evenly matched teams ever represented the University of Oregon and Oregon Agricultural College than those which meet on the Universities field this afternoon.

The University of Oregon team has developed power and punch sufficient to stamp it as one of the real leaders in Pacific Coast football circles. Its great record for the season justifies the Oregon enthusiasts in terming their football mentor, 'Shy' Huntington, a worthy exponent of Bezdek.

Coach 'Bill' Hargiss's O.A.C. eleven is a fitting opponent for Oregon. Many assert that O.A.C. has never had a stronger eleven than that developed there this season.

At Oregon Agricultural College this year Coach Hargiss has been greatly handicapped with injuries and that element classed as football 'luck.' The team has lost its two big games of the season, one at home and one on the University of California field.

However football critics are of the same opinion in stating that in both these games O.A.C. should either have won or at least tied the score. In their game against Stanford the result in all reality is classed as an O.A.C. victory. As an example of their luck every man in their backfield made more yardage than the entire Stanford team. In the California game with a little more than four minutes to play, the O.A.C. team advanced the ball from the center of the field to the three-yard line when time was called. This score would have tied the game.

Ozbun Walker, left tackle on the O.A.C. team, is one of the bright particular stars of the O.A.C. eleven. He is a remarkable defensive lineman and it is through his side of the line that most of their yardage is made. He was mentioned on Walter Camp's third all-American team in 1917.

In George Powell O.A.C. has one of the most powerful fullbacks ever seen in the Northwest. 'Butts' Reardon is one of the greatest field generals in the Northwest. Marion McCart is a worthy mate to Walker on the tackle position.

With regard to Oregon's eleven much does not need to be said. In Bartlett, Williams and Mautz they have the most powerful linemen seen in this country for many years. But the bright and shining light of the entire Oregon team is their quarterback, 'Bill' Steers. He is a cute little quarterback who tips the scales at only 185 lbs. He is as fast as they make 'em and on generalship is a wizard. His accuracy at drop-kicking is uncanny. Playing in the backfield with this great athlete are Hollis Huntington, Vinc. Jacobberger and Everett Brandenburg. 'Brick' Leslie, the the fighting center, Al Harding, right guard, and Howard and Anderson at ends give Oregon a line that, as a whole, is probably second to none in the Northwest.

Pep, dash, punch and team work have been given as the recipe of this mighty Oregon aggregation for its share of a football game. Coach Huntington has welded them into an eleven that is a fighting match for any team on the Pacific coast.

Going on the theory that a big punch must be developed for the coming game Coach Hargiss has put this team through a strenuous two weeks' program. The team that represents them on the field today will be an entirely rejuvenated eleven which has been trained to withstand any element of football luck.

This is the return of the annual interstate [sic] game after an absence of two years due to war conditions.

This contest is looked upon by all students and former students of both Oregon and O.A.C. as the one big game of the year. To win this big classic a team has completed a successful season regardless of whether all the other contests are won or not. With the two contending teams so evenly matched this year, and the spirit of rivalry greatly increased after practically being extinguished during the war, today's contest will go down in the annals of both institutions as one of the greatest contests ever played.

The University of Oregon has a much greater percentage of games won than O.A.C. has, in fact the average game won by O.A.C. is every ten years. The question arising in everyone's mind is: Will Oregon keep up that remarkable record already established or will their colors be lowered this season.[58]

Statewide interest in the game was most intense in The Dalles, because four native sons were involved, with Joe Kasberger as OAC's only representative. For Oregon, head coach Shy Huntington was described as a Bob Murray and Hugo Bezdek protégé who "has developed a powerful eleven this fall." Giving Oregon its horsepower were two players from TDHS, Bill Steers and Hollis Huntington. Continuing his skills as a kicker in the college game, "Bill Steers always kicks off for Oregon." For points after touchdowns, Shy has younger brother Hollis as another kicker who "converts goals." Besides kicking, Steers and Huntington were formidable in the Oregon backfield, with Bill Steers capping off his illustrious football career with an All-American season.[59]

William Steers, quarterback is one of Coach Murray's products from The Dalles, Oregon. Steers is a good punter, good line plunger and a bear at running back punts. He is 23 years of age, weighs 185 pounds and is a senior in college.

His equally famous teammate was described as follows:

Hollis Huntington, fullback another Dalles product and a former member of the 1916 team. Hollis played with the famous Marine team of 1917. Hollis is playing his last year of varsity football. He weighs 175 pounds, is 5 feet 11 inches, and 24 years of age.[60]

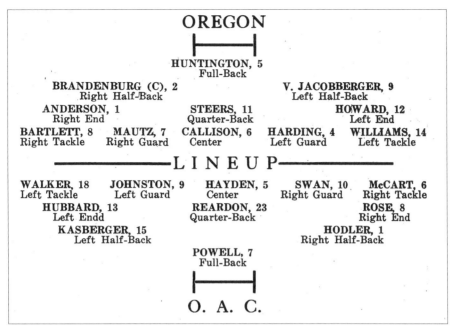

1919 OAC vs. U of O lineup.

Oregon was accustomed to playing in big games dating back to the 1916 Rose Bowl win over Pennsylvania and Shy had several experienced players. "Baz Williams, Holly Huntington and Ken Bartlett are former members of the famous 1916 team which humbled Pennsylvania." Although the game did not count in Pacific Coast Conference records because of the use of military players, Oregon had "Howard, Harding, Jacobberger, Mautz and Brandenburg [who] played on last year's team which humbled O.A.C. 13 to 6."[61]

OAC was led by quarterback and team captain Henry "Butts" Reardon. Although only "150 pounds," he is "noted for his broken field running and headwork." Reardon was a versatile athlete, known as "a wizard at basketball." Joining Reardon as team leaders were a few upperclassmen, one with an unusual style, George Powell, who "always kicks off for O.A.C.," but is most conspicuous "on the football field from the fact that he never wears a headguard." Also, there was Clarence Johnson, famed from his military service as "a survivor of the Tuscania." Another OAC player knowing Bill Steers besides Joe Kasberger was Carl Lodell, who "played on the famous Marine team with Bill Steers last year."[62]

Against arch-rival Oregon in Eugene, the Beavers lost their fourth-in-a-row, 0-9. The losing streak ended in Portland against Washington State when the Beavers won 6-0. The finale was in Corvallis, and OAC defeated Gonzaga 50-0 to salvage a sorry season.

In conference competition, Oregon and Washington tied for the championship with 2-1-0 records, followed by California and Washington State with 2-2-0 records. Stanford finished at 1-1-0 and OAC was last at 1-3-0. A 1921 *Beaver* "Review of the Season" discussed the 1919 football season, with a picture of Joe.

The story emphasized the parity among teams that was demonstrated by close scores and "breaks which decided the victory." The style of play in the conference is not described, but the story suggests that all teams employed a "universal style." The story ended with the notion that wins and losses should not be the only criteria for judging the team.

> From the standpoint of consistent, even play, and unusually strong defensive work, and yet handicapped by injuries even more than the closest followers realized, the record made is commendable.[63]

Joe's athletic career was, remarkably, injury-free. Yet, his OAC career coincided with the suggestion that conditioning and sports-injuries were a recurring problem. As the OAC season progressed, injuries took a toll without a "competent trainer and conditioner." The loss of several key players, including team captain Reardon, precipitated the hiring of additional football staff. "Toward the end of the year a professional trainer was employed and the record and work of the team from this time was remarkable." This account opined "that O.A.C. had the strongest team in the conference at the close of the season." Thus, it was believed that "future Aggie teams will have the advantage of being in excellent condition, which is second only to efficient coaching." [64]

Despite the setbacks in 1919, the future looked bright for OAC. Virtually the entire 1919 OAC team would return along with a promising group of players from the freshman team. It was expected that "O.A.C. next year will make a high bid for the Coast honors in football."[65] Regrettably for Coach Hargiss, he did not return to benefit from the young squad he had developed. The 1919 season turned out to be Coach Hargiss' second and last at OAC. The reason for the coaching change is not known. Some player profiles from the 1921 *Beaver* provide an insight into Joe's teammates on the 1919 football team.

> Joseph 'Joe' Kasberger - Left Halfback: His 180 lbs. and 5 ft., 10 in., plus a ton of inherent football ability and fight has made him a fixture in the Beaver backfield.
> Carl 'Lody' Lodell - Plays left halfback and quarterback. One of the best kickers in football. Lody weighs 180 lbs. and if he were one inch taller he would be 6 feet.
> Clyde 'Cack' Hubbard - Captain elect, left end. Unanimous choice as the best end on the Pacific Coast. Weighs 165 lbs., and 5 ft. and 9 in. tall.
> Charles 'Chuck' Rose - Rose is the youth who ran through the entire California team for a touchdown. He plays right end. He is 6 feet tall and weighs 186 lbs.
> J.H. 'Butts' Reardon - Captain and quarterback, weighs 145 lbs. and is 5 ft., 6 in., tall. An injury at the first of the season prevented him from playing until near the end of the season.[66]

The 1919 football season gave Joe enough playing time for his first varsity letter, and membership in the Varsity "O" organization. The 1923 *Beaver* has a picture and caption of Joe with other members of the "VARSITY 'O' Association." It was composed of fifty active members and concerned "itself largely with the promotion of the major sports at O.A.C." Membership was exclusively "men who have been awarded sweaters for participation in one or more major sports."[67]

The 1921 *Beaver* suggests that Dec. 1919 provided much campus excitement after registration on Dec. 3 for the 2nd quarter. A week later, weather was an issue. "Final exams loom closer but we cannot be bothered. Then snow!! School closes for lack of fuel." Apparently men and women had different final examination schedules from the following account of activities on Dec. 13 and 14, respectively: "Girls leave; everything frozen; skating on Mary's river." "Boys leave and school closes for vacation." The holiday season in Oregon was focused on Pasadena and the 1920 Rose Bowl game.[68]

Despite the tie with Washington for the conference championship, the Oregon Ducks were invited to host the 1920 Rose Bowl game against Harvard. The Dalles was interested because of Oregon's new head coach, Shy Huntington, and star players, Bill Steers and Hollis Huntington. For the aforementioned participants, the Rose Bowl was not new. For Oregon's freshman football coach, Robert L. Murray, it was a special event that capped his return to coaching after the war. In "1919 he was back again, this time as frosh coach at the University of Oregon, the one and only time he coached college ball." Shy was more than a Murray protégé, so it is not surprising that Coach Bob "accompanied the Rose Bowl team of that year to Pasadena in an official capacity."[69]

For Shy and Hollis Huntington, Bob Murray was a father-figure. Shy's wife Hallie described the Huntington sons, Walter, Shy, and Hollis as "fatherless boys" after the death of their father, James Marsh Huntington in 1900, "leaving six children under 14." James Huntington had New England roots but had become successful in Oregon with a "prominent abstract office," and in insurance. [70] Fortunately his widow, Mary, "took over the operation of the office personally and supported her family." This strong woman did not neglect household affairs. Her daughter, Hazel, was 13 when her father died and in later years "she could not remember ever sitting down to a meal when they did not have a white table cloth on the table and cloth napkins. At that time, paper napkins were unheard of."[71]

With Bob Murray's coaching, Shy developed into "a gridiron star of the first magnitude." The nickname "Shy" was acquired when he was very young from a comic-strip character, "Shy-Bones." Compared to younger brother Hollis, known as "Scrub," Shy was described as an introvert.[72] Hollis played with Shy in the 1917 Rose Bowl win over Penn and duplicated his brother's heroics in 1918 to acquire personal fame.

> The following year he returned to the Rose Bowl as a fullback, this time with the Mare Island Marines. Hollis totalled 111 yards in 20 carries, helping clinch the Rose Bowl Championship and Rose Bowl Player of the Game title.[73]

The Harvard game was memorable for many reasons. Hollis is "one of only

Oregon Ducks 1919 football team – Top row: Coach Huntington, Mautz, Anderson, Naterland, Jones, Runquist, Starr, Cosgriff, Ward, Callison, F. Jacobberger, Williams, Hayward. Center row: Shattuck, Howard, K. Leslie, Harding, V. Jacobberger, Brandenburg, H. Huntington, E. Leslie, Tuerck. Bottom row: Smith, Bradeson, Gilbert, Morfitt, Steers, Manerude, Chapman, McKinney, Dresser.

three men to play every single minute in three different Rose Bowl games." Sadly, Oregon lost, 7-6, to end a remarkable three-year consecutive string for the younger Huntington. Both Huntingtons never forgot this bitter loss. Hollis may have been the only Rose Bowl participant to play for an older brother as head coach. Also, he is distinctive for playing in three-straight Rose Bowl games for two different teams, Mare Island Marines and the University of Oregon. Both Huntingtons were enshrined in the Rose Bowl Hall of Fame in 1992.[74]

The playing careers of Bill Steers and Hollis Huntington ended in this game. Hollis coached high school football in Anaconda, MT and Salem, OR before becoming a businessman. Steers went to New York's Columbia University for a doctorate in physical education that led to college teaching at California University of Pennsylvania and the University of Miami, Florida.[75]

For Bob Murray the Eugene experience may have given him ambivalent feelings about moving up a notch in competition. One observer commented that life "in Eugene would have been more than coaching." In this context, this observer further noted:

> Working with the coaching staff at Oregon could have been difficult for Bob. He was accustomed to calling the shots and he would have been an assistant there. Bob was from the developmental period in football.[76]

According to Bill Murray, his father left Eugene to return to The Dalles and rear his family. Accounts reveal that Bob took a position with the city engineering department, but he soon returned to the field of coaching.[77] Shy Huntington and Bob Murray remained lifelong friends, despite Murray's abrupt departure. Bob's modest educational credentials may have made it impossible for him to remain as Oregon's freshman coach, despite his ties to Shy – in the emerging climate of credentialism surrounding coaches and teachers that may have been born in Eugene, and spread throughout Oregon.

Joe's role in OAC basketball presents interpretation problems. The 1923 *Beaver* shows him to be active in that sport in his junior and senior years. The key to the interpretation might be that "Varsity Basketball" is not used as it is in the case with "Varsity Football." Heartwell's book on OAC basketball has no pictures or references to Joe as a member of the varsity teams in 1920-21 and 1921-22. Perhaps he was a team candidate but was not chosen for the varsity, and instead played at the "Inter-Organizational" level.

The 1921 *Beaver* revealed that Joe was one of five men selected by Ralph Coleman for the Inter-organization all-star team for the 1919-20 school year. Joe's Phi Delta Theta fraternity brother, Howard Stoddard, was also selected. Kasberger and Stoddard were also selected to the All National Fraternity Team. There are two pictures of Joe related to this story. The 1921 *Beaver* had this story on OAC's "Interorganization Basket Ball:"

> The intramural basket ball season at O.A.C. this year was the most successful ever staged. Forty teams, composed of nearly four hundred athletes, took part. These teams represented every club, fraternity and independent group in the college.[78]

Basketball was very popular at OAC, given the level of participation in this league. "A great deal of interest in the games was manifested by the various organizations." It was not only the number of players that impressed, but also the fan support. "Practically all the members were present as players or rooters." Great zeal was shown by an unidentified organization that "even brought along a jazz band to cheer their team to greater efforts." There were six different leagues whose winners then entered a championship round of play during the season's last two weeks. "Phi Delta Theta fraternity won the interorganization championship, having lost but one game during the entire season."[79]

Basketball was an important OAC activity for Joe, regardless of the level at which he played. Even if it were not for the varsity, Joe was exposed to the college game and coaches. His friendship with one OAC basketball player, Amory T. "Slats" Gill, probably began at Phi Delta Theta. Joe certainly saw, if he did not know, many of the early greats of OAC's relatively strong basketball program. Heartwell observed that: "Winning teams usually have outstanding players in their makeup and the top teams of this era were no exception." He lists the following as all-star players: "Ade Sieberts, Spike Mix, Hod Ray, Dutch Krueger, Lee Bissett, Butts Rearden [sic], Dick Stinson, Hjelte, Gill and Richards."[80]

The conclusion of the 1919-20 basketball season brought about nonathletic honors for Joe with initiation into Alpha Zeta. Membership in this national honorary fraternity for agricultural students at OAC was highly desired. At the honorary, rather than the service, level Joe was initiated into Alpha Zeta, after he was pledged to the organization as a sophomore on Feb. 25, 1920. The 1919 *Beaver* provided more detail on Alpha Zeta. On Jan. 29, 1918, OAC's "local petitioning body of agricultural students, known as Zeta Alpha [sic]," was finally rewarded for two-year's worth of "organized and constant effort" in achieving their goal. They were granted "the long coveted charter for the Oregon Chapter of the great national honorary agricultural fraternity." Alpha Zeta was founded in 1897 as "the oldest and largest agricultural fraternity in the country," making membership very prestigious. At that time, membership was more than 2,700 and included "the major share of the most distinguished leaders and investigators in agriculture in the country."[81]

As an honorary fraternity, with membership limited to twenty-six chapters at "all of the leading institutions" in the country, Alpha Zeta granted charters "only to institutions of the highest standing." Active membership was "limited to the best students" who were identified as underclassmen. Then, active membership was conferred to "the junior, senior and graduate classes." Membership included "those having the highest qualities of character, leadership and scholarship." Alpha Zeta had one guiding principle: "Leadership in the furtherance of scientific agriculture," in recognition of this vital body of knowledge.[82]

OAC's most prestigious organization was the Forum. Joe's selection on April 14, 1920 as one of 14 new Forum members was a signal honor. The results of the "Forum Convocation" were one of the highlights of every academic year. "The Student Body awaits with bated breath the results" of its decision on new members. When the selections were announced, "new pledges of the organization receive the white rose, the greatest honor that can be given a student." The 1923 *Beaver* gave this elaboration:

> The outstanding leaders and scholars among the Junior and Senior men and women who have shown by their work a wholesome and unselfish interest in the College, who have looked toward its future and who have expended time and energy in working toward the future, make up the membership of the organization.

Without a Phi Beta Kappa chapter, OAC's Forum sufficed. Its "standards are the same as those of the national honorary fraternity," and membership was very prestigious.[83]

OAC's 1920 baseball team started practice on Feb. 7, and began a spring-training tour of California on March 13. April 27 saw the "Beavers defeat University of Willamette Bearcats' in first baseball game of season."[84] Only four other baseball game results are known. On May 4, the Beavers defeated Washington State at Pullman. On May 11, OAC won a double-header from Stanford. The final opponent was Oregon in a tight game won by OAC. The final 1920 Pacific Coast Conference standings found California first with a 5-1 record. Washington was second at 8-6. The remaining teams in order were: Oregon, 7-7, Stanford, 5-5, OAC, 8-9, and Washington State, 2-7.

After the 1919-20 school year, the frustrations of OAC football may have troubled Joe as he contemplated the prospects of another football coach. The stability issue became more personal as he experienced the coaching changes.

1920-21 School Year

On Sept. 21 football practice began amid new buildings rising rapidly on campus. When registration concluded on Sept. 24, enrollment was near 3000 students. Also, there were "rush" responsibilities at Phi Delta Theta to select prospective members. The 1923 *Beaver* reported that "pledges were announced by fraternities" on Oct. 6.[85]

Phi Delta Theta membership led Joe to new contacts and networks that earned him a name at OAC. Whether Joe was induced into student government as class treasurer by Spec Keene, student body president, is not known. Joe's relationship with his Phi Delta Theta brothers was based upon mutual interest in athletics, and participation on varsity and intramural teams. In addition to his close relationships with Spec and Slats, Joe had another close Phi Delta Theta fraternity brother who would gain prominence, Wes Schulmerich. Joe's friendships with these three men were described as the closest he had in Oregon.[86]

Roy Servais "Spec" Keene was important to Joe Kasberger in a relationship that probably began at Phi Delta Theta. As fraternity president, Spec was an OAC mover and shaker. Prior to his years at OAC, Spec excelled as an athlete at Salem High School, Class of 1915, where "he had earned 13 letters – four in football as an end, four in basketball as a center, four in baseball as a pitcher-shortstop, and one in track as a sprinter."[87]

Keene's nickname, "Spec," was given him by Leon (Doc) Barrick, a baseball

Phi Delta Theta brothers in the 1923 **Beaver.**

player from Salem. "It happened one day when I was playing shortstop and he was at first base. He told me my throws looked like 'specks' coming at him." Spec enrolled at Missouri Wesleyan College at Cameron, MO, but returned to Oregon after a year and joined the National Guard. He entered active duty during World War I, serving for nineteen months with the "41st Infantry Division in Contres, France."[88]

At OAC, Spec "lettered three years in baseball as a pitcher, but skipped basketball and football because he had his sights on a pro diamond career." Spec stated, "'It didn't take me long to learn that I would get no place in baseball ... I had hurt my arm when I fell from a troop train in France, and it never came back.'" Spec gained prominence as OAC's student body president by forming "the committee which put in motion plans for the Memorial Union."[89]

In his junior year, Joe had another group on his agenda, the Greater OAC Committee. The 1923 *Beaver* described this organization, "elected by the Student Assembly," of which Joe was one of the executive committee's three members. It had responsibility for "publicity to interest students of secondary schools throughout the state in the college." In cooperation with OAC's alumni secretary, the Greater OAC Committee "organizes clubs in Oregon towns whose purpose is to promote a keener interest in the college." In a 1929 account, Joe was described as "chairman of the Greater O.A.C. Committee."[90]

KASBERGER   SCHUMACHER   BAIN

GREATER O. A. C. COMMITTEE

—

MEMBERS OF EXECUTIVE COMMITTEE

JOE KASBERGER   BENJAMIN SCHUMACHER   MARY BAIN

*1923 **Beaver** presentation of the Greater O.A.C. Committee Executive Committee.*

On April 16, 1920, Bill Hargiss was replaced by R.B. Rutherford as OAC's head football coach for the 1920 season. The 1922 *Beaver* noted that "'Red' Rutherford was elected coach of the 'fighting Aggies,'" coming to OAC from Washington University in St. Louis, where "he put out a championship team of the Missouri Valley." As a University of Nebraska player, Rutherford "was selected by Walter Camp as a member of the all-American team." Rutherford's selection was well-received, and he won "the confidence of every member of the student-body and of every loyal O.A.C. alumnus."[91]

Assisting Coach Rutherford was G.L. Rathbun, who came to OAC from Indiana, where he assisted Coach Steim, who "put out some of Indiana's best aggregations." Rathbun was described as providing experience and an ability to "understand the game and its intricacies." Also, Rathbun was seen as a coach who knew how to convey what he knew to the players.[92] Also on the 1920 OAC coaching staff was Michael Butler, who returned as team trainer. The 1922

Beaver has an individual picture of Joe, a 1920 team photo and several player profiles.

> 'Joe' Kasberger held down a variety of places on the varsity backfield last season and played good ball in every one of them. He started the season as a halfback, played quarter for a while and wound up his sojourn as a fullback where he earned Pacific Coast honorable mention.
>
> Harold 'Big' McKenna took Powell's place at full after the Washington game and held up the center of the offense mightily. His touchdown in the third quarter put the Beavers ahead of California for a while. Mac was the best yardage gainer on the squad in the Washington State game. He has two more years.
>
> Albert 'Duke' Hodler has the reputation on the coast of being one of the hardest hitting halfbacks in the game. 'Duke' made the varsity in his first year in school and has won three letters at O.A.C. He will be absent when the roll is called next fall.[93]

The 1922 *Beaver* provides the following game summaries for the 1920 OAC football team:

> 'Hail The Fighting Aggies!' After years of criticism for supposed lack of fight, Rutherford's squad earned the new title in a single year and displayed that they had the equal or superior fighting spirit to any team in the conference. Meeting reversal after reversal in the form of injuries, the Beavers kept up their morale until the final day of training. A new spirit has been born in the hearts of Beaver rooters and Beaver players that will live on through the new athletic era at O.A.C. After running in a slump for two years, the Beavers this year came through mightily, humbled Washington, held the famous California team to its hardest game of the season, and won an ethical victory over Oregon in a 0 to 0 contest.[94]

The scheduled first game against Pacific University on Oct. 8 was cancelled.

OAC-Multnomah A.C. The season opened with a game between Multnomah and the Aggies at Corvallis. Rutherford wisely sent in his second string and used only straight plays in a sea of mud. The contest was no portent of what was to come later in the year. Neither team scored in the game, for although Summers and Seely made some brilliant runs for the Aggies, they were unable to cross the 'Winged M' goal.[95]

The Multnomah Athletic Club bears the name of the county in which Portland, OR is located. It fielded athletic teams, often with players with previous collegiate experience. (Multnomah A.C. is now a prestigious social club with extensive facilities.)

OAC-Washington. "BEAVERS HUMBLE 'SUN DODGERS' 3 to 0." The next big game was with the Purple and Gold of Washington at Seattle. The 'Sun Dodgers' were given all the honors before the game but when the Seattle Chimes played 'Bow Down to Washington' and 'Hail to Old O.A.C.' at twilight the score stood 3 to 0 in our favor. It was the first time in 15 years that the Beavers had won from Washington and the campus went into ecstasies over the victory. When the heroes returned by the O.E. an enormous crowd of rooters was there to meet them and bring them up the hill. The injury that George Powell received in the last few minutes of play, kept him out of the game for the rest of the season. It was a dear victory for the Aggies.[96]

The University of Washington's athletic teams would soon be known as the "Huskies."

OAC-California. 'A Close Call for California.' The following week was marked by the California invasion. 'Andy' Smith's prodigies trotted out on the Corvallis gridiron at 2:50 and left 2 hours later 10 points to the good. The final score was 17 to 7 for California, but 7 of those points came as a direct result of a fumble on the Aggie 4-yard line and were not earned from scrimmage. Majors picked up the fumble and stepped over the goal for a touchdown.[97]

California's "Golden Bears" were thought to be the best nationally as the "wonder team."

OAC-Washington State. The Washington State game was a dope upsetter [sic]. California had beaten the Cougars 49 to 0 and the Aggies were figured as an even break with the Staters but Gillis could not be stopped and ran through the Beavers on a cold sleety Saturday in November for four touchdowns. The absence of Swan from the lineup left great holes in the right side of the Beaver line which couldn't be plugged successfully. Harold McKenna did some great line plunging in the Cougar game, as the best yardage gainer on the Beaver team.[98]

The OAC-Washington State game was played in Pullman.

OAC-Oregon. Oregon came to Corvallis on November 30 to decide the state championship but the Aggies held them to a scoreless tie before 13,000 spectators. In the final period the Beavers had the ball on the 6-inch line, and in the opinion of some of the spectators in the press box high over-head, over the goal, but when the tangled pile of legs and arms were unraveled, the referee found the ball not quite over and the great game ended scoreless. Newspapers throughout the state generally gave O.A.C. credit for a moral victory on 'fight.'[99]

In an unusual bit of scheduling, OAC opened and closed its 1920 season with the Multnomah Athletic Club. The game may have been added to the schedule to compensate for the cancellation of the Pacific University game.

OAC-Multnomah A.C. The season ended Thanksgiving day in Portland with the Multnomah Club which the Beavers won 10 to 7. The O.A.C. varsity seemed to have lost interest after the close of the season and played soggy ball. Occasional flashes of the old brilliance redeemed the game. Summers, Kasberger and McKenna were the individual stars in the Beaver backfield and Crowell and Rose starred on the line.[100]

California won the conference championship with a 3-0-0 record. Following in second place was Stanford at 2-1-0. Oregon finished third at 1-1-1. Washington State, 1-1-0, OAC, 1-2-1, and Washington, 0-3-0, brought up the rear.

The final story about the 1920 OAC football team comes from the 1922 *Beaver* with the caption "ORANGE 'O' IS AWARDED TO PLAYERS." Eighteen players earned varsity letters, while "two others missed the honor by only a few minutes." There "were no great individual stars," but the team was blessed with cooperation. "Every man put all he had into the game and shared honors with his teammates." A final summary follows:

> The winning combination seemed to be 'Husky' McKenna, quarter; Summers and Seely, halves; Kasberger, full; Rose and McFadden, ends; Swan and Crowell, tackles; Christensen and Clark, guards; and Stewart, center. Harold McKenna, 'Hi' Wood, 'Duke' Hodler, 'Gap' Powell and 'Chuck' Johnson worked well in the Beaver backfield while 'Scotty' Scott, 'Babe' McCart, 'Ted' Heyden, 'Johnny' Johnston and 'Nite' Daigh bolstered up the line.

The *Beaver* story continues with a 1921 preview, marked by the "election of 'Gap' Powell to succeed 'Chuck' Rose as captain." Only three players from the 1920 team were not expected to return in 1921. A good freshman team provided high hopes to win an elusive Pacific Coast Conference championship in 1921.

> The hard work of Coach 'Dick' Rutherford, Assistant Line Coach Guy Rathbun, and Trainer 'Dad' Butler is credited for the Beaver showing and the 'Fighting Aggie' spirit found in the team and student body this year.

The *Beaver* story concludes with laments about the departing seniors. "Captain Rose, 'Babe' McCart, 'Twister' Swan, Claire Seely and 'Duke' Hodler will be missed when the roll is called next fall."

> However, with such men as Locey, fullback of 1916, 'Cog' Campbell of the 1919 rooks, and the many players of this year's rook squad, it is believed that the team will not be handicapped for lack of material.[101]

The 1921 *Beaver* reported that on Dec. 14 "school closed for vacation," but there was no trip to sunny Pasadena for OAC's football team this New Year's Day.[102] Joe and his senior class-to-be now had to get the job done in 1921 as they ran out of time to fulfill dreams of playing in the Rose Bowl game. Fortunately, the 1921 schedule had OAC playing Southern California in the season's last game, at Tournament Park in Pasadena.

Joe had no affiliation with the OAC varsity basketball team in the 1920-21 season that produced a poor record of 6 wins and 17 losses. Yet Coach Rutherford laid the foundation for more successful future teams that were led by "material from the greatest OAC Rook team up to that time, plus a lad named Slats Gill." According to Heartwell, "before that was to happen, though, Rutherford had a tough row to hoe in 1920-21." Heartwell added that "on paper the team looked promising, but somehow it seldom clicked."[103]

The 1922 *Beaver* presented Intramural Basketball for the 1920-21 school year, with a picture of five unidentified Phi Delta Theta players, none of whom resembles Joe. "Phi Delta Theta won the school championship in intramural basketball after a long strenuous season without losing a single game."[104]

OAC's intramural program was not only a recreational activity for students, but also a testing ground for prospective varsity basketball players. The 1922 *Beaver* stated that about "40 teams participated in the series and a lot of embryo athletes were developed." This account revealed that "more than 500 men took part in this sport during the season." At the season's end there were awards. "The winners in each of the five leagues were awarded placques [sic] and the 'Phi Delts' received a silver cup for their efforts."[105]

Another varsity winter sport at OAC was wrestling. The 1922 *Beaver* noted that OAC's wrestling team salvaged a very disappointing school year for athletics. On March 3, it was reported that: "Aggies win wrestling championship by defeating Washington State."[106] This OAC wrestling squad may have provided Joe with his first exposure to the sport.

With the arrival of warm weather, the baseball season began. There are two photos of Joe as an OAC baseball player, one from 1921 as shown here. The other photo, unshown, has this caption:

> Joe Kasberger's time was divided between the pitcher's box and third base. He was a handy man at either place. He also managed to annex his share of runs.

The 1923 *Beaver* profiles some of Joe's 1921 OAC baseball teammates.

> Stanley 'Stan' Summers' usual position was left field. 'Stan' always managed to snare his portion of the fly balls. He was a handy man at the bat. 'Stan' has one more year on the varsity.
>
> Claude Booth is the outfielder and pinch-hitter who sent the Cougars down to a 2-1 defeat in the eleventh inning. He has two more years on the varsity.
>
> Hilbert 'Dutch' Tasto played his first year on the varsity. He is a dependable third baseman and we can expect great things from him next year.

1921 **Beaver** *photo of Joe .*

Val Noonan was 'Jimmie's' dark horse last year. His hitting ability entitled him to be the lead off man in the lineup. This was his first and last year on the varsity.[107]

The final 1921 Pacific Coast Conference baseball standings found California on top with a 3-0 record. Washington State finished second at 8-4 and Washington was third at 7-4. OAC led the second division at 4-7, followed by Oregon at 4-8 and Stanford at 0-3.

The school year ended for Joe with a losing baseball team and the graduation loss of Spec. Beneath Spec's picture in the 1922 *Beaver* are his many activities.

Roy Servais Keene
Phi Delta Theta
Agriculture...Salem, Ore
Varsity Baseball (1,2,3,4); Captain (3) Vigilance Association (3,4); Vigilance
Committee (2); Withycombe Club (2,3,4); Varsity "O" Association (2,3,4);
Chairman Student Rules Revision Committee; Manager Junior Week-End
Class '21; President Kappa Sigma Nu (2); President Phi Delta Theta (3);
Class Basketball (1,2,3); President Student Body (4);
Student Affairs Committee (4); Social Committee (4)[108]

Keene's outstanding performance at OAC was rewarded in the very near future by his alma mater to whom he gave so much as a student. Clearly, Spec Keene's accomplishments did not go unnoticed by the OAC administration.

A final reference to Joe in this school year came from the 1922 *Beaver,* which referred to him as "the man without a date."[109] One of OAC's traditions was "tubbing," a practice described by Pauling's biographers. One version saw it as "a prank played on men who had no date on Saturday night." This prank had the offender "held under water by friends until he could force his way back up."[110] As a big man on campus, Joe may have been immune from this tradition.

1921-22 School Year

An old MAC friend joined Joe in Corvallis during this school year when Rev. Frank P. Leipzig, after ordination, became pastor of St. Mary's Church. This was Leipzig's first stop in a rise to becoming the fourth Bishop of the Diocese of Baker, OR and MAC's most famous alumnus. The 1922 *Beaver* reference to Joe as the man without a date came from a mint copy of this yearbook from Bishop Leipzig's collection that is in the Archdiocese of Portland Archives.

In his final year at OAC, there was more than football to keep him busy. Joe also found time for the following activities: Forum, Alpha Zeta, Treasurer, varsity football, basketball, baseball, Varsity "O" and Stock-Judging Team. The reference to Joe as "treasurer" is not clear. Possibly he was treasurer of Alpha Zeta; or, he was treasurer of the student body. Yet there were other activities, including the Forum. The 1923 *Beaver* reveals Joe as treasurer of the Forum.

1923 **Beaver** *photo of Joe, upper right, as Forum treasurer as a senior.*

Shortages, due to the war effort and increased enrollments, were realities as the 1921-22 school year began. A response by OAC's administrators was reported by Pauling's biographers. Linus Pauling was unusually bright, and his talent was recognized when he began his teaching career at OAC while still an undergraduate. In Nov. 1921, "Pauling received an offer from OAC to teach quantitative analysis in the chemistry department." By today's standards this was unusual. "Pauling had only completed the course himself six months before. Now he was being asked to teach it!"[112]

Pauling was paid "$100-a-month" and given a demanding schedule.

> He supervised laboratories and gave lectures, spending a total of about 40 hours a week with students. That amounts to about four times the work of a regular college instructor today. [113]

In discussing Pauling's offer from OAC to teach, Serafini offered several explanations. First, "there really was a dearth of instructors" because of the war effort. Second, the war's conclusion brought more students to OAC. "Classrooms were overcrowded and teachers were overworked." Despite these considerations, Serafini concludes that "it was virtually unheard of for an undergraduate to occupy the lecture podium."[114]

OAC's 1921 football season is detailed in the 1923 *Beaver* with a photo of Coach Rutherford and comments about his two-year tenure. Besides coaching, Rutherford was also the director of athletics and physical education. "The name of 'Fighting Aggies' and the 'Aggies Sixty Minutes of Fight' motto have been adopted under his regime." The story also stated that as a student at the University of Nebraska, Rutherford "was on the varsity football, basketball and wrestling teams three years, and on the track and baseball teams one year each." The 1923 *Beaver* gave a glimpse of assistant coach, Guy L. Rathbun, who was finishing his second season at OAC describing him as a "valuable man not only for the work he has done with the football team but also as coach for wrestling and baseball." Bringing OAC a wrestling championship made Rathbun distinctive. Again in 1921 the OAC football coaching staff included a trainer, and the 1923 *Beaver* described this man, Michael "Dad" Butler. He was completing his third season with OAC, and his value was reported so highly that it "cannot be estimated in words or dollars." Butler was praised because "it was seldom that a

THE FIGHTING AGGIE SQUAD

Back row: left to right—1, Powell; 2, Nelson; 3, Crow; 4, Allen; 5, Romig; 6, Waring.
3rd row—1, Giebisch; 2, Kelly; 3, R. Johnson; 4, Gilbert; 5, Simons; 6, Payne; 7, Wagner; 8, Lance; 9, Garber; 10, Boyles.
2nd row—1, Coach Rutherford; 2, Kasberger; 3, Gill; 4, Hughie McKenna; 5, Johnson; 6, Reichert; 7, Miller; 8, Tousey;
  9, Hagedorn; 10, Jessup; 11, Capt. Powell; 12 Winnie ; 13, Rice.
Bottom row—1, Harold McKenna; 2, Taggert; 3, Michelwait; 4, Stewart; 5, Christensen; 6, Daigh; 7, Crowell; 8, Locey;
  9, McFadden; 10, Taylor; 11, Laughery; 12, Garity.

1921 OAC football team.

player had to be taken from the lineup."[115] The role of "Dad" Butler in Joe's OAC career is important, since he missed no playing time due to injuries.

Profiles of Joe's teammates for 1921 come from the 1923 *Beaver.*

Captain G.A. 'Gap' Powell, the husky All-American fullback, played his fourth season of football last year. He was selected by 263 coaches throughout the United States to fill a place on the All-American eleven. 'Gap's' wonderful offensive and defensive playing for the Aggies always brought results.

Captain-elect Percy Locey played fullback on the team of 1915. Last year 'Perc' was shifted to the left tackle position, to give Powell the fullback station. In almost every game that he played he was featured in the newspaper reports.

'Nite' Daigh worked on the line at guard and end. This was 'Nite's' last year for the Aggies. He got in several games for part time, at least long enough to display his spirit and fight.

'Christy' Christensen is one of the 'fightenest' [sic] individuals on the team. So much so that he has won a place on the All-Pacific Coast eleven at left guard. 'Christy' has played his last game for the Aggies and his scrappiness will be missed next year.

'Joe' Kasberger, the fleet-footed quarterback, won a place on the mythical eleven of the Pacific Coast for the second time this year. His chatter always kept the Aggie spirit predominant on the field. This is 'Joe's' last year on the team.

'Ted' Heyden certainly made good at right guard this year, making his part of the line a stone wall. This is 'Ted's' last year on the team, he having played three straight years for the Aggies. Injuries kept him out of the Oregon game, causing him to miss his last chance at the old rivals.

'Bob' Stewart, the Aggie center, was a demon to the opposing team when it came to getting through and smearing up plays. This makes his third year for the Aggies. 'Bob' is one of the last men to make four letters on an Aggie Team.[116]

Bragging rights for Joe in The Dalles were also on the line in 1921 for the last time. After a 4-0-1 start, OAC suffered through a heartbreaking run of close losses and another scoreless tie with Oregon. The 1921 season ended for OAC with a 4-3-2 record. Game summaries follow:

OAC-Rooks (OAC Frosh). 1921's first game is shown in the OAC *Media Guide* as a regular game rather than a scrimmage. OAC Varsity won 68-7 in Corvallis.

OAC-Chemawa. In the second home game, OAC defeated the Chemawa Indians 68-0, but there are no details available.

OAC-Multnomah A.C. The third consecutive home game resulted in a 7-7 tie between the Beavers and their club rivals from Portland. Game details are unavailable.

OAC-Willamette. The final non-conference game for the Beavers was in Salem against the Bearcats. The 54-0 Beaver win may have given OAC high hopes for conference play.

The next game was against the University of Washington and the official *Game Program* featured Joe Kasberger, Number 22, with an individual picture and write-up. The roster of both teams is presented in the Appendix, with revealing information about the players, especially their ages. The average age was nearly 24 years for OAC and nearly 22 years for Washington. For OAC the oldest was 26, Percy Locey, and the youngest was 19. For Washington the oldest was 27 and the youngest was 19. While all OAC players are white, Washington had one black player, Ham Green. Beginning with Fritz Pollard of Brown and Paul Robeson of Rutgers Universities, respectively, famous black college football players were on teams of this era.

OAC-Washington. Perhaps Joe was pumped up for the Sundodgers because of being featured in the *Game Program* as follows:

Joe's photo from the official OAC Game Pro-gram *of the 1921 football game against the University of Washington.*

(22). JOE KASBERGER - The dependable quarterback, who's [sic] headwork will always keep the opponents guessing. His line plunging and passing makes

"Kasberger goes over for a Touchdown," as a senior against the Sundodgers.

him the all around star of the back field. He helped [put] The Dalles on the map.[117]

Joe's career statistics at OAC have not been located, so it is fortuitous that the *Beaver* photographer caught Joe scoring at least one touchdown. The game summary was in the photo caption.

When the 'Huskies' arrived on the Aggie campus with their little contingent of rooters, little did they expect to be handed the small end of a 24 to 0 score.[118]

OAC-Stanford. The game summary is as follows:

The Aggie-Stanford game was a dope upsetter to gridiron followers on the coast. Prior to the game our team had all the edge on the Cardinal eleven but at the end of the fourth quarter the score stood 14-7 in favor of Stanford.[119]

OAC's Homecoming game against Washington State had extra meaning with the dedication of Bell Field as the new name of OAC's stadium. "It was dedicated on Armistice Day to the Reverend J. R. N. Bell, a loyal supporter of student activities for many years."[120]

OAC-Washington State. Sadly, the Beavers lost, again, 7-3.

A place kick in the first half looked like a win for the Aggies, but little Moe Sax, quarter-back of the Cougar team worked his way through the Aggie defense for the winning touchdown.[121]

<u>OAC-Oregon.</u> A game summary follows this introduction.

> Rallies, a bonfire, the Oregon game, the bag rush, a cross country run, and a soc-
> cer game, were some of the events that kept the alumnae [sic] busy during the
> last homecoming week-end. The rooks built a huge bonfire in back of the
> forestry building, which was burned the night before the game at a monster
> rally. Saturday morning O.A.C. played a scoreless tie with Oregon in soccer.
> Following this the sophomores won the annual bag rush. The big event of the
> day was the game between Oregon and O.A.C., which also ties with a 0-0 score.
> The new stadium was used, which together with the old bleachers seats more
> than 11,000 people. Just before the game the O.A.C. chanters marched around
> the field singing at the head of the alumnae [sic] varsity 'O' parade. The day
> wound up with a homecoming dance in the men's gym.[122]

Another story of the big game presents the atmosphere surrounding this
annual war between arch-enemies, whose rivalry transcended the football field
and "was based on whether a liberal arts or technical education is better!"[123]

> The Oregon game brings to white heat the ever-present rivalry between O.A.C.
> and the State University. Rallies begin early in the week, and enthusiasm reach-
> es a high pitch at the bonfire the night before the game. Even the worst caprice
> of the weather man cannot keep crowds of rooters from this game.[124]

Despite the scoreless outcome, the game was very exciting, with weather a
factor. "The field was a sea of mud making fumbles frequent on either side." In a
classic brawl, the weather may not have mattered. "Such a game of hair raising
thrills combined with '60 minutes of fight' made every rooter forget the awful
downpour of rain." Game highlights follow as the story continues.

> With the ball on the Oregon 20 yard line three plays made the score board read
> 'third down and three to go.' Powell made the yardage. On the first down with
> the goal to go Oregon recovered a fumble. 'Spike' Leslie brought the rooters to
> their feet when he missed a goal kick by inches and so the game went.[125]

<u>OAC-USC.</u> The game summary is as follows:

> The Aggie's last '60 minutes of fight' for the season was displayed at Pasadena in
> the University of Southern California game. From the start of the game until the
> final whistle the Aggies were on the aggressive, but on the breaks of luck the
> Trojans excelled. The score O.A.C. 0, U.S.C. 7, resulted from a blocked punt.[126]

Final 1921 Pacific Coast Conference football standings found California on
top with a 4-0-0 record. Washington State was second at 2-1-1 and Stanford's 1-1-
1 was good for third. OAC at 1-2-1 led the second division, followed by Oregon,
0-1-2 and Washington, 0-3-1. OAC's 4-3-2 overall record ended Joe's career without a Pacific Coast Conference championship. He was rewarded for his individual efforts, however, with post-season honors when named as a member of the

All-Conference team in his sophomore and junior years. In a 1929 account, Joe was named "all Pacific Coast half back of 1921." Known for his versatility, reportedly, Joe "played all positions in the backfield and was recognized as one of the best utility men on the squad."[127]

Again, OAC's football future looked bright with a strong freshman team in 1921. According to the 1923 *Beaver*, the freshman team coach, Clyde "Cac" Hubbard, led them to a 3-0-1 record. OAC "Rooks" defeated Columbia University, 7-3; Albany College, 39-0; and Mount Angel College, 35-7. The tie came against the University of Oregon in a 0-0 game.

With the football season over, Joe found time for another competitive activity, OAC's Stock-Judging team. This was a more successful OAC team, whose accomplishments were reported in the *Oregon Countryman* of Dec. 1921, apparently a journal from OAC's Agriculture Department. The headline was: "International Honors Won by O.A.C. Stockmen."

The story stated that "O.A.C. was well represented at the Pacific International Livestock show in Portland," and earned several awards. Prizes were won by its "judging teams" and "the college animals exhibited there." OAC's stock-judging team was actually three teams, "consisting of the most prominent students in their respective departments," coached by E.L. Potter of the animal-husbandry staff. OAC's competition came from "all over the northwest and even British Columbia." How scoring was calculated is not described. "The team made a total of 8,089 points out of a possible 10,000. Washington State college was the nearest competitor, making 7,735 points ... ."[128]

Joe, upper left, with other members of the stock-judging team.

J.C. Hogg, senior, from Salem, was high point man of the entire contest, winning by 31 points over K.K. Mundy, from Washington State college. L.C. Brown, a senior from Enterprise, was high man in the beef cattle judging.

The story continues with a list of the team members and their scores.

J.C. Hogg of Salem, 1,731; L.C. Brown of Enterprise, 1,611; G.F. Loy, Buena Vista, 1608; Joe Kasberger, The Dalles, 1,563; and Warren Daigh, Ontario, Cal., 1,531.[129]

Joe may have belonged to the Withycombe Club, "named in honor of ex-Governor Withycombe of Oregon, [which] was founded at O.A.C. in 1916." Members were "seniors and juniors majoring in animal husbandry." This club "sends livestock judging teams to the Pacific Northwest and Pacific International shows each year." The 1921 team "carried off first honors in the Northwest and third in the International."[130] An uncaptioned group photo in the 1923 *Beaver* does not appear to include Joe.

OAC's hard times in basketball came to an end with the new era that began in 1921-22. Heartwell attributes the reversal in fortunes to "Slats Gill, the player, and his teammates Dick Stinson, Mush Hjelte, Art Ross and Sunshine Richards, under Coach Dick Rutherford." Heartwell has a team photo with the caption: "1921-22 Aggies Win 21 Games of 23 Played." A portion of the text follows:

Washington officially became known as the Huskies, February 3, 1922, but when they were still playing under the title of Sundodgers in mid January, they invaded Corvallis – quite a jinx spot for Washington many of the 50 years – and handed Coach Dick Rutherford's Beavers two defeats which OAC fans will likely never forget. Later in the season when OAC, principally through the brilliance of towering Mush Hjelte, won both games at Seattle, it was an accomplishment which only two other Aggie teams have ever attained.[131]

OAC's two losses to Washington were very costly, since "they deprived OAC of the top rating in the PCC race and the NWC championship." Also, OAC's potential claim for a national championship faded. Instead of 23-0 for the season, the 21-2 record did not impress the Helm's Athletic Foundation as much as Kansas' record of 16-2. Thus, Kansas was recognized as "the leading 1921-22 college team in the country."[132]

One key member of this team, and certainly one of OAC's all-time great basketball players, was Slats Gill, a close friend of Joe. In this context, some biographical material on Slats is provided from an article by Johnny Eggers, '49, in Heartwell's *History of Oregon State Basketball*. The story is titled "Slats Gill Compiles Great Record." Amory T. Gill "came to Oregon State as a highly-touted prep star from Salem in the fall of 1920." Slats became "a brilliant player, making the all-Coast five as a sophomore and again as a senior. He set a conference scoring mark in 1923."[133]

Basketball remained very popular at OAC, with games played in the men's gym which had seating for 2,500. The 1923 *Beaver* covered Intramural

Basketball for the 1921-22 school year with a picture of five unidentified Phi Delta Theta players, none of whom resemble Joe Kasberger. Perhaps he is not pictured because he was still playing football when intramural basketball began "in October and ended December 10." Basketball lettermen were the only players excluded from league play. Thus, the league gave "every man who was interested in basketball and had basketball ability a chance to show it." More importantly, perhaps, it gave OAC "coaches an opportunity to look over the material and pick out the best." For the third consecutive year, "Phi Delta Theta won the college championship," and a special award, "the silver loving cup as a permanent trophy."[134]

Joe's final experience as a competitive athlete was on the 1922 baseball team. Complete season results are unknown, but OAC's Pacific Coast Conference finish was the best of Joe's career here. Washington's 11-3 record won the championship, followed in the upper division by California, 12-1 and Washington State, 10-6. The second division was led by OAC, 6-6, and Idaho, 5-5, with Stanford, 1-12 and Oregon, 0-12 in the basement. The 1922 baseball team may have been coached by G.L. Rathbun, in his last appearance in that role before going to a new coaching job in Oregon.

OAC's 1924 baseball team would have a new coach, Ralph Coleman, who played a key role in Joe's career. Coleman was a member of Delta Upsilon social fraternity, as was Linus Pauling. It is in Coleman's roles as director of intramural sports and professor of physical education at OAC, beginning in 1919, that Joe probably first encountered him. Also, Coleman's role as a baseball player at OAC made it possible that he and Joe were teammates. Because of Coleman's importance to Joe, a closer look at this man is necessary.

Canby, OR, not far from Mt. Angel, is where Ralph Coleman was born on Nov. 30, 1895. He was a high school baseball player and track performer, winning letters in both sports. When he graduated from high school in 1914, Coleman then enrolled at OAC and "majored in physical education courses."[135]

Not until he arrived at OAC did Ralph realize he had track talent. However, he stuck to his childhood career goals by preparing at OAC "as a teacher in physical education and kept to that decision throughout his four years of training." Athletically, Coleman devoted himself to track in his first two years at OAC. Fortunately he was able to participate in both baseball and track with much success, "winning four letters in the latter where 'he ran the half-mile, mile and two-mile. His best time in the mile was 4:20.'" As a baseball player, "Coleman won two letters as a junior and senior."[136]

Coleman enlisted in the Army after graduating from OAC in 1918 with "a Bachelor of Science degree in Agriculture." He was assigned to the "Fourth officers training camp at Camp Lewis, where he served as a second lieutenant until the close of the war." When he was discharged from the Army in Jan. 1919, there is confusion from source material available. In one account Coleman was an Instructor of Physical Education at the University of California, presumably at Berkeley. It is inferred that this was the spring semester of 1919, because Coleman is next reported to be in Corvallis in the same year.[137]

Another story states that in his first civilian job, "Coleman took over the duties of coach and instructor in physical education at Corvallis high school for the remainder of that year." In any event, in Sept. 1919 Ralph came to OAC as a physical education instructor, "given charge of intramural sports and made coach of the freshman track squad."[138]

Coleman continued playing professional baseball during the summer for the next four years. Ralph joined the baseball team "when school was out in the spring and returning to his teaching duties at the end of the baseball season in the fall." He pitched in the Pacific Coast League, spending three summers with Portland and one with Oakland. [139]

After four years of coaching OAC's freshman track team, Coleman's baseball skills were rewarded in 1924, when OAC "transferred his coaching activities to varsity baseball, a position he filled until 1931," as head coach.[140]

On June 5, 1922, Linus Pauling received his Bachelor of Science degree from OAC. Three months later, he was at California Institute of Technology to begin graduate work in physical chemistry. Arguably, he became the most famous member of the Class of 1922.

At the same commencement, Joe's undergraduate college career finally ended with much accomplished. His Bachelor of Science Degree in Agriculture, with presumed Major Field of Horticulture, was attained with straight A's. At OAC, Joe added to his impressive undergraduate record that began at MAC. In 1929, it was reported that "he won the Silver Loving cup for scholarship and athletics in his senior year."[141] At an awards ceremony on June 12, 1922, OAC presented the cup with this inscription: "To Joseph Kasberger, who during his college days, while maintaining a high standard of scholarship and of manhood has excelled in athletics."

Where Joe would emerge next was a challenge in the research. Later events in his life reveal a special place in Joe's heart for OAC, Phi Delta Theta, and the times he spent in Corvallis. Clearly, he put much time

Joe's 1923 Beaver graduation photo.

and effort into these years. It is believed that Joe received at least as much in return as he gave. The 1923 *Beaver* summarized Joe's activities at OAC.

Kasberger, Joe M.
Phi Delta Theta
Agriculture.....................................The Dalles
Forum (3,4), Alpha Zeta (3,4),Treas. (4),
Chairman Greater O.A.C. (3), Varsity Football (2,3,4),
Basketball (3,4), Baseball (2,3,4), Freshman Football (1),
Freshman Basketball (1), Freshman Baseball (1),Varsity "O" (2,3,4)
Vigilance Com. (2), Stock Judging Team (4)[142]

IV. JOE AS A COACH AT MT. ANGEL COLLEGE
"Notre Dame of the West"

When Joe graduated on June 5, there are no indications that he had secured employment. With his distinguished academic record, graduate school may have been considered. Also, the notion of professional baseball may have been an option until he had a better idea of what to do next. With the degree in agriculture, possibilities may have existed in that field as well.

The chapter of Joe's life at OAC ended happily in the summer of 1922, five years after it began amid great uncertainty. Obviously Joe's 1917 withdrawal from MAC and transfer to OAC involved no bridge-burning. Moreover, Joe's performance at OAC refined the potential that was discovered first at MAC.

Joe received an opportunity, however, that many might consider "once in a lifetime." Whether he had been in contact with MAC during his OAC career is not known. As a prominent athlete, Joe's sports exploits at OAC kept him in the public eye. It is not known what Joe did immediately after graduation, but during the summer he must have had contact with MAC. On Aug. 15, 1922 Joe entered into a contract with MAC/Saint Benedict's Abbey.

The favored son's return to his alma mater surely was a dream come true. To secure his first head-coaching position at MAC may have been a thrill, after his taste of secular life in the Army and at OAC. He, however, had a student experience at MAC with the Benedictines that was special, and his record shows that he blossomed here. Was it the influence of the Benedictines, classmates, teammates, or just the special blend of all? In any case, what greater glory could there be for such a young man?

To go back to your "spiritual home" as a leader/teacher/coach for other young men was a special call. To be invited back was a tremendous compliment to Joe and a true indication of his worth to MAC as a most favored son. Whether or not this was blind luck, conscious fruition of a personal goal, or a logical step on the part of the MAC administration is not known. As head coach in football, basketball, and baseball, Joe did not have much time to prepare his first team for the fast-approaching school year.

There was more than compatibility between Joe and MAC that created this wonderful opportunity. The premature death of Fr. Basil Schieber in 1919 may have set these events in motion. When last observed, Fr. Basil was leaving Mt. Angel to become pastor of Sacred Heart Church, Tillamook in the summer of 1917. At that time, "the parish at Tillamook, and incidentally the entire county, was given to the ministrations of the Benedictine fathers." It was an ambitious assignment because of the parish's geography, where the distances involved were substantial. Thus, Fr. Basil planned to build "two or three chapels at distant points in his wide territory, to enable him to serve his people well."[1]

Tillamook is located near the northern Oregon coast and endures a very wet climate. Neighboring Seaside, OR normally receives more than 70 inches of rainfall per year. An influenza epidemic in 1919 had deadly effects on many institu-

CONTRACT

Mr. Joseph Kasberger, The Dalles, Oregon,

and

St. Benedict's Abbey, St. Benedict, Oregon.

This _15th_ day of _August_
in the year Nineteen hundred twenty-two, I, Joseph
Kasberger, accept the coaching position offered me
by _St. Benedict's Abbey_
at the Mount Angel College, such position starting September 1st, 1922, and ending June 1st, 1923,
under the following conditions:

First; That I shall have complete charge
of all athletics, and the responsibility thereof
during my term of work.

Second; That I shall receive for this work.
starting Sept. 1st, 1922, and ending June 1st, 1923,
the sum of Twenty-four Hundred and no/100 dollars
(#$2400) to be paid in nine monthly payments of
$266.66 2/3 each and that in addition to this reg-
ular salary, I shall receive my board, room and
laundry without charge.

Entered into this _15th_ day of _August_

Joseph Kasberger

Thomas Meier OSB
Vice President St. Benedict's Abbey

Witnessed in presence of:
Victor Rassor OSB   _James W. Drum_
John McLean   _Notary Public_

Signed this 25 day of Sep. 1922   My commission expires January 25, 1924

---

*Joe's 1922 contract with St. Benedict Abbey to be athletic director and coach of football, bas-
ketball and baseball teams.*

tional populations. Even at MAC, the June 3, 1926 *Pacific Star* reported that athletics were suspended due to the flu, rather than the war. "The space for '19 must be left empty. The dire 'Flu' closed the college portals and prohibited all athletics for the year."

Fr. Basil's health became an issue on March 28, 1919, when "he was seriously ill with influenza." In response, Fr. Hildebrand "was commissioned to look after the parish work." Because of the pastor's condition, several days later "Father Prior also left for Tillamook." Fr. Basil's condition worsened, and he expired at eight o'clock on Saturday evening, April 5, 1919, in the parish house. "Death was caused by double pneumonia following an attack of influenza, which was contracted ten days before." Besides relieving Fr. Basil of "his pastoral worries," Fr. Hildebrand "provided every possible care and administered the last Sacraments four days before death came."[2]

On Monday, April 7, a solemn requiem High Mass was said for Fr. Basil in Tillamook by "Rev. P. Ambrose, O.S.B., assisted by the Rev. P. Hildebrand, O.S.B., and the Rev. P. Ildephonse, O.S.B." Fr. Basil's remains "were then taken to Mt. Angel, accompanied by a delegation of parishioners, for burial on Wednesday morning." The Mt. Angel funeral drew many. "A solemn requiem Mass was celebrated at 10 o'clock at which the Right Rev. Abbot Placidus, O.S.B., pontificated." Indicative of Fr. Basil's stature, the "funeral sermon was preached by Archbishop Christie." His remains were committed to the abbey cemetery.[3]

Fr. Basil's parents, four surviving brothers, and two sisters could not attend the services. Only Fr. Basil's sister, Agnes, was present, since she cared for "household affairs at Tillamook and spent herself in the care of her brother when he was thrown upon his bed of suffering."[4]

Thus, Rev. Basil Schieber, O.S.B., born July 20, 1886, ordained as a priest on May 31, 1909, and died prematurely on April 5, 1919, was a key figure in Joe's life. Certainly to Joe, Fr. Basil was more than a baseball coach.

At this sad time, Joe was probably deemed by MAC as the perfect man to fill a severe institutional void. Fathers Victor and Hildebrand were more than athletic coaches and had other things on their agendas. The time had come to pursue other interests, if not ecclesiastical necessities. Joe's availability provided the ideal solution. Joe's decision to accept this position was probably not very difficult.

Since Joe had left in 1917, there were other changes at MAC, beginning at the top. "Unlike Father Adelhelm, Father Placidus did not relish being an abbot." Abbot Placidus felt that the "stability and morale of the abbey seemed to be solid enough that he could resign the office on July 5, 1921." Only two structures were added during his tenure, "the post office and barn." He will be remembered, however, as an abbot who "served the community well by exemplary life and his devotion." Abbot Placidus left Mt. Angel when succeeded, and spent "some time resting at the Indian missions; then he became pastor of St. Joseph's German parish in Portland." In this capacity, he refused "the title and insignia of abbot," and "served as a wise and kind pastor" until his death in 1940.[5]

The new abbot, Fr. Bernard Murphy, was elected on Oct. 26, 1921. "Abbot

Bernard had been born in Portland, December 10, 1874." His election reflected that Mt. Angel "was now increasingly made up of native-born Americans." The decline in the Swiss influence was reinforced by a policy that "no recruits would be accepted from Europe unless they had spent at least a year in the seminary to learn the English language and American customs." Even the "German-language divine office of the lay brothers" was changed to English. Abbot Bernard's tenure began as a time of "steady growth at Mount Angel," with the school described as "progressing well." A major goal was achieved when the "junior college division was recognized by the University of Oregon." A corresponding influx of students brought the abbey desperately needed revenue and "Abbot Bernard started saving funds to replace the ramshackle chapel."[6]

The only new building project undertaken was directed by Fr. Victor. He had students help build a "cement wall along the south side of the hilltop, to prevent players and balls from tumbling over the edge of the playing field." A visitor today sees "this picturesque wall," which is "one of the few surviving physical tokens of that era."[7] Perhaps Fr. Victor as MAC's rector, may have advocated Joe as the man who could provide continuity in the athletic traditions.

Rev. Victor Rassier

There were academic responsibilities for Joe. The 1923 Mount Angel College *Catalog* lists his name with "Coaching, Typewriting, and Shorthand" duties, but it is not known whether he had similar roles in 1922.[8] With these obligations, Joe appeared very busy, and was thought to live on campus or in the town of Mt. Angel. He was close enough to The Dalles to visit during the school year and to return home in the summer. With so many siblings at home, Joe was not needed and could pursue his career.

The term "Notre Dame of the West" was first heard while researching at Mt. Angel. It was explained as a reputation or aspiration in the minds of those close to MAC at that time.[9] The impetus for such an ambition is not clear. Perhaps it was Abbot Bernard or Father Thomas Meier, MAC's president, who planted the seed in the minds of subordinates. Notre Dame had not yet arrived as a national athletic power, despite being on the verge of this status. A more likely college for MAC to emulate was the "Galloping Gaels" of St. Mary's College in Moraga, CA. They made headlines, with their wins over bigger schools from a campus ten miles east of Berkeley.

This was a time for little colleges with big ambitions to make a national mark through football. Washington & Jefferson College of Washington, PA gave small colleges a tremendous boost with its 1921 Rose Bowl tie with the mighty University of California Golden Bears. Similarly, the "Praying Colonels" of tiny Centre College in Danville, KY had the same impact with an upset victory over Harvard.[10] And, there was Notre Dame now becoming the ultimate in obscure small schools making the big time. The Irish were only now making their move and were not much further along than MAC. The evolutionary march to national recognition for both athletics and academic programs appeared to be joined.

Growth was perceived as good for colleges, and sports were reasoned by some as the vehicle by which small colleges could gain in academic stature and prosper economically. Since colleges and football were both in their relative infancy, much of today's atmosphere was only taking shape in the early 1920s. Joe's Pacific Coast Conference experiences at OAC may have taught him some lessons.

As athletic director, Joe probably reported directly to Fr. Thomas Meier. There had to be congruence in their ideas about MAC's sports future. How effective would Joe be in developing a league in which his teams could compete? Initially, this could have been the key to any long-term success that he might enjoy. In evaluating his situation, Joe was probably pleased with MAC's location and facilities, as well as its athletic traditions – vital as an intangible factor. MAC, despite its relative youth, was very conscious of its history, as described in a June 3, 1926 *Pacific Star* story.

Joe and MAC president, Fr. Thomas Meier, who would become abbot.

> About every college campus there linger traditions that are handed down from generation to generation of students and are prized as something distinctive and something of great value, to be jealously guarded and preserved by each succeeding class.

The story continues with a suggestion of institutional vision.

> ... around the old grey walls on the hilltop there go whispers of former days and former deeds, while glories of the past are pointed out as landmarks for the future.

The story concludes with appreciation, bordering on reverence, for the accomplishments of those who started these traditions.

> The peculiar excellencies of the now 'Old Grads' are made the desired goals for the present and the records they established in work, in play, in sport and study, remain to be ever maintained and if possible surpassed.[11]

Joe was part of this tradition and his appointment to direct MAC's athletic fortunes insured continuity. The facilities and academic philosophy had a great impact on the athletic director, coaches, teams, and players. It seems important, therefore, to better understand the situation Joe faced on the hilltop with these parameters. The 1924 Mount Angel College *Catalog* provides some insights.

> The Gymnasium: is an imposing structure on the North Campus, one hundred twenty-nine feet by sixty feet in area. The building is two stories high containing on its upper floor a massive basket-ball court 84 X 44 ft., an elevated banked running track, a boxing arena, and a large handball alley. On its lower floor are located large departments for senior and junior students, shower and dressing-rooms, billiard rooms, reading rooms, equipment room, and large room for corrective exercises. It is needless to say that it is provided with all appliances necessary for physical training.[12]

The Gymnasium

MAC's playing fields were equally important assets for athletics.

> The Playgrounds: extend over an area of ten acres situated on the peak of the butte overlooking the rich Willamette Valley and contain two football fields, two baseball fields, two tennis courts and plans for a track to extend around the entire field.[13]

Not all MAC students were varsity athletes and provision was made for everyone to engage in some form of athletic exercise. It is important to understand, therefore, that Joe's role in physical education might be viewed by some as being as important as his role as a coach and athletic director. Thus, all "students must enroll in physical culture classes."[14] The logic of this requirement was implicit in the liberal arts philosophy of MAC.

The term "physical culture" appears to have pertained to a variety of games that "are encouraged during periods of recreation." Also significant appears to be the priority given athletics on the hilltop: "we do not permit athletics to become a detriment to that scholarship and moral training which Mt. Angel College stands for." In implementing this principle, the *Catalog* adds the following: "We try to regulate the time and relative importance of play and study for the best interest of the student."[15]

Competitive sports at MAC were divided into the intramural and intercollegiate. At the intramural level, there was this approach: "During the various seasons of the year, leagues are organized in all branches of sports giving every student an opportunity to take part in games." Intercollegiate sports, however, were given a more detailed presentation: "Representative teams, under the training of

Field on the hilltop at Mt. Angel.

the athletic Coach, will compete in the various sports with other institutions."
This subject is elaborated on with conditions pertaining to applicants "to any
varsity team." First, the student athlete: "Must carry at least three full subjects
beside one elective;" second, "Must have a passing average in each of the
required subjects for the quarter note; and, finally, "Must be . . . in good standing
at the institution in regard to conduct."[16]

The *Catalog* continues with the paragraph heading: "TO PARENTS OR
GUARDIANS."

Parents or guardians who desire to intrust their sons or wards to our institution, should send them at the beginning of the school year; for a long and general experience has taught us that those scholars only who come at the beginning and stay to the end of the term without interruption show a uniform and
satisfactory progress during the course. Those who join the class when it is
under way but too often interfere with the steady advancement of the whole,
and, for the time being, prove a drawback to their classmates and an extra burden to their professors. We cannot urge this point too strongly; and we would,
therefore, impress on all students the necessity of being on hand when the class
work begins. Their own interest and the progress of the class require an early
attendance. Late comers are not to expect that, for their accommodation, their
class fellows should be checked in their progress.

The *Catalog* continues with the paragraph heading: "STUDIES."

After the student has decided upon his course of studies, he will be required to
attend all the classes belonging to the course, unless different arrangements
have been made beforehand. Parents are respectfully reminded that the management of the classes belongs to the authorities of the institution, as the latter

generally know best what is to the advantage of the student. We also request that students should not be withdrawn from the school before the completion of the school year. Latecomers and those leaving before the close of school are not eligible for any scholastic honors. The decision in this matter rests with the Director of Studies.[17]

MAC held expectations that students would participate spiritually. "The Catholic boys are expected to go to the sacraments at least once a month." MAC designated one day as the time to fulfill this requirement. "The day of General Communion is the first Friday of each month, a day chosen to instill into their lives a devotion to the Sacred Heart."[18]

1922-23 School Year

Football was Joe's first task so it is fortunate that he already knew the 1921 coach, Fr. Victor. It is unlikely that he saw that team play despite the fact that the 1921 Angel football team lost to the OAC "Rooks," 7-35 in a game at Corvallis on Nov. 26. Joe was with the OAC varsity in Los Angeles on that date. Thus, improving the football team's 2-3-0 record was Joe's first challenge. The 1922 football team appears to have included Francis Pashek, the younger brother of Gregory Pashek. The 1923 Mt. Angel *Catalog* notes only four returning members of the 1921 team. Joe's first squad in 1922 approximated 16 players, with Clarence Ziegenhagen as fullback and team captain.[19]

The season began Oct. 1 at home with a 44-0 win over Highland Park. The next two games were losses, 0-7 to University of Oregon Frosh, at home, and a devastating 0-67 loss to Pacific University in Forest Grove. Joe's team came back and won the next game at home 31-7 against North Portland Clinic. The Angels lost the season's finale in Corvallis 0-6 against OAC Frosh. Joe's football coaching career record now stood at 2-3-0. There was little time to fret about football since the basketball season started in five weeks.

It was in basketball that MAC's athletic tradition manifested itself most proudly. A June 3, 1926 *Pacific Star* story has a paragraph heading, "Basketball a Tradition," with the following text.

Let us say then that excellence in basketball is a Mt. Angel tradition – that the Gold and White quintets have a past record of which we are justly proud. To trace their work with inquiring finger through the lapse of years is to mark a long line of victories and to view but a few, though honorable, defeats.[20]

By capitalizing on basketball's tradition, therefore, Joe might make his initial mark. The June 3, 1926 *Pacific Star* recalled some Angel basketball memories in a story with the heading "Highest Scores in '20." One of the most startling records was the 1920 basketball team's "netting the ball for 102 points in one contest alone." While the victim of this onslaught is not revealed, this Angel team scored big against virtually everyone and held the college's all-time scoring record for one season. "When 19 games had been played, with four defeats, the season's total score reached 1071 of which but 333 belonged to opponents."[21]

The story continues, mentioning that Fr. Victor coached the 1920-21 basketball team to a successful 11-3 season. Presumably he replaced Fr. Hildebrand when he went to Tillamook. Unfortunately, the Angels did not win them all due to a colorfully-named foe, "The Hoo Doo Toothpullers." This was Pacific Dental, "the only winning opponents, taking the long ends of two games." Despite the losses, thirteen other games "were victories and the Angels closed the season whetting their teeth for Dental next year."[22]

The 1921-22 MAC basketball season was not as good, with a 10-6 record, but "5 of the 6 losses were by close scores." The Angels still had problems with the Hoo Doo Toothpullers. "Pacific Dental held on to their jinx, winning each game by a lone basket margin." For the season's composite total score, "M.A.C. was credited with 430 points while opponents took 273."[23] Joe knew that only one or two new players could help his eight returning players from the 1921-22 team. The veteran Angels were led by team captain and center Henry Kropp. The other standout player returning was the versatile Charles Spear.

After winning the opener, the Angels lost two in a row before rebounding with five straight wins. The next game was a loss, but the season ended with a five-game win streak. Included in the last five victories was a 41-31 win over the Aggie Rooks. The June 3, 1926 *Pacific Star* accounts of the 1922-23 basketball team noted Joe's debut as basketball coach. "The cooperation of fast team and new coach brought another record to Alma Mater." As a basketball coach, Joe brought immediate success with a record of 11-3, and MAC "captured the Non-Conference Championship of Oregon." The most gratifying win, however, was over Pacific Dental Clinic (P.D.C.). "P.D.C. was not among the winners this year; their 'HooDoo' was broken at last." For the season's total cumulative results, the Angels outscored opponents 426 to 297 over the fourteen games played. [24]

Joe's attention now shifted to baseball. The 1922 MAC baseball team, coached by Fr. Victor, had a 23-game schedule, but the season record is unknown. Joe's first baseball team in 1923 faced an 18-game schedule, with results unknown. It is known, however, that the 1923 roster was so lean that Joe was shown as both head coach and shortstop. Only two players returned from the 1922 squad so the remaining seven players had plenty of playing time. Joe's catcher and captain was Emanuel Hudson, one of the two men who played on the 1922 team.[25]

Joe's debut as a coach in MAC's 1922-23 school year was quite positive. Despite the absence of baseball results, Joe's combined football and basketball results were 13-6, an improvement over the 1921-22 school year's combined results of 11-11. With such a performance, MAC may have extended Joe's contract but there are no details.

In preparing for the 1923-24 school year, Joe benefited from MAC's recent accreditation by the State of Oregon as a two-year, degree-conferring institution. Such status was not unlike that of the junior colleges that we know today. Also, increasing enrollments brought greater course offerings to the college and made MAC more attractive to prospective students.

1923-24 School Year

Joe had three players returning from his first football squad, including fullback and captain, Edwin Stockton. Charles Spear returned to play end and Kenneth Hardin was back at guard. Nineteen players greeted Joe, a pleasant increase from the sixteen players he had in 1922. Joe had to evaluate the newcomers quickly since the season opener against the MAC Alumni team was on Oct. 6.[26]

The 1923 squad developed rapidly after a 6-0 opening win. The defense was outstanding as the Angels won their first five games and allowed only one touchdown. The perfect season was marred by a 6-6 tie in the finale for one of the best records in Angel history and a foundation for future successes. Joe's career football coaching record now stood at 8-3-1. The last game was on Nov. 25 and he had nearly two months to prepare the basketball team for a season opener on Jan. 18. There are no game summaries available for the 1923 Angel football season. The Appendix lists the results by opponent.[27]

The 1923-24 MAC basketball squad returned four players from the successful 1922-23 season and expectations were high. Charles Spear was the team captain and one of the starting guards. Gilbert Scott was the center, while John Arrighi and Francis Meyers returned as forwards.

The Angels opened with four wins at home, en route to seven consecutive wins before losing to "C. Portland "[sic]. The next five games were wins, including the fifth against Columbia U., in Portland, 27-24. Columbia U. became the University of Portland, managed by the Holy Cross Fathers who also operated the University of Notre Dame. MAC and Columbia U. battled for the 1924 Non-Conference championship right down to the wire. The rematch was played at MAC, where Columbia U. won, 29-24, to set up a rubber game for the championship at a neutral site, Salem, where the Angels won a nail-biter, 28-27. This game completed their 13-2 championship season on March 20. Joe's career bas-

Joe with Mt. Angel players. From an anonymous source at the Mt. Angel archives the same photo is headed "State Non-Conference Champs '23-'24." Individual names are handwritten as follows: "Top Left – "Chuck" Spear, Captain-Guard; Top Center – Coach Joe Kasberger; Top Right – J. Arrighi, Forward; Bottom Left – "Pep" Mann, Forward; Bottom Center – G. Gray, Guard; Bottom Right – "Gil" Scott, Center.

ketball coaching record now stood at 24-5.[28]

The June 3, 1926 *Pacific Star* summarized the 1923-24 MAC basketball season, highlighting the "Non-Conference Championship of the state" for the second consecutive year. "We were forced to taste defeat from two teams but won the other 13 games. Opponents garnered but 345 of the 879 points for this season."[29] There was little time to enjoy the basketball championship, since baseball's season-opening game was scheduled for April 5. As in basketball, hopes were high for the 1924 baseball team with five returning players from the 1923 squad. Team captain, Emanuel Hudson, was back to catch along with Lawrence Greene as pitcher and third baseman. Other returners were shortstop William Bowley, first baseman Charles Coovert, and second baseman Gilbert Scott. The Angels faced a 13-game schedule that ended on June 4. 1924 season results are unknown, but Joe never had a losing season in any sport while coaching at MAC.

As the 1924 school year closed, Joe may have had doubts about his future. Fortunately, former OAC head coach and Notre Dame alumnus, Sam "Rosey" Dolan, influenced Joe's life at this uncertain time. Also significant may have been MAC faculty member, Dan Nolan, a Notre Dame chemical-engineering graduate, Class of 1923. Possibly Nolan discussed Rockne and Notre Dame football with Joe. Dolan, however, wrote an important letter on Joe's behalf.

OREGON STATE AGRICULTURAL COLLEGE

W. J. KERR, PRESIDENT

DEPARTMENT OF CIVIL ENGINEERING

CORVALLIS

May 27, 1924

IN REPLYING PLEASE ADDRESS

S. M. Dolan

Mr. K. K. Rockne,
Director of Athletics,
Notre Dame University,
Notre Dame, Indiana

Dear Mr. Rockne:

While at Mount Angel yesterday Joe Kasberger suggested that he would like very much to take a terms work in Physical Education. He is extremely anxious to be with you for a football season in order to get real football at first hand.

Joe graduated from this Institution two years ago, played football, basketball and baseball for four years, is now physical director at Mt. Angel, a little Benedictine college of some 175 students. The authorities want to sign him up for three more years, but he feels that he should learn something more about football before deciding definitely to stay in the coaching game. He is a very fine young chap, can pay his own way and would like to be around you, help if possible, if not simply be permitted to look on during all of your work with the team. If there is any way such a plan could be worked out I would greatly appreciate your helping him in the matter.

With very best wishes for yourself and old Notre Dame - I am

Yours very truly,

Sam. "Rosey" Dolan.

SMD-C

Rockne's response to Joe or Dolan has not been revealed, but the inference is that he was invited to South Bend as requested. A question remains, however, about the length, of his stay since Joe coached the 1924 MAC baseball team through June 4, 1924. Joe is known, also, to be MAC's basketball coach in Dec. 1924, or Jan. 1925.

The 1925 *Catalog* notes a lecture delivered by Mr. J. M. Kasberger, Coach, on "Student Spirit." Also, there was a "Kasberger Athletic Scholarship Medal," donated by Dan P. Nolan which went to George Gray of Bend, OR. A missing edition of the *Pacific Star* may give clues about what happened next in Joe's MAC career.[30]

The summer of 1924 was important for Joe. After spending time at home, he journeyed to South Bend, IN for the Knute Rockne football-coaches school. When Joe departed for the Midwest is not known, but the 2,000-mile train trip required several days.

The photo and caption of MAC's 1924 football team do not include Joe. In his absence, Assistant Coaches Fr. Norbert and Dan Nolan, were MAC's co-head coaches. There is no explanation for this development. Joe's status with MAC, therefore, was either a sabbatical or leave of absence.[31]

By offering Joe a multi-year contract, MAC officials may have accommodated Joe's desire to take this leave. Afterwards, the time and experience might determine if coaching were in fact best for him and MAC. This episode was more than a summer-camp excursion for Joe. It is believed that he was at Notre Dame at least from mid-August through late November. The Rockne Coaches School in 1924 began Aug. 18 and lasted for two weeks. Then, preseason football drills started before the regular season schedule.

Knute Kenneth Rockne, born March 4, 1894 in Voss, Norway, was only two years older than Joe. He was doing interesting things with Notre Dame football, revolutionizing the college game, and Joe was anxious to learn everything he could. The legend of Joe Kasberger tells of him spending "one year at Notre Dame with Knute Rockne." Lloyde Glicken's version of the legend saw Joe declining to play in a freshman game for Notre Dame. On the eve of the game, Joe reportedly told the Irish freshman team coach, George Keogan, that he could not play since he had used up his college eligibility, or words to that effect. [32]

Joe was now 28 years of age and had already played for two seasons at MAC, one season at Camp Lewis, and four seasons at OAC. Maybe Joe was young-looking for his age. What is known about Joe's stay at Notre Dame? Little, except for his letter thanking Rockne for the special favor that he had been extended. Notre Dame's archives and sports information offices have been searched fully in pursuing Joe Kasberger in 1924. There is no documentation that Joe was either a student or a faculty/staff member. Dormitory records reveal no Joe Kasberger in residence. It is possible, however, that missing enrollment rosters for Rockne's football-coaches school might contain Joe's name. There is a photo of Rockne's coaching school, not presented here, that is believed to have been taken in South Bend during the summer of 1924. The photo has this caption.

Knute Rockne, football coach of Notre Dame, and Dr. W.E. Meanwell, basket-ball coach at Wisconsin University, direct activities in a course in which 245 coaches from 36 schools are enrolled.[33]

The Notre Dame campus was filled with football players and coaches for the Rockne school, providing an opportunity to learn and make contacts in the coaching fraternity. The most important contact at the time, of course, was with Knute Rockne himself. His ideas were shared openly with other coaches and they spread throughout the country. Much of Rockne's popular appeal lay in his skill as a showman. Michael Steele noted that Rockne recognized that "football was primarily entertainment and his talk was to guarantee a good show for all concerned."[34] For those in attendance, Rockne's 1924 coaches school featured ideas in the classroom and demonstrations on the practice field.

Notre Dame, however, had never won a national championship. Respect was not easily achieved and the Irish had to prove themselves as more than an obscure Catholic college team seeking the big time. The 1924 Notre Dame foot-ball team's preseason, therefore, was important. It is known that Joe met Frank Milbauer at this time. Frank, a Notre Dame football player, was recalled to have been on the campus in the summer of 1924. At the time of their initial encounter, Joe may have been taken with Frank's size. The huge Notre Dame tackle was a member of the Notre Dame Class of 1925, but does not appear to have been on Rockne's 1924 squad. The 1924 Notre Dame football team was composed of the following players, per the 1994 Notre Dame *Media Guide*:

LE-*Chuck Collins, 6-0, 177; *Clem Crowe, 5-9, 169; Joe Rigali, 5-9, 147
LT-*Joe Bach, 5-11, 186; *Joe Boland, 6-0, 215; *John McMullan, 6-0, 204
LG-*John Weibel, 5-9, 165; *Charles Glueckert, 5-11, 185; *Vince Harrington, 5-8, 175
C-*Adam Walsh, 6-0, 187 (Captain); *Joe Harmon, 5-9, 165; *Joe Maxwell, 6-1, 180
RG-*Noble Kizer, 5-8, 165; *Dick Hanousek, 5-10, 177
RT-*Edgar (Rip) Miller, 5-11, 180; *John Wallace, 6-0, 178; *John McManmon, 6-2, 202
RE-*Ed Hunsinger, 5-11, 172;* Wilbur Eaton, 5-8, 165
QB-*Harry Stuhldreher, 5-7, 151; *Eddie Scharer, 5-8, 145; *Gene (Red) Edwards, 6-1, 160; *Frank Reese, 5-10, 152
LH-*Jim Crowley, 5-11, 162; *Max Houser, 6-1, 170; *Harry O'Boyle, 5-9, 160
RH-*Don Miller, 5-11, 160; *Ward (Doc) Connell, 5-10, 168
FB-*Elmer Layden, 6-0, 162; *Bill Cerney, 5-9, 165; *Bernie Livergood, 5-10, 175; *Tom Hearden, 5-9, 156; *John Roach, 6-0, 139
Reserves
E-Larry Keefe, Clarence Reilly; G-Joe Dienhart, Herb Eggert; C-Russ Arndt; HB-Bernie Coughlin, Oswald Geniesse, Gerry Miller, Joe Prelli
(*) Denotes monogram winners[35]

Rockne's coaches school probably concluded by the end of August, so that most participants could resume their coaching responsibilities. Joe, however, remained in South Bend for the 1924 football season in an unknown capacity. It is not known whether Joe traveled with the team.

Notre Dame played its home games on campus at the 30,000 seat Cartier Field. The 1924 schedule had nine games, four at home, three away, and two at neutral sites. The Irish opened at home with two consecutive wins over Lombard and Wabash by scores of 40-0 and 34-0, respectively. The next game, however, was the big test in New York City's Polo Grounds against Army. Before 55,000 fans, Notre Dame defeated the Cadets 13-7. Notre Dame remained on the road the following week with a 12-0 victory over Princeton. The next contest was Homecoming against Georgia Tech and a milestone win, 34-3, over the Yellow Jackets – that was Notre Dame's 200th victory in its football history. The next game was in Madison against Wisconsin, another impressive win, 38-3. The season's home finale saw Notre Dame defeat Nebraska, 34-6. The season concluded with two road games. At Chicago's Soldier Field, Northwestern fell to the Irish, 13-6. The last game was in Pittsburgh on Nov. 29 against Carnegie Tech. The Irish received a Rose Bowl bid after a 40-19 win, to set the stage for a national championship game against Stanford University.[36] Pop Warner's Indians won the Pacific Coast Conference title with a 3-0-1 conference record, and 7-1-1 overall. Stanford's star was Ernie Nevers.

Notre Dame, conversely, had given birth to multiple stars during the 1924 season. The "Four Horsemen" and "Seven Mules" became nationally known after the Army game. Sportswriter Grantland Rice had a way with words, and new national heroes were born. The four horsemen were: "Harry Stuhldreher, quarterback, weight 154; Don Miller, weight 162, and Jimmy Crowley, weight 164, halfbacks; Elmer Layden, weight 162, fullback."[37] Notre Dame's less famous "Seven Mules" were important against Stanford in the Rose Bowl game on a hot afternoon, with temperature at game time 89 degrees. Stanford won the statistical battle, but beat themselves with costly errors. The final score, 27-10, earned Notre Dame its first national championship in football.

Joe was familiar with Stanford from OAC. Is it possible that he helped Rockne prepare Notre Dame for the Stanford game? Also unknown is whether Joe attended the Rose Bowl game on Jan. 1, 1925.

1924-25 School Year

While Joe was at Notre Dame, the Angels prepared to play their season without the media attention focused on Notre Dame. The 1924 Angel football squad that Coaches Norbert and Nolan welcomed had 21 players, one of the largest football squads in MAC history.[38] The Angels may have had enough players now to emulate Rockne's famous "shock troops" approach to the game, a strategy that required lots of players. While Joe was not present, physically, his presence was felt through at least one of the co-coaches.

Coach Norbert was Joe's old Angel teammate, with the frequently misspelled last name, Guy "Guisto" Matteucci, who was now Frater Norbert. The proper appellation for Coach Norbert is vague. The *Pacific Star* always refers to coaching clergy as "Coach" without a religious designation such as father, brother, or deacon. The *Tap-A-Lam-A-Ho*, the 1922 MAC yearbook, has the following biography for "Frater Norbert Matteucci, O.S.B., A.B.:"

President of the Class of 1922. It is proverbial that southern blood and a congenial disposition are always associated. Thus it is with Frater Norbert whose cradle stood on the shores of sunny Italy. Truly a happier, more genial and sociable character could hardly be found. The fact that he has developed not a little executive ability as assistant prefect of the college no doubt won the choice as class president.[39]

Although Coach Norbert did not receive his degree until 1922, he "took his religious vows at St. Benedict's Abbey, Mt. Angel, September 8, 1920." Coach Norbert "was ordained a priest June 6, 1925." His background appeared unusual for a football coach. An undated story from an anonymous newspaper revealed that he was born in Marlia, Italy on Nov. 6, 1893. At the age of sixteen, he came to the United States and performed "manual labor in a Portland lumber mill while learning the language and furthering his education in preparation for entering the monastery."[40]

Coach Norbert had four sisters and seven brothers, one of whom, Silvio, also became a priest. Silvio was reported to have served as pastor in a small village near the family town in Italy. How Coach Norbert came to Oregon is unexplained, arriving with two brothers, Mario and Albino. The Matteuccis had a global spread with George and Peter remaining in Italy with Silvio, while Alfred went to Brazil and Orlando to Holland.[41]

Coach Nolan was MAC faculty member, Dan Nolan. There is no indication that he played varsity football for the Irish. Possibly he was experienced from high school play. The 1923 Notre Dame yearbook, *Dome*, provides what little is known about Dan Nolan. Below his picture are the following campus activities:

Daniel P. Nolan, Ch. E.
Bellows Falls, Vt.
Chemist Club; Knights of Columbus;
New England Club

The yearbook reveals that Nolan had two "alias" names: "Red" and "Rodney St. Clair." He "scorned Dartmouth which is very near his home to be a Fighting Irishman and a chemist." Nolan was fine student in his field of study and gave a campus talk in his junior year on "The Chemistry of Paper." In recognition, the yearbook wrote that Dan "had it all down on paper," and he was awarded "the annual prize."[42] A final Notre Dame yearbook reference to Dan Nolan follows:

All Badinites remember how Red was washed out of home and property in that frigid abode. Now Rodney is unique in that, though he is past sweet sixteen, still (he says) he has never been kissed.[43]

There was no captain indicated for the 1924 Angel football squad. Leadership, however, came with eight returning players from the outstanding 1923 Angel team. They knew that Joe and his co-coaches had high hopes for the 1924 season. Despite the unusual coaching situation, they were expected to perform. Perhaps Joe had overscheduled this squad. Or, they had difficulty adjusting to co-coaches and Joe's absence.

The 1924 season's results must have been disappointing. Despite a big opening win against the MAC Alumni, the offense had problems scoring. In only one other game did it click. Against the Chemawa Indians, the Angels won convincingly. With the exception of the Oregon Frosh game, the defense played very well. The Angels played close games all season, but the record for 1924 was 3-5-0. The season ended with two consecutive losses to Columbia U. and TDHS.

A June 4, 1925 *Pacific Star* story about the 1924 football team has the headline: "Football Season of Past Year a Success – Though But Few Games Were Won, Season Acted as Training Block for This Year's Team." Despite the disappointing record, the 1924 team was characterized as "well coached" in fundamentals and possessing fight. The season is recapped as follows:

> The first game of the year was against the Alumni, in which the College men defeated the former football stars, 39 to 6. Next on the schedule came the Highland Park Athletic Club of Portland. A hard fought battle, waged on a mud-soaked field, ended with the Angels trailing 7 to 6. Ten days later, the Hilltoppers handed Chemawa one of the worst defeats in years. The score at the end of this decisive battle was 32 to 0. The next schedule game was with the Oregon Frosh. The 'Babes,' from Eugene, outweighed the Fightin' Angels 20 pounds to the man, and the Angels fell once more, 19 to 7. The game was played in a sea of mud, which did much to slow up the Hilltoppers' backfield. The next game played on the local field was with the Oregon Agricultural College 'rooks' who came out on the long end of a 6 to 0 score. The Fightin' Angels were at their best that day, completing 19 out of 27 attempted forward passes, and the 'rooks' were lucky to win. Next on the list came a practice game with Independence in which every man on the squad was given a chance to play. The Angels won 7-6 against some unexpectedly strong opposition.[44]

The story concluded with Oregon's "little big game" on Dec. 6, when the Angels met Columbia U. of Portland on "the Multnomah field." It was described as one of "the fastest games seen in Portland in years." The Angels lost an exciting game, summarized here.

> From the kick-off until the final gun the play was an ever-varying assortment of ultra-modern football tactics. The Angels scored in the first quarter on a trickery pass, Walsh to Spear, followed by Teter's quarterback sneak. Columbia came back in the third quarter with a great rally and pushed over two touchdowns to win, 12 to 6.[45]

The Angels' final game was played Dec. 13 to assist Ted Gibson of TDHS. It was a "benefit game against The Dalles at that city," with the Angels " losing the

TDHS versus MAC football game at Amaton Field in 1924.

contest by a 7 to 0 score." Bill Murray offers several valuable insights about this game and Ted Gibson.

> Ted had played tackle in the state championship game of 1923 and was badly injured, sustaining a broken back. A smaller player, he weighed only 140 pounds. The benefit game capped the season in a battle with Mt. Angel. The Mt. Angel team travelled at their own expense to maximize the benefit. The Dalles won by a score of 7 to 0. The points were scored in the last five minutes of the game. Henry Cramer, right guard, scooped up a fumble and ran fifty yards for the touchdown.[46]

The MAC versus TDHS football game story in the Dec., 1924 issue of TDHS' student annual, *Steelhead for December,* is in the Appendix. The story did not mention the relationships involved. Undoubtedly, this game was not a coincidence, possibly because Joe knew Ted Gibson. Also, Joe may have scheduled the game to test his Angels against the defending Oregon high school champions. Bob Murray had scheduled college teams frequently. Thus, the chance to play a team coached by a fellow townsman, under the circumstances, may have been an easy decision for both men. Coach Murray may have felt that his team had the talent to compete with the older Angels. Bill Murray provides a perspective on this powerful team from TDHS.

> The 1924 team, successors to the football championship team of 1923, could not be said to have a hard act to follow because virtually all players were members of the preceding year's championship eleven. They won seven scheduled games by imposing scores.[47]

Murray's football teams at TDHS did not take long to reach the top after the war. In 1920, TDHS was state champion "for the area outside of Portland." The 1920 season for TDHS had two controversial games and Bob Sanders gave some

Bob Murray and the 1924 or 1925 The Dalles High School Football Team. Front row: Coach Bob Murray, Ernie Moras, Dave Parmentier, Ken Cole, Fred Lemke, Ron Stone, Delbert Glavey, Fred Cyphers; Back row: Fred Dexter, Frances Pattee, George Cobb, Bun Stadelman, Pots Glavey, Fat Dizney and Victor Wolfe.

insights. "When we played Salem they won 13 to 6 because they cut down the quarters without notifying The Dalles, to 12 minutes." Sanders added that the game was protested to no avail, so TDHS "refused to acknowledge the game as lost because they had 3 more minutes to play and could have tied easily.'" In a game at Everett, WA, Sanders recalled the loss as "90 to 6 because Everett had older and heavier players much like our 1914 team."[48]

TDHS did not enjoy another championship football team until 1923. Jack Cross gave an account of the Indians who "scalped the best in the state, downing Corvallis for the state championship." Murray's team in 1923 had a great player, Jules "Zuck" Carlson. At the next levels of competition Carlson excelled and became an "all-time Oregon State great." Then, Carlson "played eight years of professional ball with the Chicago Bears." After his pro career, "Carlson eventually wound up as coach at West Virginia."[49] The picture shown here is believed to be from this game and comes from Joe's personal photo album.

The 1924-25 MAC basketball season opened on Jan. 24. Joe's team captain and guard, Charles Spear, returned but the only other veteran from 1923-24 was John Arrighi. The 1924-25 schedule included new foes and distant places for Joe's ambitious program, due to the inauguration of two new athletic conferences in which MAC now competed.

The Willamette Valley Conference was formed in the late fall of 1924 for competition in three sports, football, basketball, and baseball. The new conference began with league play in basketball and baseball during the 1924-25 season. Officers of the conference were "President, H. Dodds of Oregon Normal; Vice-Pres. and Treasurer, G.R. Schlauch of Linfield." Other conference schools were: "Albany College, Albany; Linfield College, McMinnville; North Pacific, Portland; Oregon Normal, Monmouth; Pacific College, Newberg; and Mt. Angel College, St. Benedict, Ore."[50] With conference competition now established, Joe's Angels faced a challenging, but promising, future.

MAC's nickname reflected a new competitive atmosphere with the addition of "Fightin'" to the traditional Angel label. What is not clear, however, was the reason that MAC and the other members of this new conference did not join the established Northwest Conference, with Willamette University and several other smaller colleges and universities.

Joe began the 1924-25 basketball season with a ten-game winning streak. The first loss was inflicted by Seattle College in an away game. The Angels won the next game on the Seattle trip, but lost the final two games of the season to Columbia U. In the first against Columbia U. in Portland, the Angels lost, 28-32. In the re-match with Columbia U. at MAC, the Angels were blown out, 16-42. The 11-3 record was outstanding for this inexperienced team and Joe's career basketball coaching record now stood at 35-8.

The June 4, 1925 *Pacific Star* summarized the 1924-25 basketball season with the headline: "Angels Have Fair Year in Basketball – Inexperienced Team, Though Scoring Many Victories, Falls Before Ancient Rival." The story asserts that MAC was "rated among the leading hoop squads of the state." This performance seems exceptional. "The team won ten of thirteen games, scoring 405 points to 269 for their opponents." The story continues as follows:

> Two brilliant victories that the students won't forget, Portland Tournament All-Stars, 30 to 21, and the other over College of Puget Sound, helped to offset this. The latter battle was one which will go down in the history of Mt. Angel College as one of the most nerve-wracking contests ever staged in the Hilltop gym. At half-time the Loggers led, 20 to 10, but in the second half, the Angels held them to one lone free-throw while they piled up 16 points to win 26 to 21.

Joe's squad had the following players: "Arrighi, Schroeder, Sullivan, and Keber, forwards; Otjen, center; Capt. Spear, Hardin, and Cranston, guards."[51] There are conflicting accounts of the season record. Contrary to what was presented previously, another story gives a final record of 11-3 with 436 points scored by MAC and 285 by their foes. This account also states that the home game against Columbia U. resulted in "one of the highest scores ever chalked against her, 16-42, at this time."[52] Hopes for 1925-26 basketball already ran high, since many players were expected to return.

The basketball season ended Mar. 15 and Joe had to prepare his baseball squad for the 1925 schedule of 11 games beginning April 7 and concluding June 3. The schedule included Seattle College, but it is not known if this was at home or away. Joe and other athletic directors must have struggled with schedules and budget constraints for travel. Creating a workable conference for schools of similar size was neither easy nor cheap.

Why it took Joe so long to correspond with Knute Rockne about the 1924 Notre Dame football season is unknown. Perhaps he was overwhelmed with MAC affairs when he returned. Regardless, the following letter from Joe to Knute Rockne answers questions about the experience. Rockne responded to Joe's letter on May 1, 1925, acknowledging receipt of "your very kind letter of April 26th." Rockne then referred to his Coaches School in Corvallis for the two-week period at the end of June and in early July of 1925. "I trust that I shall be able to see you at Oregon Aggies, and with every good wish, I am Yours sincerely, K.K. Rockne, Director of Athletics."[53]

The results of the 1925 MAC baseball season are not known. The Angels had

---

MT. ANGEL COLLEGE
ATHLETIC ASSOCIATION

JOE KASBERGER
DIRECTOR

St. Benedict, Ore.
April 26, 1925.

Mr. K. K. Rockne,
Director of Athletics,
Notre Dame University,
Notre Dame, Ind.

Dear Coach Rockne:-

Accept my heartiest congratulations on your New Years achievement and the laurels it brought; the National Football Championship.

Before my final departure from South Bend I called at your Office and also at your home and was informed that you would not be back for a few days. This occurrence I regretted very much.

I wish at this time to express my deep appreciation and thanks for the valuable information received under your guidance and permission, last fall. You can rest assured that the time spent at Notre Dame will be a lasting memory. A season under a "Wonder Coach" and at a school of "He-men", with a perfect functioning football eleven, is an honor and favor not extended to every man.

Indications point to a very large enrollment at Oregon State Agricultural College for your short course in Football this summer. I hope to attend said school and have the great pleasure of attending your lectures.
Again I wish to thank you for the great favors rendered in my behalf and with kindest personal regards, I remain
Sincerely,

Joe Kasberger.

The 1925 MAC Baseball Team photo from the June 4, 1925 Pacific Star has the following caption "From left to right-Kopp, Reiling, McGrath, McCarthy, Holmes, Kligel, mascot, Dyer, Bowley-Back row-Meyers, manager, Schlesinger, Greene-capt., Teters, Schroeder, Barr, Keber, Saunders, Kasberger-coach."

15 players, led by Captain Green who was listed as a pitcher and fielder. Saunders the catcher and Bowley at third base returned from the 1924 team.

The June 4, 1925 *Pacific Star* had one last reference to Joe in the 1924-25 school year. An article about the faculty had the headline: "College Faculty Is Increased This Year." There is a statement that Joe, "the athletic coach is a graduate of O.A.C," but the article also refers to his MAC student career and coaching style.

> He was an outstanding athlete on the campus during his student days, but above all he has always been known for his clean sportsmanship and manly character.[54]

As the 1924-25 school year ended, Joe may have thought about the issues facing MAC as his athletic program matured. College athletics had changed greatly in the decade since Joe enrolled at MAC. Also, he is believed to have attended the Corvallis summer-school session taught by Knute Rockne to learn more about contemporary trends.

Preparations in Corvallis for Rockne's coaches school began in the fall of 1924. Since Joe's graduation from OAC, the school's name was changed to Oregon State Agricultural College. In correspondence dated Oct. 29, Paul J. Schissler, Oregon State's head football coach, wrote Rockne to confirm the great coach's intent to teach the course. Schissler also requested that Rockne "send out a few pictures for publicity purposes." Rockne was sent a follow-up letter on Nov. 8, 1924 by M. Ellwood Smith, Dean of Oregon State's School of Basic Arts and Sciences, Director of the College's Summer Session. Smith provided Rockne with the following activity plans for his approval:

> It is my understanding that you will be here for the first two weeks of our Summer Session, running from June 22 to July 3, and that the compensation is to be $1000.00. Registration is to occupy the whole of June 22. Consequently it will probably be necessary for your classes to be given on Saturday the first week, whereas ordinarily there is no work given on that day. This would make your work coming, if this arrangement is as you have understood, from Tuesday to Saturday inclusive of the first week, and from Monday to Friday inclusive of the second week.

Smith's letter to Rockne concluded with the expectation that Coach Schissler "should follow up your two weeks work with additional work, but that is detail dependent upon your plan."[55] This consideration was inserted because the Summer Session courses were set up on a six-week basis. On Nov. 21, 1924, Rockne returned correspondence to Schissler with the requested publicity photos. Rockne advised Schissler that a 1925 game between Notre Dame and Oregon State in Chicago was not feasible "as our schedule is practically completed." Also, Rockne requested that Schissler return the Nebraska scouting reports that he had loaned his friend for the game that the Beavers lost 0-14 in Lincoln. Notre Dame defeated Nebraska 34-6 earlier in 1924 at South Bend. Rockne closed by stating that "I like to save that stuff for my files."[56]

Paul J. Schissler, a University of Nebraska alumnus, was the reason for Rockne's appearance in Corvallis. Schissler had succeeded Joe's former head football coach, Dick Rutherford, for the 1924 season. Since Joe's last season at OAC, Rutherford struggled through two losing seasons, 3-4-0 in 1922 and 4-5-2 in 1923, before being replaced. It was in 1921 that Rutherford had his only winning season, 4-3-2, during his four years at OAC. Schissler's debut in 1924 was not impressive, with a 4-5-2 record. Rockne's previous relationship to Schissler is not known, but as Oregon State's coach, Schissler was honored to have Rockne in Corvallis. Spec Keene was an assistant to Schissler during the 1924 football season and it is likely that Joe saw him in Corvallis that summer.

In addition to Rockne's relationship with Schissler, there were historic ties between Notre Dame and its Oregon alumni. Among the first Oregonians at Notre Dame were Sam "Rosey" Dolan from Albany, Art Sharp from The Dalles and Raleigh "Rollo" Stine from Astoria, who played for Rockne in 1917-18. With the Notre Dame influence in Oregon, Rockne may have enjoyed being with old friends and spending time in a lucrative way.

Rockne returned correspondence to Dean Smith on Dec. 14, 1924, concurring with what was proposed for the 1925 Corvallis summer session. Rockne was busy preparing his team for the Rose Bowl game against Stanford, and concluded his letter as follows:

> I shall do all I can to make the course a success. As soon as I return from Pasadena, after the first of the year, I shall send you fullest details of the plans I have in mind.[57]

As promised, Rockne finalized his syllabus for Corvallis in the spring of 1925. His schedule was tight, with a one-week course in Williamsburg, VA that ended a week prior to beginning in Corvallis.

> What I have in mind is to lecture every day from 8:00 to 10:30 and then to don suits and go out in the field until noon. As I find it necessary I can put on some work in the afternoon at a time when it will not conflict with anything else. I am anxious to put on a complete course – and hard work is my middle name.[58]

Rockne arrived on time and began the course as planned. Correspondence from Schissler to Rockne in Sept., 1925 indicated that Rockne's coaches school in Corvallis was a success.

> The boys are still talking about the coaching school out here and the business men down town occasionally discus [sic] the feed out at the Game Farm. They are all hoping that you will be with us again next summer and Emma [Mrs. Schissler] and I would like you and Mrs. Rockne [Bonnie] to plan on spending an extra week or two with us.[59]

Schissler concluded that the prospects for the upcoming 1925 Beaver team were "fairly good." Sure enough, the Rockne magic may have helped Schissler's team produce a 7-2-0 record, one of the best in Oregon State's history. The only losses were to Stanford and USC, which dashed Rose Bowl hopes again. Rockne responded to Schissler's letter in mid-September with modest expectations for the new Irish season. "Prospects don't look very good – we hope to hold 'em, however. Lot [sic] of splendid young men." Apparently Rockne was pleased with Corvallis in 1925 and advised Schissler that he was "planning on coming out next year in June" so that preparations could be made in advance.[60]

Rockne's defending national champions were a marked team in 1925 and finished with a 7-2-1 record. Both losses were shutouts, 0-27 versus Army at Yankee Stadium and 0-17 versus Nebraska at Lincoln. The tie came against Penn State in a 0-0 game. Despite Notre Dame's mediocre season it is likely that Joe attended Rockne's second coaches school in Corvallis. It was an opportunity for Joe to renew old acquaintances in the coaching fraternity as well as learn the latest Rockne innovations. Spec Keene probably attended the school with Joe and may have come to know Rockne at that time. Now, as an athletic director and coach, Joe must have had a different perspective after so much exposure to Rockne in the last twelve months.

1925-26 School Year

MAC's new athletic affiliations were major news stories as the school year began. The June 3, 1926 *Pacific Star* has the headline, "Hilltoppers Play in Two Conferences – Gold and White Athletes Compete With Eleven Colleges During Year. New Group Unnamed, Oregon-Washington Conference Newly Organized; Elections to be Held." This *Pacific Star* story provides details about the founding of the Oregon-Washington Conference.

The story noted that while "the four charter members of the Oregon-Wash. Conference are Catholic institutions, the circuit directors have decided not to limit membership to any one denomination." The story speculated that "two or four more colleges" would join the conference "for the next scholastic year." The four member schools were: "Mt. Angel College, Columbia University, St. Martin's College, and Seattle College." For its first season, the story gave these "temporary officers of the association: President, Rev. Fr. Edward H. Martin, O.S.B., of St. Martin's; Secretary, Coach Harrington of Columbia U." Other business was deferred "until the near future." Then, "regular officers will be chosen." Also deferred were schedules, policies, and the "name of the association."[61]

The following incomplete story is provided with what is available, from the June 3, 1926 *Pacific Star* under the headline, "Honors go to Angel Eleven for Season '26 – Coach Joe Kasberger's Gridsters Plough Through Successful Season – Win State Honors – Gold and White Football Team Piles Up Big Score Against Opponents." The story revealed that eight starters from the 1924 team returned, while Coach Joe had brought to the Hilltop "much new material." It is no wonder that the 1925 Angels were "a powerful grid machine whose later record has gone down as one of the most successful and brilliant football teams in M.A.C. sports history."[62]

The talented Angels won six games and lost but once, for a cumulative total score of 199 points to 35 scored by its foes. Thus MAC, "by reason of its victories laid claim successfully to the Non-Conference Title of Oregon and Washington for schools of similar standing." The story continued with the paragraph heading: "Win First Game 9-0."

> As a curtain raiser for the season the Angels tackled the Corvallis Hi aggregation on College Field, Oct. 3. In the previous season their opponents had held the state title, but the strength of the M.A.C. line was clearly shown when it made yardage against this heavy team eleven times to the visitors' once and took the game by a shutout score, 9-0. The aerial attack featuring later games was not as yet working smoothly but that the team was strong on both offense and defense could be easily seen.
>
> Regarding the next two games played on the Angel home field little need be said; the scores indicate sufficiently the general run of play in the contests. The Pacific squad was unable to hold the plunging and rushing Angels and a large one-sided score, 72-0, was the result. In the third game of the season against Oregon Normal a better class of football was displayed but the visitors were unable to stop the locals when the latter made up their minds to carry the ball down the field for a touchdown.[63]

MAC's 1925 team was shown in the June 3, 1926 **Pacific Star** *with headline "Non-Conference Football Champions, Season '26 [sic]." The caption below was "Reading from left to right: back row: Coach Kasberger; Berger, end; Teters, quarter; Haynes, full; Spear, Captain and half; Walsh, full; Whitley, half; Medlock, half. First row: Line, McGowan, Hardin, Green, Hutton, center; Salvi, Busch and Johnson."*

Four days after the Oregon Normal game, the Angels were in Seattle for a game with Seattle College on October 25. In an incomplete *Pacific Star* story it is reported that the Angels trounced the Chieftains, 37-0. The Angels remained in the Puget Sound area for a contest six days later in Olympia against St. Martin's College. MAC fans were euphoric when they learned the Angels remained undefeated, untied, and unscored upon after the 29-0 whitewash of the "Martians." The scene was now set for "Oregon's Little Big Game." Joe's schedule gave him two weeks to prepare the Angels for Columbia U and "trained furiously for the grid classic of the year." How the label "Oregon's Little Big Game" evolved is not revealed, but for this game "Coach Kasberger made great and many preparations." The game was described as follows:

> When the 22nd dawned bright and clear – real football weather – a record breaking crowd was expected nor were hopes disappointed. Before some two thousand spectators on College Field the M.A.C. Squad triumphed over the Cliff Dwellers from Columbia U. by a score of 16-7. It was as pretty an exhibition of ultra-modern football, with passing, running, and line bucking, as the most ardent sports fan could desire. Standing out as the star of the game was 'Chuck' Spear, Captain and right half of the Angel Varsity. At the half the score stood 10-0 favoring the Angels. In the third quarter Columbia made a series of rapid thrusts that carried them across the line for a lone touchdown, making the score 10-7. A sensational run by Spear was the climax to what had become a fast and close contest and ended the scoring for the game. The season's last grid appearance was the Angel's sixth victory and marked a fitting close to a new and glorious page in sports history for the Gold and White.[64]

Another story in the June 3, 1926 *Pacific Star* has the headline: " 'Chuck' Spear Hero on Field and Court." Spear, from Seaside, OR, was captain of the 1925 football and 1925-26 basketball teams. He was a MAC sports hero whose "prowess on both field and floor is well known." The story concluded as follows: " 'Chuck' has long been the idol of Angel rooters and to the succeeding captains leaves a page of achievement not easy to surpass."[65]

The June 3, 1926 *Pacific Star* featured another player with a headline "George 'Shy' McGowan is Football Captain" and story. McGowan, from Lebanon, OR, was captain-elect for the 1926 Angel football team. "Persistent grit and enthusiasm make George a real fighting football player, and a highly commendable captain." The story concluded by mentioning that "Mac" was a second year student "in the College of Arts and Science and has played end on the team for two consecutive years, earning the 'A' sweater this spring."[66]

The fine 1925 football season pushed Joe's career coaching record to 14-4-1, excluding the results of the 1924 season. With the football season now history, Joe's focus shifted to basketball. A preseason story gives a sense of high hopes with three lettermen returning from the 1924-25 team. Thirty players tried out for the team, but after roster cuts the squad was "soon reduced to fourteen." With a nucleus of three lettermen, "Captain 'Chuck' Spear, guard, Harold Schroeder and John Sullivan, forwards," Joe sought a guard and a center. These positions would be filled from "a host of new material in Heenan, Price, Cardinal, Teters [sic], Burger [sic], Butler, Johnson, Hardin, and Roalson."[67]

After three weeks of preseason drills, the Willamette Valley Conference opening game was played on Dec. 18 against Pacific College. The Angels won, 43-16, then began their Christmas vacation. Before resuming regular season play, the

THE PACIFIC STAR

"Fightin' Angels"—Willamette Valley Conference Basketball Champions.

Mt. Angel College Basketball Squad, 1926. Reading from left to right; top row, Coach Joe Kasberger, Sullivan, guard, Teters, forward, Berger, guard, McGowan, guard; bottom row, Capt. 'Chuck' Spear, guard, Price, forward, Cardinal, center, Heenan, forward, and Schroeder, guard.

Angels played two practice games against the MAC Alumni and the Northwestern Bank of Portland with unknown results. The next two games were played against Willamette Valley competition. Linfield College and Albany College posted consecutive wins over the Angels. The poor Willamette Valley Conference start was soon rectified as Joe fired up his team and went through the remainder of this conference's schedule undefeated. The Angels "won the Championship at McMinnville on March 11, when they defeated Albany College 34-21." Results of Willamette Valley Conference play are as follows:

> Those teams falling before the Angel attack were: Oregon Normal, twice, 26-21 and 49-41; Pacific College, twice, 43-16 and 52-26; Linfield College, 20-13; and Albany College, twice, 47-20 and 34-21.[68]

The schedule sequence is not clear for the 1925-26 basketball season. A June 3, 1926 *Pacific Star* account suggests that the Willamette Valley Conference schedule was mixed with Oregon-Washington Conference competition. The Angels did not start Oregon-Washington Conference play any better than they did in the other conference, but they finished as the runnerup. The Angels were "still in third place in the Willamette Conference when they went north to play St. Martin's and Seattle College." The trip was disappointing when MAC "lost two heart-breaking games to the Northerners." The story is as follows:

> St. Martin's took the Angels into camp 37-16, and the next night the Seattle boys won 37-35. In the St. Martin's game the Varsity was badly off form and the home team took advantage of all the Angel misplays and converted also practically all their free throws. Mt. Angel led by eight points with four minutes to go in the Seattle game but the Coast City hoopsters came through with a whirlwind finish and won by two points.[69]

The Angels had a chance to redeem themselves against these same foes a week later at home. Against Seattle, Joe's squad "playing a steady and consistent game, nosed out the visitors 45-42." The season's conclusion featured several exciting games to decide the Oregon-Washington Conference championship. The Angels had an intense rivalry with Portland's Columbia University and late in the season, MAC beat the Cliffdwellers 28-13. The next game, though, was frustrating when MAC squandered a huge halftime lead.

> On Feb. 26 St. Martin's came south and from them the Varsity took a 48-20 victory. At the end of the first half the score stood 28-1 in favor of M.A.C. but in the latter part each made about an even number of points. The Angels wound up their conference schedule a week later in Portland by taking the second game from C.U. 40-29.[70]

At season's end, the Angels won the Willamette Valley Conference championship. A disappointing second place finish in the Oregon-Washington Conference may have been offset by the team's fine overall record of 14-4. The

Pacific Star wrote that the basketball team's "admiring sattelite [sic] pointed with just pride to their accomplishment." Another story appeared in the June 3, 1926 *Pacific Star* with the headline: "Mt. Angel Has Banner Season in Basketball – Varsity Hoopers Defeat Albany College in Willamette Valley Championship Game – Next Year is Promising – No Lettermen Graduate from Quintet and 26-27 Looks Bright."

> The Mt. Angel Hoopsters of '25-'26 were not to be outdone by the grid squad in the matter of titles. This year Mt. Angel finished one of her most successful basketball seasons by winning the Willamette Valley Conference Title in a post-season game with Albany College and by securing second place, a margin of only one game from the winners, in the Oregon-Washington Conference. [71]

The story concluded with the belief that the 1925-26 Angel basketball schedule "was one of the toughest ever faced by a M.A.C. hoop five," and the 14-4 record was satisfactory. The best part of the 1925-26 season was MAC winning with so many underclassmen, so hopes for the 1926-27 season were already high. "No members of the '26 team graduate this year and hence prospects for a winning team next winter are very bright." There were no guarantees, however, that all players would return.

> Should all of the nine first string men return for another conference schedule there will be no stopping the Angel onslaught in '27 and few will have better chances for titles than M.A.C.[72]

Joe's career basketball coaching record now stood at 49-12. His success as a football and basketball coach in 1925-26 put the baseball Angels under scrutiny. Joe's baseball team delivered to complete one of MAC's most athletically successful school years, ever.

Pacific Star accounts of MAC baseball are limited. Fortunately, the 1926 season is the best documented for the period of Joe's tenure as baseball coach. The 1926 Angel baseball team had a story in the June 3, 1926 *Pacific Star* with headline: "Angels Take Title in Valley Circuit – Clean Sweep of Schedule Gives Varsity Willamette Valley Honors." Portions of the text that are available reveal that MAC won the Willamette Valley Conference championship. The Angels were undefeated in this league's play "when they defeated Linfield College and Oregon Normal, 7-2, 13-4 last week." The final standings for the 1926 Willamette Valley Conference were as follows:

	Won	Lost	Pct.
Mt. Angel	8	0	1000
Albany College	6	2	750
Oregon Normal	4	4	500
Linfield College	2	6	250
Pacific College	0	8	000 [73]

Angel baseball in 1926 dominated Willamette Valley Conference competition with only Oregon Normal and Albany College giving Joe's team close games. "In the game against Linfield, the visitors never had a chance." A key to MAC's success was pitching.

> Beck hurled the whole game for Mt. Angel and let Linfield down with two hits and one walk, meanwhile establishing a strikeout record for Mt. Angel teams. Twenty-three of the opponents went back to the bench via the strikeout route.[74]

The previous MAC record for strikeouts is unknown. Yet the Angel squad appears to have been well rounded with hitting and defense.

> Outside of Beck's pitching, Saunders was the star of the day, gathering three hits one of them a triple and catching a fine game. Sandy picked quite a few of Beck's hooks out of the dirt that would have advanced a runner if not stopped.[75]

Phil Gallagher pitched for the Angels in the last conference game against Oregon Normal. While he did not duplicate Beck's strikeout performance, the *Pacific Star* stated that he "pitched a fine heady game," described as follows:

> While allowing the teachers nine hits he was practically airtight in the pinches, striking out but two and giving one free pass, when there were men on Phil bore down and the hitting stopped.[76]

Joe as MAC baseball coach with an unidentified player.

Angel bats delivered fifteen hits, and the Normal pitcher hurt himself by issuing five walks. MAC's "Bud Greene was the hitting star of the day getting four hits out of five up."[77]

The June 3, 1926 *Pacific Star* had two baseball stories that cannot be read in their entirety. The most legible has the headline: "Angel Team Takes 3-1 Victory from St. Martin's Squad – Homecoming Day Ball game on College Field Draws Large Crowd." There is no account of the three consecutive losses that preceded this game, a milestone event in Joe's baseball coaching career. Regardless, it was Homecoming Day and MAC beat St. Martin's College, 3-1. The contest "attracted a large crowd of old graduates" and was "the largest crowd of fans that has witnessed a game on the College Butte this year."

Air-tight pitching by Bud Greene and fine support by his team-mates were the

MAC's sports fields in spring 1926.

big factors that caused the defeat of the team from Lacey, Washington. Greene retired twelve batters by striking them out. He was especially effective in the pinches and the St. Martin's crew were able to collect only five scattered hits from his delivery. In only one inning during the entire contest was he ever in danger, and that was in the fifth frame when the visitors scored their lone run.[78]

A final baseball story from the June 3, 1926 *Pacific Star* is headlined: "Homer in Eleventh Frame Breaks Up Close Contest – Seattle College Wins." Presumably MAC's 1926 baseball season ended with a loss to Seattle College. Coupled with the three losses that are referenced above, before the win over St. Martin's College, it is inferred that the Angels had problems in the Oregon-Washington Conference. This point is important because in 1929 the following story appeared about Joe's 1925-26 athletic teams at MAC:

> While coaching at Mt. Angel a splendid record was made in athletics, during the 1925-26 season, his football squad won seven out of eight games played. In basketball the team won fifteen out of 19 games, and seventeen out of eighteen games played in baseball. All were played in the Willamette Valley Conference.[79]

The school year's end brought student awards ceremonies. The June 3, 1926 *Pacific Star* has this headline and story: "Walsh Wins First Blanket Given in History of College – '26 Graduate Merits Most Coveted Award for Athletic and Scholastic Work."

> Among the many classes graduating from Mt. Angel College the Class of '26 claims a distinctive honor not held by others, for to one of its members, Allen L. Walsh of New York, will be awarded shortly before the day of his graduation the award for special accomplishment in scholastic and athletic endeavor, the Official College Blanket.[80]

Interestingly, the award was first formulated several years earlier in the MAC Student Body Constitution, but "no one has qualified until this year to receive this mark of special honor." Thus, Al Walsh was featured in a *Pacific Star* story. To earn the award, Al graduated with academic distinction from Pre-Engineering while playing varsity football for three years, two in the Junior College and "one in the 4th Academic year." His MAC football career began as a spare on the 1924 team. On the 1925 and 1926 teams, Al was MAC's "regular fullback," earning him the "A" sweater. In concluding this story, the *Pacific Star* writer added the following about this exceptional student-athlete:

> Perhaps no member of the '26 team has labored more energetically and faithfully, not only in the field but also in scholastic work, than Allen Walsh. Although enrolled in one of the most difficult of courses, the Pre-Engineering, he has, by reason of special effort and application, been able to meet both scholastic and athletic requirements for the College Blanket. May he, upon his leaving Alma Mater, preserve unsullied not only the white blanket she will shortly confer upon him, but also the high ideals and standard of conduct taught during the years he earned the 'College Blanket' at 'good old M.A.C.'[81]

Thus, Al "merited this enviable distinction and has the further honor of being the first man to qualify for the same." The award was described as follows:

> Constructed as designed in the constitution it will be made of beautiful white fabric, decorated with a small gold border. In the centre [sic] is placed a large, 'gold Block A,' artistically set off by the snowy background. In dimensions the blanket measures five feet by six.[82]

Allen Walsh came to MAC from what appears to be a great distance and Mt. Angel archives provide additional insights into his background.

> He was a twin (sister was Alice), born in Wisconsin. His mother died, probably of TB, when he was four years old. His father seems to have travelled a lot. When Allen first started at MAC, his father, William James Walsh, lived in New York City, then here and there, then in Newport, Oregon. Allen was always a boarder at MAC. I know nothing about him after he left, although he was in pre-engineering. We have some letters from his unmarried sister, Gladys, and by 1953, when his father died in Tacoma, Allen was already dead. Why he came to Oregon I don't know.[83]

The June 3, 1926 *Pacific Star* had a story about student awards with the headline, "Rules For Awards - Mt. Angel College Student Body Association, Constitution, Section II. Emblems and Awards Part One. Athletics." The significance of the story lies in MAC's belief that both athletes and non-athletes should be awarded the Gold Block "A." There is a technical description of requirements for the awards, ranging from emblem to sweater to blanket. The qualifying activities reflected the many roles available to students. The major sports teams of football, basketball and baseball were rewarded, as well as "Yell-Leaders," the equivalent of today's cheerleaders. Similarly, awards were given for "Literary, Music, Dramatics, Debating, and Star Work."[84]

The June 3, 1926 *Pacific Star* presented a story on Joe concluding the 1925-26 school year, with the headline: "Angel Mentor Turns Out Champion Teams – Coach Joe Kasberger Directs All Major Sports At M.A.C." The story began with Joe's coaching accomplishments in his few years with the Angels: "two State Non-conference and one Conference Championship Basketball team, a Non-conference Championship Football team, and two baseball teams of no mediocre athletic brilliance."[85]

The story continued, referring to "'Joe,' as he is known on campus," being a MAC alumnus "having attended here from '15 to '17." Having received "due preparation at Mt. Angel he took up his scholastic endeavors at the Oregon Agricultural College, graduating from that institution with a Bachelor of Science Degree." The story continued by noting Joe's feats at OAC where he "merited eleven out of the possible twelve athletic awards." The story concluded with mention of Joe's taking "a coaching course at Notre Dame University, Indiana, under the direction of Knute Rockne." Thus he was characterized as "thoroughly fitted to guide the destinies of the athletic teams from M.A.C."[86]

Such a glowing assessment of his work may have sent Joe home for the summer with personal satisfaction. The 1926-27 school year gave every indication of Joe taking Angel athletic teams to an even higher level of success. As a possible recruiting aid, MAC prepared a new information brochure. Excerpts of this publication, dated 1926, follow, and it is likely that Joe authored portions.

One of the most obvious indicators of MAC's well-being was the quantity and quality of faculty and staff. While the Benedictines remained the dominant force in the classrooms, increasing enrollments required additional lay teachers.

> With the recent expansion in collegiate work, however, it became necessary to engage a number of lay-professors for some of the departments. All of them are graduates of either the Mid-western or Western universities. By bringing men of recognized institutions together, we feel that more progress can be made in a constructive educational policy. Many of our Fathers have attended Universities and Benedictine colleges in Europe, while the Universities of Notre Dame, Oregon and Washington are represented among the employed professors. Ours is not an endowed institution. Our income is limited. Our buildings are not as spacious and complete as we hope them to be in the near future. Our faculty, however, has always consisted of selected men devoted to their work. Inspiration and encouragement from the teacher is a most influential factor in efficient education. During the past few years a number of promising young men have joined our community and special attention is being given to their training as future educators.[87]

With increased size came new course offerings in response to student demands.

> In recent years there has been a great demand, on the part of students, for college courses that would prepare them more directly for the professional school.

We would prefer to have every student complete the classical course before entering the institution that is to give him his specialized equipment for his life's work. However, since this is often prohibited by the limited means of the student, Mt. Angel College has recognized the demand. A number of two-year pre-professional courses are offered such as pre-medics [sic], pre-law, dental, engineering, etc. The first two years of the four-year journalism and commerce curricula are also given in our Junior College.[88]

MAC was subject to oversight as an accredited educational institution.

Mt. Angel has for years enjoyed the esteem and co-operation of the University of Oregon and Oregon Agricultural College. In order to safeguard our graduates also in other states and private institutions, application was made for recognition to the Northwest Association of Secondary and Higher Schools. After due inspection our request was granted and all the work offered in the Junior College department is now accredited by the above mentioned association.[89]

MAC filled an important educational niche for secondary school students. Serving this market certainly benefitted the college when the preparatory school students began their college search. MAC's Academic Department supervised this school so it is apparent that their graduates were ready for college-level work. This aspect of Mt. Angel's educational complex is a carry-over from Joe's student days when secondary students were noted.

Many parents realize that for our high school boys, particularly in this age, the boarding school offers the best opportunities for real training and study. No better appreciation of true democracy can be given to our youth than to bring the sons of all nationalities, the rich and the poor, together under the same roof. The lessons taught by Christian community life are a splendid preparation for an efficient citizenship in our American Commonwealth. Three curricula are offered in the Academic Department: the Classical, the Science and the Commercial. The work given is accredited by the State of Oregon as well as by the U.S. Bureau of Education.[90]

The Seminary may have been Mt. Angel's most important educational component to serve Catholics in the Pacific Northwest. Its close ties to the Archdiocese of Oregon City were important in securing the funding necessary to meet the expensive demands of the educational complex that Mt. Angel became.

From the earliest foundation of this Benedictine Community in Oregon, our seminary has been the object of special care and attention. While we are devoted to the education of laymen that will prove an asset to their Church and their Country, we consider it still more our mission to prepare young Levites for an active career in the Vineyard of the Lord. A separate building houses the candidates for the priesthood. They are under the guidance of a man especially selected for this important work.[91]

MAC had progressed beyond what Joe remembered as a student. Certainly some credit belonged to the successful sports teams and athletics as an integral part of the MAC student experience. The perspective on athletics may have been written by Joe. Given the verbiage devoted to this topic, it appears that in publicizing MAC, athletics was seen as significant.

The place of inter-collegiate sport in the curriculum is a matter of careful consideration. It is not the dominant feature of the college life, nor are studies subordinated to it in any way; it is moderately encouraged, nevertheless, because of the indisputable benefits it certainly contains. Conference rules and the additional college rules are strictly enforced.

Intra-mural sports are especially encouraged. The college authorities are fully aware of the tendency in modern sport to develop the few and neglect the many. Such a condition does not exist at M.A.C., and because of the size of the enrollment, the physical instructors are enabled to give personal attention and supervision in athletic instruction. A Physical Education unit is a requisite in collegiate work and compulsory in the high school course. To care for this need of exercise Senior and Junior intra-mural leagues are held in basketball and baseball; (football playing, because of the average parent's wishes, is entirely optional), and in addition, facilities are provided for individual play in handball, tennis, and the various track events.

It may be mentioned here that basketball has been for years the outstanding sport at M.A.C., and a winning team is almost traditional. In the last four years the Angel Basketeers have won three titles; in '23 and '24 the Non-Conference Title of Oregon, and in '26 the Valley honors.

A special class of corrective and development exercises for those requiring extra attention is being supervised by Mr. George A. Dembinski of New York, World's Champion Weight Lifter in the feather weight class and Physical Culture expert. Any student may enter these exercises in addition to those specially assigned there. There is no charge for this instruction beyond the athletic fee paid by all students.

Two baseball diamonds are at the disposal of students. The Varsity field has a 35 foot back-stop, a grass infield, a fielding patch and baseline of sanded and rolled soil, and an outfield of wide extent. It may be said without exaggeration that there are few equals to this diamond among the schools of Oregon.

To sum up the entire athletic viewpoint and schedule in a few words: inter-collegiate athletics are considered good in moderation and encouraged to that extent; they are always subservient, however, to studies and scholastic standing. The intra-mural exercises are considered vital for health promotion and their conduction cannot fail to meet instant approval. The outside games are also valued as a helpful means to vary the student routine of recreation, especially since the great majority of students are confined as boarders within the college boundaries. Suitable awards are given for athletic participation but these are not placed on a par with intellectual prizes. To epitomize the whole athletic and scholastic situation, the Mt. Angel College ideal is "the sound mind in a sound body."[92]

This brochure noted other student activities: "Associated Student-Body, Collegiate Student-Body Association, M.A.C. Senate, M.A.C. Dramatic Club,

[and] Alumni Association."

The educational center on the hilltop that housed these many activities had a positive impact on the town below.

> The little city of Mt. Angel, about one mile west of St. Benedict's Abbey, holds a position unique and interesting among college towns. It is in Mt. Angel that the beautiful St. Mary's Church is located – one of the most inspirational and imposing churches in Oregon, a source of justifiable pride to the town and of gratification to Catholics in the state. It is in Mt. Angel that St. Mary's School is situated – the largest parochial school in Oregon. The institution is modern in its methods, and thorough and complete in its curricula. The city also can boast of Mt. Angel Academy and Normal, a boarding school for girls and young women, located a short distance south on the Pacific Highway. At the Academy, a four-year standard high school course is offered, as well as a two-year Normal course. Benedictine Sisters conduct the Mt. Angel Academy, and assist in the parochial school. Mt. Angel can well be proud of its distinction as being the greatest seat of Catholic education for its size in the West.[93]

Despite Mt. Angel's activity and success, monks did not forget the spiritual.

> Next to the chanting of the Divine Office and observance of the various feasts of the ecclesiastical year with the complete ceremonies of the liturgy, education has been for centuries the chief work of the Benedictines. Mindful of the heroic examples of the great Benedictine missionaries of the Middle Ages, work on the missions and parishes has not been neglected. Not all the young men joining our Order have the natural ability or the inclination to be teachers. The Benedictine Order by its constitution and traditions, is not restricted to any definite work. Accordingly those of our Fathers who feel an inclination to work on the missions are given every opportunity. Since its earliest history this community has taken an active part in the missionary and parish activities of the diocese. Some of our priests are engaged among the Indians of Oregon. A boarding school for Indian children, with ninety-five pupils enrolled, is conducted by the Fathers and Sisters of Mt. Angel on our missions on the West Coast of Vancouver Island. Some of our Rev. Professors use their vacation time to preach missions and retreats. Every summer a three day retreat is given at Mt. Angel College for the Catholic laymen of the archdiocese. Non-Catholics are invited.[94]

Joe probably planned to attend Rockne's Corvallis coaches school during the summer. Being identified with Rockne was very desirable for young coaches, according to Michael Steele.

> In becoming familiar with the facts of Knute Rockne's life, one must be impressed by the accolades the man received from all quarters. He was almost universally perceived by people of his era as a saint, a national father figure to youth, a prototypical 'man's man.' He stood for all that seemed right about America and the game that came to express so much about the myth of the American experience. One searches almost in vain for the discouraging word. There were very few written or said about the man. [95]

159

Rockne's scheduled appearance in Corvallis for the 1926 coaches school, however, created a furor in Eugene. To his few detractors, Rockne was a coach who corrupted the game. A University of Oregon economics professor, Glenn Hoover, led an outcry by writing "a vitriolic denunciation of the professional coaches who, in his view, plagued college campuses." Hoover gave his views in the April 14, 1926 *New Republic,* as summarized here by Steele.

He would have decreased the salaries of coaches to make them seem less important than college presidents. He urged that physical education departments be observed closely since they were 'mere shams to cloak the expenditure of funds for coaches and athletic directors' in their attempts to avoid public outcry by donors and taxpayers. Such people, Hoover alleged, hide behind their calls for improved public health and sound bodies and minds even as they look for 'leading attractions for their summer sessions.' Not surprisingly, 'the man in America who was perhaps in greatest demand and received the highest salary was that great educator and public health expert, Knute Rockne of Notre Dame, coach of the Four Horsemen.' All of this adds up to economist Hoover as 'quasi-embezzlement of trust funds,' a charge that must have seemed outrageous to Rockne.[96]

Steele's response to Hoover suggests that the University of Oregon's rivalry with Oregon State may have had more to do with the furor than Rockne himself.

Hoover would probably have known of Rockne's plans to conduct a summer coaching clinic at Oregon State University in Corvallis, only forty miles north of the University of Oregon. While the overemphasis issue dragged on for years and even has residual traces today, Hoover's charge against Rockne's activities was never made in a public forum. There is no record that Rockne responded to it. Hoover's viewpoint made him a minority of one.[97]

Nationally, Steele reported that Rockne's economics, possibly in conjunction with his coaches schools, brought detractors from some quarters. "Westbrook Pegler thought Rockne wanted to make as much money as possible while in the fickle public's spotlight; Francis Wallace agreed." These criticisms, however, were described by Steele as "a far cry from the acid remarks made by Hoover."[98] The rationale for the criticism directed at Rockne may have reflected the college game's increased emphasis on winning. Hoover's views, also, may have influenced Oregon's "Murray Law of 1929."

The 1926 version of the school was similar to 1925, with Rockne receiving "a minimum guarantee of $1000.00 for the two weeks with an optional arrangement of $15.00 for every student registering." Due to the success of 1925, Oregon State wanted assurances that Rockne would "not conduct any other coaching school during the summer in the northwest." Their rationale was that "to split up the clientele would result in disaster."[99]

Student cost was set at $25 for the course which was conducted June 21 through July 3. Oregon State's concerns about competition did not materialize. In the autumn of 1925, Rockne wrote that his "school at Corvallis will be the only one west of the Mississippi" and proposed changes for the syllabus.[100]

Despite the flack, Rockne was in Corvallis for the second consecutive summer. Material that follows is from Oregon State's *"Preliminary" Bulletin* for the 1926 Summer Session.

> **Knute Rockne of Notre Dame** discussed football last summer with upwards of 120 school men at the O.A.C. Summer Session. He returns this summer. Because of former associations with Coach Schissler, it has been possible to bring him to the Coast. This will be the only course Rockne will give in the Northwest this summer. Whether it will be possible to bring him West again is uncertain.
>
> Rockne is a great coach. He has proved himself also a great teacher.
>
> The course given this summer will be interesting both to the men who were in class last summer and to those who were not. Rockne writes that he plans to treble his field work and increase his lecture work.
>
> It means something to say that one has had work with Rockne, but that is not the main thing. Rockne teaches football, and men leave the course with full notebooks and a wealth of practical instruction. They also leave it enthusiastic, for Rockne is a humorist and a personality.[101]

The text mentioned favorable national publicity after the 1925 summer session.

> Characterized in the April issue of the *American Educational Digest* as a 'Notable Summer Session,' O.A.C. last summer witnessed a 40 percent increase in regular Campus registration over the previous summer. This was partly due to the magnetism and power of Knute Rockne; but 40 percent of this increase consisted of women. These were engaged in various fields – Commerce, Vocational Education, Physical Education, and especially Home Economics. They came not for one feature but for many.[102]

Oregon State's administrators capitalized on Rockne's popularity for the 1926 session. Conversely, there was concern that those attending in 1925 might not return for more of the same. Thus, the summer session was designed for more than football coaches.

> Last summer 356, or about half of the regular full-term resident students at the Summer Session were teachers, principals, or superintendents, a group dominated by a fine professional enthusiasm.[103]

The text did continue, however, with suggestions that there were others besides Rockne who might be attractive to sports practitioners in physical education.

> The work is organized around that of Knute Rockne, but the presence of W. A. Kearns, Coach Schissler, 'Bob' Hager, Ralph Coleman, Robin Reed, and Lewis Kuehn means the best in coaching in all fields of sport which the high school teacher is called upon to direct.[104]

In 1926 Rockne was accompanied to Corvallis by his wife, Bonnie. The school was so successful for all concerned that plans were made on July 12, 1926 for Rockne to return in 1927. Attending the 1926 session was Bob Murray. Rockne's impact on Murray was so great that he wrote a very moving essay on this experience several years later.

Also, a 1929 story on Joe revealed that he attended the Rockne coaches school in Corvallis on two occasions out of the four that were offered. Joe's summer was difficult since his mother was sick and may have undergone a surgical procedure. 1926, therefore, may have been one of the two years that he did not attend. For Joe there were more important family matters requiring his time. Joe's mother "almost never went away from home." Social calls always took place at her home. If anyone wanted to see her, "they went to her home." The Dalles developed sufficiently for two hospitals to be built. Yet, when Anna Kasberger required an operation, it was done at her home where the physician was assisted by "neighbor ladies holding lamps for light." She died in August at the age of 67.[105]

Anna Kasberger, ca. 1925.

Surely Joe and his siblings were busy after her funeral with family matters. The values inculcated in her household about family responsibilities appear to have endured for Joe's lifetime. The inspiration for the Kasberger children's devotion to the home probably began with their mother, the homemaker. The family home remained special to virtually all of her children, perhaps in part because all but Willie were born there.

Over the years, a sense of family and fond memories permeated this residence for the Kasberger children. As they matured, the "spartan strength in that household" continued and would bring them home. The great love and respect that existed was apparent to one observer who noted that "it was exchanged through feeling rather than through words." Another unifying Kasberger trait was an aversion to change. "That aspect of life was probably the hardest burden for all of them. They would have liked things to stay just the way they were."[106] What happened to Joe's siblings as they aged?

John Kasberger, Sr., ca. 1926.

Joe's oldest brother, Willie, was the only Kasberger child "who ever left home." He "went to Seattle, married, became a meat cutter and only returned home for parents' funerals." Fortunately for Joe's career, his brother John never left home. His presence at home provided a stabilizing force for the family and he "became a fireman and then engineer

John Kasberger, Sr. at his home, ca. 1926.

for the railroad." John's economic role in the family was also important, as "the breadwinner of the household all of his working years."[107]

Joe's brother George stayed home, too. Joe and George had a special relationship in maintaining the family home. "George spent his working years on farms in the neighborhood." George had suffered sunstroke as a young man, the "resulting illness precluded the possibility of his making much headway in other directions." Joe's brother Philip left home for a house directly across the street from 917 West Tenth Street, when he married his wife, Josephine. He "worked in meat markets all his working life." Max, Joe's youngest brother, remained in The Dalles as a successful banker. Yet, he never really left home either, but "really branched out and made a home about six blocks away."[108]

Joe's oldest sister, Anna Kasberger Sandoz, left home when she married Julius Sandoz. There was a special bond between Anna, as the oldest daughter, and her mother. Yet, Joe's mother had difficulty leaving her home to visit others, even Anna. After Anna married and moved five miles away, it took great persuasion for Mrs. Kasberger to visit. Thus, "only once in her remaining six years" did she make the trip.[109]

Audie married, also, and remained close to Joe. In looking back at the Kasberger children as adults, the influence of their parents remained intact.

Mill Creek Valley and Sandoz Family farm.

Because of the legend surrounding Joe, the reputation of his parents, as overbearing and protective, emerged. Bud Sandoz refuted this notion.

> Lots of people thought that my Kasberger grandparents were terribly strict and oppressive parents. My mother and my aunt and uncles did not feel that way. They held them in reverence and respect. Never once in my life have I heard any of them alter from that stance. No matter at what stage of life, I've heard different ones of them refer to the childhood years as the really happy ones.[110]

Joe with his sister, Audie.

In the case of Joe, he was unique among the Kasberger children. He was both a gifted athlete and student. None of his siblings were known for athletics, nor did any of them attend college. Joe was observed as special because "his inner drive, strength, and stamina and disciplined hard work brought him great success in his field of work." Joe was the second of the Kasberger children to leave home. Yet he remained "a 'home' person and returned there each summer, usually as soon as possible after the school year was over."[111]

Joe's bachelor status, strong religious orientation and association with the Benedictines raises questions about a religious vocation. Did Joe ever profess religious vows? Bud Sandoz shared these thoughts. "Joe never aspired to become a priest or a monk, but in many ways he lived like one." Regarding marriage and family aspirations, there is no opinion that "he ever fell in love and aspired to have his own family."[112] There are photos, however, of Joe as a young man with attractive young women.

There is no indication that Joe ever found a true love who he might desire as a

Joe, in overcoat, with a date and friends.

Joe and an unnamed young lady, undated, with anonymous caption.

She never Sensed him all

marriage partner. Yet it is believed there were "at least four ladies who were strongly interested in him as a husband but the magic did not mature."[113] The photos presented here come from the Mt. Angel archives with anonymous captions that are undated. It is possible they came from Bishop Leipzig's collection or from Bill Krebs.

1926-27 School Year

Joe probably returned to Mt. Angel in September. What had appeared in June to be a promising 1926-27 school year was off to a bad start. An anonymous story dated Sept. 17, 1926, possibly from the Salem *Journal,* is headlined: "Mt. Angel's Grid Outlook Gloomy."

> Chances for Mt. Angel to repeat last year's victorious clean up on the gridiron are not as bright as they should be, Coach Joe Kasberger stated upon his arrival on the campus Tuesday. The Gold and White machine will sustain several heavy losses, among them 'Chuck' Spear, 1925-26 captain; Hardin, tackle; Busch, guard; Teters, quarter, and Roalsen, tackle.[114]

This story mentioned that the Angels' "Captain-elect George McGowan, end, of Lebanon, Ore., will have only three other lettermen to build his team around this season." The other three lettermen were: "Walsh, full; Salvi, tackle, and Berger, end." The story added that "Coach Kasberger cannot begin regular practice until next week." The story concluded pessimistically. "Angel rooters may expect hard sledding in both the Willamette Valley and Oregon-Washington conferences."[115]

Joe was preparing the 1926 football team for the inaugural year of Oregon-Washington Conference football. The road game in Seattle, at the end of October, was a chance to see his brother Willie. There was excitement on the weekend before classes began as students returned to campus. Despite the unexpected loss of key starters, the Fightin' Angels were expected to have a good season. With a little luck, this could be a breakthrough year. The Seattle games might be the first in ambitious future schedules in major cities.

OREGON-WASHINGTON CONFERENCE
Football Schedule for '26-'27
October 30 - St. Martin's at Columbia U; Mt. Angel College at Seattle College.
November 13 - Mt. Angel College at Columbia U.
November 14 - Seattle College at St. Martin's.
November 20 - Columbia U. at Seattle College.
November 21 - St. Martin's at Mt. Angel College.[116]

Despite the plans of many, there was no 1926 football season for MAC. "During the night of September 20, 1926, twenty-three years after it was first occupied, the entire abbey and school complex burned to the ground." A short version of the Mt. Angel fire follows:

During the night of September 20, 1926, twenty-three years after it was first occupied, the entire abbey and school complex burned to the ground. The fire began in a wooden garage between the carpenter shop and the gymnasium. The night was rainy and windy when the night watchman sounded the alarm at 11:30. The fire soon caused a power outage, so that there was no way to pump water to the hilltop. Abbot Bernard retired to the little chapel in the cemetery to pray. The next morning nothing was left standing except the press and adjoining post office building, and these were endangered by sparks from the smoldering ruins. A pump truck from Salem kept their roofs wetted down, and they were saved. They became the means by which the now homeless monks would appeal for help to Catholics throughout the country.[117]

Some photos presented in this book were saved from the fire, reportedly, by Joe and players. Several have scorch marks from the flames. Also recalled were Joe and the players trying to save athletic equipment, since there was no water with which to fight the flames.

A longer version of the fire story is presented in the Appendix. A related story from the Salem, OR *Capital Journal's* Tuesday, Sept. 21 edition, with the headline "ARCHBISHOP IN MT. ANGEL ON VISIT," follows.

Archbishop Edward D. Howard left for the scene of the fire immediately upon receipt of the first news from Mt. Angel. Plans for the immediate relief of the famous old school will be discussed with Father Morris, the archbishop stated before his departure. He expressed the belief that ways and means would be found for rebuilding.[118]

Joe's success in building on the foundation for "Notre Dame of the West" is thought to have made some uncomfortable. The notion of MAC becoming an athletic powerhouse was not unanimously favored. There were many questions to be answered about Mt. Angel's future in the grim days that followed.

V. AFTERMATH OF THE FIRE

"His School Is Ruined But Not His Spirit."

Joe Kasberger spent so many years on the East Coast, a casual observer might think he was born there. The questions: why did he come, and under what circumstances, appear important. Certainly the 1926 Mt. Angel fire was a cataclysmic event in his life. What is the sequence of events that followed? It is hoped that this chapter will set the record straight.

1926-27 School Year

Initially for Joe and his colleagues at MAC, athletics were not a priority at all. Even rebuilding the school in the first days after the fire was only a secondary concern. The first priority was the necessities of life, food and shelter, for all who were displaced. Mt. Angel was in a survival mode.

The community went to the parish church in Mount Angel to pray the morning office; they would hold community prayers there for the next eighteen months. The monks took up residence in some rented houses and the old parish school. The seminary was moved to two large private houses, but no non-seminary boarders were accepted into the college after the fire. Monastic and school life

Aerial photo of Mt. Angel after the fire.

167

were soon reconstituted on a makeshift basis, but there remained the massive task of rebuilding.[1]

Mt. Angel's 1982 fire provided valuable lessons, especially for Abbot Bernard and Prior, Fr. Jerome Wespe. Having survived that trial, they were experienced on how to proceed, since they "were determined to rebuild the monastery as soon as possible." Because of the abbey's delicate financial condition, costs were put under tight control, and "all expendable assets were sold, except for the farm land which was kept inviolate as a basis for the future."[2] Despite these measures, external help was essential.

The community sent out appeals to the readers of the abbey's publications, and several of the monks, including Fathers Gabriel Morrisoe (d. 1962), Michael Reilly (prof. 1928) and Alcuin Heibel (prof. 1917), traveled around the country to collect money.[3]

Joe's first priority was working with the others to restore the community. Regarding those anxious and chaotic days, there are no accounts of Joe's role other than rebuilding and fund-raising. Within a month, Joe received media attention that was wanted and needed, since Mt. Angel required publicity, in the quest for outside assistance.

The fire was a major story in Oregon, and Joe was good copy in several publications. The insights provided in these stories are valuable in assessing his character and values. A story from *The Salem Journal,* with the handwritten date of 9/26/26, has the headline: "Football Hopes at Mt. Angel College Blasted by Fire." The story byline was: "Temporary Headquarters, Mt. Angel College, Mt. Angel, Or., Sept 25," with the following text:

'Smiling Joe' Kasberger, athletic mentor at Mt. Angel college, witnessed the destruction of his hopes for a brilliant football record this fall when Mt. Angel burned to the ground last Tuesday morning, but he is still smiling.

Coach Kasberger wasn't enthusiastic over the prospects for this season when 'Chuck' Spear, ex-Angel captain, went to Georgetown U., Washington, D. C. and Kenneth Hardin, veteran tackle, decided to give Gonzaga some of his football ability, but his hopes went sailing again when Bert Busch, Tony Berger, Schroeder, Al Walsh, Denny Hennan, Shy McGowan, and a few other veteran stars turned out on the first day of practice the day before the big fire. This season was a big opportunity to repeat last year's smashing victories on the gridiron, and it was destroyed along with the entire institution.

In the meantime, Kasberger is one of the busiest men at the scene of the catastrophe, working for the temporary relief of the Benedictine Fathers. He has already received several offers in the state to coach football teams, but 'Smiling Joe' replies to the offers, 'I don't want to talk football contracts until I have helped the Fathers get settled. After I am in a position to accept your offer, I will let you know.'[4]

HIS SCHOOL IS RUINED BUT NOT HIS SPIRIT

Joe's photo which accompanies the story about the fire appeared in the October 10, 1926 **Sunday Oregonian.**

Oregon's largest paper wrote about Joe as recounted here.

When fire recently wiped out Mount Angel college, Joe Kasberger, football coach, was temporarily out of a job. He was swamped with offers from high schools and small colleges throughout the northwest, but flatly refused every offer with the statement: 'Can't talk football contracts with the school in distress and me able to help it rebuild.' Joe's athletic career has been lengthy and sensational. He attended Mount Angel, playing on all four major sports teams and then entered O.A.C. He played for the Aggies for three years and in '21-22 was named all-coast halfback. After graduating, Joe assumed duties as coach at Mount Angel and never failed to develop a winning team in any sport.[5]

The story is repeated in the Oregon State alumni newsletter, *Beaver Tales.* Certainly Joe had accomplished much in his four-year MAC tenure with a record that speaks for itself and tantalizes the imagination. What might have become the Notre Dame of the West was now a shattered dream. As noted in the January 16, 1942 *Pacific Star:*

Joe left this coaching record at M.A.C.: two State Non-conference and one Conference Championship Basketball teams, a Non-conference Championship Football team and two basketball teams of no mediocre athletic brilliance.[6]

Left unreported was Joe's Willamette Valley Conference baseball championship in 1926.

Larger questions of where, when, and how this test would be passed remained to be answered, and his character was tested. Now, more than ever before, the strength of friendships formed in the past became important.

With MAC's total destruction, accounting for Joe during this period is difficult. It is believed that he stayed at Mt. Angel for the entire 1926-27 school year. In a letter dated Aug. 23, 1988, Rev. Martin Pollard, O.S.B., recalled Joe.

> It is now long ago and Mount Angel College at that time was not well known. It obtained full recognition for junior college work in 1923-24 and then in 1926 all burned to the ground. It never recovered and we simply changed the emphasis. Kasberger was coach up to 1926; he stayed on for about one year helping with the drive for funds but was really looking for an opening and found Newark. Since I left for Europe in September 1927 and did not return until August 1933 I knew little about his move.[7]

Important to Fr. Martin was the fact that Joe "was already formed as a fine coach; his character was settled and it remained the same; his personal qualities were well known." Joe "had great influence on those he coached." In Fr. Martin's view, Joe succeeded equally as a winner of games and as a role-model. "A word from him about not drinking or smoking or swearing was worth five sermons from another." Thus, Joe's "human qualities . . . made his record possible."[8]

Plans were made by the monks to rebuild their home.

> After long discussions, it was decided to rebuild on the top of the hill, but the abbey was to be located on the back side of the hill to assure the community seclusion and quiet. The design of the building was influenced by the memory of the fires which had twice destroyed the community's home. The buildings would not form a tight medieval enclosed square, but would be far enough apart so that a fire in one would not doom the others. A large free-standing water tank would be erected, and the power lines would be arranged for maximum safety. The buildings would be of concrete, with brick facing.[9]

Several months after the fire, construction "began on the new abbey building in the spring of 1927." Fund-raising was only partially successful and initial plans to build a four-story structure to house one hundred monks, were revised to build a three-story facility. Thanks to a church building fund that Abbot Murphy had started before the fire, there was enough capital "to build the sanctuary for a new church, to which was added a temporary nave that could seat about one hundred people." All of this activity "placed a heavy financial strain on the community, and two decades would be required to pay off the debts." Also, the response to the national appeal for aid put Mt. Angel back on its feet. In gratitude, the monks "pledged themselves to celebrate the daily community Mass perpetually for the benefactors, who made the rebuilding possible."[10]

The next known event concerning Joe transpired in June, 1927. While there is little material about Joe's mother, the following story about the father might be useful in comprehending the son. The Aug. 1927 *Union Pacific Magazine* had the following article entitled "The Dalles, Oregon," by J.M. Gale.

> Hostler John Kasberger, was retired on June 30, after 42 years in engine service. At noon on June 29, the shop employees held a very impressive ceremony in his honor.

The story continues with Howard Selleck speaking for the "shopmen." He told of "the deep friendship which existed here for Mr. Kasberger and the joy it gave us to see him receive the reward for his faithful services." After Selleck concluded his remarks, with "wishes for the years to come were happy ones," W.T. Doran spoke as Union Pacific's master mechanic. He knew Mr. Kasberger "much longer than the majority of the employees," and made many points by recalling:

> . . . the many years of honest endeavor and conscientious loyalty to the company and to his fellow workers; of the wonderful family he has raised, each successful in his particular undertaking; of his unexcelled character which we who have to continue on the road that leads to peaceful retirement and fond memories may take as our example to follow, so that we may finish with a smile and clear conscience if we have played our part the way Mr. Kasberger has done his.

Mr. Doran concluded by holding up "a gold watch chain" and speaking of its symbolism for friendship. The many links represented John Kasberger's many friends at Union Pacific "who had joined in purchasing the chain." It was then presented to Mr. Kasberger "as a token of sincere friendship formed under various conditions and circumstances." It was hoped that it would "always be a memory to Mr. Kasberger of the boys who respected, honored, and loved him as a father and fellow worker." A final retirement gift from Mr. Doran was a box of cigars. John Kasberger "thanked the boys in words deeply felt by all, after which he was personally greeted and congratulated by everyone." The story concluded with mention of others present: "H.F. Schinaman, road foreman of engines, and J.J. Bowen, yard-master." The story may provide an objective insight into the father as one of the most important influences in the lives of his children.[11]

The summer of 1927 probably found Joe in Corvallis for the Rockne coaches school. These were heated times for athletics in Oregon. Professor Hoover's views at the University of Oregon may have been reinforced by the arrival of John J. McEwan from West Point as the Ducks' new head football coach. In his 1926 inaugural season, Oregon had a dismal 2-4-1 record. Conversely, Schissler's Aggies in 1926 had an amazing 7-1-0 season, including a 16-0 win over their archrivals. Only a 17-7 loss to USC kept Oregon State out of the Rose Bowl. In correspondence dated May 5, 1927 from Schissler to Rockne, some insights into the tempest emerge.

> McEwan has been off on his golf game recently and for that reason has gone on a rampage to eliminate spring football in the Coast Conference colleges. It would help the situation out here some if you would issue an opinion as to the value of spring football and you believe that it is helpful rather than detrimental to the academic activities in the schools in which it is being held.
>
> Personally, I think Mac is too lazy to work all spring and they have a new wild-eyed president over there who loves to break into the columns of the press under any pretense. Their plan is to bring the matter up at the Conference meet this spring, and as ridiculous as it is, it might find friends among some of the

boys out here if a little sensible propaganda is not put up to kill it.[12]

Schissler's remarks that follow, may refer to public sentiment about Rockne returning to Corvallis for his third consecutive coaches school in 1927.

The Coast is clear otherwise, the atmosphere having cleared up decidedly in the past two months. It seems that the administration sees the light and so I am taking my three squares and a good flop a day with the rest of the natives.[13]

Rockne responded to Schissler, announcing that he was coming to Corvallis on June 21 from Dallas, TX. Regarding spring football, Rockne wrote:

McKewan [sic] and his Spring football give me a big laugh. As soon as I get time I will get out a little propaganda on Spring practice, as you mention. However, I wouldn't worry about it – I don't believe any of the other schools feel like McEwan. He must have some ulterior motive up his sleeve.[14]

The 1927 coaches school in Corvallis was another success. In correspondence dated July 20, 1927, Schissler quantified the impact of Rockne.

Here at Oregon State we have attracted over three hundred high school and college coaches from this section of the country the past three years and it gives these men an insight on the situation here, which they could not secure in any other way. It has helped bring many new students here.[15]

Knute Rockne remained a big draw in Corvallis since his school was well-publicized. Posters were printed and distributed widely for the 1927 summer session. An excerpt stated that "Knute Rockne was one of several prominent visiting faculty from other Institutions. Rockne, Director of Physical Education and Coach of Athletics at the University of Notre Dame," was a powerful attraction.[16] The fact that he came to Corvallis so often proved his two-week course was popular with high school and college coaches.

Bringing Rockne to Oregon State was not without cost. "Registration Fee of $10 admits to all regular classes. Rockne's work $10 additional. Rockne alone $15." The 1927 *Catalog* for the Summer Session at Oregon State Agricultural College provided the following biographical material for "Knute Rockne, B.S.:"

Director of Physical Education and Coach of Athletics, Notre Dame University – Who will give his Football Coach Course, June 20-July 2 in a two-weeks unit course including Coach Hager's 'Percentage Basketball.'[17]

The 1927 Summer School *Catalog* provides the following introduction and course-description for Rockne:

The department of Physical Education and Athletics for Men supplies a constantly growing demand for men in coaching and physical education positions.

The work given in the Summer Session for athletic coaches will be of exceptional value to those who expect to qualify for either full time or part time coaching and physical education. The courses offered will meet the demands of those who wish to brush up and get a new angle on all courses as well as of those in part-time teaching and coaching situations.

Note: The work has been arranged so that it may be taken in units of *two, three, or six weeks.* Rockne, Schissler, and Hager, Football and Basketball make a *two-weeks unit;* Football, Basketball, and Track make a *three weeks unit* with preliminary work in Baseball. For those who can stay six weeks, in addition to the Football, Basketball, Track, and Baseball, there is Promotion of Intramural and Class Activities besides all the other six weeks' courses.[18]

COURSES

1. **Football (Knute Rockne's Method)** (PEm 331s). The theoretical work will take up the rules from the standpoint of coach, players, and officials; the several styles of offense and defense with consideration of their special strengths and weaknesses; generalship and strategy. The practical work will include training, conditioning, and player's equipment; punting, the various kinds of kicking, tackling dummy and charging sled; special drills for linemen, ends, and backs; interference and team work; fundamental plays, freak plays, and signal systems. The course has been varied to be of use both to those who took the work last summer and to those taking Rockne's course for the first time. Coach P. J. Schissler will cooperate with Rockne in both lecture and practice work.

Two credits; 8:00-11:00 daily with conferences from 11:00 to 12:00, first two weeks. Ag 329 *Knute Rockne* [19]

Preparations soon began to bring Rockne back in the summer of 1928.

The spring and summer of 1927 brought enough stability in the town of Mt. Angel for a baseball season to be played, a welcome diversion from the grim rebuilding of the last eight months. Later accounts of this period state that Joe coached the Mt. Angel Townies baseball team. Joe's contract with MAC may not have been renewed at its assumed expiration in June 1927. Possibly, he had a multi-year contract extending beyond the end of the 1927 school year. In either event, Joe appears free from any contractual obligations with MAC.

Thus, Joe may have taken a position in Salem with the Oregon Motor Vehicle Agency with time to be a part-time coach. Joe is thought to have remained in Mt. Angel and commuted to Salem. The following account may support this conjecture. A June 11, 1967 *Star Ledger* story by Lloyde S. Glicken stated that Joe's degrees included a "master's in accounting from Mt. Angel" with no date indicated.[20] While it is possible that Joe did the coursework before the fire, it seems more likely that his workload precluded this academic endeavor. Fr. Hugh Feiss suggests that MAC may have had a master's program at this time.

The second scenario, from a May 9, 1940 *Pacific Star* story based on an interview with Joe, is believed to refer to the spring and summer of 1927 at the earliest. Possibly, it refers to subsequent spring and summers in 1928 and 1929, when a town baseball team, the Mt. Angel Townies, was managed by Joe.[20]

1927-28 School Year

What transpired next is almost hard to believe. Joe's experience as a player for MAC against Willamette University in the notorious forfeit loss of 1916 was thought to have been unpleasant. While geographically close, Salem and Mt. Angel probably collided culturally. The big-town state capital and the small rural village may have presented conflicts. Despite this perceived incompatibility, the 1927 football season at Willamette is the next documented focal point for Joe's activities. Furthermore, it is inferred that Willamette's athletic director and head football coach, Spec Keene, was the reason that Joe took the position. Presumably this was a part-time assistant-coach position that would allow Joe to coach at Mt. Angel Academy and Normal School in the 1927-28 basketball season. Also, Willamette's location allowed Joe to work for a state agency.

Located about 15 miles southwest of Mt. Angel, Willamette University was first known as the Oregon Institute and has the distinction of being the oldest institution of higher learning in the West. One of the most important stops in Joe's career was the time spent at Willamette. The university was important not only to Joe as a job, but also to many New Jersey athletes as the locus of their college careers.

The specifics of Joe's joining Spec at Willamette in 1927 are not known. Yet it seems logical to conclude that the move was based on friendship developed at OAC. The bottom line is that, of all the options after the fire, Joe selected Spec, the friendship outweighing any negatives that lingered concerning Willamette. The decision to hire Joe seems important for Spec since he was not as experienced as a football player or coach. Moreover, Joe had an indirect "Rockne pedigree," thought to be valuable then. College coaching positions were opening up to Rockne players, or those who knew his ways of coaching. Joe as an assistant was a very beneficial addition for Willamette.

Spec's academic degree from OAC was in animal husbandry and considered having a cattle ranch until an alternative appeared. "Fortunately, Corvallis High needed a combination football-basketball-baseball coach and a head man for physical education. Keene was the choice." In explaining his decision, Spec gave the following rationale: "I guess I went into coaching because I liked athletics and working with growing kids."[21] It was not long before Spec returned to OAC. When presented an opportunity to be OAC's freshman football coach, Spec consulted with a significant-other before making his decision, his future wife, "Marie, whom he'd met at school." The future Mrs. Keene was an important part of Spec's life and career. "At the time, she was teaching in Everett, Wash., and she counseled him to take the OSU [then OAC] position."

Thus Spec took the position and "eventually served as assistant to Paul Schissler with the varsity gridders." Spec remained in Corvallis until the spring of 1926, when given the chance to return to his home town with a position at Willamette. His responsibilities were similar to those of Joe at MAC. "He coached football, basketball and baseball the first two years and served as athletic director and head of the PE department."[22] The problems Spec faced were many. The addition of Joe to his staff provided Spec an experienced and successful perspective that he could trust in rebuilding the Cardinal and Old Gold's football program.

Willamette had begun playing football in 1894 with no recognized coach, and there was no winning tradition to speak of. Moreover, there was a multitude of coaches, suggesting instability. Ironically, Spec succeeded Joe's former assistant coach from OAC, Guy L. Rathbun, who became Willamette's head coach in 1923, posting a 2-5-1 record. In the next two seasons, Rathbun did not produce a winning record, due partially to mismatches against the Pacific Coast Conference. Rathbun's 1923 team suffered a 0-54 loss to the University of Washington. In 1924 Rathbun's team went 1-5-1, again humiliated by the University of Washington in a 0-57 loss. The final straw, either for Rathbun or the Willamette administration, was the 1925 season, a fiasco with a record of 2-7-0. Two losses were gruesome: 0-108 to the University of Washington, and 0-51 the next week to OAC.[23]

Obviously, Spec faced a major challenge in 1926 with his first football team and the inauguration of Northwest Conference play. The Bearcats responded with another losing season, but the 2-4-0 record offered a glimmer of hope. Unfortunately, the inaugural game of Spec's Willamette career was a 0-44 loss to the University of Oregon. The bullies from the University of Washington were held to a 0-28 win in the second game of the season.[24]

Joe Kasberger's arrival as Willamette's line coach for the 1927 season, was possibly just what Spec needed. Also it is possible that former MAC football players enrolled at Willamette, since it is not known what happened to them after the 1926 fire. Suddenly Spec was about to do something that had not been done since 1920. A Willamette football team would have a non-losing season record. The last Willamette coach to accomplish this feat was R. L. Mathews with a 3-1-1 record in 1920. He was the infamous coach of MAC ire, who was held

Uncaptioned photo of 1927 Willamette University football team with Joe (upper left) as assistant coach.

responsible for the Angels' forfeit-loss to the Bearcats in 1916.

Spec's 1927 football season began with a 6-32 loss to the University of Washington. The results of the 1927 football season suggest Willamette was caught in a big school-little school identity problem. Willamette did not have enough students to compete successfully with big schools, especially in the Pacific Coast Conference. The 3-3-2 season in 1927 showed improvement after the Washington game, with the Bearcats playing well defensively. Sadly, the defense failed in a 7-31 season-finale loss to Whitman College.

The 1928 Willamette yearbook, *Wallulah,* stated that the "football team went through a fairly successful season, losing only to Idaho and Whitman in Northwest Conference games." By past performance standards, it was a major improvement in athletic fortunes. "The Bearcats were rated third in the conference with a record of two games won, two lost, and one tied."[25] College of Idaho and Whitman College finished first and second, respectively, in conference play. Willamette's third place finish was followed by Puget Sound, Linfield, and Pacific. Willamette's season summary is presented in the Appendix.

The 1928 *Wallulah* also had a story about the coaching staff. Spec was recognized for arriving "when the athletics of the University were at a low ebb," but now had reversed past trends. Thus he was praised for having "developed successful teams for the last two years until now the name, 'Bearcat,' is one to be respected by any athletic squad in the Northwest." In addition, Keene's versatility in coaching all of Willamette's major sports successfully was noted.

The Cardinal and Gold colors have become firmly fixed among the leaders in all major sports of the Northwest Conference as a result of 'Spec's' efficient tutelage.[26]

1928 Willamette University football coaching staff.
Kneeling: **Head Coach Spec Keene;** *Standing:* **Ken Denman, Les Sparks and Joe Kasberger.**

Spec's assistant football coaches were also recognized for the 1927 season. Joe was described as a "former O.A.C. star and a man with three year's experience as coach at Mt. Angel College [1922,23,25], [who] served as football line coach this year." Another assistant football coach was Kenneth "Red" Denman, also a former OAC player and Phi Delta Theta, who served as the backfield coach. Denman was described as "one of the best backs turned out by the State college in recent years," after Kasberger and Keene had graduated. Spec's third assistant coach in football, Lestle [sic] J. Sparks, had the title "Graduate Manager." In addition to football duties, he was Willamette's freshman basketball and varsity track coach. Spec had another assistant, Bill Ashby, without football responsibilities. He was described as an "ex-Salem High and University of Oregon basketball player," who "had charge of the basketball squad during the first of the season while 'Spec' was supervising the football squad."[27]

At the end of Willamette's 1927 football season, Joe became a women's basketball coach at Mt. Angel Academy and Normal School. According to the Commencement 1928 issue of *The Old Gold and White* newspaper, Joe coached the team to ten victories in an eleven-game season. What is not clear from this source is whether the rigor of competition was at the college or high-school level. From this source, in a section titled "Athletic Activities 1927-28," comes the following story:

> Early in October a large class of enthusiastic girls began to practice basketball. A championship team was their aim. Miss Alice Walsh of the normal department was chosen athletic manager. Of the fifty girls who started, twenty were chosen for Coach Kasberger's class. Under the able direction of Miss Walsh and Coach Kasberger, the basketball season was a most successful one.[28]

The members of Joe's women's basketball team are listed in the Appendix. The story continued with the following sentence that creates confusion regarding Joe's role and the composition of the team: "Other exciting games: Normal vs. High School and the Eighth Grade vs. First Year High." Note that the "M.A.C." heading is presented in context despite a later reference to "M.A.A." – which seems more appropriate.[29]

The story concludes with a suggestion that baseball was played at Mt. Angel Academy and Normal School. Perhaps women's softball, thought to have originated in the early 1920s, was a sport at the Academy.

> During these beautiful spring days at M.A.A., with roses, roses everywhere, the gymnasium is practically deserted. Activities have been transferred to the tennis courts and baseball diamond.[30]

The interest of Joe possibly coaching a women's or girls' baseball team is overshadowed by another reference. In the "Chronicle" section of this edition of *The Old Gold and White*, a paragraph reveals information about Mt. Angel, indicating that the hilltop campus was rebuilt. This allusion seems important since it indicates that baseball was again being played by male students.

For the first time since the disastrous fire the Academy girls were invited to climb the hill to witness a baseball game between the Mt. Angel high school boys and the Molalla team. Although both teams played well, Molalla was victorious.[31]

A final reference to Joe appeared in the same "Chronicle" section as follows:

The members and the coach of the basketball team were guests at a banquet, which was given in their honor in the Junior Home Room in April. The players were presented with letters by Coach Kasberger, and the Coach, in turn, was presented with an old gold and white pillow.[32]

These insights into Joe's presence in the town of Mt. Angel during the 1927-28 school year answer some questions. Also, it is likely that Joe was there on "the Feast of St. Joseph, May 19, 1928," when "the community celebrated Mass in the parish church in Mount Angel," as a prelude to another celebration. After Mass, "a procession was formed and moved joyously up the hill to the new abbey which stood proudly amid a sea of mud and construction debris." It did not take long for other facilities to reappear.

The abbey schools also returned to the hilltop. The seminary was squeezed into the south end of the abbey building; day students were being taught in the basement. This overcrowded situation was not tolerated for long. In spite of the abbey's debts and the onslaught of the depression, some generous benefactors were found. Construction was hurried along, and what is today Aquinas Hall was sufficiently completed for partial occupance in September, 1930.[33]

Joe and Lolita Byrd (left) with his sister, Audie, and J. Francis Connell at their wedding in 1928.

Joe is known to have been in The Dalles during the summer of 1928 for Audie's wedding. This marriage was short-lived, as she "was a widow early and shortly moved back home."[34] Also, Joe probably attended Rockne's 1928 coaches school in Corvallis.

Rockne conducted three coaching schools during the summer of 1928 – in Dallas, TX; Hastings, NB; and Corvallis – before going to the Summer Olympics in Berlin. Indicative of the closeness of their friendship, Rockne invited Schissler and his wife Emma Lou to join him and his wife in Europe. Schissler's 1927 football team had a 3-3-1 record, including a noble 21-7 win over Coach McEwan's Ducks.

Knute Rockne's Coaches School at Oregon State, 1928. Joe is standing with his back to camera, far right.

Apparently Schissler and McEwan had settled their differences and Rockne blessed the friendship with the following words in a letter dated Dec. 7, 1927: "I am glad to hear that McKeon [sic] is coming along fine and that you and he are becoming good friends. Give him my regards when you see him."[35] Rockne's 1928 coaches school in Corvallis is recorded in Oregon State's alumni magazine, *The Alumnus*. Excerpts from the July 1928 issue are in the Appendix. The 1928 coaches school is significant as the last one conducted in Corvallis.

1928-29 School Year

Joe returned to Willamette for the 1928 season. Spec's shaky start in the 1926 and 1927 seasons, led to a more competitive team to stabilize the floundering program. The 1928 football schedule included Northwest Conference competition primarily, but both the Universities of Oregon and Washington appeared as well. Willamette's season record in 1928 was 3-5-0, due to a porous defense.

Despite the less than spectacular start to his football coaching career, Spec "was inducted into the Oregon Sports Hall of Fame in 1982 for his coaching." The reason for Joe leaving Willamette after the 1928 football season is not known. After Joe's departure, however, Spec's career began to soar. It is inferred that Joe had ambitions to head his own program. Being an assistant football coach for a fraternity brother was expedient but it was not a long-term solution .

Spec Keene is called the father of Willamette athletics, but Joe Kasberger played a role at both the beginning of, and throughout, Spec's tenure. He proved to be not only a grateful, but also a loyal, friend to Spec. Joe, therefore, might be seen as Willamette's generous uncle in the not-too-distant future. Oddly, Joe's tenure at Willamette is poorly understood.

The school year included Joe, again, coaching the women's basketball team at Mt. Angel Academy and Normal School. Other than the picture presented here, there is no additional information about the team and its record.

The summer of 1929 for Joe and other coaches did not include Knute Rockne in Corvallis. Why the Rockne coaches school was not conducted is not clear. In Sept. 1929, Rockne wrote Schissler with plans to be in Corvallis from June 16-28, 1930. In closing, Rockne referred to the Oregon State - Oregon rivalry. "It looks like McEwan has the men this year but that's all the more glory for you if you can knock

1928-29 Women's basketball team at Mt. Angel Academy and Normal School. The caption reads: "Grace Smith Aman (middle girl), Marie Flerchinger Antoine (third girl from right), Pauline Saalfeld (last girl on right), Joe Kaspberger [sic], coach."

'em off."[36] Rockne was prophetic, as Oregon defeated the Aggies 16-0. Joe is documented to have been a 1929 summer-session student at Oregon State in physical-education.

Bob Murray's last year as a football coach was 1928. Ironically, TDHS played their home games in this year "on Murray Field which had just recently been named for him." It was a good year despite a crushing conclusion. After winning six and losing one, the Indians were destroyed at home by Medford HS, 42-0, "before a local record crowd of 5,000 spectators. The game was summed up as a good big team against a good little one."[37]

Bob Murray coached the 1928-29 basketball team at TDHS to the Mid-Columbia District championship, earning the Indians a place in the state tournament at Willamette University. TDHS played well but did not appear to win the state title. Bob Murray's coaching record was now complete. Fortunately, Bob's son, Bill, has written on this complex subject.

One way of showing the record for all time is to quote Bob's total score as computed by himself. He has always claimed that his teams had won 882 games, lost 21 and tied 6. The Dalles scored 2,763 points to opponents, 651. These totals are so outstanding that they may be a composite of points from more than football games.[38]

The 1928-29 school year has events that are difficult to understand and link. Bill Murray writes about one event, handicapped by a paucity of records, that may have pertained to Joe as a prospective coach at TDHS.

Sometime in 1928 my father was showing dissatisfaction with his salary. In early 1929 he had submitted written resignation from his position as instructor and football coach. According to a representative of the office of the superintendent of public schools in a letter to the Forum of the Dalles *Daily Chronicle* , Mr. Murray had submitted his resignation at that time. He had been offered a $200 increase and refused it, claiming other more favorable opportunities. The Board indicated in its letter that he had been encouraged to accept their offer over a period of several weeks, but to no avail, also stating that he had not spoken to them after their offer.[39]

Besides Murray's 1929 resignation, there was a tragedy in The Dalles which involved Joe's baseball coach at TDHS, A.E. Gronewald, that may have impacted his career thinking.

On August 14, 1915, Allie married Hazel Huntington, a teacher at the West End School in The Dalles. Hazel was the older sister of Walter, Shy, and Hollis Huntington. Allie and Hazel had two chil-

Allie Gronewald, ca. 1929.

dren, Jerrold Alvin and Marilyn Rose, as well as one child who died at birth, Edward Herman. Allie was described by his daughter, Marilyn, as "a popular teacher who was a good example for his students." In addition, he was "soft spoken, honest, good-natured and thoroughly enjoyed working with young people." Not unlike the Kasbergers, Allie "viewed profanity as a sign of a deficiency of vocabulary which prevented accurate expression of true feelings."[40]

Allie did not serve during World War I, possibly because of his educational career. He did become involved in public affairs, however, when he "was appointed to the unexpired term of Wasco County School Superintendent. . . ." In this capacity, "his association with children continued with visits to county schools." Allie drove a little "Ford run-about," that enabled him to "faithfully visit all the schools in Wasco County at least twice a year – and there were a lot of one and two room schools in the teens and early twenties." In this capacity, Allie took a special interest in teachers. "He interviewed the candidates for teaching positions before they went to the local school boards. He often said, 'More language is caught than is taught.' He wanted a good example for his students." A story from a former student who observed Allie on a visit to a little school says much about his rapport with youngsters. As Allie "walked toward the building, he tossed a ball to the boys." The story continues:

They couldn't believe their luck and they played as hard and as fast as they could during recess and lunch time. When it was time for him to leave, with sad faces they brought the ball to him to take with him. He said 'Oh no! That is for you to keep!' They were the luckiest kids in the county that day and the memory and joy of that day endured.[41]

Allie's daughter, Marilyn G. Ericksen, was told this story by Kenny Kortge, whose "face reflected the emotions of those youngsters." Clearly, Allie enjoyed his work and his constituents rewarded him with reelection to the position in subsequent years. Besides teaching, Allie enjoyed farming since he was reared in a farming community. In pursuit of this interest, Allie became rather successful.

He brought 20 acres up 'Whiskey Gulch' (now re-named 'Orchard Road') SW of The Dalles. Part of it was planted to cherries and part of it he used for starting nursery stock for new cherry orchards. He raised Purebred White Wyndotte chickens and entered them in shows and laying competitions all over the Northwest. He had trap-nests in the chicken house which had a door that went shut when the chicken got into the nest to lay an egg. Each bird was identified by a numbered band on the leg, so he could keep accurate production records. He shipped fertile eggs to other chicken fanciers as well as operating a large incubator himself.

His cherries were raised 'dry-land' which made a firm sweet fruit of excellent quality. But the trees had to be planted 40 feet apart on the square so there would be enough moisture for the trees. Watermelons are also superior if they are 'dry-land' so he always had a good melon crop coming in between the rows of trees. He never had any trouble getting the high school kids to pick fruit for him because they knew after cherry season when the melons were ripe they would be invited to share a feast of the choice parts of the melons.[42]

Motivated by his interests in both education and farming, Allie "recognized the advantages of the 4-H program for youth and promoted those groups." Still he had time to remain involved with sports and was "always ready to referee sporting events and was accepted by all comers in the mid Columbia region as an unprejudiced, careful, fair, sporting official." As a religious man, Allie "was an active member of the Congregational church where he sang in the choir and taught a boy's Sunday School class." There were secular interests as well, especially the Kiwanis Club, where Allie "sang with the Kiwanis Quartet for club and community events." Completing this well-rounded man's activities was Allie's role as "one of the organizers of the Cherry Marketing Co-op which stabilized the cherry business."[43]

With so many activities it is surprising that Allie had time for a hobby. "He didn't do any hunting, but he was an ardent fisherman – and a remarkably successful one, "until one fateful day.

On July 14, 1929 he went fishing on the Deschutes River with his son and some friends. They were packing up to come home when Jerrold went to the bank to 'cast one more time.' His summer tennis shoes had lost their tread and he slipped off the wet rock into the churning, treacherous water near Sherar's Bridge. Allie heard him call and without stopping to remove boots or clothing, dived in to save him. He reached his son. He was a fine swimmer but was not able to get out of the whirlpools. The friends tried to extend poles to him, but they could not quite reach. It was a day of heartbreak for the whole community – the kids, the service clubs, the educational personnel, sports groups, the church, the orchardists – all felt the loss of their friend.

The bodies were not found readily. The trains traveling the banks of the Deschutes were ordered to travel slowly so all the personnel could watch carefully for any sign of a body. After a couple of weeks they spotted Allie's body but Jerrold's never surfaced. An evening graveside service was held for them at The Dalles IOOF cemetery late in July.[44]

In the fall, Allie's widow attended Monmouth Normal School for her teaching certificate. "She taught two and a half years at Falls City, Polk County, OR then returned to The Dalles in 1934 and taught first and/or second grades until she retired for health reasons in 1947."[45] Given the mood of The Dalles in the wake of these events, perhaps, Joe's next move was not all that unusual.

Presumably, Oregon high-school athletes were thought by some to be coached best only by those with college degrees. Was such a policy a measure of vengeance against Bob's successful teams? Or, was it a vendetta to "get" Murray as a person? In any case, this public policy may have been more broadly aimed than described by the accounts presented here. Two accounts of this episode follow. First, it is reported that: "In 1929 Murray retired as athletic director for the high school as a result of academic standards requiring coaches to have a college degree in education." The second account follows.

> . . . Bob Murray left The Dalles high school as coach in 1929. As soon as Murray left the coaching staff a law was enacted, 'requiring high school coaches to have a college degree in education.' As Murray was the only high school coach in Oregon without such a degree this legislation was in reality directed against him, which shows how much the teams he produced were feared by officials of opposing schools.[46]

Conversely, Bob may have engaged in brinksmanship and lost. "Bob had been grandfathered into his position under 1921 rules requiring certification in teaching on the part of all coaches."[47] For a spectacularly successful coach with only an eighth-grade education, he may have been treading on thin ice in an evolving public debate about coaches and the role of athletics in Oregon. Yet Murray had his supporters, especially after his unidentified successor was unsuccessful in the 1929 football season. In response to his friends, and perhaps coming to his senses, Murray reapplied for his old job.

> The School Board, perhaps under pressure to meet the needs of the school calendar, had expressed its intention to renew the contract of the preceding year with Bob's successor. The Board's response to the reapplication was negative. The reapplication was followed by a petition for reinstatement by over two hundred supporters, including many from the business community and presented by local lawyer, Francis Galloway, Wasco County District Attorney. The petition clearly had no effect. The Monday morning quarterbacks had lost their fight.[48]

On the surface, what appears to be a local matter may have suddenly shifted to statewide politics and education policy in the State of Oregon. The assertion that there was a "Murray Law," aimed to get only Bob Murray, appears related to the following facts provided by Bill Murray:

The clamor for reinstatement may have been the result of word that the Oregon State High School Athletic Association (OSHAA) was showing some indication that it might make exceptions to its rule established at its meeting of December, 1929. At that time it had passed an amendment to its rule stipulating 'no school shall be a member of the Oregon State High School Athletic Association if the athletic coach, director or instructor is not a full time teacher in the regular school, and no part of the salary or pay is to come from any other source than the school organization employing him.'

As would be expected, the ruling at the meeting of December, 1929, recorded no names of anyone at whom the rule was aimed or intended. However, it was clear that with this ruling my father's career in high school coaching had ended – at least in the state of Oregon! It is difficult to understand the political dynamics of such a rule in the life of the Athletic Association, but one may speculate about them as did many in The Dalles. Standards of education and pay of coaches in our high schools and colleges had been the subject of discussion and concern for several years.[49]

Perhaps there is more to the Bob Murray story. Bill Murray's research into available documentation finds a vacuum of knowledge that has yet to be filled.

I have no knowledge that the business community was proposing or planning to subsidize an increase in Bob's salary. It of course could be that the State Superintendent of Public Instruction was interested in elevating the standards of education for coaches with other situations in mind. The superintendent had the power of appointment to the Board of the State Association.

In any case, Bob was barred from application to any high school in the state by its action of December, 1929. At age 49 he had a critical problem. In my opinion we still have the problem of learning the truth about it.[50]

Regrettably, the impact was not benign for Bob Murray and his family.

I believe it was in the aftermath of all this that I began to listen to the whispered family talk about possible moves to such places as Nampa, Idaho and Pomona, California. The moves never occurred as my parents assumed responsibility for my grandparents who in their old age and ill health had come to live with us. Clearly we were in no state to move anywhere.[51]

In spite of this episode, Bob Murray remained a visible and active role-model for the youth of The Dalles. Equally important, perhaps, Murray remained in The Dalles as a respected and beloved citizen. The fact that neither Joe Kasberger, nor Hollis Huntington, nor any other former TDHS player succeeded Bob as head coach appears important as a sign of their solidarity about this event.

1929-30 School Year

Astonishingly, the 1929 football season found Joe in Ashland, OR as an assistant football coach to Roy W. McNeal, at Southern Oregon Normal College, founded in 1926. This institution's evolution was erratic, since its predecessor opened as a private school in 1869. The school was refounded as a state normal school in 1882. The original teacher's school closed in 1909, but reopened again in 1926 as Southern Oregon Normal College. With this as background, Joe arrived for the third football season in the school's history.

Ashland is located close to Medford near the Oregon-California border, more than 200 miles from Joe's familiar territory around the Willamette Valley. Ashland is described as spectacular, in the shadow of 7,500-foot Mount Ashland. Nearby attractions include the rugged Rogue River and remarkable Crater Lake. Ashland is not far from Jacksonville, the town that first attracted Fr. Adelhelm to Oregon because of the natural beauty around the Rogue River. The alpine setting at the base of the Siskiyou Mountains made for a superior quality of life. Perhaps the natural beauty brought Joe to Ashland. More likely, it was a potential head-coaching opportunity.

The aging Coach McNeal may have been looking for an heir in a few years. Without question, Joe came to Ashland highly recommended. It is possible that Joe and McNeal were acquainted. McNeal had coached at Albany College from 1917-22 before going to Portland's Lewis and Clark College. The next coaching stop was at the College of Puget Sound in Tacoma from 1922-27. Coach McNeal was a graduate of the University of Arizona and had other roles besides coaching, including teaching geography.

Before McNeal coached Southern Oregon's first football team in 1927, there was work to do. The *Media Guide* described McNeal as "the school's lone physical-education instructor," with many hats. He "was entrusted with the demanding task of starting the program." McNeal was versatile at the task of creating facilities for the football team.

Despite limited resources, McNeal was successful in creating an 8-by-30-foot dressing room and shower facility. Next, he convinced a highway construction crew working on the Old Siskiyou Highway to utilize their machinery after work to level out a playing field.[52]

Despite the availability of heavy machinery, manual labor was needed. McNeal enlisted students and faculty with "picks and shovels to put the finishing touches on a dirt-and gravel-based field," with a flaw. Reportedly, "the field had a definite slope from end to end," which made it unique. Capitalizing on this defect, "teams winning the coin toss always chose the uphill end of the field because, naturally, it was easier to run downhill."[53]

McNeal's inaugural team, the Red and Black Raiders as they were known, was outstanding. Sept. 26, 1927 was the first day of practice with 25 players on hand. The Raiders "won all three of its scheduled games, a record that would

Southern Oregon Normal's 1929 Football Squad

Reading from left to right front row: Truelove, Mgr., Pruitt, Callan, Howe, Brown, Conrad, Schneiderman (captain), Barrett, Johnson, McNeal (coach).
Second Row: Eri, Hines, Wilson, McDonald, McGee, Ayer, Hunsaker, Iverson, Reams, Brandon, Tucker, Prowse, Moe, Kasberger (assistant coach).

Joe (far right) as assistant football coach with the 1929 Southern Oregon Normal State College team.

stand until 1946." The 1927 season saw two shutout victories, 21-0 against Lewis and Clark and 32-0 against Humboldt State (CA), to open the season. The final game was a 19-12 victory over Western Oregon of Monmouth, OR.

McNeal's 1928 season ended in a 1-3-1 record, including a 0-6 loss to Oregon State Frosh and a 0-0 tie with the University of Oregon Frosh in the opening games. The season concluded with a 9-38 loss to Chico State (CA); 31-12 victory over Humboldt State; and a 0-12 loss to Western Oregon in the finale. The performance of McNeal's first two teams must have given Joe encouragement as the 1929 season began.

Joe was the subject of a flattering and revealing story in the Oct. 1929 student newspaper, *Siskiyou.* The writer, Gil Moe, was a Southern Oregon Normal football player. The story had a picture of Joe, who may have been wearing the 1918 Camp Lewis football uniform. The story had the headline: "Kasberger Commended as Player." The text follows:

> Joe Kasberger, all Pacific Coast half back of 1921 while playing on O.S.C. football team, former director of athletics at Mt. Angel College, and for the last two years assistant to 'Spec' Keene, coach of Willamette University, has been employed as assistant at the Southern Oregon Normal School.
>
> Kasberger comes to the local school highly recommended both as a coach and player.
>
> Joe Kasberger claims The Dalles as his native home. At Mt. Angel College he played on the major teams in baseball, football, and basketball and made an excellency medal in commerce and received a teaching certificate in shorthand.

The story continues with the assertion that Joe had two degrees from Oregon

State. Joe has only the 1922 degree per Oregon State University archives.

> The scholastic record made by Mr. Kasberger at Oregon State College from which he graduated in 1922 with a B.S. Degree in Agriculture and M.A. Degree in Commerce, was equalled by his record in football.
> He played all positions in the backfield and was recognized as one of the best utility men on the squad.
> In addition to his football record he won the Silver Loving cup for scholarship and athletics in his senior year and the cup given by the Stock Judging team in the Portland International Livestock show. He was elected to Forum, the highest Agricultural Honorary. He was also chairman of the Greater O.S.C. Committee.
> During the World War he played Quarterback on the Army team at Camp Lewis and in 1924 attended Notre Dame University being on the same squad as the 'Four Horsemen,' later attending the two football schools at O.S.C.
> After graduating from O.S.C. he accepted a position of director of athletics at Mt. Angel College, continuing for two years until the college burned down in the fall of 1926, at which time he took the position at Willamette University.
> While coaching at Mt. Angel a splendid record was made in athletics, during the 1925-26 season, his football squad won seven out of eight games played. In basketball the team won fifteen out of 19 games, and seventeen out of eighteen games played in baseball. All were played in the Willamette Valley Conference.
> Southern Oregon Normal should feel proud to be able to employ a man with such a successful background. It also shows the progress the school is making not only in scholastic fields but also on the athletic field.[54]

California schools dominated Southern Oregon's 1929 schedule, a situation with sorry results. The season began with consecutive home losses to Menlo Park JC (Junior College), 12-20 and Marin JC, 6-19. After an away game tie, 0-0 at Western Oregon, there was a severe road loss, 7-62 to Sacramento JC. The season ended with three home games: a 20-7 win over Chico State.; a 27-7 win over Humboldt State; and finally, on Nov. 30, a 12-18 loss to Modesto JC. What is known next about Joe comes from his 1929 Christmas cards.

In Salem, Spec's 1929 season was successful with a 6-2-0 record. One very credible observer of the 1929 team was Joe's replacement as Willamette's line coach, Emil Hauser. He was also known as "Wauseka," an All-American for Pop Warner at Carlisle Institute. In Hauser's view, "the 1929 champions were the best all-around football team Keene ever fielded." Hauser added that this team "had the best combination of any of a powerful offense and a rockbound defense." Willamette had turned the corner in football, and the groundwork was in place for future successes. In addition, Spec's basketball and baseball teams in 1929 "swept the conference in every major sport."[55]

The next sequence of events remains vague. Apparently, Joe made a monumental decision during the fall of 1929, to pursue a master's degree in physical education at Columbia University in New York City. It is possible that at this time, also, Joe received an offer to coach in California that may have been contingent upon Joe obtaining his master's degree. Possibly the coaching offer was a result of California contacts made by Joe during the 1929 football season. What is not documented is the assertion that Joe was headed to UCLA (University of California at Los Angeles) after graduate school at Columbia. The 1942 "Greg's Gossip" column in the *Oregonian* validated the notion, vaguely, that California and teaching were on Joe's future agenda.

Linking Joe to Columbia University is Ralph Coleman. The baseball field at Oregon State has been in continuous existence since 1906 and is now known as Coleman Field, a tribute to Ralph, who influenced not only Joe but other young men. In 1923, OAC "transferred his coaching activities to varsity baseball, a position he filled until 1931," presumably as head coach. Coleman's tenure as Beaver baseball coach lasted from 1923 to 1931 with one interlude. In 1928, Coleman left Corvallis "to go back to Columbia University in New York City to work and obtain his master's degree in physical education."[56] It may be noted in passing that during the interim period when Coleman was not Oregon State's baseball coach, Slats Gill filled in.

As Oregon State's baseball coach, Coleman produced several professional players.

> Among these are Wes Schulmerick [sic], now a pitcher with Philadelphia in the National League; Ed Coleman, a brother, now with the Athletics and making good in a big way as a hard-hitting outfielder; Howard Maple, who in addition to playing baseball was a star quarterback on the football team at Oregon State, and is now with Chattanooga in the Southern League as a catcher; Laurence Baker, now with Jersey City in the International League; and 'Red' Bouton, now with Omaha in the Western League.[57]

Joe's decision to attend Columbia University was a major one. Tuition was expensive and living costs in New York City were exorbitant, compared to those in Oregon. There appears to be no single cogent reason for the decision that he made. Perhaps a World War I bonus check or veterans benefits made the decision financially feasible. It is speculated that he spent the holiday season at home, and prepared for the great East Coast adventure upon which he embarked.

Joe's 1929 Christmas card to Frank Milbauer is the first documentation that he was coming East. Frank's subsequent response began another chain of events that proved fortuitous for many as they unfolded. When Frank received his annual Christmas greeting from Joe, it had the arresting news that he was coming to New York City in January. Moreover Joe wanted to visit and renew their friendship. Frank's sister, Claire, wrote his Christmas cards, and was familiar with Joe's name. Joe was always at the top of Frank's Christmas card list, the two men having exchanged season's greetings annually since 1924.[58]

At 6' 3" and 285 pounds, Frank Milbauer was a huge man by standards of his day. In 1924, Frank dwarfed his smaller Notre Dame teammates and surely stood out. Joe Kasberger, at 5'10" and 180 pounds, was of average size for football players in that era. The size differential between these men was humorously captioned by Joe in a photo of the two together, in his personal photo album. How Frank and Joe became acquainted is unclear, but the relationship made in 1924 lasted for the rest of their lives. The initial link between Joe and Frank was a mutual interest in agriculture. Frank's Notre Dame degree was in agriculture, and after graduation he returned to Newark and took a position in the insurance industry. In that role, Frank spent much time with Southern New Jersey farmers, managing insurance agents with farmers for clients.

Frank's education until the sixth grade took place at Sacred Heart Grammar School in Newark's Vailsburg neighborhood. As he grew, the school's desks became too small. Frank's mother, Louise, had two cousins who were Benedictine monks, Rev. William Koellhoffer and Rev. Maurus McBarron, both assigned to St. Benedict's Prep (SBP). Louise and her husband, Frank W., were familiar with SBP because they attended functions at the "Casino," adjacent to the SBP campus. This facility was a landmark for Newark's German-community which was then focused on St. Mary's Church. The Casino served dual purposes: as a gym for SBP; and as a social center for the parish. Frank went to SBP's lower division to complete his primary education. He remained at SBP for his secondary education and graduated in 1921, known for his size and athletic prowess.[59]

Little is known about Frank's SBP football career, except that he was big at 269 pounds. He was described as a "mountain of strength," and named to the all-state football team as a guard.[60] More is known about his performance as a shot-putter on the track-and-field team. Frank won two gold medals in 1921, to provide a clue to his skill in this event. The first gold medal was in the shot-put at SBP's Field Day. The second was won at the New Jersey Interscholastic Athletic Association Track and Field meet at Stevens Institute of Technology, Hoboken, on April 4, 1921 – with the twelve-pound shot. In later years, he continued as a shot-putter and hammer-thrower with even heavier weights. Having attracted the attention of college coaches, Notre Dame was next!

Besides Frank Milbauer, SBP's Class of 1921 produced another great athlete for Notre Dame. The classmate who accompanied Frank to South Bend was Bernard Shanley, Jr. Both men were influenced in their decision by Bernard Shanley, Sr. The young Shanley captained SBP's undefeated state-championship basketball team that was the first to play in the new Shanley Gymnasium. Bernard, Jr. made the all-state team as a guard in basketball, and lettered in baseball. His father, Bernard Shanley, Sr., SBP's Class of 1888, was the donor of Shanley Gymnasium. Bernard, Jr. did not remain at Notre Dame, and had the distinction of having two teammates, one at SBP and one in college, who became major-leaguers. He returned East and gained fame at Columbia University as a baseball player, best remembered as Lou Gehrig's roommate.[61]

As a prize football recruit for Knute Rockne, Frank was recalled to have never gotten any bigger or thinner at Notre Dame. Frank's arrival in South Bend, as a member of the Class of 1925, brought him into contact with an outstanding crop of Rockne players who became Notre Dame's first national championship team. From this talented group of athletes, emerged the storied "Four

Horsemen" and "Seven Mules." Their coach, Knute Rockne, was just now achieving national fame. Most importantly, perhaps, these great men gave Notre Dame a national reputation that the small Catholic school coveted.[62]

Frank played tackle on the 1921 freshman team. As a sophomore in 1922, he was a reserve tackle on the varsity, playing behind the following upper classmen: Forrest (Fod) Cotton, 6-1, 182; Gus Stange, 6-2, 195; Jack Flynn, 6-1, 195; Gene Oberst, 6-4, 203; Tom Lieb, 6-0, 195; and Edgar (Rip) Miller, 5-11, 177. By the 1923 season, Frank was a starter as a junior, and clearly the largest man on this squad.[63] His name, however, does not appear with the 1924 squad. Whether he had sustained a career-ending injury, or was, perhaps, too big for the Rockne style of play, is not known. Apparently Frank's football career was over, but the 1924 Notre Dame team won the national championship anyway.

According to the 1925 Notre Dame yearbook, *Dome*, Frank Augustine Milbauer graduated in 1925 with an agriculture degree, belonging to several campus organizations:

New Jersey Club, 1. Knights of Columbus, 3. Varsity Football, 3. Freshman Football. Varsity Track, 3. Monogram club, 2.[64]

Frank Milbauer in track uniform at Notre Dame, ca. 1924.

Frank will always remain prominent as a member of Rockne's football teams. It was in field events, however, that he really excelled under Notre Dame's track-and-field coach, Knute K. Rockne. The research by Frank's grandson, Christopher Seelen, is presented here. He is the son of Frank's oldest daughter, Mary Jean. Christopher gathered this material as a Notre Dame student, after seeing Frank's plaque in their Hall of Fame.

Another distinction for Frank was being one of twenty-four "monogram men" on Rockne's 1924-25 indoor and outdoor track-and-field team. Notre Dame's first outdoor meet was on April 5 against DePauw University in Greencastle, IN. A story of the meet mentioned Frank as follows:

The strong arm of Milbauer was in excellent condition, and the portly shot putter put the shot close to forty-one feet, far enough to win first place in the event.[65]

The only other references to Frank's performance as a Notre Dame shot-putter come from summaries of events for the top three places. Winning distances reveal that Frank improved from the indoor season to the final meet of the outdoor season. In the Indiana State Track Championships, at Notre Dame's Cartier Field on May 24, 1925, Frank won first place with a heave of 43 feet and 1 inch. This effort was probably the highlight of his Notre Dame shot-putting career, but was not his personal best in the 1924-25 season. His best came on May 9, 1925 in Delaware, OH, against Ohio Wesleyan, when Frank won the event by putting the shot 43 feet and eleven and one-half inches.[66] After returning to Newark, he remained active in shot-putting and hammer-throwing under the guidance of SBP's track and field coach, Jim Cavanagh. Frank competed as a member of the New York Athletic Club (NYAC) through 1930 and won two gold medals at the New Jersey Athletic Association Championships. The first gold medal was with the 35-pound hammer; the second was with the 50-pound hammer.

Joe's decision to attend CTC for his master's degree in physical education culminated a turbulent life-phase. Ever since the 1926 fire, Joe appeared to be adrift. The chance to assist Spec was a convenient interim career move. The move to Ashland in 1929 must not have satisfied Joe, and the coaching position at TDHS does not appear to have been of interest under the circumstances surrounding the vacancy. Joe had grown more mature and pragmatic now that the MAC opportunity was lost. It was a once-in-a-lifetime arrangement that was now over. The college was not going to restore intercollegiate athletics, so he needed to get on with his life elsewhere – but where? Coaching was in his blood, or else he would not be so determined to get back on a full-time basis. After having such a superior situation at MAC, finding an acceptable position of comparable stature and potential would be very difficult. Probably not lost in Joe's thoughts, also, was the Great Depression which had just begun.

CTC admitted Joe for the semester that began in Feb. 1930. Also he received Frank's Christmas card with detailed instructions for the trip to New York City. In late January, Joe left The Dalles and followed his friend's advice. Since Joe may have never been east of South Bend, IN, traveling to New York and getting settled was a challenge. To have a friend in New Jersey ready to help certainly made the trip infinitely easier. When his train arrived in Washington, DC, Joe wired Frank as instructed. Joe advised that he was arriving on the "B and O" (Baltimore and Ohio) Railroad at the Elizabeth station, and Frank was there to meet him. The two then toured in and around Newark. The vast urban area may have been an impressive sight to Joe's eyes. The 1920s are described as Newark's golden years, and the city was big, busy and crowded by Oregon standards. The full impact of the Wall Street crash of 1929 was not yet felt in Newark.[67]

In 1930, Newark was at its zenith, in population, and in prosperity as a famous manufacturing city. Strategically located as a port and rail center,

Newark was an economic powerhouse, the envy of many other cities. There was much for Joe to see in the few days that were available. Then he had to hit the books as a full-time graduate student, in a very demanding and prestigious atmosphere. Joe arrived at the Milbauer home on his 34th birthday, Jan. 31, 1930, traveling with only one suitcase and a typewriter. A steamer trunk was forwarded directly to his dormitory. Joe stayed with the Milbauers for about one week, before Frank drove him to New York and the last stop of his trip. With Frank's assistance, Joe moved into his assigned room at 507 Furnald Hall.[68]

The 1930 *Catalog for Teachers College of Columbia University* advised that graduate-degree candidates were given placement tests. The results determined the scope of the course work required for the degree. Joe's academic background in business and agriculture, rather than education, may have created a problem from the very beginning. Also, there was fine print about residency requirements for graduate degrees. An academic year in residence was not an unusual requirement at CTC by today's standards. Why did Joe think that he could complete his degree requirements in the spring and summer semesters? Perhaps when Ralph Coleman attended CTC, the requirements were different from those now in place. Or maybe Joe misunderstood or misread the *Catalog*.[69]

For whatever reason, Joe planned to head west at the end of the summer term, master's degree in hand, and report to UCLA as an assistant football coach. That is what Joe was thought to be thinking on Jan. 31, 1930 as recalled vividly by Claire Milbauer. The UCLA job may have been contingent upon Joe's having a master's degree from CTC. Joe's decision to attend CTC appears related to its national prestige as the best graduate physical-education program – that attracted the best students nationally. Knute Rockne may have been Joe's link to UCLA and Bill Spaulding, recently named as UCLA's head coach, with Rockne's recommendation.[70] As a Midwesterner, it is possible Spaulding became acquainted with Joe through Rockne, possibly at the 1924 coaches school in South Bend. With its high academic aspirations, UCLA may have had a policy that all coaches would have master's degrees.

Joe may have thought his education and experience immunized him from certain requirements. CTC, however, had strict requirements for all candidates without exceptions and Joe did not receive any waivers. He was soon settled into his dormitory room located on Broadway between West 115th and 116th Streets. Almost immediately, he could not resist the temptation to ride the famous New York subway. As "a railroad person," Joe was naturally attracted by the subway, especially with the Columbia University Station across the street from his dorm room. Joe rode the subway to the end of the line at the southern tip of Manhattan. From there, he did what he loved to do, and began walking the nearly seven miles back to Columbia. Joe's only complaint was the absence of drinking fountains, which were common at home.[71]

The graduate course load was heavy and there are no indications of Joe becoming involved with Columbia athletics other than attending campus events as a spectator. It is believed that he visited the Polo Grounds, Yankee Stadium, Ebbets Field, and Madison Square Garden, the major sports venues of New

York. Joe managed, however, to spend "virtually every weekend"at the Milbauer home. He "would bring his typewriter and books," and often accompanied Frank Milbauer to Benedict Field, where he observed him training in track-and-field events. When not with Frank or studying, Joe "enjoyed working in the Milbauer garden as a diversion from his studies."[72]

At one of Frank's workouts, Joe became acquainted with Jim Cavanagh – who, by one account, had been appointed as SBP's athletic director. Cavanagh had a reputation for generating state-championship track-and-field teams in Newark. When the head football-coach position became vacant is unknown, but SBP was looking for a replacement for George "Dewey" Hines as head football coach for the 1930 season. It is not clear when, and under what circumstances, Hines left SBP. Surely Joe must have known of the opening through his relationship with Frank. Around this time, also, Knute Rockne was in Newark to recruit Hugh Devore, SBP's star football player from the 1929 team.[73]

The question of timing in the spring and summer of 1930 seems very important for SBP. A football coach was needed at a rather late point in the year. Presumably, they would have liked to have had someone under contract when the school-year ended in June of 1930. Incredibly, in late July, with preseason practice only six weeks away, their head football-coaching position was still open. Also, SBP needed someone to teach freshman English. With SBP's situation understood, what questions concerned Joe? Was he still intent on going to UCLA when CTC's summer term began in June? It is recalled that Joe told the Milbauers some "bad news" at the end of July, announcing that his degree requirements could not be met at the end of the summer term. There was a residency requirement, necessitating an additional course in the fall semester.[74]

It is not known if Joe contacted Bill Spaulding to withdraw from the UCLA position. Perhaps it was understood that Joe could not fill the position without the graduate degree. Possibly UCLA advised Joe that the position was closed to him without the master's degree. It is possible, however, that UCLA would hold the assistant coaching position open until he completed the master's degree. UCLA probably needed a coach at the end of August or early September, and Joe might no longer be expected. There are no answers to these nagging questions.

Upon hearing Joe's "bad news," Frank Milbauer took immediate action on his behalf. "It was at that time that he talked things over with Frank Milbauer who knew that St. Benedict's Prep had an opening for a coach/teacher in September." Apparently Joe expressed enough interest for Frank to take the next step. "That week Frank made arrangements at St. Benedict's to take Joe to the school for a conference when he returned the next weekend."[75] Adding to the difficulty were the effects of the Depression, which were becoming more pronounced. Perhaps any job was a good one for a graduate student a continent away from home. Joe probably became acquainted, or at least familiar, with several SBP and other New Jersey players while at Notre Dame. In addition, Joe probably knew that Rockne recruited in New Jersey, as demonstrated by his Newark visit to recruit Hugh Devore. Obviously it was a state with football talent.

SBP had gained a reputation for having these fine football players. Certainly

Joe discussed the matter with Frank to get insights into the current instability in the SBP athletic program. It is possible, but thought unlikely, that Joe prepared a vita or resumé for Frank to show SBP's headmaster, Rev. Boniface Reger, O.S.B.

As headmaster since 1926, Fr. Boniface knew what the school wanted. Then there was Abbot Ernest Helmstetter, who was so important in SBP's development during his tenure as president, who had to be consulted. With these considerations, the Abbot of St. Mary's Abbey and the headmaster of SBP were important since they controlled the SBP's budget and made the major personnel decisions.

It would not be surprising if Abbot Ernest had more than a passing interest in any prospective coach. He probably had strong opinions about the background of a candidate, understanding the importance of sports to SBP and the character of the teams' coaches. It is likely that Fr. Boniface and Abbot Ernest discussed Joe's credentials and may have contacted Mt. Angel for references, since Joe's background made him an ideal candidate. Joe's pending CTC degree certainly carried lots of

Rev. Boniface Reger, Joe's first headmaster, served from 1926 to 1943 and was prior from 1940 to 1944.

clout, especially when combined with his experience, success and strong recommendations. Joe may have been too good to be true, possibly appearing overqualified.

SBP offered Joe the football coaching position, with the additional responsibility of teaching five classes of freshman English. In addition to the salary, SBP offered Joe housing. Thus, he "was to have a room in the field house as long as he wanted to live there."[76] The two-year contract offered to Joe, as described by Glicken, suggests great interest on SBP's side and they may have been more interested in Joe than he was in them. This inference is based on Glicken's account that Joe only wanted a one-year contract, since he did not know whether he would like SBP, or it would like him.[77] After accepting SBP's offer, Joe wrote his father to advise him of the decision. The salary was believed to be $3,300 per year but there is no evidence that there was ever a formal contract with SBP.[78] The Depression made everyone pragmatic. SBP may not have been what Joe wanted, but he must have been grateful for what was available.

Joe, on paper, does not appear at first glance

Abbot Ernest Helmstetter, elected in 1910, was in that position when Joe first came to St. Benedict's.

to be the perfect match for a Newark prep school. The initial suggestion of incompatibility between SBP and Joe was further aggravated by the appearance of instability in the athletic department at the end of the 1930 school year. Ernest "Prof" Blood would relinquish his state-championship baseball team of 1930 to Joe, under unknown circumstances, and SBP suddenly had three very successful coaches. A question may have arisen as to whether they could work together.

Culturally and geographically, Newark was far from The Dalles. Joe's six months in New York City may not have prepared him for Newark as much as one might think. The only reason for the potential success of a long-term relationship in this equation was the Benedictines. With the monks of St. Mary's Abbey, Joe was getting a known commodity, not unlike what he had known at Mount Angel. In this context, Joe may have used the resources available to him at Columbia to learn more about Newark and SBP.

St. Mary's-Newark Abbey Prior to 1930

Joe's familiarity with the Swiss Benedictines at Mt. Angel helped him in his relationship with the Bavarian Benedictines in Newark. There were differences, however, in these two communities. The Newark Benedictine root system extended through St. Vincent's Abbey in Latrobe, PA to the Bavarian Abbey of Metten. The Newark Benedictines were then, and remain today, a unique community. Despite their agrarian origins, they are not farmers, and their monastic home in a city was and is very unusual. The Benedictine presence in Newark is one of the oldest in the United States, stemming from 1836 when Rev. Nicholas Balleis, O.S.B. arrived in Newark from St. Peter's Abbey in Salzburg, Austria. This sole Benedictine responded to a call from New York Bishop John DuBois for priestly help to serve the 1830 German immigration wave. Fr. Balleis first ministered to Newark's German immigrants at St. John's Church on Mulberry Street. In later years, he served them at St. Mary's Church on High Street.[79]

This pioneering monk was followed by a formal Benedictine presence in the United States more than a decade later. The official Benedictine entry into the United States appears related to the recommendation of another Catholic religious order, the Redemptorist Congregation of Priests and Brothers, with American headquarters in Baltimore, MD. The Redemptorists assisted German immigrants to America through their network in the major European cities when the immigration process began. Upon arrival in the United States, the Redemptorists helped immigrants settle in an unfamiliar urban environment. A German immigrant group of families in Philadelphia and Baltimore proposed to settle in rural Elk County, PA. Religious persecution in Philadelphia and Baltimore had made the Germans determined to relocate to a refuge of their own. The Redemptorists, however, declined a request to accompany them West. Their persistence led to the assignment of Rev. Alex Czitkovicz for temporary aid. Fr. Alex was versatile and surveyed the virgin Pennsylvania forest before platting the town site of St. Mary's, PA. Next, he designed a church and prepared rules for the community. Then he arranged for them to receive new German immigrants who might arrive in Baltimore. Finally, Fr. Alex advised that they appeal to German Benedictines since "they are farmers" and could help.[80]

By 1846, Abbot (then Father) Boniface Wimmer, O.S.B. arrived in the United States and established a monastic community of fifteen members at what became St. Vincent's Abbey in Latrobe, PA. They came from the Bavarian Abbey of Metten. Immediately, Abbot Wimmer, a "missionary at heart," sent monks to serve German immigrants including two to assist Father Nicholas in Newark: Fr. Placidus Doettl, O.S.B., who came in 1846 and served until 1849 when replaced by Fr. Charles Geyerstanger, O.S.B.[81] Abbot Wimmer had an agrarian mindset, and saw his mission as one of following immigrants to rural areas in the West. However, there was another plea to serve German immigrants in an Eastern city that was deemed inconsistent with his vision and the Benedictine tradition.[82]

Rome established The See of Newark, NJ in 1854 and its new Bishop, James Roosevelt Bayley, needed priests to serve his flock. Bishop Bayley began a persistent effort to convince Abbot Wimmer that his monks were needed by the German immigrants in his city. Fr. Nicholas, was nearing burnout with the demands of his ministry at St. Mary's Church, then operated by the Redemptorists, taking a toll. The final straw, probably, was violence inflicted upon that church during a "Know-Nothing" riot in 1851 – which may have led to Fr. Nicholas' request for reassignment. In this atmosphere, Bishop Bayley intensified his campaign to procure Benedictines, but Abbot Wimmer had a manpower problem himself. He had already sent most of his monks to missions and parishes in four states and was opposed to Newark for two reasons. First, he was "ambivalent, if not fearful of urban life."
Second, he felt that going West was a higher priority for his community.[83]

Bishop Bayley was displeased with Abbot Wimmer's reasoning and responded: "I cannot understand what East or West has to do with the matter when the question is salvation of souls . . . . " In terms of sheer numbers to be served, Abbot Wimmer was probably swayed by Bishop Bayley's profound argument supporting his request for Newark. "There are in this city some six thousand German Catholics and the number is increasing." In Sept. 1854, Abbot Wimmer was swayed by Bishop Bayley, and responded by writing: "I am very willing to do anything in my power to satisfy a good Bishop." Shortly thereafter, Abbot Wimmer sent Fr. Valentine Felder to replace the Redemptorist at St. Mary's Church. A week later, Abbot Wimmer sent Eberhard Gahr, a subdeacon. Within a month, Fr. Rupert Seidenbusch was sent to begin the formal Benedictine commitment to

Archabbot Boniface Wimmer, 1809-1877.

Newark. As Abbot Wimmer anticipated, the urban Benedictines experienced tensions emerging from the diverse workload that they confronted. In Newark, they were asked to serve schools and parishes, give daily and weekend help to diocesan churches, convents and hospitals, all of which made living the monastic life difficult.[84]

For the Bavarian monks, it was a new and enlightening experience for which they were unprepared. Perhaps it was this first episode that sharpened the issue of defining American Benedictinism. Unlike the Benedictine commitment in Bavaria, the active versus the contemplative life in America represented a challenge. To some it was more than a challenge. It was a threat to the vocation that many of the monks chose. Nevertheless, the small Newark community of Benedictines grew quickly into a priory. In 1868 they founded St. Benedict's College, and the original intent to serve German immigrants soon changed as they served everyone. Much of this had to do with the vocations that they received in Newark. Reportedly, "less than half the men who entered the community during these years were of German descent." At St. Benedict's College, the monks taught all classes in English as a common language to reach the students who represented the many ethnicities in Newark. "As early as 1873, the school catalog listed a student body with a variety of immigrant names, only a minority of which were German."[85]

St. Benedict's College was so successful that the priory was elevated to abbey status in 1884, probably due to the graduation of 300 students in college preparatory and business programs. On July 22, 1885, Rev. James Zilliox was installed as St. Mary's Abbey's first abbot. Seventeen years after the founding of their college, the Newark Benedictines had become autonomous. The new abbey soon faced difficulties. After serving for only 18 months, Abbot James died of pneumonia and was succeeded in 1887 by Abbot Hilary Prfaengle. Despite this setback, the monks continued their work. In addition to teaching at the college, more than twenty members of St. Mary's Abbey performed other duties, including taking responsibility for many parishes and mission stations.

St. Mary's Abbey and St. Benedict's College in the early 1900s.

These included St. Mary's and St. Benedict's in Newark, Sacred Heart in Elizabeth, St. Leo's in Irvington, St. Mark's in Rahway, St. Boniface's in Paterson, St. Francis' in Trenton, and missions in Plainfield, Basking Ridge, Bound Brook, Stoney Hill, Westfield, Stirling, Summit, and Paterson.[86]

This expanding network brought more students to St. Benedict's College. Increasing enrollments led to more vocations at St. Mary's Abbey, and the growth of the community by 1886 extended beyond New Jersey. Soon added to its network were Sacred Heart Church in Wilmington, DE and St. Raphael's in Manchester, NH. Even before he was blessed as second abbot of St. Mary's Abbey in 1887, Abbot Hilary received word from Bishop Denis M. Bradley of Manchester, NH requesting a Benedictine foundation in his diocese. Abbot Hilary made an exploratory trip to Manchester to investigate the matter.[87]

After returning to Newark, Abbot Hilary sought the wisdom of Archabbot Wimmer about such an endeavor. The elderly Wimmer's response in 1887 was very important as advice to Abbot Hilary, then, and appears relevant now in understanding subsequent events at St. Mary's Abbey. Over the next eight decades, the archabbot's words appear increasingly prophetic. Archabbot Wimmer wrote Abbot Hilary as follows, regarding Manchester. The day school that is mentioned, of course, is St. Benedict's.

> The place in Manchester seems really [to] be acceptable, if only care of souls is the ambition, and a day school left to your good will; only I beg leave to remark, it might be a little premature, since you have so few priests . . . your day school there must be your main care, since your abbey depends chiefly on its grand standing.[88]

The Manchester visit impressed Abbot Hilary, and Wimmer's response seemed supportive. Despite some opposition during 1889-91, the Newark community voted favorably on the Manchester proposal. St. Mary's Abbey purchased the land, and began first phase construction for a college and seminary to serve the poor first- and sec-

Saint Anselm College building as it appeared in 1893.

ond-generation immigrant youth of New England.[89]

The rationale for founding the Manchester college was to train young monks for St. Mary's Abbey. The increasing number of monks in the Newark community made the decision plausible. The geography of this venture, however, seemed questionable, since Newark and Manchester were separated significantly by distance. Possibly there were cultural differences between Newark and Manchester as well. In Sept. 1893, in the middle of a national economic depression, St. Anselm's College was opened. The new college was placed under the patronage of the English Benedictine by that name. As planned, the new Manchester community provided St. Mary's Abbey with a college and school of theology. By the early 1920s the St. Anselm's community grew sufficiently for talks to begin about its independence. In the summer of 1927, St. Anselm's became an abbey and thirty monks of St. Mary's Abbey transferred their stability to Manchester.[90]

To compensate for St. Anselm's expected independence, plans were made in Newark. Abbot Ernest Helmstetter, the third abbot of St. Mary's Abbey, succeeded Abbot Hilary on his death in 1909. Abbot Ernest began looking in early 1925 for a new site to train young monks. According to accounts, two sites were of interest: "the Darlington estate in Mahwah and the Delbarton site in Morris Township, both in New Jersey." The decision-making process by the Abbot and the Newark community is not well documented.

> Few records exist suggesting the reasons for the eventual choice of the Delbarton site, and no discussion regarding the selection can be found in the written minutes of the chapter.[91]

Regardless, "Delbarton was selected on August 18, 1925 by chapter vote of a significant majority."[92]

The transaction was consummated quickly and a monastic community was established during the summer of 1926. St. Anselm's students and members of the Newark community were soon working at the new acquisition to expedite the establishment of a monastery. Documentation of the decision-making process to choose this site is not the only question associated with this estate. There appears to have been an ecclesiastical question as well.

> It is not known when the monastery in Morristown was canonically established as a dependent priory of St. Mary's Abbey. Since no records of this existed in the abbey or diocesan files, authorities later presumed that Bishop O'Connor and Abbot Ernest made a verbal agreement in 1926.[93]

Morristown affairs were a factor throughout Joe's Newark career. SBP was influenced by events that transpired within St. Mary's Abbey and this episode sets the monastic scene at the time of Joe's arrival.

St. Benedict's Prior to 1930

Unquestionably, the religious, educational and sports life of Newark was broadened by the 1868 founding of St. Benedict's College. From modest beginnings, St. Benedict's College and St. Mary's Abbey experienced impressive growth. Alumni of the successful college made many things possible for St.

Mary's Abbey. Immigrant sons distinguished themselves and their school upon entering the professional, technological and business ranks throughout the country. The leadership of Abbot Hilary Prfaengle appears to have been exceptional. Also important was the appointment in 1905 of Fr. Ernest Helmstetter as St. Benedict's fifth headmaster.

Athletics were significant in the school's development and may be the primary reason for its reputation, locally and nationally. Football became popular at the college level toward the end of the century and was soon played at the secondary-school level. St. Benedict's first sports team appears to have been football, when a club was formed in 1899 with 12 players and a manager. Initially there were problems with small enrollment and low interest. The first baseball team was fielded in 1906, but its record is not known. When Abbot Hilary died in 1909, St. Benedict's student body numbered 200. In 1910, Fr. Ernest succeeded Abbot Hilary as third abbot of St. Mary's Abbey. Also in 1910, St. Benedict's discontinued the college program; and then in 1917 changed its name to Prep. Coinciding with the name-change was the arrival of formal athletic programs. A baseball series began with Newark Central HS in 1912, but little is known about baseball's early years.[94]

In 1913, Rev. Valarian Kanetzky founded and coached the first varsity football team to a record of 4-3-0. The Sept. 30, 1941 *Benedict News* stated that the 1914 football team was winless, with record and competition unstated. In 1915, Fr. Augustine Wirth coached the football team to a 1-2-0 record. By 1916 Al Smith was the new football coach, but no competition or scores were given. The game's date is unreported, but SBP's largest football victory-margin ever was set as 81-0 against All Hallows HS of New York, in a year prior to 1930.[95]

Football and baseball are the sports of interest for this research. It should be noted, however, that SBP produced exceptional teams in basketball, cross-country, and track-and-field. Even soccer was played prior to 1930. SBP's growth led to the introduction of more lay faculty members. In 1919, a SBP alumnus, James Cavanagh, arrived from Newark Barringer HS as basketball and track coach, and was immediately successful.

His cross-country teams were state champions for the first fifteen years after he came to Saint Benedict's and four of his runners at one time held world marks.[96]

Shortly after Cavanagh's arrival, SBP began to develop facilities.

On March 21, 1919, the feast of Saint Benedict, Mr. Bernard M. Shanley, Jr. [sic] presented the school a large gift for the purpose of building a new gymnasium. The monastic chapter voted to buy the Halsey property adjoining the school. The acquisition of this property resulted in a decision to build a large addition to the school and a new gymnasium on the Halsey property. These additions were necessitated by the inadequacy of the existing building to accommodate the increasing number of students and by the lack of proper gymnastic facilities. The frame buildings on the property were torn down and the new buildings were erected, with the gymnasium being named in honor of the donor's father, Bernard M. Shanley, Sr.[97]

In 1920, Jack Fish became SBP's baseball coach, serving in that role through the 1925 season, winning a state championship in 1922. The 1920 football team was undefeated, but scores and competition are unknown, except for two teams. The season turned tragic when SBP player, Joe Carangelo, died from injuries suffered against Trenton Catholic HS. SBP played a postseason game against Newark South Side HS to pay his funeral expenses.[98]

In 1921, SBP's state-of-the-art Shanley Gymnasium was dedicated. Also in this year, famous athletes were graduating and moving on to the college level and beyond. Frank Milbauer and Bernard Shanley, Jr. were not the only famous athletes in the Class of 1921. Another classmate was Owen "Ownie" Carroll, who set a school pitching record of 49-2. He entered Holy Cross College and won 50 of 52 games that he pitched. Carroll played for nine years in the major leagues with several teams, before becoming Seton Hall University's baseball coach for 25 years, where he compiled a record of 341-188-6.[99]

Outdoor sports were next on the agenda of facility development under the direction of headmaster Fr. Cornelius Selhuber. He was instrumental in the early 1920s, organizing a fund-raising effort to acquire an athletic field. SBP's athletic teams played previously at "Asylum Field" in Newark. "This highly successful campaign culminated in 1925 with the purchase of four acres of property at Third Avenue and North Fifth Street."[100]

On April 18, 1925 Benedict Field was dedicated before 2,500 fans. SBP's opposition, in an 11-7 loss, was St. John's Prep from Danvers, MA.

That Fall, the first football game was played at Benedict Field, one of the most complete and modern athletic fields of the time, consisting of a baseball diamond, football field, tennis courts, and a quarter-mile track. The field had accommodations for 7,000 people for football and 2,000 people for baseball.[101]

1925 brought an outstanding basketball coach to SBP, Ernest "Prof" Blood, who had previously coached the Passaic, NJ High School "Wonder Team." SBP's "basketball team prospered under Prof's' leadership winning state championships for the next five years."[102] Coach Blood also coached baseball from 1926-30, winning a state championship in 1930 – after replacing Jack Fish, who coached baseball for the previous five years.

One of the most important headmasters in SBP's history was Fr. Boniface Reger. In 1926, he succeeded a legendary headmaster in his own right, Fr. Cornelius, who retired to Belmont Abbey in North Carolina. Both men are very important in SBP's history in terms of philosophy and stability enjoyed by the school, and its athletic programs.[103]

Once establishing Al Smith as SBP's football coach in 1916, it is not clear who held the position until the 1928 season. In that season, George D. "Dewey" Hines was the head coach with a 5-2-1 record, defeating archrival Seton Hall

Prep. In 1929, with Hines as the coach and Hugh Devore as team captain, SBP had a 4-4-0 record and lost to Seton Hall Prep. Jack Fish's position at SBP was presumed to be athletic director. In 1930, however, Fish became Seton Hall Prep's athletic director and it is unclear who may have replaced Fish as SBP's athletic director.[104]

Despite the urban setting, Joe probably found the Newark Benedictines akin to the sports-loving monks he knew in Oregon. Thus, the adaptation to be successful may have required an understanding and appreciation for the urban environment that was his new home. The Newark that Joe knew then differs considerably, of course, from the city of today.

The City of Newark Prior to 1930

Newark is the third oldest major city in the United States, founded in 1666 by thirty Puritan families from Connecticut. Led by Captain Robert Treat, they came in search of religious freedom and cheap farmland. The first Newarkers purchased most of what is now known as Essex County from the Lenni Lenape Indians in 1667 for $750-worth of weapons, powder, clothing, liquor, and supplies. The city was named Newark in honor of their pastor, Rev. Abraham Pierson – whose original home, was Newark-on-Trent, England. The early settlement of Newark was closely connected with the church known as Old First Presbyterian. Queen Anne granted the community a charter in 1713 and Newark became an incorporated town. As the population increased, diversity led to a second church in 1730, now known as Trinity Episcopal Cathedral, providing an alternative to strict Puritan ways. Population was estimated to be 1,000 at the time of the American Revolution in 1776. The war was divisive in Newark, but George Washington retreated through it in November en route to the Delaware River for his army's winter headquarters. In response, the British attacked and occupied Newark. Subsequent American independence led to Newark's rapid growth.[105]

With a critical population mass in place, an economic boom from local industry attracted waves of immigrants. An influx of immigrants in the early 1800s was important in the city's development. They were Irish and German in the 1830s and 1840s, followed by Italians and East Europeans toward the end of the century. Immigration provided the manpower necessary to build Newark's infrastructure, accomplishments that served Newark well for many generations. First, there was the Morris Canal, that started Newark on the path to becoming a transportation hub – completed in 1831. Then railroads were built to tie Newark's port and manufacturing muscle to distant markets. Success came with a cost, in terms of quality of life, with the best and worst of American-style capitalism emerging in this bustling city. By 1836, 20,000 residents were estimated to live in Newark. Education was significant in Newark's emergence as an economic force. The founding of Newark HS in 1838 gave its 91 students the distinction of attending New Jersey's first public high school, and the third in the nation. More schools followed in response to population increases. In 1840, Newark's population was estimated at 17,290.[106] The people were densely settled within the city's 24 square miles that abutted industrial land-uses. This feature of Newark created uncomfortable living conditions for many.

Newark's core, at Broad and Market Streets, began to develop retail, office, and government centers. These new activities changed the city's character from religious to commercial. In 1853 Newark HS moved into a new building, with an enrollment of 498 boys and girls.[107] For many Newark children, however, the alternative was not school but work. Child labor was cheap but vital for many families to survive economically.

The Civil War created an economic boom in Newark's manufacturing plants, which supplied both North and South. Newark, prior to the war, was a favorite trading city for Southern states, so the Civil War was a mixed blessing. Post-Civil War Newark in 1870 had a population of 105,059, quadrupling the 1840 population. By 1880, population increased by more than one-third to 143,225, and Newark's growth rate did not slow. By 1890, the population reached 181,390; and in 1900, Newark's population was estimated at 246,070.[108]

Tremendous population growth rates kept education officials busy. In 1899 Newark HS moved to a new building in North Newark. The name was changed to Barringer HS in 1907 to honor Newark's school superintendent, Dr. William N. Barringer. In response to Newark's 1910 population, estimated at 347,469, other new high schools were built. In 1912 Newark Central and Newark East Side High Schools opened, followed in 1913 by the opening of Newark South Side HS. Newark's 1920 population was estimated to be 414,524, creating a need for still more schools. In 1926 Newark West Side HS opened and was soon followed in 1928 by Newark Arts HS, SBP's neighbor, when it was built on the site formerly used by Newark Academy. In 1929 the Depression began, but Newark's population reached an all-time high of 442,337 in 1930.[109]

New Jersey Secondary School Football Prior to 1930

Little has been revealed from this research about New Jersey high school baseball prior to 1930. There is, however, much material on high school football, from Lloyde S. Glicken. In a Sept. 6, 1989 *Star-Ledger* story, Glicken wrote about the greatest New Jersey high school football teams of yesteryear. These select teams, in terms of their record, were the few that were unbeaten, untied and unscored upon. They are few in number, and must have been exceptional, even by standards of today. With such strict criteria it is not surprising that there are so few, but such teams vanished by the end of the 1930s.

Newark's status as New Jersey's largest city made it home to the first of these powerhouses. It is not surprising, therefore, that SBP's former neighbor, Newark Academy, was New Jersey's earliest dominant football team. The original Newark Academy was built in 1774 and occupied several sites in Newark over the many years of its existence, and is now in Livingston, NJ. Beginning with its 1904 team, that was 10-0-0 and outscored opponents 164-0, Newark Academy won 23 straight games before being scored upon. This is a state record that may never be broken. Their 1905 team was 9-0-0 and the Minutemen outscored opponents 209-0. Their 23-game streak lasted four games into the 1906 season before yielding a point. St. Benedict's decision to form its first team in 1899 may have been due to its successful High Street neighbor.[110]

SBP produced its first dominant team in 1917, with a season record of 6-0-0, outscoring opponents 139-0. In 1920 Newark Academy produced a 6-0-0 record while outscoring opponents 92-0. Newark Academy's last hurrah came in 1931, with a 6-0-1 record while outscoring opponents 109-0. It is not known whether Newark Academy and St. Benedict's played each other before the 1930 season. The potential for a fierce rivalry existed, but St. Benedict's and Newark Academy did not become long-term rivals. In the early 1900s, however, the Minutemen were the dominant team, and the Gray Bees, as SBP's teams are known, were just evolving. Newark's first public high school, Barringer, became the first of many great public high school teams that Newark generated.[111]

While Newark produced a large share of the state's great teams, beyond its borders there were also excellent teams. In the early years of interscholastic football, it was the prep schools that dominated, since public education was in its infancy and their athletic programs were only beginning. Two prep schools, in particular, would be Joe's early rivals, Wenonah Military Academy and Pennington School. Wenonah no longer exists, but its 1922 team had a 6-0-0 record and outscored foes 168-0. In 1928, the Wenonah team produced a 3-0-0 record while outscoring foes 74-0. The period 1929-31 had no dominant schools that were undefeated, untied, and unscored upon.[112]

The preceding provides the backdrop for the stage which Joe first trod in Sept. 1930 – when he moved to St. Benedict's Preparatory School at 528 High Street, Newark, New Jersey. His duties as a football coach and English teacher began in Sept. 1930, while enrolled at CTC for one course to complete his degree requirements.

It had taken nearly four years for Joe to complete this strange journey, with several stops along the way. Now, time would tell if this was the solution sought when it began.

VI. THE POST-GRADUATE (PG) ATHLETIC ERA

"Why in the world would Joe want to live anyplace else?"

Joe's Newark story has many components, as the context that shaped his life and teams. He did not perform in a vacuum. Realities of St. Mary's Abbey, the City of Newark, and the Milbauer family profoundly touched Joe and SBP. Personally, Joe's Newark career has two distinct phases: first, the period while he resided with the Milbauers at 17 Halstead Street in Newark's Vailsburg section; second, the period afterwards. Professionally, it was SBP's Post-Graduate (PG) era; and afterwards. Temporally, they nearly coincide.

At first glance, Joe and Newark appeared to be incompatible. Most people from Oregon, especially small-town Oregon, might feel uncomfortable with living in this city, since there is no comparison when it comes to natural beauty. Conversely, Newark was a cash cow that even Oregon farmers could appreciate, especially if one were willing to pay the price of living in a less than desirable physical environment. Also required was a willingness to tolerate a more complicated and stressful lifestyle, inherent in such a relatively big and dense city. Joe's answer was to keep his lifestyle very simple.

In September, Joe occupied his new quarters in the Benedict Field residence, several miles north of SBP's campus near downtown Newark. For an Oregonian freshly arriving from living on Broadway in upper Manhattan, Benedict Field was a haven. Joe had direct access to adjacent Branch Brook Park's natural beauty, making Benedict Field an attractive place to live. The fieldhouse was probably shared with John Ford, Benedict Field's superintendent, as well as SBP's soccer coach. The structure resembled a conventional home, and was probably quite comfortable after dorm living.

Benedict Field residence.

Also landing on his feet four years after the disastrous Mt. Angel fire of 1926 was Dan Nolan. The Notre Dame *Scholastic* of Oct. 3, 1930 revealed that Daniel P. Nolan, Ch.E. '23, "returned to Notre Dame as an instructor in the department of Chemistry and is continuing with his studies for an advanced degree."[1]

1930-31 School Year

Expectations for the 1930 football season may not have been high for the unknown coach from Oregon, a distinct advantage in Joe's favor. Dewey Hines' replacement fielded his first football team since 1925 with some notoriety. When Joe began at SBP, Abbot Martin Burne was a student, and he recalled that his hiring was regarded as something of a "ploy." Abbot Martin, also, may have meant "coup." Joe's reputation apparently made his arrival in 1930 something special.[2] It is not apparent, however, that Joe brought with him any particular technical football innovations.

During this era, SBP's teams were successful largely due to sheer numbers of PG athletic talent. Definitionally, PGs tended to be athletes in their fifth year of secondary school after completing a conventional four-year secondary school curriculum in a public or parochial high school. At SBP, it was a *quid pro quo* relationship that saw young men with athletic ability enhancing their prospects for college with additional preparatory courses, that Joe explains more eloquently later in the book.

In football, Joe's was not a unique system of West Coast offense or defense that befuddled East Coast foes. Joe's emphasis was on the fundamentals of the game, likely executing to perfection the "Notre Dame Box" offense. And, Joe's defense was prepared to stop the same offense, run by opponents. There was nothing fancy on the part of Joe and SBP, just simple, hard-hitting football played at a level of near-perfection by superior players. The 1930 team photo reveals Frank Milbauer to be Joe's assistant coach.

The 1930 football season, given the complex situation, was not bad for Joe. The big SBP game that Joe experienced for the first time was against Seton Hall Prep (SHP). In a story anonymously written thirty years later, a history of this rivalry was presented as follows:

> What is a rivalry?
> The dictionary tells us it is a state of competition, the effort of one to equal or outdo another.
> The record books tell of it coldly and impersonally in the scores of past games, but can never give the color or drama.
> The thrill of a long run, a perfectly executed pass, a goal line stand – those are the things that spell rivalry, memories always fresh in the minds of those who played or watched.
> Thus it is with St. Benedict's and Seton Hall.
> It was toward the close of the first decade of this century that the Gray Bees and Pirates became rivals. But instead of shoulder pads and helmets it was bats and gloves. The score of that game is lost over the the years but it doesn't matter. The important thing is that it was the start.
> It was on Thanksgiving Day in 1924 that the first meeting on a football field was held. St. Benedict's won 39-0, and again the following year by 25-13, this time before a holiday crowd of more than 12,000.
> In '26 the Pirates broke into the win column, rolling to a 25-0 victory but St. Benedict's came back in the next clash to prevail 26-0.
> Seton Hall put identical 13-6 victories back-to-back to close out the 1920s.[3]

Joe's first SBP Football team in 1930: First Row: J. Bolles, J. Crecca, F. Schatzman, W. Murphy, W. Smith, M. Musconi, Capt. J. Walter, Coach J. Kasberger, P. Gawalis, S. Stankavich, G. Lupo, J. Oravec, J. Boylan; Second Row: J. McDonough, D. Harkins, D. Leonard, G. Sheridan, C. Koopman, W. Kennedy, F. Varni, C. Smith, L. Lagoda, D. Mills, S. Moretti, P. Ford, F. Sussman, J. Donnelly; Third Row: C. McGuire, J. Walsh, J. Sheik, F. Mulligan, G. Wolf, H. George, S. Tedesco, J. Campbell, T. Dowd, C. Vanderweigh, J. Golvan, B. Conklin. Fourth Row: Manager W. Byrne, B. McClorry, H. Struck, N. Ciccone, W. Brady, J. Steib, G. Shaedel, J. Bradley, Ass't. Coach F. Milbauer, W. Glaccum, J. Kennedy, Ass't. Manager, F. Boetner.

With this historical perspective, Joe was under pressure to break the 3-3-0 deadlock in the series record. By most reasonable standards, a winning record of 5-2-0 and beating SHP might have been enough. Joe's team began the season with four-straight wins, followed by a 1-2 record in the next three games. The season highlight was an 18-0 win over SHP, and Joe must have been pleased. The results encouraged SBP's officials and vindicated Frank Milbauer. Joe's first team's winning percentage, however, ranked below his career average. The team photo reveals a player named J. Oravec, who did not return to SBP for his senior year. Oravec became one of Joe's most famous football players when he played collegiately, far from New Jersey.

When the 1930 football season ended, Joe had no coaching responsibilities until March when baseball season began. Through mid-December, he attended classes on Monday nights at Columbia to complete his degree requirements. The opportunity to take a few months of rest was welcome after the long and tedious grind of completing his master's degree requirements. As Joe looked forward to the 1931 baseball season, this challenge may have been greater than football since he inherited Prof Blood's defending state champions. When and under what circumstances Joe became baseball coach is unknown.[4]

Before the baseball season began, Joe and many others were devastated by the tragic news on April 1, 1931, that Knute Rockne had died in a plane crash near Bazaar, Kansas. It did not take long for Rockne's protégés to be in demand by football-playing institutions all over the country. Because of his premature death, "Rockne's most important influence on American popular culture came through the men he coached." Rockne biographer Michael R. Steele reckoned that Rockne "had five or six hundred players each year" at Notre Dame and concluded that he "can be credited with having some direct contact with more than ten thousand athletes at Notre Dame from 1914 to 1931."[5]

Joe and Frank Milbauer enjoying a light moment on Easter Sunday, 1931.

With so many football players during Rockne's Notre Dame career, it is unsurprising that not all played at the varsity level. Steele stated that "the majority of these men saw little or no varsity playing time," but did learn some football from the master. Perhaps more was learned under Rockne from the sidelines than on the playing field, and Steele noted that "a very significant number went into coaching."[6]

An indicator of Rockne's successful protégés came in 1969, college football's centennial year. Rankings were based on "the highest winning percentages. . . computed for coaches with more than ten years' service." The results are revealing to Rockne fans.

> Rockne's .897 led the field, but three of his players placed high also – Frank Leahy of Notre Dame, second, Frank Thomas at Alabama ninth, and Jim Crowley at Fordham eighteenth.[7]

Leahy, Thomas, and Crowley were just the tip of an iceberg of Rockne players in college coaching. Steele listed the following coaches as Rockne men:

> Gus Dorais . . . Detroit, Charlie Bachman at Florida, Jim Phelan at Washington, Slip Madigan at St. Mary's, Harry Mehre at Georgia, Hunk Anderson at Notre Dame, Harry Stuhldreyer at Villanova and Wisconsin, Elmer Layden at Notre Dame, Don Miller at Ohio State, Noble Kizer at Purdue, Adam Walsh at Yale, Clipper Smith at St. Mary's [Gonzaga], Eddie Anderson at Oklahoma, Rex Enright at South Carolina, as well as others such as Dutch Bergman, Glenn Carberry, Clem Crowe, Pete Dwyer, and Buck Shaw.[8]

There are other coaches, including Joe, who played for Rockne or attended his coaching school, who succeeded at the secondary school level. After Rockne's death, Coach Robert L. Murray of The Dalles was moved to write this essay, that spoke for many.

A successful football coach must have personality, enthusiasm, technical knowledge, sense of fair play, sympathy for the player, and yet be a strict disciplinarian. The late Knute Rockne possessed all these qualities. In addition, he had tact, for he always said the right thing at the right time. He knew when the situation called for sarcasm, humor, praise, or silence. Rockne was a driver, but he never became abusive. He was an insistent master, but an understanding one; an uncompromising demander of discipline and adherence to rules of training, eligibility, and method. He was quick to adapt himself to any new method of play. For example, when the 'Full Stop' rule (which was aimed directly at the Notre Dame shift) became effective, he immediately changed his methods to fit the new rule, and in the game with U.S.C., showed a style of attack previously not used by the Notre Dame teams.

In my personal contact with this nationally known coach, both in private conversation, and in the class room, I had an opportunity to observe some of his characteristics. He was a man with a fine personality, dynamic energy, (and) a wonderful pedagogue. He held the strict attention of over one hundred men in a three hour conference with only one ten minute intermission. On the practice field he would don a uniform, and give practical demonstrations of football fundamentals. So enthused was he in this work that he would often take from fifteen to thirty minutes over his allotted time. He had the power of firing his listeners with his enthusiasm. 'Rock' was a coach who played to win, and in a conversation with me used these words, 'There is no such thing as a good loser, but you can lose like a gentleman.'

In the eyes of the general public Knute Rockne was known as the wonder coach of the fighting Irish. But to the students and alumni of Notre Dame, and to [the] coaching profession, football was not his greatest achievement. To the students he was known for his sympathy and understanding, to the alumni for

Joe's first SBP Baseball team from the Telolog in 1931. Top Row: T. Millman, T. DeMaria, J. Murphy, E. Edelen, L. Lagoda, W. Whalen, S. Stankavich, N. Lombardi, J. Oravec, A. Piechowski; Sitting: T. Dial-Manager, E. Sheridan, F. Harriman, J. Walter, F. Stavella, J. Kasberger-Coach, G. Keller, D. Mills, J. Hoch.

his true friendship and guidance, and to the coaching profession for his high ideals of sportsmanship and character building. Not only has the death of Rockne been a very great loss to Notre Dame, but to the nation as well. These words of a Notre Dame alumnus expressed the thoughts of others who knew

Joe's first SBP baseball team, from his personal memorabilia.

him: 'I wonder if there lives a man who believes the great spirit of Rockne is dead. He is gone from us, but his spirit still lives.'[9]

Joe's first baseball team in 1931 had an 8-2-0 record with no indication, however, that SBP repeated as state champions. The captioned team photo indicates that J. Oravec played varsity baseball. From a story about the 1931 baseball team in the 1931 SBP yearbook, *Telolog*, it is inferred that Oravec was a junior who played as an outfielder in 1930.[10] It is believed that Oravec later spent the 1931-32 school year at Rockaway, NJ High School, from which he graduated in 1932.

On the personal side of Joe's life, the sequence of events pertaining to his first year in Newark is important. Frank Milbauer married in May 1930, and before the year was out, Joe asked the Milbauers if he could have Frank's third floor room at 17 Halstead Street. Joe and the Milbauers originally thought this arrangement would last until he went home in June 1931. However, without further discussion, this housing arrangement continued. Joe left Newark when classes ended in June and returned in September for football practice.[11]

Joe's 1931 Telolog photo.

Joe attended the Columbia University commencement exercises on June 6, 1931 and received his long-awaited A.M. degree in Physical Education. Then he went home after an absence of eighteen months and remained there through the Labor Day weekend, as became his custom. Having a master's degree from CTC made Joe a valued prospect and there is no telling how many offers he had to return West.[12]

The allure of SBP, Newark and the Milbauer household, evidently, combined to bring Joe back. It must have been a relief for SBP to see their new coach return, since there is no evidence that they had anything more than the gentlemen's agreement, a handshake. There was never a written contract between Joe and SBP. Apparently the Gray Bees liked him, and he liked them enough to return. Joe still might have the challenge of facing freshman English classes, but he was more familiar with his environment. Familiarity, however, did not necessarily mean comfort – culture shock in Newark for "Oregon Joe" may never have ended – but he had survived, probably the most difficult of all years, the first.

1931-32 School Year

The school year began with a very successful football team's 8-0-1 record. The opening game tie with a powerful Pennington School team was the only blemish. The most important game, for many, was another victory over SHP, 14-0, thanks to SBP's "hard running backs, Tony Troisi and Pat Tortorella. . . ."[13]

SBP coaches were blessed with a very supportive headmaster in Fr. Boniface, who was interested in more than athletics in the school's development. As SBP became more prominent, he "saw to it that this reputation for greatness would extend to academic and cultural areas." In 1931, Fr. Boniface organized a school band "for the purpose of 'adding zest to many of the school activities, especially in the field of sports.'" The *Pacific Star* influence may have reached Newark, through Joe, when Fr. Boniface "launched the official school newspaper, *The Gray Bee*."[14]

Life with the Milbauers on Halstead Street gave Joe the best of two worlds. He was in the city, with the benefits a city then offered, while close to work. The Milbauer home also had a suburban flavor and "park-like" yard that surely made Joe feel at home. Benedict Field, of course, provided Joe with something of the pastoral atmosphere that he needed. While it was not a perfect fit, the benefits must have outweighed the negatives – or Joe would not have stayed as long as he did. Joe's benefactors, the Milbauers, were exceptional hosts.

Joe was very popular with the Milbauer neighbors, who knew him as a visible and successful coach, and as one who was always helpful in neighborhood activities. One of the things Joe enjoyed doing most was serving as an examiner for the Boy Scouts of America. In this capacity, Joe received young scouts at the Milbauer home and determined how

Frank and Louise Milbauer enjoying a granddaughter, Marie Claire Milbauer, 18 months old. Claire and Joe were her godparents.

well a youngster knew the prescribed material for a merit badge. Joe was especially handy in the winter when it snowed, and was relied on for shoveling, a very arduous task because of the 75-foot distance from garage to street. Joe loved hard work, and snow shoveling kept him fit during the winter. It was in the spring and fall, however, when Joe worked in the Milbauer garden, that he was happiest.[15]

Joe was always helpful to the Benedictines. One night a carload of them arrived in the Milbauer driveway with a flat tire. Since their home was only 185 feet from busy South Orange Avenue, unsurprisingly they picked the Milbauer driveway to change the flat. Before the monks could begin, Joe took over and changed the tire while the monks had coffee and visited with the Milbauers. Joe's religious practice was exemplary as an active parishioner at Sacred Heart Church

Milbauer residence at 17 Halstead Street. In this photo taken in 1943, the two Milbauer grandchildren are shown. The top awning was on the window of Joe's third-floor room.

in Vailsburg, where he regularly attended the 7 AM mass. Some students did not think Joe was a Catholic, a perception that arose from observing Joe at St. Mary's Church on campus. He did not take communion at the later mass at St. Mary's, because he had done so earlier in the morning.[16]

The second school year concluded even more successfully for Joe than the first. The 1932 baseball team's 12-3-0 record included a state championship. With June graduations, it was an important time for students making decisions about their futures, despite the Depression. At Rockaway HS, in a distant suburb of Newark, former SBP play-

Claire Milbauer captioned this picture as "Always ready to dig us out." Joe was getting ready to clean the gutters on the roof. He put electric wires in the gutters to prevent icing.

er John Oravec was making a courageous decision to head West.

John "Scooter" Oravec was the first of Joe's star football and baseball players who moved on to Willamette University. To what extent Joe influenced Oravec's decision is not known. Spec Keene, however was forever grateful to Joe for this New Jersey athletic pioneer, who blazed the trail to Oregon. It did not take long for others to follow. Awaiting Oravec was Spec and his top assistant, Lestle [sic] Sparks, and other coaches:

> Howard Maple, former Oregon State athlete who coached the backfield; Paul Ackermann, former Northwest Conference all-star; Jessie Deetz, former Willamette backfield man; and Eric Hauser, former All-American guard, who was head line coach.[17]

Spec set high standards at Willamette, and after six years the 1932 Willamette yearbook had glowing praise, reporting that he "won a place of respect for himself in the hearts of the Willamette students and alumni." Equally important to Joe, as a potential college mentor for his players, were Spec's ethics. "His teams have been representative of our school, and have stood for the best qualities of inter-collegiate sports."[18]

At St. Mary's Abbey, Abbot Ernest experienced health problems. "Failing eyesight forced him to leave day-to-day administration to Prior Anselm Kienle."[19] Fortunately Fr. Boniface remained as headmaster to provide stability at SBP despite the abbot's ill health. Before Joe knew it the school year was over and he was on the train west. After some time with his family, he probably rode another train south to Los Angeles for the 1932 Olympics.

What was once the University of California Southern Branch, was now UCLA. As opposed to an institution occupying high-school-level facilities, UCLA was now maturing into a thriving and respected university, located in the Westwood section of Los Angeles. The trip to Los Angeles provided Joe several opportunities since his last visit in November 1921. Did Joe visit Coach Spaulding at UCLA while there? UCLA was developing promising athletic teams which may have interested Joe, because it was not long before the Bruins became a national power. Did UCLA remember Joe? There are no answers to these questions here. Yet this may have been his last chance to join UCLA.

The University of Southern California was still familiar to Joe as USC in south-central Los Angeles. The new Rose Bowl stadium and the Coliseum enhanced USC's powerful teams. Also, the natural rivalry between USC and UCLA made Los Angeles a hotbed for football that aided both in becoming national forces. The facilities and fan support in the growing city of Los Angeles must have been impressive to Joe, as well as the spectacular 100,000 seat Coliseum that was built for the Olympics. As the summer of 1932 ended, Joe returned to Newark and brought commemorative Olympic coins to show his family and East Coast friends. The potential in the Los Angeles trip for Joe to coach elsewhere appears to have never materialized. The summer of 1932 appears pivotal in Joe's career thinking and life, when he decided to return to

Newark. Perhaps Joe was preoccupied with thoughts about his SBP football team and the big game against Pennington School.

1932-33 School Year

The 1932 football team had a 6-1-0 record to begin the school year. Pennington School lived up to its expectations, and perhaps more. It was one of New Jersey's all-time dominant teams with a 7-0-0 record. In addition to being undefeated, Pennington was also unscored upon, outscoring its foes 168-0. It was the next to last New Jersey team to accomplish this feat. One of its victims was SBP in a 6-0 game at mid-season, that snapped Joe's first major football win-streak at 13 in a row. Pain from the Pennington loss may have been eased by an otherwise fine record. SBP's punishing victory over SHP, attributed to "a heavier, more rugged Bee squad [that] wore down the Pirates, 42-0," ended the season that surely made everyone happy.[20]

But all was not well. The Depression was now well underway, and it affected virtually everyone. Newark was a city of immigrant neighborhoods, surrounded by more prosperous suburbs to which many aspired to move when their economic fortunes improved. Newark was a grim and tough environment for many youths, but Joe benefited as a coach from the large and deep pool of talent. Athletic success for a young man was viewed as a way out of his economic dead end. Joe demonstrated an ability to both win, and help young student athletes achieve their aspirations at the college level.

The large number of talented athletes with dreams and potential was somewhat reduced by the economic reality of the times. In many families, children had to work for the family's survival. Compulsory education was still several years away. For too many young men, an SBP education was a luxury they could not afford. Attending even a public high school was a privilege denied to the poor, especially in Newark. Many felt that Newark, at that time, had the best public schools in New Jersey. On the prep-school circuit, where SBP competed, social distinctions were obvious. Also, the religious affiliations of the schools in New Jersey's economic and educational hierarchy were apparent. To many, SBP was the prep-school equivalent of Notre Dame, with ethnic athletes coached by Joe, Prof Blood, and Jim Cavanagh – all of whom were very competitive.

Many barriers to socio-economic acceptance fell on the fields of New Jersey prep-school athletic competition. Sons of the Anglo-Protestant establishment, representing prep schools of the elite, found worthy competitors in Newark at SBP. Complete acceptance may have been grudging and infeasible on both sides. There was however, an opportunity for mutual respect among the young competitors to be realized. Athletic competition, emphasizing sportsmanship and gentlemanly behavior, may have produced unexpected benefits in New Jersey over the long term. Great improvements in social and economic development emerged in the state after the Depression. This phenomenon may have been, to some extent, associated with sports.

SBP's implicit mission was to serve the youth of Newark and its environs. It was, however, a private school that did not receive public or diocesan funding. Operated as a prep school, with only a few lay teachers to supplement the teaching monks, SBP required tuition to operate and maintain the school, as well as pay teachers' salaries. Tuition was relatively low compared to the other boarding and nonboarding prep schools. This was a difficult economic time for almost everyone as the Depression worsened.

With almost three school years under his belt, Joe may have begun to feel comfortable in Newark. The longer he stayed, the less likely it appeared that he would leave – as the baseball and football teams more closely reflected his style and personality. PG and conventional student athletes surely wanted to attend SBP because of its success in athletics. It was a winning environment, and a proud tradition growing stronger.

Prohibition was repealed on April 7, 1933, and may have been the major news story of the year in Newark and elsewhere throughout the country. Champagne toasts were now legal for those who celebrated SBP's athletic successes. The first chance came when Joe's baseball team did not disappoint its fans. The 1933 baseball team won Joe another state championship with an 11-4 record, to conclude the school year. Joe headed home for the summer, bringing the Milbauers with him. Besides the beautiful scenery, they saw how difficult the economic situation had become – after the local bank closed during the infamous "Bank Holiday" in the spring. The impact of the Depression may not have been as great in The Dalles, as it was in larger cities, but it was serious.

The Depression came at a bad time for a coach without a job and lots of mouths to feed. Bob Murray, however, was determined to remain in The Dalles. "Bob was secretary of The Dalles Boxing Commission from 1930 to 1937," which kept him involved in athletics, but the first years of the Depression were not easy.

> For approximately two and a half years after he left DHS Bob worked at jobs around the town and county of any description he could find. He worked as a census enumerator in the fall of 1930, as a construction laborer, and for a time at short term surveying jobs for Wasco County. These were difficult times for him. Four years were to pass between Black Tuesday of September [sic], 1929 and the bank holiday of the spring of 1933.[21]

Despite the hard times, Bob found a "survival mechanism" in 1932 that was a godsend for his family. At last, he found a "full time position as a law enforcement officer with The Dalles City Police Department." It was not always a pleasant job but Bob was well-qualified to do what needed to be done.[22]

The Milbauer family's visit gave both families the long-awaited opportunity to better know each other. After several years of hearing about Joe's family, friends, neighbors, and beautiful hometown, they were able to judge for themselves. The Kasberger family had "ways of doing things," as the Milbauers observed. The Sunday dinners were served at 2 P.M., and everyone gathered at 917 West 10th Street. Joe's sister, Anna Sandoz, lived a few miles out of town and she attended 7 A.M. Mass at St. Peter's Church, before spending the rest of the morning helping her sister Audie prepare dinner. Although the mother was no longer alive, her routines continued.[23]

The Sandoz farm's herd of Black Angus cattle was often discussed at dinner. Joe's interest in the breed came from his stock-judging at OAC. In New Jersey Joe visited farms with Black Angus cattle and in later years acquired several. Joe's father was the perfect host with a gentle disposition, portrayed as soft-spoken and easy-going, intent on making his honored Newark guests comfortable. Loving and warm relationships developed between Milbauer and Kasberger families after this trip, only natural because of Joe's role in their lives.[24]

The chemistry between the East and West Coast families could not have been better. Joe had a home with the Milbauers in Newark that his kin in The Dalles could understand and love as much as he did. Kasberger family acceptance of the Milbauers by this trip was made clear and may have removed any misgivings Joe had about his Newark career. Over the years, Claire Milbauer made many more trips to The Dalles and considers it her second home. Her relationship with the Kasberger family extended beyond Joe, to Audie in particular, who became very close to Claire. Claire recalls an uncanny communication link between them. The bond included thinking similar thoughts to buying identical coats, but in different colors, at stores a continent apart.[25]

Also of interest to Joe in the summer of 1933 was the head football coaching change at Oregon State. Paul Schissler, as Oregon State's head football coach from 1924-32, had a career record of 48-30-2, a substantial improvement over Rutherford – but there was not yet a Rose Bowl for the Beavers. In 1933, Oregon State again found its new head football coach, Alonzo L. (Lon) Stiner, to be a Nebraska alumnus. Stiner was an All-American player and team captain for the Cornhuskers before becoming Schissler's assistant coach.[26]

Joe was probably too young in 1933 to be a candidate for the Oregon State head coaching position. His alma mater appears to have sought candidates with big-college experience. It is not known how much involvement Joe had with Oregon State athletics while in Newark prior to World War II. Perhaps Joe was preoccupied with Willamette's athletic fortunes, because of Spec Keene and the New Jersey players going to Salem.

1933-34 School Year

Joe had an added burden when he returned to Newark for the 1933-34 school year. Frank Milbauer lost his lucrative position in Newark's usually stable insurance industry and was moving back home, to 17 Halstead St., with his wife and child until conditions improved. This bad news was softened as Frank was able to continue as Joe's assistant football coach, a position he held for several years while working as a Newark probation officer. This crowded living arrangement continued until the spring of 1934, when an apartment became available in Frank's wife's family home on Gladstone Avenue. The couple lived there until a home in Millburn was purchased after the Depression ended.[27]

Despite the Depression, there was optimism regarding Newark's future. The city continued to add public high schools with the opening of Weequahic High School in 1933. At SBP, the school year began favorably with the football team producing a 7-1-1 record. The schedule featured another dominant Pennington team that tied the Gray Bees 7-7, ending Joe's ten-game win streak that began immediately after the 1932 loss to Pennington. In the following game, that concluded the season, SBP lost to Allentown Prep of Pennsylvania, 0-6. John Bateman was the team captain and made the all-state team with Dick Weisgerber. For an unknown reason SBP and SHP did not compete.

The disappointment of the tie and defeat, after seven consecutive wins to begin the season, was put in perspective when Joe experienced a deep personal loss with heartrending implications. In Nov. 1933 John Kasberger, Sr. died and Joe certainly gave thought to returning home to be with his siblings at this sad time. However, he was in an unenviable position because of the distance involved and time required for such a trip. Thus Joe was unable to attend his father's funeral, and became stoical and somber. Even in death, John Kasberger, Sr. was generous and caring for his children. The provisions of his will mandated that the homestead remain in the family until the last of his children was dead. Due to his father's bequest, Joe felt an even greater responsibility to return each summer and insure that 917 West Tenth Street was in the condition that his father desired. Also, this bequest gave the Kasberger children a home that would always be there for them.[28]

The 1934 baseball team won another state championship with a 10-3-0 record to conclude the school year. Joe would always remember the Class of 1934 as an exceptional group that produced two of his most famous players, John Bateman and Dick Weisgerber, both of whom became nationally known. Joe's most famous athlete, ever, is thought by John Bateman to be Dick Weisgerber. Bateman and Weisgerber were baseball and football teammates, and the former recalled Weisgerber competing in field events for the track team while playing a baseball game at Benedict Field. In addition to being the state champ for the discus and shot-put, Weisgerber lettered in basketball.[29]

Arguably, the most famous future coach that Joe ever mentored was John Bateman. While Bateman went to Columbia, Weisgerber joined John Oravec at Willamette, where "Scooter" was making quite a name for himself. When Weisgerber arrived for the 1934 season, he saw his fellow New Jerseyan, Oravec, become nationally prominent. Spec Keene was suddenly blessed with two sensations. With Oravec's success, Keene may not have realized at the time that Weisgerber would become,

John F. Bateman, Ph.D., former Rutgers University head football coach, SBP '34.

probably, his most exceptional athlete.

John Bateman recalled his teammate, Dick Weisgerber, as one of the greatest athletes he ever saw. As former head football coach at Rutgers University, Dr. Bateman speaks with great authority in his assessment. It is not surprising, then, that this superior four-sport athlete became a college and professional star. Important to Spec, Weisgerber in tandem with Oravec made Willamette teams "the scourge" of the Northwest Conference.[30] Joe gave Spec and Willamette payback in spades very quickly. The personal kindness and professional courtesy that had been extended to him after the 1926 fire was not forgotten. Joe continued repaying this debt with generous installments over the next few years.

While in Oregon for the summer, Joe probably visited Mt. Angel. This was a time of transition in the monastic community headed by Abbot Bernard Murphy, worn out by the strain of the fire and rebuilding. Moreover his physical health had suffered and he was now totally blind. Realizing his limitations, Abbot Murphy "decided that he should relinquish his office to a more robust man." Fr. Thomas Meier was elected as his successor on Aug. 1, 1934. Joe's dear friend was described as "a forty-seven year old priest of Swiss ancestry, who had lived in Oregon almost all his life."[31]

The new abbot was prepared for his duties, having served previously as "novice master, cleric master and subprior; he had visited European monasteries and Conception Abbey." There were personality traits that made Abbot Thomas a fine choice, since he was characterized as a "strong-willed man," with a vision for the future. With youth and good health, "he quickly set about formulating and implementing a wide range of projects."[32] Significant to Joe and the Milbauers, Abbot Thomas soon established Mt. Angel's "junior abbey" in Newark at 17 Halstead Street. The Milbauer home was not only hospitable, but large, with accommodations that could sleep eleven, and housed twenty-eight, Oregon monks over the years. A partial list of the monks who stayed, included Fathers Robert Keber, Victor Rassier, Hildebrand Melchior, and Thomas Meier. Abbot Thomas sent others from Mt. Angel when traveling to and from Europe, or on abbey business.[33]

Another of the Oregon monks to visit Newark was Rev. Jerome Wespe, Prior at St. Benedict's Abbey. He was Mt. Angel's librarian during the 1926 fire, and reportedly had an interesting visit to Newark. When he arrived from Oregon, there was no room at the Milbauers or St. Mary's Abbey. Thus, Fr. Jerome stayed at the rectory of St. Benedict's Church in Newark's Ironbound section, a few miles from the "junior abbey." When he returned to Newark from Europe, the Prior was given a choice of housing options, and chose Halstead Street because he wished "to stay with the boys." Prior Jerome's East Coast adventure was made rewarding by Frank Milbauer, who took him to rare book stores in Newark and New York City. At these locations, acquisitions were made to replenish the Mt. Angel collection that was lost in the fire.[34]

Joe knew most of the visiting monks as old friends, so there was no inconvenience in sharing his spacious quarters. The third floor had two large double beds, perfect for housing the guests. In addition to the Oregon Benedictines,

Bishop Leipzig was reunited with Joe at Halstead Street. In this male bastion, Claire and Louise at least had Louise Milbauer's sister in residence, occasionally, to even up the odds.

1934-35 School Year

Joe made a bigger name for himself with his 1934 football team. The season record was 7-0-1, but the team is noteworthy for outscoring foes 139-0. The sole blemish was the 0-0 tie against Allentown Prep of Pennsylvania, Joe's last loss or tie until a 6-6 tie with Bordentown Military Institute (BMI) in 1937. In the period between those games, there was a 23-game win streak. SHP was back on the schedule after not playing against SBP in 1933. The season finale against the Pony Pirates, as SHP came to be known, resulted in a 6-0 Gray Bee victory.

Fr. Boniface continued balancing SBP's athletics with more cultural offerings. Sometime during 1934, "at the Headmaster's urging, the Glee Club made its debut, affording, in his words, 'an opportunity for enjoyment of music and the appreciation of art.'"[35] After his experiences at MAC with a similar philosophy, Joe probably had few problems with Fr. Boniface's ideas – which did *not* include a minstrel production.

One of the best views on Joe that anyone ever had comes from a little girl who recorded her impressions. A paper entitled "Remembrances of Joe Kasberger" by Kathleen Milbauer O'Hare gives insights into Joe. Kathleen was Frank Milbauer's oldest daughter, lovingly known to Joe as "Kewp," a diminutive form of Kewpie, as in the "Kewpie Doll." Life in the Milbauer household became more crowded and complex as the Depression worsened. This was a time of sacrifice, and by Kewp's account the Milbauer grandchildren were immune. "It was the Depression and times must have been pretty tough, but we never knew it." Kewp may have been Joe's first encounter with children, and her memories of Joe as "an integral part of my grandparents' household" are priceless in understanding Joe as a human being. "He was never Uncle Joe. He was Joe Kasberger. The man who came to dinner and stayed for all those years."[36]

SBP athletics influenced Kewp's childhood with a special perspective of Joe.

After all these years, I can still remember being allowed to sit on the bench with the players. But I had to earn that spot just as the players did. It was always a joy being with my Dad and Joe. On a few occasions I can remember spending time at the field (but never allowed in the field house) – 'Guys only!'

Kewp recalled Joe as both a perfectionist and a workaholic around the Milbauer home.

Dad and Joe always had some project going – digging up the lot next door and turning it into a gorgeous lawn and garden at our home in Millburn, or working at Halstead Street. My grandparents were avid gardeners and every spare moment was spent tending the gardens, and of course Joe would be out there helping and/or constructing something! In those days, no one ever seemed to sit down. There was always work to be done.[37]

Louise Milbauer and Joe became very close. Soon Joe was calling Louise Milbauer "Katrinka," as an indication of the closeness that existed. Apparently, Joe had read a novel with a character named Katrinka that he thought resembled Louise. Joe did more than pay for room and board; he had responsibilities in the household.

One of Joe's chores at Halstead Street was to be certain that 'Skip' and 'Katrinka's' (his nicknames for my grandparents) coal bin was maintained at all times. I swear that coal dust was the enemy – that place gleamed! Anyhow, Joe said if I would help him sweep it out really well, he would take me to Oregon with him. That never happened, but you can bet that I was down there working like a dynamo. You have to understand that I was only about five or six at the time.[38]

"Kewp" – Kathleen Milbauer O'Hare

Dealing with children, when they are not your own, requires special skills. For Joe, Kewp was a wonderful learning experience and opportunity to practice what he learned at CTC.

The poor man never got a minute's peace, because I was always underfoot trying to earn 'good girl points.' I don't ever recall him losing his patience, but I do remember if we got out of line he would become very silent and you knew you had crossed the line. Thank God he had a short memory and never held a grudge! He always greeted my brother Frank and I as 'Bun' and 'Kewp' 'til the day he died. I can't remember being called anything else by him. Even my mail would be addressed as 'Kewp.'[39]

Kewp's recall on Joe and her grandmother is keen. "Joe adored my grandparents, especially Nana. She made him part of the family and that was that." The depth of Joe's relationship with Louise Milbauer appears to have had much to do with Joe spending more years with Louise than he spent with his own mother. Louise gave Joe a special place in the Milbauer home that did not preclude Joe from maintaining personal privacy.

The entire third floor of the house was his! No one dared to go up unless invited by Joe himself. Nana's rule, not his! I can remember the decor. A moose head over the stairs, (nightmare material right there), woven Indian blankets as wall hangings, trophies, gadgets and cartoon posters. Joe had a great sense of humour but talk about dead-pan! He had the true poker face when he wanted. He also had the greatest smile and what a laugh – almost a hoot! And his voice – it just boomed.[40]

One of the problems in the Milbauer household was the plethora of Franks. Thus, Skip Milbauer's grandson, Frank, Jr., who was Kewp's older brother, became known as "Bun." Bun was an abbreviated form of "Bunny," since he was thought to be as cute as a bunny as a child. Bun remembered the nights spent in Joe's "third floor suite" during winter. These were special times for Bun who recalled Joe loving cold weather – and a room without heat was no problem. Moreover, Joe believed this was "very healthy for anyone to get a good night's sleep (provided you ran quick and jumped into bed with blankets up to your nose)." Needless to say, Joe and Bun "slept very well."[41]

Louise's husband, Frank, Sr. had a nickname, too. He was "Skip," in defer-ence to his authority as skipper of the Milbauer family ship. There were other nicknames around the Milbauer home, but Joe appears to have remained just "Joe." The deep mutual love and respect that existed in the Milbauer home was special to experience. There were times, however, when household sanity was stretched – but accepted due to the home's role as a focal point of SBP-related activities.[42]

"Bun" – Frank Milbauer, Jr.

Some nights before games there were players and coaches going over game plans, talking strategy, and drawing "Xs and Os." Yet, there was little discussion of SBP affairs in the home. What is vividly recalled is Joe and Frank ministering to athletic injuries sustained by players. After games, the Milbauer kitchen often resembled an athletic training room. One recipient of sports medicine was Kewp, whose recall of one incident might indicate the treatment administered to injured players.

> I can remember jumping off a wall and really spraining my ankle. Well Joe and Dad were right there with the instant cure. Bucket of ice and bucket of hot water. 'Don't worry Kewp, we'll have you good as new in no time.' Between the two of them, I thought they were going to break my leg. There they were, with their huge hands on this seven year old's limb, plunging it into the ice, then heat and so on. Two men on a mission. This little kid was going to mend and mend fast. After that process, the ace bandage! Joe, it's too big for her, cut it. No!

No, we'll tape it! I must have truly unnerved them by screaming the entire time. Well they got the tape on and turned to me quite pleased with the excellent job they had done and actually said, 'O.K. Kewp, now walk on it.' I thought they were crazy. Surely they weren't serious, but they were and walk I did. The pain was horrible, but I was told, 'Walk it off! You've got to play in pain! Don't favor it! Don't limp, you'll make it worse! Come on, Kewp, you'd swear you were crippled!' I loved those two so much and didn't want to let them down, and so I braved it out and of course 'time is a great healer' (another adage I got from them): I mended in no time.[43]

Joe and Frank's technique did more than treat sprains, it was a style that developed character.

You know, I think being with those two did more to shape my character than anything else. That seemed to be their entire philosophy on life. Walk it off – Play in pain – I never once saw them defeated – No matter what happened in their lives – They played in pain – They walked it off – and time was always a great healer.[44]

Joe and Frank's approach for treating sprains may have had an impact on Louise Milbauer, who was an avid believer in the power of votive candles. She lighted them before SBP games with the prayer that no players would be hurt.

The 1935 baseball team's 9-2-0 record ended the school year and is memorable because Nutley HS scored the most runs ever allowed in Joe's SBP career. The irony was that the Gray Bees defeated Nutley 9-7 in the previous game. The 9-16 loss to Nutley was followed in the next game by another pounding loss to Pennington, 11-12.

1935-36 School Year

The 1935 football team won the state championship with 6-1-0 record to begin the school year. The only loss was to Pennington, 3-7 at mid-season. The 1935 season did not include arch-foe SHP. Joe, however, was assembling the talent for next year's team that many thought was Joe's and New Jersey's greatest ever in secondary school football.

Joe was pleased that Spec's Willamette football squad had a great season.

A hard driving Willamette football team raced to its second consecutive Northwest Conference championship during the 1935 campaign, turning back the challenges of four conference elevens, and whipping Dud DeGroot's powerful San Jose State College Spartans.[45]

The only defeats came from Pacific Coast Conference teams, Oregon State and Washington State. If Joe got his college-coaching kicks through Spec, 1935 was a very good season, as he completed a decade of coaching Willamette football. Spec had now won the Northwest Conference championship four times, and at 1935 season's end the Bearcats had a 13-game win-streak against conference foes.

Good teams have good players and Spec had several in 1935. Leading the list of stars was John Oravec, his "150 pound halfback," who "concluded four brilliant years by being chosen on the Associated Press' Little All-American." Additional honors came to Oravec. "He was also given honorable mention on the AP and UP all-coast teams." "Scooter," a consistent performer, "was a four year all-conference man and this season served as honorary captain." It was in 1934 when he first achieved national fame as: "the second highest scorer in the nation, runner up to Shepard of Western Maryland University."[46]

Willamette University's "Touchdown Twins" from New Jersey, Dick Weisgerber and John Oravec.

Oravec had help en route to his individual success, especially from Weisgerber who headed five other Willamette players named to the 1935 Northwest Conference all-star team. Weisgerber was a "crunching 210 pound fullback," with great versatility whose national recognition grew from his skill in kicking points after touchdowns, successful in 32 tries out of 41 attempted in 1935. Also, Weisgerber "booted the first field goal of his college career in the Whitman game." In running the ball, Willamette had its greatest success, with an offensive "juggernaut" led by a rugged line. With "Ole Olson, Carl Rhoda, and Bill Stone running interference, Oravec and Weisgerber, famed Touchdown twins, cracked off most of the yardage."[47]

In the 1935 season, Oravec was a classic all-around player, despite his diminutive size.

> Oravec piled up 582 yards in 167 scrimmage plays, 373 yards on 31 punt returns, 160 yards on six returned kick-offs, and 87 yards with five intercepted passes; punted 14 times for a 40 yard average, best game being in the rain against Pacific with 44 yards on six kicks.[48]

Primarily a blocker for Oravec, Weisgerber had great statistics when he touched the ball.

Weisgerber grabbed-up 351 yards on 78 assaults at the line, averaged 37 yards on 43 punts, 50 yards on eight kick-offs, converted 10 out of 12 kicks for point after touchdown, and collected one field goal.[49]

Due to the touchdown twins, it is no wonder that other New Jersey athletes followed.

Gardening in the Milbauer yard was a common thread that made Joe a revered son rather than an honored boarder. Joe's degree in horticulture was a big help when he discussed the Latin names for the plants, and the soil chemistry required for growth. Joe, however, was not a theoretician but a practitioner who might have had a rewarding career in landscape architecture. With the Milbauers, Joe had the perfect place to practice his gardening. Yard space was at a premium in

Joe, cleaned up the garden in the spring before leaving for The Dalles.

Newark but the Milbauer's had a fairly large yard on four city lots. Spatially, there was room for Joe to be creative.

Joe, however, had to be cautious, because Skip was no slouch when it came to gardening. He was a career Prudential man and would spend forty years with this mainstay of the Newark economy. Gardening was his most important hobby, and Joe's assistance made a great yard even greater. Before Joe's arrival, Skip had distinguished himself as an award-winning gardener with 57 varieties of irises. Invariably he won the Prudential Insurance Company annual gardening awards.[50]

Louise Milbauer soon learned that Joe could perform any household chore and fabricate almost anything out of nothing, or very little. It was in the garden, however, where Joe was happiest. By the time he left for the summer, he had the Milbauer garden in perfect shape. When Joe returned, he immediately cleared summer weeds and prepared the garden for the autumn season.

Joe's relationship with Mr. Milbauer was nearly jeopardized in a bizarre episode. For some reason, Joe received credit for the Urban Gardening Contest Award in 1936 from the New York *Herald Tribune*. It is part of Joe's legend that during his greatest coaching season, he also developed an award-winning garden. Skip was annoyed since it was his garden and not Joe's! To whom the

The award-win-ning garden viewed from Joe's window. The barn on the right is on the property next door and cars at rear are on Telford Street.

award should have been made is not clear. It is hard to imag-ine Joe want-ing credit for a garden belonging to Skip. Possibly, bad journalism came into play to create an interesting wrinkle on a slow news day. Fortunately, the inci-dent was forgotten and the fallout minimal. The award is now at Newark Abbey.[51]

Joe had a similar problem with his brother George. The Kasberger home received rave reviews for its landscaping by Joe. George was not pleased, since he did most of the work nine months of the year. Finally he decided that if Joe were going to get the credit, then he could do all the work. Joe arrived to find the yard not up to his standards and exploded at George. After cooling off, Joe got the yard right as only he could.[52]

The 1936 baseball team's 13-2-0 record concluded the school year. With graduation, there were losses and this year it was Peter Carlesimo, who became Joe's most famous protégé as a college athletic direc-tor at Scranton and Fordham Universities. After his Fordham playing career ended, Peter assisted Joe

Peter Carlesimo

before becoming Scranton University's head coach and athletic director.

The Willamette yearbook lamented the graduation of their star football play-er. Accompanying his full-size picture, in varsity letter sweater, is the following text:

JOHN ORAVEC. Meet Willamette's bid for All-American. Four years of Johnny are going to be hard to replace. New 'Joisey' is the state to thank for him along with a prayer to please send us another Scooter![53]

Little did Willamette students know that generous "Uncle Joe" heard their prayers. All Spec had to do was hang on until the next batch of stars arrived! Actually, Dick Weisgerber returned to Willamette for a Little All-American season so there was no need to panic. Yet fans are spoiled by success, and the 1935 Willamette football team was seen by some to be their best. Oravec's graduation, however, ended the Touchdown Twins era.

1936-37 School Year

Joe's 1936 football team was described as perhaps the best in New Jersey high school history, with a record of 9-0-0. What made this team noteworthy was its complete domination, outscoring foes 245-0, and allowing only 13 first downs for the entire season. Unfortunately, the Gray Bees did not play nearby Bloomfield HS in football this season. Bloomfield's 1936 football team, also, was described as one of New Jersey's best, with a 9-0-0 record, and was unscored upon. SBP and SHP did not compete.

Joe was the first to acknowledge that great teams have great players. His 1936 SBP roster produced more college football players than any other teams of his career. One player in particular, Larry Cabrelli, may have accomplished more than any former Kasberger player before his career ended. Peter Carlesimo recalled Larry as a star at Colgate and a great end collegiately and professionally. He was also a very personable and compassionate person, as well as a superb

1936 SBP Football team. First Row: Conti, Dunn, Spiegal, Ondiro, Ostinato, Drury, Reilly, Ruberti, Kolb, Yankaukas, Weiner; Second Row: Kasberger (Coach), McCarthy (Mgr.), Parker, Lonergan, Froelich, Applegate, Klukosovsky, Brown, Bolger, Cabrelli, Barker, Dahl, Milbauer (Asst. Coach); Third Row: Sullivan (Mgr.), Miller, Kaseman, Ellis, Hanlon, Theobald, Collins, Wasserfus, McIntyre, Carr, Norton.

player. As team captain and All-pro with the Philadelphia Eagles, he set a standard of excellence for future SBP players. Three players from this team went to Spec next in their football careers. The dispersion of this talent tells much about Joe's relationship with Spec Keene.

Possibly the first of the Mt. Angel Benedictines to visit Joe in Newark was Fr. Victor Rassier, whose career since 1926 had brought many different assignments. Joe's old coach had remained at Mt. Angel after the fire, serving as the Choir Master for St. Benedict's Abbey until 1927. There were other duties, such as serving as editor of *Our Patron* from 1927-29, and editor of *St. Joseph* magazine from 1925 to 1929. Finally, Fr. Victor left Mt. Angel in 1929 to become principal of the Christian Indian School in British Columbia, serving in that capacity until 1934. Ill health forced him to retire in 1935. Because of Fr. Victor's interest in music, Abbot Thomas Meier sent the ailing monk to Europe where he "began studying plainchant in the Abbeys of Clairvaux and Solemnes." From 1936 to 1937 he became an expert in Gregorian Chant, and returned to St. Benedict's Abbey as Professor of Gregorian Chant.[54]

Newark was a great baseball town, and the Triple A farm team of the New York Yankees, the Newark Bears, had much to do with the city's interest. The Bears set a record of excellence in 1937, winning the International League pennant by 25 games. To cap off this spectacular season, the Bears defeated the Columbus Red Birds to win the Little World Series. Joe Gordon of the Bears became a good friend of Kasberger's. Joe is recalled seeing Gordon play at Ebbets Field in Brooklyn and Chicago's Wrigley Field when changing trains.[55]

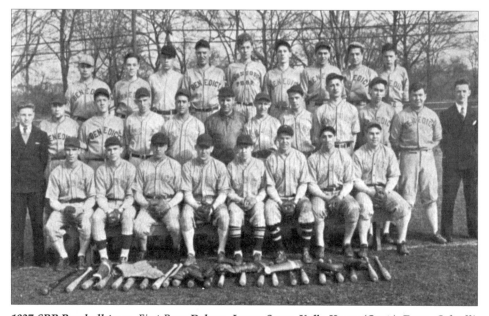

*1937 SBP Baseball team. First Row: **Delany, Lowe, Seery, Kolb, Hearn (Capt.), Dunn, Cabrelli, Drury;** Second Row: **Morrison (Ass't. Mgr.), Coyle, Carr, Applegate, Conti, Kasberger (Coach), Zazzali, Lonergan, Bolger, Keary, Parker, Slowinski (Mgr.);** Third Row: **Norton, Zannetti, McIntyre, Collins, Maloney, Rafter, Brown, Ostinato, Mindnich.***

SBP's 1937 baseball team may have had its success overshadowed by the Bears. Joe's career record in baseball through the 1937 season rose to 82-16 when the 1937 baseball team won the state championship to cap off a 19-0-0 season. It is hard to compare teams of different eras and Joe is not known to have expressed an opinion. But Joe's football and baseball teams of the 1936-37 school year were truly awesome and set records that were never equalled at SBP or very many other schools.

The summer of 1937 brought change at St. Mary's Abbey, when Abbot Ernest died of a heart attack on July 6, at the age of 77. Under his leadership SBP had passed through an important era of development to become an established presence in Newark and New Jersey. Abbot Ernest left behind a student body of 600, with enviable facilities, a proud legacy and a secure future. His successor was well placed to prepare for a future strengthened by its past. Also, St. Mary's Abbey appears to have been well situated at this time.

> The community flourished under his leadership, with most of the vocations coming out of Saint Benedict's Prep. The loss of personnel occasioned by the independence of Saint Anselm had reduced the Community of Saint Mary's from 105 to 71, but over the next ten years professions continued to outpace deaths and departures, so that, at the time of Abbot Ernest's death, the *Ordo* gave the membership of Saint Mary's Abbey as 85.[56]

Abbot Ernest's successor was Rev. Patrick O'Brien, Pastor of St. Joseph's Church in Maplewood, NJ when he was elected – the fourth Abbot of St. Mary's

Abbot Patrick M. O'Brien, elected August 11, 1937.

Abbey. Abbot Patrick spent thirteen years at SBP as "an instructor in algebra." From the very beginning of his tenure as abbot, health was a concern.

At his doctor's recommendation Father Patrick had been excused from the election chapter and was convalescing in Glen Falls, New York, when notified of his nomination. His good friend, Bishop Thomas Walsh of Newark, was at his side when the call came and exhorted him to accept this sign of God's Will.[57]

Abbot Patrick's election coincided with a promotion for Bishop Walsh. Shortly after Abbot Patrick succeeded Abbot Ernest, the Holy See made Newark an archdiocese. Simultaneously, Rome made "Bishop Walsh its first archbishop and the first metropolitan of the newly created Ecclesiastical Province of Newark."[58] Being a close friend of the new archbishop made Abbot Patrick's election interesting, despite his shallow Newark roots.

A native of Manchester, NH, Edward Raphael O'Brien completed his last two years of high school at St. Anselm Prep. Because of poor health, however, college was a struggle.

Only with difficulty did he finish his junior year at Holy Cross College, which he had entered upon graduation from Saint Anselm Prep. He spent the next two years caring for his health, and then entered Saint Anselm College, but had to drop out once again because of ill health.[59]

The young O'Brien taught Latin and history at St. Joseph's School in Manchester. At the age of 28, he entered the novitiate at Saint Vincent Archabbey in Latrobe, PA in June 1914, taking the double name, Patrick Mary.

In July of 1915, after pronouncing simple vows before Abbot Ernest, he returned to Saint Anselm to complete college and study theology. He made his solemn profession of vows in 1918 and was ordained a priest on May 29, 1920.[60]

Fr. Patrick is pictured in the 1931 *Telolog*, and may have served at SBP until his next assignment. His health, reportedly, was still a concern in 1933 when "Abbot Ernest asked him to assume the position of Pastor of Saint Joseph's in Maplewood." When Abbot Patrick succeeded Abbot Ernest, "Bishop Walsh presided at the formal abbatial blessing in the Abbey Church on November 1, 1937."[61]

It did not take long for the new abbot's agenda to be made known. "Abbot Patrick informed the chapter that he was determined to develop the Morristown property." How much discussion ensued is not known, but this account indicated there was none. "He was convinced of the need for a Catholic boarding school for boys in northern New Jersey."[62] The new president of SBP made his first move decisively.

Despite his frail appearance, Abbot Patrick was pictured as a baseball player at St. Anselm's College. It is only natural that there is tension in educational institutions between sports and academics. At SBP, Abbot Patrick may have had a different view than his predecessor. The only thing worse than losing, perhaps, is winning too often, and Joe may have had that problem after the 1936-37 school year. It is well that Fr. Boniface stayed as headmaster while Abbot Patrick acclimated himself to his new position.

1937-38 School Year

The 1937 football team posted a 6-0-1 record. The only blemish was a 6-6 tie with Bordentown Military Institute (BMI), a nemesis in the making. The Cadets/Little Army tormented Joe for the rest of his career. The Seton Hall rivalry resumed after a two-year hiatus with an exciting SBP win. A close game was decided by a SHP fumble on their own 25 yard line. SBP capitalized when "Bee quarterback George Conti pitched ten yards to Maurice Longeran for the 6-0 victory."[63] After the 1937 season, Joe's SBP career football record was 54-5-4.

These successes, perhaps, added fuel to the idea that the Benedictines could operate a boarding prep school of academic and athletic quality. This notion came to fruition, apparently, as events unfolded in 1938. Most SBP alumni and students were pleased with athletic prominence. There also may have been a minority sentiment that the Gray Bees were too good, and the presence of PG student-athletes may have become a matter of debate.

St. Mary's Monastery, Morristown, built in 1937.

The oversight of St. Mary's Abbey in formally establishing a priory at Delbarton was rectified in 1938 when the Diocese of Paterson was created to include this site. This account indicates that Abbot Patrick and Bishop Thomas McLaughlin of Paterson were the principals in an arrangement made to formally establish a Benedictine priory under the aegis of St. Mary's Abbey. As early as 1930, theological students from St. Mary's Abbey were transferred from Manchester to Delbarton. Thus, Rev. Vincent Amberg became the first prior of St. Mary's monastery at Delbarton when it was completed in 1938.[64]

This development, however, may have been the first sign that Delbarton's presence would soon be felt with the new abbot. It did not take long for secondary events to occur in Morristown that had a profound impact on SBP, and the Newark Benedictine community, committed to its urban tradition. According to accounts, the following transpired:

In 1938, Bishop McLaughlin, who for some years had served as secretary to Bishop Walsh of Newark, was named the first chief shepherd of the newly created Diocese of Paterson.

In the following months he expressed concern to Abbot O'Brien that "his diocese was inadequately supplied with Catholic schools."[65] Having only one bishop to satisfy was not a luxury enjoyed by Abbot Patrick. "Bishop Griffin of the Diocese of Trenton voiced the same concerns for his own diocese." Thus, the price of ecclesiastical success that St. Mary's Abbey enjoyed was not insignificant.

Both men stated that they would like to see a Catholic boarding school for boys established to compete with The Lawrenceville School, The Peddie School, Blair Academy, and the traditional boarding schools of New England.[66]

Competing with these long established boarding prep schools was a daunting task. How much diocesan support would be provided is unknown.

In the midst of these events, the 1938 baseball team had an 11-5-0 record to end the school year. In the season's second game, a 4-2 win over Don Bosco Prep of Ramsey, Joe coached the 100th game of his SBP career with a winning record of 84 percent. Snyder HS of Jersey City ended SBP's 31-game winning streak in the season's sixth game. SHP defeated the Gray Bees, 4-8 in the next game, the Pony Pirate's first victory in baseball or football over Joe. Three additional losses followed to end Joe's worst baseball season in Newark.

SBP was the proud flagship of St. Mary's Abbey for many years. Surely it would continue to be nurtured. Investments should be made in its future to maintain its standing in New Jersey academic and athletic circles. Yet the baseball and football teams of 1937-38 were less successful than those of the previous year. Perhaps a trend of decline, or de-emphasis of athletics, had begun. Subsequent years found winning records more modest through 1943. Perhaps this was due in part to changes in philosophy at St. Mary's Abbey. Or, there was more competitive balance among the secondary schools.

1938-39 School Year

The school year began with the football team producing a modest record of 4-1-1. In the season's second game, BMI tied the Gray Bees 7-7. The season finale saw SHP finally defeat Joe in football as described by an anonymous writer.

> When St. Benedict's took the field in 1938 it boasted a 23 game win streak [sic]. It was a lightning fast Bee team against a heavy, power-laden Hall squad. The game is one of the greatest in the annals of both schools. Boasting names who were to become known on collegiate gridirons, the Hall smashed across two scores to win 14-0. Mike Holovak, a piston legged fullback who went on to make All American at Boston College, provided the charge.[67]

Noteworthy this season was a relatively limited schedule, but the reason for fewer games is not known.

The 1938 football season produced New Jersey's last undefeated, untied, and unscored upon football team with Lodi HS's 8-0-0 record achieved while outscoring opponents 167-0.[68] Significantly, Lodi HS's prowess under Coach Stan Piela was attributed to its regional student body, coming from several nearby Bergen County towns. This arrangement deepened the Rams' talent pool and was a precursor of things to come in secondary school athletics. The implications were not lost on Joe, who would address this issue.

While Joe experienced a tough year, Spec coped with the loss at graduation of Dick Weisgerber to the Green Bay Packers. Three more talented SBP athletes were in Salem filling the void. None of these, however, achieved the fame of Oravec and Weisgerber – who were Oregon folk heroes. Joe, however, kept Spec well supplied with athletic talent, but Willamette's use of New Jersey prep school athletes was controversial.

The baseball season was highlighted at midseason with a 9-3 win over St. Mary's HS of South Amboy for Joe's 100th career win at SBP, giving him a winning record of 81 percent. The school year ended with the baseball team's 17-4 season to bring Joe's career record in the 1930s to 110-25-0. The April 17, 1946 *Benedict News* wrote about the Gray Bees' forty years of baseball history. Through the 1939 season, SBP in its history had a record of 442-100-0 for a winning record of 81 percent. In a series with Newark Central HS dating to 1912, SBP led 16-5.[69]

Joe was home for the summer with much to ponder. Looking back at his record, Joe saw great performances by his teams. Now he looked ahead to war clouds on the horizon. In addition to international conflict, Joe saw new threats to SBP posed by emerging public and parochial high-school athletic programs. Even now Vince Lombardi's name was heard as co-coach at a small Englewood, NJ high school, St Cecilia's. Lombardi's style and influence on high school football became formidable. In Newark and its suburbs, more big, public high schools competed for the young men that Joe needed for his teams. These concerns, however, were unimportant should war come for the United States.

One of the gaps in this research is establishing SBP's hierarchy for athletics. The athletic director, by one account, was Jim Cavanagh, a disputed notion that remains unresolved. Thus the headmaster, Fr. Boniface Reger, appears pivotal in dealing with the famous coaches. By all accounts, Fr. Boniface did an excellent job with these men who had and were achieving legendary status: Blood, Cavanagh, and Kasberger. Not many schools were big enough to house so much talent. Fortunately, egos were not a problem with these superior coaches who collaborated in the

Prof Blood, Joe and Jim Cavanagh.

changing environment of high/prep school sports. PG students were a staple at prep schools, but were not permitted at the high schools. This problem would require attention, but the war threat postponed immediate action.

In May 1939 Bishop McLaughlin discussed with Abbot O'Brien the feasibility of a Catholic boarding school. The result was a proposal for a school to open in September at Delbarton. The St. Mary's Abbey community approved by a strong majority their desire for a residential high school. Thus, "the original Koontz

Clericate of St. Mary's Abbey-Delbarton, 1939. Kneeling: **Ignatius Kohl, Adrian McLaughlin, Mark Confroy, Alfred Meister, Frederick Muench;** Standing: **Edmund Nugent, Jerome Fitzpatrick, Leo Beger, Gilbert Crawford, Leonard Cassell, William Fagen, Kenneth Mayer.**

mansion was given over to Delbarton School," and alterations were made for the school to open in Sept. 1939 with 12 boarding students in Grades 7 and 8. Former SBP football coach in 1915, Fr. Augustine Wirth, was its first headmaster.[70]

The summer of 1939 found Claire Milbauer in The Dalles, and she noticed that the Depression had lost its grip there as well as in Newark. Employment in war-related industries, as well as in agriculture, improved conditions for everyone. The Milbauer and Kasberger families knew from the World War I experience how much life was changed at such times, as World War II drew closer.[71]

One of the New Deal's public works projects created an opportunity that was perfect for Bob Murray. The Dalles had built a new 150-meter swimming pool to AAU standards. In addition to the natatorium, there was a new convention center and Bob Murray "assumed the position of manager of both," remaining in this role until his retirement.[72] In his new job, Murray continued to make a tremendous impression on the boys and girls of The Dalles. Joe may have been especially pleased to return to Newark knowing that Bob had survived the Depression and was rewarded for his faith in their home town.

1939-40 School Year

By the time World War II began in Sept. 1939, the school year was underway. It was business as usual at SBP and in the Milbauer home. Yet there was an underlying unease as the conflict widened and intensified. Mobilization for United States entry into the war accelerated and government-imposed restrictions on normal lifestyles began with rationing. Since Joe loved to walk, gas rationing was not a personal hardship. With Newark's superior public transit, there was no great inconvenience.

Joe's legend in Newark often mentions his walking, to the exclusion of driving. Perhaps he was uncomfortable with city-driving in Newark. Bud Sandoz suggested that Joe never relinquished his Oregon driver's license when he went East, even though he was rarely observed driving in Newark. Joe was recalled taking Sunday hikes to faraway places such as Livingston, several miles over the

Joe read the paper on the sun porch every evening. Claire Milbauer captioned this photo "Solid comfort." Note carpentry tools on the radiator.

mountains west of Newark. It was not Oregon, but the South Mountain Reservation was a challenge for hikers. Bun recalled that some of his "best memories of Joe K were Sunday afternoon walks to the Newark/South Orange line." These walks followed dinner "at my Grandmother's house." For a youngster of seven or eight years of age, the "two-mile round-trip walk" was an opportunity to listen to Joe's views on a variety of subjects. On the subject of walking, "Joe explained that it was never too early to start on getting in shape and walking was very healthy."[73]

Maybe Joe walked more to take his mind off a disappointing 1939 football season's 3-3-2 record. One of the ties was of the scoreless variety against SHP before a crowd reported at 5,000. Yet Joe's career football record of 61-9-7 for the decade of the 1930s at SBP was outstanding. Unquestionably, Joe's football schedule was tougher, with more college freshman and junior-varsity teams as opposition that had begun in 1936.

Montclair State College's junior-varsity team was the first college-level team that Joe faced in 1936, defeating the collegians 6-0. In 1937, the Gray Bees defeated the Manhattan College frosh 6-0. While there were no college teams on his 1938 schedule, the 1939 season found two college teams, Villanova College frosh, a 0-6 loss and Columbia University frosh, another loss, 14-20. The level of competition may account for the poor record. The 1939 football season ended in a 0-0 tie with SHP. Unfortunately, the saddest incident of Joe's entire coaching career occurred during this season when SBP football player, "Rip" Collins, sustained a very serious leg injury. His condition worsened and the leg was amputated by Dr. Paul A. "Bucky" O'Connor, SBP's team physician. Dr. O'Connor was not an SBP alumnus, but a Notre Dame football star in 1929 and 1930.[74]

The following document, written by Joe, is undated and appears to be an outline for a speech or paper. Joe's success as a football coach may have generated requests for advice. Because of his record in the thirties, it is very possible it was written at this time. The title is "YOUR SON SHOULD PLAY FOOTBALL," and the text is as follows:

1. If he really wants to.
2. If his physical condition permits it.
3. If he plays under the proper kind of coaching and supervision.
4. If his school provides the right kind of equipment and sanitary conditions.

5. If he is willing to go faithfully and daily through the drudgery that practice can sometime be.

6. If he knows the meaning of obedience and does as he is told.

7. If he abides by the training and conditioning rules of diet, cleanliness and sleep.

8. If he understands the necessity of using an antiseptic on cuts and of reporting injuries.

9. If he can maintain an acceptable average in schoolwork.

10. If he is well balanced emotionally.

11. If he is unselfish and thinks of the boys on the team.

12. If he wants to do something constructive and worth while during his spare hours during the afternoon.

The next two paragraphs continued on the same page:

> Urge boys to participate. First of all, participation makes them hungrier and healthier, subdues their egos and gives them a sense of fair play; and, for another thing, it keeps them occupied from 4:00 until 6:00 – the two most dangerous hours in an adolescent's afternoon.
>
> The football field is one place where democracy really works and a boy is judged by his ability and his effort, not by his color, his circumstances or his creed.

The next paragraphs are on another page but appear to be a continuation of the above.

> Proficiency in an individual sport will help the boy to make valuable contacts when he enters the business or professional world. But the team work he learns from football will be an even greater asset to him. In tennis and golf a boy plays for himself. In football he plays for a team. There is no such thing, K. Rockne once said, as a ten-and-one team. It has to be an eleven-man organization, and the different parts must work in unison to make up the finished whole. If a boy is to be a worthy member of this organization, he must bow to the will of his coach; he must keep himself in topnotch condition; he must put the team's interest ahead of his own. In short, he must learn team play – and team play is the chief essential for success in any field of endeavor today.
>
> In learning team play a boy needs more than capable hands, nimble feet, a controlled body. He needs a level head and the kind of temperament that adjusts well. How does your son qualify?[75]

Newark's 1940 population was 429,760 which included the in-migration of large numbers of Southern blacks.[76] They took jobs in defense-related manufacturing, and their numbers in the 1940 Census approximated 45,760. This racial group was a new variable in what was, virtually, an all-white city. Blacks, in 1940, remained a relatively small percentage of Newark's total population, but their presence became more noticeable.

The 1940 baseball team had a 17-3-0 record to complete the school year. As in football, college teams moved onto the schedule. The first college baseball team appeared on Joe's schedule in 1937, when SBP defeated the Newark University junior-varsity team 5-0 in that milestone game. College teams did not appear again until the 1940 season, when the Gray Bees played the Rutgers University frosh and Columbia University frosh, winning both games by scores of 17-8 and 11-6, respectively.

With the Depression ended, automobiles were in demand. For folks in The Dalles, getting the latest beauty from Detroit was facilitated by Joe. By one account, Joe left Newark for The Dalles via Detroit where he picked up a sporty two-door 1940 Chevrolet for Tom Dixon and drove it home. At the time, such a car retailed for about $730, so Tom saved money on transportation charges and Joe had a chance to test-drive the vehicle and see the sights on the road west.[77]

1940-41 School Year

A first clue to the mystery surrounding the identity of SBP's athletic director(s) during Joe's first decade in Newark appears in 1940. Thanks to Joe Hellberg's recall, it was learned that Fr. John Doyle had this role, assisted by a lay faculty member, Larry Keefe.

Joe's 1940 football team's 6-2-1 record began the school year. An account of the game against SHP is provided by an anonymous writer.

> Frank Dempsey and Len Bonforte provided the perfect pass combination as the Bees downed a scrappy Hall eleven 13-6. Late in the last period Seton Hall drove to the Bees three, but lost the ball on downs.[78]

Rev. John Doyle, O.S.B., SBP athletic director.

Getting more publicity than the SHP game was the contest against Columbia University frosh earlier in the season. One of the most famous personalities to ever compete against SBP was Jack Kerouac. More famous later as a writer, Kerouac was a highly-recruited high school star from Lowell, MA, who spent a prep school year at Horace Mann. His football career, however, ended in a game against the Gray Bees while playing for the Columbia University frosh. This obscure football game, that ended in a 13-13 tie, has a footnote in literary history that surrounds Kerouac.

The game's real drama was Kerouac returning the opening kickoff 90 yards, with Columbia head coach Lou Little and Dartmouth head coach Red Blaik in attendance. These famous coaches were there to see Kerouac perform after hearing of his exploits a week earlier against the Rutgers University frosh. Fate was not kind to Kerouac's Columbia football career on this date against SBP. While returning a punt Kerouac injured his leg and his football career ended – which led to his becoming a writer. Kerouac's classic novel, *On the Road*, made him famous as a key figure in the "Beat Generation."[79]

Joe Hellberg was a PG player for SBP from New Brunswick, NJ who remembers the game but neither Kerouac nor his injury. Joe recalls being preoccupied with Columbia's "Big Moose" Hasselman, but performing well enough that day to earn All-Metropolitan honors and scholarship offers from Syracuse, Florida and Oregon State. His decision to attend Oregon State and study forestry was unusual for SBP players who traditionally went to Willamette. Thus, Joe Hellberg has the distinction of being Joe Kasberger's first New Jersey player to attend his alma mater.[80]

The 1941 baseball team concluded the school year with a 16-1-2 record. Joe's 8-4 victory over SHP widened SBP's historical margin in this rivalry to 32-10, in a series begun in 1910. Ties are unusual in baseball, and the two that marred SBP's record came in the season's last four games.

1941-42 School Year

Despite the tensions of a world at war, St. Mary's Abbey appears concerned with other matters. What were the expectations when the boarding school at Delbarton was initiated? Certainly the economics of this grand experiment were debated fully before its implementation by the monastic community. In Sept. 1941, Delbarton's enrollment had grown to 20 boarding students, hardly a break-even enrollment by today's standards.[81] The monks may have depended on their main cash cow, SBP, to subsidize its country brother while needs in Newark were deferred or postponed.

In Newark, SBP's 1941 football team began the school year with a 6-3-0 record. The SHP game was cancelled due to the bitterness of the rivalry exceeding civil bounds. Thus SBP's 1940 victory over the Pony Pirates was the last game between these foes for nearly two decades. Joe's handwritten scores on the 1941 schedule that he sent to Joe Hellberg vary from results published in the *Telolog*, as noted in the Appendix by the designation (#). This schedule confirms Fr. John Doyle as SBP athletic director.

Spec Keene's late night phone calls to Joe on recruiting and other matters disrupted the entire Milbauer household.[82] In late 1941, it is likely they discussed the amazing Oregon State Beavers, who finally won the Pacific Coast Conference football championship and were invited to host the Rose Bowl. Their fraternity brother and former teammate, Percy Locey, became Oregon State's athletic director earlier in 1941 and could arrange good tickets for the game in Pasadena for a wonderful reunion. Also, Spec and Joe probably discussed Willamette's Hawaii trip for a pre-Christmas bowl game.

When Joe heard the news on Dec. 7 from Pearl Harbor, his first reaction must have been fear. This Willamette football squad was in the wrong place at the wrong time. Pearl Harbor, and the United States entry into World War II, became a personal concern for Joe. Inadvertently thrust on the scene in Hawaii was Tony Fraiola from New Jersey, who played for Spec's Bearcats. Fraiola was thought to have been from Newark and a former Kasberger player at SBP. Actually, Tony was from suburban New Providence where he attended Summit HS. His journey to Salem was via the United States Marine Corps and San Diego, where Spec discovered him. Fraiola was attracted to Willamette, how-ever, by Spec's SBP players, but never met Joe until after he came to Salem. The March 1995 *Willamette Quarterly Athletics Newsletter* has the following story headlined: "Yesterday's Heroes, Football trip transplants Fraiola." The story featured Tony as "part of a long line of New Jersey athletes who found their way to Willamette in the 1930s." Although unnamed in this story, the "good friend" was certainly Joe.

> Bearcat coach Spec Keene had a good friend who worked at a Catholic school in New Jersey – which is probably the only way to explain how a full-blooded Italian from the East Coast could end up in sleepy little Salem, Ore.[83]

It is not surprising that a young man from New Jersey was homesick in Salem. "Fraiola remembers struggling through his early years at Willamette, and twice contemplated quitting school." Since Spec and his wife Marie were very considerate and respected, "Keene talked him out of it, and Fraiola couldn't be more thankful." Fraiola was one of the last New Jersey players before the war. Earlier in the decade there was, "thanks in large part to the New Jersey connec-tion," a dynasty that continued until World War II.[84]

In 1940, "Willamette was so good, in fact, Keene got his Bearcats to play in an event in the Shrine Bowl in Honolulu." By today's standards, this was an unusu-al arrangement of round-robin play among three teams. "Willamette, San Jose State and the University of Hawaii were to play each other over a period of weeks in December of 1941." Luke Gill, Hawaii's head coach was a Phi Delta Theta fraternity brother from OAC, so Spec had a personal incentive for the trip, despite the outcome. Willamette's first game on Dec. 6 was a loss to Hawaii, 6-20. The loss was quickly forgotten on the next day when "Japan bombed Pearl Harbor and suddenly the United States, along with the Willamette football team, was thrust in the middle of World War II." The story continued with Fraiola reminiscing that the bombs "ruined the whole trip." The Willamette contingent "stayed on the island of Oahu for almost three weeks before leaving for the mainland just before Christmas."[85]

Who would ever dream that after a football game, they would awaken "to the sound of falling bombs and antiaircraft gunfire the next day." Fortunately, Spec and his players were unharmed and they performed "guard duty in Honolulu before it was considered safe for them to zig-zag home on the President Wilson." In retrospect, Fraiola "still can't wash away the memory of what Willamette football might have been had the war not broken out, when he was just a sophomore." Fraiola noted sadly, "if we had stayed together, what a team we would have had."[86] Despite the unexpected event on the Hawaiian trip, Fraiola remains fond of Willamette. To some, this was Spec's best Bearcat foot-ball team, but Pearl Harbor effectively ended the program under Keene.

Despite Joe's best arguments to the contrary, Spec's coaching brethren in the Northwest Conference put an end to PGs at Willamette. The controversy did not end in Oregon until World War II when college football was curtailed by man-power shortages. Oregon State, among many other schools, did not play during the 1943 football season. World War II had its impact on everyone, and it ended the Newark-Salem pipeline of talent.

Lon Stiner's career record of 72-50-17 at Oregon State was not spectacular, but he is distinguished for leading the Beavers to the 1941 Pacific Coast Conference championship and the school's first Rose Bowl invitation. Despite the Beavers' accomplishment, it was unlikely that Joe could get to Pasadena for a traditional Rose Bowl game on New Year's Day – since he spent the holidays in Newark. Strange circumstances, however, provided Joe a New Year's Day treat; and the opportunity to see the Beavers play was highly unusual because of the circumstances. The 1942 spectacle was the first and only Rose Bowl game not played in Pasadena. The key individual with regard to the 1942 Rose Bowl was Percy Locey, whose persistence in salvaging the game is a real story.

Military officials on the West Coast cancelled the game despite the 65,000 tickets that were sold for the Pasadena stadium. Due to the war, military author-ities felt that the game posed a danger – the possibility of more Japanese attacks. Given the little time available after the cancellation, Locey became very innova-tive because of the game's great significance for Oregon State fans, who had suf-fered and waited too long for this moment. In their minds, the game had to be played. Locey's coordination and implementation of a contingency plan was one of the best jobs ever done by a college athletic director.[87]

Oregon State's 7-2 record in 1941 was not exceptional, however good enough to set the stage for one of the most unique New Year's Days in college football history. The folks in Corvallis were outraged when the game was cancelled; Locey went to work to salvage it. As the host team, Oregon State had the choice of an opponent, and wanted to play the best team available. In 1941, the num-ber-one-ranked team was Minnesota, but playing the game in Minneapolis was prohibitive because of the weather. The second-ranked team was Duke, whose location and climate prompted Locey to call Duke head coach, Wallace Wade, familiar with the Rose Bowl tradition as the former head coach at the University of Alabama. His Crimson Tide teams participated in the 1926, 1927, and 1931 games, winning twice and tying once. Also, Wade had played in the 1916 game for Brown University in a 0-14 loss to Washington State College.[88]

Possibly relevant to our story was Wade's successor at Alabama, who may have been known by Joe and was probably known by Frank Milbauer as a team-mate. The University of Alabama's president, Mike Denny, replaced Wade with an unheralded, but highly recommended, assistant coach from the University of Georgia, Frank Thomas. The new Tide head football coach from East Chicago, IN was a quarterback on Rockne's 1920-21-22 teams. At Alabama, Thomas pro-duced an outstanding record that was overshadowed only by his protégé, Paul "Bear" Bryant, who attributed much of his success to the influence of Coaches Thomas and Rockne.[89]

After a brief discussion, Duke accepted the Oregon State challenge, and Locey arranged for the game to be played on the Duke campus in Durham, NC.

Duke players voted repeatedly against playing the game because of the holidays. Wade, however, finally prevailed upon his players by allowing them to go home for Christmas, in a decision that may have backfired. The 1941 Duke team was undefeated at 9-0-0, with a prolific offense that made them heavy favorites against the Beavers. The Oregon State team was enthusiastic about both the game and the opportunity to see the country. After a cross-country train journey through Chicago and Washington, DC, they arrived at their training site in Chapel Hill on the University of North Carolina campus. While the Duke players went home for Christmas, the Beavers worked hard. Accordingly, Oregon State may have been more physically and emotionally prepared for the game.[90]

Duke's stadium had a normal capacity of 35,000. With permission from Wallace Wade and the Duke administration, Percy Locey added 21,000 temporary seats. Locey then sold the tickets and promoted the game to make the Durham Rose Bowl a commercial success. Blessed with relatively good weather in Durham on New Year's Day, Oregon State fans were fortunate since there were awful conditions that afternoon in Pasadena. The Beavers stunned the Blue Devils 20-16 and Oregon State fans were delirious. On what had promised to be a bleak New Year's Day, had the game not been played, the Beaver faithful were rewarded. Locey took no chances in selecting game officials, including the timekeeper, Joe Kasberger, who was not a factor in the outcome.[91]

This improbable game had two immediate results for Joe. First, he was able to rekindle old friendships. Second, Oregon media coverage focused attention on Joe and his SBP career. In a multifaceted story, Joe was reintroduced to Oregon after more than a decade in Newark. The following story appeared Jan. 10, 1942 in the admired and widely read "Greg's Gossip" in the *Oregonian*, written by Sports Editor L.H. Gregory. His column was gospel in Oregon to sports fans. Gregory remembered everything, and often pulled a lot of material, past and present, together.

Joe Kasberger came down from St. Benedict's school in Newark, N.J., for the game at Durham and Lon Stiner pressed him into duty as timer. He meant to drive and there was to be quite an automobile caravan from Newark. But along came the news that no ordinary citizen can buy tires any more, and Joe says that scared them all out. He came by train . . . Joe, that rarity, a straight A student, used to quarterback at Oregon State, first under Bill Hargiss, then with Dick Rutherford as coach in '20 and '21. After his graduation in '22 he coached at Mount Angel, until the big fire in '26. Then for two or three seasons he helped Spec Keene at Willamette – meanwhile, in 1924, having taken a year off to go to Notre Dame to learn football under Knute Rockne as sort of unofficial assistant – that was the year of the Four Horsemen, so Joe not only had quite an experience, but made valuable acquaintances . . . After assisting

Joe's photo which appeared in "Greg's Gossip" column.

in football at Southern Oregon Normal in '29, he meant to go to California to teach, but Ralph Coleman talked him into getting himself one of those master of arts degrees at Columbia. While there in '30, he was offered the coaching job at St. Benedict's, a big prep school with 600 boys, at Newark, and took it, meanwhile working nights and Saturdays to finish up with that master of arts degree. Been at St. Benedict's ever since.

The story continues with the paragraph heading "83 Games Won."

For 12 seasons in football Joe's teams have won 83 games, tied 7 and lost only 14, and in baseball for 11 seasons his boys have taken 144 games and lost only 28. As you can guess, Joe has no immediate coaching worries.

Every now and then one of his St. Benedict's boys used to come out to Willamette. Dick Weisgerber, who at fullback helped Willamette start that long string of Northwest conference victories (he's now a baseball unpire), was one. Another was little Johnny Oravec – they called the pair 'the touchdown twins,' which was nice and poetic, except that one twin weighed around 212 and the other, Oravec, never scaled more than 145 – not very twin-like.

Still another was Vincent Herriman [sic], who later took up shortstopping in the Western International. Joe is still turning out fine athletes. Matt Bolger, the sensational Notre Dame pass-catching end, who grabbed the pass that beat Northwestern 7-6, is one of Joe's boys. So is Joe Hellberg, a promising freshman football end at Oregon State.

The story goes on with the paragraph heading "Not a Junior College."

Some of the Northwest conference schools used to get pretty mad about the boys from St. Benedict's on Willamette teams. It went so far as an attempt to have them declared junior college transfers, so as to limit their eligibility, but the move got side-tracked after Spec Keene made an eloquent plea that a 'prep school' in the East is nothing like a junior college.

Joe tells me there is no similarity with a junior college. That a St. Benedict's boy like Bolger can enter Notre Dame with freshman standing is strong confirmatory evidence.

'Nothing on the Pacific coast is quite like these prep schools of the East,' Joe explains. 'A prep school really is just a sort of extra-special high school. Many of our prep school boys have had four years of high school, others only three, but still they are not able to enter college and the prep school gets them ready. Prep school boys are not, however, prepared for anything higher than freshman collegiate standing.'[92]

When advised of the story, Bolger responded that he was a conventional, not a post-graduate, student at SBP. Moreover, Bolger was a neighbor on Halstead Street and had known Joe since childhood. Gregory concluded the story with a reference to a *New York Times* story by Allison Danzig. The Danzig story dealt with freshman eligibility during World War II and the extraordinary measures needed to keep the college game alive. High schools/prep schools were the essential incubators for players as war-related shortages became acute and college sports were in jeopardy.

Joe needed to say nothing in the Milbauer household about his work and accomplishments because they were common knowledge. In Oregon, however, it appears that virtually nothing was known of Joe's achievements. Thus the stories appearing in Portland and at Mt. Angel after the 1942 Rose Bowl were important communication sources in learning about Joe. Joe's nephew, Bud Sandoz, remarked that the first he ever knew of his Uncle Joe's coaching fame was during World War II. Bud recalled being in the Philippines when he met a soldier from East Orange, NJ who played against Joe's SBP teams.[93]

The Jan. 16, 1940 *Pacific Star* had the following story about Joe:

Joe Hellberg in Oregon State football uniform.

Next to Pearl Harbor the Rose Bowl has been the center of the national spotlight. Sitting right out in front as time-keeper at that game was Joe Kasberger '17. ... Greg's Gossip on January 10 carried a story and a picture about Joe.[94]

This brief note led to the May 9, 1942 *Pacific Star* story with the headline, "Kasberger Sets Great Record – Feels Kindly Toward M.A.C."

Have you heard about the coach whose football team copped eight state championships in ten seasons, at one time streaking to victories for seven straight years without losing a game, whose baseball nine at one time chalked up 30 consecutive victories, and who at the end of this amazing record admitted that 'it's the players that make the coach?'

'Give the world's worst coach a team of players made up of men like Grange, Thorpe, and Nagurski, and I am certain he could teach them wrong, yet they could go out, do everything right, and make him a winner,' was the blunt opinion of Coach Joseph Kasberger in a recent cross-country interview on the 'cause of my success.'

Kasberger, former Mt. Angel college coach from 1922 to 1926 set the amazing record quoted above at St. Benedict's preparatory in New Jersey. In the written interview Kasberger still felt keenly toward Mt. Angel. He wrote on old Mt. Angel College Athletic Association letterhead paper.

The story continues with the heading, "Started two Notre Dame Captains."

As many as 18 players a year have gone on to successful college football careers from Joe's St. Benedict's teams. Notre Dame picked two of its football captains off the St. Benedict's campus, 'Bill' Smith, captain of the 1936 Notre Dame team, and Hughie Devore.

But we can't forget the two 'All-Americans' that Kasberger sent to Willamette university. Johnny Oravec, little 'All-American' halfback and second highest scorer in the nation in 1935; and 'Dick' Weisgerber, little 'All-American' fullback and second highest scorer in the nation in 1936 are both Kasberger's products. For the past two years Weisgerber has played for the Green Bay Packers, champions of the Professional Football league last year.

The story continues with the heading, "Was Headache To Umpire." Note that the nickname "Kash" for Joe probably arose when his name was misspelled in a news story as "Kashberger" – when he was a MAC player and selected to the all-star team.

> Very few of today's Hilltop students remember Kasberger. Your writer was seven years old when Joe coached the Mt. Angel Townies. 'Kash' was the idol of every Mt. Angel boy, the talk of every player in the league, and the headache of every umpire in the Valley.
> Students and athletes of '26 remember Joe as the man who was all set to put Mt. Angel college on the map. Then came the fire of 1926.
> 1936 was perhaps Joe's greatest year at St. Benedict's. In that season his football team knocked over nine opponents, ending the season with an uncrossed goal line, and leaving the nine opponents with a total of 13 first downs to divide among themselves. Figuring this out, one finds that the opposition scored about one first down in each game. St. Benedict's scored 245 points.

The story concludes with the heading: "Watch Spiegel Next Year!" The *Pacific Star* noted that Willamette fared as well as SBP's nearby universities, Fordham and Columbia.

> Here is a tip direct from 'Kash' on who to watch next year in college circles. Keep an eye on Adam Spiegel! He is a comer at fullback for Columbia university. Look for these names in next year's college lineups and think of Joe Kasberger, their high school coach! Ted Ruberti, Columbia university, center; Jimmy Hearn, halfback, Pete Carlesimo, guard, and Hugh Addonizio, quarterback, all at Fordham; 'Horsey' Lonergan, John Kolb, and Larry Drury at Willamette. Altogether at least 24 of Joe's boys will play college football next year at Notre Dame, Villanova, Manhattan, and you name it.
> 'My share of good material, a fair knowledge of the game, the fact that I am a stickler on fundamentals, and the rabbit's foot in my pocket account for most of our victories,' in Joe's own words.
> The *Star* is saving Kasberger's 'advice to would-be coaches' for a later issue.[95]

The previous sentence is enticing, but this material has not been located.

Due to World War II, 1942 was a tough year for young men facing the draft. Even many coaches were affected and the sports scene was altered. Joe turned 46 in Jan. 1942 and it is unlikely that at his age he would be drafted. Yet within the year, Spec was on active duty. As a commissioned Army officer during World War I, it is surprising that Spec now served in the Navy as a Lieutenant Commander. His military duties may have been appropriate for many coaches, even Joe. Spec was "in charge of physical fitness programs for the 12th Naval District (California, Nevada, Utah, Colorado)."[96] Joe is not believed to have volunteered for, or been solicited for, a service commission to perform similar functions. The fact that Joe held no previous commission as an officer may have kept him from being called to active duty during World War II.

Surprisingly, there were enough players for the 1942 baseball season to be played. Joe's 1942 team had a 19-1-0 record to conclude the school year. The spoiler was Pennington School in the season's finale by a score of 8-3, to end a streak of 28 straight games without a loss, and 20 consecutive wins.

The Appendix does not agree with a Thursday, May 28, 1942 Newark *Evening News* caricature of Joe by Bill Crawford that states "44 school wins in a row." The Appendix does concur with a story in that paper on that date, that SBP's win over St. Mary's HS of South Amboy was the 18th in a row for the 1942 season, extending a non-losing streak of 27 games, including two ties during the 1941 season. The 19-game win-streak began in the last game of the 1941 season against SHP. Possibly, records were kept separately for

"schools" and other foes such as secondary and college teams. In response, Joe sent the story to Joe Hellberg with the following handwritten note:

> I don't like this – always a jinx – thanks a million for the picture, Joe. I'll take care of it when I see you in Corvallis this summer. My best to all – always, Joe[97]

While Joe was in Oregon, the summer proved eventful at St. Mary's Abbey. Joe returned to Newark and learned that in August, 1942 Abbot O'Brien chose Rev. Stephen Findlay as Delbarton's headmaster due to the poor health of Rev. Augustine Wirth. [98]

1942-43 School Year

Joe's 1942 football team had enough players and competition to win another state championship. SBP's perfect 7-0-0 record began the school year, including wins over two college teams. The midseason saw Joe coach his 100th career football game in a 13-0 win over Admiral Farragut Academy for a winning record of 79 percent. The Nov. 22, 1942 Newark *Sunday Call* headlines the team's reward, "New Jersey's Prep School Championship Goes to St. Benedict's." The story had two sub-paragraphs: "Holy Cross Cup To Local School" and "Lawrenceville Refuses to Play Gray Bees for State Title."

State championship honors in the major prep school football ranks go this year to St. Benedict's of Newark. As the New Jersey State Interscholastic A.A. does not rate the big prep school teams, the award is made here independently.

Winners of all their games, the Gray Bees show victories over New Brunswick, LaSalle, Manhattan Freshmen, Columbia Freshmen, Farragut, Blair and Bordentown.

Lawrenceville, also undefeated, conquered Newark Academy, Haverford Prep, Princeton third team, Hill, Choate and Peddie. The St. Benedict's team played a more difficult schedule and won by more decisive margins.

To settle the issue on the field, if possible, the Newark team challenged Lawrenceville to a postseason game. The answer from Lawrenceville was 'We have put our uniforms away for the season.'

Gray Bee Grid Coach Congratulates Captain

"Joe Kasberger, coach of St. Benedict's (right), congratulates Al Malekoff, captain of the team, when informed the Gray Bees have been selected as prep school football champions of New Jersey and winners of Holy Cross College trophy."

This year Holy Cross College offered a state championship trophy to the outstanding prep school team. The cup is hereby awarded to St. Benedict's. Comparing the records of the contending teams, there is no cause for questioning the decision.[99]

While Joe was doing the expected in Newark, Vince Lombardi became the head football coach of St. Cecilia HS in Englewood. The impact may have been felt, or at least noticed, in Newark. More apparent to Joe was the dwindling number of football players and teams. Joe saw the problem in The Dalles, where "4-fers" became a common term to describe athletes physically unfit for military service. How could any football coach continue without physically fit athletes?

The 1943 baseball team had a 16-1-0 record to conclude the school year. Rebounding from the 1942 season-ending loss, the 1943 baseball team began another win-streak. An early season rout of Pennington School, 15-0, was Joe's 200th career baseball game at SBP with a winning record of 84 percent.

Some hard decisions were required at SBP and other secondary schools regarding PGs and the issue of scholarships for athletes. The "position paper" begun by Joe in 1943 appears prophetic, as interscholastic sports coped with the disruption of World War II. New Jersey's competitive environment was changing, with Vince Lombardi and aggressive young coaches of a new breed – who now emerged. The summer of 1943 gave Joe time to compose the document which he finished in 1944. It appears later in the text.

1943-44 School Year

The school year began with a war-limited schedule; and the issue of how many "sanctioned" games were played by SBP arises. The findings are that only two games appear valid for Joe's record. Accordingly, a season record of 2-0-0 for the 1943 football season is given for Joe's career totals. The two were against Harrison HS, a 12-0 victory for the Gray Bees, and a win over Columbia University frosh by an unknown score.

SBP was a no-nonsense environment, and a few freshmen traditionally challenged the monks before they learned how to behave. Under war conditions, military drills and discipline may have made Joe think of his own experience in OAC's SATC and ROTC programs. For many SBP students, the line was fine between Benedictine and military discipline – perhaps due to some monk's military experiences, before or after entering the monastery. World War II brought a degree of militarism to civilian life. Even at a highly disciplined school like SBP, the military flavor may have exceeded traditional norms.

> Because football activities were curtailed 'for the duration,' a Commando Course was set up for the Seniors at Casino Field. The program, which intended 'to prepare the boy for what is ahead of him in the armed forces' was under the supervision of Mr. Joseph Kasberger.[100]

Fr. Malachy McPadden began his SBP career as a freshman in 1943 and provides valuable insights into the mood at the Hive during a very stressful period. Several monks from St. Mary's Abbey were now on active military duty: Fathers Maurus McBarron, George Sherry, Eugene Polhemus, Dunstan Smith, Philip Hoover and Martin Burne. Also, SBP students were prepared for military service. "Don't you know there's a war on?" was a common expression in the

246

fall of 1943. To prepare the students, the field at the Casino was "converted into an obstacle course for military training," with the intent to "toughen up the Seniors for Service." The commando course was described as a "complicated arrangement of walls, fences, barricades, tunnels and traps."[101]

In lieu of a normal gym class, the seniors went across the street "kicking and screaming," and prepared with something in mind. "The idea was they would go from graduation into one of the Armed Services." Not all seniors in the Class of 1944 were so lucky. Fr. Malachy recalled that some "were already gone by Christmas." It was not until the war ended in 1945 that normalcy returned to SBP. Fr. Malachy also recalled Casino Hall, "where certain displaced monks from Europe were living, refugees from Hitler's war." Some European monks taught classes at SBP. Fr. Malachy recalled three in particular, Fathers Sigmund and Ansgar from Austria, and Father Willibald.[102]

The 1944 baseball team produced a 16-0-1 record to conclude the school year. After fourteen-straight wins, extending back to the 1943 season, Joe was tied 2-2 by LaSalle Military Academy. There were no college teams on the schedule, probably due to college curtailment of athletics by war-related shortages. Baseball scheduling did not appear to present the same problems as those in football at the secondary school level.

Versions of the Kasberger legend speak of Joe spending his summers in The Dalles at the Sandoz Ranch. The impression for many is that Joe was a gentleman farmer, rancher, or cowboy. "This may sound great, but is not true." To clarify this subject, Bud Sandoz recalled his Uncle Joe at home during the summers. "When Joe left New Jersey, usually on the last day of the school year, he went straight to 917 West 10th Street in The Dalles." Joe was close to his sister Anna Sandoz and her family, and he frequently visited them at their property as a "welcome and fun visitor." Joe did not, however, spend his summers at the "Sandoz Ranch." The Sandoz property was a farm, not a ranch, as Bud explains.

> The word ranch usually implies wide spaces with fields of grain or herds of cattle. My father's place was in a relatively narrow valley, with orchards on the hillside and vegetables on the bottomland.

Concluding this point, Bud added that Joe's summers "were not quite as exotic as 'spending the summer on the Sandoz Ranch' might imply."[103] Now that it is clear what Joe did not do during his summers in The Dalles, the question is: What did he do? Joe's summers were centered around his home where he "would work as only he knew how, to put the grounds into a well-kept state." Joe also cared for the property of Mrs. Yaekel, a neighbor and family friend, after she became a widow.[104] Msgr. Stone recalled evenings with Joe at the local ball field, where Joe was watching, coaching or umpiring American Legion games in the 1940s. During this era, Msgr. Stone described a flamboyant and gregarious Joe, who was very popular with youngsters.

Joe was also recalled by Msgr. Stone, discussing the difficulty that he had in fielding teams in Newark during World War II. In one anecdote, Msgr. Stone recalled Joe telling a joke on himself. World War II was a problem not only in Newark, but also in The Dalles, when it came to football. There are some insights, as follows, that pertain to TDHS:

> There was no baseball nor track events during the war period from 1942 to 1946. Basketball was kept alive and football all but perished, on account of any young man qualified to play football was generally classified by the draft board as good military material; and a football team composed of 4-fers just couldn't be a winner even though it was against 4-fers from other schools.[105]

The war impacted sports, from the professional to the high-school level. Baseball was not curtailed because "4-fers" could possibly play it, but not football.

1944-45 School Year

Fr. Boniface was selected as Prior of St. Mary's Abbey in 1944. He will be remembered for many accomplishments, perhaps the most important in the realm of accreditation. "During Father Boniface's tenure, Saint Benedict's successfully underwent its first evaluation for membership in the Middle States Education Association."[106]

Fr. Boniface was replaced as headmaster in Sept. by Fr. Charles Carroll. The school year began with another limited football schedule and a 2-2-0 record. The Gray Bees opened with consecutive losses before rebounding to end the season with a two-game winstreak.

The document that follows, believed to be written by Joe, is three-pages, single-spaced and typed. SBP always had an identity problem regarding its role as private, prep, or parochial when it came to athletics. Joe clarifies many points, and puts into historical perspective the affiliations and competition available to

In 1944 Father Charles Carroll left parish work to become headmaster and prior. He held both positions until 1946.

SBP's teams. The document had no title, but there are three headings. The first is "NEED OF A PREPARATORY SCHOOL," with the following text:

> Over twenty-five (1919) years ago the N.J.S.I.A.A. classified St. Benedict's as a Preparatory School. The school was not satisfied with this classification and through Fr. Cornelius, the Headmaster, petitioned the N.J.S.I.A.A. to classify us as a High School pointing out that our courses were only four years in length, and thus making it unfair to expect us to compete with boarding Preparatory Schools which always included a large number of Post Graduates on their squads. The answer from the N.J.S.I.A.A. was that St. Benedict's is not a Public High School but a Private School, therefore, it must be classified with Preparatory Schools. As a result, we were denied admission into the Newark City

School High School League. We found that if we were to compete in athletic competition with the Preparatory Schools, we had no alternative but to allow Post Graduate students on our squads.

A Preparatory School prepares boys for college. Many boys graduated from public and parochial high schools have not the required credits for college, hence they must 'prepare' by going to another school (since their own high school will not admit them) to gain the necessary additional requirements for college. These boys are classified as Post Graduate students and should not be confused with scholarship boys. A Post Graduate is a boy who has graduated from a secondary school (either St. Benedict's or otherwise), who wishes to complement his course of studies to gain admission to a particular college. We as a Preparatory School, admit this type of boy providing he meets fully the Academic and Financial requirements of our institution.

St. Benedict's is such a school. Its graduates have done very well in college, scholastically, socially and athletically. Through the publicity it has gained through athletics, St. Benedict's is known throughout the entire nation. We hold an enviable position – scholastically, socially, and athletically. St. Benedict's is under the direction of an Order – exempt Religious. The only School of its kind in the State, Archdiocese, etc., which is able to hold its own with the great Non-Catholic Preparatory Schools. This standard we achieved through the years – [by means of] painstaking care of Faculty and the success of our Athletic Teams supervised by superb coaching.

The fact that the other Preparatory Schools in this and other States, (and rightly so), admit Public High School Graduates gives St. Benedict's the same opportunity because St. Benedict's is a Preparatory School. If we turn such boys away they have no alternative except attending one of the private Preparatory Schools. Some of these schools are conducted under Protestant auspices, and the fact is, most of these boys are Catholics. We should not entertain the thought that we necessarily are lowering our standards by admitting Post Graduate students.

These are turbulent times. The future of St. Benedict's under ordinary conditions seems assured. The trend towards Catholic Central High Schools, [and] the migration of races towards the Metropolitan area, seems to indicate that our High School Department is in jeopardy. Hence we should maintain, preserve and foster our Preparatory status.

Since St. Benedict's is a Preparatory School it should always be prepared to admit a representative number of Post Graduates and give them the opportunity to complete their preparation for college.

CONCERNING PUBLIC AND PAROCHIAL HIGH SCHOOLS.

But under no circumstances should St. Benedict's play under High School regulations. The competition would be too strong. The Public High School not only has two and three times the male enrollment but they get a different type of boy. We all must recognize that our boys are of the sheltered type, and to use plain words – 'Soft and undeveloped.' Practically all are from the Parochial Grammar Schools where physical training and facilities are 'Nil.' We also 'SCREEN' them according to their I.Q's.

It would be suicide to place ourselves on the level with Parochial High Schools . . . due to lack of organization and policy of said schools; find it very difficult to maintain friendly relations; usually lack a definite athletic program due to small or no salaried coaches; and the sportsmanship shown is not of the highest caliber. We are a Private School, hence our students deserve and expect that which is above the ordinary.

It took us many years of hard effort to build our school to achieve the athletic prominence we now enjoy in the Metropolitan section. It would be a very easy matter to step down the ladder, but entirely another matter to regain prominence, after we had realized our step was in the wrong direction.

ATHLETIC SCHOLARSHIPS

We must make a clear distinction between a Post Graduate and a Scholarship boy. See paragraph two for the definition of a Post Graduate. A Scholarship boy is a graduate or undergraduate boy of this or any other secondary school, who receives free tuition, for services rendered athletically or otherwise.

All Preparatory Schools and Colleges see the advantages of having Scholarship boys, e.g., Newark Academy, Cartaret [sic] School, Peddie, Blair, Lawrenceville, Notre Dame, Georgetown, Princeton, Columbia University, etc. They find that the proper use of a Scholarship boy is correct – the abuse is wrong.

Why not help a deserving boy with athletic ability? Nobody thinks it bad for ambitious, talented students to be given scholarships to college. In fact, Americans are in the habit of making a big fuss about the aid that is available to worthy young people seeking an education. And well we might brag about a system which does not deny to the poor the educational advantages that are available to the rich.

But why do so many people look horrified when you suggest assistance be rendered needy young men who wish to trade their athletic ability for an education? The boy who is giving his time to a major sport deserves scholarship aid just as much as the boy who shows promise in chemistry or civil engineering, band or forensics.

I don't believe in giving a boy an athletic scholarship unless the school is convinced that he needs it. But if he does need it, and can't get that all important education without it, then by all means give him help. He deserves it.

We must remember and realize that the qualities that make a good athlete are certainly not those which should disbar him from scholarship aid. On the contrary, they are in many cases the very qualities which make the school eager to give him scholarship aid. We should not make a barrier which would block educational opportunities to young men of athletic ability whose only drawback is that they lack money.

As far as scholarships are concerned, a number should be given. They would be an economic means of school advertising. Whether or not a school likes to admit it, it cannot afford to pay for the advertising elsewhere in the newspaper, that it is possible to receive on its sports page, e.g., Notre Dame, Michigan, Yale, etc. Who does not hear the names of these Colleges and think they are fine institutions?[107]

Possibly Coaches Blood and Cavanagh wrote on this topic at the request of the administration. Joe's moral stature at SBP appears to have exceeded his relative rank in the overall organization. The paper is one of the most revealing writings extant by Joe on how he felt about many issues. Since Joe was a candidate to become athletic director, it may have been reassuring to Fr. Charles that Joe expressed himself so well.

The 1945 baseball team's 9-2-0 record concluded the school year. Pennington School, in the season's third game, ended two of Joe's streaks that began in 1944. The twenty-one straight wins without a loss and the six consecutive wins were now over. Near season's end, a 5-4 win over Newark West Side HS was Joe's 200th win in his SBP baseball career, for a winning record of 85 percent.

Joe returned home for a vacation that possibly included Mt. Angel, to visit his sister Audie and her husband, Alois Keber, who resided there. The summer was concluded by the end of World War II on Sept. 2, 1945. Arriving on the East Coast in the midst of victory celebrations, Joe may have faced a squad surrounded by distractions.

Joe in Mt. Angel with his sister, Audie, and her husband, Alois Keber and his brother, Joe, ca. 1940-45.

1945-46 School Year

With the war's end, the football team played a bigger schedule. Sadly, the Gray Bees finished with a 3-3-0 record to begin the 1945-46 school year. Joe's two worst back-to-back career losses began the season. First, the United States Military Academy (West Point) Plebes annihilated the Gray Bees 0-33. There was no relief in the next game as LaSalle Military Academy defeated SBP by the identical score.

Joe was not used to losing, especially by such margins, and could not have been happy with the results. Was he overscheduled? Were his players not up to standard? Or, was Joe not keeping up with changes in the game? If Joe had any college-coaching aspirations, now appeared to be the time to pursue them, with the game's revival after the war. Approaching his fiftieth year, however, age became a factor. As former coaches returned from the war, vacancies were probably scarce at the colleges. Joe had a great situation in Newark; therefore college coaching may not have been of professional interest. Yet Joe might listen to the right offer, by the right person, at the right school.

Joe loved Christmas. Not being in The Dalles was difficult, but the Milbauers made the holidays special for Joe. Christmas of 1945 may have been the most festive one that Joe experienced on the East Coast. Dining with Joe at the Milbauers was recalled to be memorable, by Kewp, for his recitation of Grace.

> I asked my siblings about Joe remembrances and we all came up with the family dinners when Joe and Sister Georgita (Dad's cousin who was a

Joe's Christmas card to Fr. Jerome Fitzpatrick, O.S.B., ca. 1945.

Dominican Sister) would vie for the 'Pope's Nose,' and when, after a devout family Grace before meals, he would delight us with his 'Good bread, good meat, good God let's eat!'[108]

Perhaps the baseball team showed so much promise that college dreams were non-existent for Joe. The 1946 baseball team had a 14-3-0 record, losing the next to last game of the season to Roselle Park HS in the Greater Newark Tournament (GNT), 5-6. The season ended, however, with a 7-0 win over St. Mary's HS of Elizabeth – to begin the fabled 64-game win-streak. At the end of the 1946 baseball season, Joe's career record in Newark was 217-36-3.

As Joe anticipated the 1946-47 school year, his academic role as head of the commercial department would end when SBP decided to offer exclusively college-prep courses. Thus the more vocational courses in typing and shorthand which Joe taught were terminated. Joe Grum recalled being a student in Joe's business classes, where it sounded as though he were a pioneer in the field of business ethics. Grum mentioned Joe teaching the "Golden Rule," and that a man's handshake on a deal was worth more than a contract.[109] Clearly business law, as it is taught today, was not part of Joe's syllabus! Also recalling Joe's heading of SBP's commercial department was Kewp, a retired Business Education teacher.

> I wonder, how in the world did Joe ever teach typing to those boys? Do you recall the size of those old Underwood manual typewriter keys? One of Joe's fingertips probably could have spanned two or three keys.

In recalling Joe, Kewp said that the "man continues to amaze me even to this day."[110]

1946-47 School Year

If there were critics who thought that Joe was losing something as a football coach after the 1945 season, they were soon silenced. The 1946 football team began the school year with a 7-0-0 record and another state championship, with World War II veterans possibly accounting for SBP's success. Two stellar players were Sam Cavallaro and Billy Conn, who both went on to Georgetown University. As a prep performer, Conn was recalled by John Allen as one of the very finest all-around athletes to ever perform at SBP, as well as one of New Jersey's finest. Both men would be reunited with their mentor after college.

According to the *Benedict News,* it was SBP's 33rd team and the historical record was now 167-62-15. It is inferred, therefore, that for the period from 1914-29, before Joe, SBP's record was 72-44-7. The *Benedict News'* totals do not agree with the figures compiled in the Appendix for Joe's career. Before the 1947 baseball season, the *Benedict News* wrote that SBP's record since its first team in 1906 was 458-98-6, which does not concur with research compiled in the Appendix. Regardless, the 1947 baseball team was state champion with an 18-0-0 record. The streak just began as it reached nineteen in a row over two seasons.[111]

Joe's annual summer train rides to and from Oregon often led to a day at Wrigley Field or Comiskey Park. With commercial aviation becoming more routine, it is recalled that Joe did not like flying, an aversion partially related to Knute Rockne's tragic death. Riding the train and driving a car were preferred.

An experienced passenger recalls the transcontinental train-ride as a "major production." On regular trains, it was five nights and four days. On the streamliner, introduced in the 1930s, it was four nights and three days. Joe probably rode the Union Pacific, since it stopped in The Dalles. In Chicago, there was really no layover, so Joe may have arranged his itinerary to include one. Normally, a passenger took "Parmelee Transfer" from one station to another and quickly resumed the journey. Parenthetically, this passenger opined that "all wise people preferred the train!"[112]

Meanwhile, back in Oregon interesting things had transpired when Spec Keene left the Navy after the war, but did not return to Willamette. It is revealing to review Spec's complete record with the Bearcats to gain insights into the contributions that Joe and the New Jersey players made. During that golden age of Willamette athletics, "the Bearcats won 10 football titles in 17 years, and in his final season, WU captured the league grid, basketball, and baseball titles."[113]

The Navy was described as great for Spec's future job on another career path. First, however, he returned to Salem and entered the sporting goods business. Spec, reportedly, said with a chuckle, "Maybe I should have stayed with it. I'd have made more money." As with Joe, Spec apparently was not motivated by money. When their alma mater called, "Keene made his final move in the spring of 1947," for the career opportunity of his life. "He was named Percy Locey's successor as [Oregon State's] athletic director and arrived on campus to make accommodations for Slats Gill's NCAA regional-bound basketball team."[114]

Spec as Beaver athletic director appears to have been a perfect match, since he was characterized as "an Oregon Stater from the word go."[115] Keene was an obvious choice to replace Percy Locey, having paid his dues with his ticket punched at all the right stops in his career trajectory. What a wonderful opportunity the position presented to this versatile man. Would he remember those who helped him along the way? Spec was in the right place at the right time as the war's end brought a flood of veterans to college campuses with the "GI Bill."

College athletic programs expanded with pent-up demand for deferred athletic facilities. The times required athletic administrators to have management skills that were learned not only on the playing fields, but also in the military and business worlds. Also, Spec was known by virtually everyone in Oregon, and reportedly "has more friends than anybody connected with athletics at OSU."[116]

As the new athletic director, Spec had to cope with the problems and opportunities inherent in "a natural expansion trend in athletics." Capitalizing on his popularity, Spec "demonstrated administrative sharpness," which was the key to "developing Oregon State's vast athletic program into one of the finest in the nation." Spec was prepared and his response was soon apparent when he built OSU Coliseum for basketball in 1949 and Parker Stadium in 1953.[117]

Spec may have considered a football-coaching change if Oregon State's 1947 season was not successful. This sequence of events raises the question, was Joe interested in the Beaver job? And was Spec interested in Joe? Since Joe had close friends in high places, his name surely was mentioned, if not considered. Certainly Joe's success in Newark, shared with Spec, may have made him a candidate. If Joe ever wanted a college job, it is speculated that Oregon State was his top choice. Conversely, Joe may have decided that the college game was not for him, and that he was content in the coach-heaven that he had in Newark.

1947-48 School Year

The 1947-48 school year saw Fr. Gerald Flynn arrive as headmaster to replace Fr. Charles Carroll, who was "forced by his health to retire."[118] After 13 years of great stability in the headmaster's office, Joe now had his third headmaster in five years.

The 1947 football team's 6-1-1 record was capped by a 39-6 win over Scranton College frosh near season's end. It was Joe's 100th win in his SBP football career, for a winning record of 79 percent. Attention shifted to the 1948 baseball team and the 19-game win-streak.

The fall of 1947 was eventful in Corvallis as Spec faced a football-coach problem. After a successful 7-1-1 season in 1946, Lon Stiner's Beavers struggled to a 5-5-0 record in the 1947 season. A football- coaching change occurred after the 1947

Rev. Gerald Flynn, O.S.B.

season, with Lon Stiner replaced by Kip Taylor from the University of Michigan. Had Joe and Spec discussed the Oregon State head football coaching situation? Joe was now nearly 52, and age may have been an issue, along with no major college-coaching experience. Despite his successes at SBP, Joe was not known to have ever been offered a college job.[119] Spec, however, knew Joe best as the source of many star players. Some might suggest that Joe's players from Newark put Willamette on the map, and gave Spec the success that may have led to the Oregon State position as athletic director. Most important, though,

Gray Bee coaching staff, 1947: Buzz McGlynn, Joe, Dick DeStefano and Ed Nittoli.

was their longtime friend-ship.

Bob Murray remained a significant figure in The Dalles. Besides his full-time job at the natatorium and convention center, "Bob's athletic interests in post DHS years moved him into vol-unteer work, especially with American Legion baseball." Also, Bob kept active in football. "Under DHS coaches Mark Temple, Dick Sutherland and others he did some scouting for the DHS football teams." Coach Murray remained "noted for his keen power of analysis, especially in football."[120]

The end of 1947 brought retirement to Bob Murray, marking the end of an era. Murray had "no equal in producing better sportsmanship and citizenship in the community." To historians in The Dalles, Bob ranked "among the first 50 of the most outstanding citizens in the 100 years of Wasco County history!" His many interests kept him busy after being forced out as a coach nearly two decades earlier. Bob Murray "officially retired Dec. 31, 1947, but continued for a time as supervisor of the Natatorium." After retirement "he also served for years as local swim coach." There were other roles that he filled in The Dalles after retirement. Bob "entered into a career of mentoring learn-to-swim programs, and community and American legion baseball teams."[121] It is with American Legion baseball that some in The Dalles recall Joe Kasberger and Bob Murray, together, during the summer.

The new year brought a technological revolution to Americans that most educators and many parents agree is the greatest distraction to students, the television set. Television did not become an issue in most American homes until the Dumonts began to appear in 1948. Television's popularity spread like wild-fire and the new household necessity became known as the TV. The Milbauer home was no exception to this national craze. Joe was quite enchanted with this innovation. Sports programming became a staple of family life, and replaced Joe's previous attachment to the radio. Louise was especially fond of watching auto racing, despite an aversion to riding in a vehicle unless placed in the back seat, for fear of oncoming cars.[122] If Joe had worries, previously, about his play-ers' distractions, now he found the TV influenced him as well.

The 1948 baseball season followed a 19-game winning streak from the previ-ous two seasons. The team did not disappoint Joe and its fans, by finishing the season with a 20-0-0 record to bring the streak to 39 consecutive wins over three seasons. College teams returned to the 1948 baseball schedule, making the win-streak even more significant. Graduation losses in 1948 were severe with two players in particular, Walter Szot and John Thomas, who would excel at higher levels.

At St. Mary's Abbey a bigger event than the streak at SBP occurred. The Delbarton School, which had not developed rapidly, at last had its first graduating class of twelve preparatory students in June 1948. This milestone appears to be a modest yield for the effort expended, but Abbot Patrick was very pleased.[123]

"Skip" and "Katrinka" on their anniversary in Atlantic City, ca. 1947.

This eventful school year ended sadly with Frank W. Milbauer's death. It is a Milbauer family joke that Joe was a guest who came for dinner and stayed for twenty-five years. This beautifully-enduring relationship seems all-important when assessing Joe's Newark career. His decision to remain at SBP in his early career came when his Newark roots were fragile. "Skip" Milbauer, as the head of the household, deserves recognition for both his hospitality and contribution to Joe's life and career.[124]

1948-49 School Year

This school year was significant in SBP's sports history because it marked the end of an era that was characterized by long-tenured coaches with incredible records. Also the issue of a new athletic director at SBP may have become a consideration with the pending retirements of Jim Cavanagh and Prof Blood.

The 1948 football team produced a 7-1-1 record. The Gray Bees opened with six consecutive wins to extend the winning and non-losing streaks begun in 1947. Joe's football-coaching touch survived the war years

Christmas dinner, 1948. Joe, Kathleen (Kewp), Frank and Louise.

and it was business as usual. Christmas with the Milbauers, however, was somber without Skip.

The eventful school year ended with the 1949 baseball team's 22-0-0 record to extend the win-streak to 60 games, elevating Joe's career baseball record at SBP to a spectacular 277-36-3. An early season 7-3 win over Carteret Academy was Joe's 300th SBP career baseball game with a gaudy winning record of 87 percent.

1949-50 School Year

Rev. George Sherry, O.S.B., athletic director.

The sequence of events in 1949 is not clear, but two significant appointments were made at SBP. What makes the scenario presented below unclear is a 1950 *Telolog* picture of Fr. George Sherry with the caption "athletic director." Joe was appointed athletic director in 1949. When the appointment was effective is not clear, but it is assumed to have been at the start of this school year. Surely Joe was rewarded for his consistent success as a coach when named to this position. He deserved the promotion, but it had been 23 years since he held the same post at MAC. Was he prepared, however, for the other demands of this position in the post-war environment? With access to Spec Keene, Joe knew that the athletic director faced major issues. In addition to hiring and firing coaches, Spec was dealing with fundraising and facilities-development to remain competitive. Would Joe be comfortable dealing with these issues at SBP? Fortunately, the new headmaster appears to have been the ideal new boss for the new athletic director.

The second major event was Rev. Philip Hoover succeeding Fr. Gerald as headmaster.[125] Fr. Philip, SBP Class of 1930, was a former basketball star, Dartmouth College alumnus, and Naval-chaplain veteran of World War II. He was an athletic, personable and handsome young man known as "Honey" during his student days. What more could Joe ask? Some suggest that former New Jersey Senator Bill Bradley and Fr. Philip had a strong resemblance. When Fr. Philip became headmaster, both baseball and football teams were

Rev. Philip Hoover, O.S.B., headmaster.

back on top with outstanding prospects for the future. Clearly Fr. Philip was a sports enthusiast who any coach or athletic director would be grateful to have as a boss. Fr. Philip was a very popular headmaster during his tenure. As with Joe, Fr. Philip was faced with a challenge in facilities-development in the postwar era. As athletic director, Joe had new responsibilities that could take his attention away from coaching.

Also facing the new athletic director was the unenviable job of replacing a legend. Prof Blood was already of heroic stature in national basketball circles before coming to SBP in 1925. During the period 1919-25, Blood coached the Passaic, NJ High School "Wonder Team" to 159 consecutive wins. The invincible Indians finally lost "in the 13th game of the 1924-25 season when Hackensack won 39-35."[126] After twenty-five years of coaching at SBP, Prof Blood retired in 1949 with "10 state titles" won by his Gray Bees in basketball. With Prof Blood's retirement, how much interest did Joe have in succeeding that legend as basketball coach? Joe may have been curious to see whether he still had the winning touch in basketball. Instead, SBP selected Harry Singleton as head basketball coach, with his work cut out for him. Singleton faced practice and play in Shanley Gym, rapidly becoming obsolete.

SBP was blessed with two extraordinary coaches before Joe's arrival. Now he faced the future without his former friends and colleagues – because Joe also had to replace a superior coach for track and cross-country teams. Jim Cavanagh was not an easy act to follow, having "coached 16 state indoor championship teams and 15 cross-country titlists."[127] Cavanagh's replacement in track is unknown.

Joe began the school year with an outstanding football team, whose 9-0-0 record included a "challenge game" win in Rochester, NY over Aquinas

1949 FOOTBALL SQUAD
FRONT ROW: R. Sherry, R. Lasher, T. Ripa, M. Zoppi, J. Castagno, R. White, Captain; A. Charette, J. Coppola, J. D'Amiano, E. Schiller. SECOND ROW: A. Testa, E. Hanbicki, E. Vroom, R. Kempton, D. Perrin, G. Parozzo, V. Barone, L. Cassella, M. Mantz. THIRD ROW: G. Christenson, A. Saner, T. Kerwin, J. Grum, A. Miller, R. Davies, R. Ondillo, D. Schiller. FOURTH ROW: M. Warner, W. Gurkas, A. O'Connor, P. Prester, B. Serra, V. Crisafi, P. Calcagno, Assistant Coach. BACK ROW: V. Cannestro, Assistant Coach; B. Geraghty, Assistant Coach; W. Burger, S. Arbes, R. Spawn, W. McHugh, J. Kasberger, Head Coach.

ART CHARETTE

Institute. The season-ending tie with Aquinas in 1948 may have led to the rematch and large turnout of more than 24,000 Rochester fans. The competition was a formidable team, representing the Basilian Fathers who operated high schools with great sports traditions throughout the country. The 25-9 SBP win made the long trip a pleasant one. SBP's teams traveled extensively, but seldom as far as Rochester – about 375 miles from "Paris on the Passaic" to the shores of Lake Ontario. As athletic director, Joe may have received a healthy share of the gate receipts to finance the trip. Certainly Joe was experienced in these matters. Perhaps he even considered bringing the Gray Bees to Houston, TX to try another Basilian powerhouse of that era, St. Thomas HS. With Joe as athletic director, there were many new possibilities for SBP's teams.

Many players from that team contend it was Joe's and SBP's finest. How members of Joe's 1936 football team would view such opinions might make for an interesting discussion. Joe's football career record now stood at 117-20-10. Despite the greatness of the 1949 football season, attention was directed to baseball and the 1950 squad. Many of the baseball players competed in football and were a confident group after their successful season. The baseball team, however, was playing before a level of media attention previously unseen at SBP since its win-streak was of both local and national interest.

Post-World War II prosperity in New Jersey had a paradoxical impact on Newark. Suburban sprawl accelerated and living in the new housing enclaves away from the city became the American dream. New roads were built and autos made getting to many formerly-distant towns feasible. The peace was short-lived, and in June 1950 the Korean Conflict began with United States intervention. The population of The Dalles remained comparatively small, 7,676 in 1950, and social change was certainly less than in Newark.

SBP always enjoyed a competitive advantage because of Newark. It was relatively easy for the students to commute into it from considerable distances due to excellent public transit. During the 1950s, the postwar boom made Newark more prosperous, and attracted new

A view of St. Benedict's Prep and St. Mary's Abbey and Church as they appeared around 1950.

populations seeking economic opportunity. The impact of the newcomers soon became an issue. The external environment Joe now faced made his 1944 position paper prophetic. Newark's total population in 1950 was 438,776, a modest increase from the 1940 total of 429,760. Yet it remained below the 1930 level of 442,337.[128] Most noteworthy was the 60 percent increase in black population, that grew from 45,760 in 1940 to 74,965 in 1950.

With a tradition of serving Newark's youth, SBP faced a radically changing demographic situation as the 1950s began. Also, ending the PG era became a major challenge. Remaining competitive in sports, while retaining its academic reputation, was mandatory at SBP. Maintaining a proud tradition of balance was not a simple matter. Joe as athletic director was most important, as Fr. Philip steered the course from the headmaster's office. Both men may have given thought to the school's aging physical plant and the future.

The spring of 1950 brought an old friend to New York, Slats Gill – now nationally famed as Oregon State's basketball coach. With Spec as his athletic director, Slats had come a long way with Beaver basketball, as he "saw his favorite sport grow from a recreational project to a world-wide venture." Slats' role was pivotal at Oregon State, despite poor facilities and player material in his early career. With the new coliseum, Slats was seen as "the man responsible" for basketball's success. Joe Kasberger, Spec Keene and Slats Gill all had an uncanny ability to relate well with the young men they coached. Also, each was a "stickler on fundamentals." The parallels do not stop there, based upon a description of Gill's coaching style: "He believes that building character is every bit as important as winning ball games." Slats was also lauded by rival coaches and players for teams that "conduct themselves as gentlemen at all times."[129]

After graduation from OAC, Slats took his first job as a teacher at the YMCA in Oakland, CA. From there he went on to an Oakland high school, where he was an immediate coaching success when he won the city championship. This accomplishment was rewarded by Oregon State, where he returned as freshman basketball coach for the 1926-27 season. "After two good years as Rook tutor, Slats was upped to the varsity post in 1928-29." That appointment marked a new era in Beaver basketball. Slats was fortunate to be in a friendly environment with patient fans, since success was not immediate. It was not until 1933 that Slats produced his "first really great club." After that breakthrough, Slats went on a roll. "In a 10-year span, from 1940 through 1949, the records list 197 victories and 103 defeats." After twenty-four years as Beaver head-coach, Slats had a record of "401 wins and 272 losses." This performance-level in the Pacific Coast Conference "was accomplished against some of the stiffest opposition in the land."[130]

In recognition of his accomplishments, Slats now reaped national honors. In the spring of 1950, he received two significant awards for his success and popularity. "He was chosen to coach the west all-stars against the east in Madison Square Garden." Also, the Helms Athletic Foundation of Los Angeles "added the name of Slats Gill to the Helms basketball hall of fame – a select group of 20 outstanding coaches of America."[131] It is not known if Slats visited with Joe on this trip to New York, but it seems likely, since Joe was proud of his old friend and fraternity brother. Surely Joe had vivid memories of OAC's old men's gymnasium that seated 2,500, where Slats began his playing career. Now Slats and

Spec had a modern coliseum for 10,500 fans because of the program's success.

There was other news from the West Coast in April. On Tuesday, April 18, 1950, Joe's former MAC football teammate and assistant coach, Fr. Norbert Matteucci, died in San Diego. His Benedictine career, after ordination on June 6, 1925, took him away from Mt. Angel. After saying his first mass at St. Michael's Church in Portland, Fr. Norbert became "assistant pastor at St. Mary's church in Mt. Angel." He served there until moving to Portland after his "appointment as pastor of St. Agatha's parish in 1934" – where he served for more than a decade. Illness forced Fr. Norbert to California, "when on doctor's advice, he came to San Diego in 1945." After a brief stay at Mercy Hospital, "Fr. Norbert was transferred to the priest's residence for convalescence." Upon regaining his health, "he was appointed chaplain to the hospital by His Excellency, the Most Reverend Bishop."[132]

Another source stated that Fr. Norbert came to San Diego in 1943, "where he was appointed chaplain of Mercy hospital. This office he held until six months before his death." Before his remains left San Diego, it is reported that "His Excellency and the priests of San Diego recited the Office of the Dead for the repose of his soul in St. Joseph's Cathedral." The story noted that "Father Norbert's body was taken to Mount Angel for interment in the cemetery of the abbey there." Another story adds these details:

> Solemn requiem high mass without the body present will be sung at St. Agatha's church at 9 a.m. Saturday. The funeral mass will be at 10 a.m. Monday at St. Mary's parish church in Mt. Angel.[133]

SBP's baseball team did not lose again until BMI ended the New Jersey-state-record 64-game win-streak on April 19 in the fourth game of the 1950 season. The team rebounded to conclude the season with a 19-3-0 record. At the time, the 64-game win-streak was thought to be a national

BMI Snaps Benedicts' 64-Game Streak

Scoring probably the most impressive baseball victory ever recorded at Bordentown Military Institute, the varsity baseballers snapped a 64-game winning streak compiled by St. Benedict's Prep School at the Little Army diamond Wednesday afternoon by a 5-3 score.

On Saturday afternoon, the charges of Coaches Marvin O. Borst and Albert Verdel posted an easy 12-1 victory over Valley Forge Military Academy, also at the BMI field.

Arena Wins 2

Cadet Vince Arena from Atlantic City, N. J., was the winning hurler in both contests for the Borstmen, although Warren Rutledge took over for awhile in Saturday's game.

Opposing Arena on the mound for St. Benedict's was young right-hander Tom Bujonski, who suffered his 1st defeat in 15 wins recorded both in high school and prep school. Hurling for Bayonne's unbeaten team last year, Bujonski outpitched Gus Keriazakos, recently signed by the Chicago White Sox for a $67,000 bonus price.

Trailing 3-2 after 7 complete innings, the Cadets put together 3 straight singles by Forstsoffer, Tindall and Faust, scoring 1, then when 3rd baseman Undilla threw Sokolowski's hard smash wildly to 1st base, Tindall tallied with the tie-breaker. The cushion run came a moment later on a balk by relief twirler Frank LaStella.

Bujonski recorded 13 strikeouts during his 7 1/3 innings, while Arena posted 10 in going the route.

St. Benedict's (3)

	A.B.	R.	H.	O.	A.
Boob, ss	3	0	0	0	1
Schiller, rf	3	0	1	0	0
Charette, cf	4	0	1	0	0
White, c	4	0	1	12	0
Bujonski, p	4	0	0	1	3
Undilla, 3b	4	0	1	1	0
Warner, 3b	0	0	0	0	0
Malk'us, 2b	3	0	1	0	2
Picarilli, lf	3	1	1	0	0
La Str'la, p	0	0	0	0	0
Manz, 1b	3	2	1	10	1
aBaker	1	0	0	0	0
Totals	29	3	7	24	7

BMI (5)

	A.B.	R.	H.	O.	A.
Cittadino, cf	4	0	1	2	0
Moglia, 2b	4	0	0	4	2
Forsthoffer, ss	4	2	2	1	4
Tindall, c	4	1	1	11	0
A. Faust, 3b	4	1	1	0	1
Sokolowski, rf	3	1	2	1	1
Brennan, 1b	4	0	1	8	0
R. Faust, lf	4	0	0	0	0
Arena, p	3	0	0	0	1
Totals	34	5	8	27	9

aFlied out for Manz in 9th.

St. Benedict's 002 000 100 3
BMI 000 011 03x 5

E—Brennan, Moglia, Forsthoffer, Undilla 2. RBI—Charette, Manz, Cittadino, A. Faust, Sokolowski. 2B—Brennan, White. 3B—Sokolowski, Picarilli. SB—Malkus, Cittadino. DP—Forsthoffer, Moglia, Brennan, Sokolowski and Brennan. Left—St. Benedict's 8, BMI 8. SO—Arena 10, Bujonski 13, La Strella 1. BB—Arena 4, Bujonski 1, La Strella 2. Balk—La Strella. Hits—Bujonski 8 and 5 in 7 1/3, La Strella 0 and 0 in 2/3. Loser—Bujonski. Time of game—2:43. Umpires: Gotch, Carty.

record, giving SBP and Joe media attention that perhaps was unwanted. On a more positive note, two games after the BMI loss, the Bees routed Newark Vo-Tech HS, 14-0, for Joe's 300th SBP career win, with a winning record of 87 percent. Regrettably, the presence of PG players prevented the Gray Bees from appearing in the GNT during the streak. Losing was inevitable but in reviewing the sports history of SBP, is there a greater feat by any of its teams?

Summarizing this accomplishment in numbers detracts from a more personal treatment. In the absence of any writings on the streak, however, the numbers will have to suffice. For the 64 games in the streak, the Gray Bees scored 650 runs to the opposition's 102 runs. The average score was 10-2. SBP won 19 games by shutout, and 19 were won allowing only one run. There were twenty-six different opponents, the most frequent being Newark Vo-Tech HS. The Gray Bees scored the most runs, 22, against Immaculate Conception HS of Montclair in the last win before the loss. The most runs scored against SBP were 7 by Newark Central HS. The closest win was 1-0 over BMI in the fifty-seventh game.

The streak's end may have been the impetus to dismantle, once and for all, SBP's PG athletic program. Competition was changing in the post-war era beyond the traditional prep circuit. Local public and parochial opponents were not always available when SBP used PGs. Change was inevitable to rectify this awkward situation.

Two players from the 1950 baseball team, captain Art Charette and Bob Buob, enrolled at Oregon State after their SBP careers ended. Following the lead of Joe

"John Thomas was an all-coast catcher and all-star end who went both ways on the football team at Oregon State in 1952."

Hellberg and John Thomas, both pledged Phi Delta Theta fraternity and were treated well by Spec Keene and baseball coach, Ralph Coleman. Art Charette played both football and baseball. According to the Oregon State *Media Guide* and Pacific Coast Conference *Record Book*, he lettered as a defensive back and quarterback for the Beavers in 1951. Perhaps both recruits were important to Oregon State's baseball team that was becoming nationally ranked, led by their fellow New Jerseyan, Beaver star John Thomas.

As the school year concluded, the Korean Conflict began with United States intervention. Joe returned to The Dalles for the summer, where he may have drafted an essay on baseball and his winning ways. The paper may have been Joe's response to requests for more insights into his coaching that followed publicity associated with the streak. The paper entitled, "Advice to Baseball players," and attributed to Joe, is typed but undated.

The first duty of a student is to STUDY. Dig in and beat those books. Feed your mind, and work your mind and will till they grow to giant size. Make your school proud of you. The first glory of any school is a line of ideal graduates, gentlemen with character, personality, and apostolic zeal, who will be socially successful and real citizens.

Think about giving rather than getting . . . and at the same time you will be getting what money cannot buy. You cannot expect your school to put you on the map unless you put your school on the map. Remember, you get out of school just what you give and very little more. An ounce of loyalty is worth a pound of cleverness.

Boys, just keep in mind, you are only going to be as good as you think you are. You've got to have a target to aim at in baseball and also life. Why not make the target the TOP! Go out and at all times, be in condition and give your best, nothing else matters . . . but to make certain it is your BEST. It isn't a crime to fail, the crime is not to have given your best.

What made Babe Ruth so great? It was his competitive spirit that made him a joy to watch. He loved the game and gave everything he had every minute. You must have a burning desire to play the game at its BEST.

Competitive spirit!! That's the thing. Believe and have confidence in yourself and then play the game for all you're worth, every minute you're in it. Have no fear but go out on every play and never quit HUSTLING! Whether you are studying, running a machine, or doing any one of the thousand and one jobs out in the world, have faith in your ability and give your job all that you have within you, but make certain it is always your BEST.

Professional baseball. If you have the ability, go into baseball not as a future itself, but to use as a helpful stepping stone to something else kept definitely in mind. Your education FIRST, to the majority, baseball at its best is a short career.

Qualifications. If a boy can throw well and run fast, has a strong limber body, and shows signs of ultimately having first-class co-ordination, he's the kind of fellow we're looking for . . . So are the Leagues!

Tip to pitchers! Baseball scouts may differ in a number of things but in one particular they all agree . . . they hate to see a young player throwing a knuckle ball. So if you have a knuckler that you're proud of and see some scout in the stands, stow it in your hip pocket, and, instead, display the best fast ball and curve ball wares you have. That's the stuff, along with control, that catches a baseball scout's eye and interest.

Control! The pitcher with the best control will be the most effective. Control does not mean throwing the ball over the center of the plate . . . It means the ability to pitch the ball where you want to, at the time you want, after having decided where the ball should be pitched. With control you make the batter hit the ball you want him to hit. Control can only be acquired by PRACTICE! PRACTICE! AND MORE PRACTICE! When throwing for control in batting practice, always make it a rule to take about five minutes throwing to the batters as if there were men on bases.

To get a Hop or Sail on a fast ball, hold it loosely but NOT tightly! Work will win – Wishing won't! Hustle on and off the field. Hustle![134]

There is a sheet of handwritten notes and quotes that may have been used as a draft for the typed version, shown above, that are not presented here.

In August 1950, Abbot Thomas stepped down as the head of Mt. Angel Abbey with much accomplished. "Throughout his years in office, existing debts were paid off, and a fund to complete the church building was built up." By 1950, "there was sufficient capital to begin work," and in the spring construction began. "It was decided to build an underground church beneath the new nave; this crypt would be available for the needs of retreatants and seminarians." Accompanying these successes were health problems. "He suffered from high blood pressure and glaucoma." After losing one eye, Abbot Thomas followed physicians advice, and "decided to give up the abbatial duties, which were putting such a strain on him." He remained at Mt. Angel for another eleven years, "mellowing with the years and esteemed for the wide-ranging accomplishments of his sixteen years as abbot."[135] During his tenure, many of his Mt. Angel monks were in Newark on business to sell the monastery's crop of hops to Newark breweries.[136]

1950-51 School Year

Joe had a new academic role, head of driver's education, assisted by Mr. Cassell. It was a theory, rather than practice, course – described as follows:

> The course (for upperclassmen) featured lectures, pamphlets, and motion pictures, all designed to impress upon the new drivers a feeling of responsibility, not the mechanics of automobile driving.[137]

Perhaps the new course took Joe's mind off other changes on the horizon as a dominant 1950 football team responded with a 6-0-1 record.

Joe turned 55 to begin the second half of the school year as a notoriously healthy man with a defiance of Newark's winter cold. His tough-it-out attitude added to his legendary status as an immortal in the minds of many impressionable young students. Only Joe could, or would, walk Newark's frigid winter streets without an overcoat. Yet in 1951, Joe's older brother, John, Jr. died at the age of 63.[138] John was the the head of the Kasberger household in The Dalles. Without him, care of the family home may have fallen more heavily upon Joe. As a handyman, Joe would have to make the necessary repairs and improvements associated with home-ownership. Now, as Joe grew older, his ties to The Dalles appear to have intensified.

John Kasberger, Jr. was the family breadwinner and a source of stability and strength to his siblings. John's career, as a Union Pacific Railroad engineer, took him away from home often. Yet he was acknowledged as the family head.[139] Now Joe and his siblings faced the future with their own mortality more profoundly apparent. The question of why Joe returned to The Dalles so faithfully can be answered as his family ties. His strong sense of family was never abandoned. In Newark, Joe's adopted family, the Milbauers, made him more cognizant of his family at home. Without parents to maintain the sense of family, it was incumbent on Joe and his siblings to remain true to their heritage, traditions and bonds.

The 1951 baseball team had a 16-2 record to bring Joe's career record to 312-41-3. The season began with three consecutive wins, extending a new winning streak to ten games, that had begun at the end of the 1950 season. BMI ended this streak, too – 1-2, in the season's fourth game. In the next game, Panzer College frosh defeated the Gray Bees, 9-10. The remainder of the season was all wins and a thirteen-game win-streak was in progress for next year's team.

Excerpts from a story by Andrew Purcell shed much light on Joe and his PG players as this era was coming to a conclusion:

> As a prep school coach for his first 20 years or so at St. Benedict's, Kasberger had a job unlike that facing high school mentors. The latter had to weld a bunch of young, untested adolescents into a football or baseball team. Kasberger more often had to deal largely with an assortment of athletes who brought established reputations with them as they enrolled at Benedict's. While this gave Kasberger some good material, it was not without its peculiar drawbacks. The high school hero was often in need of what Kasberger called 'cranial deflation' before he could fit into the style of excellence Joe demanded. At the start of every spring and fall, when baseball or football practice was getting underway, the sports writers would pay their customary visit to Benedict Field to ask Joe about the collection of all-staters he had trying out for the team.[140]

Purcell astutely describes Joe's ability in turning talented individuals into winning teams.

> The material, during those years, was no doubt there; but it was material brought up on different systems of play, strangers one to another and, not infrequently, in need of Kasberger's cranial deflation. The job of welding this material, this collection of 'you individuals,' into a team fell to Joe K., and the coach carried out this assignment in splendid fashion.[141]

There was sadness in Newark after Joe left for his vacation when Jim Cavanagh died on June 24, at the age of 56. Summers in The Dalles for Joe were opportunities to be with family and friends in a place he loved. Yet little is known about Joe's friends, either in The Dalles or Newark. He appears to have been a man with close family members, devoted former students and players, but very few close friends in his later years. This point is baffling since he appears to have had so many close friends, fraternity brothers and teammates in his youth. What happened to these formerly close relationships? Were they outlived by Joe? Or had Joe become a recluse? This point seems increasingly relevant as Joe grew older.

1951-52 School Year

An important fund-raising affair began the school year. The first indication of this drive appeared in the 1951 *Telolog* several months earlier when it was proclaimed that $455,000 could build a new SBP.[142] On "Reunion Night" of the Alumni Association, "during the week of September 28, a Building drive for an auditorium for St. Benedict's" was reported.

This school year saw the last appearance of PG athletes at SBP. The 1951 football team's 4-2-0 season deserves a closer look at its competition. It began with a 34-7 win over a Fort Dix, NJ Army team. Next was a 21-0 win over Fordham University's junior varsity. Lehigh University's frosh were the third-straight victims, 28-0. Finally, SBP lost, 0-7, to Princeton University's frosh. Aquinas Institute avenged the 1949 loss with a 0-7 win. SBP's PG-era in football and season ended in a 27-6 win over Columbia University's frosh. Joe's career football totals at SBP stood at 127-22-11, a winning record of 79 percent.

The school year was concluded with a relatively successful baseball team that had a 13-5-0 record. The season began with three consecutive victories, including a 19-0 drubbing of BMI. The season's finale was an 11-3 win over Pennington School and there were no more PG teams at SBP. Joe's career baseball record at SBP stood at 325-46-3, an 87 percent winning record.

Joe's lofty winning percentages in football and baseball reflect highly on PG athletes and his rapport with them. The Appendix provides highlights for both football and baseball teams during the PG era. In retrospect, it seems unbelievable that Joe's teams were so talented that they won so often against the level of competition they faced. In subsequent years, Joe's teams were marked by an effort by both old and new foes to even-up the records that were set in the past.

Fr. Jerome Fitzpatrick has a unique perspective on PGs, both as a classmate and as a former teacher of them. He has shared his recollections as follows:

> They were graduates from a high school. It could be the same school or from another high school. They came to SBP to satisfy college academic requirements in which they were lacking, and also to up grade their athletic prowess so as to be more acceptable to college coaches. Most, but not all, who came to SBP were athletes. Our coaching staff in the 30's, 40's and 50's attracted many by reputation. Many paid full tuition on their own; others sought financial aid which was given to all students in need. They were full-time students, attending class all day. They were subject to the same academic requirements, as well as attendance rules. No differentiation was made for them because they were athletes. SBP followed the pattern of other preparatory schools of the era. Generally well accepted by the faculty and fellow students, some athletically inclined students resented their presence – the number of first team spots were limited by their presence.[143]

For conventional SBP student-athletes, there would be the challenge to follow in very big footsteps. For SBP's coaches, there would be the challenge of preparing younger and less experienced players.

VII. COACHING WITHOUT POST-GRADUATES (PGs)

"Think – Hustle – Win !"

With the milestone 1951-52 school year over, Joe may have had an uncertain summer. The stress of preparing the 1952 football team in the new competitive environment may have weighed heavily. Joe was probably confident that he could compete without PGs, but only time would tell. The dilemma Joe faced stemmed from his inability to play as many underclassmen as he might have liked during the last year of the PG era. Without formal coaching in their early development, the first coach they encountered had to be a patient teacher.

There were many talented athletes at SBP, but there is no substitute for game experience. Moreover, Joe was never a developmental coach who worked with the talented but inexperienced young athlete. Joe's career as a coach had always seen him molding the more mature and experienced athlete. Vince Lombardi's coaching at St. Cecilia HS was frustrating for some young players because demands were made that could not be satisfied. Until Lombardi learned the limitations of the younger athlete, he had problems that are well-documented.[1] The summer may have given Joe time to think about dealing with the talented but inexperienced, and Bob Murray may have been a valuable resource. Even Bob's thirty-year-old textbook on football fundamentals may have been read to refresh Joe on coaching youngsters.

1952-53 School Year

Football and baseball season expectations were probably less demanding than previously. The unthinkable finally happened when the 1952 football team posted a 3-4-0 record, Joe's first losing team in his SBP career. As athletic director, he had only himself to blame if this team were overscheduled. This was a valiant group of relatively young Gray Bees, possibly undermanned and certainly inexperienced, playing against foes seeking vengeance for losses inflicted by prior SBP teams loaded with PGs. Lessons learned from this trying season, however, led to future successes as players matured.[2]

On Nov. 8, 1952 there was a celebration at Willamette University as part of homecoming activities. It was Spec Keene Day and there was great publicity for this event. An *Oregonian* story by Paul Hauser provides useful insights into Spec, who was remembered fondly.

> College athletic coaches are sometimes given testimonial dinners and praise heaped high over the chicken a la king after a winning season, but it is a rare thing, indeed, when an ex-coach is called back to the campus for a day in his honor.[3]

Despite leaving Willamette, Spec Keene remained a beloved figure there. "In nine years many colleges can all but forget an ex-coach, but at Willamette they couldn't forget Spec Keene if they tried." Spec was seen as "tall, quiet, and easy-going." He was also recalled for the great athletes who came to Willamette during his seventeen-year tenure. Some were in attendance to honor Spec, known to them as a "worrier." He began worrying "about high school graduation time, when the struggle for promising freshmen started, and kept right on through the schedule until the last down of the last game."[4] Without Joe, Spec might have suffered a nervous breakdown!

Spec's Willamette accomplishments were memorable. "His over-all Northwest Conference record for 17 years is one for coaches to shoot at – 66 wins against 16 losses and 3 ties." It was gratifying for Spec to know that leaving Willamette after the war had caused no hard feelings. "Win, lose, or draw, Keene became a part of Willamette." While taking the position in Corvallis, Spec was still something of a home boy in Salem – even if he felt "pretty young to be a legend" at Willamette.[5]

Sentiments were expressed about the intangibles of Spec's career. "As many of his former players testify, Keene was a real character-builder – not by preaching, but by example." Also Spec's affection for his players was well known. "'Some had more natural ability than others,' Keene said recently, 'but in my book all are great.'" With modern NCAA rules, a head football coach today cannot be as fatherly. Spec "went beyond the concern every coach has to see that his players eat regularly, go to bed at a decent hour and keep their studies up." Hauser offered this insight. "'Spec was real good to the kids,' a onetime coaching assistant said not long ago. 'Sometimes he was too good. He helped a lot of them financially out of his own pocket.'"[6]

Spec's wife was equally popular. She was known to the athletes as Marie, not Mrs. Keene, possessing a style as "informal and kindly" as that of her husband, who "was always just Spec to everybody." As a coach's wife, it is not surprising that she knew football, including an ability "to diagnose a play – [she'd seen] enough of them worked out with catsup bottles, tumblers and salt cellars on her dining room table." It was off the playing field, however, where Marie Keene was best remembered "as a second mother to many of the boys." With two daughters of her own, she probably enjoyed having Spec's players as adopted sons. "Many of them recuperated from illness or injury with the beneficial aid of the Keene guest room and Marie's cooking." With so many players from distant places, the hospitality that she afforded was especially appreciated. "When holiday periods found a lad far from home and with no place to go, the welcome mat was out at the Keene home."[7]

In 1934, Loren Grannis from Peoria, IL became Willamette's first Little All-American. "The only year between 1934 and 1941 when someone failed to make it was 1940." [This may be an error – 1939 may be the only year, because Tony Fraiola said he was named Little All-American in 1940 and 1941.] The Associated Press selected the Little All-American teams, annually, "from the ranks of the smaller colleges." The list of Spec's Willamette Little All-Americans impresses for its consistency:

Following Grannis came halfback John Oravec in '35; Dick Weisgerber, fullback, '36; guard Elliott Becken in '37; end George Abbot, '38; and, two more guards, Joe Holland, now coach at Portland State, and Anthony Joe Fraiola in '39 and '41.[8]

Spec was diplomatic when it came to his best players and teams. "Keene doesn't even try to pick the best, just as he won't pick the best team he ever had." Spec's players were special, "they all were good boys and good teams."[9]

There is irony in Spec's success coaching football, basketball, and baseball. It was the latter sport that he loved best. As a former pro pitcher with the Portland Beavers, Spec "had a chance to go with the New York Giants," causing him to have "a high regard for pitchers and catchers." Unsurprisingly, Spec's baseball teams won five Northwest Conference championships during his tenure. In basketball, Spec won four outright Northwest Conference championships, and one co-championship. "Even with baseball as his love, it was on the gridiron where Keene's name and fame was built."[10]

Willamette University's Sports Hall of Fame includes Spec, and at least three of his players who played for Joe Kasberger at SBP: John Oravec, Dick Weisgerber, and John Kolb. Willamette's Hall of Fame citations summarize their accomplishments.

Oravec remained in Oregon, recalled by Tony Fraiola as a very bright assistant football coach at Linfield College in McMinnville. John, at this writing, lives in Salem and is remembered by many Oregonians for his exciting style and diminutive size. He was inducted Oct. 1, 1993.

JOHN ORAVEC (1932-36): John 'Scooter' Oravec still holds Willamette records for touchdowns and points scored in a game, season and career. He was a first-team Associated Press Little All America his senior year in 1935, when the Bearcats went 5-2 and outscored five small colleges 99-6. But Oravec had his best year as a junior. In 1934, he led the nation (all levels) in touchdowns scored (20) and was second in the land in points scored (120). The highlight of the season was his seven-touchdown game in a 75-0 romp over Whitman at Sweetland Field. During Oravec's four-year career the Bearcats went 17-2-1 in the Northwest Conference, including winning the last 13 games and Conference titles in 1934 and '35. Oravec also played baseball for three seasons before turning pro and joining the Vancouver Maple Leafs in Canada.[11]

Weisgerber became the mayor of Sturgeon Bay, WI after his career with the Packers ended. He was inducted Oct. 1, 1993.

DICK WEISGERBER (1934-38): Dick Weisgerber was a 1936 Associated Press Little All-America at running back and later played four years for the Green Bay Packers of the National Football League (1938-40, '42). He also made the 1936 AP All-America honorable mention list, which included all colleges and universities in the country. At Willamette, he led the nation in points-after-touchdown his freshman year (1934) and was third in the country in scoring his junior season (1936), when he started at running back. He was a four-time Northwest Conference all-star. The Bearcats were 26-8-1 overall and 18-0 against Conference opponents during Weisgerber's four years, winning NWC titles in 1934, 1936 and 1937 and sharing the championship with Linfield in 1935. He died June 1, 1984.[12]

A final member of Willamette's Hall of Fame from SBP was John Kolb, Class of 1937.

JOHN KOLB (1937-41): John Kolb lettered 12 times in football, basketball, and baseball,

John Oravec and Dick Weisgerber, ca. 1952.

winning all-Northwest Conference honors in football and basketball before graduating in 1941. He played pro baseball for the Salem Senators the summer following his graduation and in 1947 played professional basketball in Salem. Kolb later became an NCAA football official for 25 years and officiated NCAA basketball for over 20 years. Before moving into a role as an observer of Pacific-10 Conference officials, he officiated the 1971 Rose Bowl featuring Stanford's Jim Plunkett, and two East-West Shrine games. Kolb continued working as an officials observer until he died of cancer May 19, 1989, at the age of 71. Kolb was an active member of Cardinal Round Table – Willamette's athletic booster club – and was a PGA teaching professional at Oak Knoll Golf Course for 20 years.[13]

The remainder of the 1952-53 school year for Joe was troubled by unrest within St. Mary's Abbey, and monastic affairs may have become a distraction. The problems Joe faced without PGs, may have been less significant than these new matters.

With the emergence of Delbarton, it is not surprising that concerns were expressed about the unity of St. Mary's Abbey. With two distinct and active monasteries in Newark and in Morristown, unity must have been an elusive, if not impossible, goal. A few years earlier, recommendations were made by a board of Benedictine visitators. The situation was studied, with discussions following, to see how unity could be achieved, if it could! In 1953 there was again a visitation and a closing statement by the overseers reiterated the concern about unity that was expressed previously. Within the year, therefore, it was mandated that the community determine how to achieve the desired unity. Abbot O'Brien responded by forming a committee to address the concerns.[14]

The 1953 baseball team had a 16-3-0 record to salvage SBP's athletic performance for the school year. The Korean Conflict ended in July 1953, so Joe's sum-

John Thomas in College All Star Game uniform, ca. 1953.

mer provided a chance to ponder a future without war. Also, the College All-Star Football game in Chicago was of special interest.

Arguably, one of Joe's best all-around athletes from SBP was John Thomas, Class of 1948 via Newark South Side HS, now known as Shabazz HS. John initially went to the University of Maryland before realizing that College Park was not for him. After calling Joe for advice on what to do next, John got on the train for Corvallis, using Joe's steamer trunk to transport his belongings, with assurance that Spec Keene would care for him. The rest is history, as Beaver fans realized fully when John Thomas proved to be one of Oregon State's most versatile and talented athletes ever. Over his career, he won varsity letters in three sports: football, basketball, and baseball. Slats Gill allowed John to compete in baseball when the basketball and baseball schedules conflicted. The Beavers' appearance in the College World Series speaks highly of that team under "Coley," Ralph Coleman. In football, however, there were many near-misses for these talented teams surrounded by high expectations.

Also, John was a member of Phi Delta Theta, which he reckons contributed some 27 varsity athletes while he was a student. Despite John's all-around prowess, it was in football that he attracted pro scouts, and the Beaver captain was recognized for his individual performance. John may have been Joe's only former player to be honored with selection to the rosters of two post-season football classics: the East-West Shrine Game in San Francisco, and the College All-Star Game in Chicago against the Los Angeles Rams. John was drafted in the second round by the Philadelphia Eagles, but could not agree on contract terms and was traded to the Detroit Lions. When John could not agree on a contract with the Lions, he returned to baseball.[15]

1953-54 School Year

The school year began with the 1953 football team rebounding nicely from the 1952 disaster with a 6-1-0 record. After a close opening loss to Rutherford St. Mary's HS, SBP went undefeated. The last scheduled game against Fair Lawn HS was cancelled due to a snow storm. Most gratifying to Joe, perhaps, was a convincing 32-7 win over BMI at midseason – a real accomplishment, even with PGs! Joe's young Gray Bees had grown and the future was bright despite the graduation loss of Joe's diminutive quarterback, John Allen. He was known as

Joe, ca. 1953.

Joe's "mighty-mite" and a bond developed between player and coach that endured from the travails encountered by both in 1952.

Father Philip Hoover, rather than Joe, made news in the summer of 1953 by naming Joe's former baseball player, Jack Dalton, Class of 1944, to replace Harry Singleton. SBP's new basketball coach had superior credentials. After World War II, Dalton played for Prof Blood, who was the first of the three future Basketball Hall of Fame coaches who taught him the game. After SBP, Dalton went to St. John's University in Brooklyn, playing under Joe Lapchick. When Lapchick left for the New York Knicks, Dalton played for Frank McGuire. After his college career ended, Dalton coached at St. James HS in Newark.[16] Also in 1954, Fran Murphy, Class of 1946, was named as track and cross-country coach. As a protégé of Jim Cavanagh, Murphy knew the "system" and would keep the track tradition strong.

In The Dalles, there was news regarding "Bob Murray Night" at the local Elks Lodge. In appreciation for Murray's contributions, he was honored at a testimonial dinner in March, 1954. The festivities included many famous names from a wide area who came to pay tribute. In addition, "many telegrams were received from coaches and public officials." Murray's role as a coach, teacher, and mentor involved many. Jack Cross, in The Dalles *Chronicle*, noted several famous players, eight of whom played in the Rose Bowl Classic.

Charles (Shy) Huntington, who later played and coached at Oregon; George (Bun) Stadelman; Arthur (Curley) Miller; Tommy Ward; Joe Kasberger; Ariel (Cougar) Bolton; Paul Schiller; Val Gibson; Frank Devaney; Ray Ostrander; John, Fred, Rich, and Bob Cyphers; Max Bartell and Bill Martin.[17]

Bob Murray had interests beyond athletics that were recognized. "He was a past exalted ruler of Dalles Elks Lodge 303 and past president of the Old Wasco County Pioneer Association."[18]

In Newark, the remainder of the school year was relatively uneventful and the 1954 baseball team had a 15-6-0 record. An early season 24-3 win over Newark Arts HS was Joe's 400th game, for a winning record of 87 percent.

As Joe spent the summer in Oregon, Louise Milbauer's health may have been a concern, since she was a very special person in Joe's life and career.

1954-55 School Year

The 1954-55 school year was very difficult, despite the football team's 7-0-0

Late summer 1954 photo taken by Kewp to be sent to Bun on Air Force duty in England. Seated: Louise Milbauer, Mary Jean (Frank's daughter), Claire; Standing: Kathleen (Frank's wife), Claire (Frank's daughter), Frank A. Milbauer.

record. This may have been Joe's best Gray Bee team without PGs. Joe took out many frustrations with a 26-0 midseason win against BMI, a major challenge for Joe. Without PGs, SBP was at a competitive disadvantage against this powerful foe, loaded with college and professional prospects. The season ended with a 13-game win-streak, including six wins from the 1953 season.

Reasons for a successful team usually include players and coaches. In this case, Joe was doubly blessed with two all-state players, George Enderle and Ben Scotti, both of whom achieved fame at higher competitive levels. Ben was followed by his talented younger bothers, Anthony and Fred, in subsequent years. Gene has the distinction of being Joe's last former player to attend his alma mater. On the sidelines, Joe was joined by a former player, Sam Cavallaro, who brought a wealth of knowledge with him from his recent college playing career.

The issue of his successor may have never been a consideration to Joe until now. Age was not a factor as he continued to win and enjoy his work. Over the years, beginning with Frank Milbauer in the 1930s, Joe had many assistant coaches. After Frank, there was Peter Carlesimo and then Buzz McGlynn, who moved on to Metuchen and Kearny, NJ High Schools. Harry Singleton assisted Joe in baseball. Another former player, Bill Conn, became Joe's assistant, and so on.

Working for Joe was considered to be highly desirable and a great way to learn and improve resumes, possibly while attending graduate school.

Joe is honored by faculty and football team for his twenty-fifth football season. Pictured are Ben Scotti, Fr. Philip Hoover, Joe and George Enderle. His SBP football record was reported as 155-28-11.

Head-coaching positions were never easy to secure, but Joe's recommendation could only help. As one of Joe's PGs from the Class of 1947, Sam Cavallaro proved to be a very fine assistant. For those who were Sam's students, he was recalled as a tough but fair man with the ability to challenge the boy into being better as a student, athlete, and man. On the field, Sam was equally demanding, with a Vince Lombardi physical resemblance complete with style of warmth, passion and tough love.

The "Bruise Brothers" Sam and Joe.

After SBP, the East Orange native, who had earned All-City, All-State, All-County and All-Metropolitan honors as a tackle and guard, went to Georgetown University in Washington, DC. When the Hoyas dropped football, Sam transferred to Mississippi State University in Starkville. After a redshirt season in 1949, the seasoned Coast Guard veteran was toughened further by the Southeastern Conference's stiff competition. The Maroons' coach, Arthur "Slick" Morton, played the 5-11, 212 Cavallaro as a regular defensive guard, where he earned varsity letters as a junior and senior.[19] After graduation, Sam was back in New Jersey selling baby food when he saw Buzz McGlynn, and learned that Joe needed an assistant. In 1954 Sam's coaching career began as Joe's assistant. Was Sam a possible successor to be groomed by Joe?

In addition to his athletic duties, Joe remained a teacher and handyman around the school. Joe's classroom wardrobe was always a suit, starched white shirt, and tie. Claire recalled Joe opening the door at Halstead Street with one hand and removing his tie with the other. Conversely, Joe dressed as a workman when the task demanded such attire. Although he was a famous coach and athletic director, he was not above manual labor. The sight of Joe dressed as a laborer was not

Joe on Gray Bee bench, ca. 1954.

274

Still teaching Freshman English 25 years later.

missed by his nephew.

'Joe was not one to toot his own horn.' When I went to see him, if I had not known from other sources what a remarkable work he did at St. Benedict's, I probably would have thought he was the janitor. Nothing wrong with being the janitor. It's just that there was no evidence of the fine work he was doing, and had been doing for a long time. Besides, he did do the janitor's work and anything else that needed to be done.[20]

The emotional center of this year for Joe, however, was Louise Milbauer's death in Dec. 1954. Louise was "Nana" to her grandchildren, "Katrinka" to Joe, and a very special person to many in her life. Kewp lovingly recalled this wonderful woman as "a convert to Catholicism when she was 18." Her religious and human qualities made a great impression on her granddaughter. "No greater Catholic ever existed." Also, these qualities were not lost on Joe, who knew the importance of a good home life – even as an adult. "Her home was truly a loving and Christian one. Why in the world would Joe want to live anyplace else!"[21] Louise's death was mourned by the Benedictines she had hosted. Abbot Patrick attended her funeral and praised her for the kindness and hospitality that she had extended to monks over the years. Claire Milbauer now had decisions to make regarding 17 Halstead Street; to keep or sell the home would have a major impact on Joe.

At the same time, there were happenings in Corvallis that may have included Joe. From 1949 to 1954, Kip Taylor's Beavers struggled along after an impressive start of 7-3-0 in 1949. The next five years produced teams with losing records and Taylor finished with a career record of 20-36-0 in Corvallis. Spec sought another head coach after Taylor's 1954 team finished with a dismal 1-8-0 record. Again, whether or not Joe was considered is not known. Spec's choice of a new football coach, this time, proved to be a wise one. The Beavers new coach, J. Thompson (Tommy) Prothro of Duke, was known to Oregon State fans as the star of the Duke team in the 1942 Rose Bowl game.

There was more sadness in Newark, with the passing of Ernest "Prof" Blood, on Feb. 4, 1955 at the age of 82. Prof Blood's highly successful career as a basketball coach merited his selection to "Basketball's Hall of Fame at Springfield, Mass."[22] The remainder of the 1954-55 school year was stressful as Joe completed his twenty-fifth year at SBP. It is only natural that he was honored, despite his dislike of these events.

The following two stories are from the May 2, 1955 *Benedict News,* under the following headline: "TESTIMONIAL DINNER TO HONOR JOE KASBERGER TONITE AT ESSEX HOUSE." There is a huge photo of Joe under the headline. The first story is as follows:

Portrait of Joe used for the 1955 testimonial dinner to celebrate his 25 years at SBP.

Joseph M. Kasberger, athletic director and head football and baseball coach at St. Benedict's Prep will be honored tonight for his twenty-five years of service to St. Benedict's by a testimonial dinner given by the Alumni Association. The dinner, beginning at seven o'clock, is to be held in the Elizabethan Room of Newark's Hotel Essex House.

Mayor Leo Carlin, U.S. Congressman Hugh Addonizio, members of the alumni, students and friends of Mr. Kasberger are expected to attend the affair in honor of the familiar sports figure. Rev. Philip Hoover, O.S.B., Headmaster of St. Benedict's will open the dinner by giving the invocation. Following the traditional turkey dinner, toastmaster Vinnie Farrell, nationally known basketball referee and recently elected member of the Basketball Hall of Fame, will preside. Mr. Farrell will introduce the guest speaker, Mr. Peter Carlesimo, director of athletics and head football and baseball coach at Scranton University. In order to express appreciation to Mr. Kasberger for his work at St. Benedict's and for his outstanding work for New Jersey sports in general the presentation of a gift will be made by the President of the Alumni Association, Arthur O'Connor. After this ceremony, Mrs.[sic] Kasberger is expected to make a few remarks to the assembly and the testimonial dinner will draw to a close.

The story continues under the heading "Long Preparations," indicating that this may have been one of the biggest events ever sponsored by SBP.

Preparations for the dinner have been going on for months under the direction of Committee Chairman, Jack Dalton, head basketball coach here. Assisting Dalton as Treasurer was Daniel Moore. Gene Walsh took care of the various hotel arrangements while Bill Glaccum and his committee handled the printing and tickets. The speakers' committee was composed of Frank Delaney, Russ Monica and Buzz McGlynn, formerly assistant coach and intramural sports director at St. Benedict's.

The reception committee, under the chairmanship of Alumni President Art O'Connor included Frank Milbauer, Art Chautte [sic – Charette], and Bill Conn, present J.V. coach here. Publicity was handled by Bob Larkin, Ed Rockford, Bill Johnson, Ken Milsop, George Conte [sic – Conti], and Harry Durkin. Assisting dinner chairman Jack Dalton was alumni moderator Rev. Owen Hudson, O.S.B.

The story concludes under the heading "Letters Mailed," indicating that students' fathers were invited to attend with "special letters." These were mailed on March 28 with Fr. Philip and Jack Dalton giving "first public announcement

Peter Carlesimo, Joe and Abbot Patrick O'Brien at Joe's testimonial dinner.

to the student body of the proposed dinner." Honoring Joe for his twenty-five years at SBP "received immediate encouragement, demonstrating the great respect that the Director of Athletics has built up through the years."

Excerpts of the second story under the page 1 headline, referenced above, follow:

> This year Joe Kasberger celebrates his 25th season at the Bee Hive. Everyone has heard of his prowess as a grid coach who won 155 games, lost 28, and tied 11, plus six Prep School Championships. As baseball coach he also sports a fine record, but few know of the J.K. in the years before his arrival here.
>
> Joe's earlier athletic history started in 1917 when he entered Oregon State College. After taking time out for the service, he graduated with a B.S. in Agriculture in June, 1922, and later received his A.M. in Physical Education from Columbia.

After noting his college accomplishments as an athlete, the story continues under the heading "School Under Rockne" with mention of his 1924 season at Notre Dame. Then his prior coaching experiences are given: "two years at Mt. Angel College, St. Benedict, Oregon, and three years as head coach at Willamette University, Salem, Oregon." The story concludes as follows:

> The fall of 1930, saw Joe Kasberger come to the Bee Hive. His first teaching job consisted of 5 classes of Freshman English. He later was made head of the Commerce Department teaching typing and shorthand. We hope that the dinner tonight will mark not only the end of twenty-five years of service, but the beginning of twenty-five more.[23]

One of the great gaffes in *Benedict News'* history is the reference to "Mrs. Kasberger," since Joe never married. SBP's inability, as early as 1955, to get Joe's biography correct confused many subsequent stories about his life and career. Joe was very uncomfortable with this event, perhaps due to this special edition of the *Benedict News*. Since there was neither a correct story on his career nor his marital state, Joe's reaction is understandable. Joe had to be dragged, virtually, to this event by Frank Milbauer. Perhaps Joe had discussed testimonial dinners with Bob Murray and decided that these events were not for him. At this affair, the 1954 football team presented Joe with a watch, an implied message that he would be better able to keep time due to his propensity for keeping players later than they or their parents desired. Also recalled were guests autographing Joe's shirt, including Abbot Patrick who signed on Joe's collar.[24]

In that same *Benedict News*, there was the headline: "Eager Boys Try For Hive." The story was routine then, but illustrates SBP's stature.

> Four hundred and fifty boys were at the 'Bee Hive' on April 2 to take the Freshman Entrance Examination for the class of '59. One hundred and twelve schools were represented at the exam. Eighty-two Catholic schools and thirty public schools sent candidates. They came from as far north as Hasbrouck Heights and as far south as Sea Girt. Out of the 450 who took the exam only 180 were accepted.[25]

SBP rarely recruited then, and only had to select the best and the brightest for their very competitive academic environment. There must have been great satisfaction in knowing that so many young men still wanted to be Gray Bees.

The 1955 baseball team had a 16-6-0 record to conclude an ambivalent school year. Before Joe left Newark he may have discussed his housing dilemma with SBP's administrators, and possibly requested that they find him quarters for the next school year. Joe may have been the greatest of handymen around a house, but he was either unwilling or unable to cook. This episode marks the beginning of the end of the 17 Halstead Street era in Joe's career.

Claire wrote during the summer to advise Joe that she was putting 17 Halstead Street on the market She was busy with her graduate-degree requirements at Columbia that summer and needed two more terms. Also, in the fall she would be heading a new elementary school in South Orange. Claire did not need such a large home, and had found an apartment in suburban Springfield. Joe was invited to remain at 17 Halstead Street, however, until the home was sold.[26]

Joe returned to Newark and found himself alone with the furnishings at 17 Halstead Street, with prospective buyers visiting. It was lonely in such a big home with so many memories. Fortunately, there were other important matters to occupy Joe as the school year began.

1955-56 School Year

The 1955 football team had a disastrous 0-7-1 record with four losses by shutout. The highlight of the season was a 6-6 tie with Harrison HS. The nadir was inflicted by BMI, 0-47, the worst of Joe's SBP career. A postmortem by John

Joe, John Allen and Sam, taking their lumps in 1955.

Allen offered that SBP's young players were not as experienced and fully developed as their opposition.

Joe's career record now stood at 143-34-12. It probably stretches credibility to suggest that the dismal season was due to Joe's housing dilemma. Joe was heard to have said, "As the coach goes, so goes the team." Joe was not one for making excuses. Critics, however, might suggest that the problem was not Joe's housing dilemma. Rather, Joe's age was used against him in the quest for athletic talent. Perhaps he found it difficult to attract the volume of talented student-athletes that he needed. Those who once flocked to SBP were replaced by prospects with options. Any negative recruiting by rivals may have emphasized his age. Joe would not coach forever, or would he?

Without Louise, the 1955 holidays were difficult for Joe and the Milbauers. In her absence, the focal point was now in Millburn. Bun recalls Joe as "a wonderful, caring person and we were happy to have him in our lives." Bun makes it clear that Joe remained an integral part of the Milbauer family.

> Oh yes, if those dinners were at our home in Millburn, Joe never arrived with the rest of the family in the car. He walked from the Vailsburg section of Newark, to us on Bodwell Terrace, which is quite close to the Short Hills boundary. Amazingly, he was never exhausted. My sister Claire also remembered how Joe could do cartwheels and we couldn't. We tried to pinpoint his age at that time and figured maybe he was in his forties. He could have been 50 or 60 for all we knew. He just seemed ageless.[27]

In Feb. 1956, 17 Halstead Street was sold and vacated by Joe. He moved to the Casino, a wood-frame structure located at High and William Streets, directly across from SBP. This venerable facility was situated on approximately one acre, serving many purposes over the years. When Joe began living here in March, 1956, it had to be nearly one-half century old. By the mid-1950s, it included a parking lot for the faculty and fortunate students who drove cars.

At the age of 60, Joe found himself conveniently located. It is suspected, however, that the new housing arrangement did not agree with him, at least initially. As a residence for Joe's simple lifestyle, it was adequate. Bud Sandoz lived in Washington DC for more than nine years and visited Newark several times, observing Joe at both Halstead Street and the Casino. He recalled Joe's "style of living and certainly did wonder if he deliberately chose that style or if it just grew to be a habit." From Bud's accounts, the layout was very spartan though consistent with Joe's modest needs.

> He had two rooms, bare unpainted walls. He had the bare necessities, just! A bed, a chair, a chest of drawers, a closet, and a small TV set which he seldom turned on. He took meals across the street in the monastery basement. Three Benedictine sisters were the cooks, and they gave him good care and attention. He was good and thoughtful to them also.[28]

Furnishings came from 17 Halstead Street, which may may have helped him feel more at home. The where-abouts of Joe's moose head, presumably one of his few valued possessions, is not known. It was thought that Joe took it with him to his office, or the Casino, when the Halstead Street home was sold. There were no neighbors for Joe at the Casino, only monks, nuns, students, and an occasional "wino" or street vagrant. Actually, many recall

Casino Hall, Joe's residence from 1955 to 1969.

this as a very colorful neighborhood since Springfield Avenue was famed as a shopping area, especially for bridal gowns. Also, "Daddy" Grace's temple was not far away, on Springfield Avenue. Joe had proven himself as a family-oriented man who thrived with the Milbauers. Now, it seems that Joe's personality was changed by the new lifestyle.

The 1956 baseball team's 14-8-0 record concluded Joe's worst school-year per-formance by his teams. Despite the baseball team's mediocre record, it attained a place in the national record book. In a 5-2 victory over Newark Vo-Tech HS, the Gray Bees had two triple plays! In the season's finale in the GNT, SHP defeated the Gray Bees, 9-6, in their first baseball game since Joe defeated the Pony Pirates 8-4 in the 1941 season's last game. The GNT appearance was only SBP's second. Was age becoming an issue or was Joe merely in a slump? Was the slump induced by Joe's new living arrangement? Was the slump due to less tal-ent? Or, was there a generation gap between coach and players? Maybe the problem was that the athletic director overscheduled the coach. Or, was it that SBP's academic and athletic facilities did not appeal to prospective students?

Joe had much to contemplate while in The Dalles, especially his role as ath-letic director, school leader and visionary. Much is made of Joe, the baseball and football coach, whose record is clearly presented in an array of numbers. Less clearly understood and measurable is Joe's performance as an athletic director. Coaching now was only one of the demands being made upon him. His 1944 paper that alluded to "central" Catholic high schools was now prophetic. There were some serious concerns, not only for his athletic teams, but also for SBP. Would Joe's ability as an athletic director, in a more competitive secondary-school environment, equal his ability as a prophet? Now, could he position SBP's athletic programs appropriately for the future? Or was SBP already a decade late and many dollars short in providing competitive facilities?

In the post-World War II economic boom, many Newark families flocked to the suburbs. The need for new Catholic high schools was apparent. The Newark Archdiocese faced problems in suburban Bergen County with families from New York and Hudson County, as well as from Newark, creating huge growth pressures for Catholic elementary and high schools. A network of parochial, coeducational high schools was in place: St. Luke's HS in Hohokus, St. Cecilia HS in Englewood, Holy Trinity HS in Hackensack, St. Mary's HS in Rutherford, and Queen of Peace HS in North Arlington. Even with all these schools, there still was quite a challenge to meet the demand for Catholic education.

The Bergen County Catholic high schools were supplemented by Pope Pius XII HS in Passaic County, and St. Cecilia HS in Hudson County. Arguably, there was nothing wrong with these schools. Yet they did not have the aura of prestige associated with single-sex prep schools for boys, and academies for girls. In most cases, their facilities were inadequate for the new demands. Don Bosco Prep, operated by the Salesian Fathers, was the only Catholic prep school in Bergen County exclusively for boys. Its Ramsey location, near the New Jersey-New York State border, was not convenient for many. SBP and SHP, in Essex County, were more feasible options for Bergen County families with access to public transit routed to and from Newark. Similarly, St. Peter's Prep in Hudson County attracted Bergen County students with access to Jersey City public transit. Other Bergen County students went into New York City to Fordham Prep, Xavier HS, Loyola Prep, and Regis HS, since there was ample public transit from most of Bergen County.

When the first conceptual plans were made is unknown, but the Archdiocese of Newark was aided by the Christian Brothers. Their solution was a daring concept on strategically-located farmland in Oradell, near two major highways providing access to employment centers. In the mid 1950s, this sprawling parcel was developed into a modern high-school campus that became Bergen Catholic HS. It was an unusual school then, since there did not appear to be an easy way for students to reach the campus by public transit. The solution was a large school-bus fleet, routed throughout suburban towns, picking up students in the morning and delivering them home after school.

Bergen Catholic was an immediate success, and boys who normally went to the traditional Catholic prep schools in the cities were now going to Oradell. Bergen Catholic may have been short on tradition, but its founders were long on vision. Only time will tell if the Christian Brothers' bold experiment will have long-term staying power. A test of time had been passed by the older, traditional Catholic prep schools. Initially, the Christian Brothers read the market for students correctly, and their success came at the expense of the urban prep schools.

Probably the summer of 1956 found Joe thinking about these emerging challenges as he prepared for another school year. Possibly Joe discussed the matter of athletic facilities with Spec Keene when he visited Corvallis. Spec had grown beyond the "Xs and Os" of coaching and was now more concerned with dollars and cents. While Joe appeared to be struggling, Spec was on a roll in the summer of 1956. There is nothing quite like a successful football team to make the athletic director who hired the coach appear to be a genius. At Oregon State, Tommy Prothro was an immediate success with a 6-3-0 record in 1955, and his 1956 team appeared to be loaded with talent, so Rose Bowl hopes were high. In this positive atmosphere, Spec was pushing the right buttons.

Spec's duties as athletic director required personal and professional growth. He was unusually qualified, and performed his duties well because of his political skills and athletic experience, traits essential in this position. On campus, Spec was viewed favorably by the faculty for his Willamette role as an associate member of Blue Key, the senior men's honor fraternity that was active at Oregon State after his graduation. In Salem, Spec was the faculty representative to this organization. In Oregon politics, Spec was respected by the Legislature, which was important at a state university. To wit: Spec was appointed chairman of the state board of parole and probation, a significant honor, as well as other chairmanships: "chairman of the Salem City playground committee; chairman of the American Legion boxing commission; and chairman of American Legion baseball."[29]

At the national level, Spec was "very influential" as a member of the "NCAA Executive Committee for five years; a member of the NCAA television committee for a half dozen years." He also chaired "the selection committee for the western regional NCAA basketball tournament."[30] In the Pacific Coast Conference, Spec was a past-president of the Athletic Directors' Association. Spec, however, was not the one-man show that he had been at Willamette, as he managed coaches and looked at a big picture of college athletics.

The problems Spec and Joe faced had many commonalities and differences. However, Joe had access to an experienced athletic director who knew the issue of competitive-sports facilities in a new athletic age. Surely Spec would provide Joe with tricks of the trade if he were asked. Spec was credited with a major role in two significant athletic facilities on the Oregon State campus. Right after becoming athletic director in 1947, he was probably immersed in fundraising for both Gill Coliseum and Parker Stadium. Was Joe interested in these matters, or more preoccupied with coaching?

Joe had to be impressed by Spec's accomplishments which were essential for maintaining the Beavers' competitive position in athletics. Joe had to know that the same logic applied at SBP. Obviously, alumni, parents and friends were keys to successful fundraising. Despite a reputation for building things, Joe may have felt that what he had at SBP was adequate. Yet implicitly, Joe's role as athletic director appeared to call for a vision of SBP's sports future. However, none of Joe's writings, revealed to date, suggest that he had such a future vision for SBP. The visioning "thing" may not have appealed to Joe. Or, any visions he had may have been stifled. These questions are raised with the hope that more can be learned about Joe's thoughts at this critical time in SBP's evolution.

Joe's position was awkward due to the prevailing philosophy at St. Mary's Abbey. The monastic community numbered "over 120," and was active, without as sharp a focus as some might desire. The abbey was "conducting two prep schools and nine parishes, in addition to the Theologate at Delbarton." Despite appearance of surface success, all was not well in Abbot Patrick's domain. "Tensions were growing between the Morristown and Newark communities, with each feeling its growth hindered by the demands of the other."[31]

There was excitement at St. Mary's Abbey in early June with the formation of a committee. Abbot Patrick hoped to relieve tension, but was "resolute in his determination to hold the two houses together," that is Newark and Morristown. His solution was to transfer the title of Abbey from Newark to Morristown, and a vote was held on his proposal.

> The majority gave him the affirmative vote of confidence that he asked for and Saint Mary's Monastery in Morristown became 'Saint Mary's Abbey.' The Newark house reverted to the title it had borne from 1857 to 1884: Saint Mary's Priory.[32]

In July a favorable response came from Rome's Holy See on this action. Subsequently building committees were formed at both places. The decision to raise Morristown to abbey-status was a rude awakening for many associated with SBP. Perhaps the die was now cast, and the future for many in St. Mary's Abbey was at Delbarton. With this line of thinking, perhaps SBP was expendable, and no longer the focal point it had traditionally been.

Capital improvements appeared essential for SBP to remain competitive in an increasingly difficult climate of change. Joe knew there were problems with Shanley Gym. The once state-of-the-art facility was hopelessly outdated and far too small. Although "only thirty-five years old," in some minds it was obsolete but adequate. With SBP students of the new generation, however, there was disagreement, having come from parishes where the grammar-school gym and classrooms were far superior to what they saw at SBP. Benedict Field had problems, but nothing as severe as what was faced on the main campus. Capital investment was a sore need that had been deferred for many years. With SBP's 100th anniversary approaching, would this not be the time to commemorate it with major capital improvements?

Joe certainly understood the dilemma faced by Jack Dalton. SBP's great basketball tradition was linked to its home-court advantage. The noisy and cramped snakepit, Shanley Gym, was intimidating. Now, the home-court advantage was jeopardized as the game changed. Newer basketball venues, with more seating and playing area, made the competition less interested in playing at SBP. While the facility was quaint, and a great conversation piece, it was obsolete. Much of SBP's mystique was in its old facilities where tradition was seen, smelled and felt. How many other schools offered dances with monks observing student- and date-behavior from the running track suspended above the gymnasium floor! For many young women it was an incredible experience!

Joe appeared to have no appetite for fundraising, and to be content with a limited view of his role, one that gave him time to teach, coach, labor around the school, and maintain the grounds at Benedict Field. A key issue for the administration was where to put new facilities, even if the capital were raised for new construction? The SBP campus was landlocked, and acquiring adjoining sites may have been prohibitively expensive – because property values were then high. Perhaps urban-renewal funds from the City of Newark could have been procured for land acquisition. Possibly, there were no feasible options in Newark.

Other considerations were costs and the source of funds. In the postwar economic boom, many SBP alumni became affluent. With persuasive men like Joe and Fr. Philip, fundraising should not have been that difficult. How could alumni not respond generously, if approached properly? In retrospect, it appears that a more modest approach was taken by SBP. Was there sentiment that advised against investing too heavily in Newark? The prevailing mood in Newark was upbeat about its future; and New Jersey's largest city would remain viable into the foreseeable future, according to most pundits. For alumni, with sons as prospective students, however, other high school alternatives became more attractive and convenient.

Maybe an incremental course was taken, despite SBP's long-unmet needs. Was there now cautious faith in the future for one of New Jersey's premier Catholic prep schools? Or was the vision too cloudy to justify such faith? The adage of "betting with your head and not your heart" may have prevailed. In this perceived context, fundraising and new construction plans were made for $3 million worth of facilities at both Newark and Morristown. Any earlier grand schemes for SBP in Newark were replaced by more modest plans.

1956-57 School Year

The school year began with the 1956 football team's 7-2-0 record, with SBP victimized by BMI midway through the season. The school year ended with the baseball team's 14-3-0 record which may have given Joe a better summer than he had a year ago. The highlight came in the next- to-last game of the season. A 12-2-win over Pennington

Joe and the 1956 Gray Bees.

Joe on the sidelines getting an official's interpretation of a call.

School was the 400th in Joe's SBP career, for a winning record of 84 percent.

As Joe contemplated the future, the issue of retirement may have arisen. With Social Security benefits at age 62 added to the good investments that he had made, Joe's thinking about retirement would not have been unusual. SBP provided for Prof Blood's and Jim Cavanagh's retirements, and it is only logical that Joe would be afforded similar treatment. To observers then, Joe was ageless and retirement was never mentioned. Students and players probably did not realize that he was sixty years old, due to the the manner in which he conducted himself in the classroom and on the athletic field.

An observer of Joe in The Dalles was his next door neighbor, John Brookhouse, who saw a man of great physical strength, even in his older years. Recalling how Joe had built a stone wall for the home, John said Joe resembled a miniature Arnold Schwartzenegger, with bulging muscles showing through the white tee-shirt he almost always wore while working around the house. John recalled his father telling him as a youngster that Joe was a Newark school teacher. There was no mention of coaching, so John was astonished to hear that Joe was also a baseball and football coach. John was even more astounded to learn that Joe was famous enough to merit research for a biography. Joe was a man of few words in his later years, as John recalled. Around the neighborhood he was viewed as being kindly; but not gregarious, as he was described in his younger years. There was a vague remembrance of Joe as a former star athlete, but not a local hero. Joe, as a baseball and football coach with a nationally-significant record, was not known. For observers in The Dalles, there was a perception that Joe was a seasonal worker, a figure common in the American West.[33]

In The Dalles, Joe owned a red International-Harvester pickup. Whether or not this was the only vehicle Joe ever owned is not clear. Joe is known, however, to have made car trips during the summer to visit Corvallis and Mt. Angel. Coincidentally, Bud Sandoz recalled Joe's frugal ways and a "reputation for being an outrageous tightwad." Because of Joe's perceived attitude towards money, he was fortunate that he had someone to look after his interests. Joe depended upon his younger brother, Max, a banker in The Dalles, to whom he "sent the bulk of his earnings" from Newark.

In later years, when things had to be paid for out west, he told Max to take care of it. He never saw the bill and didn't know how much was paid and didn't care. The average person will usually view money as that which is needed to provide normal living-expenses, which would include a home, auto, and the endless things needed for a family life.[34]

1957-58 School Year

The author first saw "Joe K" on a beautiful Sunday afternoon in mid-Sept. 1957 at the Rutherford, NJ High School stadium. The Gray Bees met St. Mary's HS in the season opener. We registered for classes the previous Friday and would begin classes the next day. I had heard of Joe from my Corpus Christi Grammar School friend and Little League teammate, Tom Werling. Tom was two years older, and his school books became mine when he did not return to SBP. If anyone was responsible for me wanting to attend SBP, it was Tom. As an impressionable 13-year-old, with a strong interest in sports, I anticipated seeing the legendary Joe K and his fabled Gray Bees. I was not disappointed by this introduction into the reflected glory associated with SBP.

I am not sure what impressed me more about that game: the memory of Joe's coaching garb, pictured here, that I thought to be highly unusual; or SBP's running back, number 31, Frank "Rosie" Barnes, who reminded me of "Lightnin'" Lenny Moore of the Baltimore Colts. Frank appeared to me to be the only black person on the field or at the game. Barnes was a very exciting player to watch, and was made more interesting by Tom Holden from my hometown, Hasbrouck Heights, who was a St. Mary's linebacker. Rosie gave Tom and the St. Mary's defense a real workout with his

Joe with 1957 Gray Bee co-captains Rich Nazareta and Jim Scarpone.

speed and moves. Tom was a fine football player and a good guy, who went to Annapolis. Sadly, United States Marine Corps Lieutenant Tom Holden was the only resident of Hasbrouck Heights killed in Vietnam a decade later. After the game, I was better prepared for the personal adventure that began the next day and has lasted a lifetime.

Meeting new classmates was exciting for all of us members of Freshman E. By definition we were the underachievers in our otherwise cerebral group of classmates, as the bottom twenty percent of the Class of 1961. Some members of Freshman E rose to higher levels of the academic class-system, designated A through E, during our SBP career. Presumably, the administration had misdiagnosed some academic talent in the initial class assignments. For others, it became a status symbol to be confirmed "four year E-men," who walked an academic tightrope, summer school for some and a struggle to graduate for most. As we waited outside our classroom for English, it was evident that there were characters in this Freshman E class. First impressions were validated throughout the first day. Teacher after teacher was challenged to establish how far he could be pushed. Several guys speculated that we would have Joe K as our teacher. Sons of SBP alumni talked about what their fathers had told them about Joe. One story had it that he was not a Catholic As we listened intently, this legendary man appeared in the hall. Before long, we were in the classroom and Joe K was our teacher.

What a second impression! Joe K was a name only used out of earshot from him. In addressing Joe, it was always Mr. Kasberger. There was no familiarity. Joe was then 61 years old, but he appeared ageless, dressed in a double-breasted suit and starched white shirt with floral-patterned tie – more conventional than his coaching outfit. His face was tanned and it shone from a close shave that surely came from a straight-edged razor. He was not big, but very athletic and powerful in appearance. Joe's voice was deep, and he spoke with a drawl that was unique – not a Southern drawl. It was "Western" – in a part of the world accustomed to the Southern drawls of the sports broadcasters, Red Barber with the Dodgers and Mel Allen with the Yankees. Joe's drawl was distinctly different, as we trained our ears to his speech-pattern.

He made a strong impression very quickly, after some breach of behavior was not to his liking as the class began. Joe said: "Awraht . . Ah 'cept the challenge," in a voice that was not so much loud as firm. In response, however, we all kept mighty quiet as he began his lesson. I do not recall everything he said that day, but I distinctly remember two anecdotes. First, Joe taught that horses push a wagon when in harness, rather than pull, as most of us had thought. Second, we learned that you raise animals and rear children, so we must never confuse "rear" and "raise" when speaking proper English. Joe also emphasized the proper spelling and pronunciation of "athletes and athletics." Apparently he thought that many misspelled the word because it was mispronounced as "ath-a-letes and ath-a-letics." Finally, Joe insured that we understood the Latin roots of the word "suburbs." Since many of us were from the suburbs, it was nice to know that we lived in towns that were "under the city." Reading material for Joe's course is thought to have included George Orwell's *Animal Farm*, William Golding's *Lord of the Flies*, and Jonathan Swift's *Gulliver's Travels*. There seemed to be a feeling that we were privileged to have a great man as our teacher.

As a football coach, Joe did not disappoint many with a fine 1957 football team's 7-1-1 record. Only a 13-20 loss to BMI ended dreams for an undefeated season. The other blemish was a 13-13 tie with the Fair Lawn HS Cutters. The season's second game, a 27-6 win over North Arlington Queen of Peace HS, was Joe's 200th in his SBP career, for a winning record of 76 percent.

As athletic director, Joe had fine head coaches in basketball, wrestling, indoor-outdoor track and cross-country. Jack Dalton, John Allen, and Fran Murphy pro-

Sam Cavallaro, Joe and Frank Barnes.

duced state-championship teams. Also, there were minor sports programs in swimming, tennis, and golf. Joe had other responsibilities besides the football and baseball teams. Teaching academic courses was probably becoming more difficult since his time was so limited, which raises the issue of sports budgets.

To operate competitive sports programs required a fairly sizable portion of SBP's total operating budget. Ticket-sales revenue appeared modest, and probably not self-supporting, for each of the major sports. Thus, Joe's role as laborer around the main campus, and Benedict Field groundskeeper, reveals a man dedicated to keeping costs down. Or, was Joe's budget so tight that he had no choice? A workaholic by volition is different than a workaholic out of necessity! Very few athletic directors at similarly sized and situated schools probably had so many tasks. In the Newark and suburban public schools, supported by property taxes, the salaries probably exceeded what Joe received at SBP. Also, such schools had support staff to do many of the jobs that Joe performed.

This time of generational conflict and changing values was ripe for turmoil. Girls *and* cars were distractions that Joe had yet to experience in the postwar era. The age of affluence led to changing socio-economic views and a new breed of student-athlete. As Joe encountered them, perhaps a generation gap showed and young assistant coaches would be essential in helping him bridge it and navigate unknown waters. Joe was a revered, grandfather-like presence, surrounded by an aura of greatness, even if some athletes joked that SBP's Gray Bees should be renamed "Spartans," to reflect his thrifty ways. This leads to another observation about Joe by his nephew. While not all players may have liked Joe's style, he was always respected as a great man, teacher and coach.

All Kasbergers tended toward frugality, and the aphorism 'Waste not, want not' was bred into their bones. I have no doubt that Joe could have doubled or tripled his salary had he chosen to leave St. Benedict's. And I know that he was sometimes annoyed at the salary he was being paid. I've thought on this and it is my belief that money and 'things' had no meaning for Joe. He knew he had to be independent, and he was not going to be poor. But beyond that he did not have any need for money.[35]

Joe had great energy despite having a handful with Benedict Field. In the late

1950s, Joe's lifelong interest in landscaping was demonstrated at Bun's new Millburn home.

> When I married and my wife and I bought our first home, Joe was right there instructing on planting grass, and generally giving wonderful information on 'how to do it ourselves.' This sounded almost more than we could undertake, but when a project was started, he was right there until we finished. He really made it seem like fun along with work. I must say when we finished, our home really looked beautiful. We had a celebration at the end of this project with dinner and lots of laughs, and he would joke about how we seemed a little intimidated by the undertaking of the landscape project. If truth be talk we knew more about painting inside than planting outside.[36]

The bonds of friendship and family with the Milbauers never ended for Joe. The holidays were not the same without Skip and Katrinka, but they were celebrated together.

> Usually, New Year's day was our day with Joe. We would have early dinner and then football games. This was the best of times. He would always have a running commentary on the games.[37]

While Christmas was Joe's favorite holiday, one gets an impression that TV's advent changed that. Possibly New Year's Day, with televised football bowl games, emerged as his favorite holiday. New Year's Day, 1958 was special since John Thomas was home to watch the Rose Bowl, with expert commentary – as pictured here.

The school year was dominated by fundraising for a new addition to the historic school. There were student assemblies that included Newark's Mayor Leo Carlin, SBP Class of 1926. Getting SBP's entire student-body of around 600 into Shanley Gymnasium was a tight fit, and a new auditorium/theater combination was a necessity: so were new classrooms, cafeteria, and a modern school library. "Obviously, new facili-

1958 New Year's Day. John Thomas, Joe, John's father, Aloysius, and niece at the Thomas home in Newark.

ties were needed and, with this goal in mind, Father Philip launched a successful fund drive in 1957."[38]

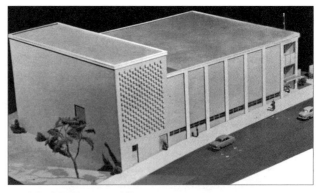

Model of SBP's new addition, ca. 1958.

Absent from the plans was a new gymnasium. Any improvements at SBP were long overdue, but a new auditorium was not a gym. Compromise was probably necessary, but core problems in old buildings still needed attention. If the monastery were in the same condition as the classrooms, improvements were needed there as well. SBP had deferred much investment during its rise to the top of the prep-school ranks. Now, the failure to act earlier had serious implications. Regardless, "ground-breaking for the new building was held on February 27, 1958."[39]

Fr. Jerome Fitzpatrick provides the following historical context for the building program in Newark that came to fruition:

> In 1945, Abbot Patrick and the Chapter (Abbey) approved a proposal to build a new SBP. This never materialized. In 1951 another proposal was undertaken to build a "Greater SBP with the Alumni Association taking the lead to raise some $450,000. The effort did not 'fly' due to limited financial potential and lack of initiative. The rendering in the 1951 *Telolog* was that of a suggested architect for the 'hoped-for' campaign, which did not materialize. In the rendering there is no drawing of a possible gym. In 1957 a plan and a fund-raiser were undertaken . . . both of which were successful. No gym was contemplated at this time. What we planned, was built and paid for by the monies raised in the campaign.[40]

A simultaneous building campaign began in Morristown for Delbarton, not a favorite school for many "Benedict's guys." One of Delbarton's problems to many was its image. SBP's students had broad socio-economic backgrounds that may have made it America at its best, with wealthy, middle-class and poor blending in a fairly egalitarian mix. It was not "where are you from" at SBP. "Where are you going" was what mattered, as Joe may have phrased it. Pretentious students did not fare well, and an attitude was adjusted or a student was gone without fanfare. Delbarton, however, was perceived as a rich boys' school, with students viewed as privileged and supercilious because of "Daddy's money." Naturally, they were ridiculed by their "less elite" SBP counterparts when paths crossed. Unsurprisingly, SBP did not schedule Delbarton's teams then. Of course, Delbarton hardly had enough athletes to field teams, a rivalry that St. Mary's Abbey could ill-afford! "Benedict's Guys" were not without attitude problems of their own. To many, SBP attitudes ranged from confidence to arrogance, with cockiness the norm. If you could do it, then it was not bragging, and SBP had a tradition of "doing a job."

Despite the success of the building programs at both locations, there remained unsolved issues within St. Mary's Abbey. The monastic concern was "that the only real answer to the question of how those in each location could sense a feeling of unity and family would be separation."[41]

Students tended to be oblivious to monastic affairs and fundraising except when the big blue Ballantine Brewery truck, with the famous golden "three-ring sign," arrived at SBP. That automatically set students to humming Ballantine's advertising jingle famed then, since Newark's Ballantine was the New York Yankees chief sponsor. So, sounds of "make the three-ring sign and ask the man for Ballantine" usually signalled an SBP fundraiser that evening, with lots of cold brew. John Allen recalls the humor of grown men, nervously drinking beer, with one eye out for Joe, lest he see former players consuming. Fr. Jerome recalls Joe to be such a straight arrow about drinking that even at Bill Meister's wedding, a few years later, all anxiously watched to see if Joe took a drink before others indulged.[42]

With the beginning of the 1958 baseball season and winter's end, Joe was happy again. Preseason drills began immediately after the basketball season. What a sight to see the aging, but still athletic, Joe hitting ground balls in Shanley Gymnasium. When it was time, he barked orders for players to run wind sprints on the gym floor, or laps around the suspended-from-the-ceiling track. It was an exhilarating time for Joe and his players when they experienced that first warm day of late winter. Then it was off to Benedict Field for the real thing. The smells of spring, the damp earth turning green, the crack of the bat, and the sound of ball on leather were a tonic for Joe.

Also, it was a time of conflict between baseball and track on the suddenly active, but very crowded, Benedict Field. With Joe as athletic director and baseball coach, baseball prevailed and trackmen learned quickly to dodge baseballs from the batting-practice cage. Benedict Field was unusual, with its oddly-shaped track of one-quarter mile, surrounding the baseball field. The batting-practice cage, however, was down the right-field line, adjacent to the track. Also, the right-field area contained a tenement home, causing the field to have an unusual configuration. The foul pole in right field, therefore, was closer to home-plate than the left-field fence, abutting the subway tracks. With the aroma of Wooten Chocolates in the air, Benedict Field was truly special. The inadequate and aging field house frustrated players anxious to clean up before catching the subway or bus for home. It was not just a problem for basketball and physical education classes at Shanley Gym. To many prospective athletes from increasingly-distant suburbs, SBP's problems may have been perfectly obvious. To Joe, it was "what does not kill you makes you stronger," or words to that effect.

Despite its warts, Joe loved Benedict Field, but deferred to track coach Fran Murphy, who lived at the field house, as Joe opted to reside at the Casino. The Bloomfield Avenue subway station was only a few short blocks away from Benedict Field and Joe could have ridden downtown and walked the relatively short distance to school. This Benedict Field oasis afforded Joe an opportunity to lovingly prepare a baseball diamond after the long winter. Appearances were not important to Joe at Benedict Field, where he was a living legend to the young men who saw him – as described by an anonymous *Benedict News* writer:

> He singlehandedly worked Benedict's Field into the proper condition each year. He raked the infield daily, before and after practice to remove the slightest pebble, put up the goalposts, painted fences and built the wall behind the backstop. He did all these things and more because of his devotion. For years Joe Kasberger never quit giving his time and work to St Benedict's. As long as this school exists, it will stand as a testimonial to Joe's loyalty.[43]

The 1958 baseball team had a 14-6-0 record to send Joe home for the summer, where he found that after many years of construction, The Dalles Dam on the Columbia River was nearing completion. Even at home, there was change for Joe to encounter, but change came at a slower pace here. On a sadder note, Joe found The Dalles in mourning after Bob Murray's death at the age of 77.

The following excerpts are from obituaries which appeared. The first is from the Tuesday evening, June 3, 1958 issue of The Dalles *Chronicle,* headlined: "Death Claims Sports Leader Robert Murray; Ex-Coach Succumbs In Local Hospital." Portions of the text follow: "An illness which required hospitalization on Sunday proved fatal yesterday evening. A heart ailment is believed to have been the cause of death."[44] The following story is from an undated, untitled, typewritten document by an anonymous writer, under the heading "Robert L. Murray;" the sentiment expressed speaks volumes about Murray:

> Robert L. (Bob) Murray, dean of athletic coaches for schools, Legion and city from 1904 to 1950 has done more in promoting fine sportsmanship among the boys and girls of The Dalles, through athletics, than any other man in the 100 years of our history![45]

Joe's loyalty to The Dalles might be construed as another linkage to Bob Murray. Joe saw Coach Murray during his summers in The Dalles, with opportunities for the mentor and protégé to discuss things of mutual interest. Of course it was coaching and Knute Rockne that they held most in common. Another topic may have been the records that each had compiled. Did Murray know that Kasberger was approaching his record? Surely, Joe knew of Bob's record and that may have motivated him to continue returning to Newark in a quest to surpass it. These questions appear profound as Joe grew older. The issue of what drove Joe in the late 1960s becomes sharper, and Murray's record may be an explanation for Joe's tenacity.

Regarding "The Dean of Athletics in The Dalles," it is important to examine Murray's truly unbelievable coaching record. The record that has been asserted does not disaggregate results by sport. Due to the relative brevity of Murray's high-school coaching career, it is not understood at all. Regardless, Cross' assertion that Murray's "record at The Dalles high will probably never be equalled" is probably valid, notwithstanding the level of competition. In a 15-year period prior to 1929, "his teams won 882 games, lost 21, and tied six. The Dalles scored 2,763 points to opponents' 651."[46]

It seems reasonable that any sports writer in The Dalles would love to hear about Joe's SBP teams, whose record was beginning to rival Coach Murray's. If Joe had tooted his own horn at home, the folks would have known that The Dalles produced not only great teams and athletes, but also coaches of whom everyone could be proud. That was not Joe's style, and maybe it was all the attention that Coach Bob received that made him determined to be obscure. The Dalles was his refuge, and the last thing Joe wanted at home was media attention. While Murray's death marked the end of an era in The Dalles, an emerging if unknown hometown legend remained a work in progress.

During the summer of 1958, the first effects of Bergen Catholic's success were felt as schools prepared to open. Some at SBP, or St. Mary's Abbey, may have trivialized Bergen Catholic's emergence as irrelevant, since not that many students came from Newark's northern suburbs. The Bergen Catholic model, however, was quickly emulated, spreading to Newark with Essex Catholic HS opening in an old Mutual Benefit Life Insurance building on Broadway. SBP's lifeblood, an almost infinite pool of qualified student athletes, was now in jeopardy. Adding insult to injury, it was not long before Union, Morris and Hudson Counties had regional Catholic high schools.

1958-59 School Year

Sam Cavallaro did not return to SBP for the 1958-59 school-year. He had secured the head-coaching position at Weehawken, NJ HS and took with him another key SBP assistant, John Allen. Sam was on the move and his next stop was at the larger Bayonne HS, where he was so successful that he was rewarded again with a New Jersey coaching plum, Bloomfield HS. Sam's predecessor, Bill Foley, had a dominant football program, respected statewide. The choice was a wise one, as Sam delivered the goods to make Joe a proud mentor. To those who knew him at SBP, it is unsurprising that Sam Cavallaro, a great man, became a very successful head coach.

Another former Kasberger player, Gene Schiller, SBP Class of 1949 and a Holy Cross College alumnus, became Joe's assistant in both football and baseball. Gene's experience in both sports at the collegiate and professional levels may have made him attractive as a prospective successor. Most ideal candidates for the position, in

Joe and new assistant coach Gene Schiller.

293

the eyes of the frugal Kasberger, were dual-sports clones who would continue his tradition. During the late 1950s, Mike Genevrino, Frank Accocella, and John Allen also assisted Joe in football. Jack Dalton, the head basketball coach, doubled as an assistant coach with Joe in baseball at the junior varsity and freshman levels. Bill Meister, another former player, coached baseball, basketball, and taught. Joe trusted them to do what he expected.

With these assistants, Joe performed groundskeeping functions at Benedict Field as a labor of love. While Joe raked the baseball diamond before games, an unknowing observer might wonder who was in charge? When it was time for pre-game infield practice, there was no doubt who was in charge! Joe liked to rake the infield, "that's all," and retirement must have been a light-year away in his mind. His healthy lifestyle made him a top candidate for becoming immortal in the minds of close observers. As an icon for SBP, surely Joe would go on forever since he did not like change. For many associated with SBP, therefore, the conventional wisdom surrounding Joe's status prevailed. "If it isn't broken, don't fix it!" Joe was getting older, but he was not broken. By all accounts, Joe never discussed retirement or succession. Yet, some things eventually were fixed at Benedict Field. The primitive facilities at the venerable field house may have been adequate for Joe, but for many players they were a hardship whose remedy was long overdue.

The 1958 football team arrived to find a new structure that brought SBP athletics into the modern age: a new Army surplus quonset hut! This structure may not have been as nice as field houses being constructed for other secondary schools in New Jersey. For a new breed of SBP athletes, however, it was a welcome improvement after nearly four decades since SBP had made such an investment for its athletes. New uniforms and equipment appeared, as well. Perhaps Joe mellowed, and responded to funds from SBP's generous Fathers' Club that wanted the best for the players. More likely, it was his younger assistant coaches who prevailed by convincing Joe that players not only expected, but needed, new uniforms and equipment. Why, Joe surely asked in disbelief. A logical response, of course, was that the old stuff had worn out! An Oregon poster that Joe brought with him to Halstead Street was prominently hung in his room with few words that say much.

> # USE IT UP
> # WEAR IT OUT
> # MAKE IT DO

While Joe's poster was not visible to players, the message was conveyed and understood.

The school year began with a fine 1958 football season's 7-1-0 record. BMI gave the Gray Bees their only loss. The Cadets still used PGs, but this was no consolation. All other foes were overwhelmed by a talented SBP squad.

There was good football news in Corvallis with a very special Beaver squad. Joe had to be very proud of the team photo, shown here, with two of his SBP players, John Thomas and George Enderle, playing prominent roles as coach and player, respectively.

OSU 1958 FOOTBALL TEAM. Front Row: Demith, James Eqpt. Mgr.; Robertson, William Asst. Coach; Swift, Derald 26; Cadwell, John 61; Anagnos, Spiro 64; Brundage, Dennis 62; Arana, Antonio 33; Horrillo, John 12; Sanchez, Sonny 68; Quinn, Jim 22; Enderle, George 65; Hall, George; Middle Row: Wenstrom, George, Mgr.; Paulson, Darnard 2; Thiel, Don 83; Doman, Jerry 80; Lukehart, Gary 27; Niko, Talisua 76; Hadraba, John 28; Rogers, Edmond 70; Dolby, Mike 66; Hadraba, Robert 50; Mason, Grimm 46; Thomas, John Asst. Coach; Back Row: Zelinka, Robert Asst. Coach; Kaohelaulii, Edward 78; Criner, Leon 40; Woodward, Earl 75; Wade, Joe 67; Parrott, Bill 82; Hogan, Howard, 72; Marsh, Amos 18; Stinnette, Jim 37; Hake, Bruce 55; Marshall, Charles 36; Farrell, Bob 23; Thomas, Aaron 89; Johnson, Roger 88.

When Joe turned sixty-three in January, he remained fit with hiking and hard work. Sunday jaunts to Springfield and Millburn were routine, and Joe's landscaping skills were tested in Montville, NJ when Claire Milbauer acquired a retirement home. Even for Joe, this was a challenge, since the site was atop a rocky hill, once a quarry. Joe came on Sundays, moved rocks around the one-acre site, then added evergreens and other vegetation to create a place of natural beauty. There was work inside and with Fred Bertoldi's help, carpentry and remodeling were done. It was like old times at Halstead Street for Joe, the workaholic, when it is realized that Sunday was his only day-off.

Possibly the biggest news story to hit SBP in nearly two decades came in mid-April.

On April 11, 1959, Rev. Philip Hoover, O.S.B., headmaster of St. Benedict's, announced jointly with Very Rev. Thomas Touhy, headmaster of Seton Hall, that the two schools would resume athletic relations. The biggest factor which led to this renewal was that St. Benedict's now adhered to strictly high school rules.[47]

An eventful school year was marked by construction activity on campus. The 1959 baseball team posted an 18-6-0 record and BMI matched their 1958 jinx by defeating the Gray Bees twice. The season's fifth game against Rutherford St. Mary's HS, a 10-4 win, was Joe's 500th career game, for an 84 percent winning record.

The author on deck as Bob Watson hits, in the game against St. Michael's of Union City, April 1959.

Coinciding with baseball was the completion of the new addition "early in May of 1959 and dedicated on May 4 by Archbishop Thomas A. Boland."[48] The Class of 1959 had the first official use for its commencement exercises.

Social change in the mid to late 1950s was real, not a figment of Joe's imagination and traditional values. Rock 'n' roll was a musical revolution and SBP students were as influenced as anyone. In August 1957, Dick Clark's American Bandstand started a daily TV diversion for the young, viewed by virtually everyone, except those playing sports or working. Also, black music was heard on one Newark radio station that featured a popular disk jockey, "Jocko," who had an eager white audience of youthful listeners. "Jocko's Rocket Ship" program, Murray the K, and Alan Freed on New York stations, drove parents and adults crazy. Peter Tripp, with the top forty hits of the week on another New York station, was mild by comparison.

Girls were the ultimate distraction as hormones raged on a busy social scene. While St. Vincent's Academy was only a few blocks from SBP, the real action was at other Catholic girls schools around Newark. Marylawn of the Oranges in South Orange, Lacordaire Academy in Upper Montclair, Mt. St. Dominic's Academy in Caldwell, and Benedictine Academy in Elizabeth, were favorites. Parties and dances made weekend studying difficult. For some players, the realization came that other activities were more relevant than sports in their lives.

Newark was great because of the retail activity that made it a bustling place to shop and watch people. Suburban shopping malls did not exist and Newark was the place where everyone shopped. Perhaps the best part of being an SBP student, if you lived in the suburbs, was the daily commute for a fascinating and stimulating change of pace. It was a mind-expanding, daily adventure to see and feel this city function. Even into the early 1960s, Newark was safe to travel by transit. Bloomfield Avenue and South Orange Avenue bus routes made getting to parties and dances feasible. Newark's suburbs, and its Forest Hill section, were focal points of weekend activity. Even after midnight it was safe downtown for the last bus or train home. Of course, in this era, most "Benedict's-guys" had highly developed "street-smarts!"

The above amenities applied before one reached the magic age of 17 – when a teenager acquired a New Jersey driver's license. Then it was off to Staten Island, Suffern, and Manhattan, New York watering holes that catered to New Jersey youth. For the very sophisticated, it was forays into Greenwich Village and the "GA" (German American) Club to rub elbows with college students and the Village Vanguard for beatniks. Jack Kerouac had touched this generation with *On the Road*. Manhattan remained an alluring place for many New Jersey high-school kids to visit. Mobility was not a problem for most SBP students.

If Joe did not understand everything he was seeing, it was not because he was blind or ignorant. The emerging lifestyles were new for everyone, as the younger generation challenged the old. Actually, this was tame stuff compared to what happened in American society ten years later. These were fundamentally good kids from good homes who were part of a changing American society – the age of affluence. It was a great time to be young, but a difficult time to be a coach, teacher or parent. This first wave of generational change in the late 1950s was only knocking on the door. Within five years the newer generation would kick the door. Within the decade, the door was knocked down and American society was never the same.

American Benedictinism faced the challenge in Newark well, with supportive and understanding monks who dealt with issues facing the young. Yet SBP had its way of doing things, and that was not changing. It was the monks' way, or the proverbial highway. It was not easy for all SBP athletes to manage time when playing for Joe. He was demanding; the teachers were demanding; and parents were demanding. It was hard, with everyone in authority so demanding of what little time there was, and sleep became a first casualty. For those who survived freshman year, most students loved SBP despite the flaws.

SBP's sports-minded students made Joe's job easy, except for times when he had to select varsity starters. He probably could have fielded two competitive varsity baseball teams. Benedict Field as a place of dreams was also a place of realization that sports were not in everyone's future. Many prospective players, therefore, opted to take advantage of the educational opportunity and forego the sports, because of demands the latter made on limited time. Joe's great players are numerous, but there is probably a host of talent who never got the chance. They could have played at other schools with lesser talent, but it just was not meant to be at SBP. Young egos, not understanding their role and accustomed to playing rather than watching, were a problem. Viewing a varsity game as a "pine brother" was not fun. Many preferred playing for the junior varsity because they were used to participating, not watching. Even the chance to be Joe's first-base coach was not much solace. Being asked to pay their dues and wait their turn for playing-time to earn a varsity letter was a message not well received by many. Soon for some, a decision was made that baseball was not worth the price. If they could not be a varsity starter, there were more interesting things than being a uniformed spectator.

For many taught by nuns in Catholic grammar schools, the monks were a dramatic departure both in style and message – no more memorizing the *Baltimore Catechism*! It amazed many students to realize how ignorant they were of Biblical teachings. Some Protestants were shocked by how little Catholic grammar school graduates knew about the Bible. Fr. Benedict Tyler was a very popular teacher in the freshman Religion class, New and Old Testament. For most students, he was a comforting and enlightening intermediary because many had never read a Bible. Fr. Benedict's patient and scholarly approach was just the right fit between the grammar school curriculum and the unique theology that awaited.

After Joe Kasberger, many students of this era might offer Fr. Ignatius Kohl as one of the most enduring personalities who was encountered. Materialism and commercialism were among the deadly secular sins that he warned against daily in the classroom. While he is not known to have had any of his thoughts published, notes from his lectures should be considered collector's items. "Iggyology" was uniquely Fr. Ignatius' view of the world. He won lasting favor with his students by emphasizing that monks were in the monastery to find God. There was little pretension that he, or all of the others had, in fact, found Him. G.K. Chesterton is recalled as one of Fr. Ignatius' favorite writers.

Fr. Ignatius was very negative about "utilitarians and utilitarianism." Also, he had a way with phrases that stuck in many minds. "You can't give what you haven't got," remains memorable, along with "the essence of a dog is doginess," and so on. A final admonition well-remembered was "Don't be a money-catcher!" Fr. Ignatius was very reassuring to many students, indeed almost revolutionary in his impact! After so many dogmatic experiences for students in parochial grammar schools, Fr. Ignatius was different and very popular. The good and self-assured diocesan priests who had found God were now replaced by monks seeking God. Of course many students had cynical young minds who often saw that those who found God best were monsignors, stereotyped as tyrants, lording it over the parish with imperial authority. Thank God for Fr. Ignatius, said many, as the realities of life became more clear. His colorful language kept many students attuned to his message.

A Benedictine presence in post-war Newark certainly made Archabbot Wimmer a prophet. As New Jersey's largest economic center, Newark's bustling commercial activity presented a legitimate problem for young minds dealing with the teachings that were heard. Before and after school, students had to transition from real world American capitalism to loftier spiritual matters predicated on denial and moderation. *The Rule of Saint Benedict* was not used as a text, *per se*. Its fundamental message of work and prayer, as well as moderation, was well understood by students. The monks led by wonderful example, and reached many students in that simple form of communication. Their dedication as teachers, while seeking God in their own unique way, was inspiring.

During this era, an influential monastic mind appeared. A redeemed Thomas Merton was now a Trappist monk at Kentucky's Abbey of Gethsemane. His classic book, *The Seven Story Mountain,* had an impact on many as one man's journey from the secular to the spiritual, but was not taught at SBP. Yet the life-story of Merton, who graduated from Columbia University, created much interest. Also germane was Merton's description of modern monastic life as a Trappist, with their stricter interpretation of *The Rule of St. Benedict.*

Finding God in a city may not have been easy for even the most determined monk. Harvard University's famous Baptist theologian, Harvey Cox, addressed this issue many years later. He suggested that contemporary monks going to the city to find God were not unlike the early monastic Desert Fathers, holy men seeking God in the wildest place of their day. St. Benedict, himself, was an urban refugee. This idea was not new to religious men and writers of romantic literature, such as Wordsworth in his classic poem, "Michael." For students at SBP, then, such themes were very poignant – but it was not easy for young students to reject the world. There was so much that a high-school-age boy had to have. Is that not why parents spent so much money to educate their sons? Only a good education could guarantee acquisitions in the future. Obviously, most students were already influenced by Madison Avenue, and serious questions emerged in young minds about the conflicting philosophies of American life and Benedictine values. The monks' message to reject, therefore, seemed strange, possibly irrelevant. The monks did plant, however, valuable seeds of wisdom in fertile minds that might one day blossom.

One of SBP's favorite coaches and teachers was Bill Meister. Joe must have been mortified (to borrow a favorite Sisters of Charity expression) when Bill bought a new car. Having a new car was probably fine, but not one that became the envy of virtually every student. Bill's 1958 Chevrolet convertible was black with a white top, clearly the students' choice for "car of the year." This gleaming beauty was parked conspicuously in the Casino parking lot, clearly visible from the classrooms across the street. It was hard to not want a 1958 Chevy convertible. Was it not possible for a student's soul to be saved even if he owned such a car? Bill was a good and reasonable man, so why not aspire to be like him – since a Chevy was much more moderate than a Corvette.

As long as secularism was done in moderation, even St. Benedict himself might concur! Yet, if we managed to minimize our other possessions, might a Corvette be acceptable? Students were warned not to be burdened by material possessions. Similar messages were learned by these same students several years later as foot soldiers in the Army and Marine Corps. Bill was young and handsome, and with those wheels must have had many girlfriends. Also, he was a great guy and possibly seen as a contemporary ideal of Benedictine education. Of course, another Benedictine ideal, Joe Kasberger, was old and he walked or rode the bus!

Bill, Class of 1948, had played for Joe and he was a solid citizen, or he would not be on the faculty or coaching staff. Given a choice between the two ideals, most students would have opted for the Bill Meister model. While Joe was very popular, he was viewed as a grandfather presence. Only Abbot Patrick commanded more respect in the halls. Bill, on the other hand, was a big brother to whom students could more easily relate. Joe was a near deity, but Bill was still young enough to be one of the guys. If you had a problem, far easier to approach Bill than Joe, in the thinking of many. There was nothing quite like riding with Bill from Benedict Field to a junior varsity game at Vailsburg Park on a beautiful spring day, with the top down. Pre-game talk was limited, with the radio on and lucky riders checking out young lovelies. The players were so energized by the ride that the opposition, usually Newark West Side HS, was annihilated. Then baseball was still fun, thanks to Jack Dalton and Bill Meister as freshman and junior-varsity coaches.

This is not to suggest that playing for the SBP varsity was not a highly desired goal. For underclassmen, it was a rare opportunity. Baseball was more business-like and serious on the varsity, with Joe wearing a game face when coaching. His visage, coupled with his voice and mannerisms, made a lasting impression. Young players soon realized that Joe played the game at a higher level, appearing to enjoy coaching with a sharp eye for details. It was his calling, and there was no room for anything less than complete concentration and dedication. It may have still been fun, but all reckless abandon and youthful exuberance appeared suppressed by the older and more mature players as a way to keep Joe off of your back.

Joe's baseball-coaching game face.

If he thought a player was inattentive or not appearing serious, there was his trademark, a loud rebuke. The coach knew what he was doing as his record indicated. Players knew that he was good, although very few knew how good, since his record was not posted. Possibly, Joe himself did not know his own record. At this time in his SBP baseball-coaching career, he was still getting the job done – even without PGs.

Joe's 1959 summer in Oregon was probably routine with the usual itinerary of visits. However, he may have thought about the big game with SHP that awaited him in the fall. Possibly in Corvallis, Joe began to prepare a game plan for the long-awaited SHP rematch with a former player, John Thomas, from whom an interesting perspective on Joe emerges.

When last mentioned, John Thomas turned to pro-baseball when pro-football contracts did not interest him. First, John served during the Korean Conflict, where he played military ball. After his Air Force stint, John signed a contract with Joe's old friend, Joe Gordon, then with the Detroit Tigers. John's professional baseball career ended in Buffalo, on a Detroit farm team. In 1956 he returned to Oregon State as a top assistant to head coach Tommy Prothro, and served through the 1958 season.[49]

George Enderle's career in Corvallis fulfilled the promise he showed in Newark. The three-year letterman was rewarded for his leadership with election as co-captain of the 1959 team. As OSU assistant football coach in 1958, John had a role in the development of George and several of his teammates who went on to play professionally. Certainly Joe was proudest of his SBP boys who performed so well so far from home at his alma mater.

George Enderle, 1959 OSU co-captain.

During this period, John was able to deal with his mentor, Joe, as a coaching colleague. Not many of Joe's former students or players had the opportunity to be with him in Oregon, one-on-one, for rare encounters to better understand what made him tick. While Joe had many former players and students, it is unlikely that more than a handful ever got to know him as a person. Perhaps it was in the classroom, rather than on the athletic fields, that young men got insights into Joe because there he had to talk. These occasions were not a time to hear Joe talk about himself. Rather, inferences were drawn about the man from the things he talked about: livestock, suburbs and doing the right thing. John's memory of being with Joe in Oregon pertains to the late 1950s.

Joe remained remote, even with one as familiar and distinguished as Thomas. He maintained a private side that few ever penetrated, as John recalls.

I did visit with Joe in The Dalles on two or three occasions, and he visited me in Corvallis four or five times. Those visits were always rather brief and when Joe was in Corvallis, he was also with 'Slats' or 'Spec' and other old cronies. The visits were never extended because Joe preferred to spend most of his summer time in The Dalles (gardening). He was basically a loner. I did meet his sister and his brother Max, and one older brother, but I have no specific memories of those visits because of brevity and circumstance.

What was Joe really like back home where he could be himself?

About the only thing I generally know about Joe K is that he was considered to be a 'real character' by his former friends and close associates. Part of that image I can only conclude stems from his voice, personal mannerisms, and the fact that he early on took on the 'bachelor' who never stood still long enough to become someone's partner stance.

John's concluding remarks may comfort those who struggle to understand Joe.

I don't think anyone really knew Joe. I have probably had as much contact as anyone in his home environment, and at the time most of our conversations related to sports and coaching. He was always asking for plays we used at Oregon State and ideas of mine related to conditioning or strategy. None of these visits were ever extended, or on what I would consider an intimate or personal level.[50]

John may have given Joe Oregon State plays and strategy for the SHP game.

1959-60 School Year

The school year's beginning was dominated by the upcoming SHP contest, to end months of great anticipation. Fortunately, Joe's 1959 squad was reloading rather than rebuilding, and began with a 6-1-0 record. The sole blemish was a crushing 7-14 loss to BMI in Joe's last football game between these teams. In the series that began with a 6-6 tie in 1937, BMI held a 8-5-3 advantage. Also, the Cadets had won the last five games against the Gray Bees. In Joe's SBP football-coaching career, the Cadets were the only team to hold a winning advantage in a series of six or more games. Only SHP's football team would face Joe's teams in as many games over the course of his career. A great rivalry ended as a new one was resumed without the PG factor.

The stage was set for a great game to conclude the season. Even the coach appeared unusually excited. It was a long time since the 1940 game, and he seemed rejuvenated, as he focused on this game. Surely, Joe's younger SHP counterpart, Tony Verducci, had his Pony Pirates ready. He had played at Newark Barringer HS and the University of Pittsburgh, and not unlike Sam Cavallaro, became a very successful coach. Some of these Gray Bees and Pony Pirates went on to play college football. For many, it was one of the biggest, if not the biggest, game they ever played.

Joe had a pep rally speech that was given annually during the football season. For anyone who ever attended SBP, one of the most vivid recollections is certainly that speech

Joe and Captain Vince Liddy in 1959.

and manner of delivery, complete with drawl. Joe was a man of few words, but he could bring down the house when he spoke – and the SHP Pep Rally was a great performance.

> 'Reverend Headmaster, members of the faculty, and buzzin' stingin' Bees!' A roar would go up from the crowd in approval of the man who spoke these words at the annual football pep rallies. This man was Joseph Kasberger, known to everyone as 'Joe K.'[51]

The legendary Joe was seemingly known to all at SBP, but not all knew him as a teacher or coach. Those privileged to have Joe in one of these roles "knew" him better, yet not even they knew him very well. Except for the annual pep-rally performance, Joe was hardly an open and approachable faculty member to the average student.

SBP and SHP students engaged in mutual dislike, and they were forewarned, under penalty of expulsion or something worse, to be on their best behavior. The game was played on a beautiful Sunday afternoon before 20,000 at Newark Schools Stadium. The game was typical of previous SBP-SHP clashes, dating back to the mid-1920s, with "tension and excitement" that made the rivalry special.

> With one minute left in the first half, Bees' quarterback Vince Liddy hit John Conforti with a 20 yard pass on a fourth down play, to put the Bees on the Hall's one. Liddy then capped the 78 yard scoring drive with a quarter-back-sneak which gave the Bees the only tally of the game. Seton Hall dominated play in the second half but the Hive defense stiffened and preserved the 6-0 lead for St. Benedict's.
>
> 1959's victory gives St. Benedict's a 10-4-1 series edge over the Hall. The Bees have amassed 207 points to the Pirates 81.[52]

SBP's win over a fine foe was thrilling from start to finish, and may have been the most publicized game Joe ever coached. The 1959 football team's 7-1-0 record brought Joe's career record at SBP to 171-39-13. There were no incidents, probably because fans were exhausted from the game's excitement. It was one of those rare games that lived up to the pre-game media hype. For those attending, it may rank as one of the best football games ever seen at any level of competition. Joe's career football record against SHP now stood at 7-1-1. In recognition of his 1959 football team, Joe was named Coach of the Year by the Archdiocese of Newark newspaper, the *Advocate*. The Gray Bees were selected as the *Advocate's* Team of the Year. While likely not Joe's top team, the 1959 squad is distinguished for winning one of the most important games in his career.

Newark's total population slipped to 405,220 in 1960, while the minority population increased dramatically. Puerto Ricans joined blacks in the expanding minority population, which spurred white flight to the suburbs. The pace of social change accelerated and Joe was not getting younger. Within the monastery, there was unrest – with some advocating relocation. Newark became dangerous, and a safer, suburban location became paramount to some before the inevitable or unthinkable transpired. No city, abbey, or school ever had a more tumultuous decade than the one they would now experience.

While the decade began positively, the situation soon deteriorated, and Newark was on a collision course with destiny. All over Newark in the late 1950s and early 1960s there was prosperity. High-rise buildings and parking garages were planned or under construction. Could so many be so wrong, considering what transpired within the decade? How much of this Joe noticed is unknown, since he was reluctant to speak about negative situations. Even those who knew him best were not privy to his thoughts as the scene was set.

Fr. Philip Hoover concluded his tenure as headmaster and was succeeded by Fr. Mark Confroy amid increasing internal and external instability. Fr. Philip experienced ill health and went to Delbarton for a well-deserved rest. SBP's new addition was thought to insure competitiveness, but the emergence of new regional Catholic high schools made it difficult. By increasing capacity from 600 to 700 students, the competition for students became more intense as recruitment, rather than selection, was a new reality.

Rev. Mark Confroy, Joe's fifth head-master, joined the faculty in 1943.

Any school's operating budget is very fragile, and the risk of increasing capacity can be a double-edged sword. Surely, the new addition was a sign of SBP's faith in Newark's future, and a reaffirmation of the school's mission. This was an important time, because Newark changed as Joe prophesied, with the balance of power among the big three Catholic prep schools under siege by the new upstarts. The big three were dominant for so long: SHP in South Orange, the oldest; St. Peter's Prep in Jersey City; and SBP.

The 1960 baseball team, however, was not distracted and became the state prep champion with a 21-5-0 record. This superior record provided a semblance of the good old days. Despite the record and state championship, however, the 1960 baseball team had a dubious distinction. Maybe Joe forgot the 1925 baseball season at MAC as ancient history. Whether or not Joe recalled is not germane. The record shows that he last lost three-straight baseball games at MAC in 1925.

Joe turned 64 in January. Was he thinking retirement? How long would he continue? Joe was aging well, but the inevitable questions arose. Did SBP have a retirement policy? Or, did Joe have a personal retirement time in mind? In a climate of changes, inside and outside SBP, some things remained constant when this school year saw Joe post a combined 27-6-0 record in football and baseball, a level of performance which silenced any critics. Yet, there were concerns that Joe's next birthday was an opportune time to call it a career. On the other hand, Joe remained remarkably durable with excellent health. Why retire a legend who still knows how to win? When working without a contract, as Joe had done for his entire SBP career, the issue was nonexistent.

Also, this was a time for Joe and many of the oldtimers on the faculty to enjoy the new facilities after so many years of making do in the old school. Hot lunches in the cafeteria were enjoyed, not only by the students, but also by the lay teachers. In addition, the new building allowed for the expansion of the library into the old cafeteria, which quickly became a popular gathering spot. Fr. Benet Caffrey did an exceptional job of making the library accessible.

> The basement of the 1910 building, which had been the cafeteria and auditorium, was renovated as a new Prep library, and the books were moved down from the old library on the first floor. The Matthew Hoehn Memorial Library was dedicated on June 9, 1960.[53]

Over the summer, SBP's Class of 1961 gave little thought to changes that the new headmaster would inaugurate in September. Fr. Mark was the guidance counselor in Fr. Philip's administration, an often thankless role, as the bearer of bad news during the college selection and recommendation process. Not all SBP students were Ivy League material, no matter what their mothers said!

Every year brought one or two new monks and lay teachers to the faculty, but the cast of veteran teachers remained. There were at SBP monks, possibly toughened from military service, who presented an image that often masked a kindlier person. Fr. Dunstan Smith, "The Duke," was a popular dean of discipline; Fathers Boniface Treanor and Francis O'Connell were his replacements. Both were likable big men who few dared to challenge. There were other monks surrounding Joe who made his coaching easier. The Dean of Studies, Fr. Nicholas Collins, was diminutive, but feared when academic progress reports and report cards were due. He was a no-nonsense Latin teacher as well. What Fr. Nicholas lacked in size, he made up for as SBP's enforcer of academic standards.

Fr. Norbert McLaughlin will forever be remembered as the sophomore geometry teacher who never exhaled cigarette smoke in class. What a distraction it was to wonder where the smoke had gone! Fr. Norbert was a slight man whose physique bore little resemblance to his namesake at Mt. Angel. Every time Joe saw Fr. Norbert, he must have been reminded of his former teammate and assistant football coach.

Fr. Anselm Murray in algebra, Fr. Basil Zusi in biology, Fr. Jerome Fitzpatrick in history, were all exceptional teachers. Fr. Gabriel Coless was a young monk who wore a beret. Naturally, he was a French teacher and popular because he gave the impression of being a Frenchman. The zaniest of all teachers was Fr. Justin Casyni, a freshman art teacher, who had paddling sticks for each student. When a swat was needed, the student assumed the position for punishment, as Fr. Justin sang "The Rain in Spain," while paddling.

For many students, however, Fr. John Browne provided the highlight of their SBP careers with his freshman music class. He had a short fuse, and was accurate when throwing keys at misbehaving students. His class trip to the old

Metropolitan Opera House in New York City to see Bizet's "Carmen" was a special, but risky, endeavor on his part. The risk came from Fr. John's belief that all students, taking unsupervised public transit, would arrive at the matinee performance as instructed. Many students will remain grateful to Fr. John for the opera experience. His love of music manifested itself in versatility. One of the great religious experiences for SBP students was Fr. John playing the organ at St. Mary's Church at the school year's opening service. With monks chanting and Fr. John playing, it was beautiful to experience and recall. As band director, Fr. John caused his charges to pump up the crowd with SBP's fight song, "Boola Boola."

The opportunity to have future abbots as teachers was something that is appreciated in retrospect. Fr. Ambrose Clark in sophomore English, and Fr. Martin Burne in senior English, made great impressions on students as learned and gifted men. For some lucky students, four years of English included not only Fathers Ambrose and Martin, but also Joe. Yet, of the four English teachers that some classes would have, Fr. Joe Barkus may have made the greatest impression. He was a large man, literally and figuratively, who taught Shakespeare to juniors with the biggest book imaginable. Fr. Joe liked to pound the book on the heads of students who were inattentive or unprepared.

Fr. Ambrose had a passion for the word "yes." Many students used the Newark vernacular "yeah," and Fr. Ambrose immediately would stop the class, while his face grew red. Then with great theatrics, he counted increasingly louder "one, two, three, YES!" It did not take long for Fr. Ambrose to change student speech patterns. Fr. Martin as a senior English teacher was memorable for a requirement to pass his course and graduate. All would memorize Lincoln's "Gettysburg Address." Then, at some time during the school year, the student stood before the class to deliver it orally. This requirement was an unusual but valuable experience, that not only gave the student a public-speaking opportunity, but also acquainted him with a body of thought that was becoming more relevant in Newark. The centennial of the Civil War was being celebrated, but many of the issues that were fought over were not yet resolved. Fr. Martin was a demanding but fair teacher. Students sensed his Marine toughness, and his course requirement was met with little argument.

Memorization was a fact of life at SBP and it is amazing how much is retained over the years. Fr. Leo Beger coached the golf team and taught sophomore Latin. He taught, and students memorized on the first day, that *Omna Gallia est divisa in partes tres.* Also he taught that: "If South Orange was on fire, would Millburn, no Maplewood!" Fr. Leo was recalled as a neighborhood youngster at the Milbauer household where he had his hair cut.

Brother Michael Scanlon had great credibility for many students over his long tenure. Trained as a nurse, he was accurate in diagnosing physical and personal problems. Brother Denis Robertson was very popular in his administrative support role with Mr. Philip Rafter.

Joe was a teacher as much as he was a coach. For many, Joe was in the same exalted category as Abbot Patrick, except more visible. When Abbot Patrick made a rare appearance, students instinctively hugged the walls with their

backs. The frail abbot was given a wide berth to insure that he was not accidentally jostled. The more robust Kasberger was treated similarly. When Joe wanted
to speak with you, there was a conversation. Otherwise, Joe was left alone,
immune from small talk in the halls.

There were other lay teachers at SBP as well. Mr. Z, Bob Zwiatowski taught
an excellent survey course, physical sciences, for the scientifically challenged.
Leo Monaco was a law student who taught civics to seniors, emphasizing class
participation in discussing current affairs and constitutional interpretations of
contemporary issues. Civil rights in the South dominated many classes as the
struggle moved North. Senator Barry Goldwater's new book, *Conscience of a
Conservative*, inspired some spirited class discussions.

There were picketers at Penn Station and the Public Service Building to
protest conditions in Dixie. For many SBP students, people of color were not
part of their lives except as athletes and musicians. Very few students, if any,
came from towns where they attended school with minorities. While SBP had a
few, it was a predominantly white environment. Many of these first and second
generation sons of immigrants were dealing with their own problems of assimilation and acceptance. SBP was still a melting-pot that brought East European,
Italian and Irish students together and succeeded in dismantling many barriers
within four years.

It was not possible to have a class with each monk at SBP. Fathers Edmund
Nugent, Columba Rafferty, Cornelius Sweeny, Theodore Howarth, Eugene
Schwartz, Owen Hudson, and others are noted in this category. By all accounts,
their classes were as special as those taught by the monks described previously.
These men had grown, in most cases, from being Joe's former students to teaching colleagues and friends. Joe must have enjoyed being with these monks, as
did the students. Joe had monk stories of his own from MAC that may have
influenced the behavior of the Newark monks. After four years, students and
monks came to know one another. It may not have been the same close relationship with monks that Joe experienced at MAC. Yet, four short years gave many
students a lifetime of memories and anecdotes about these wonderful men.

Despite the monks' best efforts, perhaps Fr. Ignatius was correct – some students were mental midgets, savages, or barbarians, and needed to be civilized. It
was not that all in the Class of 1961 were wise guys. Rather, societal changes
were now seen in this particular class. Excessive permissiveness needed rectifi-
cation. SBP needed to become more "prep-like," even if many students already
wore blazers, button-down collars and Bass Weejuns. With the Age of Aquarius
emerging within the decade, SBP's administration had a hint of future-shock.

1960-61 School Year

The 1960 football season signaled the arrival of a new competitive order for
SBP. Joe's teams had played well after the demise of the PGs, but now there
were other competitors entering the arena, who siphoned off players for their
new programs who might in the past have gone to SBP or SHP. The deep pool of

SBP 1960 FB TEAM. Front Row: Richard Kochansky, Frederick Scotti, Jerome Froelich, Robert Vinegra, Raymond Pizza, Brian Conlan, Thomas Kray; Second Row: Marshall D'Aloia, John Conforti, Frank Cosentino, William Blauvelt, William Jamieson, Joseph Kasberger (head coach); Third Row: Daniel Finn, Joseph Mirabella, Nicholas Colangelo, George Coker, Douglas Hunt, Thomas Neville, Joseph Hayden; Fourth Row: Michael Coker, Alfred Cito, John Burlick, Leonard DeMarco, Kevin Moriarty, Frank Becht; Back Row: Henry DuBois, Richard Lorenzo, Paul Ahr, David Ahr, Edward Reinoso.

talented players from which Joe drew was now drying up. With his tough scheduling, it was difficult to get underclassmen valuable playing time and experience. This problem was described by an anonymous writer in the 1960 *Game Program* for the SBP versus SHP game.

> Inexperience and injuries, the plague of football coaches from the days of the flying wedge to the present, tell the story of St. Benedict's season.
>
> And the injury jinx visited the Gray Bees with almost tragic consequences when three stars were seriously hurt in an automobile accident.
>
> In September only five lettermen greeted Coach Kasberger, faced with a major rebuilding job after the highly successful '59 campaign of seven wins and only one loss.
>
> The beginning, however, was on a note of optimism. St. Benedict's romped to a 32-0 win over West Side High. The passes of Frank Cosentino and the running of Halfback John Conforti provided the punch.
>
> New York Military Academy brought its entire cadet corps to Benedict Field but their efforts fell short with the Bees snowing them under 26-0. Again Cosentino moved the Bees through the air for three touchdowns.
>
> A Hudson County rivalry was renewed on Oct. 16 with the Bees meeting St. Michael's of Union City on the latter's home field. It marked the end of the win streak, 20-14, but more important the loss of Conforti whose collarbone was broken in the clash.
>
> In a wild, furiously fought game, St. Benedict's turned back a strong Peddie Prep club, 40-21 with Bill Jamieson racing a Peddie kickoff 80 yards to pay dirt.
>
> That night in a head-on collision, the still disabled Conforti, Guard Ray Pizza and Halfback Marshall D'Aloia were seriously injured, casting a pall over the entire student body.
>
> The traditional homecoming game was against powerful East Side High, and it was 23-6 for the Ironbound eleven, the Bees second loss.

The Bees with Coach Kasberger rebuilding his starting cast, crushed Central High 34-12.[54]

The Pony Pirates had similar problems when the season began for them.

> A green, inexperienced Seton Hall club, made up mostly of sophomores, took the field in September to start the Hall's 1960 grid campaign. It was hardly a happy beginning with Bloomfield High's strong eleven grinding out a 21-0 victory.
> But six weeks later, this same team under the coaching of Tony Verducci had matured. The early mistakes were gone; it was a hard-running, blocking and tackling unit.[55]

Compared to the 1959 game's air of excitement and anticipation, the 1960 clash between SBP and SHP did not have the same flavor. Regardless, SHP prevailed over the Gray Bees, 22-12, in the season's finale.

The *Game Program* has an essay about Joe's career and former players. The text is headlined "Joe Kasberger Identified with St. Benedict's Over Thirty Years;" and the story, by an anonymous writer, follows:

> Dean of New Jersey football coaches, a holler 'guy' from the rock 'em sock 'em football clinics of a famous Knute Rockne, Joseph Michael Kasberger has been identified with the football fortunes of Saint Benedict's Prep for over thirty years. If it's synonymous to have a name identified with an institution or noble cause, Kasberger must rate with the greatest.
> Coming to St. Benedict's via Oregon State, Notre Dame and Columbia University, Kasberger traveled across the Hudson River in 1930 to begin his present reign as head football coach. Today's game between Seton Hall and Saint Benedict's marks the 240th football contest that Kasberger has coached for the Gray Bees over a thirty-one year span. His football teams have amassed an amazing record of 185 wins, 41 losses, and 12 ties [This does not agree with the Appendix].

Seton Hall - St. Benedict's **Game Program** *photo of Joe.*

> Kasberger, whose 'Joseph Michael,' was soon to become Joe to thousands of players, coaches and friends is exceptional in many ways. He can be spotted on the Benedict bench dressed in a maroon or gray jacket, gray baseball pants and maroon socks exhorting his charges on the field of play. When not immediately spotted, his voice can be heard in the far recesses of the stadium above the noise and cheers of the fans as he bellows orders to his players with the ferocity but not profanity of a master sergeant to his platoon. No one in the coaching profession is more of a drill master in football fundamentals and conditioning than Joe. No one owns a more thorough knowledge of the game's mechanics than this

master of the gridiron sport.

Aside from an outstanding won and lost record, Joe has dozens of protégés in the coaching profession on both college and high school gridirons, the most recent being John Bateman, head football coach at Rutgers. Others include Pete Carlesimo, Scranton University; 'Whitey' Dovell, Maryland; Matt Bolger, Rutgers; John Thomas, Oregon State. High school coaches schooled in the Kasberger tradition are: 'Buzz' McGlynn, Kearny High; Sam Cavallaro, Bayonne High; Mickey Conlan, Harrison; George Conti, Metuchen High; Al Colagreco, Cliffside Park; Russ Monica, Our Lady of the Valley; Frank Farrell, Point Pleasant High; Tony Troisi, Sommerville [sic] Regional, and Joe Hellberg, Lebanon High School, Oregon.

National Football League players tutored by Joe include Ben Scotti, presently defensive halfback on the Washington Redskins; Larry Cabrelli, former captain and All Pro End of the Philadelphia Eagles; Dick Weisgerber of the Green Bay Packers, and Walter Szot, formerly of the Chicago Cardinals.

Besides a thorough knowledge of the game, Joe's chief ability lies in being able to inspire and stimulate those under his charge. He takes a sincere and active interest in his players, both as players and individuals, on and off the gridiron.[56]

Under the circumstances, Joe could be satisfied that a team with a thin roster played so well. Also pleasing must have been crowd behavior at the SHP game. The Pony Pirates were a worthy and natural rival, so mutual respect was essential for the series to continue. Moreover, the gate-receipts were substantial in supporting SBP's athletics.

Joe's 65th birthday passed uneventfully, without fanfare or birthday celebrations, at SBP. It was a low-key milestone, probably at his request. Fr. Mark probably prevailed upon Joe, however, to help him make SBP more "prep-like." Perhaps there was something wrong that needed to be fixed. Joe was a great mechanic and his athletes tended to be student-body leaders. In retrospect, they were usually all well groomed and hardly needed

Joe's former players and 1960 Gray Bee football coaches, John Allen and Mike Genevrino.

to be reminded of Joe's expectations on and off the field. What precipitated the following document is not clear, but it is dated Feb. 24, 1961 – written by Joe and addressed to "Members of St. Benedict's Athletic Teams."

Always consider it an honor to represent St. Benedict's Preparatory School. Therefore, you must not only try to present a creditable performance in your particular sport or sports, but you must also represent the school by your neat appearance, refined manners, clean sportsmanship, fair play, and above all, be a GENTLEMAN at all times.

All members of athletic teams representing St. Benedict's Preparatory School on trips are expected to present a neat and clean appearance, must be well-dressed (suit coat and slacks or matching trouser [sic], NO "T" shirts, sweaters, corduroys, denims – shoes neatly shined and a tie worn.

Take pride in your personal appearance. We should try to see ourselves as others see us.[57]

With Joe's reminder of SBP's grooming standards presumably ringing in their ears, the 1961 baseball team produced an 18-3-0 record. The highlight was a 2-0 win over BMI that may have compensated for the season's last loss in the GNT's third round,1-4, to South River HS.

This baseball team speaks volumes about the changes Joe faced as a coach and athletic director. Senioritis and attrition were always problems, but probably never to the extent seen in 1961. Graduation losses from the 1960 team were severe: John Brogan, Joe Locascio, Vince Liddy, Rich Boczon, Bob Watson, and Tom Quinn were stellar performers for Joe and they would be hard to replace as position players. Gil Hewson, Tony Candelmo, and Frank O'Brien returned as pitchers, but the only other lettermen were Bill Jamieson and Rich Kochansky at second base and right field, respectively.

During the pre-season, Hewson was deemed ineligible, so Joe had to find another pitcher. Hard-throwing senior, Gerry Clarke, looked promising but he was inexperienced.

Joe, "The Twirler," pitches batting practice. "Note the old form."

Joe may have done his best baseball coaching job, ever, by molding together a team that attained a career first for him at SBP, five consecutive shutout wins early in the season. Moreover, the Gray Bees had nine shutouts in the first fifteen games of the season, a feat unmatched in Joe's SBP career. The previous best was eight shutouts in a season. The season's success was based on senior pitchers, because it was one of the most anemic-hitting teams that Joe ever fielded. If there had been more offense and pitching depth, Joe might have won his first GNT.

Significant to this team was the performance of non-seniors. Other than Kochansky, all other position players were non-seniors. Since the end of the PG era, Joe had used juniors and an occasional sophomore. Probably a fine freshman third-baseman, Ralph Lilore, was the first, ever, to start for Joe's varsity. The fact that this senior pitching staff was caught by a sophomore, Pete Rhatican, is another sign of the times. Since the Class of 1961's sophomore year, there had not been a "transfer-in" of a talented athlete, in this case, Bob Watson, who starred in both football and baseball at Metuchen HS. This deviation from the norm allowed Joe to build the groundwork for his last famous team that may have given him what he coveted most at this stage of his career.

Saying goodbye to the graduating class of 1961 must have made Joe feel his 65-plus years. There was the realization that Fred Scotti ended the Scotti Brothers era, which had begun with Ben on that first Gray Bee team without PGs in 1952. Ben was now playing professionally for the Washington Redskins. Tony had graduated from the University of Maryland after a fine football career, but looked to a future in other kinds of entertainment, singing and acting. The

Scottis were not the only brother act that Joe would coach over his long SBP career, as evidenced by the names of his players in the Appendix. While not all common last names have been confirmed as siblings, there were at least two other families who produced three brothers as players for Joe at this point: the O'Connors, with Paul, Gerry and Brian; and the Cokers, with Jim, George and Mike. It is believed that others followed in subsequent years but their names have yet to be established.

The school year ended with a combined 23-6-0 record for Joe's football and baseball teams. If athletics were being de-emphasized, it was not yet readily apparent as he journeyed home for the 30th time in his long career.

Tony Scotti, end, University of Maryland Terrapins.

1961-62 School Year

A new school year always brought challenges, and reminders to Joe of his years. Graduation losses included Jerry Froelich, who was compensated for by the appearance of younger brother, Brian; both were sons of Dr. Jerome Froelich, Sr. from the 1936 football team. Gene Schiller mentioned in an interview with Richard Lorenzo that SBP had a "father-son" quality among students and players. The 1961 squad had another in Bill Leonard, younger brother of Tom who was a stellar performer for Joe in the late 1950s. Tom appears to have the distinction of being the first son of a former player to perform for Joe. His father, Richard, played on Joe's first SBP team in 1930. These blood relationships that Joe now experienced may help explain his success as a coach, even in his later years. Joe had a special rapport that developed into bonding over the years and transcended whatever generation gaps there were between coach and players. Kids believed that Joe was a winner and would lead them to victory despite the odds. The 1961 season gave proof to this quality.

The 1961 football team had a disappointing 3-4-0 record to begin the school year. In a recent interview, assistant coach Gene Schiller and former player, Richard Lorenzo, reminisced about a rather remarkable season despite the less than spectacular record. Not appearing in the official record for this season was a one touchdown loss to the Rutgers Frosh team in a game-like scrimmage in New Brunswick that gave the players confidence in their ability to compete. Unfortunately an already thin roster was depleted by injuries as it prepared for an over-whelmingly favored SHP team to conclude the season. It is recalled that only two-dozen Gray Bees dressed for the game and the situation was so grim that it may have been the only time Joe ever entered a game with little or no hope of winning. At halftime the Gray Bees trailed 20-0 and the game appeared out of reach. Despite Joe's dislike for change, he heeded younger advice and went to a spread offense in the second half – that SHP could not contain. The Gray Bee defense was unyielding and the offense generated 21 miraculous points for a huge upset win.[58]

Joe was never one to socialize with adults, much less players. The emotions of this win, however, led to his attendance at a victory party that night. No one can recall Joe ever doing this previously. Perhaps reflecting a mellowing for this team, Joe allowed the players to keep their game jerseys. For many, the SHP game was the only one that counted and Joe was safe for another year. The ability to beat SHP meant job-security, even at age 65. (In Nov. 1997 the squad celebrated this game with a reunion.[59])

Also on Joe's agenda was the Liberty Bowl in mid-December at Philadelphia's cavernous and cold Municipal Stadium. Oregon State's football team did not earn a Rose Bowl bid, but the Beavers had the 1960 Heisman Trophy winner, Terry Baker, as their quarterback. Joe had two reasons to enjoy this game. First, Spec and other old Oregon State friends traveled with the team and Joe may have been more comfortable socializing with his "old cronies." Second, the Beavers faced a Villanova University Wildcat team that featured one of Joe's former stars, Al Reinoso. The 6-0 Beaver victory gave the old alumnus and proud mentor a bittersweet afternoon.

The school year ended with a fine baseball team that compensated for football's disappointing season. The team's 20-3-0 record, one of Joe's best in recent years, began with eight-straight wins. This team reached the GNT's third round and season's end with a 1-6 loss to Nutley HS.

As Joe contemplated the next school year, his football schedule included a new kid on the block, Essex Catholic HS. He scheduled the fledgling Eagles for baseball in 1961 and 1962, but this would be their first meeting in football. The emergence of Essex Catholic reduced the local talent pool, and football squad depth was limited as prospects joined the opposition.

1962-63 School Year

To begin his second decade of coaching football without PGs, Joe appears to have finally gotten enough underclassmen valuable playing time and the results showed. In recalling this team, Schiller and Lorenzo mentioned uncertainty before the season began, when Joe was late returning to Newark from Oregon.

Current SBP headmaster Father Edwin Leahy, left, and Richard Lorenzo, at Benedict Field in November 1962.

At this phase of his career, it was apparent to many that Joe's other interests may have been greater than just being a coach of football or baseball.[60] Regardless, the 1962 football team's 6-1-1 record began the school year. Lawrenceville School inflicted the only loss on SBP, 13-43. The season's finale against SHP was a 7-7 tie.

Erecting and dismantling bleachers, spreading truckloads of dirt for a new baseball infield were physically demanding tasks that Joe enjoyed. For players expecting to practice football or baseball at Benedict Field, such labor for them was not seen as part of their job description. Also Joe's frugality was a bone of contention for many as he hoarded new bats and balls while nailing together and taping the old. Joe's idiosyncracies were not lost on youthful observers and generation gaps may have widened.[61]

An otherwise uneventful school year came to an exciting conclusion with a terrific 1963 baseball team that posted a 21-3-0 season. That team shared in two milestone games in Joe's SBP baseball career. In back to back games at mid-season, Joe won his 500th in a 14-6 win over Our Lady of the Valley HS. A 4-0 win in the next game against Lawrenceville School was Joe's 600th baseball game in his SBP career, with a winning record of 84 percent.

The season ended in a disappointing loss to Montclair HS, 3-8, in the GNT finals, Joe's first-ever appearance in the championship game. Despite the graduation loss of all-state Paul Thornton, many veterans would return. 1964 promised another excellent team that could finally win the elusive GNT championship. "Wait until next year" was Joe's thought during the summer of 1963.

As Joe aged and the road in Newark grew rougher, the summer at home became more than a welcome relief. The surviving nephews and nieces of Joe Kasberger came to know a different, older Joe than the younger version their parents had known. They understood little, if anything at all, about their "famous" uncle, seen as demanding, impatient and stern. Also, there was a perception that Joe lacked personal warmth, perhaps reflecting the demeanor that Joe wore in Newark – a visage and style to better deal with teenage students and players. Also, it may have been a necessary professional facade in a school climate of strict order and discipline. After all, Joe had spent his entire career dealing with young men. The difference between young men and smaller children may have been a difficult distinction for him to make. Joe was the Godfather for

Joe's 1962 Christmas card: Gerald Cerza, Bill Meister, Fran Murphy, Joe, Fr. Leo Beger, O.S.B., John Allen, Gene Schiller and Jack Dalton.

MERRY CHRISTMAS – HAPPY NEW YEAR

Hi! To wish you a Blessed Christmas and a New Year filled with Peace, Joy and Happiness.

Joe Kasberger

Frank Milbauer's daughter, Marie Claire, and he had a positive experience in the Milbauer household relating to children. Perhaps at home, at an advanced age, he did not deal well with youngsters.

1963-64 School Year

The 1963 football team's 5-3-0 record began a school year that was one of important personal losses for Joe. Also significant were the first signs of "separation" being discussed by the Newark Benedictines. Earlier in 1963, seventeen monks signed a petition to have the two communities seriously consider separation. Part of the petition read:

'The two communities have already begun to pull apart in the directions that their objectives and apostolates have taken. We feel that because of the special conditions in Newark regarding the Negro and Puerto Rican population, and the college and business area, this division will soon become even more pronounced. Such differences require different methods of training, different ideals, and different types of sacrifice.'

This petition was not approved, "but the seed of separation had taken root."[62] With Joe's dislike for change, the issue may have been personally painful.

In 1964 Joe turned 68, and in February his dear friend and coach, Fr. Victor Rassier, died. The obituary omits sports-related material that characterized his early career. Clearly, Fr. Victor was multifaceted, with achievements beyond the athletic beginnings at MAC that made him unique. Excerpts from the March 1964 issue of the *Angelus* in St. Benedict, OR follow, with the headline "Death takes Father Victor Rassier" and text by Mike Vanzandt:

On February 15, some fourteen hours before the *Motu Proprio* of Pope Paul VI went into effect, a long time patron of congregational singing and lay participation died – Rev. Victor Rassier, OSB.[63]

The story summarized the highlights of Fr. Victor's career, emphasizing his contributions in the field of church music, as how "most people would remember Father Victor." His influence extended beyond Mt. Angel after he was appointed by Archbishop Howard as the "archdiocesan director of chant." In this role, Fr. Victor was a key participant in the 1939 Centennial of the Church in Oregon, by directing "the now legendary boys' choir." This choir was so outstanding that the 1939-40 school year found Fr. Victor conducting "weekly chant classes in the Portland parochial schools," that led to another large production. He culminated this training by directing a "1000-voice choir" at a "Pontifical Mass for the CCD." The performance was so successful that "the Sisters assisting at the Mass asked for his help in instructing the chant." His help to the nuns made Fr. Victor highly respected. "Motherhouses and convents around the country remember Father Victor and express appreciation for his classes." Despite his apostolate in Sacred Music, Fr. Victor had other duties away from Mt. Angel and was appointed pastor of St. Mary's-by-the-Sea Parish in Rockaway, OR. For fourteen years he served as pastor before retiring to Mt. Angel in 1961, where he remained active. Besides reading and discussions in the ways of "liturgical participation," Fr. Victor "found time to coach seminarians in another of his talents – public speaking."[64]

Compounding Joe's personal woes was Audie's health, which was deteriorating because of cancer. Joe took a week off from his school duties to fly home to be with his beloved sister before her death, Apr. 7, 1964. With the situation in The Dalles so stressful, Joe's career in Newark may have become increasingly difficult for him to justify. At about this time, Bud Sandoz recalls visiting Joe at Casino Hall.

> It was at that time that the thought occurred to me that Joe had been working at St. Benedict's for more than thirty years, yet everything I saw made it look to me LIKE he was here on a temporary basis. I swear he could pack up everything he owned in an hour's time and be gone.

> One of Joe's most valuable possessions, therefore, was his steamer-trunk.

> The fact is, that is just about what he did once a year. He had a steamer-trunk. He did not need a steamer-trunk for clothing and personal effects. He could have traveled with an overnight bag. But the trunk could be included on his train ticket. I don't know what he filled it with on the way West, but it was very convenient to fill it with canned fruit and other good things on the way East, and it saved on the shipping cost to have these things in his trunk.[65]

The school year came to a happier conclusion than in 1963. As hoped, Joe's 1964 baseball team won the GNT, SBP's first, and the 6-5 victory over Montclair HS in the finals could not have been sweeter. The 1964 team produced a 25-3-0 record, the most wins in a baseball season for Joe's career. In recognition, he was named as New Jersey Baseball Coach of the Year by the *Star-Ledger*. Finally, Joe had accomplished in baseball everything that could be expected. Also significant as a milestone event in his SBP baseball coaching career was his 100th loss at midseason to none other than his nemesis, Bordentown Military Institute, a

1964 SBP Baseball team, GNT champions. *Front Row:* F. Casadonte, M. Petriella, R. Lilore (captain), A. DeRosa, R. Sabella; *Second Row:* J. Kasberger (head coach), R. Mason, T. Koleszar, R. Rudzonis, R. Petitti, J. McCanna, D. Farrell, R. Schnabel, E. Schiller (ass't. coach); *Back Row:* M. McAdams, D. Meehan, A. Marchese, R. Walsh, J. DuBois, T. Jakubowski.

game recalled for another reason!

One of the great stories from the research involves a star of the 1964 GNT champions, Michael "Sabby" Petriella, M.D. Joe had a problem with names as he aged, and "Sabby" became Petriella's nickname after Joe botched a preseason newspaper interview about this team's prospects. Rich Sabella, SBP's shortstop, was confused in Joe's mind with third baseman, Mike Petriella. When the newspaper story appeared, Joe referred to "Sabby" as his third baseman and the name stuck. Before jumping to any conclusions about Petriella's game-winning hit against Montclair, there is more to the story. Sabby had struggled for three years in obscurity on the Gray Bee bench, retrieving baseballs on the subway tracks behind the left-field fence as a freshman. This was Sabby's claim to fame as an underclassman, but Joe knew who Sabby was, even if he got his name wrong. Sabby stuck it out and was rewarded with possibly the greatest thrill of his life.

Sabby remembers vividly one of this team's few losses in 1964. Joe had developed a fixation about BMI, and he wanted to win this game very badly. Unfortunately, the game was scheduled to be played the day after the senior prom, at Bordentown. Sabby recalled team captain, Ralph Lilore, telling his teammates that Joe wanted prom-night activities curtailed for a good night of rest. As the team assembled the next morning for the one and one-half hour bus ride to Bordentown, one player was missing. Joe was furious and held the bus, hoping that the player would show. Finally the tardy player arrived in his prom tuxedo, and Joe went ballistic.

The Cadets capitalized on errors to win a game that SBP should have won. After blowing a lead, SBP lost on an infield misplay – a dropped ball that should have been handled easily. Joe and the team could not get back to Newark fast enough as assistant coach, Gene Schiller, drove the bus into a speeding citation on the New Jersey Turnpike. After being ticketed by the state trooper, Schiller and the players endured Joe muttering the strongest language ever heard from him for the duration of the trip. Perhaps this episode was the 1964 team's wake-up call for greatness.[66]

Joe was honored in 1964 by the Notre Dame Alumni of North Jersey. Andrew Purcell wrote the following lines concerning the award:

> Kasberger has received many honors. Among the most cherished came in 1964 when the Notre Dame Alumni of North Jersey cited three people for their contributions to education and teaching: one was the president of a women's college, another was a high school principal and the third was Joseph Michael Kasberger, English teacher, physical education instructor, football and baseball coach and athletic director.[67]

GNT champions' coach, Joe, ca. 1964, at Benedict Field.

Joe's undated essay that follows may have been prepared on the occasion of accepting this award. It is titled "My Philosophy of American Secondary Education."

(a) We should aim to prepare the boy to be a useful citizen and worthy of the ideals of our country.

(b) The curriculum should render all possible help in the preparation of a student for his future career. The curriculum should assist the students to adjust themselves better to occupational life; it should see to it that each youth is given an opportunity to assume self-direction and self-responsibility in situations which are as similar as possible to the actual conditions which prevail in the world of today. The school should keep uppermost in mind that it is educating boys who are to assume the duties and responsibilities of a useful citizenship, and who must, in practically all cases, pursue a specific calling for the purpose of gaining a livelihood.

(c) Our methods of instruction must be flexible and must serve as guides. Problems should be used as the basis of instruction and the teacher should serve as a guide rather than a dictator. The instructor should try to have the boy leave school with the desire to be a student for the remainder of his life. Teachers should keep constantly in mind that the real value of education is not the acquisition of facts but rather the establishment of character. The life of the school, recognizing no social classes and permitting special privileges to none, should approximate as closely as possible the ideal of a democratic community.

(d) Men of irreproachable character and becoming personality, with a sympathetic understanding towards the student's problem, carefully selected and adequately trained for their position should be selected. I believe we should place more stress on competency, scholarship, and character of service rendered instead of training in the selection of the teacher. The teacher should try to be the one hundred point man in everything he does. 'As a man feels in his heart, so will he teach.'[68]

One interpretation is that Joe's ideal teacher reflects many of his own character traits.

The summer of 1964 found Joe at home, possibly with a dying brother, George. Preoccupation with George may have lessened the impact of Slats Gill and Spec Keene retiring from their Oregon State positions. Certainly these events gave Joe reason to think about his own advancing age.

1964-65 School Year

The 1964 football team had a disappointing start with three consecutive losses to very difficult foes: St. Peter's Prep of Jersey City; North Bergen HS, possibly coached by New Jersey's winningest high school football coach, Joe Coviello; and East Orange HS. What was Joe thinking when he scheduled them in succession to open a season? After two straight wins, the season ended with three straight losses, for a 2-6-0 record. Adding to the football season's disappointment, the year of losses continued when George Kasberger died in Nov. at the age of 75. The funeral required a flight home to help bury his brother.

Joe began the second semester of the school year with his 69th birthday. An omen of a bad baseball season was the opening 0-10 loss to Essex Catholic. The 1965 baseball season ended with a 16-7-0 record, possibly a natural letdown after the 1964 team's graduation of key players.

The summer of 1965 in The Dalles found Joe facing his 70th birthday. Surely thoughts of retirement were in his head. With George dead, who would take care of the Kasberger home while he was in Newark? Max and Philip had their own homes in The Dalles, so the issue must have weighed heavily on Joe. As he prepared to return to Newark, there was another war on the horizon, unlike all others he had known. In Sept. 1965, the Vietnam conflict began with United States troops committed.

Awaiting Joe in Newark was a major challenge, of his own making, with the football schedule. Despite his age, he was not backing off with competition, and a formidable trio opened the season: St. Peter's Prep, North Bergen HS and East Orange HS. The first two Hudson County foes were noted for great football teams. As former coach at Memorial HS of West New York, North Bergen coach Joe Coviello was a New Jersey legend after winning 70 out of 71 games. Coviello first gained fame when his Memorial HS team smashed Vince Lombardi's St. Cecilia HS team, 43-6. St. Peter's Prep had ended Memorial's win-streak at 39 games, before it started another streak of 31 games without a loss in the late 1950s and early 1960s.

1965-66 School Year

The 1965 football team had a 6-3-0 record and recognition for Joe began to appear in many forms. The 1966 SBP *Alumni Directory* was dedicated to him, a self-evident honor to many alumni. Joe had "a strong influence on more Benedict's men than any other faculty member over the years," and Andrew Purcell wrote a story on his life with the following excerpt:

> For 35 years Joe Kasberger has been showing athletes from 520 High Street the 'right way' to do things. In the process, he has left a deep mark on literally thousands of varsity football and baseball players who came under his care. Additional thousands who knew him either [as] a teacher – or simply the man on the sidelines who wore baseball pants whatever the season – have been similarly marked.[69]

In addition to honors for Joe, there were other key events in 1966. An omen of bad things to come was news from Oregon that Slats Gill had died on April 5. At St. Mary's Abbey, there was tension on the issue of unity, and a formal request for separation into Newark and Morristown components was made to the Holy See, "but was deemed 'inopportune.'" Despite stress at the abbey, Newark was preparing for a big celebration. On May 18, 1966, Newark celebrated its 300th birthday. According to John Cunningham's book, *Newark*, the signs of problems were there, but they were ignored or not understood at the time. Cunningham describes the situation as follows:

> A thriving seaport, a booming airport, a brisk financial leadership, diversified industry, a bold new concept in urban higher education, housing planned for all economic levels, a modernized government: all of these were actualities as Newark prepared in 1966 to observe its 300th anniversary.
>
> Nevertheless, uneasiness underlay the optimism. Newark was failing to recognize the major challenge facing all Northern cities – the influx of rural Southern blacks into heavily populated areas of the North. Compounding the problem was the unmistakable fact that rapidly growing suburban populations were almost completely segregated, sometimes subtly *de facto* but more often blatantly racist.
>
> Blacks surged into Newark and other cities as the 1960s wore on. They had to occupy the worst housing, endure the gouging of slum landlords, take the most menial jobs, face the prospect of being last hired and first fired in an automated society that was eliminating the kind of jobs that always had been economic steppingstones for the downtrodden.
>
> The 1960 Census revealed that the city's 1950 population of 483,776 had dipped to 405,000. White totals were off nearly 100,000 down from 363,487 to 265,000. Concurrently, the non-white population had risen from 74,965 to 138,000 (including about 9,000 Puerto Ricans), about thirty-five per cent of the total. By 1966, the proportion of black residents was at least fifty per cent.
>
> School figures in 1960 showed that the public school enrollment was about two-thirds black. City high schools were sixty per cent non-white. Many elementary schools were all black or nearly so.

The evidences of injustice and evil were blatant enough, if anyone in the city administration dared to admit this or if the city drumbeaters – including the newspapers – had taken the trouble to investigate the worsening plight of Newark residents rather than to crow about the building boom.

Newark was a city waiting for an explosion as it reached its 300th anniversary year in 1966. Its leaders ignored the crass discrimination and deepening poverty, preferring to believe that a celebration of 300 years of existence would help insure loyalty to Newark among the poor.[70]

With these demographic and socio-economic conditions as a backdrop for the festivities, Newark celebrated with a traditional Broad Street parade under the slogan, "Pride in Newark." For those concerned with SBP baseball, the season was excruciating. The 1966 baseball team's record of 11-12-0 was Joe's first losing baseball season in his entire coaching career.

Joe headed West for the summer on what may have been a very long train ride for a 70-year-old man. Joe was unaccustomed to a losing baseball season, and questions may have arisen while he was in the relative peace of The Dalles. The foremost may have been: How much more am I able to take? Yet Joe returned to Newark in September!

1966-67 School Year

The school year began with a losing football season. Bergen Catholic HS finally arrived on Joe's schedule, and the result was a 12-19 loss to the Crusaders. Also, East Orange HS manhandled the Gray Bees, 0-45, not a pretty sight for SBP's fans. At mid-season, SBP defeated Newark Central HS 40-20, for Joe's 200th career win, and a winning record of 73 percent. The season was salvaged by an emotional 7-7 tie in the finale against favored SHP – a game televised in the New York metropolitan area.

This fitting tribute, and his team's inspired play, came in what proved to be Joe's last football game as head coach. Very few, if any, knew at the time that this would be the case. Joe's final career football record at SBP was complete, at 201-64-15, after the 3-5-1 performance by the 1966 team. His career winning record of 72 percent was in decline over the last decade.

The fall of 1966 produced addi-

Joe and his last SBP football coaching staff in 1966. Kneeling: A. Schiller, J. Kasberger, J. Visotski; Standing: E. Schiller, W. Conn, A. Reinoso.

tional significant events in Joe's life, as the stressful school year unfolded. The most significant, perhaps, occurred in early Nov. when Abbot Patrick, now 81 years old and Abbot "for more than 29 years, petitioned Rome for a Coadjutor Abbot."[71] The request was honored, and on Nov. 28 Fr. Martin Burne, Class of 1932, was elected. The new abbot was a World War II Marine Corps veteran of the South Pacific campaigns, where he had served as chaplain. "After the War he resumed his duties at Saint Benedict's, which included a deep involvement in the music programs."[72]

In early 1967, the fourth abbot of St. Mary's Abbey and president of SBP, Patrick M. O'Brien, died. A distinguishing feature of his tenure was

Post-game awards after 1966 SBP-SHP football game, Joe's last as head coach: "Flanked by Joe Kasberger and Vic Obeck, Jim Hamley receives most valuable lineman trophy after game with the Hall."

Joe's last SBP football team in 1966. Front Row: R. Mooney, J. Fonseca, J. Close, D. Cheney (Co-Captain), S. Boyd (Co-Captain), J. Wiatr, E. Perrotta, D. Desideria; Second Row: J. Kasberger (Coach), F. Crawley, R. Pami, E. Helies, M. Semler, J. Hamley, M. Schirmer, A. Lowas, R. Marasco, E. Schiller (Ass't Coach); Third Row: A. Reinoso (Ass't Coach), C. McLaughlin, R. Soriano, E. Brady, P. Flanagan, R. Tallucci, D. Mamatz, J. Serelka, J. Ryan, T. Martens; Fourth Row: R. McDonnell (Manager), T. Matthews, R. Tankoos, J. Flynn, E. Sabella, V. Peloso, G. Gaul, H. McCaffrey, J. Dischute, B. D'Amore; Back Row: J. Stanley, J. Cascarelle, R. Decker, G. Tobin, J. Connolly, S. Tafaro, J. Vespole, J. Rhatican, B. Holly.

resilience. "For most of his abbacy poor health required Abbot Patrick to be absent for long periods of time." During his absences, the Priors of St. Mary's Abbey were very important. The contributions in Newark and Morristown were recorded for these "stalwart men," acclaimed because they "kept the community on a steady keel over the years." While the Priors who served in Morristown are not listed from this source, the Newark Priors were: "Fathers Anselm Kienle, Boniface Reger, Charles Carroll, Matthew Hoehn, Martin Burne, George Sherry, and Maurus McBarron."[73] Abbot Martin took command after Abbot Patrick's death and made important decisions. With his military background, he was well prepared for this trying episode in the abbey's history. Abbot Martin was decisive at a time when this quality was sorely needed.

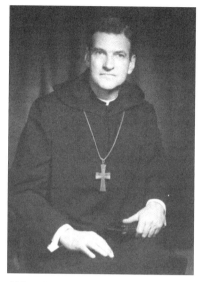

Abbot Martin Burne, elected November 28, 1966.

He knew the issues from his roles as student, teacher, prior and coadjutor.

The 1967 baseball season results are vexing, since not all game scores are given – only shown as "W" for wins and "L" for losses. A midseason win over Admiral Farragut Academy was Joe's 700th career game, with a winning record of 82 percent. It was an erratic season, but a big improvement over the 1966 disaster. The 16-7 season concluded with a 4-3 win over SHP.

Baseball and football results were dwarfed by two epic events. First, in June 1967 Joe "stepped-down" as athletic director and football coach. Second, there were other changes made by Abbot Martin. A June 11, 1967 Newark *Sunday News* story by Hugh Delano, is headlined, "Kasberger Dropping Two of Three Jobs." Story excerpts follow:

> Joe Kasberger is stepping down as football coach and athletic director at St. Benedict's Prep.
> He will continue to coach baseball at the High St. school.
> The announcement of Kasberger's partial retirement . . .was made yesterday by the Rt. Rev. Martin J. Burne, Abbot of St. Mary's, Morristown, and president of St. Benedict's.[74]

In a June 11, 1967 Newark *Star Ledger* story by Lloyde S. Glicken, there are two headlines for a story that appears on two pages. The headline for the continuation of the story stated that "Kasberger quits Benedict's posts." Excerpts from

Joe, ca. 1967.

the story follow:

> Joe Kasberger . . . is retiring as football coach and athletic director at St. Benedict's Prep.
>
> . . . Kasberger has decided to relinquish some of his responsibilities – the post of athletic director and coaching football. But he'll still coach baseball. Kasberger explains why, when someone asked when he would retire completely:
>
> 'Heck, never if I can help it. I'm a bachelor, one of those guys who never made the same mistake once. Gosh darn it, I guess I like being a coach.'[75]

Joe's successor as athletic director was Fr. Theodore Howarth, Class of 1941. The new head-football coach was Joe's assistant since 1958, Eugene Schiller, Class of 1950.

Joe was offered the groundskeeping position at Delbarton and was offended, possibly making him even more determined to remain in Newark. Joe's annoyance probably had more to do with any thought that he might leave SBP for greener pastures.[76] Yet this gesture to provide Joe an alternative to Newark appears to have been a kind one. The context of Joe's age, and his revered status among the Benedictines of St. Mary's Abbey, should not be lost in the emotions surrounding this unfortunate episode.

New SBP athletic director, Rev. Theodore Howarth, and head football coach, Gene Schiller, in Shanley Gym.

In June 1967, Abbot Martin also made a number of other changes in personnel.

He appointed Father Laurence Grassman to succeed Father Mark as Headmaster. Father Mark assumed the pastorate of Notre Dame parish in Cedar Knolls. Father Stephen was relieved of his duties as Headmaster of Delbarton School and his place was taken by Father Francis O'Connell. Father Jerome Fitzpatrick became Prior in Newark, replacing Father Maurus McBarron, who was named Pastor of Saint Mary's Parish.[77]

Joe's new status at SBP was not discussed by him with those thought to be close to him, and in whom he might confide. Neither Claire Milbauer nor Bud Sandoz knew anything about it. Nor can either recall Joe's brothers or sister mentioning this episode.

> This may surprise you, but I am confident that Joe did not tell anyone of his family on the West Coast that he had resigned as Athletic Director or as head football coach. He had a private side to him. He did not talk about unpleasant things with respect to himself, and he didn't seem to like to hear about them with respect to other people.[78]

There are no accounts of how Joe reacted to what took place in Newark while he was in Oregon in the summer of 1967. The summer was dangerous in many American cities, as domestic strife over the Vietnam conflict and civil rights was pervasive. Conditions in Newark worsened and a scene was set for the inevitable.

John Cunningham's *Newark* recapped the results of events that began on Wednesday, July 12, in the Central Ward adjacent to SBP, and continued, until the National Guard left on Monday, July 17.

> By Tuesday, most businesses reopened. The 'Newark Disorders' were over. More precisely, the bloodshed and violence were finished. City leaders, black and white, had to sort out and assess the six awesome days and nights of killing, lootings, arson and terror.
>
> There were cold, telling statistics: twenty-six dead, more than 1,500 wounded, at least 1,600 arrested and property damage of $10,251,000. More than one thousand stores and businesses were ruined, including 167 food stores. Newark and New Jersey had been stunned by the ferocity of the conflict and by the evident mishandling by law enforcement agencies.[79]

After the riots, Newark was never the same again. To many, Newark was no longer an asset to SBP – which was in serious trouble. The Newark Benedictines described their dilemma as follows:

> The Summer of 1967 was the Summer of the Newark Riots, from which the city is still recovering 25 years later. The Riots and their 'White Flight' aftermath left Newark a city that bore little resemblance to its former self. The Benedictines were forced to take a long, hard look at the meaning of their presence in the city. Saint Benedict's had always educated the sons of Catholics of European origin, who came from Newark and its environs. Though the riots left no doubt that there was a new situation to be faced, demographic changes had been going on for thirty years, ever since southern African-Americans had begun moving North in large numbers during the 1930's. They now constituted a substantial segment of the City's population.[80]

The Newark riots coincided with SBP's 100th anniversary that began in the 1967-68 school year. If for no other reason, Joe would return for the festivities.

1967-68 School Year

In Sept., when Joe returned to his residence at Casino Hall adjacent to the riot area, he was in personal danger. Joe, at age 71, was expected to coach the 1968 baseball team, and teach health and physical-education classes. The 1967 football team was coached by Gene Schiller, and Joe did not have any role with it during the season. In this environment, Fr. Laurence Grassman, Class of 1933 and a popular chemistry teacher, did not have an easy time as Joe's sixth headmaster.

The school year was one of continuing internal and external stress, with problems plaguing SBP and St. Mary's Abbey. Aggravating the situation was the national unrest over Vietnam and civil rights that continued. Despite civil-rights

Rev. Laurence Grassman, O.S.B., headmaster.

struggles in the streets of Newark, the Vietnam conflict could not be ignored – since many alumni were serving their country, and casualties became very personal.

The 1968 baseball season saw Joe defeating SHP at midseason, 9-4, for the last time. As the season dwindled to an end, there was a 1-8 loss to old friend and worthy foe, BMI. This was the last game in the series that began with a 16-7 SBP victory in 1938. Joe's career record in baseball against the Cadets was 24-15-0. His career record against BMI, in both football and baseball, was complete at 30-22-3. The Cadets were Joe's most frequent opponent in football and baseball at SBP. Only Pennington School's baseball team, with 41 appearances, faced Joe more during his career. Against this foe, his record was 30-11-0.

The Gray Bees rebounded to win two straight games, to set the stage for the season's finale and Joe's last game and trip as a coach. Against Blair Academy in Blairstown, NJ, the Gray Bees lost 7-3 to conclude the 1968 season with a 13-10-0 record. Joe's career baseball record at SBP was now complete at 593-137-3. Also in 1968, Coach Bob Murray's record for career wins apparently was eclipsed by Joe's. While his passing of Murray's career record may sadden some, these persons can solace themselves in the fact that Joe's winning percentage did not surpass Murray's. The Dalles people in general take satisfaction that Murray and Kasberger together had among the top-secondary-school coaching records in the country.

During Joe's last Oregon vacation there was turmoil over St. Peter's Church, replaced by a new structure away from downtown. Msgr. Stone noted a "near schism" that "developed over the abandonment and sale of the 80-year-old Gothic church which had been a landmark in downtown The Dalles."[81]

The summer of 1968 was difficult for most Americans. The Vietnam War, Democratic Convention turmoil in Chicago, problems in Europe, civil-rights struggles in the streets, and the recurring nightmares of political assassinations were ingredients for

At City Hall, Mayor Hugh Addonizio greets student representatives with Fathers Jerome, Laurence and Boniface.

The new St. Peter's Church, The Dalles, ca. 1967.

mass paranoia. While Joe spent the summer of 1968 in The Dalles digesting these epic events, an important event took place in Newark within the Benedictine community.

A straw vote ballot was taken in preparation for a chapter meeting to be held on Saturday, July 6, 1968. Fifty eight capitulars voted that Newark be given independent status. Seventeen voted that Newark be phased out and everyone move to Morristown. Only six voted for the *status quo*.[82]

A week of deliberation followed for the monks at this trying time.

On Saturday, July 13, 1968, approximately sixty monks attended a discussion meeting about the future of the community in Newark. A second discussion took place one week later, to be followed by still further discussion over the next several months. No doubt about it, and in spite of the dire forecasts of the doomsayers, the move was on for an independent monastery in Newark. Abbot Martin made such independence a major priority and gave his support to the movement.[83]

How much Joe knew about these events while in The Dalles is not known. All that Joe could do was pray for those he would be rejoining shortly. Prayers for wisdom and strength were probably offered by many to help the city rebuild. Yet there were other concerns.

One of Joe's three alma maters, Columbia University, remained a focal point of anti-war activity on the East Coast. Student rage over Vietnam did not surprise Joe, the veteran, who knew the terrible impact that war had on young men. All the wars of his lifetime had touched him, but this conflict was different from Joe's aging perspective. Vietnam became more personal to him in the summer of 1968, as more of

Joe and his right hand man, Fred Bertoldi, preparing Benedict Field for another season.

327

his students and players served. While most returned, Joe had already sustained two casualties from his 1960 football team. Joe mourned when Lieutenant Brian Conlan, United States Marine Corps platoon leader, was killed in action. Worse, perhaps, than Brian's definitive death was George Coker's prisoner-of-war status as a naval aviator. Which one of his boys would be next, since there was no light at the tunnel's end in the summer of 1968? As it developed, Ed Brady from the 1966 football team, had that misfortune when he was killed in action. The Tet Offensive earlier in the year made a bad situation worse, and tensions remained high.

In the late summer of 1968, Joe Kasberger approached his 73rd birthday as he packed his few belongings into his faithful trunk, for this was his 39th train journey of nearly 3,000 miles from The Dalles to Newark. Since first making this trip nearly four decades ago, he had become a regular passenger every June and September. Joe's commute to his job in Newark was a different kind of travel, but it made him predictable. The Dalles was home, but Newark was a special place. Despite an aversion to change, Joe remained very loyal.

When summer ended it was time to go to Newark and practice what he had preached. Joe followed the maxim he had taught his boys: "When the going gets tough, the tough get going." Since "Benedict's Hates a Quitter," there would be no quitting on Joe's part. In looking ahead to the new school year, there were challenges aplenty. For a nervous SBP family of teachers, students, parents, and alumni, Joe was an anchor of stability in a changing environment – and beyond that, a link of continuity for many in a troubled city and state. Joe knew that he had to be at St. Benedict's and he left The Dalles for Newark as he always had since 1931.

Most men of Joe's age and level of success were safely settled into retirement, living their "golden years" in relative peace. Such a condition was not for Joe, probably even in the best of times, since he always had things to do. Bud Sandoz recalled Joe as being in good health during the summer of 1968, although he was beginning to exhibit signs of aging.

> When he left here in September of 1968, I had no feeling that he was ill. But I did think he had a gray look, and that there were character lines on the face of a man who was beginning to age. I wondered how long he might carry on.[84]

Joe said what proved to be his last goodbyes, and headed east.

1968-69 School Year

At the age of 72, Joe arrived in Newark for yet another school year. Why did he return? Perhaps Joe had kept score and wanted to coach the 1969 baseball team for his 600th career-win and push his SBP career total in football and baseball to over 800 wins. No one seems to know what drove him to continue. Possibly Joe could not, or would not, differentiate between retiring and quitting. This seems especially true in the light of the grim environment he saw in the fall

Joe, giving a pep rally speech.

of 1968, with SBP's future growing bleaker.

Rebuilding Newark included dealing with new realities that faced its institutions. Also, there was a new headmaster, Joe's seventh, Fr. Ambrose Clark. Joe had fewer responsibilities, but there was another baseball season that required preparation: and teaching new students was always a challenge. Joe's life experiences and accumulated wisdom kept him a valuable member of the Newark community. It now needed leadership that, perhaps, only he could provide as a new Newark tried to emerge from the rubble. Thus, some might learn from Joe in dealing with the aftermath of fire and destruction.

Joe in 1968 appears to have had a leadership role, based on commitment, not involvement, and on leading by example. Joe still had enough left for one more good struggle. To younger men, Joe was an awe-inspiring presence as the personification of SBP, standing with the school at this dangerous time. Just having Joe there was reassuring, especially when they knew he could be safely away from the fray in The Dalles if he wished. Rather than exhort the boys and men of SBP from a safe distance, Joe put his body where his mouth was.

Many monks sought Joe's advice and wisdom as a respected elder of the Newark community. He had taught and coached many of those caught in the tidal wave of social change that was reshaping the city, school, and monastery. Also, he was an inspiration to the dwindling band of monks who remained committed to Newark. Joe probably saw the handwriting on the wall, and did what he could to insure SBP's survival in the face of frightening odds. When classes began, the riot's effect was seen in a lowered enrollment. SBP's 100th Anniversary required everyone to deal with change as part of a great tradition. If handled wisely, change *might* be beneficial for another century.

Joe, in profile, in his office, 1968.

Within St. Mary's Abbey, Abbot Martin continued with the transition from Abbot Patrick's long reign. The monks faced the choice between Newark and Morristown. Surely they were wanted at SBP, but the Delbarton School could not

*The Newark Abbey Community in 1968. First Row: **Justin Csanyi, Bernard Peters, Virgil Stallbaumer, Prior Jerome Fitzpatrick, Abbot Ambrose, Subprior Basil Zusi, Cornelius Sweeney, Maurus McBarron and Lucien Donnelly;** Second Row: **Nicholas Collins, Walter Lee, Maynard Nagengast, Philip Waters, Robert Reagan, Theodore Howarth, Boniface Treanor, Eugene Schwarz, Celestine Staab and Aquinas Fay;** Third Row: **Laurence Grassman, Sean Cunneen, Timothy Dwyer, Joseph Barkus, Casimir Finley, Regis Wallace, Matthew Wotelko, Declan Cunniff, Maurice Carlton and Melvin Valvano;** Fourth Row: **Denis Robertson, Antony Kovacs, John Browne, Jeremiah Cullinane, Michael Scanlon, Albert Holtz, Colman Clohosey, Edwin Leahy, Marius Meehan, Benedict Tyler and Bruno Ugliano.**

help but benefit from an influx of experienced Newark monks. There were no easy decisions in 1968. Perhaps Joe's greatest personal and professional role was now being dramatized as a stabilizing presence, bearing witness.

Those in St. Mary's Abbey who felt strongly about the proposed separation remained dissatisfied. A second petition, therefore, was made to the Holy See to separate St. Mary's Abbey into autonomous Newark and Morristown groups. Facilitation by Abbot Martin led to the separation request being granted in the fall of 1968. After meeting with his council, Abbot Martin began the tricky separation process of allocating the assets and personnel of the two locations – a process made stressful by Newark's worsening social conditions.

Amid this activity, the 1968 football team was coached by Gene Schiller to a record of 1-6-1. In the most stressful school year in SBP's history, the distractions were onerous to both students and faculty. Finally on Nov. 21, 1968, the Newark monastery was again an abbey – known as Newark Abbey, under the patronage of the Immaculate Conception. On Dec 14, 1968, the newly autonomous monks elected their first abbot, Joe's spiritual advisor, Fr. Ambrose Clark, Class of 1945. "Archbishop Boland conferred the abbatial blessing on February 22, 1969 at Sacred Heart Cathedral."[85] Fr. Jerome Fitzpatrick, Class of 1937, became head-

Joe's 1968 Christmas card photo.

master, the eighth of Joe's SBP career.

Joe's reaction to these monastic events remains unrevealed. Yet his 1968 Christmas card to Joe Hellberg provides an insight into his feelings about Abbot Ambrose, and world events. After asking about Joe Hellberg and his family in Lebanon, OR, Joe mentioned recent events in Newark as follows:

Abbey here separated from Delbarton Abbey or Morristown. Ambrose Clark, present Headmaster, former student, selected Abbot last Saturday. Smart, young (41), progressive young man and should do well.[86]

As it developed, this was Joe's last Christmas card, and the card's message of "Peace on Earth" on one side of the front may suggest Joe's sentiments about many issues plaguing the monastery, city, country and world. Moreover, it is inferred that Joe favored this picture of himself, so it is used on the cover of this book. Also, the message inscribed on his photo, "Think - Hustle - Win!" was his last message to his cards' recipients.

Sickness was a stranger to Joe and some thought him to be immortal, because he was tougher than all who knew him. With his healthy lifestyle, he would outlive everyone, since, if he had not died of pneumonia by now, he never would. Surely, after all those brutally cold Newark winters without an overcoat, Joe would never die. He was invincible! Several generations of students had seen with their own eyes Joe walking up and down South Orange Avenue, the 2.8 miles between the Milbauer home

Joe in his office, 1968.

and the school.

Christmas remained Joe's favorite holiday and the man who was never sick or injured finally began to fail. As Joe faced his 73rd birthday in a month, it seemed normal for a man of his age to finally weaken. Yet there was still New Year's Day, 1969 to be celebrated, and the feast of televised college bowl games, and dinner with the Milbauers. The latter gave Joe another chance to delight all with his prayer of thanksgiving before the meal. Then, it was game time, and commentary by Joe. Kewp shares useful insights into a failing Joe.

> I asked my sons, who are now in their thirties, just what they remembered about Joe. They each responded in a very similar fashion. They admired and respected him, however they could only picture Joe trying to watch football games, while they were playing around his feet, distracting him. They wanted him to play with them, but he was starting to slide then, and as my Dad lovingly said about my sons, 'Those O'Hare boys are enough to make a strong man cry!' So we limited the time they had with him. But his voice remained strong, even as his condition worsened.[87]

Claire noticed that Joe was not well while they were taking down the Christmas tree. There was no immediate concern with an infection from a thumb splinter and a bout with pneumonia. Certainly he would recover quickly, but after several weeks Joe's condition did not improve. While climbing the stairs to visit Fr. Laurence, Joe was observed to stumble by Brother Michael, who sensed

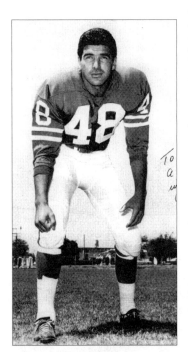

Ben Scotti, Defensive Back, San Francisco Forty Niners.

a medical problem and advised Abbot Ambrose. One of the new Abbot's first duties was to direct Joe to seek medical attention. Bud Sandoz recalled the Kasberger family being notified first of Joe's actual illness in February. In March, Joe was hospitalized for tests, and the results were not good; and he was unable to coach the baseball team, since he stayed hospitalized until the pneumonia cleared. Then, when his condition did not improve, exploratory surgery was performed at St. Mary's Hospital in Orange. SBP alumnus, Dr. George F. Hewson, Class of 1926, headed Joe's surgical team, composed of other Gray Bee alumni, and they found terminal cancer. Joe remained hospitalized to recuperate and receive treatment until the Memorial Day weekend.[88]

In May Joe's brother Max and nephew Bud visited him at the hospital, when they realized he was terminally ill. Talks were held among physicians, Joe's family and closest friends to determine where he should recuperate when discharged from the hospital. Three options were considered: the monastery in Newark, a nursing home, and Claire's Montville home. While the monks wanted Joe to return to the monastery, the physicians overruled them and the decision was made for Joe to go to Montville. Claire and Joe had had an older brother – younger sister relationship over the course of 39 years. More important to Joe's family, Claire was a close friend to them as well.

When Joe's condition became known, great concern was expressed by his former students and players. Joe's last pro-football player, Ben Scotti, flew in from California, the most dramatic response at the time because of the geography involved. With so many admirers, Joe might be a frequently visited patient. Ben recalls visiting Joe on behalf of his brothers, Tony and Fred, because of their affection and esteem for the great coach. Despite Dr. Jerome Froelich's order of "no visitors," Ben breached hospital security.

Before embarking on his professional football career, Ben played at the University of Maryland, from which he graduated in 1960. Joe's office wall prominently displayed a picture of Ben in his Redskins uniform, indicative of a close relationship between the coach and player.

Ben was fortunate to be joined at College Park by his brother, Anthony, after his SBP graduation. Collegiately, Ben "captured the spotlight in 1958 as UPI All American and First team All ACC," for the Terrapins. Professionally, Ben was selected "in 1960 as Washington Redskin of the Year."[89] The highlights of Ben's pro career were summarized on a trading card by The Ted Williams Card Company. For those who never saw Ben play as a pro, the following description gives an insight into his style:

> At 6'1", 185 pounds, Ben Scotti was hardly intimidating walking down the street. But when he ran onto a football field it was a different story. A defensive back who made the Washington Redskins in 1959 as a free agent, Scotti developed a reputation for hammering anyone who came into his area. Referred to as the Redskin's hatchet man by opponents, Scotti was a tough and dependable tackler who led the Redskins in interceptions in 1960. Acquired by the Eagles in 1962, Scotti was called the 'Hardest Hitting defensive back I ever played against,' by 260-pound All Pro Guard Jerry Kramer of the Green Bay Packers. At an emotional team meeting following the assassination of President Kennedy in 1963, Ben was insulted by the remarks of a 260-pound teammate. A battle ensued and the teammate ended up with a broken nose, a mouthful of missing teeth, and a black eye. Scotti was suspended the next day and signed with the 49ers before the 1964 season, which was his last.[90]

Despite Ben's fearsome reputation in football, there was another side to him which was manifested upon learning of Joe's grave condition. The following account is Ben's recollection of his visit with Joe:

> John Allen, a former Benedict star quarterback and coach, called and informed me that Joe was seriously ill. The news shocked all of us here in California because to us Joe was indestructible, a perfect picture of health. All the Scotti brothers had played for Joe and since I was the oldest, I came into Newark to bring the prayers of our family to him.

Claire Milbauer's home in Montville on top of the quarry, where Joe spent his last days.

When I entered the hospital, they told me that no visitors were permitted. I then identified myself and was recognized by the hospital security staff as a former Benedict man and a well known professional athlete. The fact that I flew in from California helped to impress the hospital staff and they asked me to please keep the visit brief.

Joe was very happy to see me and he told Claire Milbauer, who was present, in his joking way, 'Nobody can stop Ben from reporting to his Coach!'

We talked about positive things: sports, the entertainment business, and the fact that nothing is going to keep him down. Before I left, I told Joe I would send him an album by my brother Tony featuring classics like 'As Time Goes By,' and some country music that he requested.

A short time later, I received a letter from Claire stating that Joe had been listening to both Tony's music and the country songs the day he passed on.[91]

Claire's initial alarm was replaced by resignation to an inevitable flow of visitors who followed Ben. There was no way to keep Joe's boys from him now. Joe was very pleased by Ben's visit and the promise of albums by his brother Tony, and Joe's favorite singer, Jim Reeves.

Claire had Joe's power of attorney, a decision agreed to by Joe and his family prior to surgery. Montville insured Joe rest, quiet and comfort in his last months. Before going there, Joe visited the Casino to retrieve his belongings, and found the room ransacked. Apparently lost was Joe's gold watch, presented to

Porch of Claire's home, Joe's hideout in 1969 for peace and quiet.

Joe's sister, Anna; her daughter, Sister Helen Sandoz; and her son, Bud Sandoz.

him by the 1964 baseball team. Also lost was Joe's scrapbook that preserved news stories about his teams. Fortunately, Joe's personal photo album was found and is now at the Newark Abbey Archives. The remoteness of Montville did not deter those intent on visiting Joe.

Claire's Montville home was a special place for Joe to spend his last months during the summer of 1969. Located at an elevation with a breathtaking view, the "rock-pile," as Joe referred to it, may have made him think about Oregon. Claire recalled the summer of 1969 as a time when Joe's family from The Dalles came to be with him. Joe's sister, Anna, and niece, Sister Helen Sandoz, visited. Abbots Martin and Ambrose were regular visitors, along with Benedictines from as far away as Mt. Angel.

The loyalty of Joe's many friends prompted special commendation from Claire for the comfort it gave Joe. Especially remembered was (then) Frater Edwin Leahy who stayed with a hospitalized Joe to insure that his needs were met. Also, he was remembered for transporting Oregon visitors from the airport to Montville. When Joe needed blood, Frater Edwin arranged for the donors. Now in Joe's last months, his labors bore visible fruit with a flow of visitors bearing witness to his greatness as a man.

Perhaps 6,000 young men had been exposed to Joe at SBP over 39 years. While not all visited, the number who did remains a vivid memory to Claire. One visitor, George Koeck, Class of 1955, recalls learning about baseball from Joe, a sport he did not play at SBP. Joe was engrossed with TV coverage of the "Amazing" New York Mets as they captivated the baseball world with their improbable season. Joe's commentary while watching televised games fascinated George, who never realized that baseball was such an intellectual exercise. Joe liked George very much, for he bestowed upon him his silver loving cup from OAC as the winner of the scholar-athlete award in 1922. When recently advised of the cup's meaning by the author, George was overwhelmed – since he did not realize its significance to Joe. The procession of visitors that Joe received in Montville was one of the most moving things Claire had ever observed. She recalled never understanding the power of male-bonding, despite all the years of Joe's residence in the Milbauer household, until this phase of his life.

Ben's sentiments were the tip of a larger emotional iceberg shared by many. The illness of indestructible Joe, a specimen of clean living, now sick and dying, was a shock to almost everyone. Joe's lifestyle should have given him many more years of life. Now it was apparent that the immortal coach was just a mortal after all. Yet Joe was accorded a measure of respect, reverence and love that was normally reserved for a blood relation.

Joe, without children of his own, came to realize that he had adopted many sons over the years. As a father-figure to many, Joe reaped the harvest of his good and hard work, knowing that he was truly loved by many he had served in Newark so faithfully and for so long. Thus, Joe was comfortable in Montville with his music, and pleasure from the many visitors. By all accounts, Joe was an exceptionally good and uncomplaining patient.

1969-70 School Year

Abbot Ambrose and some St. Benedict's students.

Another school year began at SBP without Joe, a first in nearly four decades. It was a strange sensation at venerable SBP, to have school in session without the great man walking the halls. Joe missed them as much as they missed him. Fr. Jerome, as headmaster, may have felt lonely at the helm of his troubled ship, despite Abbot Ambrose keeping everyone current on Joe's condition. There was nothing to do except to pray.

For Gene Schiller and the 1969 football squad, it was difficult preparing with this distraction ongoing. The 1968 season was not good but there were hopes for improvement in 1969. The season opener was a loss to a new school, St. Joseph's HS of Montvale. The next, against Bergen Catholic HS, did not look promising for SBP either.

For this crop of SBP students, there was a different view of Joe, described now as "a Health and First-Aid teacher who had an office in the gym and lived in that landmark of Newark, Casino Hall."[92] They were too young to fully comprehend Joe's greatness. They knew that he was someone special, but the greatest impression he made was his choice of residence and his "voice." Long before these students were born, the late Bill Dougherty gave Joe this nickname which almost everyone used.

"THE VOICE"

Bill referred to him as 'The Voice,' because Joe had a

voice that could be heard blocks away at practice and during games. It is parenthetically noted that Leo the Lip Durocher was much in the news in those days. Not that Joe baited the umpires or opposing players, but because he used his vocal chords extensively, Bill's choice of a nickname was a natural.[93]

Joe to these students was nearly as old as Casino Hall, then on the verge of being "torn down and in its place will stand a [new] Newark building." How ironic that the failing legend lived in what was known by some students as "the wrestlers' clubhouse," and was not "the only landmark to reside next to the parking lot." Over the years, Joe performed many tasks at SBP and alumni are hard-pressed to nominate another who worked as hard and long as Joe. Even as a "carpenter, painter, plumber, and electrician," Joe captured their imagination as someone unique to their lives.[94]

Joe stayed at Montville until late September, when his condition worsened and he returned to St. Mary's Hospital in Orange. There Bishop Joseph A. Costello, Class of 1933, administered the apostolic blessing. Joe's last days found him positive – and "he would always say he felt fine." Joe died on Tuesday, Oct. 1, 1969.

Rev. Jerome Fitzpatrick, O.S.B., headmaster.

Fr. Jerome had the unenviable task of announcing Joe's passing to the student body, and chose the following words to convey the sad news:

God in his wisdom has seen fit to call from our company into his kingdom truly one of the great men of St. Benedict's Prep. He was to us what the redwood is to the world of trees, he was a giant among us, and we are saddened by his passing. While he was among us he showed us, in his own way, the goodness of God and the glad tidings of his Son, Jesus Christ, by the manner in which he lived. For some thirty-nine years he labored among us and he counseled, he directed, he cared deeply for us. We are in his debt, for he was a man in every sense of the word.[95]

The sadness of Joe's death was exceeded only by the shock to many, since his illness was not known to all in the far-flung network of alumni throughout the world. Hearing of Joe's death probably brought many private tears, since not all were able to visit Joe at the end. Nor were all able to pay final respects at his funeral, and benefit from shared grief. Among the mourners was SHP football coach Tony Verducci, who brought his team to pay their respects. Joe's funeral Mass at St. Mary's Church in Newark on Saturday, Oct. 5 was heavily attended by mourners, saying a final goodbye.

A *Benedict News* story eulogized, "Joe Kasberger never quit on St. Benedict's and certainly the Hive will never forget him." This account of Joe by the last generation of students to know him concludes as follows: "Benedict's hates a quitter. St. Benedict's will never quit on the memory of Joseph Kasberger."[96]

Signs at Bergen Catholic-St. Benedict's football game, October 5, 1969.

There was another opportunity to honor Joe in the afternoon at Benedict Field when the Gray Bees faced a heavily favored Bergen Catholic HS football team. SBP's football fortunes were in decline for several years, and the upstart Crusaders were just beginning a proud tradition of their own. How ironic that these two teams, going in different directions, should meet on this sad day. The fact that the game was played at all is a tribute to the players and coaches. Joe probably would have expected nothing less. Playing under such emotional circumstances creates the potential for unusual outcomes. In this case, that is what happened, with SBP's dramatic upset-win, proving to be the most inspirational game ever played by the Gray Bees.

From news accounts, it may have been SBP's greatest football victory ever – with the assistance of their "12th Man – Joe K." The sign on the field house at Benedict Field read, "Win it for Joe," according to the *Star Ledger*. The story lead read: "And that's what an underdog St. Benedict's Prep football team did yesterday in its farewell to Joe Kasberger, the famed Gray Bee mentor, who died last week." Excerpts of the story follow:

> St. Benedict's, a one-game winner in 1968, rallied for a touchdown in the fourth period and upset Bergen Catholic of Oradell, 16-14, at Newark.
> St. Benedict fans roared through the final six minutes 'do it for Joe' after

Uncaptioned photo of 1969 SBP football team: "They won it for Joe!"

338

M. Claire Milbauer

Rev. Nicholas Collins, O.S.B.

quarterback Tim Rhatican tied the game at 14-14 with a pass to John Harrington and the same pair teamed for the 2 point conversion.[97]

Joe's remains were returned to The Dalles, accompanied by Fr. Nicholas Collins and Claire Milbauer, for burial at St. Peter's Cemetery on Monday, Oct. 7, 1969 – after a Funeral Mass at St. Peter's Church celebrated by Msgr. Michael J. McMahon. Joe's final resting place is in the Kasberger family plot, in a beautiful and tranquil location. The simplicity of Joe's gravestone says much about this unique man.

Joe was the product of many coaches, whom he shared with his players. He became a coaching mosaic of those who had coached and taught him as a player and as a young coach. Joe orchestrated all these collective voices and philosophies over the years into his own. His background was broad and experiences numerous – perhaps that is why Joe was such a complex man, despite the veneer of simplicity.

The mantra most associated with Joe – "Benedict's Hates a Quitter," was a very powerful and confusing message to young and old alike. A valuable interpretation of what Joe meant comes from Gene Schiller, who may have been the one most professionally close to Joe in his last years. Gene had the honor and burden of succeeding Joe and all that it entailed. Thus, his views are very important. At a memorial service, Gene came to a realization about this message that he had first heard as a player for Joe 20 years before. But Gene now knew that it "was not for them."

> This small quote plastered all over was for only one person. It was to be a constant reminder, a thorn – a yoke – for only Joe Kasberger. Joe had put it there for himself. It was there to remind him that he must never quit. He must never quit working with boys – turning them into men. He must never quit teaching the value of manliness and sportsmanship. He must never quit doing his part in making a great St. Benedict's. No matter how he felt, what problems or hardships he had – how old and tired he got – he must never quit living his life as he knew it must be lived. And quit he never did. He often bellowed, 'A quitter never wins, and a winner never quits.' Joe Kasberger never quit life, and for that reason he has won God in heaven.[98]

It would appear, however, that Joe's favorite inspirational slogan "THINK," is equally important in remembering him. Parents of young men truly got their money's worth at SBP with Joe on the faculty. With his academic credentials and keen intellect, Joe was more than a great coach. His stature as a teacher and leader should never be forgotten as significant qualities in his success.

St. Peter's Cemetery, The Dalles.

There is little doubt that most who knew him admired his personal code of conduct as exemplary and worthy. Yet, life was neither easy nor fair to Joe and he was living proof that bad things happen to good people. But Joe's faith or intelligence made him realize that there are ups and downs that we all face, so Joe taught, as he lived, that we cannot take ourselves too seriously. He knew from his own life experiences that you never know what tomorrow will bring and one must be prepared, and think beforehand what you will do if the ball is hit to you. While this might be another one of Joe's simple sports analogies about life, for many it is a wonderful reminder to be prepared. As a coach, Joe's teams were prepared as the record indicates. As a teacher, he taught students to be equally ready for life's challenges.

Joe had few valuables before his death so what he possessed must have been cherished. His personal photo album, therefore, may be viewed as one of his few valued possessions. The fact that he left it in Newark suggests two things. First, he loved SBP enough to leave it in their care. Second, Joe may have wanted posterity to know what his life in Oregon had been like. The cryptic captions for many photos reveal Joe's personal side. His wry humor, coupled with fond memories, makes these photos very special. Not all of them are presented here, but of those that are, many captions are written by Joe.

Not everyone Joe touched wanted to be an athlete, coach, teacher or bachelor. They may have wondered what exposure to Joe might have meant as young men. Did his personal philosophy and outlook on life have an influence that is still felt many years after his death? For those who have felt Joe's touch in their personal lives, perhaps some questions are now answered. It is not surprising that Joe kept his story short and vague for fear of being misunderstood or boring people with all that he had done. Also, Joe may have wanted to minimize the risk of young men despairing at the prospect of living a life as hard as his. Still, describing Joe remains easier than defining him. Claire labeled Joe as a "man's man" and others have similar descriptions. One description on which all can agree, however, is that Joe was one-of-a-kind, since he was so many things wrapped up into one.

Closing this research on Joe is satisficing because there is probably more to be learned about his life. As a coach, however, the numbers speak for themselves and need little more elaboration. In performing that role, Joe was a very good man, one of the best ever known by many, but he was not perfect. Vince

Lombardi's biographer, Michael O'Brien, was able to portray a darker side of this legendary man as a young high school coach. Perhaps there were negatives for some about Joe as a coach, as with all successful coaches. They are not social workers, or "Dr. Feelgoods," especially Joe.

In comparing Lombardi's and Kasberger's coaching styles, it might be valid to assert that Joe was a role model when Vince began his career at St. Cecilia HS in the late 1930s. There is a recollection that Joe had an autographed picture of Lombardi in his office. As with Lombardi and other great coaches, not all players loved their coach, and Joe may have bruised some egos and hurt feelings along the way as well. Regardless of these apparently rare instances, Joe was a tough and demanding man who did not play favorites. As with Lombardi, he tended to treat all players alike and may have been verbally brusque.

While the notorious expression attributed to Lombardi, "Winning isn't everything..." might also apply to Kasberger, it seems important to emphasize the relatively poor winning records Joe endured as a player. Joe saw first-hand the unpleasant fate of coaches he knew personally who did not win, or not enough. As a coach, winning is extremely important and after Joe's experiences as a player, he must have been driven to insure that his players never endured the traumas of losing that he experienced. Joe's 1924 sojourns to be with Rockne at Notre Dame and subsequent Corvallis coaches schools, gave him an experience he never had as a player. He learned how to win by learning what it takes to win.

Countervailing any negatives about Joe's coaching style was his relationship with the Benedictines that appears extraordinary in the annals of their American evolution. They chose wisely in identifying Joe as a special young man who made their way of life better understood by generations of students. Joe reciprocated with loyalty for the remainder of his life. The pain from the Mt. Angel fire on that fateful day in 1926 never vanished. Joe did not dwell on the negative and turned it into a positive when he was rewarded with an opportunity provided by the Benedictines at another place and time. SBP was not MAC, but Newark's Benedictines were much like the Oregon monks who formed him. Joe never forgot who recruited him to be a student in 1915, gave him his first contract in 1922, and hired him in 1930. For 43 of the 47 years that he worked, Benedictines were Joe's employers, colleagues, and friends. That is mutual loyalty!

In reviewing what has been written and said about him from this research, one might conclude that Joe was a saintly man, or has been portrayed in that vein. Sister M. Georgita Milbauer, O.P., longtime observer and friend of Joe, described him as follows after his death:

> He lived a priestly life, and he could have been an example to many of the clergy with whom he lived these last ten years. [99]

To comprehend Joe it seems essential to understand Benedictines. Often lost in Benedict of Nursia's sainthood was his lay status. Benedictines, as clergy, are an evolutionary form of St. Benedict and his original followers. Joe may have followed in that early tradition by not professing vows as a lay oblate, brother or priest. For those intent on labelling him, modern labels do not fit but there is a precedent for his lifestyle.[100]

Joe brought the Newark Benedictines back to their agrarian past, teaching urban monks how to plant seeds in fertile young minds and nurture them by exemplary leadership. Joe and his monastic colleagues knew that they were not going to change young men overnight. In the course of some lifetimes, however, the seeds would grow. Then, the older and wiser former students had a gift that keeps on giving. They would know how to act and do the right thing when answers are not easy. In turn, they may influence their own children and possibly other young people in their care.

The Benedictine message was never zealous and often cryptic, with Joe, possibly, their ultimate role model for the male layman. If you do not have a vocation to profess vows, you can be like Joe! A subtle form of proselytization, based upon leadership by example, is perhaps a valid description of the Benedictine way. Joe's life-style, based upon his own interpretation of the Benedictine educational experience, was singular. Perhaps the message Joe wanted to convey was that we must make our own interpretations and live accordingly.

As a human being, Joe was misread as the "Marlboro Man," "Oregon Rancher," or other symbolic character. Appearances are deceiving and a closer look at Joe helped the author, and may help others, see him as he really was – as a group-oriented man. Legendary accounts serve a purpose but with a better understanding of his background, different impressions are formed. The author's son, Jeremy, said about Joe after hearing his story, "It is hard to believe a man such as Joe Kasberger ever lived." Many who knew him agree as his memory and influence endure over time. Joe was a paradox who gave a first impression of rugged individualism. An icon of American folklore Joe was not. He was neither a Horatio Alger nor a self-made man. He disdained individualism and had little use for those proclaiming to be self-made. He knew that such men are rarities, to be disbelieved as myth, because it took others to succeed: family, schools, friends, communities, and teams. As a coach, Joe knew an individual must be subordinated to a larger group for best results.

Many years after his passing Joe is still fondly recalled. Perhaps Ben Scotti's words speak best on what Joe meant to the many who knew him.

> If there is ever a Hall of Fame for saintly coaches Joe would be number one on the list. Just as St. Benedict left all worldly possessions to live in a cave in the 6th Century A.D. and later became the Father of Monastic life – Joe Kasberger gave up all worldly possessions to be father to students and athletes from all walks of life. His memory will forever live with those who were touched by his eternal spirit.[101]

Overall as a coach, teacher and man, Joe remains the personification of SBP to many, a role important in its history and ongoing evolution. His leadership role as a successful transcender of generations and ethnicities makes Joe a unifier for thousands as the common denominator to whom many best relate from their educational experiences as young men.

As significant as Joe is to SBP, the fire that led to Joe's arrival in Newark is not an obscure footnote in his life for those who seek to understand him. Before Joe became a Newark legend, he was MAC's favored son, and will always be famous to them. Equally important was his hometown, The Dalles, which in many ways he never left. He was reared in a culture of sports and academics that produced many great men. It is unsurprising that Joe was so deeply influenced by his home town for his life journey and kept returning home.

Joe's Oregon roots were deep, but he left much of himself in Newark. This symbolism was commemorated by a gift from Mt. Angel Abbey to their Newark brothers after Joe's death. How fitting that the Oregon monks chose one of their most visible natural resources, a redwood tree, as a living monument for those in Newark to have and nurture. The tree is in the Newark Abbey's cloister-garden, as a reminder of their original gift to Newark, Joe Kasberger, MAC, Class of 1917.

If Joe was a rarity in life when he lived, by today's standards some may see a marginal man on the fringe of contemporary American society. Joe did not write an epitaph for his gravestone. Perhaps his 1968 Christmas Card, however, has the message he wanted all to remember: "Think - Hustle - Win!" It seems, however, that the few words chosen say as much as he thought needed saying. In the immortal words of Joe K, used in captioning his Gold Medal photo from 1916, let us conclude with "Nuf Sed!"

Afterword

After his death Benedict Field was renamed "Joe Kasberger Field" with ceremonies and the unveiling of a plaque in his honor. Also, Joe was inducted into both the Newark and New Jersey Halls of Fame.

Joe's death did not the end his story in conjunction with SBP. In 1971, Rev. Leonard Cassel, Class of 1935 was elected Abbot of St. Mary's Abbey in Morristown. Abbot Martin remained at Delbarton until Abbot Leonard was blessed and then went to Canyon City, CO as an administrator at Holy Cross Abbey and returned to Morristown when his assignment was completed. Abbot Brian Clarke, Class of 1949 next succeeded Abbot Leonard as the Abbot of St. Mary's Abbey. Turning to Newark Abbey, Abbot Ambrose was succeeded

"Groundskeeper LeRoy Smith talks to Tony Sessa and Robert Rosa, l to r, outside St. Benedict's athletic field named for former great coach."

in 1973 by the second and present Abbot of Newark Abbey, Abbot Melvin Valvano, Class of 1956. In the interim, SBP closed at the end of the 1972 school year.

As with news of Joe's death less than four years earlier, there was more shock than sorrow. Initially, especially for those not close to the events that transpired after the riots, SBP was thought to be like Joe, indestructible and invincible. When SBP announced that it would "close its doors for good," the most famous living alumnus, Hugh Devore, said "I thought St. Benedict's would last forever."[102] His shocked reaction spoke for many with similar views.

> Dwindling enrollments and rising costs has [sic]led to a decision that shocked thousands of former students and athletes who helped make the Gray Bees of St. Benedict's a name connoting power in school sports.
> As a scholastic dynasty vanishes, so does a sports saga at St. Benedict's which tells of legendary coaches, national champions and Olympic stalwarts as far back as 1903. [103]

The Benedict's experience was an intense and defining moment in young lives. The emotions engendered by the forming process created strong feelings about alma mater. Its closing and subsequent reopening aroused many, positively and negatively. SBP was a school where a young man had to want to be, in order to be formed by the traditions associated with it: demanding, strict and uncompromising in its methods. Accordingly, news of the closing was not unlike news of a death in the immediate family.

SBP was never a school for everyone. To graduate required willingness to leave a piece of one's self behind. Very few forced to attend SBP completed the four years. Most students came and stayed because they loved the school and were very proud and loyal. Proof of this trait was demonstrated when SBP reopened the following year in response to great support from its friends and alumni. SBP was able to renew itself in Newark and remain an inspiration to many as a beacon of hope – despite the profound changes. Many do not recognize the same SBP from past experiences. To others it remains a symbol of the great tradition that Joe Kasberger helped to create.

The urban experiment for the Newark Benedictines remains unfinished history in the annals of this ancient religious order. Yet, the record after nearly 130 years may be pleasing to Abbot Wimmer and Bishop Bayley as SBP continues to pass, perhaps, the greatest test of all – time.

Many characters have been introduced in this account; the reader may wonder what happened to them. Accordingly, a few are mentioned here to the extent known. Shy Huntington resigned as Oregon head coach in 1923 to enter the fuel-oil business and devote his time to horses from a small farm near Eugene. Before his death in 1973, Shy served on the Oregon State Racing Commission and in the Oregon Legislature. Hollis Huntington also left coaching and became a businessman in Salem, where he died in 1969.

Fr. Hildebrand Melchior died Jan. 12, 1977 in a Mt. Angel nursing home at the age of 89. His long Benedictine career finally brought him back to Mt. Angel where he retired as assistant pastor of St. Mary's Church. In between his departure and return, Fr. Hildebrand spent a "year at the Indian Mission in Kakawis, Vancouver Island, B.C." and "sixteen years at Tillamook." His last assignment before retirement followed his role as pastor of Holy Rosary Church in Crooked Finger, OR. Upon returning to Mt. Angel, Fr. Hildebrand served on the Marion County Parks and Recreation Commission.

> Here he supervised the first addition to St. Mary's Grade School, promoted the planting of trees along Mount Angel's main street, established in 1954 the Marian Pilgrimages, which have become a tradition, attracting as many as 3,000 persons at Crooked Finger, founded the Benedictine Art Shop and the Benedictine Village Home, which was the forerunner of the Benedictine Nursing Home, helped to establish the Mount Angel Towers retirement home and served as its chaplain. [104]

Clearly, Fr. Hildebrand was not outdone in versatility by Fr. Victor!

Spec Keene died August 24, 1977 after retiring as OSU's athletic director. Frank A. Milbauer, Sr. moved to Spring Lake, NJ and retired as vice-president of industrial relations for Quinn and Boden Co., book manufacturers in Rahway, NJ. He died May 3, 1983 and was inducted post-humously into SBP's Hall of Fame, with citation received by his son, "Bun."

In recent months, several contributors to this research passed away. Rev. Martin Pollard, O.S.B. was in his nineties when he expired in March 1997. John Thomas died April 27, 1997 in Bend, OR. Joe Hellberg died June 30, 1997 in Lebanon, OR. "Bun," Frank A. Milbauer Jr., died July 7, 1997. Abbot Ambrose Clark received permission to leave the Benedictines in 1973 and resumed his given name, James. He retired in 1992 from Staten Island, NY Academy where he was the headmaster, and died July 19, 1997.

Most recently, John Bateman died on January 1, 1998 in New London NH. Enough cannot be said for the support, wisdom and encouragement that he provided in this research. Many words were written about John's life and distinguished career to make his sentiments about Joe in the Foreword all the more powerful. Joe had many great players, and John ranks among the very best for his accomplishments as a Columbia All-American football player and scholar with graduate and doctoral degrees in political science. As an assistant coach for Columbia's Lou Little and Penn's Steve Sebo, John was well prepared to be head coach at Rutgers. He was an immediate success and in 1961 gave the Scarlet Knights their first undefeated and untied season. When he retired, after the 1972 season, his record was the best in the school's long football history.

PERSONAL NOTE

The last time I saw Joe was before graduation in June 1961. I recall saying goodbye, and being wished well – a final encounter made awkward by a meeting I had with Joe in early April. He invited me into his Shanley Gymnasium office to discuss my leaving the baseball team before the season began. It was a cordial and frank conversation that left no bad feelings about him on my part. I think Joe understood that I had lost interest, and appreciated my candor. It was not easy for me to give up baseball since it was a big part of my younger life. Now I realized that I had outgrown it, as another Little League burnout.

Some of my greatest life-experiences came through baseball, with the greatest baseball thrill of them all at Benedict Field, thanks to Joe. I was a fifteen-year-old sophomore and Joe started me in a game as a varsity shortstop. I singled in my first at bat. After stealing second base, I made Joe nervous when I took third on a fielder's choice. The third baseman did not look me back to the bag, and I took off and made it in a close play. Then I scored on a sacrifice fly to manufacture a run. When I returned to the bench, Joe was more excited than I – not angry, perhaps only startled by what he had just observed. "Jawce, what are you doing out there?" I remember him asking. I do not recall how I responded. Yet, I know that he loved the effort that produced the run. Likely, he did not appreciate my aggressive style. After all, this was not a Hasbrouck Heights Little League or Babe Ruth League game. At the time, I did not know the difference. Baseball was a game to have fun. I was so charged up afterwards that my defense in the field may have suffered. While I had committed no errors, I was shaky. Joe was very relieved to see upperclassmen, Tom Quinn or Vince Liddy, finally appear around the sixth inning to substitute for me. They were probably in "jug," or detention, for some rule infraction. Probably that is the reason that Joe had started me. Fortunately, we held on to defeat St. Michael's HS of Union City in a very exciting game. I will never forget this life-moment.

When our meeting ended, I could not help but feel that I had disappointed Joe. Maybe he now hated me. If so, he never conveyed such a feeling over the next two months before graduation. I was probably not the first, and would not be the last, young baseball player he would see calling it a career. I never played again and still have no regrets.

After graduation, I went to the University of Alabama. Three months after leaving Joe, I encountered an emerging legend, Paul "Bear" Bryant, who appeared immediately to have a sports philosophy similar to Joe's. At that time, Bear had not yet arrived as a legend, but was assembling the first of his many Alabama national championship teams that would make him legendary. To be sure, there were personality and lifestyle differences between these two men. Yet, they appeared to a young observer as sharing a coaching philosophy to go with their drawling speech. It was incredible for me to realize that Joe Kasberger and Bear Bryant sounded so much alike in terms of philosophy! It would take many years for me to fully understand the linkage between Joe and Bear.

It was in Vietnam in Oct. 1969 when I read of Joe's death. My father, Anthony

Joyce, sent me the obituary, and I was stunned when I read the sad news. As an infantry officer in-country since February, I thought that I had become numbed by death. The biggest shock may have been that Joe had died at such a relatively young age. Surely, if he were not immortal, then he would at least live to be one hundred. Joe's passing ended what little remaining hope I had that maybe there was at least someone who gets out of this world alive. It was not unlike knowing where you were when President Kennedy was assassinated.

In subsequent years I waited for what I thought would be the inevitable book on Joe. There was much about Joe that I had always wanted to know. Why not start the research and get the ball rolling, was my initial thinking. Since I am not a professional writer, I never intended to write a book on anything, much less one on Joe Kasberger.

It was good to visit Joe's grave recently. I felt better to see his home and meet some of his family. The serenity that surrounds his final resting place is well deserved after the difficulties of Joe's final years. To understand him, for many of us, is to better understand ourselves. Joe's influence remains with many long after his departure. The lingering effect of exposure to Joe is one of the fascinating aspects of this man. Perhaps this characteristic validates his legendary status in the eyes and hearts of his fans. Possibly, the serious Kasberger student needs to visit the places of his formative years for a fuller understanding of the man: The Dalles, Mt. Angel, Corvallis, Salem, and Ashland.

The first step in the research was quantifying Joe's SBP baseball and football records that began in the headmaster's office in early 1988. Rev. Edwin Leahy, O.S.B. provided access to his *Telolog* collection for compiling most of Joe's football and baseball records, as an exercise in curiosity. Preliminary findings led to Rev. Augustine Curley, O.S.B. and the school library and archives for missing and new material, especially Joe's few writings.

Before any thought of a book, there was a desire to analyze Joe's numbers, and determine how good a coach was he? Once the numbers were crunched, Kansas City, where coaching records are kept, was contacted. When Joe's numbers were deemed to be nationally significant, thoughts of a book emerged.

Coincidentally, my father-in-law, Harold D. Morgan, gave me a *Serra Magazine* with a story about Mt. Angel Abbey in Oregon. I recognized it as Joe's alma mater, but thought it was extinct after the fire. I phoned and found myself speaking with an elderly monk who had a clear voice. Without hesitation, after hearing I was in New Jersey, he asked if I were calling about Joe Kasberger. I was amazed that Rev. Martin Pollard, O.S.B., was so prescient. He was very kind and tried to let me down gently. He knew Joe, but discouraged a book because everything I needed was lost in the 1926 fire.

I made more phone calls, and corresponded with Joe's family. Joe's niece, Jennifer Kasberger, in Mukilteo, WA, was very helpful at the outset, when making the right Kasberger-family contact was most difficult. Josephine Kasberger, Joe's sister-in-law, was helpful, but due to her age, directed me to Joe's nephew, Bernard (Bud) Sandoz. Bud's interest and efforts are exceptional in providing pieces of Kasberger family life during the summer of 1988, as a jigsaw puzzle, awaiting assembly.

Sam Cavallaro was my freshman history teacher at SBP. His funeral provided a chance to see Jack Dalton, who introduced me to Joe's former players, Joe Grum and Bill Johnston. Possibly the best advice I ever received was Jack's, to call Claire Milbauer, thought to know more about Joe than anyone still alive. Despite the years, her memory amazes in recalling Joe's life. By the spring of 1989, I developed health problems and the book went on hold until the early part of 1995.

Nearly three years ago I entered the Kasberger data on my personal computer to test new LOTUS software. After extensive data-entry, I ran several data sorts. I was immediately impressed by both the software and the Kasberger record. The numbers took life as information with, possibly, interesting appeal. If a book of Joe's entire life were not feasible because of destroyed material, perhaps Joe's record book would suffice. I finalized the numbers, and decided to gather as much material as I could about Joe's life. Fleshing out the numbers with what was known about Joe might make for a simple book.

The reason for calling Mt. Angel archives, again, is forgotten. It was, however, one of the most significant things that I did. Archivist Patricia Brandt has become extremely important in the research's development. She shared material about Joe at Mt. Angel, as a student and as a coach, that was thought by Fr. Martin to be lost. Her superior, Rev. Hugh Feiss, O.S.B., is commended for the support this research received. Patricia also directed me to her colleagues at Oregon State University archives, Elizabeth Nielsen and Dawn Barron, who responded with more material. Also, Patricia directed me to her cousin, Msgr. William S. Stone, formerly the historian for the Diocese of Baker, Oregon, who lived in The Dalles and knew Joe.

Msgr. Stone led me to Lorna Elliott at The Dalles-Wasco County Library, who shared historical documents relevant to Joe. Also, Lorna introduced me to Joe's former neighbor, John Brookhouse, who provided insights and advised that I call Robert M. Huntington, Ph.D. for material on his uncles, Shy and Hollis. Steve Bungum at The Dalles High School Library and his students were most helpful. Similarly, at St. Mary's Academy in The Dalles, Harriet Langfelt directed me to Sister Rosemarie Kasper, S.N.J.M., archivist of the Holy Names Sisters in Marylhurst, OR. The archives of the Benedictine Sisters in Mt. Angel, thanks to Sister Alberta Dieker, O.S.B., have yielded answers to questions that arose in telling Joe's story. Bill Murray and Marilyn Ericksen provided great material on their fathers, Bob Murray and Allie Gronewald, two important men in Joe's life. The sheer volume of Kasberger material from Oregon is overwhelming and an easy book became complex.

Joe's life in short-story form may have been recorded by Lloyde S. Glicken, in a Newark *Star-Ledger* column after his death. Much of Joe's legend is oral history, recalled by many who knew him and passed along with variations and embellishments heard from others. In researching Joe's life, Glicken was very useful in providing guideposts.

As Joe's younger years unfolded there was exponential growth in the research network thanks to others interested in Joe and the people of his era in Oregon. Once Joe's Oregon story was revealed, attention shifted to Newark friends, colleagues and students who might be able to elaborate on the personal side of Joe's life that was not well-known. As indicated in the Acknowledgements, many contributed to complete this research to date.

I. Textual Appendix

APPENDIX A - MAC GAME STORIES, 1915 FOOTBALL SEASON

<u>MAC 42-Lebanon HS 0.</u> The Nov., 1915 *Pacific Star* has this game story.

They came, they saw, but were conquered, nor was there the least semblance of a doubt after the first quarter, as to which side the tide of victory would flow. This in part tells the story of the 42-0 drubbing administered the Lebanon High School football team by the fast M.A.C. squad on the college gridiron Saturday October 16.

Lebanon won the toss and chose to receive. Kasberger kicked off and the ball went into scrimmage on Lebanon's 30 yard line. After two or three fruitless attempts at line plunging the High School lads lost the ball to Mt. Angel on a fumble. Here is where the visitors showed the only fight they displayed in the entire game; but gradually the college boys worked the ball to their opponent's goal line, where Pashek was shoved across for the first touchdown. Kronberg missed the goal. Spirited on by first blood and inspired by the sight of victory, the collegians renewed their efforts and in a short time annexed a second touchdown. This time Kronberg kicked the goal. The second quarter registered two more touchdowns for the Angels, Kronberg making one and Pashek making the other. Kronberg kicked one goal. At this stage of the game it was apparent that the High School boys were no match for their more aggressive opponents, the latter resorting almost entirely to line plunging, and seemingly tearing through their opponents' defense at will.

The timekeeper's whistle robbed the High School team of further slaughter at this junction of the game by deciding the first half, with the ball in Mt. Angel's possession on Lebanon's 2 yard line. The third and fourth quarters were more repetitious of the first two, with two touchdowns in the third and one in the fourth; while Kronberg in the last quarter to add to his former glory successfully dropped the ball over the bar from the 20 yard line to swell the total to 42 points for the Angels. The game ended with the ball in M.A.C.'s possession on the visitor's 30 yard line.

The High School lads were hopelessly outclassed, and not once during the entire game did Lebanon make their required yardage for the fourth down. And neither did they possess the ball in Mt. Angel's territory. However much credit is due to the wonderful defence [sic] supplied by our line, in particular Melchior, Mattucci, and Eckerlin who were there to interfere at every play, not forgetting our reliable center Krebs who continually tackled the quarterback before he could pass the ball. The honor of the back-field goes to Capt. Pashek who made five of the six touchdowns for the Angels. Kronberg made the other, besides kicking a drop and three of the six free chances at goal.

The lineup:

Mt Angel College	Position	Lebanon H. School
Coghlan	R.E.L.	Waters
Melchior	R.T.L.	Mills
Eckerlin, Pohndorf	R.G.L.	Simmons
Krebs	C	Budley
Engertsberger, Coombs	L.G.R.	Lawrence

Mattucci	L.T.R.	E. Caldwell, Southard
Franciscovich	L.E.R.	Scott
Kasberger	Q	Southard
Sohler	R.H.L.	C. Caldwell
Pashek (Capt.)	L.H.R.	Mackey, Curl
Kronberg	F	Millsap

MAC 7-Pacific U. 27. The Dec., 1915 *Pacific Star* has this game story.

October the 23rd witnessed the first real tragedy enacted in the blossoming hopes of M.A.C.'s gridiron career when she fell, for the first time this season, before the weightier and more experienced Pacific University eleven at Forest Grove, and succumbed to a 27 to 7 defeat.

However the comparative strength of the two teams can scarcely be judged from the score; for despite the fact that Mt. Angel was playing her first game away from home on strange grounds, her aggressive ability in line plunges did not suffer in comparison with those of her more seasoned opponents.

Pacific owes her victory largely to her success in deceiving the College boys via the aerial route, which mode of progress netted the University many yards and was twice directly responsible for touchdowns. On the other hand Mt. Angel seemed to be troubled by the omen of 'hard luck.' Twice with the ball within easy striking distance of the opponents' goal it was lost on a fumble and dreams of victory vanished with the oval as it was punted to safety.

A fumble by Mt. Angel on her 30 yard line shortly after the kickoff gave the ball to Pacific where, after a succession of end runs and line plunges, they carried the ball across the line for the first score of the game. Lucas kicked goal. This was shortly followed by Pacific's second touchdown on a 15 yard forward pass to Stanley across the goal line. Lucas again kicked goal.

However this did not dishearten the boys from Angel City. They redoubled their efforts and before the first half had ended they, by a succession of line plunges, had plowed their way from almost the center of the field to the goal line, where Pashek was shoved across for what proved to be the Angels' only touchdown.

The second half opened bright for the College boys when Sohler intercepted one of Pacific's passes on her 20 yard line. From here the College boys worked the ball to within a couple of yards of their opponents' goal, only to lose it on a fumble.

The University boys annexed their third touchdown in this quarter when Irle on an end run carried the ball across the line, Lucas again kicked goal.

In the last quarter the Angels once more experienced a thrill of pleasure with the ball on the opponents' 5 yard line; again the slippery oval chose its own course and glided to the ground where it was recovered by Pacific.

With but one minute left to play and the ball in Pacific's possession on Mt. Angel's 20 yard line Lucas started around end, where he was neatly dumped by Pashek, but recovered himself and sprinted across the line for the University's fourth touchdown, just as the whistle blew for the end of the game. This time Lucas missed goal.

An unwelcomed drizzle throughout the game made the ball slippery, and was the cause of several fumbles, which proved to be costly, especially for the Angels.

The entire backfield of Mt. Angel deserves exceptional credit for progressing the ball, while for Pacific Lucas and Irle were the bright stars.

The following is the lineup:

Mt. Angel College	Position	Pacific University
Franciscovich	R.E.L.	Stanley
Eckerlen	R.T.L.	Donaldson
Simon	R.G.L.	Rasmusen
Krebs	C	Jones
Combs	L.G.R.	Romig
Melchior	L.T.R.	Livesay
Coghlan, Rassier	L.E.R.	Wilcox
Kasberger	Q	Goodman
Sohler	R.H.L.	Lucas
Pashek (Capt.)	L.H.R.	Irlie
Kroneberg	F	Gead

MAC 20-Albany College 9. The Jan. 1916 *Pacific Star* has this game story.

Victory again crowned the efforts of our speedy aggregation on November 13, when they welcomed the stalwart Albany College eleven to this city, and treated them to an elaborate display of M.A.C. gridiron ability from which they awoke to realize the worst defeat they had sustained this season.

After receiving the kick-off in the first quarter the Angels completely surprised their opponents by the speed they displayed in tearing off long end runs and line plunges until but with six yards to go Kasberger skirted the end for the required yardage and registered the first score of the game. Kronberg failed at goal from a difficult angle.

This was soon followed by Mt. Angel's second touchdown in the same quarter when Sohler with perfect interference reeled off a 65 yard run around right end and carried the ball between the standards. Kronberg annexed another point by kicking goal.

In the second junction of the game the Southern boys took a hand at the scoring, when with the ball on Mt. Angel's 15 yard line Gildow caught the Angels off guard on a neatly executed delayed end run and had no trouble in carrying the oval across the line. French failed to convert goal.

A fumble by the locals on Albany's five yard line after Kronberg had returned one of Albany's punts about 75 yards, blasted the only scoring chance available for the Angels in this period.

A long forward pass to Coghlan on the visitors 20 yard line in the third stanza was converted into Mt. Angel's third touchdown when he sprinted across the line and placed the oval between the posts. Kronberg's perfect kick netted another point.

Albany boys succeeded in holding the Angels scoreless in the last quarter, while they annexed an additional three points to their honor, when on the 25 yard line with but two minutes left to play French succeeded in kicking a perfect goal from placement.

Long end runs by Kasberger and Sohler, and the line plunging of Pashek coupled with the stellar defensive work of Coghlan and Melchior were the features of the game for Mt. Angel, while for Albany French and Gildow were the bright stars.

The Lineup:

Mt. Angel College	Position	Albany College
Coghlan	R.E.L.	Shortiedge
Melchior	R.T.L.	Tolles
Eckerlen	R.G.L.	Martin, Jensen
Krebs	C	Hunter, Parker
Simon	L.G.R.	Lanson
Matteucci	L.T.R.	Springer
Franciscovich	L.E.R.	McKee
Kasberger	Q	Gildow
Sohler	R.H.L.	French
Pashek (Capt.)	L.H.R.	Jenkins
Kronberg	F	Gloor

MAC 20-Oregon City Reds 0. The Jan., 1916 *Pacific Star* has this game story.

Despite the handicap of weight and sloppy condition of the field on November 20th Mt. Angel College succeeded in annexing another scalp to their belt by defeating the Oregon City Red men [sic] to the tune of 20 to 0.

With the same rush and determemating [sic] spirit that characterized their former victories the College boys succeeded in piling up their first count five minutes after playing had begun when Kasberger tore around end for the last ten yards, after the ball had been advanced almost from the center of the field by the old style of play. Kronberg's trusty toe added another point.

The Angels' next score came in the second quarter when Sohler intercepted one of Oregon City's passes on their 40 yard line and succeeded in breaking away from the throng and scampering to the goal. Kronberg converted goal.

Two complete passes coupled with a series of line plunges enabled Kasberger to add another six points to the Angels score in the same stanza. Kronberg missed goal.

On account of the cold and drenched players no time was taken out between halves.

Continual rains during the early part and the already soggy condition of the field rendered it almost like a pond of mud in the second half in which it was impossible for either side to accomplish anything and the repeated fumbles proved more a source of enjoyment to the spectators than the outcome of the game.

Among the visitors we recognized our old friend Quinn who last year proved the hero of many a battle, but he met a stone wall in Simon our reliable guard who along with Franciscovich and Kasberger shared the honors of the fray.

The closing Foot-ball season marks perhaps the most successful year ever experienced by the M.A.C. in this department of our annual pastime [sic].

By virtue of their overwhelming defeat of Albany College and their rejected challenge at the hands of Willamette University, Mt. Angel College lays claim to the Non-Conference championship of the state.

Marred by but a single defeat (and this at a time when she was minus two regular men), the great record of the White and Gold for the past season stands out conspicuously for the future recognition of M.A.C. in the world of gridiron fame. The following is the lineup:

Mt. Angel College	Position	Oregon City
Franciscovich	R.E.L.	Geanelley
Matteucci	R.T.L.	Powers
Simon	R.G.L.	Quinn
Krebs	C	Gant
Eckerlen	L.G.R.	Green
Melchior	L.T.R.	Horlow
Coghlan	L.E.R.	Green
Kasberger	Q	Moss
Sohler	R.H.L.	Sherry
Pashek (Capt.)	L.H.R.	Dingy
Kronberg	F	Miller

APPENDIX B - MAC GAME STORIES, 1916 FOOTBALL SEASON

<u>MAC 2-Vancouver Athletic Club 6.</u> The Nov., 1916 *Pacific Star* has this game story.

Mt. Angel's First Team made its initial appearance on the new football field on Oct. 18, against the heavy Vancouver aggregation. The showing made by the boys banishes all fear in the minds of the skeptical as to our coach's ability to shape a winning team. The Vancouver crowd presented an aggressive team that fought from start till finish.

The game started with Mt. Angel receiving. Sohler caught the ball and advanced it 20 yards before he was downed. Captain Kasberger pulled off several classy line plunges netting 15 yards. This was followed by a series of forward passes mixed with several end runs which soon carried the ball well within our opponents' territory. Mt. Angel failed to make yardage and lost the ball. Vancouver started with a rush but could not batter down the stonewall defense offered by our boys. A fumble on their goal line resulted in a safety. After Sohler's injury the machine-like team lost some of its pep. The pigskin was exclusively confined to Vancouver's territory during the greater portion of the first half, but several long punts kept the ball from crossing the line. The quarter ended: Mt. Angel 2, Vancouver 0.

The second quarter brought no change to the score and neither team showed to advantage. It was one continual see-sawing back and forth. Pashek and Kasberger won merited praise at different intervals for really excellent plays.

Kasberger opened up the third quarter by kicking to Rooney who was downed in his tracks. Forward passes and end runs netted Vancouver some long gains and brought the ball to our 10 yard line. First down, 10 yards to go for a touchdown, looked easy for Vancouver. Four times they plunged into Mt. Angel's line and four times Mt. Angel hurled them back. Vancouver lost the ball on the 15 yard line. Then a line plunge by Pashek advanced the ball 10 yards making Vancouver take notice. It was not until the quarter was well under way that the Vancouver team made the first touchdown. Daniels forward passed to Rooney, who carried the ball 20 yards before he was tackled by Coghlan. The ball was now on our 10 yard line. The Mt. Angel squad knew what was expected from them and fought accordingly, but the beef of the Vancouver team proved too much for them, and they were forced to give way. Moyer carried the ball over the line for a touchdown. Daniels failed to kick goal, score: Vancouver 6, Mt. Angel 2.

The final quarter found both teams fighting hard. The plunging of Pashek, the twisting, wriggling, open field running of Sohler and Glatt, together with the large gains made by Kasberger featured this quarter. It was in this quarter that the Vancouver team was at its best. They put up a stubborn defense, and twice succeeded in staving off Kasberger when he was within striking distance of the goal.

The luminaries in the game for Mt. Angel were Capt. Kasberger, Sohler and Pashek, while La Caff and Noyer [sic] starred for Vancouver.

Noonan refered [sic] the game and proved himself a capable and efficient man at handling the whistle.

The teams lined up as follows:

Mt. Angel	Position	Vancouver
Coghlan	L.E.R.	Rooney
Melchior	L.T.R.	Morgen
Eckerlen	L.G.R.	VanDorer
Krebs	Center	McDonald
Schwall	R.G.L.	Dutch
Fuller	R.T.L.	Laipple
Brown	R.E.L.	Cook
Kasberger	Quarter	Daniels
Pashek	L.H.R.	Mumford
Glatt	Full.	Noyer
Sohler	R.H.L.	LaCaff

MAC 13-Pacific U. 14. The Dec., 1916 *Pacific Star* has this game story.

On October 28th the husky pigskin warriors of Forest Grove trotted over to battle against the Collegians. With the confidence of a 27 to 7 defeat which they administered to us last year, they were ready to wipe us off the map, with their old line-up of last year and the additional weight of beef. But as it was they merely snatched the game from us by a one point lead, 14 to 13.

In the most spectacular and hard fought game on the local gridiron for many a moon, the Pacific University lads plucked the victory not so much by their superior playing but because fickle fortune deserted us in the pinches. It was agreed by us that only the tender glances of Dame Fortune made it possible for P.U. to register the victory. As the spectators beheld the M.A.C. back-field plough through the line for yard after yard, it was thought that M.A.C. should have the game. But P.U. completed three brilliant forward passes and on their touchdowns kicked both goals, whereas luck was against our plucky Captain when he missed kicking a goal by a few inches.

The game started at 1:30 P.M. with Mr. De Witt, star fullback of the Multnomah Athletic Club, blowing the whistle. Taylor for P.U. kicked the ball to Capt. Kasberger who advanced it to the 20 yard line. A line plunge by Sohler placed the ball on the ten yard line. Fuller pulling off a sensational 9 yard end run, placed the ball a few inches from the line. Pashek made the first touchdown through center. Kasberger failed to kick goal by a few inches. Mt. Angel kicked the ball; it was caught by Walker who with interference made 15 yards before he was downed by Sohler. Failing to pierce the line, P.U. punted on the second down. Fuller by clever dodging and nifty sprinting carried it 15 yards. First Quarter: Mt. Angel 6; Pacific 0.

The second quarter found the ball in P.U.'s possession, Mt. Angel having failed to make yardage in the first quarter. The visitors in vain tried line plunge after line plunge. Shift formations were resorted to, which carried the ball to our 15 yard line. Here P.U. was held for downs and the Collegians had the ball. Kasberger with a pretty end run of 20 yards carried the ball out of danger. The ball kept shifting back and forth for some time during this quarter. Finally Erle, speared a forward pass and like a bullet shot away for a touchdown. Smith kicked the goal just as the whistle blew. Mt. Angel 6; Pacific U. 7.

In the third quarter Mt. Angel opened up with a series of straight line plunges that brought them to the center of the field. The game see-sawed back and forth, Mt. Angel showing her superiority by plunging through P.U.'s line for several big gains. Mt. Angel was then penalized for being off side. On a fumble by one of the visitors Coghlan, one of the niftiest players on the squad, scooped up the ball and shot away for a touchdown. The whole opposing team was after him but to no avail. Coghlan was determined to let no one touch him. Kasberger kicked goal. Mt. Angel 13; Pacific U. 7.

The last quarter saw a hard struggle, the heavy backfield of P.U. commencing to tire our line, and they made their yardage on line plunges. Fowler picked the ball out of the mass of players and made a spectacular run of 20 yards before he was downed on our 5 yard line. Right here is where M.A.C. showed their bulldog grit. Three times straight she held as a stone wall but superior beef was against her and on the fourth down P.U. had made the second touchdown. Smith kicked goal. Mt. Angel 13; Pacific University 14.

Coach Victor's prodigies showed their worth. Aside from the starring of Capt. Kasberger, Pashek, and Sohler, it is hard to name any particular star. Coghlan came into the limelight on several occasions. The line was a veritable stone wall up to the last quarter. The back field will compare with any one in the country.

Coghlan and Meehan playing at ends, won much applause and were kept in the limelight by their timely headwork in breaking up plays. Lucas, Fowler and Jones played stellar ball for Pacific University.

The Lineup:

Mt. Angel College	Position	Pacific University
Coghlan	R.E.L.	Jones, L.
Melchior	R.T.L.	Livesay
Eckerlen	R.G.L.	Roming [sic]
Krebs	C	Smith
Simon	L.G.R.	Barondrick
Glatt	L.T.R.	Walker
Meehan	L.E.R.	Jones, R.
Kasberger	Q	Fowler

Pashek	R.H.L.	Taylor
Sohler	L.H.R.	Erle
Fuller	F	Lucas

MAC 0-Willamette 1. The Dec., 1916 *Pacific Star* has this game story.

'O Lord, I thank Thee that I am not like other men' – crooked – bum sports – insipid cowards-yellow streaked artists – uncultured low-brows,' etc; thus does the Willamette *Collegian* give expression to its hypocritical ravings over the Willamette-Mt. Angel College Football Game. Like its worthy exemplar of two thousand years ago, the Pharisee, the *Collegian* has dressed itself in the garments of hypocrisy and the slime of mendacity.

Mt. Angel College Football Team journeyed to our Sister Institution to contend in honest battle with the warriors upholding the colors of Willamette University. Schmidt of Portland, Ore. blew the whistle as W.U. kicked to M.A.C. on her twenty yard line. It was a matter of four minutes until the Collegians had planted the ball on W.U.'s ten yard line. A penalty of fifteen yards on the fourth down gave the ball to Willamette. The official of the game allowed M.A.C. to carry the ball to W.U.'s ten yard line on four different occasions only to take it away from them by a penalty of fifteen yards.

During the three quarters that were played Mt. Angel College was penalized eighty-five (85) yards and Willamette University not one inch. The penalties on the M.A.C. Team amounted to forty five yards more than the yardage that W.U. made during the entire three quarters. The Captain of the Collegians kept his team under control in the face of such apparent-unfair and one-sided officialling.

With one more minute left in the third quarter, Sohler, halfback of the Collegians, intercepted a forward pass and advanced the ball twenty yards. The two teams were in a position to resume play when the head-linesman proceeded under the instructions of Coach Mathews of W.U. to call Mt. Angel College offside. Referee Schmidt tried to add insult to injury by enforcing Coach Mathew's decision but Captain Kasberger refused to accept the insult and ordered his players off the field.

The bold and hypocritical editorial in the Willamette *Collegian* is the expression of a warped mind and puny intellect. 'We must sever athletic relations with an institution that insults our spectators by walking off the field.' If the spectators were men with all the term implies then the insult was farthered by the dirty tactics used in trying to win the game and the Mt. Angel team should be commended for putting an end to such insulting crookedness. With an impartial official the score would have been very one-sided – this everyone could determine at the outset. That Willamette only advanced the ball forty yards in three quarters is evidence enough.

Mt. Angel College Football Team is characterized – yellow, quitters, afraid it would lose the game. Wake up Willamette! Don't you realize that at best you stole the game? Does it require someone to arouse your dormant sense of honor? A one to nothing forfeit is a glorious foundation for a non-conference championship.

Realizing as we do that it is in your enjoyable pleasure to engage with whomsoever you fancy, yet for the sake of peace in the neighborhood we would suggest that you contend in athletic encounters not with young blood but with some Home for the Aged or some Academy for Young Ladies. These might be mesmerized by such wholesale larceny but we of Mt. Angel College prefer to let the better team win.

Score at the end of the third quarter: Willamette 0 M.A.C. 6

Forfeited Score: Willamette 1 M.A.C. 0

There is no lineup available for this game.

MAC 3-Chemawa 0. The Jan., 1917 *Pacific Star* has this game story.

Winding up the 1916 season, the Mt. Angel squad earned a hard-fought victory over the Chemawa Indians by the score of 3 to 0. The annual encounter of 1916 proved to be the most interesting in which these two squads have ever engaged.

From the initial outset of the game the battle was a royal one. Both teams fought tooth and nail to cop the victory, for the Indians were determined to duplicate last year's victory, while the Collegians at the same time were more than determined that they would wipe out the defeat slated out to them in the 1915 season.

A somewhat cloudy day dawned for the big match, and shortly after the scheduled time the Mt. Angel squad swept upon the field amid the cheers of the Collegians. A few seconds later the Indians were nimbly practising [sic] their signals.

Chemawa kicked off and the ball was kept within our 30 yard line, two periods, play was about even with Mt. Angel showing superior class in gaining yardage. The sensational returns by Pashek at the kick-off for 20 yards, the wonderful all around playing of Sohler, the tackling of Simon and Melchior, the admirable work of Krebs at center, were features of the game. But to the stellar playing of Captain Kasberger goes the bulk of praise for this signal victory. It was his remarkable kick from placement in the last period that spelled victory, and it was his smashing attacks and line plunging alone, that made victory possible.

In the third period Kasberger, throwing off no less than five men, cleverly dodging and shifting, aided by the wonderful interference of Brown, Sohler, and Glatt, carried the ball from our 15 yard line to the opponents' 45 yard line. On the fourth down he capped the climax by kicking a field goal from the 30 yard line. Much credit must be given to Coghlan for his steadiness in holding the ball while Kasberger converted the goal from placement.

For the losers, Eder the full back [sic], was the main star of the game. By his brilliant line plunging and nifty running he added much glory to his team. Downey, the quarterback, Lane, left end, and Horchenback, right end were other star men for the Indians.

The Lineup:

Mt. Angel College	Position	Chemawa
Fuller	R.E.L.	Lane
Simon	R.T.L.	Patrovich
Schwall	R.G.L.	Dick
Krebs	C	Elk
Eckerlen	L.G.R.	Fields
Melchior	L.T.R.	Johnson
Coghlan	L.E.R.	Colby

Kasberger	Q	Downey
Glatt	R.H.L.	Tatscheme
Sohler	L.H.R.	Chamberlain
Brown	F	Eder

An anonymous story. dated Nov. 19, is headlined: "Mount Angel 3, Chemawa 0-Place Kick Brings Victory Over Indians in Hard Tussle."

A place-kick from the 38-yard line by Captain Kasberger gave the Mount Angel football team a 3-to-0 victory over the Chemawa Indians' eleven here Saturday afternoon. The lone score came in the last quarter after a hard tussle all the way through.

Stanley Borleske, coach of the Lincoln High squad of Portland, had little difficulty handling the game as referee. Few penalties were inflicted during the matinee. A return contest may be staged later in the season.

Another anonymous story for the same game, dated Nov. 21, is headlined: "Kasberger Stars in Victory Over Indians."

The skillful toe of Joseph Kasberger, captain of the college football squad, decided the victory for Mount Angel college against the Chemawa Indians by the narrow margin of one field goal, Saturday, winning the game by a score of 3 to 0. In the third quarter Captain Kasberger kicked the goal from the 37-yard line. He was the star of the game. Time after time he went through the lines of the losers for from 3 to 12 yards gain. He also pulled off several nifty end runs, netting a gain of 20 yards each time.

Throughout the game Kasberger, Coughlan, Schwall and Pashek starred for the victors. For the losers, Downey and Charles Eder were the stellars. Thurensehusen crept into the limelight with his 40-yard run.

APPENDIX C - COACH BAILEY'S 1916 ALL-STAR FOOTBALL TEAM

An anonymous news story, undated, is excerpted for Coach Bailey's 1916 all "non-conference" team.

In submitting his eleven, Coach Bailey says: 'Following compliments from the majority of the coaches of the non-conference eleven picked last season and the suggestion that as my team did not conclude the season I could make my selections from a more neutral standpoint, I have again named an Oregon non-conference team.'

In making his selections, Bailey says: 'The picking of a team this year is somewhat difficult, from the fact that the non-conference teams have not been characterized by men of exceptional ability as in a few years past. The men selected are, however, well qualified, but as a team do not present the tremendous strength that could have been found in a non-conference team of three or four years ago.'

The text continues with the paragraph heading "Willamette Man First."

'As captain of the team, and without doubt the best man on any non-conference team, I have selected Grosvenor, of Willamette. His open-field running, punting, headwork and all-around ability demonstrate clearly that he is conspicuously fitted for the position.

'At the other half I have placed French, of the Albany College team. I consider him the best punter and place-kicker on a non-conference team, as well as being a powerful plunger and great defensive player.

'Fullback goes to Lucas, of Pacific, as the greatest ground-gainer on his team and brilliant defensive player.

'The quarterback position is given to Kasberger of Mount Angel. He is a good open-field runner, good at making interference and plays good defensive ball.

'The line positions are more bitterly contested, the most conspicuous superiority going to two Willamette ends, Rexford and Ratcliffe. Rexford, in particular, is entitled to all-star selection as being, the greatest defensive player.'

The text continues with the paragraph heading "Livesay and Tobie Win."

'The tackle berths go to Livesay, of Pacific, and Tobie, of Willamette. There is little question about their superiority, both being aggressive, fast and of good weight.

'The guard positions are the hardest to fill. They are given to Krebs, of Mount Angel, and Tohles, of Albany. Krebs is the equal of any man playing in the center of the line. I have shifted Tohles from his position as tackle to the other guard. He is an exceptionally aggressive player, and used excellent headwork. During the Albany-Willamette game it was he who broke through the line, scooped up a fumble and registered a touchdown for Albany. Captain Flegel, of Willamette; Roming, of Pacific; and Eckerlen, of Mount Angel, are all good men, but fail to combine the qualities found in the two selected.

'The position at center goes to Smith, of Pacific, his 200 pounds of brawn proved to be a difficult wall for any of the backs who essayed to attack yardage through the center of the line.'

APPENDIX D - MAC GAME STORIES, 1916-17 BASKETBALL SEASON

MAC 46-Molalla 9. [sic] An anonymous news story, dated Dec. 18, is headlined "Mount Angel Defeats Molalla Team."

The Mount Angel college basketball team took the long end of a 46 to 9 score yesterday afternoon from the Molalla team on the local floor. At the outset of the game Coach Hildebrand tried out several new men and the game was slow; as soon as he shot in his first team men Mount Angel simply walked away with the losers. Spear, center, the find of the season, was one of the mainstays for Mount Angel. Classic came into prominence with his ability in shooting fouls.

The second half commenced with Mount Angel leading by a score of 46 to 5. Then Nat Schanedling, a former Lincoln high star, became the stellar man. Evading his guard at every moment of the half he managed to drop in nine pretty baskets. From every angle of the floor he shot them. For the losers, Echerd, center, and Shaver, guard, were the star men.

```
                    The Lineup
        Mt. Angel              Molalla
      Classic, 6        F      Engle, 2
      Schanedling, 20   F      Woodworth, 2
      Spear, 8          C      Echerd, 3
      Kasberger, 2      G      Palfrey, 0
      Pashek, 8         G      Shaver, 2
```

MAC 38-Woodburn AC 23. An anonymous January 9 news story is headlined: "Mt. Angel Wins From Woodburn A.C., 38-23-Continues Winning Streak
by Taking Lead at Start of Game."

Mt. Angel college quint continued its winning streak by taking the Woodburn Athletic club basketball team into camp by a score of 38 to 23 last night.
Gregory Pashek started the game by tossing a goal from the center of the floor
and a minute later Classic duplicated the feat.

This brilliant spurt seemed to dazzle the visitors, and, although they played
a hard game they were unable to overcome the lead. During the entire first half
the losers were plainly outplayed for the center landed the ball in his own territory without any difficulty and either Classic or Pashek was on the spot to
grab the ball. The first half ended with Mt. Angel leading by a score of 17 to 5.

The second half commenced with the losers determined to capture the game,
but their efforts proved futile, although they managed to cage several baskets
towards the end of the second half, when the collegians slacked in their playing.

Greg Pashek and Classic were the goal winners of the day. The latter, a
Portland lad, is showing the best of any of the new players. He is the best foul
shooter seen for some time on the local floor. Shanedling took five baskets as
his share of the points. Brost, a Portland lad, took Spear's place in the latter part
of the game. Kasberger held down his forward to two baskets, and in the meantime secured four himself.

MAC 55-Christian Brothers College 18. An anonymous January 15 news story
is headlined: "Mt. Angel College Squad Beats C.B.C."

By defeating the Christian Brothers College of Portland Saturday by the
score of 55 to 18 the Mount Angel college quintet continued its winning streak.
The visitors drew first blood, Cosgrove dropping in a foul. But Mt. Angel came
back strong when Pashek and Classic caged two baskets apiece in a few
moments. During the entire first half of the game Mt. Angel continued to lead
with the exception of the first point. Taking a brilliant spurt the collegians went
through some nifty team work and showed the best class of the season. At the
end of the first half the local lads were ahead, 20 to 8.

The second half opened strong, with the victors again showing real class.
Classic shot a spectacular basket from the 80-foot line. From that time the collegians dropped in basket after basket, whereas the losers were able to cage
only five points. Classic, for the collegians grabbed 13 points as his share of the
game. But it was Spear, center for the locals, who showed real class by caging
eight baskets, with Shanedling following with seven. For the leaders Ryan and
Cosgrove were the stellar men. Cosgrove and Ryan are the best and neatest
players seen on the local floor this season.

The Lineup:

Mount Angel		Christian Bros.
Shanedling (14)	F	Cosgrove
Classic (13)	F	Ryan
Spear (16)	C	Walsh
Kasberger (6)	G	Hoiter
Pashek (6)	G	Murnane

APPENDIX E - THE PROGRAM FOR THE 1917 MAC MINSTREL

From the March, 1917 *Pacific Star*

Endman-Bones	Charles Simon
Endman-Bones	William Spear
Endman-Tambourine	Charles Coghlan
Endman-Tambourine	Lynn Fuller
Interlocutor	Joseph Miller

CHORUS

1st Tenor

Lynn Fuller, Bernard Kropp, Lenore Davis

2nd Tenor

Chas. Simon, Chas Coghlan, William Spear, Joseph Miller

1st Bass

Stephen Rassier, James Robinson, Wilfred Rassier

2nd Bass

John Friedman, Jos. Kasberger, Adolph Glatt, Ray Sheehan

APPENDIX F - OFFICIAL PROGRAM Univ. of Oregon vs. OAC, 10-15-19

Team Statistics

OREGON

Name—	Position	Wt.	Age	Yrs. on Team	Home—
Martin Howard	L. E.	170	20	2	Portland
Bazil Williams	L. T.	185	24	3	Eugene
Albert Harding	L. G.	173	20	2	Baker, Ore.
P. Collison	Center	170	23	2	Coquille, Ore.
Carl Mautz	R. G.	195	20	2	Portland, Ore.
Kenneth Bartlett	R. T.	180	24	3	Estacada Ore.
Stan Anderson	R. E.	160	22	2	Portland, Ore.
W. Steers	Quarter	180	23	2	The Dalles, Ore.
V. Jacobberger	L. Half	165	20	2	Portland, Ore.
E. Brandenburg (C)	R. Half	165	22	2	Bandon, Ore.
H. Huntington	Full	175	24	2	The Dalles, Ore.

Line average, 176 lbs.; backs average, 171; team average, 173.

O. A. C.

"Cack" Hubbard	L. E.	158	24	3	Weiser, Idaho
Ozbun Walker	L. T.	200	25	3	Portland, Ore.
Carl Lodell	L. G.	180	24	3	Portland, Ore.
Hayden	Center	187	22	2	Pendleton, Ore.
Clarence Johnson	R. G.	160	24	2	Portland, Ore.
Marion McCart	R. T.	200	21	1	Selma, Calif.
Charles Rose	R. E.	185	24	2	Seattle, Wn.
Henry Reardon (C)	Quarter	150	25	2	Corvallis, Ore.
J. Kasberger	L. Half	175	22	1	The Dalles, Ore.
Albert Hodler	R. Half	170	22	2	Portland, Ore.
George Powell	Full	200	22	2	Portland, Ore.

Line average, 181 lbs.; backs average, 174; team average, 177.

TEAM STATISTICS
AGGIES

Name	Position	Age	No.	Home
Powell (C)	F. B.	23	1	Portland, Ore.
Kasberger	Q.	25	22	The Dalles, Ore.
McFadden	L. E.	20	9	Corvallis, Ore.
Stewart	C.	23	4	Portland, Ore.
Christensen	L. G.	22	14	Stanwood, Wash.
Heyden	R. G.	22	17	Pendleton, Ore
Locey	L. T.	26	25	Weiser, Idaho
Sommers	R. H.	20	2	Lebanon, Ore.
Crowell	R. T.	21	5	Los Angeles, Cal.
McKenna (Hugh)	Q.	24	3	Portland, Ore.
McKenna (Harold)	R. T. & F. B.	24	15	Corvallis, Ore.
Miller	L. H.	19	16	Long Beach, Cal.
Gill	R. H.	22	21	Salem, Ore.
Deigh	R. G.	25	12	Ontario, Cal.
Hagedorn	H. B.	24	11	Salem, Ore.
Jessup	H. B.	21	19	Portland, Ore.
Taylor	G.	23	27	Monroe, Wash.
Garber	Q.	21	18	Freewater, Ore.
Laughery	R. E.	22	8	Payette, Idaho
Winnie	F.	22	29	Ashland, Ore.
Taggert	E.	23	24	Hillsboro, Ore.
Richert	H. B.	21	10	San Diego, Cal.
Tousey	F.	19	30	Portland, Ore.
Michelwait	G.	20	28	Twin Falls, Idaho
Johnson	Q.	24	20	Hood River, Ore.
Garity	E.	23	23	La Grande, Ore.
Simons	E.	24	13	Shedd, Ore.
Giebisch	C.	24	26	Portland, Ore.
Clark	R. G.	22		Salem, Ore.

TEAM STATISTICS
SUNDODGERS

Name	Position		Age	No.	Home
Eckman (C)	Back	L. H.	25	28	Seattle, Wash.
Wilson	Back	Q.	22	1	Seattle, Wash.
Hill	Back	R. H.	23	2	Seattle, Wash.
Langhorn	Back	F. B.	21	3	Bellingham, Wash.
Hall	Back	Q.	20	4	Tacoma, Wash.
Clark	Line	L. T.	21	5	Spokane, Wash.
Ingram	Line	R. T.	21	6	Everett, Wash.
Hobi	Line	L. G.	23	7	Hoquiam, Wash.
Gundlach	Line	R. G.	24	8	Hoquiam, Wash.
Ferry	End	L. E.	22	9	Wallace, Idaho
Gustafson	End	L. E.	23	10	
Galligan	End	R. E.	19	11	Seattle, Wash.
Haynes	Line	C.	24	12	Everett, Wash.
Black	Back		21	13	Seattle, Wash.
Quass	Back		20	14	Wenatchee, Wash.
Smith	Back	F. B.	23	15	Spokane, Wash.
Green	Back	R. H.	19	16	Seattle, Wash.
Zeil	Back	R. H.	21	17	Seattle, Wash.
Lemon	Line	C.	20	18	Port Townsend, Wash.
Warren	Line	R. G.	25	19	Monroe, Wash.
McInroe	Line	R. G.	21	20	Bellingham, Wash.
Keinholz	Line	L. G.	22	21	Walla Walla, Wash.
Tingling	Line	L. T.	27	22	Spokane, Wash.
Ferry	Line		20	23	Seattle, Wash.
Parker	Line	R. E.	21	24	Everett, Wash.
Pitwood	Line	R. T.	21	25	Elma, Wash.
Rogge	Line	L. G.	22	26	Seattle, Wash.
Whitman	Back	F. B.	22	27	Seattle, Wash.

A story from *The Steelhead for December* 1924 is headlined: "Mt. Angel-The Dalles Game."

In one of the most exciting, hardest fought, cleanest games witnessed on the Amotan Field in many a moon, The Dalles whipped Mt. Angel college Saturday afternoon, December 13, by a score of 7 to 0.

It was a game that filled every tensely interested football partisan in The Dalles with triumphant glee. For two hours – all too short – the crowd that turned out to help Ted Gibson in his grim battle for health, reigned in a pandemonium of excitement as the two teams battled with every thing they had in order to win that great game.

Outweighed by 10 to 12 pounds, The Dalles line with perfect teamwork ripped large holes in the Angels' line through which the backs made substantial gains. In the last few minutes of the struggle it looked as if no score was to be made. Three times had The Dalles fought the ball to the Angels' very goal line, but three times they lost it on fumbles. There were three minutes to go, with the ball in Mt. Angel's possession on their own 45-yard line. They had just completed a pretty pass for 30 yards, and then came Cramer's opportunity to make himself a hero.

Mt. Angel's backfield, in attempting a delayed forward pass, got badly mixed. A Dalles lineman broke through and smashed into the man with the ball, jarring it out of his hands. Cramer in the meantime, had gotten through and saw the free ball rolling around. He made a mad scramble for it, got it, and was down the field with every ounce of energy he had for the winning score of the game. A Mt. Angel player almost caught The Dalles' flying hope, but Altermatt got quite awkward at this time and accidentally on purpose got his long, lanky frame interwoven with the other player, both going down in a heap and giving Cramer a clear field for his great chance to score. The feat, considering that Cramer is a guard, was very extraordinary. The other point came along when Cook passed over the goal line to Stone for the extra unit.

The rest of the game was replite [sic] with every football thrill imaginable, Cook was his old self again, and his kicks, twisting and finding their way through the crisp December air, were beautiful to see. Two of them sailed for 55 yards, and several others twisted their way for 45-yard gains.

Mt. Angel got a very lucky break at the very first of the game. The Dalles took the ball on their opponents' 40-yard line and started a march for the goal line. Stone started the heart-breaking attack with a 10-yard gain. Carlson then ripped off 5 yards followed with 6 more. Stone added three more and so, slowly the ball advanced down the field. Fulkerson and Carlson were doing the heavy work and had crashed their way to the 4-yard line and there a mixup in signals prevented a touchdown. [sic] Instead of kicking, Mt. Angel uncorked some brilliant running plays and soon had their goal line in safety.

The Dalles lost another chance to score just before the end of the first half. The locals took the ball on the 15-yard line when Mt. Angel fumbled and Fulkerson recovered for The Dalles. Carlson hit tackle for 5 yards and then followed with three more. The next play was disastrous when The Dalles fumbled and Mt. Angel recovered. The half ended with the ball in their possession.

The other tragedy came in the third quarter. Mt. Angel on her own 10-yard line punted to the 25-yard line. Fulkerson and Carlson carried the ball to the 15-yard line and then Cook passed to Cyphers who caught it but three Mt. Angel players struck him simultaneously knocking the ball out of his arms, thus losing another score for The Dalles.

From start to finish, Mt. Angel was outclassed. Several times they made gallant stands before the terrific smashes of The Dalles' backs but they couldn't keep it up. Only the breaks saved them from a severe drubbing and a Dalles score.

In victory The Dalles stood out as a real football aggregation. The line worked like a well-oiled piece of machinery, and the backs, regular demons on the offensive. In defeat Mt. Angel was always fighting and never giving up for points that wouldn't come.

Cook, Carlson, Fulkerson and Stone, The Dalles backfield were running the ball for good and consistent gains, but just when they got within striking distance of the goal line someone fumbled.

Mt. Angel had an excellent team. However, their only gains were made in the shadow of their own goal line, but in midfield they seemed to lack the punch.

Fumbles were very costly to The Dalles. They lost at least three touchdowns. However, it was a great team that beat Mt. Angel. They were supreme at all stages of the game.

The Lineup:

THE DALLES		MT. ANGEL
Altermatt	LE	W. Walsh
Dizney	LT	T. Buckley
Wickman	LG	A. Salvi
Stadelman	C	P. Hutton
Cramer	RG	L. Greene
Pattee	RT	K. Hardin
Cyphers	RE	McGowan
Cook	Q	Teters
Fulkerson	RH	Kearney
Stone	LH	Spear
Carlson	F	A. Walsh

Substitutions: Mt. Angel, Busch for Buckley; Wymer for Kearney; Kearney for Wymer; McGrath for Spear.

Officials: Referee, Ward; Umpire, Daigh; Head Linesman, Rice; Timekeeper, Huett.

APPENDIX I – MT. ANGEL FIRE LONG VERSION
SEPTEMBER 20, 1926

This fire story comes the Salem *Capital Journal* in its Tuesday, Sept. 21 edition. The front page headline is "MILLION LOSS MT ANGEL FIRE – College and Monastery Are In Ruins – Rare Books and Manuscripts Dating Back to 15th Century Lost – Lack of Water and Stiff Wind Render Efforts to Check Flames Futile." The story follows.

Flames, believed to have started from a short-circuit in a truck in the garage early this morning visited the second devastating conflagration in its history upon Mount Angel college and the Benedictine monastery, inflicting a loss estimated at $1,000,000 in buildings, equipment, rare manuscripts and other valuables housed in the museum and libraries.

No accurate figures as to the amount of insurance carried was available today but it is negligible compared to the loss, it was announced by Father Dominic, priest of the Mt. Angel parrish [sic], following a conference with Abbot Bernard Murphy, O.S.B., head of the institution; Father Maurus, prior of the monastery; and Rev. Alcuin rector of the college.

The story continues with the paragraph heading "BUILDING LOSS $400,000."

The loss on the buildings they estimated at $400,000 and the remainder on equipment, articles in the museum and manuscripts and books in the libraries dating back to the fifteenth century.

Discovered shortly after 12:30 o'clock as it ate its way through the roof of the garage building, the fire, fanned by a stiff south-west wind, spread rapidly to the big frame gymnasium, the nun's house, the chapel, and then to the main building through the seminary wing, reducing each in succession to ashes and heaps of twisted debris, except for the bare stone walls of the main building which today tower over the still smoldering ruins.

Lack of water and the slippery condition of the highways which seriously delayed the arrival of fire fighting apparatus from Salem, Silverton and Woodburn, left the priests, brothers, 200 students, gathered for the opening of the fall term, and hundreds of people from miles around nothing to do but rescue such effects as they could from the advancing flames and stand by and watch the buildings consumed. One three-inch line of hose fed by gravity pressure supplied the only water available.

The flames were discovered in plenty of time to give all sleeping occupants of the buildings ample opportunity to dress and save their personal belongings, except for some of the boys sleeping in the wing adjoining the gymnasium, who lost some clothing. One group of about a dozen students in the south wing slept through the early stages of the fire but were discovered and awakened before the flames had spread to the main building.

Shooting high into the air from the grouped structures on the crest of the College hill, rising 200 feet above the level of the flat valley on all sides, the spectacle of the flames attracted sightseers from the country and the roads and highways leading to the base of the hill were literally jammed with automobiles.

The story continues with the paragraph heading "SCHOOL ABANDONED."

All thoughts of attempting to continue school this year were dismissed as the extent of the damage unfolded under close investigation this morning, and the students who had gathered from all parts of the United States for registration yesterday are today making arrangements to return to their homes. The seminarians studying for the priesthood are being transferred to temporary quarters on the college dairy ranch on Crooked Finger creek in the foothills, 17 miles east of Mt. Angel, where they will continue their studies.

Temporary housing for students, priests and others are being provided in the private homes in the vicinity. The 12 nuns, who made their homes in the nuns' house have been transferred to the convent at the academy at the foot of the hill.

The garage where the fire started was a frame building with a cement floor, large enough to hold eight cars. It faced directly on the wide pavement on the north side of the seminary wing of the main building. Below the garage and reached by way of a roadway on a lower level of the hill was the laundry equipped with all modern washing machines, mangles [sic] and hot air dryers. A cement areaway led from the laundry underneath the pavement to the kitchen in the basement of the northwest corner of the main building. During the school year a total of 500 people were served daily with food cooked in this kitchen. Hundreds and hundreds of dollars in kitchen machinery – vegetable peelers, dish washers, big ranges, bread cutters – had been installed to lighten the work for the nuns who were cooks for the big establishment.

North and east of the garage, 30 or 40 feet distant, was the huge old frame three-story gymnasium, where the fire got its best start. On the first floor were the pool and billiard rooms, the shower rooms, the student body store rooms and a small gymnasium completely equipped with apparatus and mats. A single stairway led to the main basketball floor and handball alleys. A running track and balcony for spectators circled the basketball floor.

Underneath the gymnasium and reached also by a lower level roadway were the furnace rooms which contained the central heating plant for the entire institution, a well equipped bakery where bread and pastry were baked each day for the institution and for the Benedictine Sisters' academy and boarding school for girls a mile away, and a big butcher shop.

From the gymnasium the fire spread rapidly to the small two-story frame house situated in a corner of the athletic field and to one side of the gymnasium. This house was used as a home for the Benedictine nuns, twelve in all, who were cooks and who did the cleaning in the college.

At the same time that the Sisters' house started, the flames attacked the chapel which was situated directly across the roadway from the gymnasium. The sacristy of the chapel where were stored priceless old vestments and mass books, many of them brought from Benedictine monasteries in the old world, started first.

The story continues with the paragraph heading "CHAPEL TREASURERS [sic]."

As soon as it was discovered that the fire might prove serious the monks' and seminarians' first thought was for the sacristy treasures. By the time that the flames reached the chapel many of the oldest and most precious vestments, the chalices of gold, many inlaid with precious stones and equally valuable monstrances had been carried to a place of safety. In the chapel were old mass books of parchment, some of them hundreds of years old and the result of a lifetime's work of the old world monks and brothers. Some of these were saved from the fire but damaged in carrying out.

The chapel contained one of the finest pipe organs in the state. It was the gift of a wealthy New York woman whose son was formerly a student at the college. It was a complete loss as was the beautiful old main altar in the chapel. A number of valuable oil paintings also went.

The story continues with the paragraph heading "MUSEUM DESTROYED."

By the time that the destruction of the chapel was seen to be inevitable the students were busy carrying their personal effects from their rooms and dormitories which occupied the third and fourth floors of the south wing of the main building. School rooms, offices, libraries and museums occupied the first and second floor of the college wing.

The college museum was one of the most complete in the state and in the past attracted visitors from far and wide. Father Frowin, O.S.B., had been curator of the museum for a number of years and had superintended the collection and classification. A complete museum of natural history was included, one of the best collections of coins in the west, dozens and dozens of rare mounted birds, a stamp collection worth hundreds of dollars, a big collection of butterflies and all insects, a number of rare old carvings and curious [sic] from practically every nation on the globe – all went up in flames. So far as could be learned today absolutely nothing was saved from the museum.

Causing the greatest grief to the members of the religious community, however, was the loss of the library in the monastery which occupied the main wing and which was cloistered. Years had been spent in the accumulation of the library and rarely did any of the old priests visit the Benedictine monasteries in Engelberg, Switzerland, the original home of the Mt. Angel monks, the monastery in Subiaco, Monte Christe, Italy, or any of the other old world monasteries of the Benedictine order without bringing back some priceless old volumes for the Mount Angel monastery library. Manuscripts dating back to the fifteenth century, some possibly older, were included in the collection of 20,000 volumes. None were saved.

The story continues with the paragraph heading "HEAD ABBOT RECENT VISITOR."

Only a few weeks ago the Abbott [sic] Primate Felix Von Stotzingen, of Rome, Italy, head of all Benedictine monasteries in the world, was entertained on the hill. He is still in the United States and word of the disaster was sent him immediately this morning.

Local people offered the services of their trucks and cars to carry some of the things salvaged from the college wing, such as ward-robes, dressers, and a few grand pianos, from the places on the side of the hill where they had been hurriedly dumped to a place of safety in empty buildings down town.

The college and monastery were first established at the foot of the hill and were moved to the present location after a similar fire in 1892 wiped out the old buildings.

Decision on what is to be done in the matter of rebuilding will be reached at a conference to be held this afternoon, it was announced.

A related story from same paper and date has the following headline "ARCHBISHOP IN MT. ANGEL ON VISIT" and the brief story is as follows.

Archbishop Edward D. Howard left for the scene immediately upon receipt of the first news from Mt. Angel. Plans for the immediate relief of the famous old school will be discussed with Father Morris, the archbishop stated before his departure. He expressed the belief that ways and means would be found for rebuilding.

APPENDIX J - KNUTE ROCKNE AT OREGON STATE, JULY, 1928

Knute Rockne's 1928 coaches school in Corvallis was recorded by an anonymous writer for Oregon State's alumni magazine, *The Alumnus*. Excerpts from this story come from the July 1928 issue.

'Never let the other fellow know that you don't know anything,' admonished Knute Rockne to a prospective high school football coach. 'If you are not sure keep still and let the other fellow do the talking. But when you do say something say it assertively as though you knew more about it than ald [sic] man Britannica.'

The eminent Notre Dame grid mentor, who has completed his fourth summer coaching school at Oregon State, evidently had this in mind when he took on the *Alumnus* interviewer for a few verbal rounds. Coach Rockne's desk was sandwiched in the same private office along with Coach Paul J. Schissler's but that was as far as privacy went. There were always a group of coaches, would-be coaches, players and the like crowding into the 12 by 12 room along with a couple of roll-tops and a filing cabinet – and a cuspidor. And the latch string was always out. One thing about this tireless man from Indiana – he is always ready with a joke, a quick quip, a helping word or for a friendly chat. The office was an open forum every afternoon from 3 to 5.

The coach looked up as the *Alumnus* representative appeared in the doorway, and remarked that Clipper Smith and he had been worrying about getting their proper amount of publicity for the day as no reporters had shown up before.

Clipper Smith, Gonzaga university coach, played under Rockne as a guard nine or 10 years ago on a team that played practically the whole season with 11 men – only 13 letters being awarded. And so Clipper comes in for plenty of good-natured digs from 'Rock' – and some that are rather barbed. Rockne likes Smith a great deal – he must – for he is always razzing him. But he never admits his fondness. Yet with all of the razzing he is solicitous of Smith's welfare. And probably when the wily old mentor is breathing his final ozone he will accuse Clipper Smith of putting strychnine in his soup to bring about his demise.

But to get back to the details, Slip Madigan of St. Mary's was on hand also; as was Coach Schissler who was busily dictating letters and generally taking the world seriously.

'You'll have world affairs settled in no time,' Rockne fired at Schissler who with knit brows was intensely dictating.

'What are you trying to do pick a fight with me – Dear Mr. Jones, we are in receipt of your letter,' offered Schissler, addressing Rockne and the stenographer in the same breath.

About that time the *Alumnus* got a word in. 'What do you think of . . . ' began the scribe. 'What do I think of the campus?' interrupted Notre Dame's pride. 'I think it is a splendid one. And say, you know, these new buildings are surely going to put it on the map. I can notice a vast difference and improvement just in the four years that I have been coming here to teach at summer session.

'The change has not all been in the physical campus construction either. Your athletics have been building up steadily.'

Just then Dal Ward [Phi Delta Theta], stellar end in 1926, now coaching at Minneapolis, came in and was introduced.

'What is your opinion on scouting?' a happy thought struck the *Alumnus* representative.

'It's a fine thing,' declared Rockne. 'And a natural outgrowth. In any business you are anxious to find out in a square way what your competitor is doing. It helps keep the team on their toes since neither side is exactly playing in the dark. There is nothing in the world wrong with watching an opponent perform in a game.'

'Say Clipper,' turning to Smith, 'the only way in the world to get anywhere is to assert yourself. A coach can either assert himself and be boss or he can lay down and let someone else run things and when he does his days are numbered.'

Along came Lee Bissett, ex-'18 who is now coaching at Oakland Tech High, Oakland, Cal., and dragged Coach Schissler out of the picture.

Earl Peck, ex-'28 who is located at Twin Falls, Idaho, wandered in and confided that he was going to help coach football but had never once played a game in his life. Rockne was all help at once. Five minutes of earnest advice and Peck left prepared to pit his team against Idaho's best preppers.

'A very nice record your Gonzaga eleven turned in last year but don't let an affair like that happen with Mt. St. Charles again.'

And the *Alumnus* reporter departed with Coach Rockne still slinging verbal brickbats at the Gonzaga mentor.

But Rockne can be very serious and in earnest when the occasion warrants. Every morning of the two-week coaching school he worked tirelessly from 8 o'clock until 12 spending all but an hour and half of this lecturing in the class room. With room 323 at the top of the south wing of the Ag building jammed with students Rockne would hold forth cracking out the football lore and telling the how and who of it all. And he did not beg them to take it – he presented it with the confidence of one who has tried his theories and knows they will work.

Generally, he started off with a story – and he can tell stories with the natural ability of the congenital raconteur. One morning it was one as he put it 'to indicate just how long the class could expect to be in session.'

Story excerpt continues three paragraphs later.

Rockne is very much opposed to heavy scrimmage, especially early in the season. Dummy scrimmage, forward pass dummy scrimmage and fundamental drill are the things that he stresses. After the first two or three weeks of training he gives his men actual scrimmage for four or five weeks – but not too much of it. The needless pounding and bruising of excess scrimmage do not meet with favor in Rockne's coaching plan.

After the preliminary training Coach Rockne cuts his squad to about 40 men and he keeps three teams in action each evening. He watches them all. One team will be in actual scrimmage, another in forward-pass dummy scrimmage and another in dummy offensive scrimmage. His one assistant is in direct charge of the actual scrimmage but Rockne fires a stentorian command, suggestion or reproof at all three of the teams from time to time just to let them know as he puts it that he is on the job.

Freshman furnish the opposition for his varsity in actual scrimmage. They are too young and unsophisticated to know enough and not to get in and fight. They all come out wearing their high school monograms, primed to show the world what's what. The reserves and second stringers will not go up against the varsity and suffer pounding, they ease up; but the freshman dig in enthusiastically with their cleats and prepare to do or die. So Coach Rockne uses them for his varsity practice.

Knute Rockne was discussing rugby one day in class so he singled out Art Taafe, '26, who is director of athletic news for Oregon State, and asked him if a certain point were not correct. Taafe used to be quite a rugby star before he left Ireland and fell into the decline. He answered Rockne in the affirmative. 'That's fine,' said Rockne, 'now that I've got a yes-man in the crowd I can go ahead and give my lecture.'

He is always pulling jokes on someone else but they got one on Rockne concerning his golf.

Story excerpt continues two paragraphs later.

Rockne entered the golf tournament for summer session coaches and advanced a couple of rounds. He then confided that he had forfeited to Clipper Smith so that Clipper would have something in which he could say he had beaten Rockne.

Signal practice is no good, according to Coach Rockne. It does absolutely nothing to help the team since all you have is a whole lot of men running to get nowhere. Then, too, the half holds the ball longer than he would in a game and it slows up his reactions so that when he gets into a game he must entirely readjust himself.

No kid glove business figured in Rockne's work. He got into a suit and went right out on the field to actually demonstrate the men [sic].

The Rockne-Schissler course will be given for the fifth consecutive year in the 1929 summer session as Coach Rockne has signed to return.

II. STATISTICAL APPENDIX

APPENDIX A
JOE KASBERGER FOOTBALL PLAYER AT MT. ANGEL COLLEGE (MAC)
ST. BENEDICT, OR

FOOTBALL

OPPOSITION	LOCATION	STATE	FB GAME	FB WIN %	GAME DATE	GAME SITE	SCORE OAC	SCORE OPP	FOOTBALL W	L	T
LEBANON HS	LEBANON	OR	1	100%	___	AWAY	42	0	1	0	0
PACIFIC U	FOREST GROVE	OR	2	50%	10-23	AWAY	7	27	1	1	0
ALBANY COLLEGE	ALBANY	OR	3	67%	11-13	HOME	20	9	2	1	0
OREGON CITY	OREGON CITY	OR	4	75%	___	___	20	0	3	1	0
CHEMAWA?	CHEMAWA	OR	?	–	___	___	–	–	–	–	–
1916 SEASON							89	36	3	1	0
VANCOUVER A.C.	VANCOUVER	WA	5	60%	10-18	HOME	2	6	3	2	0
PACIFIC U	FOREST GROVE	OR	6	50%	10-28	HOME	13	14	3	3	0
WILLAMETTE U	SALEM	OR	7	43%	___	AWAY	0	1	3	4	0
CHEMAWA	CHEMAWA	OR	8	50%	11-18	___	3	0	4	4	0
1917 SEASON			4				18	21	1	3	0

BASKETBALL

OPPOSITION	LOCATION	STATE	BB GAME	BB WIN %	GAME DATE	GAME SITE	SCORE OAC	SCORE OPP	FOOTBALL W	L	T
MOLALLA	MOLALLA	OR	1	100%	12-17	HOME	46	9	1	0	0
WOODBURN A.C.	WOODBURN	OR	2	100%	01-08	HOME	38	23	2	0	0
CHRISTIAN BROTHERS	PORTLAND	OR	3	100%	___	___	55	18	3	0	0
1916-17 SEASON/INCOMPLETE											

APPENDIX B
JOE KASBERGER FOOTBALL PLAYER AT OREGON AGRICULTURAL COLLEGE (OAC) CORVALLIS, OREGON

OPPOSITION NAME	LOCATION	STATE	GAME	WIN %	GAME DATE	GAME SITE	OAC	OPP	FOOTBALL W	L	T
ALUMNI	CORVALLIS	OR	1	0%	___	HOME	0	0	0	0	1
ROOKS (OAC FROSH)	CORVALLIS	OR	2	50%	___	HOME	21	0	1	0	1
PACIFIC U	PACIFIC GROVE	OR	3	67%	___	HOME	46	6	2	0	1
STANFORD	PALO ALTO	CA	4	50%	___	HOME	6	14	2	1	1
CALIFORNIA	BERKELEY	CA	5	40%	___	AWAY	14	21	2	2	1
MULTNOMAH A.C.	PORTLAND	OR	6	33%	___	HOME	0	14	2	3	1
OREGON	EUGENE	OR	7	29%	___	AWAY	0	9	2	4	1
WASHINGTON STATE	PULLMAN	WA	8	38%	___	NEUT	6	0	3	4	1
GONZAGA	SPOKANE	WA	9	44%	___	HOME	50	0	4	4	1
1919 SEASON		4-4-1					143	64			
MULTNOMAH A.C.	PORTLAND	OR	10	40%	___	HOME	0	0	4	4	2
WASHINGTON	SEATTLE	WA	11	45%	___	AWAY	3	0	5	4	2
CALIFORNIA	BERKELEY	CA	12	42%	___	HOME	7	17	5	5	2
WASHINGTON STATE	PULLMAN	WA	13	38%	___	AWAY	0	28	5	6	2
OREGON	EUGENE	OR	14	36%	___	AWAY	0	0	5	6	3
MULTNOMAH A.C.	PORTLAND	OR	15	40%	___	AWAY	10	7	6	6	3
1920 SEASON		2-2-2					20	52			
ROOKS (OAC FROSH)	CORVALLIS	OR	16	44%	___	HOME	68	7	7	6	3
CHEMAWA	CHEMAWA	OR	17	47%	___	HOME	68	0	8	6	3
MULTNOMAH A.C.	PORTLAND	OR	18	44%	___	HOME	7	7	8	6	4
WILLAMETTE	SALEM	OR	19	47%	___	AWAY	54	0	9	6	4
WASHINGTON	SEATTLE	WA	20	50%	___	HOME	24	0	10	6	4
STANFORD	PALO ALTO	CA	21	48%	___	AWAY	7	14	10	7	4
WASHINGTON STATE	PULLMAN	WA	22	45%	___	HOME	3	7	10	8	4
OREGON	EUGENE	OR	23	43%	___	AWAY	0	0	10	8	5
SOUTHERN CALIFORNIA	LOS ANGELES	CA	24	42%	___	AWAY	0	7	10	9	5
1921 SEASON		4-3-2					231	42			

SUMMARY OF JOE'S OAC VARSITY CAREER

		WIN %		OAC	OPP	W	L	T
1919 SEASON		44%		143	64	4	4	1
1920 SEASON		33%		20	52	2	2	2
1921 SEASON		44%		231	42	4	3	2
TOTAL VARSITY CAREER		42%		394	158	10	9	5

APPENDIX PART C
COACH JOE KASBERGER AT MT. ANGEL COLLEGE ST BENEDICT, OR

OPPOSITION NAME	CITY	STATE	GAME	WIN %	GAME DATE	GAME SITE	MAC	OPP	CAREER FOOTBALL W	L	T
HIGHLAND PARK	HIGHLAND PARK	OR	1	100%	10-01	HOME	44	0	1	0	0
UNIV OF OREGON FROSH	EUGENE	OR	2	50%	10-14	HOME	0	7	1	1	0
PACIFIC UNIVERSITY	FOREST GROVE	OR	3	33%	10-21	AWAY	0	67	1	2	0
NORTH PACIFIC DENTAL COLLEGE	PORTLAND	OR	4	50%	10-29	HOME	31	7	2	2	0
AGGIE ROOKS (OAC FROSH)	CORVALLIS	OR	5	40%	11-20	AWAY	0	6	2	3	0
1922 SEASON			5				75	87	2	3	0
ALUMNI	MT ANGEL	OR	6	50%	10-07	HOME	6	0	3	3	0
CHEMAWA INDIANS	CHEMAWA	OR	7	57%	10-13	HOME	18	6	4	3	0
INDEPENDENCE	INDEPENDENCE	OR	8	63%	10-28	AWAY	34	0	5	3	0
HOLY NAME			9	67%	11-18	HOME	20	0	6	3	0
CHEMAWA INDIANS	CHEMAWA	OR	10	70%	11-21	AWAY	7	0	7	3	0
TOLEDO	TOLEDO	OR	11	64%	11-25	AWAY	6	6	7	3	1
1923 SEASON			5-0-1	6			91	12	7	3	1
ALUMNI	MT ANGEL	OR	N/A	64%	10-05	HOME	39	6	7	3	1
HIGHLAND			N/A	64%	10-12	HOME	6	7	7	3	1
CHEMAWA INDIANS	CHEMAWA	OR	N/A	64%	10-18	AWAY	33	0	7	3	1
STAYTON	STAYTON	OR	N/A	64%	10-25	AWAY	6	0	7	3	1
UNIV OF OREGON FROSH	EUGENE	OR	N/A	64%	10-31	HOME	7	19	7	3	1
AGGIE ROOKS (OAC FROSH)	CORVALLIS	OR	N/A	64%	11-15	HOME	0	6	7	3	1

OPPOSITION NAME	CITY	STATE	GAME	WIN %	DATE	SITE	MAC	OPP	W	L	T
INDEPENDENCE	INDEPENDENCE	OR	N/A	64%	11-22	AWAY	13	7	7	3	1
COLUMBIA U(U OF PORTLAND)	PORTLAND	OR	N/A	64%	12-06	AWAY	6	12	7	3	1
THE DALLES HS	THE DALLES	OR	N/A	64%	12-13	AWAY	0	7	7	3	1
1924 SEASON*			4-5-0			9	110	64	7	3	1
CORVALLIS HIGH SCHOOL	CORVALLIS	OR	12	67%	10-03	HOME	9	0	8	3	1
PACIFIC COLLEGE	NEWBERG	OR	13	69%	10-16	HOME	72	0	9	3	1
OREGON NORMAL	MONMOUTH	OR	14	71%	10-21	HOME	29	0	10	3	1
SEATTLE COLLEGE	SEATTLE	WA	15	73%	10-25	AWAY	37	0	11	3	1
ST MARTIN'S COLLEGE	LACEY	WA	16	75%	10-31	AWAY	29	0	12	3	1
OAC ROOKS (FROSH)	CORVALLIS	OR	17	71%	11-06	AWAY	7	28	12	4	1
COLUMBIA U (U OF PORTLAND)	PORTLAND	OR	18	72%	11-22	HOME	16	7	13	4	1
1925 SEASON			6-1-0			7	199	35	13	4	1

COACH JOE KASBERGER
AT MT. ANGEL COLLEGE
BASKETBALL RECORD

OPPOSITION NAME	CITY ST BENEDICT, OR	STATE	GAME	WIN %	GAME DATE	GAME SITE	MAC	OPP	W	L	T
PORTLAND ALUMNI	PORTLAND	OR	1	100%	12-17	HOME	20	14	1	0	0
MOLLALA LEGION	MOLLALA	OR	2	50%	01-14	AWAY	12	16	1	1	0
UNIV OF OREGON FROSH	EUGENE	OR	3	33%	01-20	AWAY	22	39	1	2	0
WOODBURN FIRE	ST PAUL	OR	4	50%	01-28	HOME	47	7	2	2	0
CHEMAWA INDIANS	CHEMAWA	OR	5	60%	02-03	HOME	50	15	3	2	0
SALEM LEGION	SALEM	OR	6	67%	02-13	AWAY	25	10	4	2	0
CHEMAWA INDIANS	CHEMAWA	OR	7	71%	02-15	AWAY	27	12	5	2	0
SILVERTON LEGION	SILVERTON	OR	8	75%	02-18	HOME	25	15	6	2	0
SILVERTON LEGION	SILVERTON	OR	9	67%	02-22	AWAY	16	32	6	3	0
AGGIE ROOKS (OAC FROSH)	CORVALLIS	OR	10	70%	02-23	HOME	41	31	7	3	0
N. PACIFIC DENTAL COLLEGE	PORTLAND	OR	11	73%	02-25	HOME	37	19	8	3	0
N. PACIFIC DENTAL COLLEGE	PORTLAND	OR	12	75%	03-02	AWAY	27	24	9	3	0
TILLAMOOK	TILLAMOOK	OR	13	77%	03-09	AWAY	43	17	10	3	0
WHEELER	WHEELER	OR	14	79%	03-10	AWAY	22	11	11	3	0
1922-23 SEASON			11-3-0			14	414	262	11	3	0
DEAF SCHOOL	————	————	15	80%	01-18	HOME	44	11	12	3	0
KNIGHTS OF COLUMBUS			16	81%	01-27	HOME	33	32	13	3	0
MONMOUTH	MONMOUTH	OR	17	82%	01-29	HOME	45	15	14	3	0
DALLAS	DALLAS	OR	18	83%	02-06	HOME	28	25	15	3	0
CHEMAWA INDIANS	CHEMAWA	OR	19	84%	02-09	AWAY	33	20	16	3	0
CHEMAWA INDIANS	CHEMAWA	OR	20	85%	02-15	HOME	38	14	17	3	0
MONMOUTH	MONMOUTH	OR	21	86%	02-16	AWAY	46	11	18	3	0
C. PORTLAND	PORTLAND	OR	22	82%	02-23	HOME	21	29	18	4	0
N. PORTLAND DENTAL CLINIC	PORTLAND	OR	23	83%	02-29	AWAY	32	30	19	4	0
N. PORTLAND DENTAL CLINIC	PORTLAND	OR	24	83%	03-02	HOME	36	31	20	4	0
SEASIDE	SEASIDE	OR	25	84%	03-07	AWAY	36	18	21	4	0
VANCOUVER STARS	VANCOUVER	WA	26	85%	03-09	AWAY	27	24	22	4	0
COLUMBIA U (U OF PORTLAND)	PORTLAND	OR	27	85%	03-13	AWAY	27	24	23	4	0
COLUMBIA U (U OF PORTLAND)	PORTLAND	OR	28	82%	03-16	HOME	29	34	23	5	0
COLUMBIA U (U OF PORTLAND)	PORTLAND	OR	29	83%	03-20	SALEM	28	27	24	5	0
1923-24 SEASON			13-2-0			15	503	345	24	5	0
DEAF MUTES	SALEM	OR	30	83%	01-24	AWAY	24	9	25	5	0
GERVAIS ACES	GERVAIS	OR	31	84%	01-26	HOME	48	16	26	5	0
OREGON NORMAL	MONMOUTH	OR	32	84%	01-29	HOME	42	11	27	5	0
SEATTLE COLLEGE	SEATTLE	WA	33	85%	02-14	HOME	22	11	28	5	0
GERVAIS ACES	GERVAIS	OR	34	85%	02-15	HOME	42	12	29	5	0
COLLEGE OF PUGET SOUND	TACOMA	WA	35	86%	02-18	HOME	26	21	30	5	0
OREGON NORMAL	MONMOUTH	OR	36	86%	02-20	AWAY	32	15	31	5	0
GRANDE RONDE			37	86%	02-22	HOME	37	14	32	5	0
WOODBURN BL.	WOODBURN	OR	38	87%	02-25	HOME	33	30	33	5	0
PORTLAND A. ST.	PORTLAND	OR	39	87%	03-01	HOME	30	21	34	5	0
SEATTLE COLLEGE	SEATTLE	WA	40	85%	03-07	AWAY	24	30	34	6	0
SEATTLE K. OF C.	SEATTLE	WA	41	85%	03-08	AWAY	32	21	35	6	0
COLUMBIA U (U OF PORTLAND)	PORTLAND	OR	42	83%	03-13	AWAY	28	32	35	7	0
COLUMBIA U (U OF PORTLAND)	PORTLAND	OR	43	81%	03-15	HOME	16	42	35	8	0
1924-25 SEASON			11-3-0			14	436	285	35	8	0
PACIFIC COLLEGE	NEWBERG	OR	44	82%	12-18		43	16	36	8	0
ALUMNI	MT. ANGEL	OR	45	82%	————	————	—	—	37	—	0
NORTHWEST BANK OF PORTLAND	PORTLAND	OR	46	83%	————	————	—	—	38	—	0
LINFIELD COLLEGE	LINFIELD	OR	47	81%	————	————	19	27	38	9	0
ALBANY COLLEGE	ALBANY	OR	48	79%	————	————	26	28	38	10	0
OREGON NORMAL	MONMOUTH	OR	49	80%	————	————	26	21	39	10	0
OREGON NORMAL	MONMOUTH	OR	50	80%	————	————	49	41	40	10	0
ALBANY COLLEGE	ALBANY	OR	51	80%	————	————	34	21	41	10	0
PACIFIC COLLEGE	NEWBERG	OR	52	81%	————	————	52	26	42	10	0
LINFIELD COLLEGE	LINFIELD	OR	53	81%	————	————	20	13	43	10	0
ALBANY COLLEGE	ALBANY	OR	54	81%	————	————	47	20	44	10	0
ST MARTIN'S COLLEGE	LACEY	WA	55	80%	————	AWAY	16	37	44	11	0
SEATTLE COLLEGE	SEATTLE	WA	56	79%	————	AWAY	35	37	44	12	0
SEATTLE COLLEGE	SEATTLE	WA	57	79%	————	HOME	45	42	45	12	0
COLUMBIA U (U OF PORTLAND)	PORTLAND	OR	58	79%	————	HOME	28	13	46	12	0
ST MARTIN'S COLLEGE	LACEY	WA	59	80%	————	HOME	48	20	47	12	0
COLUMBIA U (U OF PORTLAND)	PORTLAND	OR	60	80%	————	AWAY	40	29	48	12	0
1925-26 SEASON			13-4-0			17	528	391	48	12	0

COACH JOE KASBERGER
AT MT. ANGEL COLLEGE
BASEBALL RECORD

OPPOSITION NAME	CITY ST BENEDICT, OR	STATE	GAME	WIN %	GAME DATE	GAME SITE	MAC	OPP	W	L	T
PORTLAND ALUMNI	PORTLAND	OR	1	————	04-08	————	—	—	—	—	—
OREGON AGRICULTURAL COLLEGE (OAC)	CORVALLIS	OR	2	————	04-13	HOME	—	—	—	—	—
OREGON AGRICULTURAL COLLEGE (OAC)	CORVALLIS	OR	3	————	04-14	AWAY	—	—	—	—	—
CHEMAWA INDIANS	CHEMAWA	OR	4	————	04-27	AWAY	—	—	—	—	—
N. PACIFIC DENTAL COLLEGE	PORTLAND	OR	5	————	04-28	AWAY	—	—	—	—	—

N. PACIFIC DENTAL COLLEGE	PORTLAND	OR	6	___	04-28	AWAY	___	___	___	___
VANCOUVER BARRACKS	VANCOUVER	WA	7	___	05-05	HOME	___	___	___	___
WILLAMETTE UNIVERSITY	SALEM	OR	8	___	05-08	HOME	___	___	___	___
VANCOUVER BARRACKS	VANCOUVER	WA	9	___	05-11	AWAY	___	___	___	___
KNIGHTS OF COLUMBUS			10	___	05-13	HOME	___	___	___	___
KNIGHTS OF COLUMBUS			11	___	05-13	HOME	___	___	___	___
N. PACIFIC DENTAL COLLEGE	PORTLAND	OR	12	___	05-17	HOME	___	___	___	___
KELSO ATHLETIC CLUB			13	___	05-19	HOME	___	___	___	___
CHEMAWA INDIANS	CHEMAWA	OR	14	___	05-22	HOME	___	___	___	___
WILLAMETTE UNIVERSITY	SALEM	OR	15	___	05-24	AWAY	___	___	___	___
KELSO ATHLETIC CLUB			16	___	05-27	AWAY	___	___	___	___
N. PACIFIC DENTAL COLLEGE	PORTLAND	OR	17	___	05-30	AWAY	___	___	___	___
WOODBURN ATHLETIC CLUB	ST PAUL	OR	18	___	06-03	AWAY	___	___	___	___
1923 SEASON	**18 GAMES**									
BENSON TECH			19	___	04-05	HOME	___	___	___	___
OREGON AGRICULTURAL COLLEGE (OAC)	CORVALLIS	OR	20	___	04-11	AWAY	___	___	___	___
OREGON AGRICULTURAL COLLEGE (OAC)	CORVALLIS	OR	21	___	04-12	AWAY	___	___	___	___
CHEMAWA INDIANS	CHEMAWA	OR	22	___	04-26	HOME	___	___	___	___
PACIFIC COLLEGE	NEWBERG	OR	23	___	05-09	HOME	___	___	___	___
CHEMAWA INDIANS	CHEMAWA	OR	24	___	05-10	AWAY	___	___	___	___
COLUMBIA U(U OF PORTLAND)	PORTLAND	OR	25	___	05-14	AWAY	___	___	___	___
MULTNOMAH ATHLETIC CLUB	PORTLAND	OR	26	___	05-17	AWAY	___	___	___	___
MULTNOMAH ATHLETIC CLUB	PORTLAND	OR	27	___	05-24	HOME	___	___	___	___
PORTLAND K OF C	PORTLAND	OR	28	___	05-25	HOME	___	___	___	___
MONMOUTH NORMAL	MONMOUTH	OR	29	___	05-28	HOME	___	___	___	___
COLUMBIA U(U OF PORTLAND)	PORTLAND	OR	30	___	06-01	HOME	___	___	___	___
MONMOUTH NORMAL	MONMOUTH	OR	31	___	06-04	AWAY	___	___	___	___
1924 SEASON	**13 GAMES**									
GERVAIS BLUES	GERVAIS	OR	32	___	04-07		___	___	___	___
PACIFIC COLLEGE	NEWBERG	OR	33	___	04-24		___	___	___	___
GERVAIS BLUES	GERVAIS	OR	34	___	04-30		___	___	___	___
OREGON NORMAL	MONMOUTH	OR	35	___	05-02		___	___	___	___
OREGON STATE PEN.		OR	36	___	05-09		___	___	___	___
COLUMBIA U(U OF PORTLAND)	PORTLAND	OR	37	___	05-16		___	___	___	___
COLLEGE OF PUGET SOUND	TACOMA	WA	38	___	05-20		___	___	___	___
SEATTLE COLLEGE	SEATTLE	WA	39	___	05-23		___	___	___	___
ST MARTIN'S COLLEGE	LACEY	WA	40	___	05-24	HOME	___	___	___	___
OREGON NORMAL	MONMOUTH	OR	41	___	05-29		___	___	___	___
COLUMBIA U(U OF PORTLAND)	PORTLAND	OR	42	___	06-03		___	___	___	___
1925 SEASON	**11 GAMES**									
ALBANY COLLEGE	ALBANY	OR	43				___	___	___	___
OREGON NORMAL	MONMOUTH	OR	44				___	___	___	___
LINFIELD COLLEGE	McMINNVILLE	OR	45				___	___	___	___
PACIFIC COLLEGE	NEWBERG	OR	46				___	___	___	___
ALBANY COLLEGE	ALBANY	OR	47				___	___	___	___
OREGON NORMAL	MONMOUTH	OR	48				___	___	___	___
LINFIELD COLLEGE	McMINNVILLE	OR	49				___	___	___	___
PACIFIC COLLEGE	NEWBERG	OR	50				___	___	___	___
1926 SEASON/INCOMPLETE/UNSEQUENCED	8+ GAMES?						___	___	___	___

JOE KASBERGER CAREER SUMMARY - MAC

1923 BASEBALL	18 GAMES
1924 BASEBALL	13 GAMES
1925 BASEBALL	11 GAMES
1926 BASEBALL/INCOMPLETE-OUT OF SEQ.	8+ GAMES?
TOTAL 1923-26 RECORD	

JOE KASBERGER CAREER SUMMARY - MAC

		W	L	T
1922 FOOTBALL RECORD	40%	2	3	0
1923 FOOTBALL RECORD	83%	5	0	1
1924 FOOTBALL RECORD*	44%	4*	5*	0*
1925 FOOTBALL RECORD	86%	6	1	0
TOTAL RECORD 1922,23,25 RECORD	72%	13	4	1

JOE KASBERGER CAREER SUMMARY-MAC

		W	L	T
1922-23 BASKETBALL	79%	11	3	0
1923-24 BASKETBALL	87%	13	2	0
1924-25 BASKETBALL	79%	11	3	0
1925-26 BASKETBALL/NOT IN SEQUENCE	77%	13	4	0
TOTAL 1922-26 RECORD	80%	48	12	0

JOE KASBERGER CAREER SUMMARY - MAC

	W	L	T
1922,23,25 FOOTBALL	13	4	1
1922-26 BASKETBALL	48	12	0
1923-26 BASEBALL			
TOTAL 1922-26 RECORD	61	16	1

APPENDIX D
**JOE KASBERGER HEAD BASKETBALL
COACH AT MT ANGEL ACADEMY & NORMAL SCHOOL**

SCHOOL - OPPOSITION	CITY	STATE	GAME	WIN %	GAME DATE	GAME SITE	MAA	OPP	W	L	T
MOLLALA HIGH	MOLLALA	OR	1	100%	___		20	13	1	0	0
MOLLALA HIGH	MOLLALA	OR	2	100%	___	HOME	46	34	2	0	0
MOLLALA HIGH	MOLLALA	OR	3	100%	___	AWAY	36	13	3	0	0
SCIO HIGH			4	100%	___	HOME	31	21	4	0	0
GERVAIS	GERVAIS	OR	5	100%	___	AWAY	27	12	5	0	0
GERVAIS HIGH	GERVAIS	OR	6	100%	___	HOME	58	15	6	0	0
ST HELEN'S HALL			7	100%	___	HOME	36	13	7	0	0
HOLY CHILD ACADEMY	PORTLAND	OR	8	100%	___	HOME	74	7	8	0	0
OREGON CITY WOOLEN MILLS	OREGON CITY	OR	9	100%	___	HOME	26	24	9	0	0
OREGON CITY	OREGON CITY	OR	10	90%	___	AWAY	15	30	9	1	0
1927-28 SEASON							369	182	9	1	0

JOE KASBERGER ASS'T FOOTBALL COACH
AT WILLAMETTE UNIV FOR SPEC KEENE — SALEM, OREGON

OPPOSITION NAME	CITY	STATE	GAME	WIN %	GAME DATE	GAME SITE	WU	OPP	W	L	T
WASHINGTON	SEATTLE	WA	1	0%	___	___	6	32	0	1	0
OREGON NORMAL	MONMOUTH	OR	2	50%	___	___	28	0	1	1	0
PUGET SOUND	TACOMA	WA	3	33%	___	___	6	6	1	1	1
COLLEGE OF IDAHO	CALDWELL	ID	4	25%	___	___	0	6	1	2	1
CHEMAWA	CHEMAWA	OR	5	20%	___	___	6	6	1	2	2
PACIFIC	FOREST GROVE	OR	6	33%	___	___	13	7	2	2	2
LINFIELD	McMINNVILLE	OR	7	43%	___	___	12	6	3	2	2
WHITMAN	WALLA WALLA	WA	8	38%	___	___	7	31	3	3	2
1927 SEASON	3-3-2						78	94			
WHITMAN	WALLA WALLA	WA	9	33%	___	___	0	45	3	4	2
LINFIELD	McMINNVILLE	OR	10	40%	___	___	36	0	4	4	2
PUGET SOUND	TACOMA	WA	11	45%	___	___	25	18	5	4	2
PACIFIC	FOREST GROVE	OR	12	42%	___	___	0	6	5	5	2
COLLEGE OF IDAHO	CALDWELL	ID	13	38%	___	___	6	44	5	6	2
OREGON	EUGENE	OR	14	36%	___	___	6	38	5	7	2
WASHINGTON	SEATTLE	WA	15	33%	___	___	0	28	5	8	2
ALBANY	ALBANY	OR	16	38%	___	___	38	6	6	8	2
1928 SEASON	3-5-0						111	185			

JOE KASBERGER ASS'T FOOTBALL COACH
AT SOUTHERN OREGON STATE COLLEGE — ASHLAND, OR
FOR ROY MCNEAL - OPPOSITION

OPPOSITION	CITY	STATE	GAME	WIN %	GAME DATE	GAME SITE	SON	OPP	W	L	T
MENLO PARK JUNIOR COLLEGE	MENLO PARK	CA	1	0%	___	HOME	12	20	0	1	0
MARIN JUNIOR COLLEGE	MARIN	CA	2	0%	___	HOME	6	19	0	2	0
WESTERN OREGON	MONMOUTH	OR	3	0%	___	AWAY	0	0	0	2	1
SACRAMENTO JUNIOR COLLEGE	SACRAMENTO	CA	4	0%	___	AWAY	7	62	0	3	1
CHICO STATE	CHICO	CA	5	20%	___	HOME	20	7	1	3	1
HUMBOLDT STATE	HUMBOLDT	CA	6	33%	___	HOME	27	7	2	3	1
MODESTO JUNIOR COLLEGE	MODESTO	CA	7	29%	___	HOME	12	18	2	4	1
1929 SEASON							84	133	2	4	1

APPENDIX G - SUMMARY OF FOOTBALL AND BASEBALL RESULTS BY SCHOOL YEAR, JOE KASBERGER, ST. BENEDICT'S PREP, NEWARK, NJ

School Year	TOTAL			FOOTBALL			POINTS		BASEBALL			RUNS	
	Win	Lose	Tie	Win	Lose	Tie	SBP	OPP	Win	Lose	Tie	SBP	OPP
1930-31	13	4	0	5	2	0	110	22	8	2	0	104	30
1931-32	20	3	1	8	0	1	189	19	12	3	0	110	59
1932-33*	17	5	0	6	1	0	165	13	11	4	0	137	73
1933-34	17	4	1	7	1	1	204	20	10	3	0	106	54
1934-35	16	2	1	7	0	1	133	0	9	2	0	122	50
1935-36	19	3	0	6	1	0	120	19	13	2	0	128	42
1936-37	28	0	0	9	0	0	245	0	19	0	0	230	60
1937-38	17	5	1	6	0	1	143	13	11	5	0	126	56
1938-39	21	5	1	4	1	1	67	32	17	4	0	188	103
1939-40	20	6	2	3	3	2	78	33	17	3	0	187	44
1940-41	22	3	3	6	2	1	119	46	16	1	2	166	75
1941-42	25	4	0	6	3	0	91	42	19	1	0	200	39
1942-43	23	1	0	7	0	0	206	19	16	1	0	121	21
1943-44*	18	0	1	2	0	0	12	0	16	0	1	143	20
1944-45	11	4	0	2	2	0	44	44	9	2	0	93	27
1945-46	17	6	0	3	3	0	69	100	14	3	0	136	57
1946-47	25	0	0	7	0	0	245	38	18	0	0	153	28
1947-48	26	1	1	6	1	1	221	45	20	0	0	200	35
1948-49	29	1	1	7	1	1	199	32	22	0	0	240	36
1949-50	28	3	0	9	0	0	308	48	19	3	0	241	37
1950-51	22	2	1	6	0	1	192	57	16	2	0	183	43
1951-52	17	7	0	4	2	0	129	46	13	5	0	121	55
1952-53	19	7	0	3	4	0	76	123	16	3	0	124	44
1953-54	21	7	0	6	1	0	174	54	15	6	0	130	51
1954-55	23	6	0	7	0	0	210	44	16	6	0	198	61
1955-56	14	15	1	0	7	1	33	207	14	8	0	94	59
1956-57	21	5	0	7	2	0	285	65	14	3	0	149	51
1957-58	21	7	1	7	1	1	217	88	14	6	0	117	59
1958-59*	25	7	0	7	1	0	211	82	18	6	0	177	91
1959-60	28	6	0	7	1	0	162	53	21	5	0	163	78
1960-61	23	6	0	5	3	0	182	98	18	3	0	96	39
1961-62	23	7	0	3	4	0	169	194	20	3	0	188	64
1962-63	27	4	1	6	1	1	193	107	21	3	0	149	61
1963-64	30	6	0	5	3	0	192	113	25	3	0	232	66
1964-65	18	13	0	2	6	0	92	176	16	7	0	146	86
1965-66	17	15	0	6	3	0	141	96	11	12	0	109	69
1966-67*	19	12	1	3	5	1	120	149	16	7	0	31	19
1967-68	13	10	0	-	-	-	-	-	13	10	0	149	90
TOTAL	793	202	18	200	65	15	5746	2337	593	137	3	5687	2032

*Incomplete game scores

APPENDIX H - JOE KASBERGER'S RECORD AT ST. BENEDICT'S PREP, NEWARK, NJ - WITH AND WITHOUT PGs AND FOR HIS CAREER

Football With PGs 1930 - 1951

WINS: 126
LOSSES: 23
TIES: 11
SEASONS: 22
WINNING PERCENTAGE: 79%
POINTS SCORED: 3289
POINTS ALLOWED: 688
AVERAGE SCORE: 21-4
SHUTOUTS FOR: 88
SHUTOUTS AGAINST: 16
BEST WIN-LOSS SEASON: 9-0-0/1936
MOST POINTS SCORED/YEAR-FOR: 308/1949
MOST POINTS SCORED/YEAR-AGAINST: 100/1945
BEST WINNING PERCENTAGE SEASON: 100%/1936, 42, 43, 46, 49
WORST WINNING PERCENTAGE SEASON: 38%/1939
LONGEST WIN STREAK: 13/1935-37
LONGEST LOSS STREAK: 2/1939, 45
GAMES WITHOUT SCORE KNOWN: 2/1932, 43
STATE CHAMPIONSHIPS: 4/1934, 35, 42, 46
MOST FREQUENT OPPONENT: 9/Bordentown Military Institute, Bordentown, NJ
WORST LOSS MARGIN: 0-33/1945-LaSalle Military Academy, Oakdale, NY and USMA Plebes, West Point, NY in consecutive games
LARGEST WIN MARGIN: 75-0/1937-Lincoln College Prep, Location Unknown
AVERAGE SEASON WINS: 6
AVERAGE SEASON LOSSES: 1
AVERAGE SEASON TIES: 1
MOST GAMES/SEASON: 9/1931, 33, 36, 40, 41, 48, 49
LEAST GAMES/SEASON: 2/1943
MOST POINTS SCORED/GAME-FOR: 75/1937-Lincoln College Prep, Location Unknown
MOST POINTS SCORED/GAME-AGAINST: 33/1945-0-33/1945-LaSalle Military Academy, Oakdale, NY and USMA Plebes, West Point, NY in consecutive games
NUMBER OF DIFFERENT OPPONENTS: 68
AVERAGE SCORE WHEN SBP WON: 25-3
AVERAGE SCORE WHEN SBP LOST: 3-14
AVERAGE SCORE WHEN SBP TIED: 5-5

APPENDIX I - JOE KASBERGER'S RECORD AT ST. BENEDICT'S PREP, NEWARK, NJ - WITH AND WITHOUT PGs AND FOR HIS CAREER

Baseball With PGs 1931 - 1952

WINS: 325
LOSSES: 46
TIES: 3
SEASONS: 22
WINNING PERCENTAGE: 87%
RUNS SCORED: 3435
RUNS ALLOWED: 1044
AVERAGE SCORE: 9-3
SHUTOUTS FOR: 89
SHUTOUTS AGAINST: 7
BEST WIN-LOSS SEASON: 22-0-0/1949
MOST RUNS SCORED/YEAR-FOR: 241/1950
MOST RUNS SCORED/YEAR-AGAINST: 103/1939
BEST WINNING PERCENTAGE SEASON: 100%/1937, 47, 48, 49
WORST WINNING PERCENTAGE SEASON: 69%/1938
LONGEST WIN STREAK: 64/1947-50
LONGEST LOSS STREAK: 5/2 consecutive losses in 1932, 34, 35, 38, 51
GAMES WITHOUT SCORE KNOWN: 0
STATE CHAMPIONSHIPS: 6/1931, 32, 33, 34, 37, 47
MOST FREQUENT OPPONENT: 26/Pennington School, Pennington, NJ
WORST LOSS MARGIN: 2-10/1934/Dickinson HS, Jersey City, NJ
LARGEST WIN MARGIN: 28-0/1937/Arts HS, Newark, NJ
AVERAGE SEASON WINS: 15
AVERAGE SEASON LOSSES: 2
AVERAGE SEASON TIES: 0
MOST GAMES/SEASON: 22/1949, 50
LEAST GAMES/SEASON 10/1931
MOST RUNS SCORED/GAME-FOR: 28/1937/Arts HS, Newark, NJ
MOST RUNS SCORED/GAME-AGAINST: 16/1935/ Nutley HS, Nutley, NJ
NUMBER OF DIFFERENT OPPONENTS: 74
AVERAGE SCORE WHEN SBP WON: 10-2
AVERAGE SCORE WHEN SBP LOST: 3-6
AVERAGE SCORE WHEN SBP TIED: 4-4

APPENDIX J - JOE KASBERGER'S RECORD AT ST. BENEDICT'S PREP, NEWARK, NJ - WITH AND WITHOUT PGs AND FOR HIS CAREER

Football Without PGs 1952 - 1966

WINS: 74

LOSSES: 42

TIES: 4

SEASONS: 15

WINNING PERCENTAGE: 62%

POINTS SCORED: 2457

POINTS ALLOWED: 1649

AVERAGE SCORE: 20-14

SHUTOUTS FOR: 20

SHUTOUTS AGAINST: 10

BEST WIN-LOSS SEASON: 7-0-0/1954

MOST POINTS SCORED/YEAR-FOR: 285/1956

MOST POINTS SCORED/YEAR-AGAINST: 207/1955

BEST WINNING PERCENTAGE SEASON: 100%/1954

WORST WINNING PERCENTAGE SEASON: 0%/1955

LONGEST WIN STREAK: 5/1962

LONGEST LOSS STREAK: 4/1955

GAMES WITHOUT SCORE KNOWN: 0

STATE CHAMPIONSHIPS: 0

MOST FREQUENT OPPONENT: 12/Central HS, Newark, NJ

WORST LOSS MARGIN: 0-47/1955-Bordentown Military Institute, Bordentown, NJ

LARGEST WIN MARGIN: 46-0/1956-Queen of Peace HS, North Arlington, NJ

AVERAGE SEASON WINS: 5

AVERAGE SEASON LOSSES: 3

AVERAGE SEASON TIES: 0

MOST GAMES/SEASON: 9/1956, 57, 65, 66

LEAST GAMES/SEASON: 7/1952, 53, 54, 61

MOST POINTS SCORED/GAME-FOR: 54/1956-Pingry School, Martinsville, NJ

MOST POINTS SCORED/GAME-AGAINST: 48/1961-Lawrenceville School, Lawrenceville, NJ

NUMBER OF DIFFERENT OPPONENTS: 33

AVERAGE SCORE WHEN SBP WON: 27-8

AVERAGE SCORE WHEN SBP LOST: 10-25

AVERAGE SCORE WHEN SBP TIED: 8-8

APPENDIX K - JOE KASBERGER'S RECORD AT ST. BENEDICT'S PREP, NEWARK, NJ - WITH AND WITHOUT PGs AND FOR HIS CAREER

Baseball Without PGs 1953 - 1968

WINS: 268
LOSSES: 91
TIES: 0
SEASONS: 16
WINNING PERCENTAGE: 75%
RUNS SCORED: 2252
RUNS ALLOWED: 988
AVERAGE SCORE: 6-3
SHUTOUTS FOR: 66
SHUTOUTS AGAINST: 11
BEST WIN-LOSS SEASON: 25-3-0/1964
MOST RUNS SCORED/YEAR-FOR: 232/1964
MOST RUNS SCORED/YEAR-AGAINST: 91/1959
BEST WINNING PERCENTAGE SEASON: 89%/1964
WORST WINNING PERCENTAGE SEASON: 48%/1966
LONGEST WIN STREAK: 11/1964
LONGEST LOSS STREAK: 4/1966
GAMES WITHOUT SCORE KNOWN: 1/1959; 16/1967
STATE CHAMPIONSHIPS: 1/1960
MOST FREQUENT OPPONENT: 22/Bordentown Military Institute,
 Bordentown, NJ
WORST LOSS MARGIN: 0-10/1965-Essex Catholic HS, East Orange, NJ
LARGEST WIN MARGIN: 28-2/1958-St Rose HS, Belmar, NJ
AVERAGE SEASON WINS: 17
AVERAGE SEASON LOSSES: 6
AVERAGE SEASON TIES: 0
MOST GAMES/SEASON: 28/1964
LEAST GAMES/SEASON: 17/1957
MOST RUNS SCORED/GAME-FOR: 28/1953-Eastern Military Academy, Cold
 Spring Harbor, NY and 1960-St. Rose HS, Belmar, NJ
MOST RUNS SCORED/GAME-AGAINST: 15/1954-Bordentown Military
 Institute, Bordentown, NJ
NUMBER OF DIFFERENT OPPONENTS: 59
AVERAGE SCORE WHEN SBP WON: 8-2
AVERAGE SCORE WHEN SBP LOST: 2-5
AVERAGE SCORE WHEN SBP TIED: N/A

APPENDIX L - JOE KASBERGER'S RECORD AT ST. BENEDICT'S PREP, NEWARK, NJ - WITH AND WITHOUT PGs AND FOR HIS CAREER

Football Career 1930 - 1966

CAREER WINS: 200
CAREER LOSSES: 65
CAREER TIES: 15
CAREER SEASONS: 37
CAREER WINNING PERCENTAGE: 72%
CAREER POINTS SCORED: 5746
CAREER POINTS ALLOWED: 2337
CAREER AVERAGE SCORE: 21-8
CAREER SHUTOUTS FOR: 107
CAREER SHUTOUTS AGAINST: 27
CAREER BEST WIN-LOSS SEASON: 9-0-0/1936, 49
CAREER MOST POINTS SCORED/YEAR-FOR: 308/1949
CAREER MOST POINTS SCORED/YEAR-AGAINST: 207/1955
CAREER BEST WINNING PERCENTAGE SEASON: 100%/1936, 49, 54
CAREER WORST WINNING PERCENTAGE SEASON: 0%/1955
CAREER LONGEST WIN STREAK: 13/1935-37, 1953-54
CAREER LONGEST LOSS STREAK: 4/1955
CAREER GAMES WITHOUT SCORE KNOWN: 3/1932, 41, 43
CAREER STATE CHAMPIONSHIPS: 4/1934, 35, 42, 46
CAREER MOST FREQUENT OPPONENT: 16/Bordentown Military Institute, Bordentown, NJ and Seton Hall Prep, West Orange, NJ
CAREER WORST LOSS MARGIN: 0-47/1955, Bordentown Military Institute, Bordentown, NJ
CAREER LARGEST WIN MARGIN: 75-0/1937-Lincoln College Prep, Location Unknown
CAREER AVERAGE SEASON WINS: 5
CAREER AVERAGE SEASON LOSSES: 2
CAREER AVERAGE SEASON TIES: 0
CAREER MOST GAMES/SEASON: 9/1931, 33, 36, 40, 41, 48, 49, 56, 57, 65, 66
CAREER LEAST GAMES/SEASON: 2/1943
CAREER MOST POINTS SCORED/GAME-FOR: 75/1937-Lincoln College Prep, Location Unknown
CAREER MOST POINTS SCORED/GAME-AGAINST: 48/1961-Lawrenceville School, Lawrenceville, NJ
CAREER NUMBER OF DIFFERENT OPPONENTS: 87
CAREER AVERAGE SCORE WHEN SBP WON: 26-4
CAREER AVERAGE SCORE WHEN SBP LOST: 7-21
CAREER AVERAGE SCORE WHEN SBP TIED: 6-6

APPENDIX M - JOE KASBERGER'S RECORD AT ST. BENEDICT'S PREP, NEWARK, NJ - WITH AND WITHOUT PGs AND FOR HIS CAREER

Baseball Career 1931 - 1968

CAREER WINS: 593
CAREER LOSSES: 137
CAREER TIES: 3
CAREER SEASONS: 38
CAREER WINNING PERCENTAGE: 81%
CAREER RUNS SCORED: 5687
CAREER RUNS ALLOWED: 2032
CAREER AVERAGE SCORE: 8-3
CAREER SHUTOUTS FOR: 157
CAREER SHUTOUTS AGAINST: 18
CAREER BEST WIN-LOSS SEASON: 22-0-0/1949
CAREER MOST RUNS SCORED/YEAR-FOR: 241/1950
CAREER MOST RUNS SCORED/YEAR-AGAINST: 103/1939
CAREER BEST WINNING PERCENTAGE SEASON: 100%/1949
CAREER WORST WINNING PERCENTAGE SEASON: 48%/1966
CAREER LONGEST WIN STREAK: 64/1947-50
CAREER LONGEST LOSS STREAK: 4/1966
CAREER GAMES WITHOUT SCORE KNOWN: 17/1959,1967
CAREER STATE CHAMPIONSHIPS: 6/1932, 34, 35, 38, 47, 60
CAREER MOST FREQUENT OPPONENT: 41/Pennington School, Pennington, NJ
CAREER WORST LOSS MARGIN: 0-10/1965-Essex Catholic HS, Newark, NJ
CAREER LARGEST WIN MARGIN: 28-0/1937-Arts HS, Newark, NJ
CAREER AVERAGE SEASON WINS: 16
CAREER AVERAGE SEASON LOSSES: 4
CAREER AVERAGE SEASON TIES: 0
CAREER MOST GAMES/SEASON: 28/1964
CAREER LEAST GAMES/SEASON: 10/1931
CAREER MOST RUNS SCORED/GAME-FOR: 28/1937,53,58-Arts HS, Eastern Military Academy, and St Rose HS
CAREER MOST RUNS SCORED/GAME-AGAINST: 16/1935-Nutley HS
CAREER NUMBER OF DIFFERENT OPPONENTS: 101
CAREER AVERAGE SCORE WHEN SBP WON: 9-2
CAREER AVERAGE SCORE WHEN SBP LOST: 3-6
CAREER AVERAGE SCORE WHEN SBP TIED: 4-4

JOE KASBERGER AT ST. BENEDICT'S PREP
BASEBALL & FOOTBALL — NEWARK, NJ

	OPPOSITION NAME	LOCATION	STATE	TOTAL W	L	T	BASEBALL W	L	T	FOOTBALL W	L	T
1	Admiral Farragut Academy	Pine Beach	NJ	34	1	1	28	1	1	6	0	0
2	Allentown Prep	Allentown	PA	1	1	1	0	0	0	1	1	1
3	Alumni	Newark	NJ	5	0	0	5	0	0	0	0	0
4	Aquinas Institute	Rochester	NY	1	1	1	0	0	0	1	1	1
5	Archbishop Walsh HS	Irvington	NJ	6	0	0	6	0	0	0	0	0
6	Archmere Academy	Claymont	DE	2	0	0	0	0	0	2	0	0
7	Arts HS	Newark	NJ	4	1	0	4	1	0	0	0	0
8	Barringer HS	Newark	NJ	13	2	0	11	2	0	2	0	0
9	Bayley Ellard HS	Madison	NJ	5	0	0	4	0	0	1	0	0
10	Bayonne HS	Bayonne	NJ	0	1	0	0	1	0	0	0	0
11	Belleville HS	Belleville	NJ	4	3	0	4	3	0	0	0	0
12	Bergen Catholic HS	Oradell	NJ	1	3	0	1	2	0	0	1	0
13	Blair Academy	Blairstown	NJ	14	4	0	8	2	0	6	2	0
14	Bloomfield HS	Bloomfield	NJ	1	0	0	1	0	0	0	0	0
15	Bloomfield Tech HS	Bloomfield	NJ	3	0	0	3	0	0	0	0	0
16	Bordentown Military Institute	Bordentown	NJ	29	23	3	24	15	0	5	8	3
17	Brown Prep	Philadelphia	PA	8	0	0	1	0	0	7	0	0
18	Bullis School	Potomac	MD	0	2	0	0	0	0	0	2	0
19	Camp Kilmer	New Brunswick	NJ	1	0	0	0	0	0	1	0	0
20	Carteret Academy	Short Hills	NJ	13	1	1	11	1	0	2	0	1
21	Central HS	Newark	NJ	21	4	0	10	3	0	11	1	0
22	City College of NY Frosh	New York	NY	1	0	0	0	0	0	1	0	0
23	Columbia University Frosh	New York	NJ	8	2	1	3	1	0	5	1	1
24	Concordia Prep			1	1	0	1	1	0	0	0	0
25	Cook Academy	Upper NY State	NY	0	1	0	0	0	0	0	1	0
26	Curtis HS		NY	0	0	1	0	0	0	0	0	1
27	Dickinson HS	Jersey City	NJ	16	4	0	14	4	0	2	0	0
28	Don Bosco Prep	Ramsey	NJ	8	3	0	8	2	0	0	1	0
29	East Orange HS	East Orange	NJ	13	3	0	12	0	0	1	3	0
30	East Side HS	Newark	NJ	13	8	0	8	5	0	5	3	0
31	East Stroudsburg College JV	E Stroudsburg	PA	2	0	1	0	0	0	2	0	1
32	Eastern Military Academy	Cold Spring Harbor	NY	9	2	0	6	1	0	3	1	0
33	Essex Catholic HS	East Orange	NJ	14	6	0	11	4	0	3	2	0
34	Fair Lawn HS	Fair Lawn	NJ	2	1	1	0	0	0	2	1	1
35	Ferris HS	Jersey City	NJ	2	0	0	2	0	0	0	0	0
36	Florence HS	Florence	NJ	1	0	0	1	0	0	0	0	0
37	Fordham University JV	Bronx	NY	1	0	0	0	0	0	1	0	0
38	Fort Dix	Fort Dix	NJ	1	0	0	0	0	0	1	0	0
39	Good Counsel HS	Newark	NJ	1	0	0	1	0	0	0	0	0
40	Hanover Park HS	Hanover Park	NJ	1	0	0	1	0	0	0	0	0
41	Harrison HS	Harrison	NJ	11	0	1	6	0	0	5	0	1
42	Hillside HS	Hillside	NJ	1	0	0	1	0	0	0	0	0
43	Hofstra College Frosh	Hempstead	NY	3	0	0	0	0	0	3	0	0
44	Holy Trinity HS	Hackensack	NJ	1	0	0	1	0	0	0	0	0
45	Hun School	Princeton	NJ	3	1	0	1	0	0	2	1	0
46	Immaculate Conception HS	Montclair	NJ	6	1	0	6	0	0	0	1	0
47	Irvington HS	Irvington	NJ	7	0	0	7	0	0	0	0	0
48	Kingsley School	Brooklyn	NY	3	0	0	2	0	0	1	0	0
49	LaSalle Military Academy	Oakdale	NY	8	3	1	5	1	1	3	2	0
50	Lawrenceville School	Lawrenceville	NJ	5	5	0	5	3	0	0	2	0
51	Lehigh University Frosh	Bethlehem	PA	1	0	0	0	0	0	1	0	0
52	Lincoln College Prep			1	0	0	0	0	0	1	0	0
53	Livingston HS	Livingston	NJ	2	0	0	2	0	0	0	0	0
54	Lyndhurst HS	Lyndhurst	NJ	5	0	0	5	0	0	0	0	0
55	Mackenzie School		NY	2	0	0	1	0	0	1	0	0
56	Madison HS	Madison	NJ	1	0	0	1	0	0	0	0	0
57	Manhattan College Frosh	New York	NY	3	1	0	0	0	0	3	1	0
58	Marianapolis Prep	Thompson	CT	3	1	0	0	0	0	3	1	0
59	Montclair Academy	Montclair	NJ	10	1	0	8	1	0	2	0	0
60	Montclair HS	Montclair	NJ	1	1	0	1	1	0	0	0	0
61	Montclair State Coll Frosh	Upper Montclair	NJ	1	0	0	1	0	0	0	0	0
62	Montclair State College JV	Upper Montclair	NJ	7	0	0	6	0	0	1	0	0
63	Mt. St. Michael Prep	Bronx	NY	3	0	0	0	0	0	3	0	0
64	Muhlenberg College Frosh	Allentown	PA	1	0	0	0	0	0	1	0	0
65	New Brunswick HS	New Brunswick	NJ	3	0	0	1	0	0	2	0	0
66	New York Military Academy	Cornwall-on-Hudson	NY	10	1	0	4	0	0	6	1	0
67	Newark Academy	Livingston	NJ	10	1	0	8	1	0	2	0	0
68	Newark College of Eng Frosh	Newark	NJ	3	0	0	3	0	0	0	0	0
69	Newark University JV	Newark	NJ	1	0	0	1	0	0	0	0	0
70	Newark Vo-Tech HS	Newark	NJ	24	0	0	24	0	0	0	0	0
71	Newman School	Lakewood	NJ	4	0	0	4	0	0	0	0	0
72	North Bergen HS	North Bergen	NJ	0	3	0	0	1	0	0	2	0
73	Nutley HS	Nutley	NJ	4	4	0	4	4	0	0	0	0

JOE KASBERGER AT ST. BENEDICT'S PREP
BASEBALL & FOOTBALL — NEWARK, NJ

	OPPOSITION NAME	LOCATION	STATE	TOTAL W	L	T	BASEBALL W	L	T	FOOTBALL W	L	T
74	NY Stock Exchange	New York	NY	0	1	0	0	1	0	0	0	0
75	Orange HS	Orange	NJ	5	1	0	5	1	0	0	0	0
76	Oratory Prep	Summit	NJ	2	0	0	0	0	0	2	0	0
77	Our Lady of the Valley HS	Orange	NJ	25	3	0	23	3	0	2	0	0
78	Panzer College Frosh	East Orange	NJ	2	1	0	2	1	0	0	0	0
79	Parsippany HS	Parsippany	NJ	1	3	0	1	3	0	0	0	0
80	Peddie School	Hightstown	NJ	23	4	0	17	3	0	6	1	0
81	Pennington School	Pennington	NJ	35	13	1	30	11	0	5	2	1
82	Perkiomen School	Pennsburg	PA	3	0	0	2	0	0	1	0	0
83	Phillipsburg HS	Phillipsburg	NJ	1	0	0	0	0	0	1	0	0
84	Pierce School	Philadelphia	PA	1	0	0	0	0	0	1	0	0
85	Pingry School	Martinsville	NJ	6	3	0	4	2	0	2	1	0
86	Pope Pius XII HS	Passaic	NJ	10	0	0	8	0	0	2	0	0
87	Princeton Prep	Princeton	NJ	3	0	0	0	0	0	3	0	0
88	Princeton University Frosh	Princeton	NJ	0	1	0	0	0	0	0	1	0
89	Queen of Peace	North Arlington	NJ	4	1	0	0	0	0	4	1	0
90	Rahway HS	Rahway	NJ	1	0	0	0	0	0	1	0	0
91	Red Bank Catholic HS	Red Bank	NJ	1	0	0	1	0	0	0	0	0
92	Roselle Catholic HS	Roselle	NJ	4	2	0	4	2	0	0	0	0
93	Roselle HS	Roselle	NJ	2	0	0	2	0	0	0	0	0
94	Roselle Park HS	Roselle Park	NJ	0	1	0	0	1	0	0	0	0
95	Rutgers Prep	Somerset	NJ	2	0	0	2	0	0	0	0	0
96	Rutgers University Frosh	New Brunswick	NJ	3	0	0	2	0	0	1	0	0
97	Rutgers University JV	New Brunswick	NJ	1	0	0	0	0	0	1	0	0
98	Rutherford HS	Rutherford	NJ	1	0	0	1	0	0	0	0	0
99	Salesian School	Goshen	NY	3	0	0	3	0	0	0	0	0
100	Salesianum Prep	Wilmington	DE	1	0	0	0	0	0	1	0	0
101	Samuel Johnson Academy		CT	3	0	0	0	0	0	3	0	0
102	Scarborough School	Scarborough	NY	3	0	1	3	0	1	0	0	0
103	Scranton College Frosh	Scranton	PA	2	0	0	0	0	0	2	0	0
104	Seton Hall Prep	West Orange	NJ	22	8	3	13	4	0	9	4	3
105	Snyder HS	Jersey City	NJ	2	2	0	2	2	0	0	0	0
106	South River HS	South River	NJ	0	2	0	0	2	0	0	0	0
107	South Side HS	Newark	NJ	20	4	0	15	0	0	5	4	0
108	St Basil HS	Stamford	CT	1	0	0	0	0	0	1	0	0
109	St Cecelia HS	Englewood	NJ	2	0	0	0	0	0	2	0	0
110	St Dominic's HS	Oyster Bay	NY	1	0	0	0	0	0	1	0	0
111	St Francis Prep	Fresh Meadow	NY	2	0	0	0	0	0	2	0	0
112	St. Francis Xavier Prep	Brooklyn	NY	1	0	0	0	0	0	1	0	0
113	St Ignatius HS	Brooklyn	NY	3	0	0	0	0	0	3	0	0
114	St James HS	Newark	NJ	2	0	0	2	0	0	0	0	0
115	St John's Prep	Astoria	NY	3	0	0	3	0	0	0	0	0
116	St Joseph's HS	Montvale	NJ	3	0	0	3	0	0	0	0	0
117	St Mary's HS	South Amboy	NJ	24	0	0	23	0	0	1	0	0
118	St Mary's HS	Rutherford	NJ	33	7	0	25	4	0	8	3	0
119	St Mary's HS	Perth Amboy	NJ	3	1	0	3	1	0	0	0	0
120	St Mary's HS	Elizabeth	NJ	8	1	0	8	1	0	0	0	0
121	St Mary's HS	Manhasset (?)	NY	3	0	0	3	0	0	0	0	0
122	St Michael's HS	Union City	NJ	4	2	0	3	1	0	1	1	0
123	St Michael's HS	Newark	NJ	6	0	0	6	0	0	0	0	0
124	St Patrick HS	Elizabeth	NJ	7	1	0	7	1	0	0	0	0
125	St Peter's HS	New Brunswick	NJ	9	0	0	9	0	0	0	0	0
126	St Peter's Prep	Jersey City	NJ	14	12	0	12	9	0	2	3	0
127	St Rose HS	Belmar	NJ	8	0	0	8	0	0	0	0	0
128	Thomas Jefferson HS	Elizabeth	NJ	7	10	0	7	10	0	0	0	0
129	Trenton Catholic HS	Trenton	NJ	5	1	0	0	0	0	5	1	0
130	Union Catholic HS	Union	NJ	2	0	0	2	0	0	0	0	0
131	Union HS	Union	NJ	8	6	0	8	6	0	0	0	0
132	Upsala College Frosh	East Orange	NJ	3	0	0	2	0	0	1	0	0
133	US Military Academy Plebes	West Point	NY	0	1	0	0	0	0	0	1	0
134	US Military Academy Prep	Fort Monmouth	NJ	3	1	0	2	1	0	1	0	0
135	Vailsburg HS	Newark	NJ	3	0	0	3	0	0	0	0	0
136	Valley Forge Military Acad	Wayne	PA	2	0	0	0	0	0	2	0	0
137	Villanova College Frosh	Villanova	PA	0	2	0	0	0	0	0	2	0
138	Weequahic HS	Newark	NJ	2	1	0	2	1	0	0	0	0
139	Wenonah Military Academy	Wenonah	NJ	2	0	0	0	0	0	2	0	0
140	West Chester College Frosh	West Chester	PA	1	0	0	0	0	0	1	0	0
141	West Orange HS	West Orange	NJ	1	0	0	1	0	0	0	0	0
142	West Side HS	Newark	NJ	15	4	0	13	4	0	2	0	0
143	Woodbridge HS	Woodbridge	NJ	1	1	0	1	1	0	0	0	0
144	Xavier Prep	New York	NY	1	0	0	0	0	0	1	0	0
	TOTAL BASEBALL & FOOTBALL			793	202	18	593	137	3	200	65	15

JOE KASBERGER AT ST. BENEDICT'S PREP - NEWARK, NJ
BASEBALL CAREER RECORD, 1931 TO 1968

OPPOSITION NAME	CITY	STATE	GAME	CAREER BASEBALL WIN %	SEASON BASEBALL SBP	RUNS OPP	CAREER BASEBALL W	L	T
BAYLEY-ELLARD HS	MADISON	NJ	1	100%	12	0	1	0	0
ST MARY'S HS	SOUTH AMBOY	NJ	2	100%	13	4	2	0	0
NY STOCK EXCHANGE		NY	3	67%	2	3	2	1	0
PEDDIE SCHOOL	HIGHTSTOWN	NJ	4	75%	14	0	3	1	0
MACKENZIE SCHOOL		NY	5	80%	7	4	4	1	0
DICKINSON HS	JERSEY CITY	NJ	6	67%	2	4	4	2	0
DICKINSON HS	JERSEY CITY	NJ	7	71%	17	8	5	2	0
PENNINGTON SCHOOL	PENNINGTON	NJ	8	75%	11	0	6	2	0
ST JOHN'S PREP	ASTORIA	NY	9	78%	13	4	7	2	0
BROWN PREP	PHILADELPHIA	PA	10	80%	13	3	8	2	0
	1931 SEASON		10		104	30	8	2	0
DICKINSON HS	JERSEY CITY	NJ	11	82%	10	7	9	2	0
EAST SIDE HS	NEWARK	NJ	12	75%	3	5	9	3	0
SETON HALL PREP	WEST ORANGE	NJ	13	77%	5	1	10	3	0
CONCORDIA PREP			14	79%	10	1	11	3	0
PENNINGTON SCHOOL	PENNINGTON	NJ	15	80%	12	5	12	3	0
ST JOHN'S PREP	ASTORIA	NY	16	81%	7	1	13	3	0
ST JOHN'S PREP	ASTORIA	NY	17	82%	6	4	14	3	0
PEDDIE SCHOOL	HIGHTSTOWN	NJ	18	83%	13	3	15	3	0
SETON HALL PREP	WEST ORANGE	NJ	19	84%	7	5	16	3	0
ROSELLE HS	ROSELLE	NJ	20	85%	11	0	17	3	0
ST PETER'S HS	NEW BRUNSWICK	NJ	21	86%	10	7	18	3	0
ROSELLE HS	ROSELLE	NJ	22	86%	8	4	19	3	0
DICKINSON HS	JERSEY CITY	NJ	23	83%	0	3	19	4	0
NUTLEY HS	NUTLEY	NJ	24	79%	1	8	19	5	0
SALESIAN SCHOOL	GOSHEN	NY	25	80%	7	5	20	5	0
	1932 SEASON		15		110	59	12	3	0
ST MARY'S HS	RUTHERFORD	NJ	26	81%	10	3	21	5	0
ST MARY'S HS	RUTHERFORD	NJ	27	81%	4	2	22	5	0
WOODBRIDGE HS	WOODBRIDGE	NJ	28	79%	2	4	22	6	0
SALESIAN SCHOOL	GOSHEN	NY	29	79%	21	3	23	6	0
WOODBRIDGE HS	WOODBRIDGE	NJ	30	80%	9	8	24	6	0
SOUTH RIVER HS	SOUTH RIVER	NJ	31	77%	3	8	24	7	0
PENNINGTON SCHOOL	PENNINGTON	NJ	32	78%	11	5	25	7	0
PENNINGTON SCHOOL	PENNINGTON	NJ	33	79%	5	3	26	7	0
SALESIAN SCHOOL	GOSHEN	NY	34	79%	16	3	27	7	0
NUTLEY HS	NUTLEY	NJ	35	80%	8	0	28	7	0
DICKINSON HS	JERSEY CITY	NJ	36	78%	13	14	28	8	0
NUTLEY HS	NUTLEY	NJ	37	78%	12	4	29	8	0
CONCORDIA PREP			38	76%	2	6	29	9	0
DICKINSON HS	JERSEY CITY	NJ	39	77%	11	5	30	9	0
BLAIR ACADEMY	BLAIRSTOWN	NJ	40	78%	10	5	31	9	0
	1933 SEASON		15		137	73	11	4	0
ST PETER'S HS	NEW BRUNSWICK	NJ	41	78%	15	2	32	9	0
GOOD COUNSEL HS	NEWARK	NJ	42	79%	16	4	33	9	0
EAST ORANGE HS	EAST ORANGE	NJ	43	79%	12	5	34	9	0
ST PETER'S HS	NEW BRUNSWICK	NJ	44	80%	12	4	35	9	0
PENNINGTON SCHOOL	PENNINGTON	NJ	45	80%	7	1	36	9	0
DICKINSON HS	JERSEY CITY	NJ	46	80%	2	0	37	9	0
PENNINGTON SCHOOL	PENNINGTON	NJ	47	79%	4	5	37	10	0
BLAIR ACADEMY	BLAIRSTOWN	NJ	48	79%	8	5	38	10	0
DICKINSON HS	JERSEY CITY	NJ	49	78%	2	10	38	11	0
NUTLEY HS	NUTLEY	NJ	50	76%	8	9	38	12	0
BARRINGER HS	NEWARK	NJ	51	76%	6	4	39	12	0
PEDDIE SCHOOL	HIGHTSTOWN	NJ	52	77%	10	3	40	12	0
NUTLEY HS	NUTLEY	NJ	53	77%	4	2	41	12	0
	1934 SEASON		13		106	54	10	3	0
ADMIRAL FARRAGUT ACADEMY	PINE BEACH	NJ	54	78%	15	4	42	12	0
MONTCLAIR ACADEMY	MONTCLAIR	NJ	55	78%	20	0	43	12	0
ADMIRAL FARRAGUT ACADEMY	PINE BEACH	NJ	56	79%	13	1	44	12	0
NUTLEY HS	NUTLEY	NJ	57	79%	9	7	45	12	0
NUTLEY HS	NUTLEY	NJ	58	79%	9	16	45	13	0
PENNINGTON SCHOOL	PENNINGTON	NJ	59	76%	11	12	45	14	0
MONTCLAIR ACADEMY	MONTCLAIR	NJ	60	77%	10	0	46	14	0
ST MARY'S HS	RUTHERFORD	NJ	61	77%	3	1	47	14	0
ST MARY'S HS	RUTHERFORD	NJ	62	77%	10	2	48	14	0
DICKINSON HS	JERSEY CITY	NJ	63	78%	7	1	49	14	0
EAST ORANGE HS	EAST ORANGE	NJ	64	78%	15	6	50	14	0
	1935 SEASON		11		122	50	9	2	0
ADMIRAL FARRAGUT ACADEMY	PINE BEACH	NJ	65	78%	20	0	51	14	0
ORANGE HS	ORANGE	NJ	66	79%	7	5	52	14	0
ST MARY'S HS	RUTHERFORD	NJ	67	79%	7	4	53	14	0
SOUTH SIDE HS	NEWARK	NJ	68	79%	4	2	54	14	0
EAST ORANGE HS	EAST ORANGE	NJ	69	80%	3	0	55	14	0
ORANGE HS	ORANGE	NJ	70	79%	3	6	55	15	0
ST MARY'S HS	RUTHERFORD	NJ	71	79%	7	0	56	15	0
MONTCLAIR ACADEMY	MONTCLAIR	NJ	72	78%	4	6	56	16	0
NEWMAN SCHOOL	LAKEWOOD	NJ	73	78%	9	0	57	16	0
ADMIRAL FARRAGUT ACADEMY	PINE BEACH	NJ	74	78%	17	1	58	16	0
PENNINGTON SCHOOL	PENNINGTON	NJ	75	79%	7	2	59	16	0
KINGSLEY SCHOOL	BROOKLYN	NY	76	79%	8	1	60	16	0
SOUTH SIDE HS	NEWARK	NJ	77	79%	7	5	61	16	0

OPPOSITION NAME	CITY	STATE	GAME	CAREER BASEBALL WIN %	SEASON BASEBALL SBP	BASEBALL RUNS OPP	CAREER BASEBALL W	L	T
CARTERET ACADEMY	SHORT HILLS	NJ	78	79%	16	4	62	16	0
DICKINSON HS	JERSEY CITY	NJ	79	80%	9	6	63	16	0
1936 SEASON			15		128	42	13	2	0
ARTS HS	NEWARK	NJ	80	80%	28	0	64	16	0
ST MARY'S HS	RUTHERFORD	NJ	81	80%	22	2	65	16	0
ORANGE HS	ORANGE	NJ	82	80%	4	3	66	16	0
NEWARK UNIVERSITY JV	NEWARK	NJ	83	81%	5	0	67	16	0
DICKINSON HS	JERSEY CITY	NJ	84	81%	9	2	68	16	0
CARTERET ACADEMY	SHORT HILLS	NJ	85	81%	17	5	69	16	0
IRVINGTON HS	IRVINGTON	NJ	86	81%	11	5	70	16	0
NEWMAN SCHOOL	LAKEWOOD	NJ	87	82%	26	7	71	16	0
RUTHERFORD HS	RUTHERFORD	NJ	88	82%	6	2	72	16	0
ST PETER'S HS	NEW BRUNSWICK	NJ	89	82%	14	4	73	16	0
KINGSLEY SCHOOL	BROOKLYN	NY	90	82%	10	7	74	16	0
ORANGE HS	ORANGE	NJ	91	82%	17	4	75	16	0
MONTCLAIR ACADEMY	MONTCLAIR	NJ	92	83%	13	1	76	16	0
PENNINGTON SCHOOL	PENNINGTON	NJ	93	83%	7	5	77	16	0
EAST ORANGE HS	EAST ORANGE	NJ	94	83%	3	0	78	16	0
DICKINSON HS	JERSEY CITY	NJ	95	83%	12	5	79	16	0
MONTCLAIR ACADEMY	MONTCLAIR	NJ	96	83%	14	3	80	16	0
SOUTH SIDE HS	NEWARK	NJ	97	84%	3	0	81	16	0
PENNINGTON SCHOOL	PENNINGTON	NJ	98	84%	9	5	82	16	0
1937 SEASON			19		230	60	19	0	0
ST PATRICK'S HS	ELIZABETH	NJ	99	84%	24	3	83	16	0
DON BOSCO PREP	RAMSEY	NJ	100	84%	4	2	84	16	0
PEDDIE SCHOOL	HIGHTSTOWN	NJ	101	84%	10	3	85	16	0
DICKINSON HS	JERSEY CITY	NJ	102	84%	10	3	86	16	0
BORDENTOWN MILITARY INSTITUTE	BORDENTOWN	NJ	103	84%	16	7	87	16	0
SNYDER HS	JERSEY CITY	NJ	104	84%	3	4	87	17	0
SETON HALL PREP	WEST ORANGE	NJ	105	83%	4	8	87	18	0
ST PETER'S HS	NEW BRUNSWICK	NJ	106	83%	8	5	88	18	0
PENNINGTON SCHOOL	PENNINGTON	NJ	107	82%	0	1	88	19	0
BORDENTOWN MILITARY INSTITUTE	BORDENTOWN	NJ	108	82%	11	5	89	19	0
SNYDER HS	JERSEY CITY	NJ	109	83%	8	0	90	19	0
PENNINGTON SCHOOL	PENNINGTON	NJ	110	82%	0	3	90	20	0
NEWMAN SCHOOL	LAKEWOOD	NJ	111	82%	5	0	91	20	0
DICKINSON HS	JERSEY CITY	NJ	112	82%	13	3	92	20	0
WEST SIDE HS	NEWARK	NJ	113	81%	6	7	92	21	0
THOMAS JEFFERSON HS	ELIZABETH	NJ	114	82%	4	2	93	21	0
1938 SEASON			16		126	56	11	5	0
ST PATRICK'S HS	ELIZABETH	NJ	115	81%	5	10	93	22	0
ST PATRICK'S HS	ELIZABETH	NJ	116	81%	24	5	94	22	0
DICKINSON HS	JERSEY CITY	NJ	117	81%	8	5	95	22	0
DICKINSON HS	JERSEY CITY	NJ	118	81%	8	1	96	22	0
SCARBOROUGH SCHOOL	SCARBOROUGH	NY	119	82%	3	1	97	22	0
NEWARK ACADEMY	LIVINGSTON	NJ	120	82%	7	6	98	22	0
WEST SIDE HS	NEWARK	NJ	121	81%	1	5	98	23	0
CENTRAL HS	NEWARK	NJ	122	81%	6	0	99	23	0
ST MARY'S HS	SOUTH AMBOY	NJ	123	81%	9	3	100	23	0
SETON HALL PREP	WEST ORANGE	NJ	124	81%	13	7	101	23	0
WEEQUAHIC HS	NEWARK	NJ	125	82%	13	9	102	23	0
NEWMAN SCHOOL	LAKEWOOD	NJ	126	82%	14	0	103	23	0
ST PETER'S HS	NEW BRUNSWICK	NJ	127	82%	11	7	104	23	0
NEWARK ACADEMY	LIVINGSTON	NJ	128	82%	2	1	105	23	0
BORDENTOWN MILITARY INSTITUTE	BORDENTOWN	NJ	129	82%	5	3	106	23	0
THOMAS JEFFERSON HS	ELIZABETH	NJ	130	82%	8	1	107	23	0
SNYDER HS	JERSEY CITY	NJ	131	82%	6	1	108	23	0
ADMIRAL FARRAGUT ACADEMY	PINE BEACH	NJ	132	82%	14	15	108	24	0
ST MARY'S HS	SOUTH AMBOY	NJ	133	82%	5	3	109	24	0
PENNINGTON SCHOOL	PENNINGTON	NJ	134	82%	19	7	110	24	0
SETON HALL PREP	SOUTH ORANGE	NJ	135	81%	7	13	110	25	0
1939 SEASON			21		188	103	17	4	0
ST MICHAEL'S HS	NEWARK	NJ	136	82%	18	2	111	25	0
CENTRAL HS	NEWARK	NJ	137	81%	0	1	111	26	0
ST MICHAEL'S HS	NEWARK	NJ	138	81%	15	0	112	26	0
SCARBOROUGH SCHOOL	SCARBOROUGH	NY	139	81%	12	0	113	26	0
DICKINSON HS	JERSEY CITY	NJ	140	81%	22	2	114	26	0
ST PETER'S HS	NEW BRUNSWICK	NJ	141	82%	13	0	115	26	0
RUTGERS UNIVERSITY FROSH	NEW BRUNSWICK	NJ	142	82%	17	8	116	26	0
ST MARY'S HS	PERTH AMBOY	NJ	143	81%	2	5	116	27	0
ST PATRICK'S HS	ELIZABETH	NJ	144	81%	8	4	117	27	0
PENNINGTON SCHOOL	PENNINGTON	NJ	145	81%	3	4	117	28	0
WEEQUAHIC HS	NEWARK	NJ	146	81%	3	2	118	28	0
COLUMBIA UNIVERSITY FROSH	NEW YORK	NY	147	81%	11	6	119	28	0
BORDENTOWN MILITARY INSTITUTE	BORDENTOWN	NJ	148	81%	5	1	120	28	0
ADMIRAL FARRAGUT ACADEMY	PINE BEACH	NJ	149	81%	3	1	121	28	0
ST MARY'S HS	SOUTH AMBOY	NJ	150	81%	9	0	122	28	0
ST MARY'S HS	SOUTH AMBOY	NJ	151	81%	9	4	123	28	0
PENNINGTON SCHOOL	PENNINGTON	NJ	152	82%	2	1	124	28	0
ST MARY'S HS	PERTH AMBOY	NJ	153	82%	3	2	125	28	0
ST PATRICK'S HS	ELIZABETH	NJ	154	82%	23	0	126	28	0
SETON HALL PREP	WEST ORANGE	NJ	155	82%	9	1	127	28	0
1940 SEASON			20		187	44	17	3	0

JOE KASBERGER AT ST. BENEDICT'S PREP - NEWARK, NJ
BASEBALL CAREER RECORD, 1931 TO 1968

OPPOSITION NAME	CITY	STATE	GAME	CAREER BASEBALL WIN %	SEASON BASEBALL SBP	RUNS OPP	CAREER BASEBALL W	L	T
DICKINSON HS	JERSEY CITY	NJ	156	82%	8	3	128	28	0
ST MARY'S HS	SOUTH AMBOY	NJ	157	82%	11	6	129	28	0
ST MARY'S HS	SOUTH AMBOY	NJ	158	82%	12	4	130	28	0
SCARBOROUGH SCHOOL	SCARBOROUGH	NY	159	82%	6	5	131	28	0
HILLSIDE HS	HILLSIDE	NJ	160	83%	2	1	132	28	0
PENNINGTON SCHOOL	PENNINGTON	NJ	161	83%	16	0	133	28	0
RUTGERS UNIVERSITY FROSH	NEW BRUNSWICK	NJ	162	83%	11	4	134	28	0
ST MICHAEL'S HS	NEWARK	NJ	163	83%	10	0	135	28	0
CENTRAL HS	NEWARK	NJ	164	83%	14	8	136	28	0
COLUMBIA UNIVERSITY FROSH	NEW YORK	NY	165	82%	4	8	136	29	0
BORDENTOWN MILITARY INSTITUTE	BORDENTOWN	NJ	166	83%	7	0	137	29	0
ST MARY'S HS	PERTH AMBOY	NJ	167	83%	8	3	138	29	0
WEST SIDE HS	NEWARK	NJ	168	83%	15	7	139	29	0
ST PETER'S HS	NEW BRUNSWICK	NJ	169	83%	14	8	140	29	0
ST MICHAEL'S HS	NEWARK	NJ	170	83%	5	0	141	29	0
SCARBOROUGH SCHOOL	SCARBOROUGH	NY	171	82%	3	3	141	29	1
ST MARY'S HS	PERTH AMBOY	NJ	172	82%	5	4	142	29	1
ADMIRAL FARRAGUT ACADEMY	PINE BEACH	NJ	173	82%	7	7	142	29	2
SETON HALL PREP	WEST ORANGE	NJ	174	82%	8	4	143	29	2
1941 SEASON			19		166	75	16	1	2
ST PATRICK'S HS	ELIZABETH	NJ	175	82%	16	0	144	29	2
ST MICHAEL'S HS	NEWARK	NJ	176	82%	10	0	145	29	2
NEW BRUNSWICK HS	NEW BRUNSWICK	NJ	177	82%	6	4	146	29	2
HOLY TRINITY HS	HACKENSACK	NJ	178	83%	13	2	147	29	2
HARRISON HS	HARRISON	NJ	179	83%	5	1	148	29	2
ST MARY'S HS	SOUTH AMBOY	NJ	180	83%	10	2	149	29	2
COLUMBIA UNIVERSITY FROSH	NEW YORK	NY	181	83%	4	0	150	29	2
IMMACULATE CONCEPTION HS	MONTCLAIR	NJ	182	83%	22	4	151	29	2
LA SALLE MILITARY ACADEMY	OAKDALE	NY	183	83%	13	7	152	29	2
ST PETER'S HS	NEW BRUNSWICK	NJ	184	83%	15	0	153	29	2
BARRINGER HS	NEWARK	NJ	185	83%	13	3	154	29	2
ST MICHAEL'S HS	NEWARK	NJ	186	83%	10	1	155	29	2
LA SALLE MILITARY ACADEMY	OAKDALE	NY	187	83%	19	1	156	29	2
CENTRAL HS	NEWARK	NJ	188	84%	2	1	157	29	2
HARRISON HS	HARRISON	NJ	189	84%	9	1	158	29	2
ADMIRAL FARRAGUT ACADEMY	PINE BEACH	NJ	190	84%	7	1	159	29	2
PENNINGTON SCHOOL	PENNINGTON	NJ	191	84%	11	1	160	29	2
ST MARY'S HS	SOUTH AMBOY	NJ	192	84%	8	0	161	29	2
WEST SIDE HS	NEWARK	NJ	193	84%	4	2	162	29	2
PENNINGTON SCHOOL	PENNINGTON	NJ	194	84%	3	8	162	30	2
1942 SEASON			20		200	39	19	1	0
ST MARY'S HS	ELIZABETH	NJ	195	84%	7	0	163	30	2
ST PATRICK'S HS	ELIZABETH	NJ	196	84%	15	1	164	30	2
ST MARY'S HS	RUTHERFORD	NJ	197	84%	6	1	165	30	2
OUR LADY OF THE VALLEY HS	ORANGE	NJ	198	84%	2	0	166	30	2
SOUTH SIDE HS	NEWARK	NJ	199	84%	4	1	167	30	2
PENNINGTON SCHOOL	PENNINGTON	NJ	200	84%	15	0	168	30	2
IMMACULATE CONCEPTION HS	MONTCLAIR	NJ	201	84%	11	1	169	30	2
ST PATRICK'S HS	ELIZABETH	NJ	202	84%	5	3	170	30	2
ST MARY'S HS	RUTHERFORD	NJ	203	84%	13	1	171	30	2
COLUMBIA UNIVERSITY FROSH	NEW YORK	NY	204	84%	4	0	172	30	2
HARRISON HS	HARRISON	NJ	205	84%	5	0	173	30	2
ST MARY'S HS	ELIZABETH	NJ	206	84%	7	3	174	30	2
CENTRAL HS	NEWARK	NJ	207	85%	4	2	175	30	2
HARRISON HS	HARRISON	NJ	208	85%	14	0	176	30	2
OUR LADY OF THE VALLEY HS	ORANGE	NJ	209	84%	0	4	176	31	2
OUR LADY OF THE VALLEY HS	ORANGE	NJ	210	84%	5	2	177	31	2
FLORENCE HS	FLORENCE	NJ	211	84%	4	2	178	31	2
1943 SEASON			17		121	21	16	1	0
HARRISON HS	HARRISON	NJ	212	84%	12	0	179	31	2
LA SALLE MILITARY ACADEMY	OAKDALE	NY	213	85%	4	3	180	31	2
SOUTH SIDE HS	NEWARK	NJ	214	85%	7	1	181	31	2
ST MARY'S HS	ELIZABETH	NJ	215	85%	10	1	182	31	2
ST MARY'S HS	ELIZABETH	NJ	216	85%	16	2	183	31	2
ORANGE HS	ORANGE	NJ	217	85%	3	0	184	31	2
CENTRAL HS	NEWARK	NJ	218	85%	11	2	185	31	2
ST MARY'S HS	RUTHERFORD	NJ	219	85%	15	7	186	31	2
WEST SIDE HS	NEWARK	NJ	220	85%	1	0	187	31	2
PENNINGTON SCHOOL	PENNINGTON	NJ	221	85%	3	0	188	31	2
ST MARY'S HS	RUTHERFORD	NJ	222	85%	7	0	189	31	2
OUR LADY OF THE VALLEY HS	ORANGE	NJ	223	85%	23	0	190	31	2
LA SALLE MILITARY ACADEMY	OAKDALE	NY	224	85%	2	2	190	31	3
HARRISON HS	HARRISON	NJ	225	85%	12	1	191	31	3
OUR LADY OF THE VALLEY HS	ORANGE	NJ	226	85%	4	1	192	31	3
BORDENTOWN MILITARY INSTITUTE	BORDENTOWN	NJ	227	85%	11	0	193	31	3
PENNINGTON SCHOOL	PENNINGTON	NJ	228	85%	2	0	194	31	3
1944 SEASON			17		143	20	16	0	1
DON BOSCO PREP	RAMSEY	NJ	229	85%	16	1	195	31	3
OUR LADY OF THE VALLEY HS	ORANGE	NJ	230	85%	8	3	196	31	3
PENNINGTON SCHOOL	PENNINGTON	NJ	231	85%	2	3	196	32	3
ADMIRAL FARRAGUT ACADEMY	PINE BEACH	NJ	232	85%	6	5	197	32	3
OUR LADY OF THE VALLEY HS	ORANGE	NJ	233	85%	24	1	198	32	3

JOE KASBERGER AT ST. BENEDICT'S PREP - NEWARK, NJ
BASEBALL CAREER RECORD, 1931 TO 1968

OPPOSITION NAME	CITY	STATE	GAME	WIN %	CAREER BASEBALL SBP	SEASON BASEBALL RUNS OPP	CAREER BASEBALL W	L	T
ADMIRAL FARRAGUT ACADEMY	PINE BEACH	NJ	234	85%	10	0	199	32	3
CENTRAL HS	NEWARK	NJ	235	85%	1	2	199	33	3
WEST SIDE HS	NEWARK	NJ	236	85%	5	4	200	33	3
DON BOSCO PREP	RAMSEY	NJ	237	85%	7	2	201	33	3
BORDENTOWN MILITARY INSTITUTE	BORDENTOWN	NJ	238	85%	7	3	202	33	3
PENNINGTON SCHOOL	PENNINGTON	NJ	239	85%	7	3	203	33	3
1945 SEASON			11		93	27	9	2	0
DON BOSCO PREP	RAMSEY	NJ	240	85%	16	4	204	33	3
NEWARK VOCATIONAL-TECH HS	NEWARK	NJ	241	85%	7	6	205	33	3
ADMIRAL FARRAGUT ACADEMY	PINE BEACH	NJ	242	85%	8	0	206	33	3
UNION HS	UNION	NJ	243	85%	0	2	206	34	3
LA SALLE MILITARY ACADEMY	OAKDALE	NY	244	85%	5	3	207	34	3
ORANGE HS	ORANGE	NJ	245	85%	9	2	208	34	3
DON BOSCO PREP	RAMSEY	NJ	246	85%	19	2	209	34	3
EAST ORANGE HS	EAST ORANGE	NJ	247	85%	4	3	210	34	3
NEWARK VOCATIONAL-TECH HS	NEWARK	NJ	248	85%	10	9	211	34	3
OUR LADY OF THE VALLEY HS	ORANGE	NJ	249	85%	11	7	212	34	3
BARRINGER HS	NEWARK	NJ	250	85%	3	2	213	34	3
ADMIRAL FARRAGUT ACADEMY	PINE BEACH	NJ	251	85%	18	0	214	34	3
POPE PIUS XII HS	PASSAIC	NJ	252	85%	5	2	215	34	3
BORDENTOWN MILITARY INSTITUTE	BORDENTOWN	NJ	253	85%	5	1	216	34	3
LA SALLE MILITARY ACADEMY	OAKDALE	NY	254	85%	4	8	216	35	3
ROSELLE PARK HS	ROSELLE PARK	NJ	255	85%	5	6	216	36	3
ST MARY'S HS	ELIZABETH	NJ	256	85%	7	0	217	36	3
1946 SEASON			17		136	57	14	3	0
NEWARK ACADEMY	LIVINGSTON	NJ	257	85%	17	0	218	36	3
CARTERET ACADEMY	SHORT HILLS	NJ	258	85%	1	0	219	36	3
MONTCLAIR ACADEMY	MONTCLAIR	NJ	259	85%	11	0	220	36	3
ADMIRAL FARRAGUT ACADEMY	PINE BEACH	NJ	260	85%	9	1	221	36	3
ST MARY'S HS	RUTHERFORD	NJ	261	85%	12	4	222	36	3
NEWARK VOCATIONAL-TECH HS	NEWARK	NJ	262	85%	13	1	223	36	3
NEWARK ACADEMY	LIVINGSTON	NJ	263	85%	7	0	224	36	3
POPE PIUS XII HS	PASSAIC	NJ	264	85%	2	1	225	36	3
LA SALLE MILITARY ACADEMY	OAKDALE	NY	265	85%	7	5	226	36	3
ST MARY'S HS	RUTHERFORD	NJ	266	85%	17	6	227	36	3
NEWARK VOCATIONAL-TECH HS	NEWARK	NJ	267	85%	10	1	228	36	3
POPE PIUS XII HS	PASSAIC	NJ	268	85%	8	1	229	36	3
BLAIR ACADEMY	BLAIRSTOWN	NJ	269	86%	13	3	230	36	3
MONTCLAIR ACADEMY	MONTCLAIR	NJ	270	86%	6	0	231	36	3
BORDENTOWN MILITARY INSTITUTE	BORDENTOWN	NJ	271	86%	2	1	232	36	3
EAST ORANGE HS	EAST ORANGE	NJ	272	86%	5	0	233	36	3
CENTRAL HS	NEWARK	NJ	273	86%	6	3	234	36	3
ST MARY'S HS	ELIZABETH	NJ	274	86%	7	1	235	36	3
1947 SEASON			18		153	28	18	0	0
CARTERET ACADEMY	SHORT HILLS	NJ	275	86%	13	2	236	36	3
NEWARK COLLEGE OF ENGR FROSH	NEWARK	NJ	276	86%	9	1	237	36	3
MONTCLAIR ACADEMY	MONTCLAIR	NJ	277	86%	11	2	238	36	3
OUR LADY OF THE VALLEY HS	ORANGE	NJ	278	86%	8	3	239	36	3
PENNINGTON SCHOOL	PENNINGTON	NJ	279	86%	7	2	240	36	3
RUTGERS PREP	SOMERSET	NJ	280	86%	10	2	241	36	3
NEWARK VOCATIONAL-TECH HS	NEWARK	NJ	281	86%	13	0	242	36	3
NEWARK COLLEGE OF ENGR FROSH	NEWARK	NJ	282	86%	11	2	243	36	3
POPE PIUS XII HS	PASSAIC	NJ	283	86%	19	3	244	36	3
NEWARK ACADEMY	LIVINGSTON	NJ	284	86%	8	0	245	36	3
NEWARK VOCATIONAL-TECH HS	NEWARK	NJ	285	86%	7	0	246	36	3
LYNDHURST HS	LYNDHURST	NJ	286	86%	13	0	247	36	3
POPE PIUS XII HS	PASSAIC	NJ	287	86%	5	4	248	36	3
CENTRAL HS	NEWARK	NJ	288	86%	12	7	249	36	3
LYNDHURST HS	LYNDHURST	NJ	289	87%	11	2	250	36	3
MONTCLAIR ACADEMY	MONTCLAIR	NJ	290	87%	11	0	251	36	3
BORDENTOWN MILITARY INSTITUTE	BORDENTOWN	NJ	291	87%	8	1	252	36	3
EAST ORANGE HS	EAST ORANGE	NJ	292	87%	12	2	253	36	3
ST MARY'S HS	ELIZABETH	NJ	293	87%	5	1	254	36	3
NEWARK ACADEMY	LIVINGSTON	NJ	294	87%	7	1	255	36	3
1948 SEASON			20		200	35	20	0	0
NEWARK COLLEGE OF ENGR FROSH	NEWARK	NJ	295	87%	15	0	256	36	3
LYNDHURST HS	LYNDHURST	NJ	296	87%	13	0	257	36	3
LYNDHURST HS	LYNDHURST	NJ	297	87%	4	2	258	36	3
BORDENTOWN MILITARY INSTITUTE	BORDENTOWN	NJ	298	87%	12	1	259	36	3
ST PETER'S PREP	JERSEY CITY	NJ	299	87%	6	3	260	36	3
CARTERET ACADEMY	SHORT HILLS	NJ	300	87%	7	3	261	36	3
RUTGERS PREP	SOMERSET	NJ	301	87%	14	2	262	36	3
NEWARK VOCATIONAL-TECH HS	NEWARK	NJ	302	87%	15	1	263	36	3
NEW YORK MILITARY ACADEMY	CORNWALL-ON-HUDSON	NY	303	87%	20	4	264	36	3
MONTCLAIR STATE COLLEGE FROSH	UPPER MONTCLAIR	NJ	304	87%	16	6	265	36	3
OUR LADY OF THE VALLEY HS	ORANGE	NJ	305	87%	7	0	266	36	3
LYNDHURST HS	LYNDHURST	NJ	306	87%	12	0	267	36	3
THOMAS JEFFERSON HS	ELIZABETH	NJ	307	87%	21	1	268	36	3
POPE PIUS XII HS	PASSAIC	NJ	308	87%	7	1	269	36	3
NEWARK VOCATIONAL-TECH HS	NEWARK	NJ	309	87%	13	0	270	36	3
CARTERET ACADEMY	SHORT HILLS	NJ	310	87%	10	3	271	36	3
OUR LADY OF THE VALLEY HS	ORANGE	NJ	311	87%	12	0	272	36	3
BORDENTOWN MILITARY INSTITUTE	BORDENTOWN	NJ	312	88%	1	0	273	36	3

APPENDIX O

JOE KASBERGER AT ST. BENEDICT'S PREP - NEWARK, NJ
BASEBALL CAREER RECORD, 1931 TO 1968

OPPOSITION NAME	CITY	STATE	GAME	CAREER BASEBALL WIN %	SEASON BASEBALL SBP	BASEBALL RUNS OPP	CAREER BASEBALL W	L	T
EAST ORANGE HS	EAST ORANGE	NJ	313	88%	9	0	274	36	3
NEW YORK MILITARY ACADEMY	CORNWALL-ON-HUDSON	NY	314	88%	5	4	275	36	3
ST MARY'S HS	MANHASSET	NY	315	88%	9	1	276	36	3
ST MARY'S HS	MANHASSET	NY	316	88%	12	4	277	36	3
	1949 SEASON		22		240	36	22	0	0
MONTCLAIR STATE COLLEGE JV	UPPER MONTCLAIR	NJ	317	88%	10	1	278	36	3
EAST SIDE HS	NEWARK	NJ	318	88%	18	1	279	36	3
IMMACULATE CONCEPTION HS	MONTCLAIR	NJ	319	88%	22	1	280	36	3
BORDENTOWN MILITARY INSTITUTE	BORDENTOWN	NJ	320	88%	3	5	280	37	3
ST PETER'S PREP	JERSEY CITY	NJ	321	88%	6	4	281	37	3
CARTERET ACADEMY	SHORT HILLS	NJ	322	88%	6	0	282	37	3
NEWARK VOCATIONAL-TECH HS	NEWARK	NJ	323	88%	13	3	283	37	3
PERKIOMEN SCHOOL	PENNSBURG	PA	324	88%	16	0	284	37	3
PANZER COLLEGE FROSH	EAST ORANGE	NJ	325	88%	8	0	285	37	3
OUR LADY OF THE VALLEY HS	ORANGE	NJ	326	88%	24	0	286	37	3
ST MARY'S HS	SOUTH AMBOY	NJ	327	88%	22	1	287	37	3
THOMAS JEFFERSON HS	ELIZABETH	NJ	328	88%	1	3	287	38	3
POPE PIUS XII HS	PASSAIC	NJ	329	88%	12	0	288	38	3
BARRINGER HS	NEWARK	NJ	330	88%	5	4	289	38	3
CARTERET ACADEMY	SHORT HILLS	NJ	331	87%	4	8	289	39	3
PANZER COLLEGE FROSH	EAST ORANGE	NJ	332	87%	7	1	290	39	3
BORDENTOWN MILITARY INSTITUTE	BORDENTOWN	NJ	333	87%	10	1	291	39	3
EAST ORANGE HS	EAST ORANGE	NJ	334	87%	6	0	292	39	3
MONTCLAIR STATE COLLEGE JV	UPPER MONTCLAIR	NJ	335	87%	14	2	293	39	3
POPE PIUS XII HS	PASSAIC	NJ	336	88%	6	1	294	39	3
NEW YORK MILITARY ACADEMY	CORNWALL-ON-HUDSON	NY	337	88%	10	0	295	39	3
NEW YORK MILITARY ACADEMY	CORNWALL-ON-HUDSON	NY	338	88%	18	1	296	39	3
	1950 SEASON		22		241	37	19	3	0
MONTCLAIR STATE COLLEGE JV	UPPER MONTCLAIR	NJ	339	88%	10	4	297	39	3
UPSALA COLLEGE FROSH	EAST ORANGE	NJ	340	88%	10	0	298	39	3
IMMACULATE CONCEPTION HS	MONTCLAIR	NJ	341	88%	18	0	299	39	3
BORDENTOWN MILITARY INSTITUTE	BORDENTOWN	NJ	342	87%	1	2	299	40	3
PANZER COLLEGE FROSH	EAST ORANGE	NJ	343	87%	9	10	299	41	3
NEWARK VOCATIONAL-TECH HS	NEWARK	NJ	344	87%	14	0	300	41	3
PERKIOMEN SCHOOL	PENNSBURG	PA	345	87%	6	0	301	41	3
US MILITARY ACADEMY PREP	FORT MONMOUTH	NJ	346	87%	10	3	302	41	3
MONTCLAIR STATE COLLEGE JV	UPPER MONTCLAIR	NJ	347	87%	12	0	303	41	3
ST MARY'S HS	SOUTH AMBOY	NJ	348	87%	15	7	304	41	3
THOMAS JEFFERSON HS	ELIZABETH	NJ	349	87%	13	2	305	41	3
UPSALA COLLEGE FROSH	EAST ORANGE	NJ	350	87%	9	0	306	41	3
BARRINGER HS	NEWARK	NJ	351	87%	5	0	307	41	3
US MILITARY ACADEMY PREP	FORT MONMOUTH	NJ	352	88%	8	4	308	41	3
NEWARK VOCATIONAL-TECH HS	NEWARK	NJ	353	88%	12	2	309	41	3
EAST ORANGE HS	EAST ORANGE	NJ	354	88%	8	0	310	41	3
BARRINGER HS	NEWARK	NJ	355	88%	12	8	311	41	3
ST MARY'S HS	SOUTH AMBOY	NJ	356	88%	11	1	312	41	3
	1951 SEASON		18		183	43	16	2	0
MONTCLAIR STATE COLLEGE JV	UPPER MONTCLAIR	NJ	357	88%	2	0	313	41	3
ALUMNI	NEWARK	NJ	358	88%	3	1	314	41	3
BORDENTOWN MILITARY INSTITUTE	BORDENTOWN	NJ	359	88%	19	0	315	41	3
EAST SIDE HS	NEWARK	NJ	360	88%	0	7	315	42	3
ST PETER'S PREP	JERSEY CITY	NJ	361	88%	5	0	316	42	3
BARRINGER HS	NEWARK	NJ	362	87%	5	6	316	43	3
MONTCLAIR STATE COLLEGE JV	UPPER MONTCLAIR	NJ	363	87%	10	8	317	43	3
PENNINGTON SCHOOL	PENNINGTON	NJ	364	87%	5	4	318	43	3
THOMAS JEFFERSON HS	ELIZABETH	NJ	365	87%	0	4	318	44	3
EASTERN MILITARY ACADEMY	COLD SPRING HARBOR	NY	366	87%	14	1	319	44	3
ST MARY'S HS	SOUTH AMBOY	NJ	367	87%	13	7	320	44	3
EASTERN MILITARY ACADEMY	COLD SPRING HARBOR	NY	368	87%	1	3	320	45	3
BORDENTOWN MILITARY INSTITUTE	BORDENTOWN	NJ	369	87%	4	2	321	45	3
US MILITARY ACADEMY PREP	FORT MONMOUTH	NJ	370	87%	3	4	321	46	3
ST MARY'S HS	MANHASSET	NY	371	87%	5	2	322	46	3
BARRINGER HS	NEWARK	NJ	372	87%	12	3	323	46	3
EAST ORANGE HS	EAST ORANGE	NJ	373	87%	9	0	324	46	3
PENNINGTON SCHOOL	PENNINGTON	NJ	374	87%	11	3	325	46	3
	1952 SEASON		18		121	55	13	5	0
ALUMNI	NEWARK	NJ	375	87%	11	10	326	46	3
ST MARY'S HS	RUTHERFORD	NJ	376	87%	6	0	327	46	3
ARTS HS	NEWARK	NJ	377	87%	5	0	328	46	3
BORDENTOWN MILITARY INSTITUTE	BORDENTOWN	NJ	378	87%	11	2	329	46	3
NEWARK VOCATIONAL-TECH HS	NEWARK	NJ	379	87%	5	2	330	46	3
ST PETER'S PREP	JERSEY CITY	NJ	380	87%	2	4	330	47	3
EASTERN MILITARY ACADEMY	COLD SPRING HARBOR	NY	381	87%	28	3	331	47	3
PENNINGTON SCHOOL	PENNINGTON	NJ	382	87%	6	0	332	47	3
THOMAS JEFFERSON HS	ELIZABETH	NJ	383	87%	1	4	332	48	3
ST MARY'S HS	RUTHERFORD	NJ	384	86%	1	2	332	49	3
ST MARY'S HS	SOUTH AMBOY	NJ	385	86%	1	0	333	49	3
ADMIRAL FARRAGUT ACADEMY	PINE BEACH	NJ	386	87%	9	3	334	49	3
NEWARK VOCATIONAL-TECH HS	NEWARK	NJ	387	87%	4	0	335	49	3
BORDENTOWN MILITARY INSTITUTE	BORDENTOWN	NJ	388	87%	5	0	336	49	3
HUN SCHOOL	PRINCETON	NJ	389	87%	8	2	337	49	3
EAST ORANGE HS	EAST ORANGE	NJ	390	87%	5	0	338	49	3
ADMIRAL FARRAGUT ACADEMY	PINE BEACH	NJ	391	87%	6	3	339	49	3

JOE KASBERGER AT ST. BENEDICT'S PREP - NEWARK, NJ
BASEBALL CAREER RECORD, 1931 TO 1968

OPPOSITION NAME	CITY	STATE	GAME	CAREER BASEBALL WIN %	SEASON BASEBALL SBP	BASEBALL RUNS OPP	CAREER BASEBALL W	L	T
UNION HS	UNION	NJ	392	87%	7	3	340	49	3
PEDDIE SCHOOL	HIGHTSTOWN	NJ	393	87%	3	2	341	49	3
	1953 SEASON		19		124	44	16	3	0
ALUMNI	NEWARK	NJ	394	87%	9	3	342	49	3
ST MARY'S HS	RUTHERFORD	NJ	395	87%	5	3	343	49	3
BAYLEY-ELLARD HS	MADISON	NJ	396	87%	9	0	344	49	3
BORDENTOWN MILITARY INSTITUTE	BORDENTOWN	NJ	397	87%	7	15	344	50	3
BLOOMFIELD TECH HS	BLOOMFIELD	NJ	398	87%	3	0	345	50	3
ST PETER'S PREP	JERSEY CITY	NJ	399	86%	0	1	345	51	3
ARTS HS	NEWARK	NJ	400	87%	24	3	346	51	3
PENNINGTON SCHOOL	PENNINGTON	NJ	401	87%	4	3	347	51	3
EASTERN MILITARY ACADEMY	COLD SPRING HARBOR	NY	402	87%	11	1	348	51	3
ST MARY'S HS	SOUTH AMBOY	NJ	403	87%	6	0	349	51	3
PINGRY SCHOOL	MARTINSVILLE	NJ	404	86%	1	2	349	52	3
NEWARK VOCATIONAL-TECH HS	NEWARK	NJ	405	86%	5	1	350	52	3
ST MARY'S HS	RUTHERFORD	NJ	406	86%	2	3	350	53	3
BORDENTOWN MILITARY INSTITUTE	BORDENTOWN	NJ	407	86%	7	3	351	53	3
UNION HS	UNION	NJ	408	86%	0	2	351	54	3
ST MARY'S HS	SOUTH AMBOY	NJ	409	86%	3	0	352	54	3
ADMIRAL FARRAGUT ACADEMY	PINE BEACH	NJ	410	86%	3	1	353	54	3
NEWARK VOCATIONAL-TECH HS	NEWARK	NJ	411	86%	20	2	354	54	3
PEDDIE SCHOOL	HIGHTSTOWN	NJ	412	86%	4	1	354	54	3
PENNINGTON SCHOOL	PENNINGTON	NJ	413	86%	5	6	355	55	3
SOUTH SIDE HS	NEWARK	NJ	414	86%	2	1	356	55	3
	1954 SEASON		21		130	51	15	6	0
ALUMNI	NEWARK	NJ	415	86%	13	4	357	55	3
BLOOMFIELD TECH HS	BLOOMFIELD	NJ	416	86%	13	0	358	55	3
EASTERN MILITARY ACADEMY	COLD SPRING HARBOR	NY	417	86%	8	0	359	55	3
BORDENTOWN MILITARY INSTITUTE	BORDENTOWN	NJ	418	86%	2	3	359	56	3
ST PETER'S PREP	JERSEY CITY	NJ	419	86%	4	7	359	57	3
PENNINGTON SCHOOL	PENNINGTON	NJ	420	86%	6	2	360	57	3
ARTS HS	NEWARK	NJ	421	86%	3	4	360	58	3
ST MARY'S HS	RUTHERFORD	NJ	422	86%	25	1	361	58	3
ST MARY'S HS	RUTHERFORD	NJ	423	86%	11	0	362	58	3
BAYLEY-ELLARD HS	MADISON	NJ	424	86%	4	3	363	58	3
SOUTH SIDE HS	NEWARK	NJ	425	86%	16	0	364	58	3
NEWARK VOCATIONAL-TECH HS	NEWARK	NJ	426	86%	13	4	365	58	3
PINGRY SCHOOL	MARTINSVILLE	NJ	427	85%	5	6	365	59	3
BORDENTOWN MILITARY INSTITUTE	BORDENTOWN	NJ	428	86%	8	1	366	59	3
UNION HS	UNION	NJ	429	85%	3	6	366	60	3
NEWARK VOCATIONAL-TECH HS	NEWARK	NJ	430	85%	13	4	367	60	3
BAYLEY-ELLARD HS	MADISON	NJ	431	85%	10	0	368	60	3
ADMIRAL FARRAGUT ACADEMY	PINE BEACH	NJ	432	85%	6	1	369	60	3
EASTERN MILITARY ACADEMY	COLD SPRING HARBOR	NY	433	85%	8	3	370	60	3
PEDDIE SCHOOL	HIGHTSTOWN	NJ	434	85%	2	4	370	61	3
ST MARY'S HS	SOUTH AMBOY	NJ	435	85%	4	2	371	61	3
PENNINGTON SCHOOL	PENNINGTON	NJ	436	85%	21	6	372	61	3
	1955 SEASON		22		198	61	16	6	0
FERRIS HS	JERSEY CITY	NJ	437	85%	5	2	373	61	3
ALUMNI	NEWARK	NJ	438	85%	4	3	374	61	3
BLOOMFIELD TECH HS	BLOOMFIELD	NJ	439	85%	10	2	375	61	3
ST MARY'S HS	RUTHERFORD	NJ	440	85%	4	0	376	61	3
BORDENTOWN MILITARY INSTITUTE	BORDENTOWN	NJ	441	85%	0	6	376	62	3
ST PETER'S PREP	JERSEY CITY	NJ	442	85%	5	4	377	62	3
NEWARK VOCATIONAL-TECH HS	NEWARK	NJ	443	85%	12	0	378	62	3
ARTS HS	NEWARK	NJ	444	85%	3	0	379	62	3
PENNINGTON SCHOOL	PENNINGTON	NJ	445	85%	5	1	380	62	3
ST MARY'S HS	RUTHERFORD	NJ	446	85%	2	6	380	63	3
SOUTH SIDE HS	NEWARK	NJ	447	85%	8	1	381	63	3
PINGRY SCHOOL	MARTINSVILLE	NJ	448	85%	5	4	382	63	3
NEWARK VOCATIONAL-TECH HS	NEWARK	NJ	449	85%	5	2	383	63	3
BORDENTOWN MILITARY INSTITUTE	BORDENTOWN	NJ	450	85%	0	2	383	64	3
UNION HS	UNION	NJ	451	85%	0	1	383	65	3
ADMIRAL FARRAGUT ACADEMY	PINE BEACH	NJ	452	85%	5	2	384	65	3
PEDDIE SCHOOL	HIGHTSTOWN	NJ	453	85%	1	5	384	66	3
ST MARY'S HS	SOUTH AMBOY	NJ	454	85%	3	2	385	66	3
PENNINGTON SCHOOL	PENNINGTON	NJ	455	85%	1	2	385	67	3
EASTERN MILITARY ACADEMY	COLD SPRING HARBOR	NY	456	85%	9	2	386	67	3
THOMAS JEFFERSON HS	ELIZABETH	NJ	457	84%	1	3	386	68	3
SETON HALL PREP	WEST ORANGE	NJ	458	84%	6	9	386	69	3
	1956 SEASON		22		94	59	14	8	0
FERRIS HS	JERSEY CITY	NJ	459	84%	14	0	387	69	3
ST ROSE HS	BELMAR	NJ	460	84%	11	2	388	69	3
ST MARY'S HS	RUTHERFORD	NJ	461	84%	5	0	389	69	3
ST PETER'S PREP	JERSEY CITY	NJ	462	84%	8	1	390	69	3
ST MARY'S HS	SOUTH AMBOY	NJ	463	84%	15	1	391	69	3
ST ROSE HS	BELMAR	NJ	464	84%	7	6	392	69	3
PENNINGTON SCHOOL	PENNINGTON	NJ	465	84%	1	8	392	70	3
ST MARY'S HS	RUTHERFORD	NJ	466	84%	6	7	392	71	3
IMMACULATE CONCEPTION HS	MONTCLAIR	NJ	467	84%	6	0	393	71	3
PINGRY SCHOOL	MARTINSVILLE	NJ	468	84%	7	3	394	71	3
WEST SIDE HS	NEWARK	NJ	469	84%	3	2	395	71	3
NEWARK VOCATIONAL-TECH HS	NEWARK	NJ	470	84%	20	9	396	71	3

JOE KASBERGER AT ST. BENEDICT'S PREP - NEWARK, NJ
BASEBALL CAREER RECORD, 1931 TO 1968

OPPOSITION NAME	CITY	STATE	GAME	CAREER BASEBALL WIN %	SEASON BASEBALL SBP	RUNS OPP	CAREER BASEBALL W	L	T
ST MARY'S HS	SOUTH AMBOY	NJ	471	84%	17	4	397	71	3
ADMIRAL FARRAGUT ACADEMY	PINE BEACH	NJ	472	84%	6	0	398	71	3
PEDDIE SCHOOL	HIGHTSTOWN	NJ	473	84%	9	2	399	71	3
PENNINGTON SCHOOL	PENNINGTON	NJ	474	84%	12	2	400	71	3
THOMAS JEFFERSON HS	ELIZABETH	NJ	475	84%	2	4	400	72	3
1957 SEASON			17		149	51	14	3	0
ST ROSE HS	BELMAR	NJ	476	84%	28	2	401	72	3
ST MARY'S HS	RUTHERFORD	NJ	477	84%	9	2	402	72	3
BORDENTOWN MILITARY INSTITUTE	BORDENTOWN	NJ	478	84%	2	6	402	73	3
ST MARY'S HS	SOUTH AMBOY	NJ	479	84%	9	0	403	73	3
ST PETER'S PREP	JERSEY CITY	NJ	480	84%	5	7	403	74	3
OUR LADY OF THE VALLEY HS	ORANGE	NJ	481	84%	4	1	404	74	3
ST ROSE HS	BELMAR	NJ	482	84%	7	1	405	74	3
PENNINGTON SCHOOL	PENNINGTON	NJ	483	84%	7	0	406	74	3
ST MARY'S HS	RUTHERFORD	NJ	484	84%	8	3	407	74	3
IMMACULATE CONCEPTION HS	MONTCLAIR	NJ	485	84%	3	1	408	74	3
BORDENTOWN MILITARY INSTITUTE	BORDENTOWN	NJ	486	84%	1	5	408	75	3
UNION HS	UNION	NJ	487	84%	6	5	409	75	3
ADMIRAL FARRAGUT ACADEMY	PINE BEACH	NJ	488	84%	5	3	410	75	3
BELLEVILLE HS	BELLEVILLE	NJ	489	84%	1	6	410	76	3
PEDDIE SCHOOL	HIGHTSTOWN	NJ	490	84%	4	1	411	76	3
PINGRY SCHOOL	MARTINSVILLE	NJ	491	84%	9	5	412	76	3
ST PETER'S PREP	JERSEY CITY	NJ	492	84%	1	5	412	77	3
PENNINGTON SCHOOL	PENNINGTON	NJ	493	84%	1	4	412	78	3
THOMAS JEFFERSON HS	ELIZABETH	NJ	494	84%	3	2	413	78	3
NEWARK VOCATIONAL-TECH HS	NEWARK	NJ	495	84%	4	0	414	78	3
1958 SEASON			20		117	59	14	6	0
ST ROSE HS	BELMAR	NJ	496	84%	9	1	415	78	3
ST MICHAEL'S HS	UNION CITY	NJ	497	84%	7	3	416	78	3
ST MARY'S HS	SOUTH AMBOY	NJ	498	84%	7	2	417	78	3
BORDENTOWN MILITARY INSTITUTE	BORDENTOWN	NJ	499	84%	3	10	417	79	3
ST MARY'S HS	RUTHERFORD	NJ	500	84%	10	4	418	79	3
ST PETER'S PREP	JERSEY CITY	NJ	501	84%	12	11	419	79	3
ST MICHAEL'S HS	UNION CITY	NJ	502	84%	8	7	420	79	3
OUR LADY OF THE VALLEY HS	ORANGE	NJ	503	83%	3	6	420	80	3
OUR LADY OF THE VALLEY HS	ORANGE	NJ	504	83%	1	3	420	81	3
WEST SIDE HS	NEWARK	NJ	505	83%	6	4	421	81	3
NEWARK VOCATIONAL-TECH HS	NEWARK	NJ	506	83%	15	0	422	81	3
ST MARY'S HS	RUTHERFORD	NJ	507	83%	8	1	423	81	3
ST ROSE HS	BELMAR	NJ	508	83%	21	3	424	81	3
BORDENTOWN MILITARY INSTITUTE	BORDENTOWN	NJ	509	83%	9	14	424	82	3
UNION HS	UNION	NJ	510	83%	4	3	425	82	3
DON BOSCO PREP	RAMSEY	NJ	511	83%	4	0	426	82	3
ST MARY'S HS	SOUTH AMBOY	NJ	512	83%	8	1	427	82	3
ADMIRAL FARRAGUT ACADEMY	PINE BEACH	NJ	513	83%	15	1	428	82	3
BELLEVILLE HS	BELLEVILLE	NJ	514	83%	4	8	428	83	3
PENNINGTON SCHOOL	PENNINGTON	NJ	515	83%	4	2	429	83	3
IRVINGTON HS	IRVINGTON	NJ	516	83%	4	2	430	83	3
PEDDIE SCHOOL	HIGHTSTOWN	NJ	517	83%	7	0	431	83	3
PENNINGTON SCHOOL	PENNINGTON	NJ	518	83%	8	5	432	83	3
ST PETER'S PREP	JERSEY CITY	NJ	519	83%	?	?	432	84	3
1959 SEASON			24		177	91	18	6	0
ST MICHAEL'S HS	UNION CITY	NJ	520	83%	4	2	433	84	3
ESSEX CATHOLIC	NEWARK	NJ	521	83%	4	3	434	84	3
ST MARY'S HS	RUTHERFORD	NJ	522	83%	9	0	435	84	3
SETON HALL PREP	WEST ORANGE	NJ	523	83%	10	3	436	84	3
BORDENTOWN MILITARY INSTITUTE	BORDENTOWN	NJ	524	83%	2	1	437	84	3
WEST SIDE HS	NEWARK	NJ	525	83%	6	10	437	85	3
ST PETER'S PREP	JERSEY CITY	NJ	526	83%	0	3	437	86	3
ST MICHAEL'S HS	UNION CITY	NJ	527	83%	1	2	437	87	3
OUR LADY OF THE VALLEY HS	ORANGE	NJ	528	83%	4	1	438	87	3
PEDDIE SCHOOL	HIGHTSTOWN	NJ	529	83%	13	5	439	87	3
ST ROSE HS	BELMAR	NJ	530	83%	9	8	440	87	3
LAWRENCEVILLE SCHOOL	LAWRENCEVILLE	NJ	531	83%	4	2	441	87	3
NEWARK VOCATIONAL-TECH HS	NEWARK	NJ	532	83%	17	2	442	87	3
IRVINGTON HS	IRVINGTON	NJ	533	83%	6	3	443	87	3
ST MARY'S HS	RUTHERFORD	NJ	534	83%	12	6	444	87	3
BORDENTOWN MILITARY INSTITUTE	BORDENTOWN	NJ	535	83%	10	0	445	87	3
UNION HS	UNION	NJ	536	83%	1	4	445	88	3
PENNINGTON SCHOOL	PENNINGTON	NJ	537	83%	6	2	446	88	3
ADMIRAL FARRAGUT ACADEMY	PINE BEACH	NJ	538	83%	6	3	447	88	3
BELLEVILLE HS	BELLEVILLE	NJ	539	83%	6	2	448	88	3
EAST SIDE HS	NEWARK	NJ	540	83%	3	2	449	88	3
PENNINGTON SCHOOL	PENNINGTON	NJ	541	83%	9	4	450	88	3
THOMAS JEFFERSON HS	ELIZABETH	NJ	542	83%	3	1	451	88	3
BLAIR ACADEMY	BLAIRSTOWN	NJ	543	83%	6	0	452	88	3
BAYONNE HS	BAYONNE	NJ	544	83%	5	9	452	89	3
ST ROSE HS	BELMAR	NJ	545	83%	7	0	453	89	3
1960 SEASON			26		163	78	21	5	0
ESSEX CATHOLIC	EAST ORANGE	NJ	546	83%	6	2	454	89	3
BORDENTOWN MILITARY INSTITUTE	BORDENTOWN	NJ	547	83%	2	0	455	89	3
WEST SIDE HS	NEWARK	NJ	548	83%	6	1	456	89	3
ST PETER'S PREP	JERSEY CITY	NJ	549	83%	7	4	457	89	3

JOE KASBERGER AT ST. BENEDICT'S PREP - NEWARK, NJ
BASEBALL CAREER RECORD, 1931 TO 1968

OPPOSITION NAME	CITY	STATE	GAME	CAREER BASEBALL WIN %	SEASON BASEBALL SBP	RUNS OPP	CAREER BASEBALL W	L	T
ESSEX CATHOLIC	EAST ORANGE	NJ	550	83%	1	0	458	89	3
BARRINGER HS	NEWARK	NJ	551	83%	0	5	458	90	3
PEDDIE SCHOOL	HIGHTSTOWN	NJ	552	83%	3	0	459	90	3
NEWARK VOCATIONAL-TECH HS	NEWARK	NJ	553	83%	19	0	460	90	3
DON BOSCO PREP	RAMSEY	NJ	554	83%	3	2	461	90	3
IRVINGTON HS	IRVINGTON	NJ	555	83%	2	1	462	90	3
ARCHBISHOP WALSH HS	IRVINGTON	NJ	556	83%	2	0	463	90	3
UNION HS	UNION	NJ	557	83%	5	0	464	90	3
SOUTH SIDE HS	NEWARK	NJ	558	83%	2	0	465	90	3
ADMIRAL FARRAGUT ACADEMY	PINE BEACH	NJ	559	83%	5	0	466	90	3
BELLEVILLE HS	BELLEVILLE	NJ	560	83%	5	0	467	90	3
SETON HALL PREP	WEST ORANGE	NJ	561	83%	8	7	468	90	3
THOMAS JEFFERSON HS	ELIZABETH	NJ	562	83%	1	2	468	91	3
UNION HS	UNION	NJ	563	83%	4	3	469	91	3
EAST SIDE HS	NEWARK	NJ	564	83%	7	4	470	91	3
SOUTH RIVER HS	SOUTH RIVER	NJ	565	83%	1	4	470	92	3
EAST SIDE HS	NEWARK	NJ	566	83%	7	4	471	92	3
1961 SEASON			21		96	39	18	3	0
ARCHBISHOP WALSH HS	IRVINGTON	NJ	567	83%	16	6	472	92	3
ESSEX CATHOLIC	EAST ORANGE	NJ	568	83%	7	2	473	92	3
WEST SIDE HS	NEWARK	NJ	569	83%	18	0	474	92	3
ESSEX CATHOLIC	EAST ORANGE	NJ	570	83%	2	1	475	92	3
BARRINGER HS	NEWARK	NJ	571	83%	6	4	476	92	3
PEDDIE SCHOOL	HIGHTSTOWN	NJ	572	83%	18	3	477	92	3
ST PETER'S PREP	JERSEY CITY	NJ	573	83%	4	1	478	92	3
LAWRENCEVILLE SCHOOL	LAWRENCEVILLE	NJ	574	83%	4	6	478	93	3
ARCHBISHOP WALSH HS	IRVINGTON	NJ	575	83%	8	1	479	93	3
IRVINGTON HS	IRVINGTON	NJ	576	83%	6	2	480	93	3
VAILSBURG HS	NEWARK	NJ	577	83%	7	1	481	93	3
SOUTH SIDE HS	NEWARK	NJ	578	83%	6	4	482	93	3
ADMIRAL FARRAGUT ACADEMY	PINE BEACH	NJ	579	83%	15	1	483	93	3
UNION HS	UNION	NJ	580	83%	7	4	484	93	3
BELLEVILLE HS	BELLEVILLE	NJ	581	83%	1	0	485	93	3
EAST SIDE HS	NEWARK	NJ	582	83%	4	5	485	94	3
SETON HALL PREP	WEST ORANGE	NJ	583	83%	10	3	486	94	3
THOMAS JEFFERSON HS	ELIZABETH	NJ	584	83%	10	2	487	94	3
BORDENTOWN MILITARY INSTITUTE	BORDENTOWN	NJ	585	83%	5	3	488	94	3
BLAIR ACADEMY	BLAIRSTOWN	NJ	586	83%	14	3	489	94	3
RED BANK CATHOLIC HS	RED BANK	NJ	587	83%	3	1	490	94	3
UNION HS	UNION	NJ	588	84%	16	5	491	94	3
NUTLEY HS	NUTLEY	NJ	589	83%	1	6	491	95	3
1962 SEASON			23		188	64	20	3	0
WEST SIDE HS	NEWARK	NJ	590	83%	2	1	492	95	3
ARCHBISHOP WALSH HS	IRVINGTON	NJ	591	83%	9	0	493	95	3
ESSEX CATHOLIC	EAST ORANGE	NJ	592	83%	6	3	494	95	3
OUR LADY OF THE VALLEY HS	ORANGE	NJ	593	83%	6	3	495	95	3
BORDENTOWN MILITARY INSTITUTE	BORDENTOWN	NJ	594	83%	0	7	495	96	3
ROSELLE CATHOLIC HS	ROSELLE	NJ	595	83%	7	0	496	96	3
ESSEX CATHOLIC	EAST ORANGE	NJ	596	83%	7	1	497	96	3
BARRINGER HS	NEWARK	NJ	597	83%	12	7	498	96	3
PEDDIE SCHOOL	HIGHTSTOWN	NJ	598	83%	14	6	499	96	3
OUR LADY OF THE VALLEY HS	ORANGE	NJ	599	83%	14	6	500	96	3
LAWRENCEVILLE SCHOOL	LAWRENCEVILLE	NJ	600	84%	4	0	501	96	3
IRVINGTON HS	IRVINGTON	NJ	601	84%	8	4	502	96	3
VAILSBURG HS	NEWARK	NJ	602	84%	3	1	503	96	3
UNION HS	UNION	NJ	603	84%	4	1	504	96	3
BELLEVILLE HS	BELLEVILLE	NJ	604	83%	1	4	504	97	3
EAST SIDE HS	NEWARK	NJ	605	83%	7	2	505	97	3
ADMIRAL FARRAGUT ACADEMY	PINE BEACH	NJ	606	83%	7	1	506	97	3
SETON HALL PREP	WEST ORANGE	NJ	607	84%	4	1	507	97	3
ST PETER'S PREP	JERSEY CITY	NJ	608	84%	4	0	508	97	3
BLAIR ACADEMY	BLAIRSTOWN	NJ	609	84%	3	0	509	97	3
BLOOMFIELD HS	BLOOMFIELD	NJ	610	84%	7	0	510	97	3
HANOVER PARK HS	HANOVER PARK	NJ	611	84%	11	4	511	97	3
LIVINGSTON HS	LIVINGSTON	NJ	612	84%	6	1	512	97	3
MONTCLAIR HS	MONTCLAIR	NJ	613	84%	3	8	512	98	3
1963 SEASON			24		149	61	21	3	0
ARCHBISHOP WALSH HS	IRVINGTON	NJ	614	84%	11	2	513	98	3
ESSEX CATHOLIC	EAST ORANGE	NJ	615	84%	6	1	514	98	3
WEST SIDE HS	NEWARK	NJ	616	84%	27	2	515	98	3
OUR LADY OF THE VALLEY HS	ORANGE	NJ	617	84%	15	2	516	98	3
ROSELLE CATHOLIC HS	ROSELLE	NJ	618	84%	7	2	517	98	3
PARSIPPANY HS	PARSIPPANY	NJ	619	84%	4	3	518	98	3
BARRINGER HS	NEWARK	NJ	620	84%	5	3	519	98	3
PEDDIE SCHOOL	HIGHTSTOWN	NJ	621	84%	4	0	520	98	3
LAWRENCEVILLE SCHOOL	LAWRENCEVILLE	NJ	622	84%	12	4	521	98	3
VAILSBURG HS	NEWARK	NJ	623	84%	13	4	522	98	3
ARCHBISHOP WALSH HS	IRVINGTON	NJ	624	84%	10	0	523	98	3
UNION HS	UNION	NJ	625	84%	3	4	523	99	3
OUR LADY OF THE VALLEY HS	ORANGE	NJ	626	84%	7	0	524	99	3
BORDENTOWN MILITARY INSTITUTE	BORDENTOWN	NJ	627	84%	5	6	524	100	3
BELLEVILLE HS	BELLEVILLE	NJ	628	84%	9	4	525	100	3
EAST SIDE HS	NEWARK	NJ	629	84%	3	1	526	100	3
ADMIRAL FARRAGUT ACADEMY	PINE BEACH	NJ	630	84%	11	3	527	100	3

JOE KASBERGER AT ST. BENEDICT'S PREP - NEWARK, NJ
BASEBALL CAREER RECORD, 1931 TO 1968

OPPOSITION NAME	CITY	STATE	GAME	CAREER BASEBALL WIN %	SEASON BASEBALL SBP	SEASON BASEBALL OPP	CAREER BASEBALL RUNS W	L	T
SETON HALL PREP	WEST ORANGE	NJ	631	84%	7	2	528	100	3
THOMAS JEFFERSON HS	ELIZABETH	NJ	632	84%	1	4	528	101	3
ST PETER'S PREP	JERSEY CITY	NJ	633	84%	5	0	529	101	3
BLAIR ACADEMY	BLAIRSTOWN	NJ	634	84%	14	2	530	101	3
ESSEX CATHOLIC	EAST ORANGE	NJ	635	84%	10	2	531	101	3
SOUTH SIDE HS	NEWARK	NJ	636	84%	5	0	532	101	3
IRVINGTON HS	IRVINGTON	NJ	637	84%	8	3	533	101	3
WEST ORANGE HS	WEST ORANGE	NJ	638	84%	5	2	534	101	3
MADISON HS	MADISON	NJ	639	84%	12	0	535	101	3
LIVINGSTON HS	LIVINGSTON	NJ	640	84%	7	5	536	101	3
MONTCLAIR HS	MONTCLAIR	NJ	641	84%	6	5	537	101	3
1964 SEASON			28		232	66	25	3	0
ESSEX CATHOLIC	EAST ORANGE	NJ	642	84%	0	10	537	102	3
NORTH BERGEN HS	NORTH BERGEN	NJ	643	84%	1	5	537	103	3
WEST SIDE HS	NEWARK	NJ	644	84%	8	5	538	103	3
OUR LADY OF THE VALLEY HS	ORANGE	NJ	645	84%	15	1	539	103	3
PARSIPPANY HS	PARSIPPANY	NJ	646	83%	1	6	539	104	3
PEDDIE SCHOOL	HIGHTSTOWN	NJ	647	83%	3	2	540	104	3
NEWARK ACADEMY	LIVINGSTON	NJ	648	83%	6	3	541	104	3
OUR LADY OF THE VALLEY HS	ORANGE	NJ	849	84%	21	0	542	104	3
ADMIRAL FARRAGUT ACADEMY	PINE BEACH	NJ	650	84%	6	1	543	104	3
LAWRENCEVILLE SCHOOL	LAWRENCEVILLE	NJ	651	83%	1	2	543	105	3
ST JAMES HS	NEWARK	NJ	652	83%	15	1	544	105	3
ST PETER'S PREP	JERSEY CITY	NJ	653	83%	9	6	545	105	3
CENTRAL HS	NEWARK	NJ	654	83%	8	5	546	105	3
BARRINGER HS	NEWARK	NJ	655	84%	5	4	547	105	3
BORDENTOWN MILITARY INSTITUTE	BORDENTOWN	NJ	656	84%	1	0	548	105	3
CARTERET ACADEMY	SHORT HILLS	NJ	657	84%	12	2	549	105	3
EAST SIDE HS	NEWARK	NJ	658	84%	9	2	550	105	3
ROSELLE CATHOLIC HS	ROSELLE	NJ	659	83%	4	11	550	106	3
SETON HALL PREP	WEST ORANGE	NJ	660	83%	6	5	551	106	3
SNYDER HS	JERSEY CITY	NJ	661	83%	1	3	551	107	3
THOMAS JEFFERSON HS	ELIZABETH	NJ	662	83%	8	9	551	108	3
SOUTH SIDE HS	NEWARK	NJ	663	83%	5	3	552	108	3
BLAIR ACADEMY	BLAIRSTOWN	NJ	664	83%	1	0	553	108	3
1965 SEASON			23		146	86	16	7	0
ESSEX CATHOLIC	EAST ORANGE	NJ	665	83%	5	7	553	109	3
WEST SIDE HS	NEWARK	NJ	666	83%	10	0	554	109	3
CENTRAL HS	NEWARK	NJ	667	83%	0	1	554	110	3
ROSELLE CATHOLIC HS	ROSELLE	NJ	668	83%	7	2	555	110	3
PARSIPPANY HS	PARSIPPANY	NJ	669	83%	1	10	555	111	3
ESSEX CATHOLIC	EAST ORANGE	NJ	670	83%	2	5	555	112	3
PEDDIE SCHOOL	HIGHTSTOWN	NJ	671	83%	0	3	555	113	3
NEWARK ACADEMY	LIVINGSTON	NJ	672	83%	5	0	556	113	3
LAWRENCEVILLE SCHOOL	LAWRENCEVILLE	NJ	673	83%	17	4	557	113	3
ST JAMES HS	NEWARK	NJ	674	83%	8	0	558	113	3
SOUTH SIDE HS	NEWARK	NJ	675	83%	3	2	559	113	3
ST PETER'S PREP	JERSEY CITY	NJ	676	83%	1	2	559	114	3
OUR LADY OF THE VALLEY HS	ORANGE	NJ	677	83%	7	6	560	114	3
BERGEN CATHOLIC HS	ORADELL	NJ	678	83%	2	3	560	115	3
CARTERET ACADEMY	SHORT HILLS	NJ	679	83%	9	1	561	115	3
EAST SIDE HS	NEWARK	NJ	680	83%	1	2	561	116	3
DON BOSCO PREP	RAMSEY	NJ	681	82%	2	3	561	117	3
SETON HALL PREP	WEST ORANGE	NJ	682	82%	3	6	561	118	3
BORDENTOWN MILITARY INSTITUTE	BORDENTOWN	NJ	683	82%	1	3	561	119	3
OUR LADY OF THE VALLEY HS	ORANGE	NJ	684	82%	3	0	562	119	3
ST JOSEPH'S HS	MONTVALE	NJ	685	82%	7	3	563	119	3
BLAIR ACADEMY	BLAIRSTOWN	NJ	686	82%	5	6	563	120	3
ADMIRAL FARRAGUT ACADEMY	PINE BEACH	NJ	687	82%	10	0	564	120	3
1966 SEASON			23		109	69	11	12	0
WEST SIDE HS	NEWARK	NJ	688	82%	1	2	564	121	3
CENTRAL HS	NEWARK	NJ	689	82%	6	0	565	121	3
PINGRY SCHOOL	MARTINSVILLE	NJ	690	82%	?	?	566	121	3
EAST SIDE HS	NEWARK	NJ	691	82%	?	?	567	121	3
BORDENTOWN MILITARY INSTITUTE	BORDENTOWN	NJ	692	82%	?	?	567	122	3
ST PETER'S PREP	JERSEY CITY	NJ	693	82%	2	1	568	122	3
PEDDIE SCHOOL	HIGHTSTOWN	NJ	694	82%	5	4	569	122	3
CARTERET ACADEMY	SHORT HILLS	NJ	695	82%	?	?	570	122	3
ESSEX CATHOLIC	EAST ORANGE	NJ	696	82%	11	5	571	122	3
LAWRENCEVILLE SCHOOL	LAWRENCEVILLE	NJ	697	82%	?	?	571	123	3
UNION CATHOLIC HS	UNION	NJ	698	82%	?	?	572	123	3
SOUTH SIDE HS	NEWARK	NJ	699	82%	?	?	573	123	3
ADMIRAL FARRAGUT ACADEMY	PINE BEACH	NJ	700	82%	?	?	574	123	3
ST MARY'S HS	ELIZABETH	NJ	701	82%	?	?	575	123	3
WEEQUAHIC HS	NEWARK	NJ	702	82%	2	4	575	124	3
ROSELLE CATHOLIC HS	ROSELLE	NJ	703	82%	?	?	575	125	3
ST JOSEPH'S HS	MONTVALE	NJ	704	82%	?	?	576	125	3
BERGEN CATHOLIC HS	ORADELL	NJ	705	82%	?	?	577	125	3
NEWARK ACADEMY	LIVINGSTON	NJ	706	82%	?	?	577	126	3
THOMAS JEFFERSON HS	ELIZABETH	NJ	707	82%	?	?	577	127	3
DON BOSCO PREP	RAMSEY	NJ	708	82%	?	?	578	127	3
OUR LADY OF THE VALLEY HS	ORANGE	NJ	709	82%	?	?	579	127	3
SETON HALL PREP	WEST ORANGE	NJ	710	82%	4	3	580	127	3
1967 SEASON			23		31	19	16	7	0

JOE KASBERGER AT ST. BENEDICT'S PREP - NEWARK, NJ
BASEBALL CAREER RECORD, 1931 TO 1968

OPPOSITION NAME	CITY	STATE	GAME	CAREER BASEBALL WIN %	SEASON BASEBALL SBP	RUNS OPP	CAREER BASEBALL W	L	T
WEST SIDE HS	NEWARK	NJ	711	82%	20	4	581	127	3
CENTRAL HS	NEWARK	NJ	712	82%	17	3	582	127	3
CARTERET ACADEMY	SHORT HILLS	NJ	713	82%	26	0	583	127	3
PARSIPPANY HS	PARSIPPANY	NJ	714	82%	3	10	583	128	3
ST PETER'S PREP	JERSEY CITY	NJ	715	82%	6	7	583	129	3
PEDDIE SCHOOL	HIGHTSTOWN	NJ	716	82%	7	3	584	129	3
ESSEX CATHOLIC	EAST ORANGE	NJ	717	82%	4	2	585	129	3
EAST SIDE HS	NEWARK	NJ	718	81%	1	4	585	130	3
LAWRENCEVILLE SCHOOL	LAWRENCEVILLE	NJ	719	82%	5	1	586	130	3
ST MARY'S HS	ELIZABETH	NJ	720	81%	2	8	586	131	3
ESSEX CATHOLIC	EAST ORANGE	NJ	721	81%	1	10	586	132	3
SETON HALL PREP	WEST ORANGE	NJ	722	81%	9	4	587	132	3
ST JOSEPH'S HS	MONTVALE	NJ	723	81%	10	4	588	132	3
ADMIRAL FARRAGUT ACADEMY	PINE BEACH	NJ	724	81%	3	0	589	132	3
BERGEN CATHOLIC HS	ORADELL	NJ	725	81%	1	2	589	133	3
UNION CATHOLIC HS	UNION	NJ	726	81%	8	2	590	133	3
SOUTH SIDE HS	NEWARK	NJ	727	81%	12	0	591	133	3
THOMAS JEFFERSON HS	ELIZABETH	NJ	728	81%	2	3	591	134	3
DON BOSCO PREP	RAMSEY	NJ	729	81%	1	3	591	135	3
BORDENTOWN MILITARY INSTITUTE	BORDENTOWN	NJ	730	81%	1	8	591	136	3
OUR LADY OF THE VALLEY HS	ORANGE	NJ	731	81%	7	4	592	136	3
ROSELLE CATHOLIC HS	ROSELLE	NJ	732	81%	2	1	593	136	3
BLAIR ACADEMY	BLAIRSTOWN	NJ	733	81%	1	7	593	137	3
	1968 SEASON		23		149	90	13	10	0

END OF FILE

JOE KASBERGER AT ST. BENEDICT'S PREP - NEWARK, NJ FOOTBALL CAREER RECORD, 1930 TO 1966 OPPOSITION NAME	CITY	STATE	GAME	CAREER FOOTBALL WIN %	SEASON FOOTBALL SBP	POINTS OPP	CAREER FOOTBALL W	L	T
SAMUEL JOHNSON ACADEMY		CT	1	100%	7	6	1	0	0
RUTGERS UNIVERSITY FROSH	NEW BRUNSWICK	NJ	2	100%	12	0	2	0	0
PRINCETON PREP	PRINCETON	NJ	3	100%	34	0	3	0	0
DICKINSON HS	JERSEY CITY	NJ	4	100%	33	0	4	0	0
PEDDIE SCHOOL	HIGHTSTOWN	NJ	5	80%	6	12	4	1	0
COOK ACADEMY		NY	6	67%	0	4	4	2	0
SETON HALL PREP	WEST ORANGE	NJ	7	71%	18	0	5	2	0
1930 SEASON			7		110	22	5	2	0
CURTIS HS		NY	8	63%	0	0	5	2	1
ST MARY'S HS	SOUTH AMBOY	NJ	9	67%	33	0	6	2	1
PIERCE SCHOOL	PHILADELPHIA	PA	10	70%	13	6	7	2	1
BARRINGER HS	NEWARK	NJ	11	73%	34	0	8	2	1
DICKINSON HS	JERSEY CITY	NJ	12	75%	34	0	9	2	1
PEDDIE SCHOOL	HIGHTSTOWN	NJ	13	77%	14	7	10	2	1
SAMUEL JOHNSON ACADEMY		CT	14	79%	33	6	11	2	1
SETON HALL PREP	WEST ORANGE	NJ	15	80%	14	0	12	2	1
SOUTH SIDE HS	NEWARK	NJ	16	81%	14	0	13	2	1
1931 SEASON			9		189	19	8	0	1
MT ST MICHAEL PREP	BRONX	NY	17	82%	47	0	14	2	1
PRINCETON PREP	PRINCETON	NJ	18	83%	30	0	15	2	1
SAMUEL JOHNSON ACADEMY		CT	19	84%	26	7	16	2	1
PENNINGTON SCHOOL	PENNINGTON	NJ	20	80%	0	6	16	3	1
PEDDIE SCHOOL	HIGHTSTOWN	NJ	21	81%	?	?	17	3	1
WENONAH MILITARY ACADEMY	WENONAH	NJ	22	82%	20	0	18	3	1
SETON HALL PREP	WEST ORANGE	NJ	23	83%	42	0	19	3	1
1932 SEASON			7		165	13	6	1	0
PHILLIPSBURG HS	PHILLIPSBURG	NJ	24	83%	18	0	20	3	1
BLAIR ACADEMY	BLAIRSTOWN	NJ	25	84%	27	0	21	3	1
BROWN PREP	PHILADELPHIA	PA	26	85%	29	0	22	3	1
PRINCETON PREP	PRINCETON	NJ	27	85%	47	7	23	3	1
ST FRANCIS PREP	FRESH MEADOW	NY	28	86%	26	0	24	3	1
WENONAH MILITARY ACADEMY	WENONAH	NJ	29	86%	35	0	25	3	1
HUN SCHOOL	PRINCETON	NJ	30	87%	15	0	26	3	1
PENNINGTON SCHOOL	PENNINGTON	NJ	31	84%	7	7	26	3	2
ALLENTOWN PREP	ALLENTOWN	PA	32	81%	0	6	26	4	2
1933 SEASON			9		204	20	7	1	1
SALESIANUM PREP	WILMINGTON	DE	33	82%	12	0	27	4	2
MACKENZIE SCHOOL		NY	34	82%	13	0	28	4	2
PENNINGTON SCHOOL	PENNINGTON	NJ	35	83%	16	0	29	4	2
BARRINGER HS	NEWARK	NJ	36	83%	40	0	30	4	2
ST FRANCIS PREP	FRESH MEADOW	NY	37	84%	13	0	31	4	2
ADMIRAL FARRAGUT ACADEMY	PINE BEACH	NJ	38	84%	33	0	32	4	2
ALLENTOWN PREP	ALLENTOWN	PA	39	82%	0	0	32	4	3
SETON HALL PREP	WEST ORANGE	NJ	40	83%	6	0	33	4	3
1934 SEASON			8		133	0	7	0	1
ST MARY'S HS	RUTHERFORD	NJ	41	83%	18	6	34	4	3
BROWN PREP	PHILADELPHIA	PA	42	83%	22	0	35	4	3
XAVIER PREP	NEW YORK	NY	43	84%	7	0	36	4	3
ADMIRAL FARRAGUT ACADEMY	PINE BEACH	NJ	44	84%	20	0	37	4	3
PENNINGTON SCHOOL	PENNINGTON	NJ	45	82%	3	7	37	5	3
MONTCLAIR ACADEMY	MONTCLAIR	NJ	46	83%	20	6	38	5	3
ALLENTOWN PREP	ALLENTOWN	PA	47	83%	30	0	39	5	3
1935 SEASON			7		120	19	6	1	0
ST MARY'S HS	RUTHERFORD	NJ	48	83%	28	0	40	5	3
ST. FRANCIS XAVIER PREP	BROOKLYN	NY	49	84%	29	0	41	5	3
KINGSLEY SCHOOL	BROOKLYN	NY	50	84%	18	0	42	5	3
MONTCLAIR STATE COLLEGE JV	UPPER MONTCLAIR	NJ	51	84%	6	0	43	5	3
PENNINGTON SCHOOL	PENNINGTON	NJ	52	85%	6	0	44	5	3
LA SALLE MILITARY ACADEMY	OAKDALE	NY	53	85%	33	0	45	5	3
BROWN PREP	PHILADELPHIA	PA	54	85%	32	0	46	5	3
ADMIRAL FARRAGUT ACADEMY	PINE BEACH	NJ	55	85%	34	0	47	5	3
EAST SIDE HS	NEWARK	NJ	56	86%	59	0	48	5	3
1936 SEASON			9		245	0	9	0	0
ST MARY'S HS	RUTHERFORD	NJ	57	86%	20	0	49	5	3
LINCOLN COLLEGE PREP			58	86%	75	0	50	5	3
BORDENTOWN MILITARY INSTITUTE	BORDENTOWN	NJ	59	85%	6	6	50	5	4
ARCHMERE ACADEMY	CLAYMONT	DE	60	85%	14	7	51	5	4
PENNINGTON SCHOOL	PENNINGTON	NJ	61	85%	16	0	52	5	4
MANHATTAN COLLEGE FROSH	NEW YORK	NY	62	85%	6	0	53	5	4
SETON HALL PREP	WEST ORANGE	NJ	63	86%	6	0	54	5	4
BROWN PREP (X)	PHILADELPHIA	PA	X		X	X	X	X	X
1937 SEASON			7		143	13	6	0	1
ARCHMERE ACADEMY	CLAYMONT	DE	64	86%	13	0	55	5	4
BORDENTOWN MILITARY INSTITUTE	BORDENTOWN	NJ	65	85%	7	7	55	5	5
ST CECILIA HS	ENGLEWOOD	NJ	66	85%	21	6	56	5	5
BROWN PREP	PHILADELPHIA	PA	67	85%	14	7	57	5	5
PENNINGTON SCHOOL	PENNINGTON	NJ	68	85%	12	0	58	5	5
SETON HALL PREP	WEST ORANGE	NJ	69	84%	0	12	58	6	5
1938 SEASON			6		67	32	4	1	1

JOE KASBERGER AT ST. BENEDICT'S PREP - NEWARK, NJ
FOOTBALL CAREER RECORD, 1930 TO 1966

OPPOSITION NAME	CITY	STATE	GAME	CAREER FOOTBALL WIN %	SEASON FOOTBALL SBP	POINTS	OPP	CAREER FOOTBALL W	L	T
ST CECILIA HS	ENGLEWOOD	NJ	70	84%	13	0	59	6	5	
VILLANOVA COLLEGE FROSH	VILLANOVA	PA	71	83%	0	6	59	7	5	
BORDENTOWN MILITARY INSTITUTE	BORDENTOWN	NJ	72	82%	0	0	59	7	6	
COLUMBIA UNIVERSITY FROSH	NEW YORK	NY	73	81%	14	20	59	8	6	
BULLIS SCHOOL	POTOMAC	MD	74	80%	6	7	59	9	6	
PENNINGTON SCHOOL	PENNINGTON	NJ	75	80%	12	0	60	9	6	
BROWN PREP	PHILADELPHIA	PA	76	80%	33	0	61	9	6	
SETON HALL PREP	WEST ORANGE	NJ	77	79%	0	0	61	9	7	
1939 SEASON			8		78	33	3	3	2	
ST BASIL HS	STAMFORD	CT	78	79%	12	7	62	9	7	
VILLANOVA COLLEGE FROSH	VILLANOVA	PA	79	78%	0	7	62	10	7	
WEST CHESTER COLLEGE FROSH	WEST CHESTER	PA	80	79%	14	0	63	10	7	
COLUMBIA UNIVERSITY FROSH	NEW YORK	NY	81	78%	13	13	63	10	8	
MUHLENBERG COLLEGE FROSH	ALLENTOWN	PA	82	78%	7	0	64	10	8	
MANHATTAN COLLEGE FROSH	NEW YORK	NY	83	78%	23	0	65	10	8	
BORDENTOWN MILITARY INSTITUTE	BORDENTOWN	NJ	84	77%	0	13	65	11	8	
BROWN PREP	PHILADELPHIA	PA	85	78%	37	0	66	11	8	
SETON HALL PREP	WEST ORANGE	NJ	86	78%	13	6	67	11	8	
1940 SEASON			9		119	46	6	2	1	
NEW BRUNSWICK HS	NEW BRUNSWICK	NJ	87	78%	3	0	68	11	8	
MARIANAPOLIS PREP	THOMPSON	CT	88	78%	8	0	69	11	8	
LA SALLE MILITARY ACADEMY	OAKDALE	NY	89	79%	21	0	70	11	8	
MANHATTAN COLLEGE FROSH (#)	NEW YORK	NY	90	78%	6	13	70	12	8	
COLUMBIA UNIVERSITY FROSH	NEW YORK	NY	91	78%	7	6	71	12	8	
SCRANTON COLLEGE FROSH	SCRANTON	PA	92	78%	14	0	72	12	8	
BLAIR ACADEMY	BLAIRSTOWN	NJ	93	77%	0	7	72	13	8	
bORDENTOWN MILITARY INSTITUTE (#)	BORDENTOWN	NJ	94	77%	6	16	72	14	8	
BROWN PREP (#)	PHILADELPHIA	PA	95	77%	26	0	73	14	8	
SETON HALL PREP (X)			X		X	X	X	X	X	X
1941 SEASON			9		91	42	7	2	0	
NEW BRUNSWICK HS	NEW BRUNSWICK	NJ	96	77%	13	0	74	14	8	
LA SALLE MILITARY ACADEMY	OAKDALE	NY	97	77%	41	13	75	14	8	
MANHATTAN COLLEGE FROSH	NEW YORK	NY	98	78%	21	0	76	14	8	
COLUMBIA UNIVERSITY FROSH	NEW YORK	NY	99	78%	26	6	77	14	8	
ADMIRAL FARRAGUT ACADEMY	PINE BEACH	NJ	100	78%	13	0	78	14	8	
BLAIR ACADEMY	BLAIRSTOWN	NJ	101	78%	52	0	79	14	8	
BORDENTOWN MILITARY INSTITUTE	BORDENTOWN	NJ	102	78%	40	0	80	14	8	
BROWN PREP	PHILADELPHIA	PA	X		X	X	X	X	X	X
1942 SEASON			7		206	19	7	0	0	
HARRISON HS	HARRISON	NJ	103	79%	12	0	81	14	8	
COLUMBIA UNIVERSITY FROSH	NEW YORK	NY	104	79%	?	?	82	14	8	
1943 SEASON			2		12	0	2	0	0	
LA SALLE MILITARY ACADEMY	OAKDALE	NY	105	78%	0	18	82	15	8	
TRENTON CATHOLIC HS	TRENTON	NJ	106	77%	6	26	82	16	8	
BORDENTOWN MILITARY INSTITUTE	BORDENTOWN	NJ	107	78%	20	0	83	16	8	
MONTCLAIR ACADEMY	MONTCLAIR	NJ	108	78%	18	0	84	16	8	
1944 SEASON			4		44	44	2	2	0	
US MILITARY ACADEMY PLEBES	WEST POINT	NY	109	77%	0	33	84	17	8	
LA SALLE MILITARY ACADEMY	OAKDALE	NY	110	76%	0	33	84	18	8	
TRENTON CATHOLIC HS	TRENTON	NJ	111	77%	8	6	85	18	8	
BORDENTOWN MILITARY INSTITUTE	BORDENTOWN	NJ	112	76%	7	21	85	19	8	
SOUTH SIDE HS	NEWARK	NJ	113	76%	32	7	86	19	8	
COLUMBIA UNIVERSITY FROSH	NEW YORK	NY	114	76%	22	0	87	19	8	
ADMIRAL FARRAGUT ACADEMY	PINE BEACH	NJ	X		X	X	X	X	X	X
1945 SEASON			6		69	100	3	3	0	
ST MARY'S HS	RUTHERFORD	NJ	115	77%	40	12	88	19	8	
TRENTON CATHOLIC HS	TRENTON	NJ	116	77%	30	7	89	19	8	
POPE PIUS XII HS	PASSAIC	NJ	117	77%	26	6	90	19	8	
ADMIRAL FARRAGUT ACADEMY	PINE BEACH	NJ	118	77%	31	13	91	19	8	
BORDENTOWN MILITARY INSTITUTE	BORDENTOWN	NJ	119	77%	21	0	92	19	8	
NEWARK ACADEMY	LIVINGSTON	NJ	120	78%	33	0	93	19	8	
SOUTH SIDE HS	NEWARK	NJ	121	78%	64	0	94	19	8	
1946 SEASON			7		245	38	7	0	0	
ST IGNATIUS HS	BROOKLYN	NY	122	78%	48	0	95	19	8	
MARIANAPOLIS PREP	THOMPSON	CT	123	77%	6	13	95	20	8	
TRENTON CATHOLIC HS	TRENTON	NJ	124	77%	41	6	96	20	8	
POPE PIUS XII HS	PASSAIC	NJ	125	78%	35	0	97	20	8	
BLAIR ACADEMY	BLAIRSTOWN	NJ	126	78%	20	0	98	20	8	
SCRANTON COLLEGE FROSH	SCRANTON	PA	127	78%	39	6	99	20	8	
NEWARK ACADEMY	LIVINGSTON	NJ	128	78%	25	13	100	20	8	
CARTERET ACADEMY	SHORT HILLS	NJ	129	78%	7	7	100	20	9	
1947 SEASON			8		221	45	6	1	1	
EAST STROUDSBURG COLLEGE JV	EAST STROUDSBURG	PA	130	78%	33	0	101	20	9	
MARIANAPOLIS PREP	THOMPSON	CT	131	78%	7	6	102	20	9	
BLAIR ACADEMY	BLAIRSTOWN	NJ	132	78%	19	0	103	20	9	
CARTERET ACADEMY	SHORT HILLS	NJ	133	78%	39	0	104	20	9	
CITY COLLEGE OF NY FROSH	NEW YORK	NY	134	78%	63	0	105	20	9	

JOE KASBERGER AT ST. BENEDICT'S PREP - NEWARK, NJ
FOOTBALL CAREER RECORD, 1930 TO 1966

OPPOSITION NAME	CITY	STATE	GAME	CAREER FOOTBALL WIN %	SEASON FOOTBALL SBP	POINTS OPP	CAREER FOOTBALL W	L	T
HOFSTRA COLLEGE FROSH	HEMPSTEAD	NY	135	79%	25	13	106	20	9
BULLIS SCHOOL	POTOMAC	MD	136	78%	0	6	106	21	9
VALLEY FORGE MILITARY ACADEMY	WAYNE	PA	137	78%	6	0	107	21	9
AQUINAS INSTITUTE	ROCHESTER	NY	138	78%	7	7	107	21	10
1948 SEASON			9		199	32	7	1	1
CAMP KILMER	NEW BRUNSWICK	NJ	139	78%	26	7	108	21	10
EAST STROUDSBURG COLLEGE JV	EAST STROUDSBURG	PA	140	78%	53	0	109	21	10
ST IGNATIUS HS	BROOKLYN	NY	141	78%	46	6	110	21	10
NEW YORK MILITARY ACADEMY	CORNWALL-ON-HUDSON	NY	142	78%	39	7	111	21	10
MARIANAPOLIS PREP	THOMPSON	CT	143	78%	20	7	112	21	10
HOFSTRA COLLEGE FROSH	HEMPSTEAD	NY	144	78%	39	0	113	21	10
PERKIOMEN SCHOOL	PENNSBURG	PA	145	79%	26	0	114	21	10
AQUINAS INSTITUTE	ROCHESTER	NY	146	79%	25	9	115	21	10
CARTERET ACADEMY	SHORT HILLS	NJ	147	79%	34	12	116	21	10
1949 SEASON			9		308	48	9	0	0
EAST STROUDSBURG COLLEGE JV	EAST STROUDSBURG	PA	148	78%	7	7	116	21	11
UPSALA COLLEGE FROSH	EAST ORANGE	NJ	149	79%	35	13	117	21	11
NEW YORK MILITARY ACADEMY	CORNWALL-ON-HUDSON	NY	150	79%	20	7	118	21	11
ST IGNATIUS HS	BROOKLYN	NY	151	79%	48	0	119	21	11
US MILITARY ACADEMY PREP	FORT MONMOUTH	NJ	152	79%	20	12	120	21	11
HOFSTRA COLLEGE FROSH	HEMPSTEAD	NY	153	79%	13	6	121	21	11
RUTGERS UNIVERSITY JV	NEW BRUNSWICK	NJ	154	79%	49	12	122	21	11
PERKIOMEN SCHOOL	PENNSBURG	PA	X		X	X	X	X	X
1950 SEASON			7		192	57	6	0	1
FORT DIX	FORT DIX	NJ	155	79%	34	7	123	21	11
FORDHAM UNIVERSITY JV	BRONX	NY	156	79%	21	0	124	21	11
LEHIGH UNIVERSITY FROSH	BETHLEHEM	PA	157	80%	28	0	125	21	11
PRINCETON UNIVERSITY FROSH	PRINCETON	NJ	158	79%	0	7	125	22	11
AQUINAS INSTITUTE	ROCHESTER	NY	159	79%	19	26	125	23	11
COLUMBIA UNIVERSITY FROSH	NEW YORK	NY	160	79%	27	6	126	23	11
1951 SEASON			6		129	46	4	2	0
ST MARY'S HS	RUTHERFORD	NJ	161	78%	0	25	126	24	11
HUN SCHOOL	PRINCETON	NJ	162	78%	0	28	126	25	11
EASTERN MILITARY ACADEMY	COLD SPRING HARBOR	NY	163	78%	18	12	127	25	11
ST DOMINIC'S HS	OYSTER BAY	NY	164	78%	39	6	128	25	11
BLAIR ACADEMY	BLAIRSTOWN	NJ	165	78%	0	27	128	26	11
BAYLEY-ELLARD HS	MADISON	NJ	166	78%	7	6	129	26	11
IMMACULATE CONCEPTION HS	MONTCLAIR	NJ	167	77%	12	19	129	27	11
1952 SEASON			7		76	123	3	4	0
ST MARY'S HS	RUTHERFORD	NJ	168	77%	19	20	129	28	11
HUN SCHOOL	PRINCETON	NJ	169	77%	42	0	130	28	11
EASTERN MILITARY ACADEMY	COLD SPRING HARBOR	NY	170	77%	14	7	131	28	11
BORDENTOWN MILITARY INSTITUTE	BORDENTOWN	NJ	171	77%	32	7	132	28	11
TRENTON CATHOLIC HS	TRENTON	NJ	172	77%	20	7	133	28	11
QUEEN OF PEACE HS	NORTH ARLINGTON	NJ	173	77%	26	0	134	28	11
HARRISON HS	HARRISON	NJ	174	78%	21	13	135	28	11
FAIR LAWN HS	FAIR LAWN	NJ	X		X	X	X	X	X
1953 SEASON			7		174	54	6	1	0
ST MARY'S HS	RUTHERFORD	NJ	175	78%	31	7	136	28	11
EASTERN MILITARY ACADEMY	COLD SPRING HARBOR	NY	176	78%	26	0	137	28	11
HARRISON HS	HARRISON	NJ	177	78%	26	12	138	28	11
BORDENTOWN MILITARY INSTITUTE	BORDENTOWN	NJ	178	78%	26	0	139	28	11
FAIR LAWN HS	FAIR LAWN	NJ	179	78%	33	6	140	28	11
TRENTON CATHOLIC HS	TRENTON	NJ	180	78%	27	12	141	28	11
QUEEN OF PEACE HS	NORTH ARLINGTON	NJ	181	78%	41	7	142	28	11
1954 SEASON			7		210	44	7	0	0
ST MARY'S HS	RUTHERFORD	NJ	182	78%	6	20	142	29	11
QUEEN OF PEACE HS	NORTH ARLINGTON	NJ	183	78%	0	8	142	30	11
EASTERN MILITARY ACADEMY	COLD SPRING HARBOR	NY	184	77%	0	19	142	31	11
HARRISON HS	HARRISON	NJ	185	77%	6	6	142	31	12
BORDENTOWN MILITARY INSTITUTE	BORDENTOWN	NJ	186	76%	0	47	142	32	12
PINGRY SCHOOL	MARTINSVILLE	NJ	187	76%	14	34	142	33	12
FAIR LAWN HS	FAIR LAWN	NJ	188	76%	7	47	142	34	12
CENTRAL HS	NEWARK	NJ	189	75%	0	26	142	35	12
1955 SEASON			8		33	207	0	7	1
ST MARY'S HS	RUTHERFORD	NJ	190	75%	35	6	143	35	12
QUEEN OF PEACE HS	NORTH ARLINGTON	NJ	191	75%	46	0	144	35	12
ADMIRAL FARRAGUT ACADEMY	PINE BEACH	NJ	192	76%	34	0	145	35	12
HARRISON HS	HARRISON	NJ	193	76%	42	6	146	35	12
BORDENTOWN MILITARY INSTITUTE	BORDENTOWN	NJ	194	75%	6	20	146	36	12
PINGRY SCHOOL	MARTINSVILLE	NJ	195	75%	54	14	147	36	12
FAIR LAWN HS	FAIR LAWN	NJ	196	76%	28	0	148	36	12
CENTRAL HS	NEWARK	NJ	197	76%	27	0	149	36	12
SOUTH SIDE HS	NEWARK	NJ	198	75%	13	19	149	37	12
1956 SEASON			9		285	65	7	2	0
ST MARY'S HS	RUTHERFORD	NJ	199	75%	20	13	150	37	12
QUEEN OF PEACE HS	NORTH ARLINGTON	NJ	200	76%	27	6	151	37	12
HARRISON HS	HARRISON	NJ	201	76%	33	12	152	37	12

JOE KASBERGER AT ST. BENEDICT'S PREP - NEWARK, NJ
FOOTBALL CAREER RECORD, 1930 TO 1966

OPPOSITION NAME	CITY	STATE	GAME	CAREER FOOTBALL WIN %	SEASON FOOTBALL SBP	POINTS OPP	CAREER FOOTBALL W	L	T
BORDENTOWN MILITARY INSTITUTE	BORDENTOWN	NJ	202	75%	13	20	152	38	12
BLAIR ACADEMY	BLAIRSTOWN	NJ	203	75%	26	0	153	38	12
RAHWAY HS	RAHWAY	NJ	204	75%	26	12	154	38	12
FAIR LAWN HS	FAIR LAWN	NJ	205	75%	13	13	154	38	13
PINGRY SCHOOL	MARTINSVILLE	NJ	206	75%	26	12	155	38	13
CENTRAL HS	NEWARK	NJ	207	75%	33	0	156	38	13
1957 SEASON			9		217	88	7	1	1
ST MARY'S HS	RUTHERFORD	NJ	208	75%	32	6	157	38	13
OUR LADY OF THE VALLEY HS	ORANGE	NJ	209	76%	43	13	158	38	13
PEDDIE SCHOOL	HIGHTSTOWN	NJ	210	76%	19	0	159	38	13
BLAIR ACADEMY	BLAIRSTOWN	NJ	211	76%	26	7	160	38	13
BORDENTOWN MILITARY INSTITUTE	BORDENTOWN	NJ	212	75%	6	19	160	39	13
CENTRAL HS	NEWARK	NJ	213	76%	34	12	161	39	13
MT ST MICHAEL PREP	BRONX	NY	214	76%	30	12	162	39	13
ST MICHAEL'S HS	UNION CITY	NJ	215	76%	21	13	163	39	13
1958 SEASON			8		211	82	7	1	0
NEW YORK MILITARY ACADEMY	CORNWALL-ON-HUDSON	NY	216	76%	14	6	164	39	13
OUR LADY OF THE VALLEY HS	ORANGE	NJ	217	76%	14	7	165	39	13
PEDDIE SCHOOL	HIGHTSTOWN	NJ	218	76%	33	7	166	39	13
MT ST MICHAEL PREP	BRONX	NY	219	76%	14	12	167	39	13
BORDENTOWN MILITARY INSTITUTE	BORDENTOWN	NJ	220	76%	7	14	167	40	13
CENTRAL HS	NEWARK	NJ	221	76%	41	7	168	40	13
ORATORY PREP	SUMMIT	NJ	222	76%	33	0	169	40	13
SETON HALL PREP	WEST ORANGE	NJ	223	76%	6	0	170	40	13
1959 SEASON			8		162	53	7	1	0
WEST SIDE HS	NEWARK	NJ	224	76%	32	0	171	40	13
NEW YORK MILITARY ACADEMY	CORNWALL-ON-HUDSON	NY	225	76%	26	0	172	40	13
ST MICHAEL'S HS	UNION CITY	NJ	226	76%	12	20	172	41	13
PEDDIE SCHOOL	HIGHTSTOWN	NJ	227	76%	40	21	173	41	13
EAST SIDE HS	NEWARK	NJ	228	76%	6	23	173	42	13
CENTRAL HS	NEWARK	NJ	229	76%	34	12	174	42	13
ORATORY PREP	SUMMIT	NJ	230	76%	20	0	175	42	13
SETON HALL PREP	WEST ORANGE	NJ	231	76%	12	22	175	43	13
1960 SEASON			8		182	98	5	3	0
WEST SIDE HS	NEWARK	NJ	232	76%	33	20	176	43	13
LAWRENCEVILLE SCHOOL	LAWRENCEVILLE	NJ	233	76%	38	48	176	44	13
ST PETER'S PREP	JERSEY CITY	NJ	234	75%	13	26	176	45	13
EAST SIDE HS	NEWARK	NJ	235	75%	21	37	176	46	13
CENTRAL HS	NEWARK	NJ	236	75%	22	12	177	46	13
NEW YORK MILITARY ACADEMY	CORNWALL-ON-HUDSON	NY	237	75%	21	31	177	47	13
SETON HALL PREP	WEST ORANGE	NJ	238	75%	21	20	178	47	13
1961 SEASON			7		169	194	3	4	0
ST PETER'S PREP	JERSEY CITY	NJ	239	75%	40	18	179	47	13
LAWRENCEVILLE SCHOOL	LAWRENCEVILLE	NJ	240	75%	13	43	179	48	13
ESSEX CATHOLIC HS	NEWARK	NJ	241	75%	38	13	180	48	13
CENTRAL HS	NEWARK	NJ	242	75%	38	13	181	48	13
EAST SIDE HS	NEWARK	NJ	243	75%	13	7	182	48	13
SOUTH SIDE HS	NEWARK	NJ	244	75%	14	6	183	48	13
NEW YORK MILITARY ACADEMY	CORNWALL-ON-HUDSON	NY	245	75%	30	0	184	48	13
SETON HALL PREP	WEST ORANGE	NJ	246	75%	7	7	184	48	14
1962 SEASON			8		193	107	6	1	1
NEW YORK MILITARY ACADEMY	CORNWALL-ON-HUDSON	NY	247	75%	41	7	185	48	14
EAST ORANGE HS	EAST ORANGE	NJ	248	75%	14	33	185	49	14
CENTRAL HS	NEWARK	NJ	249	75%	40	19	186	49	14
PEDDIE SCHOOL	HIGHTSTOWN	NJ	250	75%	40	13	187	49	14
EAST SIDE HS	NEWARK	NJ	251	75%	19	7	188	49	14
SOUTH SIDE HS	NEWARK	NJ	252	75%	13	14	188	50	14
ESSEX CATHOLIC HS	EAST ORANGE	NJ	253	75%	13	7	189	50	14
SETON HALL PREP	WEST ORANGE	NJ	254	74%	12	13	189	51	14
1963 SEASON			8		192	113	5	3	0
ST PETER'S PREP	JERSEY CITY	NJ	255	74%	20	40	189	52	14
NORTH BERGEN HS	NORTH BERGEN	NJ	256	74%	0	19	189	53	14
EAST ORANGE HS	EAST ORANGE	NJ	257	74%	7	21	189	54	14
CENTRAL HS	NEWARK	NJ	258	74%	25	12	190	54	14
EAST SIDE HS	NEWARK	NJ	259	74%	13	12	191	54	14
SOUTH SIDE HS	NEWARK	NJ	260	73%	7	19	191	55	14
ESSEX CATHOLIC HS	EAST ORANGE	NJ	261	73%	13	32	191	56	14
SETON HALL PREP	WEST ORANGE	NJ	262	73%	7	21	191	57	14
1964 SEASON			8		92	176	2	6	0
ST PETER'S PREP	JERSEY CITY	NJ	263	73%	7	21	191	58	14
NORTH BERGEN HS	NORTH BERGEN	NJ	264	72%	13	21	191	59	14
EAST ORANGE HS	EAST ORANGE	NJ	265	72%	19	7	192	59	14
CENTRAL HS	NEWARK	NJ	266	73%	34	13	193	59	14
SOUTH SIDE HS	NEWARK	NJ	267	73%	19	7	194	59	14
VALLEY FORGE MILITARY ACADEMY	WAYNE	PA	268	73%	12	0	195	59	14
ESSEX CATHOLIC HS	EAST ORANGE	NJ	269	72%	0	13	196	60	14
EAST SIDE HS	NEWARK	NJ	270	73%	19	7	196	60	14
SETON HALL PREP	WEST ORANGE	NJ	271	73%	18	7	197	60	14
1965 SEASON			9		141	96	6	3	0

JOE KASBERGER AT ST. BENEDICT'S PREP - NEWARK, NJ
FOOTBALL CAREER RECORD, 1930 TO 1966

OPPOSITION NAME	CITY	STATE	GAME	CAREER FOOTBALL WIN %	SEASON FOOTBALL SBP	POINTS OPP	CAREER FOOTBALL W	L	T
ST PETER'S PREP	JERSEY CITY	NJ	272	73%	20	0	198	60	14
BERGEN CATHOLIC HS	ORADELL	NJ	273	73%	12	19	198	61	14
EAST ORANGE HS	EAST ORANGE	NJ	274	72%	0	45	198	62	14
CENTRAL HS	NEWARK	NJ	275	72%	40	20	199	62	14
DON BOSCO PREP	RAMSEY	NJ	276	72%	13	19	199	63	14
EAST SIDE HS	NEWARK	NJ	277	72%	14	26	199	64	14
SOUTH SIDE HS	NEWARK	NJ	278	72%	7	13	199	65	14
ESSEX CATHOLIC HS	EAST ORANGE	NJ	279	72%	7	0	200	65	14
SETON HALL PREP	WEST ORANGE	NJ	280	71%	7	7	200	65	15
	1966 SEASON		9		120	149	3	5	1

(X) = CANCELLED GAME
= 1941 SEASON VARIANCE DUE TO JOE K
    NOTATION OF SCORES & RESULTS ON
        SCHEDULE TO JOE HELLBERG
OTHER SOURCE RESULTS AS FOLLOWS
SBP 7 - MANHATTAN COLL FR 13
SBP 16 - BMI 7
SBP 26 - BROWN PREP 0
END OF FILE

III. JOE KASBERGER'S PLAYERS APPENDIX

APPENDIX A - JOE'S PLAYERS AT MT. ANGEL COLLEGE (MAC), 1922-26

Arrighi, John - 1922-23, 1923-24, 1924-25 Basketball

Barr, _____ - 1925 Baseball

Beck, Robert - 1926 Baseball

Becker, Henry - 1923-24 Basketball - 1924 Baseball

Berger (Burger), Tony - 1925 Football

Blackwell, James - 1922 Football

Bowley, William - 1923, 1924 Baseball

Bowley, _____ - 1924 Baseball - 1925 Baseball

Brack, Joseph - 1922 Football*

Buckley, _____ - 1923, 1924 Football

Busch, Bert - 1924 Football

Butler, Bancroft - 1923 Football

Butsch, Joseph -1922 Football*

Capet, John - 1923-24 Football

Cardinal, Edwin - 1924-25 Basketball - 1925 Baseball

Caughell, John 1922 Football

Coovert, Charles -1922-23 Basketball - 1923 Baseball - 1923 Football - 1924 Baseball

Cranston, Walter 1922 Football* - 1922-23 Basketball

Cranston, _____ - 1924-25 Basketball

DeLasaux, Cecil - 1922 Football

Druffel, _____ - 1923, 1924 Football

Duffy, _____ - 1923 Football

Duerst, Henry - 1923 Football - 1924 Football

Dyer, Carl - 1923-24 Basketball - 1925 Baseball

Farley, John - 1922-23 Basketball

Gray, George -1923 Football - 1923-24 Basketball

Green, _____ - 1924 Football

Greene (Green), Lawrence - 1923-24 Baseball* - (Captain) - 1925 Baseball

Hardin, Ken - 1922,* 1923, 1924 Football - 1923-24, 1924-25 Basketball

Heenan (Hennan), Denny - 1925 Football

Holmes, _____ - 1925 Baseball

Hudson, Emanuel (Capt.) - 1923,* 1924 Baseball - 1923-24 Basketball

Hutton, _____ - 1924 Football

Inwalle, _____ - 1923 Football

Johnson, _____ - 1925-26 Basketball

Kearney, _____ - 1924 Football

Keber, Carl - 1924-25 Basketball - 1925 Baseball

Kinney, _____ - 1923 Football

Kinney, G. - 1924 Football

Kinney, R. - 1924 Football

Kohler, Ernest - 1922 Football

Kopp, _____ - 1925 Baseball

Koppert, Raymond - 1923* Baseball

Kropp, Henry (Captain) - 1922*-23 Basketball

Lyness, _____ - 1923 Football - 1924 Baseball

Mann, ___"Pep" - 1923-24 Basketball - 1924 Baseball

McCarthy, _____ - 1925 Baseball

McGowan, George - 1924 Football

McGrath, Arthur - 1924 Football - 1925 Baseball

Meyers, Francis - 1922-23, 1923-24 Basketball

Otjen, Lawrence - 1924-25 Basketball

Overton, _____ - 1923 Football

Pashek, Francis - 1922 Football

Ployhart, Peter - 1922 Football - 1922-23 Basketball

Price, A. Elmer - 1925-26 Basketball

Reiling, _____ - 1925 Baseball

Roalson (Roalsen), William - 1925-26 Basketball

Salvi, Anthony - 1924 Football

Saunders, John - 1924, 1925 Baseball

Schlesinger, _____ - 1925 Baseball

Schroeder, Harold - 1924-25 Basketball - 1925 Baseball

Scott, Gilbert - 1922-23, 1923-24 Basketball - 1923, 1924 Baseball

Spear, Charles - 1922, 1923, 1924, 1922-23* (Captain) - 1923-24, 1924-25 Basketball

Stockton, Edwin - 1922, 1923 Football (Captain) - 1924 Baseball

Sullivan, John - 1924-25 Basketball

Teare, _____ - 1924 Football
Tennant, Richard - 1922 Football
Teters (Teter), Paul - 1924 Football -
1925 Baseball
Towner, Elwood - 1923 Baseball
Traynor, Louis - 1923 Baseball
Tuma, Carl - 1923 Baseball
Tuning, O - 1923, 1924 Football
Umbaugh, _____ - 1923 Football
Walsh, Allen - 1923, 1924 Football
Walsh, W. - 1924 Football
Watson, John - 1922 Football

Wernmark, Kneut -1922 Football
Woodward, _____ - 1924 Baseball
Wymer, _____ - 1923, 1924 Football
Ziegenhagen, Clarence (Captain) - 1922
Football

* 1921-22 School Year Lettermen

1925 MAC FOOTBALL TEAM N/A
1925-26 MAC BASKETBALL TEAM
N/A
1926 MAC BASEBALL TEAM N/A

APPENDIX B - JOE'S PLAYERS AT MOUNT ANGEL ACADEMY
AND NORMAL SCHOOL, 1927-28

1927-28 BASKETBALL TEAM
Alice Walsh - athletic manager and for-
ward
Dorothy Ford - forward
Dorothy Patemore - center
Florence Kosydar - center

Vernice Mickel - guard
Reta Burns - guard
Marie Flerchinger - substitute
Helen Smith - substitute
Margaret Pennett - substitute
1928-29 BASKETBALL TEAM N/A

APPENDIX C - JOE'S BASEBALL AND FOOTBALL
PLAYERS AT ST. BENEDICT'S PREP, 1930-68

Accocella, Frank (AC*) 1958,59* F
Ackerman, Albert   1950 F
Adair, Gene   1941 F
Adamkowski, Francis 1932 B
Addonizio, Hugh   1934 F
Ahr, David   1960 B,1958-60 F
Ahr, Paul   1959,60 F
Alexander, Frank   1935 F
Alger, George   1961,62 F
Allen, John (AC*)   1952,53,55,56,59,62-64*
                     F, 1953-54 B
Allen, Russell   1963 F
Allen, Thomas   1947 F
Allena, Andrew   1941 F
Alvino, Oreste   1938 B,F
Anderson, James   1947,48 F
Andreola, Frank   1963 F
Antanaitas, Richard (CC*) 1952*,53 F
Antonovsky, George 1940,41 F
Apicelli, Salvatore 1952 F
Applegate, Milton   1936 F,1937 B
Arbes, Sam   1940 F
Arbes, S   1949 F
Atkinson, Burr   1954 B
Aulisi, Joe (AC*)   1951,63* F
Baker, John   1950 B
Bakum, Walter   1960 F
Baldaccini, Philip   1953 F

Bannon, David   1953-55 F,1955-56 B
Barker, Lawrence   1936 F
Barkowski,_____   1934 B
Barnes, Frank   1956,57 F
Baran, Walter   1937*F
Bataille, Wilfred   1938 F
Bateman, John   1933 F, 1934 B
Bauer, Theodore   1939 F
Becht, Frank   1960 F
Beekman, Philip   1947 F
Belber, George   1946 F
Bellew, Robert   1934 B
Bendokas, John   1962-64 F
Bergeur, John   1936 B
Beriont, Wally   1941 F
Bermann, Richard   1961 F
Bertelli, Michael   1961-63 F
Biancone, R   1950 F
Bien, Edward (Mgr*) 1937,38*F,1938 B
Billack, John   1966 B
Bishop, Robert   1944,45 F
Blauvelt, William   1959-61 B,1959-60 F
Blazak, John   1937 F, 1938 B
Blood, Ben   1931 B
Boczon, Richard   1958-59 B
Boettner, Frank (Mgr*) 1930,31* F
Boland, Joseph   1950 F
Bolger, Frank   1945 F

Bolger, James 1954-56 F, 1956,57 B
Bolger, John 1940,41,44 F
Bolger, Matthew (Cap*) 1936,38,39* F, 1937-39 B
Bolles, John 1930 F
Bonavolonta, Julius 1958 B
Bonforte, Eugene 1941 F
Bonforte, Len (AC*) 1940,50,51* F, 1941 B
Bost, Douglas 1961 F
Bower, Neil 1940,41 F
Boyd, Ronald 1950,51 F
Boyd, Steven (CC*) 1964-66* F
Boylan John (AC*) 1930,38* F
Boylan, Jack 1953 F
Boyle, John 1944 F
Bradley, John 1930 F
Brady, Charles 1950 F
Brady, Edward 1965,66 F
Brady, William 1930 F
Breen, Edward 1941 F
Breunig, Joseph 1945-47 F, 1947 B
Brewster, Robert 1948 F
Briante, Nick 1953-54 F, 1953-55 B
Briante, Patsy 1961-63 F,1962-63 B
Broderick, James 1945 F
Brogan, Charles 1945 B
Brogan, John (Cap*) 1957-60* B
Brogan, Peter (CC*) 1953-56* F, 1955-57 B
Brophy, Francis 1936 B
Brothers, Tom 1958-59 F
Brown, John 1936 F, 1937 B
Brown, Theodore 1963 F
Brown, Thomas 1954,55 F
Browne, Joseph 1963 F
Brueno, Raymond 1947 F
Bruinooge, Tom (Mgr) 1959 B
Bruno, Leon 1959 F
Brzozowski, Thomas 1954,55 B
Bubnis, Vincent 1939 F
Budzleski, Albert 1941 F
Bujnowski, Tom 1950 B
Buob, Robert 1950 B
Burger, Charles (AM*) 1961* B
Burger, Walter (Mgr*) 1949,50* F
Burke, Harry 1961,62 F
Burke, John (CC*) 1962-64* F
Burke, Michael 1954-56 F
Burke, Adrian 1938 B
Burlick, John 1960,61 F
Burnett, Lawrence 1932 B
Burns, Alan 1961 F
Burns, Richard 1944-47 F
Burton, Donald 1945 F
Bury, Vincent 1954 F
Burzynski, Michael 1955 F
Butera, Stephen 1950 B, F
Butfiloski, Joseph 1955 B
Butkus, Peter (AC*) 1941,50* F,1943 B
Butler, Ed 1939 F,1940 B
Byrnes, Alan 1961 F
Byrne, John 1955 F
Byrne, Walter (Mgr*) 1930* F
Cabrelli, Larry 1936 F, 1937 B
Cadigan, Richard 1953 B

Caffrey, James 1938 F
Cahill, Peter 1958 B
Caine, William 1939 F
Calcagno, Peter (AC*) 1939,49,50* F
Callahan, James 1934 F
Callan, Robert 1934,35 F
Calo, Vincent 1941 F
Cameron, Edward 1937 F
Campbell, John 1930 F
Campbell, Robert (Mgr*) 1939* B
Candelmo, Tony (CC*) 1958-61*B
Cannarozzi, Albert 1957-58 F
Cannestro, Anthony (AC) 1948,49* F
Cannestro, Vic 1934,35 F,1935,36 B
Cappock, William 1953 F
Caprio, Ray 1960-62 F
Carbone, Gary 1938 B
Cardillo, Joseph (Cap*) 1948* F
Carey, Thomas 1953 F
Carlesimo, Peter (AC*) 1938 B,1934,35* 40*,41*F
Carlin, Ed 1943 B
Carney, Harold 1944-46 F
Carolan, Robert 1955 F
Carr, James 1938 F
Carr, James 1959-62 F, 1961,62 B
Carr, James P. 1936, F,1936,37 B
Carr, J. Peter 1937 F
Carriero, William (Mgr*) 1945* B
Carroll, Joseph 1956-58 F
Carroll, Walter 1958 B
Carton, Edward 1934 B
Caruso, Marno 1941 F
Caruso, Thomas 1952 F
Casadonte, Frank 1964,65 B
Cascarelle, J 1966 F
Casey, Joseph 1940,41 B
Cashill, William 1957 F
Cassell, John (AC*) 1947* B,1951*F
Cassella, Louis 1949 F
Cassino, Joseph 1941 F,1942 B
Castagno, Joseph 1949 F
Castellano, Gerald (Mgr*) 1968* B
Catino, Robert 1962,63 F
Cavallaro, Sam (AC*) 1946,54-57* F
Cavanaugh, Gerard 1938-40 B
Cavanaugh, James 1950 F
Cavanaugh, William 1938 B
Cecere, Lawrence 1945 B
Cerza, Jerry (AC*) 1962,63*F
Chagnon, Joseph 1944 F
Charette, Art (Cap*)1948,49 F,1949,50* B
Cheney, Douglas (CC*) 1964-66* F
Chilton, Forrest (Mgr*) 1959 F,1959-60* B
Christenson, George 1949 F
Ciampaglio, Alphonse 1950 F
Cibelli, Christopher 1937 F
Ciccia, Anthony 1941 B
Ciccone, Nicholas 1930 F
Cito, Alfred, Sr. 1935,38-40 B
Cito, Alfred, Jr. 1960,61F
Ciurczak, Anthony 1963 B
Clark, Joseph 1938 F
Clarke, Gerald 1961 B

Cleary, James	1931,34 F, 1932 B	D'Aloia, Marshall Jr.	1959-60 F,1962 B
Close, James	1964-66 F	D'Alonzo, Frank	1951 F
Clyne, John	1956,57 F	Dalton, Jack (AC*)	1955-59* B
Cogan, John	1951,55 F	Dalton, Jerome	1958 F
Coker, George	1958-60 F	Daly, Thomas	1944 F
Coker, James	1953,55,56 F	Damasco, John	1940,41 F
Coker, Michael	1959-61 F	D'Amato, Peter	1958 B
Colagreco, James	1947 F	D'Amiano, Joe	1949 F
Colangelo, Nicholas	1959-61 F	D'Amore, Beni	1966 F,1968 B
Coles, Allan	1938 B	Dankowski, Walter	1948 F
Collins, Edwin "Rip"	1936-38 F, 1937-39 B	Dargin, John	1938 F
Collins, Joseph	1966 B	Dashuta, John	1938-40 F
Collins, Paul M.	1959 F	Dauenheimer, Charles	1941 F
Collins, Paul J.	1935 F	Davies, John	1949 F,1950 B
Colton, Frederic	1954,55 B	Deacon, Robert	1947 F,1948 B
Columbo, William	1961-64 F	Dean, Gerald (Mgr*)	1936 *B
Commercio, Vincent	1956 F	DeCapua, Michael	1964 F
Conaton, Daniel	1960,61 F	Decker, Richard	1966 F
Confalone, Samuel	1960,61 F	DeCosta, Leo	1956 B
Confessore, Ralph	1945 F	Degnen, John	1961 F
Conforti, John	1958-60 F	Degnen, William	1947 B
Confroy, Thomas	1947 F	DeGoria, Patsy	1950 F
Conklin, Frank	1950 B	Dehmer, Peter	1963 F
Conklin, Jack	1930 F	DeJianne, William	1932 B
Conlan, Brian	1958-60 F	Del Favero, John	1952,53 F
Conn, William (Cap*)(AC*)	1944-46*,52,53* F,1945-47 B	Del Tufo, Louis (CC*)	1937,38*F
Connell, James	1944,45 F	Delany, Francis	1934-37 B
Conner, Andrew	1954 F	Deleot, Robert	1940 B
Connolly, John	1966 F	Deleot, Charles	1934 F
Connors, Francis	1935,36 B	Della Fera, Joseph	1959 F
Connors, Ralph	1941-43 B	Del Vescovo, Anthony (AC*)	1958,64* F
Conti, George	1935-37 F, 1937 B	Del Vescovo, Gerard	1963,64 F
Conti, George B.	1963,64 F	DeMarco, Leonard (CC*)	1960-62* F
Cooney, Robert	1953,54 F	DeMaria, Joseph	1931 B
Coppola, Joseph	1949 F	DeMartino, Joseph	1958 F
Corcoran, Joseph	1952,53 F	DeMarzio, Frank	1962 F
Corrigan, Peter	1934 F	DeMasi, Joseph	1959 F
Corrubia, Nick	1941 F	Demeter, Albert	1952,53 B
Cortese, Harold	1966 B	Dempsey, Andrew	1955 F
Cosentino, Frank	1959-61 B, F	Dempsey, Frank	1940 F, 1941 B
Cosentino, Robert	1966 B	Dennis, Charles	1947 B
Cosgrove, Frank	1934,35 F, 1935 B	deNourie, Bert	1952,53 F
Coughlin, Roger	1951 F	DePalma, Joseph	1962,63 F
Covino, Robert	1964 F	DePalma, Warren	1942 B
Coyle, George	1936,37 B	Depretz, George	1935 F, 1936 B
Crawley, Francis	1965,66 F	Dermody, William (Cap*)	1944 F,1945*B
Cray, John	1945 F	DeRosa, August	1962-65 B,1962-64 F
Crecca, Joseph	1930 F	DeSheplo, Louis	1931 F
Crelin, Wilbur	1938,39 F	Desiderio, James	1964-66 F, 1966 B
Crisafi, Vincent	1949 F	DeStefano, Dick (AC*)	1939,40,47*,50* F, 1940,41 B
Crocco, Charles	1938 F	DeVito, Eugene	1947 F,1948 B
Cronin, John	1953,54 B	Devlin, James	1941 F
Crosby, William	1953 F,1954-57 B	Devore, James	1945 F
Crum, E	1939 F	Devore, Paul	1935 F
Cullen, William	1941 F	Dial, Thomas (Mgr*)	1931* B
Cummings, Robert	1948 F,1949 B	Diamente, Frank	1937 F, 1938 B
Cyron, Wayne	1962 F	Dick, Thomas	1959 F
Czerniach, Bohdan	1960 F	DiGirolamo, L. Henry	1938-41 F, 1940 B
D'Agostini, Charles	1964,65 F	DiGiulio, James	1964 F
D'Agostini, Norman	1963,64 F	DiIorio, Joseph	1963,64 F
Dahl, Werner	1934-36 F	DiLorenzo, Vince	1940 F
D'Alia, Francis	1945 F	Diloria, J	1954 F
D'Aloia, Marshall Sr.	1939 F,1939,40 B	DiMasi, Mario	1959 F

DiPizzo, Daniel   1947 F
DiQuollo, Carmen   1963 F
Dischute, J   1966 F
Doby, Gregory   1963 F
Doherty, Brian   1963-65 F
Donnelly, James   1930 F
Donnelly, Thomas   1954 F
Dougherty, John   1947 B
Dougherty, Joseph   1934 F
Dougherty, Thomas   1950 F
Dour, ____   1954 F
Dovell, "Whitey"   1947 F
Dowd, Kevin   1955 F
Dowd, William   1940 B
Dowd, Thomas   1930,31 F
Downey, John   1944, F,1945 B
Downey, William   1945-47 B,1945,46 F
Drew, Paul   1960,61 F
Drotos, Frederick   1938 F
Drumm, Joe   1939 F
Drury, Larry (CC*)   1935,36* F,1936,37 B
DuBois, Henry   1960-62 F,1963 B
DuBois, John   1964,65 B
Duerbig, Alfred   1961 B
Duff, Joe   1942 B
Duffy, John   1963-65 F
Duhig, John   1953,54 F
Dunham, M. Francis   1966 B
Dunn, Edward   1935, F,1936,37 B
Dunn, James   1965 B
Durand, Bernard   1945,46 B
Durkin, Harry   1946-49 B
Durkin, Richard   1941 F,1943 B
Durkin, Robert   1952,53 F
Durkin, Tom (AC*)   1939,41,48* F,1943 B
Dziuban, Eugene   1934,35 F
Edelen, Earl   1931,32 B
Edelen, Richard   1945 F
Egan, Thomas   1934 F
Ehrhardt, William   1960-62 B
Eisenberg, Edwin   1941 F
Ellis, Shannon   1935-37 F
Emmett, Bob   1941,43 B
Enderle, George (CC*)(AC*) 1952-54*,55* F
Engelken, Albert   1955 F
Ensenat, Bart   1963,64 F
Euston, Frank   1965 F
Fachet, Louis   1932 B
Fairbanks, Joseph   1939,40 B
Fallon, Peter   1935,36 B
Farley, Matthew   1931 F
Farquhar, Robert   1952,53 F
Farrell, Frank   1943,44,46 F
Farrell, Robert   1963 F,1964 B
Farrell, Thomas   1941 F
Farrell, Thomas   1951-53 F
Fay, Bernard W.   1944 F
Fee, Charles (Mgr*)   1950* B
Feehan, John   1945-48 B
Feeney, Robert   1941 F,1943 B
Fehrenbach, Edward   1938,39 B
Fernicola, James (Cap*) 1965,66* B
Feury, Thomas   1945 F
Finan, Oliver   1946 B

Fine, Robert   1956 B
Finn, Daniel   1959-61 F
Fiore, John   1966 B
Fischer, Charles   1941 F
Fisher, Alan   1962 F
Fitzpatrick, James   1952,53 B,1954 F
Flanagan, Paul   1966 F
Flanagan, Robert (Mgr*) 1948* B
Flood, John   1932,34 B
Flynn, John   1966 F
Foley, Adrian Sr.   1938 F
Foley, Adrian Jr.   1961-63 B,1961-63 F
Foley, Brendan   1946,47 F
Fonseca, Joseph   1964-66 F
Ford, John (AC*)   1939* F
Ford, Pat   1930 F
Forlenza, Lawrence   1955,56 F
Foster, Frederick   1932 B
Fouser, Edward   1934 B
Fox, Andrew   1931 F, 1932 B
Frederick, R   1950 F
Freeze, Phillip   1961 F
Frezza, Louis   1937 F, 1938 B
Friederick, Peter   1944,45 F
Fritzsche, Carl   1954,55 F
Froelich, Brian   1961-63 F
Froelich, Jerome Sr.   1934-36 F
Froelich, Jerome Jr.   1959-60 F
Fuccello, Charles   1952 B
Furey, Jim (AC*)   1950,51* F
Furlong, Bill   1963 F
Furlong, George   1958 B
Fuschino, Francis   1953 F
Gabriel, Daniel   1965,66 B
Gallagher, Hugh   1948 B
Gallagher, James   1938,39 F
Gallucci, Michael   1962,63 B
Garafola, Anthony   1947 F
Garrigan, Walter   1945 B
Garrubbo, Mario (CC*) 1955-58* F,1956-58 B
Gaul, Gilbert   1966 F
Gawalis, Cifert   1930 F
Gemeiner, Richard   1939,41 B
Genevrino, Mike (Cap*) (AC*)1940 F,
                       1941,42*,45* B
Gentempo, Joe   1955-57 F
George, Harry   1931 F
Geraghty, B (AC*)   1949* F
Ghegan, John   1963,64
Giacobbe, Robert   1952 F
Gibbons, John   1938 F
Gilligan, Richard   1953,55,56 B
Gilligan, Thomas   1948,49 B
Gilligan, Walter   1954,55 B
Gilsenan, John   1934 F
Giovan, John   1930,31 F, 1932 B
Glaccum, William   1930 F
Glancy, Robert   1944-46 F
Gleason, Bob   1942 B
Golden, Brian   1963-65 F
Golembiewski, Sigismund 1932 B
Golgosky, Alexander   1932 B
Golgosky, Bill   1935,36 B
Gonzalez, Valentine   1941 B

Gorman, John (AM*) 1958* F
Gormley, James 1958-59 B
Gorski, Joseph (Mgr*) 1946* B
Gottfried, Philip 1938 F
Govette, Norman 1943 B
Gowalis, Joe 1940 F
Graham, David 1963-65 F
Grant, Robert 1945,46 B
Graul, Albert 1938 F
Greco, Frank 1941 F
Green, Richard 1944 F
Greig, Donald 1948 F
Grieco, Albert 1951 F, 1952 B
Griffith, Ed 1951 F
Griggs, John 1945 F
Grinc, Alan 1963 F
Grinsted, Francis 1931 B
Grischuck, William 1941 F
Groome, Eugene 1935,36 B
Groome, Frank 1935,36 B
Grum, Edward 1941,44 F
Grum, Joe (Cap*) 1945-47* F,1945,47 B
Grum, John 1946,47 F
Guenther, Robert 1960 F
Guida, Nicholas 1949 B
Gurkas, William 1949 F
Guzzo, Joseph 1960-62 F
Gyorgydeak, Joe 1939 F,1940 B
Haesler, Richard 1945,46 F
Hahn, Robert 1945 F
Hak, Gerald 1938 F
Hak, Warren (Mgr*) 1949* B
Hamley, James 1966 F
Hammill, George (AC*) 1939*,40* F
Hanbicki, Edward 1949 F
Handerhan, Robert 1939 B
Haney, William 1939 F
Hanlon, Edmund 1935-37 F
Hanlon, Thomas 1941 F
Harkins, David 1930,31 F
Harriman, Vincent 1931,32 B
Harty, Matthew 1935 B
Hastings, Charles (Mgr*) 1933* F
Hattersley, Carl 1952,53 B
Hayden, Joseph 1959-61 F
Hayes, Charles 1955,56 F
Hayes, Edward 1931 F, 1932 B
Hayes, Gerard 1952,53 F
Hayes, William 1939 F
Healy, Vincent 1934 F
Hearn, James (Cap*) 1936,37*,39 B,1939 F
Hearn, Michael 1934 B, 1934 F
Heffernan, Ray 1953,54 F
Helies, Edward 1966 F
Hellberg, Joe 1940 F,1941 B
Helmstetter, Jacob 1945 B
Henczynski, George 1951 F
Henderson, ____ 1938 B
Hennessy, Daniel 1958-59 B
Herbert, Richard 1957 F
Herrmann, August 1953,54 B
Heurich, Charles 1940,41 B
Hewson, Gilbert 1957-60 B
Hewson, Robert 1949 B

Higgins, Frank 1942 B
Higgins, Paul 1939 F
Higgins, Richard 1947 F
Hines, Arthur 1940,41 B
Hinrichsen, Carl 1939 B
Hock, Joe (Cap*) 1931,32,34* B
Hoffer, Ernest 1958 B
Holly, B. John 1966 F
Hooper, Donald 1950 B
Hoover, Raymond 1953 F
Hopkins, John 1968 B
Hornig, Ernest (Mgr*) 1934* B
Howell, John 1956 F,1957 B
Huber, John 1959 F
Hughes, Eugene 1934 F
Hughes, Michael 1940 B
Hull, Gerald 1954 B
Humencki, Edmund 1934 F
Hunt, Douglas 1959-60 F
Hurle, Raymond 1945 B
Hurley, Pat 1961-62 B
Huysse, Joseph 1940 B
Iamundo, Ernie 1954,56,57 F
Immerso, Joseph 1955 F
Inglis, Thomas 1941 B
Innis, Anthony 1947 F
Ivanicki, Casmir 1940 B
Jacquin, Don 1954 F,1955 B
Jakubowski, Theodore 1964 B
Jamieson, Bill 1959-62 B,1959-61 F
Janowski, Henry 1932,34 B
Janson, Richard 1953 F
Jarvis, Harold (Mgr*) 1961 *B
Jellovitz, John 1959 B, F
Jernick, William 1938,41 F
Johnson, James 1938 F, 1940,41 B
Johnson, Robert 1941 B
Johnston, William 1939 B,1939 F
Jones, John 1938 F
Jovnik, Joseph 1945 F
Joyce, Dennis 1959 B
Judge, Charles (Mgr*) 1934,35* B
Kania, Joe 1940,41 F
Kanter, Louis 1938 B
Kaplan, Gregory 1966 B
Kaplowitz, Seymour 1947 F
Karczewski, Henry 1939 F
Kardash, Peter 1968 B
Kaseman, G. Wesley 1936 F
Kavanagh, Charles 1962 F
Kawalec, Vic 1946-48 B
Kazary, Al 1939 F
Kearney, John (Mgr*) 1957-58* B
Keary, Bob 1937 B
Keegan, Robert 1932 B
Kelleher, Gerard (Cap*) 1945,46 B, 1944,45* F
Kelleher, William 1946,48 F
Keller, Alfred 1949 B
Keller, George 1931 B
Keller, Joseph (Cap*) 1934,35* B
Kellett, William 1946 F
Kelly, Jack 1938-40 F
Kempton, Alan 1949 F
Kennedy, Jerome (AM*) 1930* F

Kennedy, William 1930,31 F
Kerr, Robert 1941 F
Kershaw, Julius 1938,39 B
Kerwin, Michael 1944-46 F
Kerwin, Thomas 1948,49 F
Kiernan, John 1952,53 B
Kimler, Charles 1934,35 F
King, Edward 1940,41 B
Kinney, Michael 1936 B
Kirby, James 1948 F
Kirby, John 1956 F
Kircher, Rudolph 1939 F
Klein, John 1955 F
Klemm, Jerome 1955 B
Kline, Richard 1952,53 F
Klukosovsky, Joseph 1935-37 F
Knowles, Stanley 1934 F
Kochansky, Richard (CC*) 1957-60 F,
                      1958-61* B
Kochel, Charles 1931 B
Koechlein, Donald 1931 F
Koeck, George 1952-54 F
Koellhoffer, Hubert 1932,34 B
Kohl, B. John 1957-59 F
Kohl, Peter 1956,57 F,1958 B
Kolb, John 1935,36 F,1936,37 B
Koleszar, Thomas 1963,64 B
Koopman, Christopher 1930 F
Korn, Peter (CC*) 1951* F
Kossack, Kenneth 1952 F
Kozak, Stephen 1932 B
Kraemer, Robert 1940,41 B
Kray, Thomas 1959 B,1958-60 F
Krevetski, Paul 1944,45 F
Kriznauskas, Paul 1966 B
Kuchinski, Chet 1939 F
Kull, M. "Al" 1940 F
Lagoda, Louis 1930 F, 1931 B
Lakos, Thomas 1941 F,1942,43 B
Lally, Michael 1958 F
LaMorgese, Michael 1952 F
Lampariello, Joseph 1940 B
Landers, Peter 1968 B
Landgraf, William 1944,45,47 F
Lang, Michael 1961 F
Lardieri, Peter 1958,59 F,1959-62 B
Larkin, Robert 1940 B
Lasher, Robert 1947-49 F
LaStella, Jack 1950 B
Lauber, Edward 1946,47 F
Laughna, Michael 1968 B
Laurie, Donald 1958-59 F
Lavin, Thomas 1946 F
Lawless, William 1953 B
Lawrence, Richard 1951 F
Leahy, Dennis 1960-62 F
Leary, Jerome 1947 F
LeCompte, Eugene 1938 F
Leehive, Dennis 1961,62 B
Leffler, Al 1939,40 F, 1940 B
Lehmann, Charles 1948 F
Lenox, Alfred 1952-54 F
Leonard, John 1952 B
Leonard, Richard 1930,31 F

Leonard, Robert 1959 B
Leonard, Thomas (CC*) 1955-58* F
Leonard, William 1960 B
Leonard, ___ (AC*) 1940*B
Leonhardt, Francis 1945 F
Leslie, John 1947,48 F
Liddy, Vince (Cap*) 1957-59* F,1959-60 B
Lilore, Ralph (Cap*)1961-64* B,1962,63 F
Linnett, Robert 1947 F
Linsley, David 1953 F
Lister, George 1944-46 F,1946-47 B
Loba, ___ 1951 F
Lobo, Walter 1945 B,1945 F
Locasacio, Joseph 1958-59 B
Lockie, Thoms 1931 F, 1932 B
Lombardi, Nicholas 1931 B
Lonergan, Maurice (Cap*) 1936,37* F,
                      1937,38*B
Long, Edward 1945,46 F
Lorenzo, John 1963 F
Lorenzo, Richard 1960-62 F,1961-63 B
Loughery, J. Robert 1946,47 F
Loughridge, Richard 1955 F
Lowas, Albert 1965,66 F
Lowe, Louis 1937 B
Lunz, William 1931 F
Lupo, Gerard 1930 F
Lupton, Robert 1965 B
Luthy, Alfred 1958 B
Lynch, David 1954-56 F, 1956 B
Lynch, Donald 1950 B
Lynch, Robert 1944 F
Lyon, Peter 1949 B
Lyons, Raymond 1931,35 F
MacCauley, James 1944 F
MacClymont, William 1939 B
MacInnes, David 1945 F
Mackessy, John 1957-59 F
Madura, Jerome 1951 F
Maffongelli, Joe (Mgr*) 1961* F
Magliaro, Eugene 1941 F
Maguire, Frank 1934 F
Maher, Edward 1940 B
Mahon, Joseph 1941 B
Mahoney, Timothy 1954,55 B
Mahoney, Walter 1941 F
Malekoff, Al (Cap*) 1941,42* F, 1942 B
Malizia, Francis 1947 F
Malkiewicz, R 1950 F
Malkmus, Robert 1950 B
Mallack, Robert 1952,53 B
Malloy, Terrence 1960 F
Maloney, Brian 1952,53 F
Maloney, Joseph 1937 B
Mamatz, Dennis 1966 B, 1966 F
Mangin, Nicholas 1944 F
Manhardt, John 1946,48 B
Mantz, Maurice 1949 F
Manzella, Blaise 1959 F
Marasco, Robert 1966 F
Marchese, Andrew 1964,65 B
Marchitto, Fred 1948 F
Marck, Kenneth 1941 F
Marra, Allen 1959 B,1958-59 F

Marsh, Robert 1955,56 F
Martens, Theodore 1966 F
Mason, Robert 1963,64 B
Matthews, Edwin 1961 F
Matthews, Thomas 1966 F
Mattia, Peter 1965 F
Maurer, Mark 1941 F, 1942 B
Mazzei, John 1934 F,1935 B
McAdams, Michael 1961-63 F
McCabe, Thomas 1945 F
McCaffrey, Harry 1966 F
McCann, John 1937 F
McCanna, James 1964,65 B
McCarthy, John (Mgr*) 1936* F
McCauley, Bernard 1941 F
McClorry, Robert 1930 F
McCloushy, ____ 1954 F
McCormick, Frank 1941 F
McCosker, James 1934 F
McCourt, James 1941 F
McCoy, Nicholas 1946 F
McCudden, Walter 1957-59 F
McCue, Thomas (BB/AM*) 1948 B*, F
McDonald, Eugene 1945 F,1948 B
McDonald, Patrick 1956,57 B,1955 F
McDonnell, Michael 1955 B
McDonnell, Robert (Mgr*) 1964-66* F
McDonnell, Thomas 1963-65 F
McDonough, Chris 1957-58 F
McDonough, Francis 1930 F
McDonough, George 1945 B
McDonough, Joseph 1938-40 B
McDowell, Robert 1961-63 B
McGarry, Robert 1965,66 F
McGarry, Robert (AM*) 1950 B,1952* F
McGarvey, James 1947 F
McGeehin, John 1948 B
McGinley, Conde 1938,39 F
McGinnis, R 1940 F
McGlynn, Leo (AC*) 1945-48,52,53* F,
        1946-491952-55* B
McGoldrick, Jack 1940 F
McGonigle, John 1931 F
McGovern, Edward 1938,40 F
McGovern, Timothy 1952 F
McGowan, Joseph 1950 F
McGowan, Thomas 1956 F
McGrath, John 1952 B
McGuinness, Bernard 1940 B, 1941 F
McGuinness, John 1941 B, 1941 F
McGuire, John 1930,31 F
McHugh, Francis 1939 B
McHugh, Patrick 1953 F
McHugh, William 1949 F
McIntyre, Lawrence 1935,36 F,1937 B
McKendricks, John 1938 B
McKenzie, James 1952-55 F
McKeon, John 1963 F
McLaughlin, Charles 1964-66 F
McLaughlin, John 1963 F
McLaughlin, William 1938 F, 1939 B
McLeod, Thomas 1951 F, 1952,53 B
McNally, Donald 1948 B
McNicholas, Thomas (Mgr*) 1954* F

McNulty, Matthew 1932 B
Meade, John 1935 B
Meccia, Carmine 1938 F, 1940 B
Meccia, Matthew 1955 F
Medici, Anthony 1938 F, 1939 B
Meehan, Arthur 1952,53 B
Meehan, Daniel 1963-65 B
Meister, William (AC*) 1948, 1958,66* B
Merola, Raymond 1950 F
Merrigan, Francis 1934 F
Merrill, Peter 1956 F
Metz, Helmer 1945-47 F
Middleton, Thomas 1956-59 B
Mikinis, L 1941 F
Milbauer, Frank Sr. (AC*) 1930,31,36,37,* F
Milbauer, Frank Jr. 1945 F
Miller, Charles 1945 F
Miller, Joseph 1949 F
Miller, Peter 1966 B
Miller, William 1935-37 F
Millman, Thomas 1931 B
Mills, Edwin D. 1930,31 F, 1931,32 B
Mills, John 1939 F, 1940 B
Milsop, Kenneth 1935 F
Mindnich, Al 1940,41,43 B
Mindnich, Jerome 1938 B
Mindnich, John 1937 B
Mindnich, John D (Cap*) 1939* B
Mindnich, J.W. (Cap*) 1938-41* B
Mindnich, Paul 1950,52 B
Minnefor, Anthony 1953-55 B
Mirabella, A "Mike" 1939 F
Mirabella, Joseph 1959,60 F
Mocco, Peter 1957-59 F
Molinaro, Anthony 1965 F
Molitor, Bernard 1938 B
Mollek, Joseph 1932 B
Molner, George 1941 F
Monaco, Frank 1938 F
Monaco, William 1950,51 F
Monica, Russ (Cap*) 1934* F
Mooney, Richard 1966 B
Mooney, Robert 1965,66 B,1965,66 F
Moore, Bernard J. (Mgr*) 1950 F,1954* B
Moore, John 1939,40 F, 1940,41 B
Moran, E. Farley 1953-55 B,1953,54 F
Moran, Joseph 1935 B
Moran, Richard 1956-58 F
Moretti, Steve 1930 F
Morgan, Peter 1953-56 F
Moriarity, Kevin 1960-62 F,1961,62 B
Moro, Anthony 1960 F
Morrison, Edward (AM*) 1937,38* B
Morrissey, William 1945 F
Mosconi, Michael 1930,31 F
Moyna, Patrick 1951 F
Muller, Richard 1960 B
Mulligan, Arthur 1958 B
Mulligan, Frank 1930 F
Munch, Robert 1968 B
Murname, Oliver 1941 F
Murnane, John 1936 B
Murphy, Edward 1940 F
Murphy, George 1953,54 F

Murphy, Gerald   1931 B
Murphy, James   1963-65 F
Murphy, Jim   1943 B
Murphy, Thomas W.   1930 F
Murray, Ed   1938,39 F
Murray, Michael   1946 F
Nagy, Alek   1931 B
Napoliello, Vincent 1952 F
Nazareta, Richard (CC*) 1954,56,57* F,
                     1956-58 B
Nemick, Stanley   1934 F
Nesto, Ralph   1959 F
Neville, Thomas   1959-60 F
Newberry, Donald   1948 F,1949 B
Newhard, Howard   1947 B
Nisivocci, John   1948 F
Nittoli, Ed (AC*)   1946,47* F
Nolan, Richard   1949 B
Norton, John   1935-37 B,1935,36 F
Norton, Richard   1953 F
Oates, Kevin   1961-63 F
O'Brien, H. Frank   1958-61 B
O'Brien, Joseph (AM*) 1931*,34,35 F,1932 B
O'Brien, Louis   1952 F
O'Brien, Richard   1960-62 B
O'Connell, James   1948 B
O'Conner, Joseph (Trn*) 1954* F
O'Connor, Arthur   1947,49 F
O'Connor, Brian   1931 F
O'Connor, Brian   1955-57 F
O'Connor, Garrett   1947 F
O'Connor, Gerald   1957-59 F
O'Connor, John   1945,46 B
O'Connor, Paul   1951-54 F
O'Connor, Richard   1950 F
O'Donnell, D   1953 F
O'Donnell, John (Mgr*) 1932* B
Oelkers, Robert (CC*) 1951* F
O'Gara, Robert   1946 F, 1947 B
O'Halloran, Thomas   1934 F
O'Hara, John   1934 F
O'Hara, William   1945 F
O'Malley, Eugene   1939,41 F
O'Mara, William   1938-41 F
Ondilla, Robert   1949 F,1950 B
Ondiro, Michael (CC*) 1936,37* F
O'Neill, John   1957-58 B
O'Neill, LeRoy (Cap*)(AC*) 1946-48* B,
                     1945-47,54* F
O'Neill, M   1961 F
Oravec, John   1930 F, 1931 B
Orsini, Anthony   1941 F
Orsini, Frank   1931 F
Ort, William   1955 F
Ostinato, Marcellino 1936 F,1937 B
Palecek, Stephen   1966 B
Pami, Robert   1965 F,1968 B
Paradise, J (AC*)   1948* F
Pareti, Harold   1963-65 F
Parigian, Berge   1940,41 F,1941,43 B
Parker, Thomas   1935-37 F, 1937 B
Parozzo, George   1948,49 F
Payton, Harry   1953,54 B
Pellechia, Ralph   1951 F

Peloso, Vincent   1966 F
Penberthy, Jack   1935 F,1936 B
Pepin, George   1938 F
Perrin, David   1949 F
Perrotta, Eugene   1964-66 F
Peters, Bob   1943 B
Petitti, Robert (CC*) 1962-64* F,1963-65 B
Petriella, Michael   1963,64 B
Petrin, Henry   1949 B
Petrone, Peter (Cap*) 1963-65* F
Petruzzelli, Anthony 1954,55 F
Petry, Joseph   1963 F,1965,66 B
Piccirillo, Robert   1950 B
Piechowski, Anthony 1931 B
Piniazik, Peter   1938 B
Pizza, Raymond   1958-60 F
Pizzi, Herman   1948 F,1949 B
Policastro, James (Mgr*) 1962,63* B
Ponzo, Joseph   1952 B
Potter, Tim   1941 F
Prester, Paul   1949 F
Price, Robert   1941 F
Proulx, Henry   1941 F, 1942 B
Puchalik, Paul   1961,62 B
Quinn, Ed (Cap*)   1934-36* B,1931,34,35 F
Quinn, James   1953-55 F
Quinn, Thomas   1931 F
Quinn, Thomas   1959,60 B
Quintano, Peter   1940 B
Rafter, Edward   1938-40 B
Rafter, Joseph   1937 B
Ragold, Richard   1947 F
Raskowski, W   1948 F
Rasna, John   1935,36 B
Reagan, Charles   1944,45 B
Reagan, Robert   1952 B
Reagan, Vincent   1939 B
Rears, Richard   1956,58 B
Redden, Michael   1968 B
Reed, Francis   1938 F, 1941 B
Regan, P   1950 F
Reichart, Joe   1940 F
Reilly, E   1966 B
Reilly, John   1950 F
Reilly, John (CC*)   1936* F
Reilly, Richard   1956 F
Reilly, Richard   1965 B,1963-65 F
Reilly, Robert   1939 F
Reilly, Robert   1963,64 F
Reilly, William   1947-48 B,1945,47 F
Reinoso, Al (AC*)   1956-58,65,66* F
Reinoso, Edward (CC*) 1960-62* F
Renner, Frank   1931 F
Reynolds, Kevin   1954,55 F
Rhatican, Timothy   1966 F
Rhatican, Peter   1960-63 B,1960-62 F
Rhatican, William   1958 B
Rhoads, Thomas   1955 F
Riley, Thomas   1939 B
Rinaldi, Peter (Cap*) 1950* F
Ripa, Thomas   1949 F
Ritchings, Richard   1940 B
Rodd, Dennis   1944,45 F
Rodney, Albert   1941 F

Rogers, Brian	1960-62 F	
Rogers, Anthony	1937 F,1936,38 B	
Rooney, William	1937 F	
Ross, Sidney	1932 B	
Rothlein, Frederick	1945 F	
Rothlisberger, Robert	1940 B	
Rubas, Peter	1952,53 F,1953 B	
Ruberti, Ted (CC*)	1931,34-37* F	
Ruddy, Richard	1952 B	
Rudzonis, Robert	1964 B	
Rusak, Walter (Mgr*)	1962-64* F	
Russo, Anthony	1946 F,1947 B	
Russo, Peter	1934 F,1935 B	
Ryan, Edmond	1963-66 F	
Ryan, Francis	1932 B	
Ryan, Joseph	1947 F	
Ryan, Joseph	1966 B	
Ryan, Thomas	1940 B	
Rzemieniewski, Henry (Mgr*)	1961,62* F	
Sabella, Edward	1966 F,1968 B	
Sabella, Richard	1963-65 B,1963,64 F	
Sagitas, Walter	1952,53 F	
Saldutti, Felix	1939-41 F, 1940-41 B	
Saner, Alfred	1949 F	
SanFillipo, William	1961 F	
Santaniello, Daniel	1966 B	
Sar, John	1950 F	
Sautner, Frank	1950 B	
Savage, James	1957 F	
Savage, Lawrence	1965 B	
Sava, Nicholas	1938 F,1939 B	
Sayer, Jack	1952-55 B	
Scanzera, Irwin	1946 F	
Scardefield, William	1941 B	
Scarpone, James (CC*)	1957-58 B,1954-57* F	
Schaedel, Charles	1930 F	
Schaedel, William	1960 F	
Schatzman, Frederick	1930 F	
Schefter, Adalbert	1931 F, 1932 B	
Scheick, James	1962-64 F	
Schenk, James	1948 F	
Schiller, A (AC*)	1961* F	
Schiller, Donald	1949 F	
Schiller, Eugene (AC*)	1949,58-66* F, 1950,1959-66* B	
Schirmer, Michael	1965,66 F	
Schleck, Richard	1935 F	
Schleer, Gordon	1941 F	
Schlittenhart, Harry	1943 B	
Schmidt, Louis	1948 F,1949 B	
Schmidt, Peter	1931 F, 1932 B	
Schnabel, Robert	1964,65 B	
Schneidenbach, R	1948 F	
Schuelke, Henry (Mgr*)	1960* B	
Schultz, Carl	1932 B	
Scotti, Anthony (CC*)	1955,56* F	
Scotti, Ben (CC*)	1952-54* F	
Scotti, Frederick	1958-60 F	
Seery, John	1936,37 B	
Semler, Michael	1964-66 F,1968 B	
Sentner, H. Robert	1952,53 B	
Serika, Joseph	1966 F	
Serra, Benjamin	1949 F	
Severson, Jack	1941 F	

Shaunessy, William	1965,66 B
Sheeran, Stanley	1931 F
Sheik, John	1930 F
Sheppard, Michael (AC*)	1961 F
Sheridan, Eugene	1930 F,1931 B
Sherry, Robert	1947-49 F,1948-50 B
Short, Edward	1953,54 F
Short, Walter	1940 F
Signorelli, John	1963 F
Sikora, Fred	1961-63 B
Silva, Edward	1939 B
Siman, John	1939 B
Singleton, Harry (AC*)	1940* F,1941,50* B
Skelly, Joseph	1946 F
Slane, Robert	1941 B
Slattery, G. Brian	1953,54 F
Slevin, John	1952 F
Sloniewsky, Roman	1955 F
Slowinski, Julian	1958 F
Slowinski, Walter (Mgr*)	1935-37* B
Smith, Charles	1930 F
Smith, Eugene	1948 B
Smith, Francis	1952 B
Smith, Henry	1953,54 B
Smith, Kenneth	1953 F
Smith, Walter	1935 F, 1936 B
Smith, William	1930 F
Smith, William	1952 F
Smyka, Richard	1939,41 F,1943 B
Snyder, Frederick	1932 B
Sobocinski, Vincent	1944 F
Sommer, James	1940,41 B
Soriano, Richard	1965,66 F
Sowa, Frank (Mgr*)	1947,48* F
Spatuzzi, Frank	1935 B
Spawn, Sandford	1949 F
Speer, Raymond	1940 B
Spiegel, Adam (CC*)	1935-38*F,1936,38,39 B
Spiessbach, Joseph	1944,45 F
Spina, Philip	1940,41 F
Spinner, Charles	1952 F
Spreen, Ron	1939,40 F
Stankavich, Stanley	1930 F,1931,34 B
Stanley, John	1966 F
Starner, John	1952 B
Stavella, Charles	1931 B
Steib, John	1930 F
Stiso, Edward (Mgr*)	1957-59* F
Storff, Thomas	1934 F
Strazza, Harold	1954 F
Stroh, Ronald	1963 F
Struck, Harry	1930 F
Stypa, George	1950 F
Stypa, Joseph	1947,48 F
Sullivan, Cornelius	1935 B
Sullivan, Daniel (Mgr*)	1937* F
Sullivan, Francis (Mgr*)	1936* F
Sullivan, William (Mgr*)	1934* F
Sullivan William	1939 F
Surmonte, Charles	1950,51 F
Sussman, Joseph	1930 F
Sutton, Richard	1940 B
Swales, James	1931 F,1932 B
Sweney, Chuck	1942 B

Sweeney, William	1932,34,35 B,1934 F
Szot, Walter	1939 F
Tafaro, Stephen	1966 F
Talarico, George	1938 F
Talarico, Lawrence	1939 B
Tallucci, Raymond	1965,66 F
Tankoos, Robert	1966 F
Tarantino, Donald	1950 B
Tarrant, Richard	1958-59 B
Tauriello, Maurice	1955,56 B
Taylor, Doherty	1944 F
Tedesco, Salvatore	1930,31 F
Tellone, Arthur	1944 F
Tenpenny, Ray	1939 F
Testa, Allan	1949 F
Tevlin, T	1950 F
Theobald, John	1936 F
Theophilakos, William 1941 F
Thievan, Louis	1954 F
Thoma, Joseph	1950 F
Thomas, John	1947,48 F,1948 B
Thornton, Paul (CC*) 1961-63* B
Tidik, Stephen	1938 F
Tighe, Jack	1959 B
Tighe, Austin	1954 F,1956 B
Tighe, T	1946 F
Tobin, Gerard	1966 F
Tortorella, Pat (AC*) 1931,41* F,1932 B
Townsend, Curtis	1950 F
Toye, Frederick	1954 F
Tracy, Edward	1931 F
Traudt, Terry	1956-59 B
Trezza, William	1962,63 F
Troisi, Anthony	1931 F
Tuson, Richard (Mgr*) 1941* F
Tuson, Russell (Mgr*) 1944,45* F
Tyson, John	1961 F
Uhl, Robert	1948 F
Umschied, Don	1943 B
Valenti, Gerald	1945,46 F
Valerio, John	1959,60 F
Vandermark, Jacob 1934 B
Vandeweghe, Charles 1930 F
Van Houten, Leonard 1938,39 F
Van Volkenburgh, Richard 1968 B
Varni, Fred	1930 F
Veneri, David	1953 B
Venezia, Sabino	1950 F
Vernay, Vincent	1950 F
Verrone, Louis	1963-65 F,1965 B
Vespole, Ernest	1966 F
Vinegra, Robert	1959-61 F
Vinges, Peter	1955 F
Vroom, Eugene	1949 F
Waldele, Robert	1949 B
Waldron, James	1953,54 B
Waldron, William	1931,34 F
Walker, William	1944-46 B,1945 F
Wallace, Edward	1962 F
Wallace, Francis	1947,48 F
Wallace, Michael	1944,45 F
Walbrecker, William 1935 F
Walsh, Frank	1943 B
Walsh, James	1941,43,45 F,1943 B

Walsh, John	1930 F
Walsh, Michael	1945 F
Walsh, R (Mgr*)	1955*B,1955 F
Walsh, Raymond	1963-65 B
Walsh, Thomas	1931 F, 1932 B
Walsh, Thomas	1963 F
Walters, Rev. John (Chap*) 1939 B*, 1939* F
Walter, Arthur	1944 F
Walter, Joe (Cap*)	1930,31* F,1931 B
Walter, John	1961-63 F
Walter, Raymond	1934 B
Walter, Robert	1940 B
Ward, Hugh	1938 F
Ward, John	1936 B
Ward, William	1938-40 B
Warner, Mitchell	1949 F,1950 B
Wasserloos, Charles 1936,38,39 F
Waters, Robert	1946,47 F
Waters, William	1939 F
Watson, Robert	1958-59 F,1959-60 B
Weber, John	1963,64 F
Weiner, Bernard	1936 F
Weisgerber, Dick	1932,33 F,1934 B
Werger, Edward	1938 F
Werwezga, Stan	1942 B
Whelan, Warren	1931,32 B
White, Robert (Cap*) 1949-50 B,1949* F
Wiatr, Joseph	1964-66 F,1965,66 B
Williams, Gerard	1952 F
Wimmer, Leonard	1934 B
Winne, Frederick (Mgr*) 1945* F
Wojciak, Raymond 1961-63 F
Wolf, George	1930,31 F
Worobec, Bohdan	1960 F
Wyatt, George	1944 F
Yakimowicz, Thaddeus 1950 F
Yankaukas, Peter	1936 F
Zannetti, James	1936-38 B
Zaremba, Steven	1953,54 F
Zazzali, Victor	1937 B
Zilahy, Norman	1955 F
Zimmerman, Thomas 1950 F
Zimmerman, Z/F	1938 B
Zinckgraf, John	1950 F
Zoppi, Michael	1949 F
Zuzzio, Al	1939 F

DISCLAIMER: Names are predominantely from yearbook and team photo captions. There is great variation in first name initials in captions with student and alumni directories. If a name has been misspelled, please advise so that revisions can be made in subsequent printings. Not all teams have photos and/or captions.

BIBLIOGRAPHY

BOOKS

Bolton, Clyde. *The Crimson Tide, A Story of Alabama Football.* Huntsville, AL: The Strode Publishers, 1972.

Cunningham, John T. *Newark.* Newark, NJ: New Jersey Historical Society, 1988.

Heartwell, James C. *The History of Oregon State College Basketball 1901-02 - 1952-53.* Corvallis, OR: Cascade Printing Company, 1953.

McPadden, O.S.B., Rev. Malachy, ed. *The Benedictines in Newark 1842-1992.* Newark, NJ: Wall Street Group, 1992.

Michelson, Herb and Newhouse, Dave. *Rose Bowl Football Since 1902.* Briarcliff Manor, NY: Stein and Day, 1977.

Miers, Earl Schenk. *Football.* New York, NY: Grossett & Dunlap, 1967.

Newton, David E. *Linus Pauling-Scientist and Advocate.* New York, NY: Facts on File, 1994.

O'Brien, Michael. *Vince, A Personal Biography of Vince Lombardi.* New York, NY: William Morrow and Company, Inc, 1987.

Olson, Sherry H. *Baltimore, The Building Of An American City.* Baltimore, MD: The Johns Hopkins University Press, 1980.

Revs. Pollard, Martin O.S.B. and Feiss, Hugh O.S.B. *Mount of Communion: Mount Angel Abbey 1882-1982.* Salem, OR: Capital City Graphics, 1985.

Sargent, J. Kathryn. *The Handbook of Private Schools.* Boston, MA: Porter/Sargent Publishers, Inc., 1991.

Serafini, Anthony. *Linus Pauling-A Man And His Science.* New York, NY: Paragon House, 1989.

Sheen, Most Reverend Fulton J. *The World Book Encyclopedia.* Chicago, IL: Field Enterprises Educational Corporation, 1971.

Steele, Michael R. *Knute Rockne-A Bio-Bibliography.* Westport, CT: Greenwood Press, 1983.

Stone, Msgr. William S. *The Cross In The Middle Of Nowhere.* Bend, OR: Maverick Publications, Inc., 1993.

Woolf, Henry B., Editor in Chief. *Webster's New Collegiate Dictionary.* Springfield, MA: G. & C. Merriam Co., 1976.

_____ . *Saint Mary's Abbey-Delbarton/Newark Abbey 1884-1984.* Morristown/Newark, NJ: St.Mary's/Newark Abbey, 1984.

_____ . *Directory of Colleges and Universities.* Washington, DC: US News & World Report, Inc., 1988.

PERIODICALS

Alumni Newsletter, St. Benedict's Prep, Newark, NJ

Angelus, St. Benedict, OR

Benedict News, St. Benedict's Prep, Newark, NJ

Bordentown Register, Bordentown, NJ

Capital Journal, Salem, OR

Chronicle, The Dalles, OR

Newark News, Newark, NJ
Optimist, The Dalles, OR
Oregonian, Portland, OR
Pacific Star, Mount Angel College, St. Benedict, OR
Salem Journal, Salem, OR
Scholastic, Notre Dame University, Notre Dame, IN
Siskiyou, Southern Oregon Normal School, Ashland, OR
Southern Cross, San Diego, CA
Star-Ledger, Newark, NJ
Statesman Journal, Salem, OR
Steelhead, The Dalles HS, The Dalles, OR
The Old Gold and White, Mt. Angel Academy and Normal School, Mt. Angel, OR
The Sunday Call, Newark, NJ
Weekly Chronicle, The Dalles, OR

YEARBOOKS

Beaver, Oregon Agricultural College, Corvallis, OR
Crimson and Gray, The Dalles HS, The Dalles, OR
Dome, Notre Dame University, Notre Dame, IN
Tap-A-Lam-A-Ho, Mount Angel College, St. Benedict, OR
Telolog, St. Benedict's Prep, Newark, NJ
Wallulah, Willamette University, Salem, OR

ALUMNI DIRECTORIES

Mt. Angel College/Seminary, St. Benedict, OR
Oregon Beta Chapter List, Phi Delta Theta Fraternity at Oregon Agricultural College, Oxford, OH
St. Benedict's Prep, Newark, NJ

COLLEGE CATALOGS

Mt. Angel College, St. Benedict, OR (1915-16; 1916-17; 1921-22; 1922-23; 1923-24; 1924-25; 1925-26)
Oregon Agricultural College, Corvallis, OR (1917-18; 1921-22; 1927)
Oregon Agricultural College, Corvallis, OR (Preliminary Bulletin for 1925, 1926 Summer Sessions)
Oregon State Agricultural College, (Summer, 1927)
Teachers College of Columbia University, New York, NY (1930-31 Bulletin)

FOOTBALL MEDIA GUIDES

Mississippi State University, Starkville, MS
Notre Dame University, Notre Dame, IN
Oregon State University, Corvallis, OR
Southern Oregon State College, Ashland, OR

MAGAZINES

Mike D'Orso, "Saturday's Hero: A Beat," *Sports Illustrated*, Oct. 23, 1989, pp. Unnumbered.

Tim Frank, "Hugh Devore, The Oldest Living Irish Football Coach Returns to Notre Dame Stadium," *Notre Dame-Purdue Football Game Program,* Sep. 29, 1990, Notre Dame, IN: pp. 65-66.

J.M. Gale, "The Dalles, Oregon," *The Union Pacific Magazine,* Aug., 1927, p. 54.

Vic Kelly, Sports Information UCLA, "Peerless Bill Spaulding," *News Magazine of Western Michigan University,* Kalamazoo, MI: Winter, 1961.

Rev. Dominic Milroy, O.S.B., What it Means to be a Benedictine School Today." *Delbarton Today.* Morristown, NJ: Fall, 1997.

_____. University of Maryland, College Park, *Alumni Magazine,* College Park, MD: Winter, 1995.

_____. U of W - O.A.C. *Official Program,* Oregon Agricultural College, October 22, 1921, Corvallis, OR.

_____, *The Oregon Countryman,* December, 1921, OAC, Corvallis, OR

St. Benedict's Prep, *Game Program,* Seton Hall Prep vs. Seton Hall Prep, November, 20, 1960, Newark, NJ.

_____. University of Oregon - O.A.C., *Game Program,* Nov. 15, 1919, Eugene, OR.

_____. *Beaver Tales,* Oregon State University, Corvallis, OR.

_____. *Oregon Stater,* Oregon State University, Corvallis, OR.

PAMPHLETS AND BROCHURES

Corvallis, Benton Co. Oregon, *Community Fact Sheet,* Corvallis, OR, January, 1994.

Mount Angel Abbey, *Mount Angel College,* St. Benedict, OR, undated.

Mount Angel Abbey, untitled, St. Benedict, OR., undated.

Newark Public Information Office. *Facts About Newark,* July, 1982.

Oregon State University. *Welcome to OSU,* Corvallis, OR., undated.

Rose Bowl Hall of Fame Day. Pasadena CA: 1992.

RECORD BOOKS

National High School, Kansas City, MO.

Pacific Coast Conference, *Record Book, 1916-1957,* Undated, Los Angeles, CA.

JOE KASBERGER WRITINGS

Kasberger, Joseph M., Memorandum to Members of St. Benedict's Athletic Teams, Feb. 24, 1961.

Kasberger, Joseph M., (Typed Speech/Essay), Your Son Should Play Football, undated.

Kasberger, Joseph M., (Typed Speech/Essay), My Philosophy of American Secondary Education, undated.

Kasberger, Joseph M., (Typed Memo/Speech), Advice to Baseball Players, undated.

Kasberger, Joseph M., (Typed Memo/ Position Paper), Need of A Preparatory School, presumed to be 1944, undated.

Kasberger, Joseph M., Correspondence to Knute K. Rockne, April, 1925.

Kasberger, Joseph M., Christmas Card writings, several years.

Kasberger, Joseph M., Comments on News Clipping to Joe Hellberg.

MISCELLANEOUS

Dolan, Sam. Correspondence to Knute K. Rockne on behalf of Joe Kasberger, University of Notre Dame Archives, Notre Dame, IN.

Gronewald, Hazel Huntington. "Alvin Edward Gronewald," from her memoirs. Provided by Marilyn G. Ericksen. The Dalles, OR: July, 1997.

Murray, William C. "The Life of Coach Robert L. Murray of The Dalles." Paper for the Original Wasco County Courthouse Forum. February 20, 1988.

"Informal Information Reply" pertaining to Joe Kasberger's service record, National Personnel Records Center, St. Louis, MO.

Joe Kasberger. Biographical sheet, Phi Delta Theta Fraternity National Headquarters, Oxford, OH.

Joe Kasberger. Contract with St. Benedict's Abbey, St. Benedict, OR executed on August 15, 1922.

Joe Kasberger. Personal Photograph Album and Captions from Newark Abbey Archives, Newark, NJ.

Milbauer, Frank, Jr. untitled Manuscript on Joe Kasberger, 1996.

O'Hare, Kathleen Milbauer. Manuscript entitled "Remberances of Joe Kasberger," 1996.

Rockne, Knute K. Correspondence to Joe Kasberger, May, 1925. University of Notre Dame Archives. Notre Dame, IN.

Rockne, Knute K. Correspondence to Paul L. Schissler. University of Notre Dame Archives. Notre Dame, IN.

Rockne, Knute K. Correspondence to M. E. Smith. University of Notre Dame Archives. Notre Dame, IN.

Schissler, Paul L. Correspondence to Knute K. Rockne University of Notre Dame Archives. Notre Dame, IN.

Schissler, Paul L. Correspondence to Calvin French, Ph. D. University of Notre Dame Archives. Notre Dame, IN.

Smith, M. E. Correspondence to Knute Rockne, University of Notre Dame Archives. Notre Dame, IN.

Scotti, Ben. Biographical Sketch, Trading Card by Ted Williams Company.

Walsh, O.S.B., Rev. Leo. Transcript of audio tape regarding Rev. Basil Scheiber, undated, Mt. Angel Abbey Archives, St. Benedict, OR.

_____. Oregon State Agricultural College. Poster for Summer Session, 1927. Corvallis, OR.

_____. *Quarterly Athletic Newsletter*, Willamette University, Salem, OR.

Krier, Jean. Manuscript about The Dalles, "Columbia Gorge History," undated, The Dalles-Wasco County Library.

_____. Manuscript on Sports in The Dalles. Undated, The Dalles-Wasco County Library.

_____. Fact Sheet about Saint Mary's Academy. Undated, Marylhurst, OR.

_____. Manuscript pertaining to Rev Basil Scheiber, Mt. Angel Abbey Archives, St. Benedict, OR.

_____. Ralph Orval Coleman Biography. Oregon State University Archives,

Corvallis, OR.

_____. Manuscript "Camp Lewis, 1917-1919." Undated. Fort Lewis, WA Military Museum.

_____. Hall of Fame Citations for John Oravec, Richard Weisgerber, and John Kolb. Willamette University. Salem, OR.

ARCHIVES/LIBRARIES

Archdiocese of Portland, Portland, OR
Columbia University, Columbiana Collection-Low Library, New York, NY
Columbia University, Teachers College, New York, NY
Diocese of Baker, Bend, OR
Fort Lewis Military Museum, Fort Lewis, WA
Hall of Champions, San Diego, CA
Houston Public Library, Houston, TX
Mt. Angel Abbey, St. Benedict, OR
Multnomah County Public Library, Portland, OR
Newark Abbey/ St. Benedict's Prep, Newark, NJ
Newark Public Library, Newark, NJ
Notre Dame University, Notre Dame, IN
Oregon State University, Corvallis, OR
Queen of Angels Monastery, Mt. Angel, OR
U.S. Marine Corps, Camp Pendleton, CA
United Methodist Church, Salem, OR
The Dalles HS, The Dalles, OR
The Dalles-Wasco County Public Library, The Dalles, OR
The Sisters of The Holy Names, Marylhurst, OR

INTERVIEWS

John M. Allen, Allen Archambault, John F. Bateman, Ph.D., Joyce Baudenstill, Pat Bernard, Bill Blauvelt, Ernest Ben Blood, Matthew Bolger, Jim Booth, Lorenzo Bouie, Robert Buob, Patricia Brandt, John Bookhouse, Rt. Rev. Martin Burne, O.S.B., Tony Candelmo, Ruth Cavallaro, James P. Clark, Rt. Rev. Brian Clarke, O.S.B., Gerald Clarke, Carl Cluff, Frank Cosentino, Hugh Devore, Sister Alberta Dieker, O.S.B., Harry Durkin, George Enderle, Marilyn G. Ericksen, Rev. Hugh Feiss, O.S.B., Rev. Jerome Fitzpatrick, O.S.B., Anthony Fraiola, Jerry Froelich, Gilbert Gaul, Lloyde Glicken, Mary Grant, John Grembowiec, Joe Grum, Joseph P. Hellberg, Wiles Hellock, Alfred Helwig, M.D., Alfred Helwig, Sr., Ayne Helwig, Gilbert Hewson, Bruce Howard, Rev. Theodore Howarth, O.S.B., Robert M. Huntington, Ph. D., William Jamieson, Julia Joyce, Jennifer Kasberger, Josephine Kasberger, Sister Rosemarie Kasper, S.N.J.M., Frank Kern, George Koeck, Charles Lamb, Harriet Langfeldt, Vince Liddy, Jay Locey, Richard Lorenzo, Terence Loughery, Susan McGonigal, M. Claire Milbauer, Helen Mondell, Harold Morgan, Rosemary Morgan, Bill Murray, Richard Nazareta, Elizabeth Nielsen, Frank O'Brien, Michael Petriella, M.D., Alan Pfeifer, Rev. Martin Pollard, O.S.B., Andrew Purcell, Al Reinoso, Rich Rosenthal, Bernard Sandoz, Charles Sandoz, Goldie Sandoz, Jim Sandoz, Jim Scarpone, Gene Schiller, Ben Scotti, Msgr. William Stone, John F. Thomas, Joeseph R. Thomas, Cliff Voliva, Vincent Walsh, Rev. Joe Walter, S.J., William Wassersug.

CHAPTER NOTES

PREFACE
1. John F. Thomas, correspondence with author.
2. Paul Horowitz, *Newark News* Newark, NJ: April 14, 1972, p. E-4 .
3. Bruce L. Howard, correspondence with author.

CHAPTER 1: Joe Kasberger's Early Years

1. Robert M. Huntington, Ph.D., correspondence and interviews with author.
2. Jean Krier, "Columbia Gorge History," undated manuscript about The Dalles, OR from The Dalles-Wasco County Library.
3. Jean Krier, "Columbia Gorge History."
4. Jean Krier,"Columbia Gorge History."
5. Jean Krier,"Columbia Gorge History."
6. Jean Krier,"Columbia Gorge History."
7. Jean Krier,"Columbia Gorge History."
8. Jean Krier,"Columbia Gorge History."
9. Bernard J. Sandoz, correspondence and interviews with author.
10. Bernard J. Sandoz.
11. Bernard J. Sandoz.
12. Bernard J. Sandoz.
13. Bernard J. Sandoz.
14. Bernard J. Sandoz.
15. David E. Newton, *Linus Pauling - Scientist and Advocate*, (New York, NY: Facts on File, 1994), p. 6.
16. Bernard J. Sandoz.
17. Bernard J. Sandoz.
18. Bernard J. Sandoz.
19. Bernard J. Sandoz.
20. Bernard J. Sandoz.
21. Bernard J. Sandoz.
22. David Newton, *Linus Pauling - Scientist and Advocate*, p. 7.
23. Anthony Serafini, *Linus Pauling - A Man and His Science*, (New York, NY: Paragon House, 1989), p. 1.
24. Anthony Serafini, *Linus Pauling - A Man and His Science*, p. 2.
25. Msgr. William S. Stone, *The Cross in the Middle of Nowhere*, (Bend, OR: Maverick Publishers, Inc., 1993), p.10.
26. Msgr. William S. Stone, *The Cross in the Middle of Nowhere*, p. 10.
27. Msgr. William S. Stone, *The Cross in the Middle of Nowhere*, p. 27.
28. Msgr. William S. Stone, *The Cross in the Middle of Nowhere*, p. 29.
29. Msgr. William S. Stone, *The Cross in the Middle of Nowhere*, p. 29.
30. Msgr. William S. Stone, *The Cross in the Middle of Nowhere*, p. 30.
31. Msgr. William S. Stone, *The Cross in the Middle of Nowhere*, p. 30.
32. Msgr. William S. Stone, *The Cross in the Middle of Nowhere*, p. 33.
33. Sister Rosemarie Kasper, The Sisters of the Holy Names Archives, Marylhurst, OR correspondence to author, July 17, 1995 that includes manuscript "Notes on The Dalles, Oregon," by S. Beatrice W., dated 12-8-89.
34. Sister Rosemarie Kasper.
35. Harriet Langfeldt, St. Mary's Academy, interviews with author.
36. Anthony Serafini, *Linus Pauling - A Man and His Science*, p. 6.
37. David Newton, *Linus Pauling - Scientist and Advocate*, p. 7.
38. Anthony Serafini, *Linus Pauling - A Man and His Science*, p. 6.
39. *Crimson and Gray*, The Dalles HS 1914 Yearbook, The Dalles, OR: p. 17.
40. Marilyn G. Ericksen, *Alvin Edward (Allie) Gronewald, from the Memoirs of Hazel Huntington Gronewald*, The Dalles, OR: July 14, 1997.
41. Anonymous, *Weekly Chronicle*, The Dalles, OR: June 4, 1914, from The Dalles-Wasco County Library.
42. *Crimson and Gray*, 1914, p. 29.
43. Anonymous, *Weekly Chronicle*, The Dalles, OR: June 11, 1914, from The Dalles-Wasco County Library.
44. Anonymous, *Weekly Chronicle*, The Dalles, OR: June 18, 1914, from The Dalles-Wasco County Library.
45. Robert M. Huntington, Ph.D.

46. Anonymous, *Weekly Chronicle*, The Dalles, OR: June 18, 1914, from The Dalles-Wasco County Library.
47. Robert M. Huntington, Ph.D.
48. Bernard J. Sandoz.
49. Anonymous, Manuscript on sports in The Dalles, OR, undated, p. 73, from The Dalles-Wasco County Library.
50. Anonymous, Manuscript on sports in The Dalles, OR, p. 73.
51. Anonymous, Manuscript on sports in The Dalles, OR, p. 73.
52. Anonymous, Manuscript on sports in The Dalles, OR, p. 77.
53. Anonymous, Manuscript on sports in The Dalles, OR, p. 73.
54. William C. Murray, *The Life of Coach Robert L. Murray of The Dalles*, Paper for the Original Wasco County Courthouse Forum, Saturday, Feb. 20, 1988, p. 1.
55. William C. Murray, *The Life of Coach Robert L. Murray of The Dalles*, p. 2.
56. William C. Murray, *The Life of Coach Robert L. Murray of The Dalles*, p. 4.
57. Anonymous, Manuscript on sports in The Dalles, OR, p. 72.
58. Anonymous, Manuscript on sports in The Dalles, OR, p. 72.
59. Anonymous, Manuscript on sports in The Dalles, OR, p. 72.
60. Anonymous, Manuscript on sports in The Dalles, OR, p. 72.
61. Anonymous, Manuscript on sports in The Dalles, OR, p. 72.
62. Anonymous, Manuscript on sports in The Dalles, OR, p. 72.
63. Anonymous, Manuscript on sports in The Dalles, OR, p. 72.
64. Notre Dame University *Football Media Guide*, Notre Dame, IN: 1994, p. 271.
65. Anonymous, Manuscript on sports in The Dalles, OR, p. 72.
66. Anonymous, Manuscript on sports in The Dalles, OR, p. 72.
67. Robert M. Huntington, Ph.D.
68. Jack Cross, *Chronicle*, The Dalles, OR, story on Bob Murray, circa 1948, from The Dalles-Wasco County Library.
69. Anonymous, Manuscript on sports in The Dalles, OR, p. 72.
70. William C. Murray, *The Life of Coach Robert L. Murray of The Dalles*, p. 8.
71. Anonymous, Manuscript on sports in The Dalles, OR, p. 72.
72. Anonymous, Manuscript on sports in The Dalles, OR, p. 72.
73. Anonymous, Manuscript on sports in The Dalles, OR, p. 72.
74. Anonymous, Manuscript on sports in The Dalles, OR, p. 72.
75. Anonymous, Manuscript on sports in The Dalles, OR, p. 72.
76. *Pacific Star*, Mount Angel College, St. Benedict, OR: October, 1917, p. 25.
77. Lloyde S.Glicken, *Star-Ledger*, Newark, NJ: October 2, 1969.
78. Patricia Brandt, Mt. Angel Abbey Archives, correspondence and interviews with author.
79. Michael Vanzandt, *Angelus*, St. Benedict, OR: March, 1964, from Mt. Angel Abbey Archives.
80. Michael Vanzandt, *Angelus*.
81. Anonymous, *Capital Journal*, Salem, OR: January 14, 1977, from Mt. Angel Abbey Archives.
82. Anonymous news story, December 9, 1916, from Mt. Angel Abbey Archives.
83. Fulton J. Sheen, *The World Book Encyclopedia*, vol. 2, (Chicago, IL: Field Enterprises Education Corp., 1971), p. 195.
84. Anonymous, *Mt. Angel Abbey Brochure*, undated, Mt. Angel Abbey, St. Benedict, OR.
85. Fulton J. Sheen, *The World Book Encyclopedia*, p. 195.
86. Henry B. Woolf, Editor in Chief, *Webster's New Collegiate Dictionary*, (Springfield, MA: G. & C. Merriam Co. 1976), p. 1122.
87. Anonymous, *Mt. Angel Abbey Brochure*.
88. Anonymous, *Mt. Angel Abbey Brochure*.
89. Anonymous, *Mt. Angel Abbey Brochure*.
90. Anonymous, *Mount Angel College*, St. Benedict's Abbey School Brochure, St. Benedict, OR: circa 1926, p. 3.
91. Revs. Martin Pollard O.S.B. and Hugh Feiss, O.S.B., *Mount of Communion,1882-1982*, Mt. Angel Abbey, (Capital City Graphics, Salem, OR: revised 2nd edition, 1985), p. 1.
92. Revs. Martin Pollard O.S.B. and Hugh Feiss, O.S.B., *Mount of Communion,1882-1982*, p. 1.
93. Revs. Martin Pollard O.S.B. and Hugh Feiss, O.S.B., *Mount of Communion,1882-1982*, p. 2.
94. Revs. Martin Pollard O.S.B. and Hugh Feiss, O.S.B., *Mount of Communion,1882-1982*, p. 2.
95. Revs. Martin Pollard O.S.B. and Hugh Feiss, O.S.B., *Mount of Communion,1882-1982*, p. 3.
96. Revs. Martin Pollard O.S.B. and Hugh Feiss, O.S.B., *Mount of Communion,1882-1982*, p. 3.
97. Revs. Martin Pollard O.S.B. and Hugh Feiss, O.S.B., *Mount of Communion,1882-1982*, p. 3.

98. Revs. Martin Pollard O.S.B. and Hugh Feiss, O.S.B., *Mount of Communion,1882-1982,* p. 3.
99. Revs. Martin Pollard O.S.B. and Hugh Feiss, O.S.B., *Mount of Communion,1882-1982,* pp. 3-4.
100. Revs. Martin Pollard O.S.B. and Hugh Feiss, O.S.B., *Mount of Communion,1882-1982,* p. 4.
101. Revs. Martin Pollard O.S.B. and Hugh Feiss, O.S.B., *Mount of Communion,1882-1982,* p. 4.
102. Revs. Martin Pollard O.S.B. and Hugh Feiss, O.S.B., *Mount of Communion,1882-1982,* p. 4.
103. Revs. Martin Pollard O.S.B. and Hugh Feiss, O.S.B., *Mount of Communion,1882-1982,* p. 15.
104. Revs. Martin Pollard O.S.B. and Hugh Feiss, O.S.B., *Mount of Communion,1882-1982,* p. 15.
105. Revs. Martin Pollard O.S.B. and Hugh Feiss, O.S.B., *Mount of Communion,1882-1982,* p. 16.
106. Revs. Martin Pollard O.S.B. and Hugh Feiss, O.S.B., *Mount of Communion,1882-1982,* p. 17.
107. Mount Angel College, *Catalog,* St. Benedict, OR: 1923, p. 7.
108. Revs. Martin Pollard O.S.B. and Hugh Feiss, O.S.B., *Mount of Communion,1882-1982,* p. 17.
109. Revs. Martin Pollard O.S.B. and Hugh Feiss, O.S.B., *Mount of Communion,1882-1982,* p. 18.
110. Revs. Martin Pollard O.S.B. and Hugh Feiss, O.S.B., *Mount of Communion,1882-1982,* p. 19.
111. Revs. Martin Pollard O.S.B. and Hugh Feiss, O.S.B., *Mount of Communion,1882-1982,* p. 30.

CHAPTER 2: Joe as a Student at Mt. Angel College

1. Mount Angel College, *Catalog,* St. Benedict, OR: 1923, p. 7.
2. Anonymous, *Mount Angel College*, St. Benedict's Abbey School Brochure, St. Benedict, OR: circa 1926, p. 3.
3. Anonymous, *Mount Angel College*, p. 3.
4. Anonymous, *Mount Angel College*, p. 3.
5. Anonymous, *Mount Angel College*, p. 5.
6. Anonymous, *Mount Angel College*, p. 5
7. Anonymous, news story on Rev. Basil Schieber, O.S.B., April, 1919, from Mt. Angel Abbey Archives.
8. Anonymous, news story on Rev. Basil Schieber, O.S.B., April, 1919, from Mt. Angel Abbey Archives.
9. Rev. Leo Walsh, O.S.B., tape transcript on Rev. Basil Schieber, O.S.B., Mt. Angel Abbey Archives.
10. Rev. Leo Walsh, O.S.B., tape transcript on Rev. Basil Schieber, O.S.B., Mt. Angel Abbey Archives.
11. Anonymous, news story on Rev. Basil Schieber, O.S.B., April, 1919, Mt. Angel Abbey Archives.
12. Rev. Leo Walsh, O.S.B., tape transcript on Rev. Basil Schieber, O.S.B., Mt. Angel Abbey Archives.
13. Rev. Leo Walsh, O.S.B., tape transcript on Rev. Basil Schieber, O.S.B., Mt. Angel Abbey Archives.
14. Rev. Leo Walsh, O.S.B., tape transcript on Rev. Basil Schieber, O.S.B., Mt. Angel Abbey Archives.
15. Rev. Leo Walsh, O.S.B., tape transcript on Rev. Basil Schieber, O.S.B., Mt. Angel Abbey Archives.
16. Anonymous, news story on Rev. Basil Schieber, O.S.B., April, 1919, from Mt. Angel Abbey Archives.
17. *Pacific Star,* Mount Angel College, St. Benedict, OR: October, 1917, p. 45.
18. *Pacific Star,* Mount Angel College, October, 1917, p. 25.
19. *Pacific Star,* Mount Angel College, October, 1917, p. 25.
20. *Pacific Star,* Mount Angel College, October, 1917, p. 25.
21. *Pacific Star,* Mount Angel College, October, 1917, p. 45.
22. Anonymous, news story, handwritten date of 1918, from Mt. Angel Abbey Archives.
23. Anonymous, news story, handwritten date of 1918, from Mt. Angel Abbey Archives.
24. *Pacific Star,* Mount Angel College, October, 1915, p. 33.
25. *Pacific Star,* Mount Angel College, October, 1915, p. 33.
26. *Pacific Star,* Mount Angel College, November, 1915, p. 35.
27. *Pacific Star,* Mount Angel College, November, 1915, p. 37.
28. Robert M. Huntington, Ph.D. correspondence and interviews with author.
29. *Pacific Star,* Mount Angel College, January, 1916, p. 33.
30. *Pacific Star,* Mount Angel College, February, 1916, p. 34.
31. Anonymous, news story from Mt. Angel Abbey Archives.
32. *Pacific Star,* Mount Angel College, January, 1916, p. 28.
33. *Pacific Star,* Mount Angel College, January, 1916, p. 28.
34. *Pacific Star,* Mount Angel College, January, 1916, p. 28.
35. *Pacific Star,* Mount Angel College, February, 1916, p. 34.
36. *Pacific Star,* Mount Angel College, February, 1916, p. 34.
37. Revs. Martin Pollard O.S.B. and Hugh Feiss, O.S.B., *Mount of Communion,1882-1982,* Mt. Angel Abbey, (Capital City Graphics, Salem, OR: revised 2nd edition, 1985), p. 30.
38. Anonymous, news story, January 13, 1916, from Mt. Angel Abbey Archives.
39. *Pacific Star,* Mount Angel College, June 3, 1926, p. 6.

40. *Pacific Star*, Mount Angel College, June 3, 1926, p. 6.

41. *Pacific Star*, Mount Angel College, February, 1916, p. 34.

42. *Pacific Star*, Mount Angel College, June 3, 1926, p. 6.

43. *Pacific Star*, Mount Angel College, May, 1916, p. 73.

44. Anonymous, news story, July 27, 1918, from Mt. Angel Abbey Archives.

45. Anonymous, news story, June 17, 1916, from Mt. Angel Abbey Archives.

46. Lloyde S. Glicken, *Star-Ledger*, Newark, NJ: October 2, 1969.

47. Anonymous, news story, March 17, 1916, from Mt. Angel Abbey Archives.

48. Mt. Angel College and Seminary *Catalog*, St. Benedict, OR: 1915-16, p. 39.

49. Joe Kasberger captions in his photo album, Newark Abbey Archives, Newark, NJ.

50. Msgr. William S. Stone, *The Cross in the Middle of Nowhere*, (Bend, OR: Maverick Publishers, Inc., 1993), p. 96.

51. Anonymous, news story, September 30, 1916, from Mt. Angel Abbey Archives.

52. *Pacific Star*, Mount Angel College, October, 1916, p. 41.

53. *Pacific Star*, Mount Angel College, October, 1916, p. 42.

54. *Pacific Star*, Mount Angel College, October, 1916, p. 42.

55. Anonymous, news story, September 30, 1916, from Mt. Angel Abbey Archives.

56. Anonymous, news story, September 30, 1916, from Mt. Angel Abbey Archives.

57. Anonymous, news story, September 23, 1916, from Mt. Angel Abbey Archives.

58. *Pacific Star*, Mount Angel College, October, 1916, p. 43.

59. *Pacific Star*, Mount Angel College, November, 1916, p. 29.

60. *Pacific Star*, Mount Angel College, November, 1916, p. 28.

61. *Pacific Star*, Mount Angel College, December, 1916, pp. 36-37.

62. *Pacific Star*, Mount Angel College, December, 1916, pp. 37-38.

63. Anonymous, *Salem Journal*, Salem, OR: November 6, 1916, from Mt. Angel Abbey Archives.

64. *Pacific Star*, Mount Angel College, January, 1917, pp. 34-35.

65. Anonymous, news story, December 2, 1916, from Mt. Angel Abbey Archives.

66. Anonymous, news story, December 20, 1916, from Mt. Angel Abbey Archives.

67. *Pacific Star*, Mount Angel College, January, 1917, p. 35.

68. *Pacific Star*, Mount Angel College, January, 1917, p. 35.

69. *Pacific Star*, Mount Angel College, January, 1917, p. 37.

70. Anonymous, news story, undated, from Mt. Angel Abbey Archives.

71. *Pacific Star*, Mount Angel College, January, 1917, p. 36.

72. *Pacific Star*, Mount Angel College, February, 1917, p. 36.

73. *Pacific Star*, Mount Angel College, February, 1917, p. 36.

74. *Pacific Star*, Mount Angel College, February, 1917, p. 37.

75. *Pacific Star*, Mount Angel College, February, 1917, p. 40.

76. *Pacific Star*, Mount Angel College, October, 1917, p. 27.

77. *Pacific Star*, Mount Angel College, October, 1917, p. 27.

78. Anonymous, news story, December 8, 1916, from Mt. Angel Abbey Archives.

79. Anonymous, news story, December 8, 1916, from Mt. Angel Abbey Archives.

80. Anonymous, news story, December 9, 1916, from Mt. Angel Abbey Archives.

81. Anonymous, news story, December 9, 1916, from Mt. Angel Abbey Archives.

82. Anonymous, news story, December 9, 1916, from Mt. Angel Abbey Archives.

83. Anonymous, news story, December 9, 1916, from Mt. Angel Abbey Archives.

84. Anonymous, news story, December 16, 1916, from Mt. Angel Abbey Archives.

85. Anonymous, news story, December 18, 1916, from Mt. Angel Abbey Archives.

86. Anonymous, news story, January 9, 1917, from Mt. Angel Abbey Archives.

87. Anonymous, news story, January 15, 1917, from Mt. Angel Abbey Archives.

88. *Pacific Star*, Mount Angel College, June 3, 1926, p. 6.

89. *Pacific Star*, Mount Angel College, March, 1917, p. 58.

90. *Pacific Star*, Mount Angel College, October, 1917, p. 26.

91. Mt. Angel College and Seminary *Catalog*, St. Benedict, OR: 1916-17, p. 40.

92. *Pacific Star*, Mount Angel College, March, 1917, p. 59.

93. *Pacific Star*, Mount Angel College, March, 1917, p. 59.

94. Anonymous, news story, March 13, 1917, from Mt. Angel Abbey Archives.

95. *Pacific Star*, Mount Angel College, March, 1917, p. 59.

96. Anonymous, news story, September 14, 1918, from Mt. Angel Abbey Archives.

97. *Pacific Star*, Mount Angel College, October, 1917, pp. 41-43.

98. Anonymous, news story, July 13, 1918, from Mt. Angel Abbey Archives.

99. *Pacific Star,* Mount Angel College, October, 1917, p. 24.

100. *Pacific Star,* Mount Angel College, October, 1917, p. 26.

101. *Pacific Star,* Mount Angel College, October, 1917, p. 44.

102. *Pacific Star,* Mount Angel College, October, 1917, pp. 44-45.

103. *Pacific Star,* Mount Angel College, October, 1917, p. 45.

104. *Pacific Star,* Mount Angel College, October, 1917, p. 45.

105. *Pacific Star,* Mount Angel College, October, 1917, p. 44.

106. *Pacific Star,* Mount Angel College, October, 1917, pp. 44-45.

107. *Pacific Star,* Mount Angel College, October, 1917, p. 45.

108. Anonymous, news story, September 14, 1918, from Mt. Angel Abbey Archives.

109. Bernard J. Sandoz, correspondence and interviews with author.

CHAPTER 3: Joe at OAC Before and After the War

1. Anonymous, *Welcome to OSU,* undated, Oregon State University, Corvallis, OR.

2. Anonymous, *Welcome to OSU.*

3. Anthony Serafini, *Linus Pauling - A Man and His Science,* (New York, NY: Paragon House, 1989), pp. 12-13.

4. Anthony Serafini, *Linus Pauling - A Man and His Science,* p. 12.

5. Anthony Serafini, *Linus Pauling - A Man and His Science,* p. 14.

6. Oregon Agricultural College, *General Catalog,* 1917-18, Corvallis, OR: p. 393.

7. Oregon Agricultural College, *General Catalog,* 1917-18, Corvallis, OR: p. 394.

8. Oregon Agricultural College, *General Catalog,* 1917-18, Corvallis, OR: p. unknown.

9. Oregon Agricultural College, *General Catalog,* 1921-22, Corvallis, OR: p. 384.

10. *Pacific Coast Conference Record Book 1916-1957,* Los Angeles, CA: undated, p. 15.

11. *Beaver,* Yearbook of Oregon Agricultural College, Corvallis, OR: 1923, p. 125.

12. Elizabeth Nielsen, Oregon State University Archives, Corvallis, OR: correspondence and interviews with author.

13. *Chapter List,* Phi Delta Theta International Headquarters, Oxford, OH: undated, p. 147.

14. *Chapter List,* Phi Delta Theta International Headquarters, p. 147.

15. Robert M. Huntington, Ph.D., correspondence and interviews with author.

16. Oregon State University, *Football Media Guide,* undated, Corvallis, OR: p. 166.

17. James C. Heartwell, *The History of Oregon State College Basketball 1901-02 - 1952-53,* (Corvallis, OR: Cascade Printing Co.), 1953, pp. 23-27.

18. *Pacific Coast Conference Record Book 1916-57,* p. 29.

19. Oregon State University, *Football Media Guide,* p. 166.

20. Anonymous news story, September 14, 1918, from Mt. Angel Abbey Archives.

21. *Pacific Coast Conference Record Book 1916-57,* p. 15.

22. James C. Heartwell, *The History of Oregon State College Basketball 1901-02 - 1952-53,* p. 26.

23. James C. Heartwell, *The History of Oregon State College Basketball 1901-02 - 1952-53,* pp. 27-28.

24. James C. Heartwell, *The History of Oregon State College Basketball 1901-02 - 1952-53,* p. 27.

25. James C. Heartwell, *The History of Oregon State College Basketball 1901-02 - 1952-53,* p. 27.

26. James C. Heartwell, *The History of Oregon State College Basketball 1901-02 - 1952-53,* p. 28.

27. *Beaver,* Yearbook of Oregon Agricultural College, 1919, p. 193.

28. Anthony Serafini, *Linus Pauling - A Man and His Science,* p. 15.

29. Anthony Serafini, *Linus Pauling - A Man and His Science,* p. 15.

30. Anonymous, news story, July 13, 1918, from Mt. Angel Abbey Archives.

31. Anonymous, news story, July 13, 1918, from Mt. Angel Abbey Archives.

32. Anonymous, news story, July 13, 1918, from Mt. Angel Abbey Archives.

33. Anonymous, news story, July 27, 1918, from Mt. Angel Abbey Archives.

34. Anonymous, news story, July 27, 1918, from Mt. Angel Abbey Archives.

35. William C. Murray, *The Life of Coach Robert L. Murray of The Dalles,* Paper for the Original Wasco County Courthouse Forum, Saturday, Feb. 20, 1988, p. 8.

36. William C. Murray, *The Life of Coach Robert L. Murray of The Dalles,* p. 9.

37. *Pacific Coast Conference Record Book 1916-57,* p. 29.

38. William C. Murray, correspondence and interviews with author.

39. Anonymous news story, September 14, 1918, from Mt. Angel Abbey Archives.

40. Anonymous, Manuscript excerpt, "Camp Lewis, 1917-1919," from Fort Lewis Military Museum, Fort Lewis, WA: undated, p. 7.

41. Anonymous, Manuscript excerpt, "Camp Lewis, 1917-1919," p. 8.

42. Anonymous, Manuscript excerpt, "Camp Lewis, 1917-1919," p. 8.

43. Alan Archambault, Fort Lewis Military Museum Archivist, correpondence and interviews with author.

44. Gil Moe, *Siskiyou*, Newspaper of Southern Oregon Normal School, Ashland, OR: October 22, 1929, p. 4.

45. Herb Michelson and Dave Newhouse, *Rose Bowl Football Since 1902*, (Briarcliff Manor, NY: Stein and Day), pp. 41-43.

46. Elizabeth Nielsen.

47. Oregon State University, *Football Media Guide*, p. 166.

48. James C. Heartwell, *The History of Oregon State College Basketball 1901-02 - 1952-53*, p. 28.

49. M. Claire Milbauer, correspondence and interviews with author.

50. Bernard J. Sandoz, correspondence and interviews with author.

51. Bernard J. Sandoz.

52. *Beaver*, Yearbook of Oregon Agricultural College, 1921, p. 178.

53. *Beaver*, Yearbook of Oregon Agricultural College, 1923, p. 125.

54. *Beaver*, Yearbook of Oregon Agricultural College, 1923, p. 68.

55. *University of Oregon-O.A.C. Football Game Program*, University of Oregon, Eugene, OR: Nov. 15, 1919.

56. *University of Oregon-O.A.C. Football Game Program.*

57. *University of Oregon-O.A.C. Football Game Program.*

58. *University of Oregon-O.A.C. Football Game Program.*

59. *University of Oregon-O.A.C. Football Game Program.*

60. *University of Oregon-O.A.C. Football Game Program.*

61. *University of Oregon-O.A.C. Football Game Program.*

62. *University of Oregon-O.A.C. Football Game Program.*

63. *Beaver*, Yearbook of Oregon Agricultural College, 1921, p. 271.

64. *Beaver*, Yearbook of Oregon Agricultural College, 1921, p. 272.

65. *Beaver*, Yearbook of Oregon Agricultural College, 1921, p. 272.

66. *Beaver*, Yearbook of Oregon Agricultural College, 1921, p. 274.

67. *Beaver*, Yearbook of Oregon Agricultural College, 1923, p. 144.

68. *Beaver*, Yearbook of Oregon Agricultural College, 1921, p. 179.

69. Anonymous, *The Dalles Optimist*, The Dalles, OR: story on Bob Murray, June, 1958, from The Dalles-Wasco County Library.

70. Marilyn G. Ericksen, correspondence and interviews with author.

71. Marilyn G. Ericksen, correspondence and interviews with author.

72. Marilyn G. Ericksen, correspondence and interviews with author.

73. Anonymous, *Rose Bowl Hall of Fame Day*, Brochure, Pasadena, CA: 1992.

74. Anonymous, *Rose Bowl Hall of Fame Day*, Brochure, Pasadena, CA: 1992.

75. William C. Murray, *The Life of Coach Robert L. Murray of The Dalles*, p. 18.

76. Marilyn G. Ericksen correspondence and interviews with author.

77. William C. Murray, *The Life of Coach Robert L. Murray of The Dalles*, p. 10.

78. *Beaver*, Yearbook of Oregon Agricultural College, 1921, p. 292.

79. *Beaver*, Yearbook of Oregon Agricultural College, 1921, p. 292.

80. James C. Heartwell, *The History of Oregon State College Basketball 1901-02 - 1952-53*, p. 23.

81. *Beaver*, Yearbook of Oregon Agricultural College, 1919, p. 294.

82. *Beaver*, Yearbook of Oregon Agricultural College, 1919, p. 294.

83. *Beaver*, Yearbook of Oregon Agricultural College, 1923, p. 379.

84. *Beaver*, Yearbook of Oregon Agricultural College, 1922, p. 200.

85. *Beaver*, Yearbook of Oregon Agricultural College, 1923, p. 210.

86. John F. Thomas, correspondence and interviews with author.

87. Anonymous, "Seventeen Proud Keene Years," *Oregon Stater*, Alumni Magazine of Oregon State University, Corvallis, OR: September/October 1964, p. 10.

88. Anonymous, "Seventeen Proud Keene Years," *Oregon Stater*, p. 10.

89. Anonymous, "Seventeen Proud Keene Years," *Oregon Stater*, p. 10.

90. Gil Moe, *Siskiyou*, p. 4.

91. *O.A.C.-University of Washington Football Game Program*, Oregon State University, Corvallis, OR: October 22, 1921, p. 3.

92. *O.A.C.-University of Washington Football Game Program*, p. 3.

93. *Beaver*, Yearbook of Oregon Agricultural College, 1922, p. 351.

94. *Beaver*, Yearbook of Oregon Agricultural College, 1922, p. 358.

95. *Beaver*, Yearbook of Oregon Agricultural College, 1922, p. 358.

96. *Beaver,* Yearbook of Oregon Agricultural College, 1922, p. 358.

97. *Beaver,* Yearbook of Oregon Agricultural College, 1922, p. 359.

98. *Beaver,* Yearbook of Oregon Agricultural College, 1922, p. 359.

99. *Beaver,* Yearbook of Oregon Agricultural College, 1922, p. 359.

100. *Beaver,* Yearbook of Oregon Agricultural College, 1922, p. 359

101. *Beaver,* Yearbook of Oregon Agricultural College, 1922, p. 360.

102. *Beaver,* Yearbook of Oregon Agricultural College, 1921, p. 179.

103. James C. Heartwell, *The History of Oregon State College Basketball 1901-02 - 1952-53,* p. 30.

104. *Beaver,* Yearbook of Oregon Agricultural College, 1922, p. 397.

105. *Beaver,* Yearbook of Oregon Agricultural College, 1922, p. 397.

106. *Beaver,* Yearbook of Oregon Agricultural College, 1922, p. 212.

107. *Beaver,* Yearbook of Oregon Agricultural College, 1923, p. 270.

108. *Beaver,* Yearbook of Oregon Agricultural College, 1922, p. 89.

109. *Beaver,* Yearbook of Oregon Agricultural College, 1922, p. 142.

110. David E. Newton, *Linus Pauling - Scientist and Advocate,* (New York, NY: Facts on File, 1994), p. 13.

111. *Beaver,* Yearbook of Oregon Agricultural College, 1923, p. 378.

112. David Newton, *Linus Pauling - Scientist and Advocate,* p. 14.

113. David Newton, *Linus Pauling - Scientist and Advocate,* p. 16.

114. Anthony Serafini, *Linus Pauling - A Man and His Science,* pp. 16-17.

115. *Beaver,* Yearbook of Oregon Agricultural College, 1923, p. 247.

116. *Beaver,* Yearbook of Oregon Agricultural College, 1923, pp. 248-249.

117. *O.A.C.-University of Washington Football Game Program,* p. 11.

118. *Beaver,* Yearbook of Oregon Agricultural College, 1923, p. 254.

119. *Beaver,* Yearbook of Oregon Agricultural College, 1923, p. 254.

120. *Beaver,* Yearbook of Oregon Agricultural College, 1923, p. 70.

121. *Beaver,* Yearbook of Oregon Agricultural College, 1923, p. 255.

122. *Beaver,* Yearbook of Oregon Agricultural College, 1922, p. 211.

123. Robert M. Huntington, Ph.D.

124. *Beaver,* Yearbook of Oregon Agricultural College, 1923, p. 74.

125. *Beaver,* Yearbook of Oregon Agricultural College, 1923, p. 256.

126. *Beaver,* Yearbook of Oregon Agricultural College, 1923, p. 255.

127. Gil Moe, *Siskiyou,* p. 4.

128. *The Oregon Countryman,* Oregon Agricultural College, Corvallis, OR: Dec. 1921, p. 27.

129. *The Oregon Countryman,* p. 27.

130. *Beaver,* Yearbook of Oregon Agricultural College, 1923, p. 551.

131. James C. Heartwell, *The History of Oregon State College Basketball 1901-02 - 1952-53,* p. 31.

132. *The History of Oregon State College Basketball 1901-02 - 1952-53,* p. 31.

133. James C. Heartwell, *The History of Oregon State College Basketball 1901-02 - 1952-53,* p. 88.

134. *Beaver,* Yearbook of Oregon Agricultural College, 1923, p. 302.

135. Anonymous, *Biography of Ralph Orval Coleman,* undated, Corvallis, OR. p. 25, from Oregon State University Archives.

136. Anonymous, *Biography of Ralph Orval Coleman,* p. 26.

137. Anonymous, *Biography of Ralph Orval Coleman,* p. 26.

138. Anonymous, *Biography of Ralph Orval Coleman,* p. 26.

139. Anonymous, *Biography of Ralph Orval Coleman,* p. 27.

140. Anonymous, *Biography of Ralph Orval Coleman,* p. 26.

141. Gil Moe, *Siskiyou,* p. 4.

142. *Beaver,* Yearbook of Oregon Agricultural College, 1923, p. 125.

CHAPTER 4: Joe as a Coach at Mt. Angel College

1. Anonymous, news story on Rev. Basil Schieber, O.S.B., April, 1919, from Mt. Angel Abbey Archives.

2. Anonymous, news story on Rev. Basil Schieber, O.S.B., April, 1919, from Mt. Angel Abbey Archives.

3. Anonymous, news story on Rev. Basil Schieber, O.S.B., April, 1919, from Mt. Angel Abbey Archives.

4. Anonymous, Manuscript "R.P. Basil Schieber, O.S.B.," April 5, 1919, from Mt. Angel Abbey Archives.

5. Revs. Martin Pollard O.S.B. and Hugh Feiss, O.S.B. *Mount of Communion, 1882-1982,* Mt. Angel Abbey, (Capital City Graphics, Salem, OR: revised 2nd edition, 1985), p. 31.

6. Revs. Martin Pollard O.S.B. and Hugh Feiss, O.S.B., *Mount of Communion, 1882-1982,* p. 31.

7. Revs. Martin Pollard O.S.B. and Hugh Feiss, O.S.B., *Mount of Communion, 1882-1982,* p. 31.

8. Mount Angel College, *Catalog,* St. Benedict, OR: 1922, p. 6.

9. Patricia Brandt, correspondence and interviews with author.

10. Earl Schenk Miers, *Football*, (Grossett & Dunlap, New York, NY: 1967), pp. 26-28.

11. *Pacific Star,* Mount Angel College, St. Benedict, OR: June 3, 1926, p. 5.

12. Mount Angel College, *Catalog*, 1924, p. 14.

13. Mount Angel College, *Catalog*, 1924, p. 14.

14. Mount Angel College, *Catalog*, 1924, p. 14.

15. Mount Angel College, *Catalog*, 1924, p. 14.

16. Mount Angel College, *Catalog*, 1924, p. 15.

17. Mount Angel College, *Catalog*, 1924, p. 15.

18. Mount Angel College, *Catalog*, 1924, p. 14.

19. Mount Angel College, *Catalog*, 1922, p. 56.

20. *Pacific Star,* Mount Angel College, June 3, 1926, p. 5.

21. *Pacific Star,* Mount Angel College, June 3, 1926, p. 6.

22. *Pacific Star,* Mount Angel College, June 3, 1926, p. 6.

23. *Pacific Star,* Mount Angel College, June 3, 1926, p. 6.

24. *Pacific Star,* Mount Angel College, June 3, 1926, p. 6.

25. Mount Angel College, *Catalog*, 1923, p. 59.

26. Mount Angel College, *Catalog*, 1924, p. 62.

27. Mount Angel College, *Catalog*, 1924, p. 62.

28. Mount Angel College, *Catalog*, 1924, pp. 62-63.

29. *Pacific Star,* Mount Angel College, June 3, 1926, p. 6.

30. Mount Angel College, *Catalog*, 1924, p. unnumbered.

31. *Pacific Star,* Mount Angel College, June 4, 1925, p. 5.

32. Lloyde S. Glicken, *Star-Ledger*, Newark, NJ: October 2, 1969.

33. Earl Schenk Miers, *Football*, p. 45.

34. Michael R. Steele, *Knute Rockne-A Bio-Biography*, (Westport, CT: Greenwood Press, 1983), p. 131.

35. Notre Dame University, *Football Media Guide*, Notre Dame, IN: 1994, p. 240.

36. Notre Dame University, *Football Media Guide*, p. 219.

37. Earl Schenk Miers, *Football*, p. 47.

38. Mount Angel College, *Catalog*, 1924, p. 67.

39. *Tap-A-Lam-A-Ho*, Yearbook of Mount Angel College, St. Benedict, OR: 1922, p. 36.

40. Anonymous, news story on Rev. Norbert Matteucci, O.S.B., undated, from Mt. Angel Abbey Archives.

41. Anonymous, news story on Rev. Norbert Matteucci, O.S.B., undated, from Mt. Angel Abbey Archives.

42. *Dome*, Yearbook of Notre Dame University, Notre Dame, IN: 1923, p. 96.

43. *Dome*, Yearbook of Notre Dame University, 1923, p. 96.

44. *Pacific Star,* Mount Angel College, June 4, 1925, p. 4.

45. *Pacific Star,* Mount Angel College, June 4, 1925, p. 3.

46. William C. Murray, *The Life of Coach Robert L. Murray of The Dalles,* Paper for the Original Wasco County Courthouse Forum, Saturday, Feb. 20, 1988, p. 12.

47. William C. Murray, *The Life of Coach Robert L. Murray of The Dalles,* p. 11.

48. Anonymous, Manuscript on sports in The Dalles, OR from The Dalles-Wasco County Library, undated, p. 72.

49. Anonymous, Manuscript on sports in The Dalles, OR, p. 72.

50. *Pacific Star,* Mount Angel College, June 3, 1926, p. 6.

51. *Pacific Star,* Mount Angel College, June 4, 1925, p. 4.

52. *Pacific Star,* Mount Angel College, June 3, 1926, p. 6.

53. Knute Rockne letter to Joe Kasberger, May 1, 1925, from University of Notre Dame archives.

54. *Pacific Star,* Mount Angel College, June 4, 1925, p. 3.

55. M.E. Smith letter to Knute Rockne, November 8, 1924, from University of Notre Dame archives.

56. Knute Rockne letter to Paul Schissler, November 21, 1924, from University of Notre Dame archives.

57. Knute Rockne letter to M. E. Smith, December 14, 1924, from University of Notre Dame archives.

58. Knute Rockne letter to M. E. Smith, April 13, 1925, from University of Notre Dame archives.

59. Paul Schissler letter to Knute Rockne, September 5, 1925, from University of Notre Dame archives.

60. Knute Rockne letter to Paul Schissler, September 16, 1925, from University of Notre Dame archives.

61. *Pacific Star,* Mount Angel College, June 3, 1926, p. 6.

62. *Pacific Star,* Mount Angel College, June 3, 1926, p. 4.
63. *Pacific Star,* Mount Angel College, June 3, 1926, p. 4.
64. *Pacific Star,* Mount Angel College, June 3, 1926, p. 4.
65. *Pacific Star,* Mount Angel College, June 3, 1926, p. 4.
66. *Pacific Star,* Mount Angel College, June 3, 1926, p. 4.
67. *Pacific Star,* Mount Angel College, June 3, 1926, p. 5.
68. *Pacific Star,* Mount Angel College, June 3, 1926, p. 5.
69. *Pacific Star,* Mount Angel College, June 3, 1926, p. 5.
70. *Pacific Star,* Mount Angel College, June 3, 1926, p. 5.
71. *Pacific Star,* Mount Angel College, June 3, 1926, p. 5.
72. *Pacific Star,* Mount Angel College, June 3, 1926, p. 5.
73. *Pacific Star,* Mount Angel College, June 3, 1926, p. 4.
74. *Pacific Star,* Mount Angel College, June 3, 1926, p. 4.
75. *Pacific Star,* Mount Angel College, June 3, 1926, p. 4.
76. *Pacific Star,* Mount Angel College, June 3, 1926, p. 4.
77. *Pacific Star,* Mount Angel College, June 3, 1926, p. 4.
78. *Pacific Star,* Mount Angel College, June 3, 1926, p. 5.
79. Gil Moe, *Siskiyou,* Newspaper of Southern Oregon Normal School, Ashland, OR: October 22, 1929, p. 4.
80. *Pacific Star,* Mount Angel College, June 3, 1926, p. 1.
81. *Pacific Star,* Mount Angel College, June 3, 1926, p. 8.
82. *Pacific Star,* Mount Angel College, June 3, 1926, p. 8.
83. Patricia Brandt, correspondence and interviews with author.
84. *Pacific Star,* Mount Angel College, June 3, 1926, p. 5.
85. *Pacific Star,* Mount Angel College, June 3, 1926, p. 4.
86. *Pacific Star,* Mount Angel College, June 3, 1926, p. 4.
87. Anonymous, *Mount Angel College,* St. Benedict's Abbey School Brochure, St. Benedict, OR: circa 1926, pp. 5-6.
88. Anonymous, *Mount Angel College,* pp. 6-7.
89. Anonymous, *Mount Angel College,* p. 7.
90. Anonymous, *Mount Angel College,* p. 7.
91. Anonymous, *Mount Angel College,* p. 7.
92. Anonymous, *Mount Angel College,* pp. 17-19.
93. Anonymous, *Mount Angel College,* pp. 23-24.
94. Anonymous, *Mount Angel College,* p. 24.
95. Michael R. Steele, *Knute Rockne-A Bio-Biography,* p. 131.
96. Michael R. Steele, *Knute Rockne-A Bio-Biography,* p. 131.
97. Michael R. Steele, *Knute Rockne-A Bio-Biography,* pp. 131-132.
98. Michael R. Steele, *Knute Rockne-A Bio-Biography,* p. 132.
99. Paul Schissler correspondence to Knute Rockne, September 22, 1925, from University of Notre Dame archives.
100. Knute Rockne correspondence to M. Ellwood Smith, September 30, 1925, from University of Notre Dame archives.
101. Oregon Agricultural College, *Preliminary Bulletin for 1925 Summer Session,* Corvallis, OR: November, 1924, pp. 4-5.
102. Oregon Agricultural College, *Preliminary Bulletin for 1925 Summer Session,* p. 5.
103. Oregon Agricultural College, *Preliminary Bulletin for 1925 Summer Session,* p. 5.
104. Oregon Agricultural College, *Preliminary Bulletin for 1926 Summer Session,* p. 9.
105. Bernard J. Sandoz, correspondence and interviews with author.
106. Bernard J. Sandoz.
107. Bernard J. Sandoz.
108. Bernard J. Sandoz.
109. Bernard J. Sandoz.
110. Bernard J. Sandoz.
111. Bernard J. Sandoz.
112. Bernard J. Sandoz.
113. Bernard J. Sandoz.
114. Anonymous, news story, September 17, 1926, from Mt. Angel Abbey Archives.
115. Anonymous, news story, September 17, 1926, from Mt. Angel Abbey Archives.
116. *Pacific Star,* Mount Angel College, June 3, 1926, p. 8.

117. Revs. Martin Pollard O.S.B. and Hugh Feiss, O.S.B., *Mount of Communion, 1882-1982*, p. 32.
118. Anonymous, *Capital-Journal*, Salem, OR: September 21, 1926, p. 1, from Mt. Angel Abbey Archives.

CHAPTER 5. Aftermath of the Fire

1. Revs. Martin Pollard O.S.B. and Hugh Feiss, O.S.B., *Mount of Communion,1882-1982*, Mt. Angel Abbey, (Capital City Graphics, Salem, OR: revised 2nd edition, 1985), p. 32.
2. Revs. Martin Pollard O.S.B. and Hugh Feiss, O.S.B., *Mount of Communion,1882-1982*, p. 32.
3. Revs. Martin Pollard O.S.B. and Hugh Feiss, O.S.B., *Mount of Communion,1882-1982*, p. 32.
4. Anonymous, *Salem Journal*, Salem, OR: September 26, 1926, from Mt. Angel Abbey Archives.
5. Anonymous, *Sunday Oregonian*, Portland, OR: October 10, 1926.
6. *Pacific Star*, Mount Angel College, January 16, 1942, p. 4.
7. Rev. Martin Pollard, O.S.B., Mt. Angel Abbey Archives, correspondence with author.
8. Rev. Martin Pollard, O.S.B., correspondence with author.
9. Revs. Martin Pollard O.S.B. and Hugh Feiss, O.S.B., *Mount of Communion,1882-1982*, p. 32.
10. Revs. Martin Pollard O.S.B. and Hugh Feiss, O.S.B., *Mount of Communion,1882-1982*, p. 33.
11. J.M. Gale,"The Dalles, Oregon," *The Union Pacific Magazine*, August 1927, p. 54.
12. Paul Schissler letter to Knute Rockne, May 5, 1927, from University of Notre Dame archives.
13. Paul Schissler letter to Knute Rockne, May 5, 1927, from University of Notre Dame archives.
14. Knute Rockne letter to Paul Schissler, May 11, 1927, from University of Notre Dame archives.
15. Paul Schissler letter to Calvin French, Ph.D., July 20, 1927, from University of Notre Dame archives.
16. Oregon State Agricultural College, *Poster* for Summer Session, Corvallis, OR: 1927, p. 2.
17. Oregon State Agricultural College, *Poster* for Summer Session, p. 4.
18. Oregon State Agricultural College, *Summer Catalog*, 1927, p. 28.
19. Oregon State Agricultural College, *Summer Catalog*, 1927, p. 28.
20. *Pacific Star*, Mount Angel College, May 9, 1940, p. 4.
21. Anonymous, "Seventeen Proud Keene Years," *Oregon Stater*, Alumni Magazine of Oregon State University, Corvallis, OR: September/October, 1964, pp. 10-11.
22. Anonymous, "Seventeen Proud Keene Years," *Oregon Stater*, pp. 10-11.
23. Willamette University vs. Lewis & Clark College, *Football Game Program*, Salem, OR: October 22, 1994.
24. Willamette University vs. Lewis & Clark College, *Football Game Program*.
25. *Wallulah*, Yearbook of Willamette University, Salem, OR: 1928, p. 116.
26. *Wallulah*, Yearbook of Willamette University, p. 111.
27. *Wallulah*, Yearbook of Willamette University, p. 111.
28. *The Old Gold and White*, Mt. Angel Academy and Normal School, Mt. Angel, OR: Commencement, 1928.
29. *The Old Gold and White*, Mt. Angel Academy and Normal School.
30. *The Old Gold and White*, Mt. Angel Academy and Normal School.
31. *The Old Gold and White*,Mt. Angel Academy and Normal School.
32. *The Old Gold and White*, Mt. Angel Academy and Normal School.
33. Revs. Martin Pollard O.S.B. and Hugh Feiss, O.S.B., *Mount of Communion, 1882-1982*, p. 33.
34. Bernard J. Sandoz, correspondence and interviews with author.
35. Knute Rockne letter to Paul Schissler, December 7, 1927, from University of Notre Dame archives.
36. Knute Rockne letter to Paul Schissler, September 19, 1929, from University of Notre Dame archives.
37. William C. Murray, *The Life of Coach Robert L. Murray of The Dalles*, Paper for the Original Wasco County Courthouse Forum, Saturday, Feb. 20, 1988, p. 13.
38. William C. Murray, *The Life of Coach Robert L. Murray of The Dalles*, p. 14.
39. William C. Murray, *The Life of Coach Robert L. Murray of The Dalles*, p. 14.
40. Marilyn G. Ericksen, *Alvin Edward (Allie) Gronewald, from the Memoirs of Hazel Huntington Gronewald*, The Dalles, OR: July 14, 1997.
41. Marilyn G. Ericksen, *Alvin Edward (Allie) Gronewald, from the Memoirs of Hazel Huntington Gronewald*.
42. Marilyn G. Ericksen, *Alvin Edward (Allie) Gronewald, from the Memoirs of Hazel Huntington Gronewald*.
43. Marilyn G. Ericksen, *Alvin Edward (Allie) Gronewald, from the Memoirs of Hazel Huntington Gronewald*.
44. Marilyn G. Ericksen, *Alvin Edward (Allie) Gronewald, from the Memoirs of Hazel Huntington*

Gronewald.

45. Marilyn G. Ericksen, *Alvin Edward (Allie) Gronewald, from the Memoirs of Hazel Huntington Gronewald.*

46. Anonymous, Manuscript on sports in The Dalles, OR, undated, p. 73, from The Dalles-Wasco County Library.

47. William C. Murray, *The Life of Coach Robert L. Murray of The Dalles*, p. 15.

48. William C. Murray, *The Life of Coach Robert L. Murray of The Dalles*, p. 14.

49. William C. Murray, *The Life of Coach Robert L. Murray of The Dalles*, pp. 14-15.

50. William C. Murray, *The Life of Coach Robert L. Murray of The Dalles*, p. 15.

51. William C. Murray, *The Life of Coach Robert L. Murray of The Dalles*, p. 15.

52. Southern Oregon State College, *Football Media Guide*, Ashland, OR: 1995, p. 5.

53. Southern Oregon State College, *Football Media Guide*, p. 5.

54. Gil Moe, *Siskiyou*, Newspaper of Southern Oregon Normal School, Ashland, OR: October 22, 1929, p. 4.

55. Paul Hauser, *Oregonian*, Portland, OR: November 2, 1952, p. 7.

56. Anonymous, *Biography of Ralph Orval Coleman*, undated, Corvallis, OR, p. 26, from Oregon State University Archives.

57. Anonymous, *Biography of Ralph Orval Coleman*, p. 27.

58. M. Claire Milbauer, correspondence and interviews with author.

59. M. Claire Milbauer.

60. *Newsletter*, St. Benedict's Prep Alumni, Newark, NJ: Summer, 1983, p. 6.

61. *Newsletter*, St. Benedict's Prep Alumni, Spring/Summer, 1992, p. 15.

62. M. Claire Milbauer.

63. Notre Dame University, *Football Media Guide*, Notre Dame, IN: 1994, p. 240.

64. *Dome*, Yearbook of Notre Dame University, Notre Dame, IN: 1925, p. 101.

65. *Scholastic*, Notre Dame University, Notre Dame, IN:1925, p. 322.

66. *Scholastic*, Notre Dame University, p. 829.

67. M. Claire Milbauer.

68. "Beaver Tales," *Oregon State Monthly*, Corvallis, OR: April, 1930, p. 31.

69. *Teachers College Bulletin*, Teachers College of Columbia University, New York, NY: 1930-31, p. 209.

70. Vic Kelly, "Peerless Bill Spaulding," *News Magazine*, Western Michigan University, Kalamazoo, MI: Winter, 1961, p. 11.

71. M. Claire Milbauer.

72. M. Claire Milbauer.

73. Tim Frank, "Hugh DeVore, The Oldest Living Irish Football Coach Returns to Notre Dame Stadium," *Notre Dame-Purdue Football Game Program*, Notre Dame University, Notre Dame, IN: Sept. 29, 1990, p. 65.

74. M. Claire Milbauer.

75. M. Claire Milbauer.

76. M. Claire Milbauer.

77. Lloyde S. Glicken, *Star-Ledger*, Newark, NJ: October 2, 1969.

78. Bernard J. Sandoz.

79. Rev. Malachy McPadden, O.S.B., ed., *The Benedictines in Newark 1842-1992*, (Newark, NJ: Wall Street Group, 1992), p. 5.

80. Olson, Sherry H., *Baltimore, The Building of an American City*, (Baltimore, MD:The Johns Hopkins University Press, 1980), p. 125 quoting Sister Mary Gilbert Kelly, *Catholic Immigrant Colonization Projects, 1815-1860*, (Washington DC: U.S. Catholic Historical Society, 1939), pp. 122-29.

81. Rev. Malachy McPadden, ed., *The Benedictines in Newark 1842-1992*, pp. 6-7.

82. Anonymous, *Saint Mary's Abbey-Delbarton/Newark Abbey 1884-1984*, Newark/Morristown, NJ: 1984, p. 4.

83. Anonymous, *Saint Mary's Abbey-Delbarton/Newark Abbey 1884-1984*, p. 4.

84. Anonymous, *Saint Mary's Abbey-Delbarton/Newark Abbey 1884-1984*, pp. 4-6.

85. Anonymous, *Saint Mary's Abbey-Delbarton/Newark Abbey 1884-1984*, p. 7.

86. Anonymous, *Saint Mary's Abbey-Delbarton/Newark Abbey 1884-1984*, p. 7.

87. Anonymous, *Saint Mary's Abbey-Delbarton/Newark Abbey 1884-1984*, p. 9.

88. Anonymous, *Saint Mary's Abbey-Delbarton/Newark Abbey 1884-1984*, p. 9.

89. Anonymous, *Saint Mary's Abbey-Delbarton/Newark Abbey 1884-1984*, p. 9.

90. Anonymous, *Saint Mary's Abbey-Delbarton/Newark Abbey 1884-1984*, p. 10.

91. Anonymous, *Saint Mary's Abbey-Delbarton/Newark Abbey 1884-1984*, p. 10.

92. Anonymous, *Saint Mary's Abbey-Delbarton/Newark Abbey 1884-1984*, p. 10.

93. Anonymous, *Saint Mary's Abbey-Delbarton/Newark Abbey 1884-1984*, p. 14.

94. *Benedict News*, St. Benedict's Prep, Newark, NJ: September 30, 1941.

95. *Benedict News*, St. Benedict's Prep, Newark, NJ: September 30, 1941.

96. Rev. Malachy McPadden, O.S.B., ed., *The Benedictines in Newark 1842-1992*, p. 25.

97. Rev. Malachy McPadden, O.S.B., ed., *The Benedictines in Newark 1842-1992*, p. 25.

98. *Benedict News*, St. Benedict's Prep, Newark, NJ: September 30, 1941.

99. Anonymous, *The Sunday Call*, Newark, NJ: Nov. 22, 1942, Part II, p. 8.

100. Rev. Malachy McPadden, O.S.B., ed., *The Benedictines in Newark 1842-1992*, p. 25.

101. Rev. Malachy McPadden, O.S.B., ed., *The Benedictines in Newark 1842-1992*, p. 25.

102. Rev. Malachy McPadden, O.S.B., ed., *The Benedictines in Newark 1842-1992*, p. 26.

103. Rev. Malachy McPadden, O.S.B., ed., *The Benedictines in Newark 1842-1992*, p. 26.

104. *Benedict News*, St. Benedict's Prep, Newark, NJ: September 30, 1941.

105. *Facts About Newark*, City of Newark, Newark, NJ: 1982.

106. John T. Cunningham, *Newark*, (Newark, NJ: New Jersey Historical Society, 1988), p. 116.

107. William Gordon, "Barringer, the First 160 Years," *Star-Ledger*, Newark, NJ: January 24, 1988, Section 2, p. 1.

108. *Facts About Newark*.

109. *Facts About Newark*.

110. Lloyde S. Glicken, *Star-Ledger*, Newark, NJ: September 6, 1989, p. 56.

111. Lloyde S. Glicken, *Star-Ledger*, September 6, 1989, p. 56.

112. Lloyde S. Glicken, *Star-Ledger*, September 6, 1989, p. 56.

CHAPTER 6: The Post-Graduate (PG) Athletic Era

1. *Scholastic*, Notre Dame University, Notre Dame, IN: October, 3, 1930, p. 46.

2. Rt. Rev. Martin Burne, O.S.B., correspondence with author.

3. Anonymous, *St. Benedict's Prep-Seton Hall Prep Football Game Program*, St. Benedict's Prep, Newark, NJ: Nov. 20, 1960, unnumbered.

4. M. Claire Milbauer, correspondence and interviews with author.

5. Michael R. Steele, *Knute Rockne-A Bio-Biography*, (Westport, CT: Greenwood Press, 1983), p. 119.

6. Michael R. Steele, *Knute Rockne-A Bio-Biography*, p. 119.

7. Michael R. Steele, *Knute Rockne-A Bio-Biography*, p. 119 quoting Warren Brown, *Rockne*, (Chicago, IL: Reilly & Lee, 1931), p. 32.

8. Michael R. Steele, *Knute Rockne-A Bio-Biography*, p. 119.

9. Robert L. Murray, untitled manuscript on Knute Rockne's death, circa 1931.

10. *Telolog*, Yearbook of St. Benedict's Prep, Newark, NJ: 1931, p. 116.

11. M. Claire Milbauer.

12. M. Claire Milbauer.

13. Anonymous, *St. Benedict's Prep-Seton Hall Prep Football Game Program*.

14. Rev. Malachy McPadden, O.S.B., ed., *The Benedictines in Newark 1842-1992*, p. 26.

15. M. Claire Milbauer.

16. M. Claire Milbauer.

17. *Wallulah*, Yearbook of Willamette University, Salem, OR: 1932, p. 128.

18. *Wallulah*, Yearbook of Willamette University, 1932, p. 128.

19. Rev. Malachy McPadden, O.S.B., ed., *The Benedictines in Newark 1842-1992*, p. 27.

20. Anonymous, *St.Benedict's Prep-Seton Hall Prep Football Game Program*.

21. William C. Murray, *The Life of Coach Robert L. Murray of The Dalles*, Paper for the Original Wasco County Courthouse Forum, Saturday, Feb. 20, 1988, p. 15.

22. William C. Murray, *The Life of Coach Robert L. Murray of The Dalles*, p. 15.

23. M. Claire Milbauer.

24. M. Claire Milbauer.

25. M. Claire Milbauer.

26. Oregon State University, *Football Media Guide*, Corvallis, OR: 1995, p. 167.

27. M. Claire Milbauer.

28. Bernard J. Sandoz, correspondence and interviews with author.

29. John F. Bateman, Ph.D., correspondence and interviews with author.

30. John F. Bateman, Ph.D.

31. Revs. Martin Pollard O.S.B. and Hugh Feiss, O.S.B., *Mount of Communion, 1882-1982*, Mt. Angel Abbey, (Salem, OR: Capital City Graphics, revised 2nd edition, 1985), p. 48.

32. Revs. Martin Pollard O.S.B. and Hugh Feiss, O.S.B., *Mount of Communion, 1882-1982*, p. 48.

33. M. Claire Milbauer.

34. M. Claire Milbauer.

35. Rev. Malachy McPadden, O.S.B., ed., *The Benedictines in Newark 1842-1992*, pp. 26-27.

36. Kathleen Milbauer O'Hare, Manuscript enttitled "Remembrances of Joe Kasberger," undated, 1996, p. 1.

37. Kathleen Milbauer O'Hare, "Remembrances of Joe Kasberger," p. 1.

38. Kathleen Milbauer O'Hare, "Remembrances of Joe Kasberger," p. 1.

39. Kathleen Milbauer O'Hare, "Remembrances of Joe Kasberger," pp. 1-2.

40. Kathleen Milbauer O'Hare, "Remembrances of Joe Kasberger," p. 2.

41. Frank Milbauer, Jr., Untitled Manuscript on Joe Kasberger, undated, 1996.

42. M. Claire Milbauer.

43. Kathleen Milbauer O'Hare, "Remembrances of Joe Kasberger," pp. 2-3.

44. Kathleen Milbauer O'Hare, "Remembrances of Joe Kasberger," p. 3.

45. *Wallulah,* Yearbook of Willamette University, 1936, unnumbered page.

46. *Wallulah,* Yearbook of Willamette University, 1936, unnumbered page.

47. *Wallulah,* Yearbook of Willamette University, 1936, unnumbered page.

48. *Wallulah,* Yearbook of Willamette University, 1936, unnumbered page.

49. *Wallulah,* Yearbook of Willamette University, 1936, unnumbered page.

50. M. Claire Milbauer.

51. M. Claire Milbauer.

52. Bernard J. Sandoz.

53. *Wallulah,* Yearbook of Willamette University, 1936, p. 45.

54. Michael Vanzandt, *Angelus,* St. Benedict, OR: March, 1964 from Mt. Angel Abbey Archives.

55. M. Claire Milbauer.

56. Rev. Malachy McPadden, O.S.B., ed., *The Benedictines in Newark 1842-1992*, p. 27.

57. Rev. Malachy McPadden, O.S.B., ed., *The Benedictines in Newark 1842-1992*, p. 30.

58. Rev. Malachy McPadden, O.S.B., ed., *The Benedictines in Newark 1842-1992*, p. 30.

59. Rev. Malachy McPadden, O.S.B., ed., *The Benedictines in Newark 1842-1992*, p. 30.

60. Rev. Malachy McPadden, O.S.B., ed., *The Benedictines in Newark 1842-1992*, p. 30.

61. Rev. Malachy McPadden, O.S.B., ed., *The Benedictines in Newark 1842-1992*, p. 30.

62. Rev. Malachy McPadden, O.S.B., ed., *The Benedictines in Newark 1842-1992*, p. 31.

63. Anonymous, *St. Benedict's Prep-Seton Hall Prep Football Game Program.*

64. Anonymous, *St. Mary's Abbey-Delbarton/Newark Abbey 1884-1984,* Morristown/Newark, NJ: 1984, p. 14.

65. Anonymous, *St. Mary's Abbey-Delbarton/Newark Abbey 1884-1984,* p. 16.

66. Anonymous, *St. Mary's Abbey-Delbarton/Newark Abbey 1884-1984,* p. 16.

67. Anonymous, *St. Benedict's Prep-Seton Hall Prep Football Game Program.*

68. Lloyde S.Glicken, *Star-Ledger,* Newark, NJ: September 6, 1989, p. 56.

69. *Benedict News,* St. Benedict's Prep, Newark, NJ: April 17, 1946.

70. Rev. Malachy McPadden, O.S.B., ed., *The Benedictines in Newark 1842-1992,* p. 31

71. M. Claire Milbauer.

72. William C. Murray, *The Life of Coach Robert L. Murray of The Dalles,* p. 16.

73. Frank Milbauer, Jr., untitled manuscript on Joe Kasberger.

74. M. Claire Milbauer.

75. Joseph M. Kasberger, "Your Son Should Play Football," Newark Abbey Archives, Newark, NJ: undated, Speech/Essay.

76. *Facts About Newark,* City of Newark, Newark, NJ: 1982.

77. Marilyn G. Ericksen, correspondence and interviews with author.

78. Anonymous, *St. Benedict's Prep-Seton Hall Prep Football Game Program.*

79. Michael D'Orso, "Saturday's Hero: A Beat," *Sports Illustrated,* Oct. 23, 1989, unnumbered pages.

80. Joseph P. Hellberg, correspondence and interviews with author.

81. Anonymous, *St. Mary's Abbey-Delbarton/Newark Abbey 1884-1984,* p. 16.

82. M. Claire Milbauer.

83. Willamette University, *Quarterly Athletic Newsletter,* Salem, OR: March, 1995, p. 1.

84. Willamette University, *Quarterly Athletic Newsletter,* March, 1995, p. 1.

85. Willamette University, *Quarterly Athletic Newsletter,* March, 1995, pp. 1, 4.

86. Willamette University, *Quarterly Athletic Newsletter,* March, 1995, p. 4.

87. Herb Michelson and Dave Newhouse, *Rose Bowl Football Since 1902,* (Briarcliff Manor, NY: Stein and Day, 1977), p. 127.

88. Clyde Bolton, *The Crimson Tide, A Story of Alabama Football,* (Huntsville, AL: The Strode Publishers, 1972), p. 71.

89. Clyde Bolton, *The Crimson Tide, A Story of Alabama Football,* pp. 130-131.

90. Herb Michelson and Dave Newhouse, *Rose Bowl Football Since 1902*, pp. 129-136.

91. Herb Michelson and Dave Newhouse, *Rose Bowl Football Since 1902*, pp. 129-136.

92. L.H. Gregory, "Greg's Gossip," *Oregonian*, Portland, OR: January 10, 1942.

93. Bernard J. Sandoz.

94. *Pacific Star*, Mount Angel College, St. Benedict, OR: January 16, 1940, p. 4.

95. *Pacific Star*, Mount Angel College, May 9, 1942, p. 4.

96. Anonymous, "Seventeen Proud Keene Years," *Oregon Stater*, Alumni Magazine of Oregon State University, Corvallis, OR: September/October 1964, p. 11.

97. Joe Kasberger note to Joe Hellberg, May 28, 1942.

98. Anonymous, *St. Mary's Abbey-Delbarton/Newark Abbey 1884-1984*, p. 16.

99. *The Sunday Call*, Newark, NJ: November 22, 1942, p. 8.

100. *Benedict News*, St. Benedict's Prep, Newark, NJ: March 15, 1968, p. 5.

101. Rev. Malachy McPadden, O.S.B., *Alumni Newsletter*, St. Benedict's Prep, September, 1986, p. 2.

102. Rev. Malachy McPadden, O.S.B., *Alumni Newsletter*, St. Benedict's Prep, September, 1986, p. 2.

103. Bernard J. Sandoz.

104. Bernard J. Sandoz.

105. Anonymous, Manuscript on sports in The Dalles, OR from The Dalles-Wasco County Library, undated, p. 73.

106. Rev. Malachy McPadden, O.S.B., ed., *The Benedictines in Newark 1842-1992*, p. 27.

107. Joseph M. Kasberger, "Need of a Preparatory School," Newark Abbey Archives, Newark, NJ: undated, but presumed to be 1944 typed memorandum/essay, pp. 1-3.

108. Kathleen Milbauer O'Hare, "Remembrances of Joe Kasberger," p. 3.

109. Joseph Grum, interviews with author.

110. Kathleen Milbauer O'Hare, "Remembrances of Joe Kasberger," p. 3.

111. *Benedict News*, St. Benedict's Prep, Newark, NJ: April 17, 1946.

112. Robert M. Huntington, Ph.D. correspondence and interviews.

113. Anonymous, "Seventeen Proud Keene Years," *Oregon Stater*, p. 11.

114. Anonymous, "Seventeen Keene Proud Years," *Oregon Stater*, p. 11.

115. Oregon State University, *Football Media Guide*, Corvallis, OR: 1963, p. 20.

116. Oregon State University, *Football Media Guide*, Corvallis, OR: 1963, p. 20.

117. Oregon State University, *Football Media Guide*, Corvallis, OR: 1963, p. 20.

118. *Benedict News*, St. Benedict's Prep, Newark, NJ: March 15, 1968, p. 5.

119. M. Claire Milbauer.

120. Anonymous, *The Dalles Chronicle*, Bob Murray story, The Dalles, OR: June 3, 1958, from The Dalles-Wasco County Library.

121. Anonymous, Manuscript on sports in The Dalles, p. 73, from The Dalles-Wasco County Library.

122. M. Claire Milbauer.

123. Anonymous, *St. Mary's Abbey-Delbarton/Newark Abbey 1884-1984*, p. 16.

124. M. Claire Milbauer.

125. Rev. Malachy McPadden, O.S.B., ed., *The Benedictines in Newark 1842-1992*, p. 33.

126. Paul Horowitz, *The Evening News*, Newark, NJ: April 14, 1972, p. E5.

127. Paul Horowitz, *The Evening News*, p. E5.

128. *Facts About Newark*.

129. James C. Heartwell, *The History of Oregon State College Basketball 1901-02 - 1952-53*, (Corvallis, OR: Cascade Printing Co., 1953), p. 88.

130. James C. Heartwell, *The History of Oregon State College Basketball 1901-02 - 1952-53*, p. 89.

131. James C. Heartwell, *The History of Oregon State College Basketball 1901-02 - 1952-53*, p. 89.

132. Anonymous, *Southern Cross*, San Diego, CA: April 21, 1950, from Mt. Angel Abbey Archives.

133. Anonymous, Rev. Norbert Matteucci, O.S.B. news story, from Mt. Angel Abbey Archives.

134. Joseph M. Kasberger, "Advice to Baseball Players," Newark Abbey Archives, Newark, NJ: undated, typed speech/essay.

135. Revs. Martin Pollard O.S.B. and Hugh Feiss, O.S.B., *Mount of Communion, 1882-1982*, p. 50.

136. M. Claire Milbauer.

137. *Benedict News*, St. Benedict's Prep, Newark, NJ: March 15, 1968, p. 5.

138. Bernard J. Sandoz.

139. Bernard J. Sandoz.

140. Andrew J. Purcell, "The Joe Kasberger Story," St. Benedict's Prep *Alumni Directory*, Newark, NJ: 1966, p. 19.

141. Andrew J. Purcell, "The Joe Kasberger Story," p. 19.

142. *Telolog,* Yearbook of St. Benedict's Prep, 1951, p. 140.

143. Rev. Jerome Fitzpatrick, O.S.B., correspondence and interviews with author.

CHAPTER 7: Coaching Without Post-Graduates (PGs)

1. Michael O'Brien, Vince, *A Personal Biography of Vince Lombardi,* (New York, NY: William Morrow and Company, Inc. 1987), pp. 51-76.

2. John M. Allen, correspondence and interviews with author.

3. Paul Hauser, *Sunday Oregonian Magazine,* Portland, OR: November 2, 1952, p. 6.

4. Paul Hauser, *Sunday Oregonian Magazine,* pp. 6-7.

5. Paul Hauser, *Sunday Oregonian Magazine,* p. 7.

6. Paul Hauser, *Sunday Oregonian Magazine,* p. 7.

7. Paul Hauser, *Sunday Oregonian Magazine,* p. 7.

8. Paul Hauser, *Sunday Oregonian Magazine,* p. 7.

9. Paul Hauser, *Sunday Oregonian Magazine,* p. 7.

10. Paul Hauser, *Sunday Oregonian Magazine,* p. 7.

11. Willamette University, *Hall of Fame Citation,* Willamette University, Salem, OR: undated.

12. Willamette University, *Hall of Fame Citation.*

13. Willamette University, *Hall of Fame Citation.*

14. Anonymous, *Saint Mary's Abbey-Delbarton/Newark Abbey 1884-1984,* Newark/Morristown, NJ: 1984, p. 18.

15. John F. Thomas, correspondence and interviews with author.

16. *Alumni Newsletter,* St. Benedict's Prep, Newark, NJ: January, 1987, p. 1.

17. Jack Cross, *Chronicle,* The Dalles, OR: March, 1954, from The Dalles-Wasco County Library.

18. Anonymous, *Chronicle,* The Dalles, OR: June 3, 1958, from The Dalles-Wasco County Library.

19. Mississippi State University, *Football Media Guide,* Starkville, MS: 1951, p. 19.

20. Bernard J. Sandoz, correspondence and interviews with author.

21. Kathleen Milbauer O'Hare, Manuscript entitled: "Remembrances of Joe Kasberger," undated, 1996, p. 2.

22. Paul Horowitz, *The Evening News,* Newark, NJ: April 14, 1972, p. E5.

23. *Benedict News,* St. Benedict's Prep, Newark, NJ: May 25, 1955, pp. 1, 4.

24. M. Claire Milbauer, correspondence and interviews with author.

25. *Benedict News,* St. Benedict's Prep, May 25, 1955, p. 4.

26. M. Claire Milbauer.

27. Kathleen Milbauer O'Hare, "Remembrances of Joe Kasberger," p. 3.

28. Bernard J. Sandoz.

29. Anonymous, "Seventeen Proud Keene Years," *Oregon Stater,* Alumni Magazine of Oregon State University, Corvallis, OR: September/October 1964, p. 11.

30. Anonymous, "Seventeen Keene Proud Years," *Oregon Stater,* p. 11.

31. Rev. Malachy McPadden, O.S.B., ed., *The Benedictines in Newark 1842-1992,* p. 38.

32. Rev. Malachy McPadden, O.S.B., ed., *The Benedictines in Newark 1842-1992,* p. 38.

33. John Brookhouse, interviews with author.

34. Bernard J. Sandoz.

35. Bernard J. Sandoz.

36. Frank Milbauer, Jr., untitled manuscript on Joe Kasberger.

37. Frank Milbauer, Jr., untitled manuscript on Joe Kasberger.

38. Rev. Malachy McPadden, O.S.B., ed., *The Benedictines in Newark 1842-1992,* p. 38.

39. Rev. Malachy McPadden, O.S.B., ed., *The Benedictines in Newark 1842-1992,* p. 38.

40. Rev. Jerome Fitzpatrick, O.S.B., correspondence and interview with author.

41. Anonymous, *Saint Mary's Abbey-Delbarton/Newark Abbey 1884-1984,* p. 18.

42. Rev. Jerome Fitzpatrick, O.S.B., correspondence and interviews with author.

43. *Benedict News,* St. Benedict's Prep, Nov. 1969, p. 2.

44. Anonymous, Manuscript on sports in The Dalles, OR, undated, p. 72, from The Dalles-Wasco County Library.

45. Anonymous, Manuscript on sports in The Dalles, OR, p. 72.

46. Jack Cross, *Chronicle,* The Dalles, OR: undated, circa 1954 from The Dalles-Wasco County Library.

47. Anonymous, *St. Benedict's Prep-Seton Hall Prep Football Game Program,* St. Benedict's Prep, Newark, NJ: Nov. 20, 1960.

48. Rev. Malachy McPadden, O.S.B., ed., *The Benedictines in Newark 1842-1992,* p. 38.

49. John F. Thomas, correspondence and interviews with author.

50. John F. Thomas, correspondence and interviews with author.

51. *Benedict News,* St. Benedict's Prep, November, 1969, p. 2.

52. Anonymous, *St. Benedict's Prep-Seton Hall Prep Football Game Program.*

53. Rev. Malachy McPadden, O.S.B., ed., *The Benedictines in Newark 1842-1992,* p. 39.

54. Anonymous, *St. Benedict's Prep-Seton Hall Prep Football Game Program.*

55. Anonymous, *St. Benedict's Prep-Seton Hall Prep Football Game Program.*

56. Anonymous, *St. Benedict's Prep-Seton Hall Prep Football Game Program.*

57. Joseph M. Kasberger, "Memorandum to Members of St. Benedict's Athletic Teams," Newark Abbey Archives, Newark, NJ: February 24, 1961.

58. Eugene Schiller Audio Tape Interview by Richard Lorenzo, January 14,1998.

59. Eugene Schiller Audio Tape Interview by Richard Lorenzo, January 14,1998.

60. Eugene Schiller Audio Tape Interview by Richard Lorenzo, January 14,1998.

61. Eugene Schiller Audio Tape Interview by Richard Lorenzo, January 14,1998.

62. Rev. Malachy McPadden, O.S.B., ed., *The Benedictines in Newark 1842-1992,* p. 41.

63. Michael Vanzandt, *Angelus,* St. Benedict, OR: March, 1964, p. 1, from Mt. Angel Abbey Archives.

64. Michael Vanzandt, *Angelus,* p. 1, from Mt. Angel Abbey Archives.

65. Bernard J. Sandoz.

66. Michael Petriella, M.D., interviews with author.

67. Andrew J. Purcell, "The Joe Kasberger Story," St. Benedict's Prep *Alumni Directory,* Newark, NJ: 1966, p. 20.

68. Joseph M. Kasberger, "My Philosophy of American Secondary Education," Newark Abbey Archives, Newark, NJ: Undated, typed speech/essay.

69. Andrew J. Purcell, St. Benedict's Prep *Alumni Directory,* 1966, p. 18.

70. John T. Cunningham, *Newark,* (Newark, NJ: New Jersey Historical Society, 1988), pp. 311-312.

71. Rev. Malachy McPadden, O.S.B., ed., *The Benedictines in Newark 1842-1992,* p. 40.

72. Rev. Malachy McPadden, O.S.B., ed., *The Benedictines in Newark 1842-1992,* p. 40.

73. Rev. Malachy McPadden, O.S.B., ed., *The Benedictines in Newark 1842-1992,* p. 39.

74. Hugh Delano, *Sunday News,* Newark, NJ: June 11, 1967.

75. Lloyde S. Glicken, *Star-Ledger,* Newark, NJ: June 11, 1967.

76. M. Claire Milbauer.

77. Rev. Malachy McPadden, O.S.B., ed., *The Benedictines in Newark 1842-1992,* p. 40.

78. Bernard J. Sandoz.

79. John T. Cunningham, *Newark,* p. 325.

80. Rev. Malachy McPadden, O.S.B., ed., *The Benedictines in Newark 1842-1992,* pp. 40-41.

81. Msgr. William S. Stone, *The Cross in the Middle of Nowhere,* (Bend, OR: Maverick Publishers, Inc., 1993), p. 215.

82. Rev. Malachy McPadden, O.S.B., ed., *The Benedictines in Newark 1842-1992,* p. 41.

83. Rev. Malachy McPadden, O.S.B., ed., *The Benedictines in Newark 1842-1992,* p. 41.

84. Bernard J. Sandoz.

85. Rev. Malachy McPadden, O.S.B., ed., *The Benedictines in Newark 1842-1992,* p. 44.

86. Joe Kasberger Christmas Card to Joe Hellberg, December, 1968.

87. Kathleen Milbauer O'Hare, "Remembrances of Joe Kasberger," p. 4.

88. M. Claire Milbauer.

89. Anonymous, *Alumni Magazine,* University of Maryland, College Park, Winter, 1995.

90. *Ben Scotti Profile,* Ted Williams Trading Card Company, 1994.

91. Ben Scotti, correspondence and interviews with author.

92. *Benedict News,* St. Benedict's Prep, November, 1969, p. 5.

93. Joseph R. Thomas, correspondence and interviews with author.

94. *Benedict News,* St. Benedict's Prep, November, 1969, p. 5.

95. Rev. Jerome Fitzpatrick, O.S.B., speech notes, October 1, 1969, from Newark Abbey Archives.

96. *Benedict News,* St. Benedict's Prep, November, 1969, p. 5.

97. Anonymous, *Star-Ledger,* Newark, NJ: October 6, 1969.

98. *Alumni Newsletter,* St. Benedict's Prep, Newark, NJ: Winter, 1969.

99. *Alumni Newsletter,* Mt. Angel College, St. Benedict, OR: Winter, 1969.

100. Rev. Dominic Milroy, O.S.B., "What it Means to be a Benedictine School Today,"*Delbarton Today,* Morristown, NJ: Fall, 1997, pp. 4-9.

101. Ben Scotti, correspondence with author.

102. Paul Horowitz, *Newark News,* p. E4.

103. Paul Horowitz, *Newark News,* p. E4.

104. Anonymous, *Capital Journal,* Salem, OR: January 14, 1977 from Mt. Angel Abbey.

INDEX

444

Armorial Seal of St. Benedict's Preparatory School

The COAT OF ARMS of St. Benedict's Preparatory School may be seen in color in the auditorium lobby. On the field of black, the color of the Benedictine habit, are two gold ravens. These ravens recall the Order's founder, St. Benedict. One represents the bird that fed him when he was a hermit; the other, the raven that snatched poisoned bread from the saint's hand.

The book in the center is the *Holy Rule* of St. Benedict containing the opening words, "Listen, O my son, to the precepts of thy master." Directly above is the coat of arms of the Order of St. Benedict, a patriarchal cross mounted on the word *Pax*.

The two crescents on the upper part of the shield are symbols of the Virgin Mary; one applies to the Abbey, which has the title of St. Mary's of the Immaculate Conception; the other to the whole United States, which is under the patronage of the Blessed Virgin inder the title of the Immaculate Conception.

The school motto is taken from St. Gregory's life of St. Benedict. *Gratia Benedictus Nomine* refers primarily to St. Gregory's description of St. Benedict as "Blessed in grace and in name." To us, it means that we who are called Benedict men, or in English, "Blessed" men, should strive to be always living in the grace of God.

Dennis Joyce was educated at St. Benedict's Prep in Newark, New Jersey. Joe Kasberger was his Freshman English teacher as well as his baseball coach. The experience was so fascinating that this research resulted. Joyce is a graduate of the University of Alabama and holds graduate degrees from the University of Tennessee and the University of Baltimore.